MENZIES' REPORTS.

[NEW SERIES.]

1828–1849.

VOL. II. PART I.

DECISIONS ON SURETYSHIP.

EBDEN, HOUGHTON, & Co. *vs.* DE VILLIERS.

Guarantee.—Provisional sentence on, refused.

A letter from A directing B to furnish C with goods, in conjunction with a bill drawn by C on A in favour of B, held insufficient for provisional sentence against A. 1828. Feb. 28.

[Vol. I, p. 73.]

WITHAM *vs.* VENABLES.

Security for costs not exigible from the plaintiff, who is an incola; nor from one who, although no incola, has immovable property within the Colony. March 14.

[Vol. I, p. 291.]

DUNLEVIE *vs.* HARRINGTON AND GADNEY.

Security for costs not exigible from plaintiff, a military man in service at the Cape, he being considered an incola. March 18.

[Vol. I, p. 292.]

Maasdorp *vs.* Morkel's Executor.

Beneficium excussionis, renunciation of.

1828. March 20. *The effect of the renunciation, by the surety, of the beneficium excussionis is, that judgment obtained against such surety by the creditor may be put into execution at once by him without first taking out execution against the principal debtor. Application by such surety to restrain the creditor from execution refused accordingly.*

[Vol. I, p. 293.]

Hare, q.q., *vs.* Croeser.

Beneficium excussionis, renunciation of.—Excussion, what is sufficient.

March 27. *The renunciation, by a surety, of the beneficium excussionis makes him directly liable to the creditor, although real property specially mortgaged in security by the debtor has not been excussed. This independently of the fact that the surety was bound as co-principal debtor.*

It is sufficient excussion of such mortgaged property to show, by the confirmed final liquidation account of the principal debtor's estate, and by a certificate by the sequestrator that the debtor had no other property, that such property has been awarded to a prior preferent creditor. And this notwithstanding a pending appeal by the other creditors regarding the validity and award of such prior preference.

[Vol. I, p. 293.]

Et vide Serrurier *vs.* Langeveld, *post, p.* 3. *Et* Chase *vs.* Cloete, *post, p.* 4.

Muller *vs.* Meyer.

Beneficium excussionis, renunciation of.—Rear-surety, (Achterborg.)

June 19. *The effect of the renunciation of the benefit of excussion by a rear-surety is destroyed by his adding a clause binding himself to pay if the other sureties are unable to pay.*

[Vol. I, p. 302.]

Cases Decided in the Supreme Court of the Cape of Good Hope

(Volume II)

William Menzies,

Editor: James Buchanan

Alpha Editions

This edition published in 2019

ISBN : 9789353976972

Design and Setting By
Alpha Editions
email - alphaedis@gmail.com

CASES

DECIDED

IN THE SUPREME COURT

OF THE

CAPE OF GOOD HOPE,

AS REPORTED BY THE LATE

HON. WILLIAM MENZIES, ESQUIRE,

(SENIOR PUISNE JUDGE OF THE SUPREME COURT.)

EDITED BY

JAMES BUCHANAN,

ADVOCATE.

VOL. II.

J. C. JUTA & CO.,

CAPETOWN.
PORT ELIZABETH.
GRAHAMSTOWN.
JOHANNESBURG.
KING WILLIAMSTOWN.
EAST LONDON.
STELLENBOSCH.
DURBAN.

1903.

VAN OOSTERZEE *vs.* MCRAE, q.q. CARFRAE & CO.

1. *Sureties.—Right of action against them can only arise upon the obligation as entered into by them. Therefore, where defendants were sureties to a bond dated 20th March,* 1820, *and the mortgagor subsequently executed another bond dated 25th April,* 1825, *reciting the former bond, and varying it, and where the mortgagee of the bond of* 1820 *died, and her heirs summoned the sureties on the second bond, which had alone been assigned to them, held the sureties were not liable on such bond.* 1828. June 26.

2. *Sureties are discharged by creditor giving up the security of promissory notes under which they become sureties, without taking any other and good security in lieu thereof.*

[Vol. I, p. 305.]

Et vide DU TOIT'S TRUSTEES *vs.* DE KOCK, *post, p.* 12.

DREYER *vs.* SMUTS.

Surety to a bond binding himself for the payment of the capital sum not liable for the interest. June 30.

[Vol. I, p. 308.]

SERRURIER *vs.* LANGEVELD.

(*Confirming Hare, q.q., vs. Croeser, ante, p.* 2.)

Placaat, 21*st February,* 1564.

Surety under renunciation of the beneficia and special hypothec not entitled to claim previous excussion of the hypothec, this privilege belonging only to simple sureties; but may in execution point out goods of debtor, and insist on their being taken in execution. Sept. 11. Oct. 7.

[Vol. I, p. 316.]

[This decision followed in CHASE *vs.* CLOETE, 30th September, 1828, *post, p.* 4, and in BRINK *vs.* ANOSI.]

In Re Insolvent Estate of Buissinne.—Van der Byl and Meyer *vs.* Sequestrator and Attorney-General.

Sureties to Collectors of the Revenue.

1828. Sept. 23. *The legal hypothec enjoyed by the Government of this Colony upon the property of collectors of revenue not diminished or impaired by Government taking sureties from such collectors.*

[Vol. I, p. 318.]

[Followed in *Re* Insolvent Estate of Buissinne, Croeser *vs.* Sequestrator and Attorney-General, 5th June, 1829, vol. 1, p. 330.]

[The Tacit Hypothecation Amendment Act, No. 6 of 1861, abolishes the previous tacit hypothecs of Government on estates of auctioneers and deputy postmasters considered as collectors of the revenue.]

Chase *vs.* Cloete.

[Following Hare *vs.* Croeser, *ante, p.* 2. Serrurier *vs.* Langeveld, *ante, p.* 3.]

Surety having renounced the benefit of excussion cannot claim the prior excussion of hypothec.

Sept. 30. Chase *vs.* Cloete. This was an action against the defendant, as one of two sureties, for payment of the price of landed property purchased at vendue.

Cloete, for defendant, quoted *Van Leeuwen, Censura Forensis*, 4, 11, 12; *Voet*, 20, *tit.* 4, § 3, *in fine;* and contended that no action lay against the defendant, who was merely a security, even although he had renounced the benefit of excussion, until the lien which the vendue-master has over the property sold be first excussed; and that, in respect of the above authorities, the decision in *Hare vs. Croeser* (9th April, 1828, *ante, p.* 2) was erroneous.

Joubert referred to *Loenius* 30, *Boel's Annotation*, as directly in opposition to *Van Leeuwen*.

This case was allowed to stand over, to wait the decision in the case of *Serrurier vs. Langeveld;* and in conformity to that decision (7th October, 1828, *ante, p.* 2), the Court gave provisional sentence, as prayed.

ROUSSEAU *vs.* BIERMAN.

1. *Surety discharged by the creditor's failure to cause special mortgage of slaves to be registered. Mortgage of slaves must be enregistered in Slave Registry to be effectual. [Slave Registry abolished on emancipation of slaves.]* 1828. Dec. 21.
2. *Surety discharged by creditor taking a less effectual obligation from a co-surety than that agreed on and originally set forth in the bond.*

[Vol. I, p. 338.]

LOW *vs.* SPENGLER.

Surety, having renounced the beneficium excussionis, whether discharged by the creditors giving up a pignus prætorium obtained from the debtor. 1829. Sept. 29.

[Not decided; the Court seeing no evidence of the constitution of the *pignus prætorium.*]

[Vol. I, p. 401.]

NISBET & DICKSON *vs.* THWAITES.

Proclamation, 6*th Sept.,* 1805.

Surety not released, although special mortgage given by debtor be annulled and set aside as an undue preference under Proclamation of 6*th Sept.,* 1805. *The creditor has still a concurrent, although not a preferent obligation upon him.* Dec. 18.

[Vol. I, p. 427.]

VAN DER BYL *vs.* MALHERBE.

Surety who has bound himself only for a certain time is not liable after the expiration of that time (even though he has bound himself as joint principal debtor), when no demand was made upon the principal debtor himself, nor the principal debtor proved to have become insolvent, within such time. So held on appeal. Dec. 22.

[Vol. I, p. 430.]

Sed vide note to that page.

Executors of Morkel *vs.* The Heirs of Morkel.

1829. Dec. 22. *A wife married in community of property cannot be bound as a surety without her husband's consent.*

[Vol. I, p. 177.]

Horn *vs.* Loedolff and Uxor.

1830. Jan. 12. *Surety not released by reason of another interposing in his stead, without thereafter signing the undertaking.*

[Vol. I, p. 403.]

Meyer *vs.* Deneys.

June 15. *It will not bar objection of nullity in respect of due registration of mortgage bond in the Colonial Debt Register, that the sureties to another bond duly registered had, by a clause in such latter bond, declared themselves satisfied with the mortgage contained in the former and unregistered bond.*

[Vol. I. p. 434.]

Et vide next case.

Kotze *vs.* Meyer.

Sept. 7. *Surety, although co-principal debtor, released by the creditor having lost the special mortgage in the bond by neglect of registry.*

[Vol. I, p. 466.]

Et vide Meyer *vs.* Low, *post, p.* 8.

Cloete *vs.* Bergh.

1831. March 17. *Surety, bound as joint principal debtor, whether discharged by creditor's release of a pignus prætorium on the estate of the original debtor, whether acquired before or after the suretyship's obligation was entered into.*—[*Not decided.*]

[Vol. I, p. 516.]

SUTHERLAND *vs.* SNELL.

A judgment obtained against an office-holder for a deficiency in the accounts of his office, on his own admission in an action to which his surety was no party, is no evidence to warrant provisional sentence for the amount of such deficiency against such surety, who had bound himself for default of such office-holder. 1831. March 31.

[Vol. I, p. 69.]

OVERBEEK *vs.* CLOETE.

Surety having renounced the benefit of excussion, is not released by creditor's refusal to take a bond from him, the surety, and cede debt or discuss the debtor. March 31.

Release in this way is only the privilege of simple sureties, and not of those who have so renounced.

[Vol. I, p. 523-4.]

Et vide VAN DER BYL *vs.* MUNNIK, *post;* VERMAAK *vs.* CLOETE, *post;* EXECUTORS OF HOETS *vs.* DE VOS, *post.*

ORPHAN CHAMBER *vs.* SERTYN AND OTHERS.

Sureties signing conditions of sale, in which it was, inter alia, declared that they bound themselves under renunciation of the usual benefits, held provisionally liable. Dec. 1.

[Vol. I, p. 25.]

In Re ANDERSON.

MORRISON *vs.* ANDERSON AND STENHOUSE.

Sureties by bond for prosecuting an appeal can be condemned by rule of Court without a regular action when the bond consents, in its terms, to execution issuing on the default of appellant to prosecute appeal. June 1.

[Vol. I, p. 527.]

NEETHLING, q.q., *vs.* MINNAAR.

1831. Dec. 13. *Notice given by a surety, before having paid the debt, to debtor to pay such debt, not sufficient to enable surety, after having paid debt and obtained cession, to demand from debtor without fresh notice.*

[Vol. I, p. 535.]

BRINK *vs.* VAN DER RIET.

1832. March 13. *Co-surety not liable after rehabilitation to co-surety who paid the principal before the confirmation of the liquidation account of his co-surety, and had not then ranked on such co-surety's estate.*

SEMBLE: *The co-surety's rehabilitation is also a bar to a fresh claim thereafter by the principal debtor who had previously claimed on the insolvent estate of such co-surety.*

[Vol. I, p. 543.]

MEYER *vs.* SCHONNBERG.

March 15. *A surety indemnitatis (i.e., for deficiency after excussion of hypothecation and four personal sureties) having paid the debt, cannot, without cession of action, maintain a claim of damages against the sequestrator for negligence in executing the sentence against a preceding ordinary surety.*

[Vol. I, p. 545.]

MEYER *vs.* LOW.

June 29. Aug. 13. *Condictio indebiti; Novation; Transactio; Res Judicata: Non-registration of bond by creditor, when.*

M. was one of three sureties in solidum and co-principal debtors on a bond, dated 14th Sept., 1813, passed by Van N. for 3,000 rds., in favour of L. Van. N. surrendered. L. demanded payment of the bond from M., who paid it on cession of action; and filed his claim on the estate of Van N., but got nothing, in consequence of the default of L. in not registering the bond until Sept., 1827, by which time prior preferences were created. M. now reclaimed the amount of the bond from L. on this ground. L.

averred (and the fact was admitted by M.) that after the death of Van N., and knowing of the delay in the registration of the bond, M. made certain proposals to L. on his calling up the bond, renewing his liability in respect thereof, the result of which proposals was that M. (after having meanwhile suffered provisional sentence to go against him for the whole amount) paid one half in cash, and passed a new bond for the other half. HELD, *that these acts of M. amounted to such a novation, transaction, and res judicata as barred his present claim for condictio indebiti. The Court was of opinion* (WYLDE, C. J., *dubitante) that but for such acts, the principle laid down in* KOTZE *vs.* MEYER (*ante, p.* 6), *as to the release of the surety on the non-registration of the bond by the creditor, would have applied in this case, although the bond here was one of general mortgage, and in* KOTZE *vs.* MEYER *of special mortgage.*

1832. June 29. Aug. 13.

Meyer *vs.* Low.

The plaintiff's declaration stated that the defendant had been summoned for the restitution of a certain sum of money unlawfully paid over to him. That the plaintiff, by a notarial bond, bearing date 14th September, 1813, bound himself as surety and joint principal debtor, together with Servaas van Breda and Gysbertus van Reenen, now deceased, for Marthinus van Niekerk, in favour of the defendant, for a sum of 3,000 rds. Cape currency. That the said Marthinus van Niekerk having surrendered his estate as insolvent, the defendant officially demanded of the said plaintiff payment of the aforesaid bond by virtue of his liability *in solidum* for the said debt; and that the plaintiff did accordingly pay to the defendant upon a proper cession of action on the estate of the insolvent and his joint sureties the aforesaid sum of 3,000 rds. That having filed his claim upon the insolvent estate of the principal debtor, nothing had been awarded to him on the said claim in the distribution of the estate, confirmed by the Supreme Court. That the reason and cause why the said amount was not adjudged to the plaintiff out of the proceeds of the said estate arises from the neglect of the said defendant in duly registering the said bond, passed by the said Marthinus van Niekerk, within a reasonable time after the same had been executed by the principal debtor; the said bond being executed on the 14th September, 1813, and not registered in the public debt registry until the 29th of September, 1827, several months after the decease of the principal debtor; by reason of which neglect all hypothecations prior to the latter date have been ranked before the bond ceded to the said plaintiff. And whereas

1832. June 29. Aug. 13.

Meyer *vs.* Low.

the defendant, by reason of this neglect, has been the sole cause of the loss sustained by the plaintiff, he now brings his action *ex condictione indebiti*, claiming that the defendant be condemned to repay to the said plaintiff the sum of 3,000 rds., or £225 sterling, with interest from the 16th September, 1829, until the final payment, with costs of suit,—the plaintiff being ready and willing, upon the receipt thereof, to transfer back to the defendant the notarial bond of the said Marthinus van Niekerk, dated 14th September, 1813.

The defendant admitted the execution of the bond of 14th September, 1813, and said that no other mortgage for the said bond was given than a general mortgage of the property of the principal debtor and sureties. He further pleaded that on the 28th September, 1827, after the death of Van Niekerk, he, the defendant, had served a notice on the widow, calling up the bond, and also upon the present plaintiff. That on the 22nd September, 1827, defendant, at the special request of the plaintiff himself, caused the bond to be enregistered in the public debt registry. That the plaintiff applied to the defendant to allow him to retain the capital on interest, proposing certain sureties; to which the defendant acceded, in so far, namely, that the half of the debt should be paid in cash, whilst for the moiety a notarial bond should be passed by plaintiff, secured by two sureties. That before complying with these conditions, the plaintiff had on the 10th September, 1829, suffered a provisional sentence to be passed against him for the whole amount of his debt, upon which the plaintiff, however, on the 14th and 15th September, 1829, paid the half of the said amount, in cash, being 1,770 rds., whilst he, for the other moiety, offered a notarial bond passed by him, plaintiff, on the 10th September, 1829, and secured merely by personal suretyship, which was declined to be accepted, unless moreover secured by special mortgage, as required by defendant. That such special mortgage bond, bearing date 20th November, 1829, whereby certain slaves were mortgaged by one M. van Breda, was some months subsequently, in January, 1830, offered to the defendant, but refused for insufficiency of the slaves. That the present defendant then instructed his attorney to summon the present plaintiff for the other moiety of the bond of 14th September, 1813. The plaintiff, on the 10th June, 1830, appeared before a notary public, and there, after having in a most ample and unequivocal manner repeated his liability to the defendant on the new bond of the 10th September, 1829, renounced and gave up his right of preference as a first mortgagee on the four slaves in favour of the defendant, who then finally accepted the bond; through which acts the novation of debt entered into in September, 1829, has been contracted and confirmed as late as the month of June, 1830. That the plaintiff, since September, 1827, up to 10th June, 1830, had every opportunity of ascertaining that the debt which he partly paid and partly took over and renewed, would not, nor could not, be paid out of the estate of the Widow M. van Niekerk; which estate had, after her demise, in the month of September, 1829, been placed under sequestration, of which estate the plaintiff himself had been thereafter appointed trustee, and framed a liquidation account on the 20th July, 1830. That the plaintiff had no ground for restitution *ex condictione indebiti;* and that the plaintiff had suffered no damage through the non-registration of the bond of 14th September, 1813, because no general mortgage on the estate of the said Widow M. van Niekerk, of whatever date, had been paid or received out of the said estate; the special and legal mortgages having absorbed all the assets of the estate.

The plaintiff's replication admitted all the facts in the plea, save that he had every opportunity of ascertaining from September, 1827, &c. (*ut supra*), and said he was not barred from having his remedy against the defendant by any of the allegations therein contained, further, that a sum of 15,000*g*. from crops sold in the estate had been awarded to the oldest general mortgage.

Defendant rejoined generally.

Cloete, for plaintiff, put in bond, 14th Sept., 1813, and liquidation account of the estate of the deceased Van Niekerk and the widow, 14th Sept., 1830. And closed his case.

Hofmeyr, for defendant, led evidence in support of his plea.

Cloete, for plaintiff, quoted *Kotzé vs. Meyer* (*7th Sept.*, 1830, *ante p.* 6); and first maintained, that the fact in this case of the principal debtor having only given a general mortgage instead of a special mortgage, as in Kotzé's case, did not affect the principle upon which that decision was given. (*Pothier on Contracts, p.* 3, *c.* 1, *art.* 6, § 2.) Secondly, he maintained that if the bond had been duly registered, a certain amount would have been awarded to it out of Van Niekerk's estate. Thirdly, that his claim, to the extent which would have been so awarded out of Van Niekerk's estate, was not barred by anything in the plea founded on the *novatio debiti* alleged to have been made.

Hofmeyr, for the defendant, maintained the contrary, and quoted *Pothier, p.* 2, *c.* 6, *p.* 242, *Eng. edit.*, 1806; *Voet* 12, 6, 15; *Grotius* 3, 30, § 10.

Cur. adv. vult.

1832. June 29. Aug. 13. — Meyer *vs.* Low.

Postea (13th August).—The Court gave judgment for the defendant, on the ground that the plaintiff had no right to a *condictio indebiti,* in consequence of the principles laid down in *Voet, ut supra cit.*, as to novation transaction and *res judicata* barring *condictio indebiti,* and also that he had renounced the *beneficium actionum cedendarum* by paying without objecting.

The Court were of opinion that the principle of the decision in the case of *Kotzé vs. Meyer* was sound, and applied to a general mortgage as well as to a special mortgage. WYLDE, C. J., *dubitante* on this last point.

BUYSKES AND OTHERS, TRUSTEES OF DU TOIT, *vs.* JOSEPH DE KOCK, JACOBUS J. SMUTS, AND M. DE KOCK.

Surety, having engaged to become such under special mortgage of certain property, not bound to execute surety bond without such mortgage. Right of action against such surety dependent upon the obligation as entered into by him.

Dec. 6. — Buyskes and Others, Trustees of Du Toit, *vs.* Joseph de Kock, Jacobus J. Smuts, and M. de Kock.

The defendant J. de Kock purchased the place Brouwers Kloof from the plaintiffs. The deed of purchase contained the following clause: "The payment shall be made in the manner following, to wit, 1,000 guilders in cash at the transfer of the place, and the remainder 29,000 guilders may be taken over on interest from different persons under mortgage of the said place."

De Kock at the same time delivered to the plaintiffs the following obligation, proved and admitted to have been signed by the defendants J. J. Smuts and M. de Kock:

"We, the undersigned, do bind ourselves as sureties and joint principal debtors for Mr. J. de Kock as purchaser of the place of Mr. P. du Toit, named Brouwer's Kloof, situated at Paardeberg, for the sum of thirty thousand guilders, under mortgage of said place.

"J. J. SMUTS,
"M. DE KOCK.

"Paardeberg, 17th November, 1830."

Plaintiffs brought the action against the three defendants, praying that they may be decreed to execute a mortgage bond or bonds in their favour for the price.

The defendant J. de Kock admitted his liability, and the other two defendants denied their liability to execute such bond or bonds.

Cloete, for the plaintiffs, maintained that the obligation No. 2 entitled plaintiffs to call on defendants to sign as sureties the mortgage bond or bonds which the first defendant, Joseph de Kock, is to pass for the price.

1832. Dec. 6.

Buyskes and Others, Trustees of Du Toit, *vs.* Joseph de Kock, Jacobus J. Smuts, and M. de Kock.

Brand, for the third defendant, maintained that the effect of this deed was to bind the defendant as a surety from the moment J. de Kock passed a bond or bonds for the price under mortgage of the place, and did not bind him to do that which plaintiffs now claimed * that he should be adjudged to do, namely, to bind himself as a surety in any other deed.

The Court gave judgment against the first defendant in terms of his admission, with costs; and judgment for the second and third defendants, with costs.

Cloete *vs.* Bergh.

Surety.—Eight sureties engaging in mutual guarantee, each for one eighth share, and two of the sureties becoming insolvent, the remaining six were held bound to each other in one sixth, notwithstanding the guarantee of one eighth.

In this case, Hoffman, with eight sureties, of whom the plaintiff and defendant were two, granted a bond to A. for £550, specially mortgaging a certain house, the sureties binding themselves *in solidum*, as co-principal debtors, and renouncing the *beneficium divisionis*.

1832. Dec. 31. 1833. Feb. 1.

Cloete *vs.* Bergh.

The Orphan Chamber became the holders of the bond.

Hoffman became insolvent.

After deducting the proceeds received from the sale of the special mortgages, a balance of £415 17s. remained due in respect of the bond.

Two of the eight sureties had become insolvent. The Orphan Chamber had become the administrator of the estate of two others of the sureties. The Orphan Chamber sued the plaintiff, and recovered from him £277 4s. 8d., being the whole amount of the debt, under deduction of £138 12s. 4d., being two sixths thereof, in respect of the liability of the estates of the sureties which were under the administration of the Orphan Chamber, for each one sixth, and plaintiff obtained cession of action from the Orphan Chamber. Founding on this cession of action, plaintiff claimed provisional sentence against defendant for the whole debt, which he had been condemned to pay, under deduction of one sixth, being plaintiff's own one sixth share as surety.

* *Cons. Van Oosterzee vs. McRae, q.q. Carfrae & Co.*, p. 3.

1832. Dec. 31. 1833. Feb. 1. — Cloete *vs.* Bergh.

Cloete maintained that the insolvency of the two sureties had increased the liability of the remaining six sureties from one eighth to one sixth, and quoted *Van der Linden, Instit., B.* 1, *ch.* 14, *sec.* 9, 10, *p.* 204, 212; *Voet,* 46, 1, 29.

Brand, contra, maintained that the defendant was only liable for three eighths, and not three sixths, in respect of the following clause in the bond: "The first appearer (Hoffman) promising to hold free and harmless his said sureties in this their engagement for the whole, and they, the sureties, guaranteeing each other in an eighth share thereof."

Cur. adv. vult.

Postea (1st February, 1833).—The Court unanimously gave provisional sentence as prayed, with costs, holding that the above clause, founded on by the defendant, does not take this case out of the operation of the rule laid down by *Voet,* 46, 1, 29; *Van Leeuwen, Cens. For.,* 4, 17, 24.

WATERMEYER, q.q., *vs.* THERON AND MEYRING.

A creditor on a notarial bond containing a general mortgage loses his right of preference on the debtor's estate by non-registration of the bond, and also releases thereby the debtor's surety from preferent claim.

Feb. 12. — Watermeyer, q.q., *vs.* Theron and Meyring.

In this case, the plaintiff claimed provisional sentence against the defendant on a bond, in which the defendant was a surety and co-principal debtor.

Cloete, for the defendant, pleaded that plaintiff, by not registering the bond, which was notarial, and contained a general mortgage of the estate of the principal debtor, had lost his preference on the estate of that debtor, and had only been ranked as a concurrent debtor, and consequently had obtained, instead of his whole debt, only that percentage which he now offered to allow to the defendant in deduction, and that by so destroying the effect of the mortgage, he had discharged the defendant. And referred to *Meyer vs. Low, June* 29, 1832 (*ante, p.* 8). *and Kotzé vs. Meyer,* 7*th September,* 1830 (*ante, p.* 6). *Vide Robertson vs. Onkruydt,* 12*th January,* 1842 (*post*).

Provisional sentence refused. Costs to remain costs in the principal case.

Steytler *vs.* Saunders.

Construction of undertaking.—When a surety is considered not to have bound himself for the amount of a penalty.

Provisional sentence was claimed on the following document: 1833. Feb. 19. Steytler *vs.* Saunders.

"29th October, 1832.

"Three months after date I accept to pay Mr. J. W. Horak, or his order, a sum of 2,153 rds., for value received in sheep, without any further notice being required, binding myself, if this note should not be discharged within ten days after it becomes due, then to pay 5 per cent. besides to the agent appointed by him for collecting the said amount.

"JOHN JOHNSTONE."

"I accept to pay the amount hereof as own debt.

"Accepted, payable in Cape Town.

"JOHN SAUNDERS."

The note was not paid within ten days after it became due. After the summons was served on him, Saunders tendered the capital, interest, and expenses of summons. Plaintiff refused to receive the amount tendered unless the 5 per cent. were also paid.

The Court held that Saunders had only bound himself for the debt simply, and not under the condition as to the 5 per cent.

Judgment for plaintiff in terms of defendant's tender. Plaintiff to pay costs of the day.

Eagar *vs.* Clarke and Trustees of Harris.

Guarantee, letter of, how far binding on guarantor.

In this case, the following facts were proved or admitted by the parties. Reeves & Mills bought goods from Messrs. Borradaile, Thompson, & Pillans for £450, to be paid by a bill at eight months from 6th October, 1832. Messrs. Borradaile, Thompson, & Pillans insisted that this bill should have another name on it than Reeves & Mills. Fairclough & Eagar, in consideration of a commission of two and a half per cent., accepted a bill drawn on them by Reeves & Mills, in favour of Messrs. Borradaile, Thompson, & Pillans, for £450. Before the bill became due, Reeves & Mills claimed certain goods from Fairclough & Eagar, in consequence of a certain transaction. Fairclough & Eagar refused to deliver the goods until Reeves & Mills should Dec. 5. Eagar *vs.* Clarke and Trustees of Harris.

1833. Dec. 5. — Eagar *vs.* Clarke and Trustees of Harris.

give them a guarantee for the due payment by Reeves & Mills of said bill. Reeves & Mills, in consequence, got the defendants, Clarke and Harris, to give the following letter of guarantee:

"Cape Town, March 29, 1833.

"Messrs. FAIRCLOUGH & EAGAR.

"GENTLEMEN,—We do hereby jointly and severally agree to become responsible for the due and punctual payment of your acceptance to Messrs. Reeves & Mills's draft in favour of Messrs. Borradaile, Thompson, & Pillans for £450, due the 6th June next, or for the payment of the same, should Mr. E. Eagar's departure from the Colony take place before the same shall fall due.

"THOMAS HARRIS.
"G. CLARKE."

Reeves & Mills gave this letter to Messrs. Fairclough & Eagar, who thereupon delivered up to them the goods above mentioned. Reeves & Mills had told Harris and Clarke that they wanted this letter in order to induce Fairclough & Eagar to give them up said goods. Messrs. Borradaile, Thompson, & Pillans had never asked for any guarantee of Fairclough & Eagar's acceptance, with which they were perfectly satisfied, and were ignorant that any such letter of guarantee had been given by Harris and Clarke. Reeves & Mills became insolvent before the bill became due, and Fairclough & Eagar paid it to Messrs. Borradaile, Thompson, & Pillans, and gave due notice of its dishonour to Clarke and Harris. Eagar, under an authority from that firm, now sued the defendants for repayment of the said sum of £450. After the action was commenced, Clarke surrendered his estate as insolvent; and as a trustee had not been appointed to his estate when the trial came on, the plaintiff did not then insist against him.

The counsel for the other defendants, the trustees of Harris, contended that, as soon as the bill had been paid by the acceptors, Fairclough & Eagar, to the payees, Messrs. Borradaile, Thompson, & Pillans, the guarantee became, *eo ipso*, discharged.

But the Court gave judgment for the plaintiff, with costs.

DU TOIT *vs.* VOS.

There were twenty-five sureties for 1,000*f. each, for a sum of* 25,000*f., which sum, after a payment in reduction by the principal debtor of* 5,000*f., and by eight of the sureties of* 8,000*f., became* 12,000*f. Plaintiff, a ninth surety,* *paid this balance, took cession of the bond, and brought action against defendant, a tenth surety, for one thirteenth share of the 12,000f., being one twenty-fifth of the 20,000f. unpaid by the principal debtor, and a proportion for four insolvent sureties. Defendant tendered one twenty-fifth of the 12,000f.* **Held**, *he was liable for one twenty-fifth of the 20,000f., but not, under the stipulations of the bond, liable for deficiency caused to plaintiff by the insolvency of the four sureties.*

On the 15th July, 1819, the plaintiff, the defendant, and twenty-three other persons executed a bond as sureties (*waarborgen*) for the behalf of the plaintiff and E. A. Buyskes, who were thereafter to bind themselves as sureties and co-principal debtors for 25,000f. for G. Buyskes, in favour of the Lombard Bank. This bond of the 16th July, 1819, was in these terms: "Who declared to bind and interpose themselves as sureties for the aforesaid sum of 25,000f. and the interest in favour of both of the hereinbeforementioned sureties, and that each of them only for and to the concurrence of a sum of 1,000f. to that effect, and under promise and undertaking, as they, the appearers, by these presents promise and undertake, each of them to satisfy and pay the said sum of 1,000f. of the said value, *or so much less as shall in the course of time appear to be as yet unpaid by the aforesaid principal debtor,* with the interest then due and payable upon the whole or the balance of the abovementioned capital sum in the course of time, *each of them in the proportion of their abovementioned shares,* and that upon the first demand to the aforementioned securities, E. Buyskes and J. F. du Toit, and as soon as both the lastmentioned sureties, Buyskes and Du Toit, &c., *shall in the course of time be called upon, in virtue of the suretyship, &c., either for the entire or partial payment of the abovementioned capital of* 25,000f., *and the interest to grow due thereon.*"

1834. Aug. 28. Du Toit *vs.* Vos.

The plaintiff and E. A. Buyskes ceded this bond to the Lombard Bank on the 31st December, 1819, and on the 11th January, 1820, the plaintiff and E. A. Buyskes, in a bond executed by them and G. Buyskes, bound themselves as sureties and co-principal debtors, for and with G. Buyskes, to the Lombard Bank, for the said sum of 25,000f. Thereafter, G. Buyskes, in discharge of the bond of 11th January, 1820, paid to the Bank, on or before the 15th July, 1826, 5,000f. Thereafter, between the 30th June, 1829, and 4th October, 1832, the Bank, in virtue of the bond of 16th July, 1819, which had been ceded to them as aforesaid, recovered 1,000f. from each of eight of the

1834. Aug. 28. — Du Toit *vs.* Vos.

twenty-five persons bound as sureties (*waarborgen*) in that bond, thus reducing the capital of the debt to 12,000*f.*, whereon the interest remained unpaid from the 1st January, 1832. Thereafter, the plaintiff, on 24th December, 1832, as one of the co-sureties in the bond of 11th January, 1820, was called on by the Bank to pay, and did pay, the said balance of the capital, being 12,000*f.*, with interest thereon from the 1st January, 1832, and obtained cession from the Bank of the two bonds of 11th January, 1820, and 16th July, 1819. Four of the twenty-five sureties in the last-mentioned bond had become insolvent. Plaintiff in this action claimed from the defendant 923*f.*, as being a thirteenth share of 12,000*f.*; maintaining that he was entitled to demand from defendant not merely a twenty-fifth share of the balance unpaid by the principal debtor, but so much more as, in consequence of the insolvency of the four sureties, plaintiff was unable to recover from them, provided that he did not demand more than 1,000*f.* in all from defendant. The defendant tendered 480*f.*, being a twenty-fifth share of the balance of 12,000*f.*, maintaining that in consequence of the Bank having been paid 8,000*f.* from eight of the sureties, he was liable for no more; but the Court held that the defendant was liable for one twenty-fifth share of the balance of the debt, viz., 20,000*f.*, which had not been paid by the principal debtor, and was not liable to make good to any extent the deficiency occasioned to plaintiff by the insolvency of the four sureties, and gave judgment for plaintiff accordingly, for 800*f.*, with interest from 1st January, 1832, and costs.

Colonial Government *vs.* Sandenberg, Executors of Matthiessen, and Jan W. Klerck.

Where a bond of suretyship for the proper discharge of duty by a Government officer ("that he shall *faithfully," &c.) did not bear the date of its execution.* **Held** *that the sureties were thereby entirely discharged from liability; it being impossible for the Court to fix any date at which liability could be held to have arisen.*

Sept. 3. — Colonial Government *vs.* Sandenberg, Executors of Matthiessen, and Jan W. Klerck.

This action was brought by Government against the executors of the late C. Matthiessen, and against W. J. Klerck, to recover from them the amount of a certain sum due by the late Van de Graaff, as Vendue-master of Stellenbosch, to Government, in respect of his said office, which sum could not be recovered by Government from his estate, which had been surrendered as insolvent,—in virtue of a bond alleged to have been executed by the said Matthiessen and Klerck, whereby they constituted themselves sureties *in solidum* on behalf of His Majesty's Government of this Colony, &c., and that the said H. van de Graaff shall faithfully perform the duties of his said employment; and thereby also bound themselves that in the event of the said Van de Graaff appearing to be in any wise deficient in his said duty, they should then compensate and pay unto the said Government, &c., &c., all and every damage which shall appear to have been occasioned unto the same through the neglect or other misconduct of the said Van de Graaff to the concurrence of 10,000 rds., and which security was thereby also covenanted to stand good until his last conclusive account shall have been delivered and appointed.

1834. Sept. 3.

Colonial Government *vs.* Sandenberg, Executors of Matthiessoo, and Jan W. Klerck.

In their plea, the first defendants admitted that they were the executors of Matthiessen; and all the defendants denied all and every allegation or matter of fact as by the said plaintiff alleged, and stated that they are not liable or bound in manner and form as by the declaration alleged.

At the trial, the defendants admitted that Van de Graaff was Vendue-master of Stellenbosch from 21st June, 1816, until his death, and that his estate was not surrendered until after his death.

The *Attorney-General* put in the bond of securityship alleged to be signed by Matthiessen and Klerck. The signatures were admitted by defendants. It was then agreed that counsel should first argue on the legal validity of the bond.

Brand, for the defendants, then objected that this bond had no date, and although bearing to have been passed "*before the witnesses hereinafter named*," no witnesses were thereinafter mentioned, nor had any persons signed it as witnesses. That it was not signed by Van de Graaff, although in it it was stated that "there also appeared H. van de Graaff, who promised fully to indemnify his said securities," &c.; and that although it commenced in these terms:

"This day, being the ————————

"Before me,

"H. P. Auret,

"Chief Assistant in the Colonial Secretary's Office,"

it was not signed by Mr. Auret, before whom as tabelled it was said to be executed. He quoted *Cod.* 4, 21, *l.* 17, and maintained that, in respect of all or any of those objections, the deed was incomplete, had never been duly executed by the defendants, and therefore was not binding on them.

1834. Sept. 3. — Colonial Government *vs.* Sandenberg, Executors of Matthiessen, and Jan W. Klerck.

The Court held that as the sureties bound themselves that Van de Graaff *shall* faithfully perform the duties of his said employment, they were not bound for anything that had happened before they executed the bond; and that as the bond was not dated, there was no evidence when it was executed, so that it might have been executed only the day before his death, in which case the sureties would not have been liable for anything done or omitted to be done by him before that day; and on this ground they held that the defendants were not liable for the sum claimed, and, without deciding any other point, gave judgment for defendants, with costs.

CLOETE *vs.* EKSTEEN.

Dec. 1.

A bond-surety, who, having paid the debt due by the principal debtor, had obtained cession of the bond from the creditor, cannot sue provisionally on a deed of indemnity by the defendant holding him, the surety, harmless in case of such payment generally for whatever sum he might have to pay; the payment being incapable of proof, without evidence extrinsic of the deed of indemnity, and this although the summons alleged a payment of a specific amount on account.

[Vol. I, p. 71.]

NEETHLING *vs.* HAMMAN.

Dec. 3.

Possession of a bond by one of two sureties with an acknowledgment by the creditor, endorsed on such bond, that he had received payment of the whole from this one, is not sufficient evidence of payment by such surety to entitle him to provisional sentence against his co-surety for the moiety.

[Vol. I, p. 71.]

WILLEMS *vs.* WIDOW SCHENDELER.

A was the debtor on a bond, and B, by a separate deed, became surety and a principal debtor. The condition of the bond was notice to the debtor before payment could be demanded. The separate deed was silent as to notice. B was proceeded against as co-principal debtor only. **HELD**, *that* *on that ground, without reference to his obligation as surety, he was equally entitled to notice with A, and provision refused accordingly.*

This was an action for provisional sentence brought by the plaintiff (the creditor in a bond, which required a certain notice to be given to the debtor before payment could be demanded from him) against a person who, in a separate deed, had bound himself as surety and co-principal debtor. (This latter deed contained no stipulation about notice.)

1835. Aug. 1. „ 6.

Willems *vs.* Wid. Schendeler.

The plaintiff proved that he had given the requisite notice to the principal, but no notice had been given to the surety.

Cloete, for defendant, contended that the surety was entitled to insist upon the same previous notice as the principal debtor, and quoted *Pothier on Obligations* § 371, 380, *and l.* 7, 19, *ff. De Exceptionibus.*

The *Attorney-General* maintained that the notice to the principal debtor completely put an end to the condition as to previous notice.

Cur. adv. vult.

Postea.—The Court held that, as the defendant was bound not only as a surety, but as a joint principal debtor, and as this action was brought against him solely in respect of his obligation as joint principal debtor, and not of his obligation as surety, he was entitled to the notice stipulated in the original bond to be given to the principal debtor, with whom defendant afterwards became bound as a joint principal debtor. The Court also held that intimation conveyed to defendant of legal proceedings having been taken against the original debtor, and the property mortgaged in the bond, was not equivalent to a notice to defendant to pay, and refused provisional sentence with costs.

Churchwardens of Uitenhage *vs.* Meyer and Barnard.

Where sureties bind themselves for the due performance of a contract by their principal, who fails so to perform it, it is no answer to an action against such sureties by the party with whom the principal contracted that the sureties, having never been themselves called upon by him to perform the contract, were not further liable.

The plaintiffs and C. F. Pohl had entered into an agreement, dated 20th March, 1821, whereby, *inter alia*, it was stipulated that Pohl should build a church at Uitenhage,

Aug. 25. „ 31.

Churchwardens of Uitenhage *vs.* Meyer and Barnard.

1835. Aug. 25. " 31.

Churchwardens of Uitenhage *vs.* Meyer and Barnard.

in consideration of a certain sum to be paid him by the plaintiffs, 18,000 rds. of which were to be paid at the signing of the agreement. Pohl also bound himself to complete and finish the building on or before the 20th March, 1823, and in the event of his failing so to do, to repay the said sum to the plaintiffs.

The defendants had, by a notarial deed, dated 8th March, 1821, bound themselves as sureties *in solidum* in favour of the plaintiffs for such sum of money as the said Pohl should receive at the signing of the contract between him and the plaintiffs, in the event of his becoming liable to repay the same.

On the 21st of March, 1821, when the contract was signed, the said sum of 18,000 rds. was paid by the plaintiffs to Pohl.

Disputes took place between the plaintiffs and Pohl, in consequence of which plaintiffs, on the 4th March, 1824, instituted an action for damages against Pohl before the late Court of Justice, in which action they alleged that Pohl had failed to finish the building before the 20th March, 1823, and on that ground claimed from him repayment of the 18,000 rds., which had been advanced to him.

In this action Pohl was condemned by the sentence of the said Court, dated 16th August, 1827, to repay to the plaintiffs the said sum of 18,000 rds., received by him as aforesaid.

Against this sentence Pohl noted an appeal to the then Court of Appeal, which appeal he subsequently, in January, 1831, abandoned.

Pohl became insolvent, and on the 1st September, 1831, surrendered his estate.

While the abovementioned action was pending between the plaintiffs and Pohl, the present defendants, on the 25th of November, 1824, instituted before the late Court of Justice an action against the present plaintiffs, whereby the said defendants claimed that the suretyship bond entered into by them as aforesaid should be annulled, and they released therefrom.

In this action, the plaintiffs and defendants entered into a transaction, by which they agreed to submit to the decision of the Court, on a joint memorial, the question as to the defendants' claim to be released from their said obligation as sureties for Pohl, and renounced the right of appealing from the decision of the Court on the said question. Whereupon the said Court of Justice, on the 22nd of September, 1827, gave judgment, and declared the said defendants to be bound and liable, by virtue of the said surety bond entered into by them on the 6th of March,

1821, to continue as sureties for C. F. Pohl, in favour and in behalf of the plaintiffs, until the said C. F. Pohl shall have fully complied with the sentence dated 16th August, 1827, as aforesaid, or to repay to the said plaintiffs such sum as the said Pohl, by a final decision in the said Court of Appeal shall be condemned to repay.

1835. Aug. 25. " 31.

Churchwardens of Uitenhage *vs.* Meyer and Barnard.

The present action was brought by the plaintiffs to recover from the defendants, in virtue of the said bond, and of the said sentences of the late Court of Justice, respectively dated 16th August and 22nd September, 1827, the balance of the said sum of 18,000 rds. still due to them, after deduction of the dividend thereon which they had received out of the insolvent estate of Pohl.

The defendants pleaded first the general issue.

2ndly. That by the said deed of suretyship, they bound themselves for the due performance of the contract entered into between the said C. F. Pohl and the plaintiffs, and the defendants say that they have never been required or called upon to comply with the said contract; wherefore they say that they are discharged from their liability under the said deed of suretyship.

3rdly. That having bound themselves as sureties for the said C. F. Pohl for the construction of a church at Uitenhage, the said C. F. Pohl did, on his part, comply with the tenor of his engagement, but that the plaintiffs did unlawfully obstruct the said C. F. Pohl in the performance of the said contract, and did without any just cause prevent the said C. F. Pohl from completing the said contract; by reason whereof the said defendants say that they are further discharged from their liability under the deed of suretyship.

The plaintiffs excepted that the defendants are not entitled to plead the second and third pleas, because the same have already been decided against the defendants by a sentence of the late Court of Justice, dated the 22nd day of September, 1827, and have become a *res judicata* between the said plaintiffs and the said defendants.

This day *Brand*, for the plaintiffs, argued in support of the exception of *res judicata.*

But the Court, without calling on the defendants, held that this sentence did not decide the question now at issue between the parties, and therefore could not be pleaded as founding the exception of *res judicata* in answer to the second and third pleas of the defendants, and overruled the exception with costs.

The Court held that the only question at issue between the parties, in the action between them in which the sentence of the 22nd day of September, 1827, was given, was whether

1835. Aug. 25. " 31. — Churchwardens of Uitenhage *vs.* Meyer and Barnard.

the present defendants were *at that time* entitled to be absolutely released from their suretyship; that the sentence merely decided that they were not entitled to be *so* released, but were to continue bound as sureties until a final judgment should be given in the action between the present plaintiffs and Pohl, then under appeal, but did not decide what was to be the nature, extent, or amount of the defendants' liabilities as sureties, or bar them from any ground of defence competent to them in their character of sureties, when any claim should be made against them by the plaintiffs, in consequence of Pohl's not satisfying the judgment against him after the appeal had been determined.

Postea.—At the trial of the case, the Court, after hearing *Cloete,* for the defendants, and without calling on the plaintiffs, decided that the defence taken in the second plea was unfounded in law, and could not be maintained.

Brand, for the plaintiffs, then maintained that the judgment of the late Court of Justice of the 16th August, 1827, obtained by the plaintiffs against Pohl, was a *res judicata* against the defendants to the extent and effect of ascertaining and fixing the amount of the liability incurred by them in consequence of Pohl's failure to perform the contract. But the Court, in respect of the authority of *Voet* 42, 1, 32, held that the said judgment against Pohl was not *res judicata, sed res inter alios acta,* in so far as the present defendauts were concerned.

After hearing the evidence for both parties, the Court ultimately, by consent, gave judgment for the plaintiffs for £1,338 15s., and costs.

Trustees of Du Toit *vs.* Executors of J. J. Smuts and M. de Kock.

Sureties for the payment of the purchase amount of a farm "and all that is attached by earth and nails," not liable for movables (e.s. fustage) sold at the same time with the farm.

Where the undertaking of suretyship mentioned 30,000*f. as such purchase amount, but the declarations of sale and purchase fixed it at* 23,510*f. (the difference being for the fustage), the sureties were held liable for the lesser amount only.*

Co-principal debtors (not having renounced the benefit of division) are liable in solidum, and not pro rata.

Sureties held liable in interest from the date of the obligation of the principal debtor, and not merely from the date of demand upon them; and a tender by defendants being only "a tempore litis contestatæ," was therefore held insufficient to carry costs.

The following were the facts of this case. J. J. de Kock entered into an agreement for the purchase of a farm from Mr. du Toit, of whose insolvent estate the plaintiffs had since been appointed trustees, and executed the following deed in favour of Du Toit:

1835. Aug. 27.

Trustees of Du Toit *vs.* Executors of J. J. Smuts and M. de Kock.

"I, the undersigned, acknowledge to have purchased from Mr. P. G. du Toit, D.'s son, his farm called Browers Kloof, situate at Paardeberg, with all that '*aard en nagel vast is*,' and in its length and extension as contained in the transfer made to said Du Toit, &c., &c., and such for the sum of 30,000 guilders, Cape valuation, the interest shall take effect on the 31st January, 1831; the place can be taken possession of on the 15th January, 1831. All profits and loss shall go for account of the seller until the day of its being taken over. The payment shall be in manner as follows: 1,000*f.* in cash at the transfer of the place, and the remaining 29,000*f.* can be taken over at interest by different persons under mortgage of the aforesaid place."

J. J. Smuts and M. de Kock, who have since died, and whose executors the defendants have since been appointed, executed the following obligation in favour of Du Toit:

"We, the undersigned, bind ourselves as sureties and co-principal debtors with Mr. J. de Kock, as the purchaser of the place of Mr. P. du Toit, called Browers Kloof, situated at Paardeberg, for the sum of 30,000*f.*, Indian valuation, under mortgage of the said place.

"J. J. SMUTS.
"M. DE KOCK.

"Paardeberg, 17th November, 1830."

On the 7th May, 1831, Du Toit and J. de Kock made the usual oaths for the ascertainment of the transfer duty on the above sale of Browers Kloof before the civil commissioner for Stellenbosch, to the following effect:

"I, J. de Kock, do solemnly, in the presence of the Almighty God, profess, testify, and declare that the sum of 30,000*f.*, which shall be paid by me to Petrus G. du Toit, D.'s son, as the purchase-money for certain part of the freehold farm called Browers Kloof, together with a piece of perpetual quitrent land, containing 416 morgen and 305½ square roods, situated at the Paardeberg, in this district, together with certain goods and movable property as mentioned in the annexed certificate of the field-cornet and

1835. Aug. 27.

Trustees of Du Toit *vs.* Executors of J. J. Smuts and M. de Kock.

witnesses, to me sold on the 17th November, 1830, is the full and entire sum of me required," &c., &c. The oath was sworn on the 7th May, 1831. The articles set forth in the certificate consisted of wine, brandy, casks, stills, &c., which were valued at 6,490*f*. This sum was deducted from the 30,000*f*., and the transfer duty was paid only on the balance of 23,510*f*. Thereafter, De Kock having refused to receive transfer, Du Toit obtained a judgment against De Kock, whereby he was condemned to receive transfer, to pass a mortgage bond for 29,000*f*., and to pay 1,000*f*. to Du Toit. J. de Kock thereupon, before receiving transfer, or complying with the above judgment, became insolvent; and the plaintiffs, after giving due notice to Smuts and M. de Kock, the sureties, obtained an order from the Court to sell the said landed property, Browers Kloof, for account of De Kock and his sureties; in virtue of which order, Browers Kloof was accordingly sold, and the net proceeds thereof were placed to the credit of De Kock and his sureties in the liquidation account of the insolvent estate of the said De Kock, which account has been confirmed by the Court.

After awarding the net proceeds of Browers Kloof to the plaintiffs in diminution of the said sum of 30,000*f*., a balance of £580 6s. 5½d., with the interest thereon, from the 5th October, 1833, remained due to the plaintiffs. For this balance the plaintiffs in this action sued the defendants, and prayed that in respect of their said suretyship obligation, they should be condemned jointly and severally to pay the same to them.

In their plea, the defendants pleaded that the real price which was agreed to be paid for Browers Kloof was not 30,000*f*., but only 23,510*f*., which last-mentioned sum is the whole amount for which the said Smuts and M. de Kock were ever liable as sureties; and that the true balance thereof which still remains due to the plaintiffs is not £580 6s. 5½d., but only £384 7s. 10½d., with the interest thereon only *a tempore litis contestæ*, and that they had tendered, and still tender, each to pay the plaintiffs the proportions of the said sum of £384 7s. 10½d., for which they are liable in law by the true construction of the terms of their said obligation, viz., each the sum of £192 3s. 11¼d., with interest as aforesaid, and costs to the time when said tender was made.

Cloete, for plaintiffs, maintained that by the deed of sale De Kock became indebted to Du Toit for 30,000*f*., and that by the deed of suretyship the defendants became liable as sureties for the whole of this debt of 30,000*f*., whether it was contracted for the price of the farm itself or of the farm and the fustage.

The *Attorney-General* and *De Wet*, for the defendants, maintained that the real effect of the suretyship deed was to bind the defendants as sureties for that which was the price of the farm, and not of movables sold with the farm, and that the defendants had been deceived by the deed of the purchaser and seller as to what was the real price of the farm, and that if the deed of suretyship were ambiguous, it must, according to the established principle of law, be construed in favour of the sureties. (*Van der Linden, Inst., p.* 211; *Voet*, 46, 1, 4.)

The Court held that the terms of the deed of suretyship only bound the defendants in so far as Mr. de Kock was legally bound by the deed of purchase signed by him, and not for anything for which he was liable by any contract or agreement not appearing *ex facie* of that deed. That by the deed of purchase, De Kock was bound for nothing more but for the price of the land of the place Browers Kloof, and all "*dat aard en nagel vast is*," and not for the price of any *movables* on and sold at the same time with the farm. That although the deed of purchase stipulated 30,000*f.* as the price of the land, yet that if De Kock could have proved that this was not the real price of the place, he would not have been liable for more than had been actually agreed on between him and Du Toit, and that the oaths taken by the seller and purchaser for the ascertainment of the transfer duty, which showed that a less sum than that inserted in the deed was the actual price, were sufficient evidence that such less sum was really the price paid for the farm.

The Court therefore held that it was proved that the price of the *place* as specified in the deed of purchase was truly 23,510*f.*, and that this, under deduction of that part of the price which had been already received by the plaintiffs, was all for which the defendants were liable under the deed of suretyship.

Defendants maintained that, although bound as joint or co (*mede*) principal debtors, yet as they had not expressly renounced the *beneficium divisionis*, they were only liable *pro rata*.

But the Court, on hearing *Cloete* for the plaintiffs, and the authority of *Pothier on Contracts*, § 408 and 416, found that the effect of the words co (*mede*) principal debtors was to render them liable *singuli in solidum*.

Defendants maintained they were only liable for interest on the sum now found to be due by them from the date of the demand made on them, and not from the 1st January, 1831, from which period the original debtor, De Kock, was liable.

1835. Aug. 27. — Trustees of Du Toit *vs.* Executors of J. J. Smuts and M. de Kock.

The Court held they were liable for interest from the 1st January, 1831. The Court held that the tender which had been made by defendants was insufficient, and that under the circumstances of the case they ought to pay costs.

Judgment for plaintiffs for £413 12s. 4½d., with interest from the 25th October, 1833, and costs.

Bell q.q. Colonial Government *vs.* McDonald & Breda.

What does not amount to such a satisfaction by or release of principal debtor as will discharge the surety.

1836. May 27. June 13. — Bell q.q. Colonial Government *vs.* McDonald and Breda.

The declaration in this case set forth that J. F. R., then Commissary of Vendues, by a bond dated 13th June, 1817, signed with his hand, acknowledged himself to be truly and lawfully indebted to the Colonial Government in the sum of 150,000*f.*, being for moneys advanced out of the Government chest to the said J. F. R., in his aforesaid capacity of Vendue Commissary, renounced therefore the exception of *non numeratæ pecuniæ*, and promised and undertook to pay to the said Government the said sum of 150,000*f.*, with the interest at 6 per cent., three months subsequent to notice having been given or received to that effect; or otherwise, the said sum of 150,000*f.* was to be repaid or accounted for at the demise of the said J. F. R., or, &c., &c.

In security of the said debt, R. then mortgaged a certain house in Cape Town belonging to him.

That the said defendants did, by the said bond, bind themselves *in solidum* as sureties for and co-principal debtors of the said sum of 150,000*f.* and interest, under express renunciation of the *beneficia ordinis divisionis et excussionis.*

That on the 4th April, 1824, the said J. F. R. died, without having satisfied or paid the said sum of 150,000*f.*, or any part thereof; but on the 30th May, 1826, C. A. Fitzroy and E. A. Buyskes, who were appointed joint Commissaries of Vendues at the death of the said J. F. R., paid to the Colonial Government the sum of 90,000*f.* on account of the said bond, passed by the said J. F. R., and secured by the said defendants, together with the interest on the said sum of 150,000*f.* up to the said 30th May, 1826, thereby leaving a balance of 20,000 rds., or £1,500, due upon the said bond, which said sum of 20,000 rds., or £1,500, and interest from the said 30th May, 1826, the said defendants, as sureties *in solidum* as aforesaid, are liable to pay and satisfy to the said plaintiffs. Wherefore, &c., &c.

In their plea, the defendants admitted the execution of the bond by R. and them, and his death, as alleged in the declaration; but they deny that any balance is due to the Colonial Government by the late J. F. R., or by them, the said defendants, upon the said bond, except a sum of 10,700 rds. 3 sk. 3 st., which the executors of the estate of the late J. F. R. have tendered to pay to the said Colonial Government, but which they have refused to accept, and which tender the said defendants now again make in Court.

And that the said bond, with the exception of the aforesaid sum of 10,700 rds. 3 sk. 3 st., at the demise of the said J. F. R., or thereabout, or at the giving over of the said Vendue Office to the successors of the said J. F. R., has been paid or accounted for to C. A. Fitzroy and E. A. Buyskes, who, as joint Commissaries of Vendues, have been appointed by the said Colonial Government as the successors to the said J. F. R. in the said Vendue Office.

And, as a further plea, the said defendants say that subsequent to such accounting as aforesaid, and after the said C. A. Fitzroy and E. A. Buyskes had succeeded the said J. F. R. as aforesaid, the Colonial Government hath allowed them, the said C. A. Fitzroy and E. A. Buyskes, to remain indebted to the said Colonial Government the amount of the said bond, and to take the amount thereof upon their own liability, and have also cancelled the said bond, and have allowed the mortgage thereby given to be destroyed and annulled, and have allowed it to pass out of the estate of the said J. F. R., and have thereby made a novation of debt, and have foreclosed themselves from giving a due and legal act of cession to the said defendants upon the mortgage specially pledged and mortgaged as aforesaid, whereby the said Colonial Government hath lost all right of action against the said defendants upon the said bond.

By the documentary evidence put in by the defendants, and admitted by the plaintiff; and by the evidence of E. A. Buyskes, who had been deputy Commissary of Vendues, and after R.'s death one of the joint Commissaries of Vendues, and of J. J. L. Smuts, formerly secretary of the Orphan Chamber, and of H. Tennant, chief clerk in the Orphan Department of the Master's Office, it was proved that besides the sum of 50,000 rds. lent to R. by Government, in respect of which he and the defendants had granted the bond now sued on, another sum of 30,000 rds. had also been advanced to him by Government as a temporary loan. That he died on the 5th April, 1824, and the administration of his estate devolved on, and was assumed and entered on by the Orphan Chamber. That on the 26th March, 1824, Buyskes had made up and transmitted to R. a rough calcu-

1836. May 27. June 13.

Bell q.q. Colonial Government *vs.* McDonald and Breda.

lation of the state of the affairs of the department, which showed that, in addition to the said two loans of 80,000 rds., he was liable to make good to the department 10,700 rds. 3 sk. 3 st., and had after R.'s death, and in 1824, discovered additional items with which R. was chargeable, amounting to about 3,000 rds., and that on finally winding up the affairs of the department, Buyskes had discovered that, at the time of R.'s death, the sums then actually due by and chargeable against R., in addition to the debt of 80,000 rds., amounted (including a sum charged as interest on 20,000 rds., part of the loan of 50,000 rds., from 1st April, 1824, to 31st May, 1826) to 20,933 rds. 7 sk. 3 st. That after R.'s death, the cash-book had been made up by Buyskes to the 1st May, 1826, from which it appeared that at that date the available assets and cash in the chest of the department amounted to 192,610 rds., and that no part of this sum of 192,610 rds. had afterwards been lost or turned out unavailable. That these assets were liable for claims to a large amount which the public had against the department; and that after giving R. credit for the said sum of 192,610 rds., and debiting him with the amount of the debts due to the public, and of the two loans from Government of 80,000 rds., there was a balance against him amounting to the said sum of 20,933 rds., 7 sk. 3 st. (including the before-mentioned interest). That the Vendue department continued to be managed by Buyskes, as Deputy Commissary, from R.'s death till the 24th April, when he and Col. Fitzroy were appointed joint Commissaries, and that they managed it until its abolition in 1828. That in the course of their management they applied the said sum of 192,610 rds. in the payment of the just claims which the public had against the department at the date of R.'s death, and, secondly, in the payment to Government of 30,000 rds., in discharge of the temporary loan to R. of 30,000 rds., and of 30,000 rds. in part payment of the 50,000 rds. due by him to Government by the bond now sued on. On the 28th May, 1825, the Secretary to Government wrote to the joint Commissaries of Vendues, desiring them to inform him whether the 30,000 rds. constituting the temporary Government loan to R. had been paid by them to the Orphan Chamber as part of Mr. R.'s estate, or whether it had been taken over as part of the balance of the Commissary of Vendues, and in the latter case desiring it to be repaid into the office of the Receiver-General.

The Commissaries, on the 20th June, 1825, replied to the above letter that the said sum of 30,000 rds. was still kept in the treasury of the Commissaries of Vendues for the same purpose as R. had appropriated it to,—namely, to be more

1836. May 27. June 13.

Bell q.q. Colonial Government vs. McDonald and Breda.

prepared for a punctual discharge of the amount of vendue rolls when due, defaulters in the payment of debts contracted at public sales being so numerous. They then stated certain reasons, in respect of which they maintained that, unless they were allowed to retain both the said sum of 30,000 rds., and also the 50,000 rds. which had been lent to R. on the bond, on the same terms on which he had held them, an alteration must be made in the mode of effecting sales and giving credit to the purchasers, which they apprehended would occasion a serious defalcation in the profits of the office to Government, which had hitherto been productive of so large a revenue; and on this ground prayed to be allowed to hold both the said sums of 30,000 rds. without interest, and of 50,000 rds. at interest *from the time that the same shall have been collected from the administration of R.;* and that, although regular steps had been taken, the debts contracted at public sales under the administration of R. had not been all settled, in consequence of which it had hitherto been impossible to ascertain the amount of losses sustained by him, and therefore they had not been able to make a settlement with the Orphan Chamber, as administering his estate.

In a letter dated 30th June, 1825, the Secretary to Government informed the Commissaries that the 30,000 rds. must be paid to the Treasury without delay, but that they were authorized to detain at interest such portion of the 50,000 rds. as they might absolutely require for the purposes stated by them, on giving sufficient security for the same. The Commissaries accordingly paid 30,000 rds. to the Treasury in discharge of the temporary loan to R.

On the 10th May, 1826, the Secretary to Government wrote to the joint Commissaries, informing them that the Lieut.-Governor had authorized a loan of 40,000 rds. to be made to them, should they require it, on finding security for the same, but at the same time directing them forthwith to pay to the Receiver-General "the sum of 50,000 rds. which was advanced to their predecessor by Government in 1817, with the interest due thereon."

On the 30th May, 1826, the Commissaries stated, in reply, "that besides the great number of sentences in favour of this office lodged at the Sequestrator's office since our appointment on the 24th April, 1824, as joint Commissaries of Vendues, and still unpaid, there is a large number unsettled in favour of this office under the administration of the late Commissary of Vendues, J. F. R., which, with the other claims this office has on the estate of the late J. F. R., altogether amount to about 20,000 rds., as far as is till this moment known, for the payment of which sum we have

1836. May 27. June 13. this day applied to the Orphan Chamber, as administering his estate.

Bell q.q. Colonial Government vs. McDonald and Breda. "That we have, in the mean time, paid to the Receiver-General the sum of 30,000 rds., in part payment of the capital advanced in 1817 to our predecessor, Mr. J. F. R.

"We beg humbly to request that His Honour the Lieut.-Governor may be graciously pleased to allow an indulgence in the payment of the remaining capital of 20,000 rds., *till we* have been able to recover the same from the Orphan Chamber, as administering the estate of J. F. R."

On the 7th June, 1826, the Secretary to Government informed the joint Commissaries that the Lieut.-Governor had granted their request in giving the indulgence sought as to the 20,000 rds., but that he did so on the supposition that they would take immediate steps for recovering the said arrears.

That on the 15th May, 1824, the Orphan Chamber, as administering the estate of R., had in due form given notice to all claimants on the estate of R. to lodge their claims, and that no claim had been lodged on the bond in question, or on any other ground, either by the Government or the joint Commissaries of Vendues against R.'s estate, before November, 1827, when the liquidation account of the estate was closed by the Orphan Chamber, notwithstanding that on the 25th January, 1826, the Orphan Chamber had written to the joint Commissaries of Vendues, urging them to furnish even a provisional account of the state of account between R. and the Vendue department, and requesting them to credit R. with any outstanding unliquidated sentences due on his account, *in order that the promptest measures may be taken for effecting payment thereof.*

That on the 15th May, 1827, the Orphan Chamber had again written to the joint Commissaries, complaining of no account or information, such as they had asked, having been furnished to them, and that in consequence they had been prevented from watching over the interest of the heirs of the estate; that therefore they held the estate of R., as Vendue Master, no longer responsible for unliquidated vendue bills existing at the time of his death; and that the Orphan Chamber would, in six weeks from that date, make out a general liquidation account of the estate, with the view of settling the shares due to the respective heirs.

That on the 6th November, 1827, Buyskes, as Commissary of Vendues, wrote a letter to the Orphan Chamber, informing them that the rough statement, dated 26th March, 1824, transmitted by him to R. was incomplete, and that the Commissaries had been prevented from making out the account of R.'s liabilities to the Vendue department by the delay of the Sequestrator's department, and requesting the Orphan Chamber to postpone making up the liquidation account of the estate until the Commissaries should be able to frame a complete account between the Vendue department and R., which they expected to be able to do immediately.

1836. May 27. June 13.

Bell q.q. Colonial Government *vs.* McDonald and Breda.

On the 7th November, 1827, the Secretary of the Orphan Chamber wrote to Buyskes, informing him that the Chamber declined postponing any longer the liquidation of the estate, and that they would debit the estate with the sum of 10,700 rds. 3 sk. 3 st., shown to be due by him by the statement of the 26th March, 1824.

On the 27th June, 1827, the landed property, which, in the bond now sued on, had been mortgaged to Government in security of the 50,000 rds., and which had been sold by the Orphan Chamber, was duly transferred to the purchaser.

On the 19th April, 1830, Buyskes, on the part of the late joint Commissaries of Vendues, wrote to the Orphan Chamber, enclosing an account of the claims of the Vendue department on the estate and heirs of R., showing the before-mentioned balance of 20,933 rds. 7 sk. 3 st., to be due, and calling for the immediate payment thereof with interest.

That, on the 25th September, 1830 (*vide Colonial Government vs. Fitzroy, 15th October*, 1830, *Vol.* 1, *p.* 492), the plaintiff, on the part of the Colonial Government, had sued Colonel Fitzroy as one of the joint Commissaries of Vendues for 20,000 rds., as the balance of the sum of 50,000 rds. due to Government by virtue of the bond in respect of which the defendants were sued, which had not been paid to Government by the joint Commissaries as above mentioned, and that the Court had found that Colonel Fitzroy was not liable for any part of the said sum of 20,000 rds. originally due by R., in respect that the Government had failed to prove any *laches* on the part of the joint Commissaries of Vendues to recover that sum from R.'s estate, or that the non-recovery of any part of that balance was owing to any neglect or fault of the joint Commissaries.

Brand, for the defendants, contended that the cash and assets stated in Mr. Buyskes' statement as being in the Vendue chest on the 26th March must be considered as applicable in the first instance to the discharge of the capital of the bond for 50,000 rds. and the other 30,000 rds. advanced by Government, and that as the amount of the cash and assets greatly exceeded the amount of this capital of 80,000 rds. advanced, the amount of the bond for 50,000 rds. now sued on must be held and taken to have

1836. May 27. June 13.

Bell q.q. Colonial Government *vs.* McDonald and Breda.

been completely accounted for to Government on the demise of Mr. R.; and consequently that as the defendants, as sureties in the bond, were not liable to account for deficiencies incurred without reference to the bond, the claim of the Government against the sureties became discharged on the death of Mr. R., and argued that, from the conduct both of Government and the successors of Mr. R., it was evident that the Government recognized this principle and acted under it.

He maintained that the Government had by their conduct, by construction, delegated the right to recover the debt to Buyskes and Fitzroy, and that their proceedings were such as to amount to a sufficient accounting by R. to them for the contents of the bond.

To show that the Government had admitted and made themselves parties to, and homologated the application of the amount of the bills and cash in the Vendue chest to the settlement of the bond for 50,000 rds., he referred to the account made up by Buyskes of the amount due by R.'s estate to the Government, and which account was afterwards founded on in the action instituted by the Government against Fitzroy and Buyskes.

2nd. He contended that the Government, by not filing their claim on the estate of R. before its liquidation and distribution among the heirs, had weakened their power of recovering the debt from the representatives of the principal debtor, and consequently had impaired the sureties' power of recovering against the principal debtor, if the sureties should now be made to pay the debt to the Government, and thereby discharged their claim against the sureties *pro tanto*, and quoted the cases of *Kotze vs. Meyer, 7th September*, 1830 (*ante, p.* 6); *Meyer vs. Low, 29th June*, 1832 (*ante, p.* 8); *Watermeyer vs. Theron & Meyring, 5th February*, 1833 (*ante, p.* 14); *Orphan Chamber vs. Breda, September*, 1832; *Leyser, Meditationes ad Pandectas, vol.* 7, *p.* 877. And maintained that as the extent to which the sureties' right of recourse had been impaired could not be ascertained until the heirs of R. were excussed, the plaintiff must first excuss the heirs.

3rd. He maintained that as 10,700 rds. were set apart by the Orphan Chamber out of the estate of R. to meet this claim of the Government, and the Government ought to have demanded and received payment of this reserved sum, a deduction corresponding to the interest of this sum ought to be made from the interest now claimed by Government.

The *Attorney-General* argued *contra*.

Cur. adv. vult.

Postea (13th June, 1836).—The Court gave judgment for the plaintiff, as prayed, with costs, upon cession of action to defendants against estate and representatives.

1836. May 27. June 13.

Bell q.q. Colonial Government *vs.* McDonald and Breda.

The Court held that the defendants had failed to show that the amount of the bond had ever been paid or accounted for to Government, or to R.'s successors on behalf of Government, and that nothing which the Government had done or omitted to do had destroyed or in any way impaired their right now to recover from the defendants, notwithstanding their being sureties as well as co-principal debtors, the amount of the bond.

VERMAAK *vs.* CLOETE.

It is no defence to a provisional claim on a bond against a surety and co-principal debtor who has renounced the beneficium divisionis et excussionis, that the creditor had made no claim on the estate of the debtor, who subsequently became insolvent, and was therefore unable to give cession of action; the debtor's estate being admittedly insufficient to have met any preferent claim that might have been made upon it.

Aug. 31.

Vermaak *vs.* Cloete.

In defence against a claim for provisional sentence on a bond by Hoffman in favour of plaintiff against defendant, one of two sureties bound as joint-principal debtors, and having renounced the *beneficia divisionis et excussionis*,

Cloete, for defendant, maintained, that as the estate of the principal debtor had been placed under sequestration in 1826, and had been wound up in 1829, without the plaintiff having made any claim on that estate, plaintiff could not now give defendant an effectual cession of action against the principal debtor, and therefore had lost his recourse against defendant. It was averred by plaintiff, and not denied by defendant, that the estate of Hoffman had been insufficient to pay the preferent creditors, and that nothing could have been obtained in payment of the bond sued on, even if a claim had been made on Hoffman's estate.

The Court repelled the defence and gave provisional sentence. [Same found, *vide Overbeek vs. Cloete, 31st August*, 1830, *Vol.* 1, *p.* 523.]

MENZIES, J., stated that his judgment was given without reference to whether anything might or might not have been recovered from Hoffman's estate, if a claim had been made in respect of this bond.

The Court refused provisional sentence in the case of the *Executors of Hoets vs. De Vos* (1st February, 1837), and

1836. Aug. 31. — Vermaak *vs.* Cloete.

left the plaintiff to his remedy in the principal action, in a nearly similar case, except that in the latter the principal debtor had been rehabilitated.

But *postea,* in the principal case (24th August and 8th September, 1837, *post,* p. 53), gave judgment for the plaintiff with costs.

In re the Partnership Estate of Wolff & Bartman.—Sureties of *vs.* Trustees of.

W. & B., partners in business as auctioneers, took out individual licences as auctioneers, and afterwards surrendered both partnership and private estates. Government was ranked preferently on the separate estate of B. for auction dues on sales held by him under his individual licence. The separate estate being insufficient, the Government claimed preference on the partnership estate. The trustee rejected the claim as not being for a partnership debt. The sureties for B.'s separate estate appealed to the Court, who upheld the decision of the trustee.

Nov. 22. — *In re* the Partnership Estate of Wolff and Bartman—Sureties of *vs.* Trustees of.

Wolff and Bartman had each separate licences granted to them individually as auctioneers, under the Ordinance No. 31, but they carried on this business as auctioneers in partnership, although in holding sales only one of them acted as auctioneer.

They became insolvent, and their joint and separate estates were placed under sequestration. The Colonial Government were ranked as preferent creditors on the separate estate of Bartman, for duties to Government in respect of sales held by Bartman as auctioneer, under the licence held by him individually. The separate estate of Bartman, not being sufficient to discharge those duties, the Government claimed to be ranked as preferent creditors for those duties in the joint or partnership estate of Wolff and Bartman. In the liquidation account, the trustee of the said joint estate rejected the claim, and refused to rank Government at all as creditors under that estate, on the ground that the debt claimed on was a private debt due by Bartman, and not a partnership debt.

Against this decision of the trustee, Bartman's sureties to Government for the duties, with which as auctioneer he should become chargeable to Government, appealed to the Court under the provisions of the 34th section of Ordinance No. 64.

The Court dismissed the appeal, with costs, holding that, under the Ordinance No. 31, the Government had no claim for auction duties against any person or estate except the person who, under the licence, held the sale as auctioneer, and his sureties, and his and their estates.

1836. Nov. 22.

In re the Partnership Estate of Wolff and Bartman—Sureties of *vs.* Trustees of.

Brand, for the trustees, then moved for and obtained confirmation of the distribution account.

[The Tacit Hypothecations Amendment Act, 5 of 1861, abolishes the hypothec of Government on estates of auctioneers from that date.]

Wolhuter *vs.* De Villiers and Others.

Sureties, action to compel performance of undertaking by.

Nov. 24. 1837. Feb. 7. „ 14.

Wolhuter *vs.* De Villiers and Others.

The declaration in this case set forth that the plaintiff was the creditor of one Hamman, who had surrendered his estate as insolvent, and that the defendants had been bound as sureties and co-principal debtors for and with Hamman for certain debts due by Hamman, and for which his place Klein Libertas was mortgaged, and that in consideration of the plaintiff's consenting that the said place should remain unsold, the defendants executed a written engagement, dated 28th February, 1829, whereby they bound themselves, so soon as the estate of the said Hamman should be liquidated by the Sequestrator, to pass and execute in favour of the plaintiff a first mortgage bond over the said place for 4,500 rds., being the amount of the debt due by Hamman to the plaintiff. That the estate of Hamman had long since been liquidated, and the defendants called on to execute the said bond, which they had refused to do. That a payment received by plaintiff from Hamman's estate had reduced plaintiff's debt to £187 2s. 9¾d. Wherefore he claimed that the defendants should be adjudged to execute in favour of the plaintiff a mortgage bond for £187 2s. 9¾d. over Klein Libertas, in terms of the said written engagement.

After hearing the counsel for the parties, the Court gave judgment for the plaintiff, as prayed, with costs.

Postea (7th February, 1837).—The plaintiff summoned the defendants to show cause why a decree of civil imprisonment should not be granted against all the defendants for non-performance of the judgment of the 24th November, 1836.

Defendants offered to pay the principal, but refused to pay interest or to grant any bond for it.

The case was postponed until the 14th instant.

1836. Nov. 24. 1837. Feb. 7. „ 14. — Wolhuter *vs.* De Villiers and Others.

(14th February, 1837).—The Court (KEKEWICH, J., absent) adjudged that the defendants were liable in the interest from the 10th of May, 1831, and gave decree of civil imprisonment as prayed, to be stayed for seven days.

ROGERSON, N.O., *vs.* MEYER AND BERNING.

Bartman, by bond, bound himself in a sum of £500, and M. and B. bound themselves as sureties for £250 each. B. was summoned individually for £250, without mention of M. in the summons. M. was separately summoned in the same way, without mention of B. The declaration was filed against both as if they had been co-defendants in one summons. Exception was taken to the declaration on the ground of variance, and sustained by the Court.

Joint sureties may be sued in one action: so may a principal debtor and sureties, even when they have renounced the benefit of excussion; or a principal debtor and sureties bound by separate deeds.

The exception "ineptæ cumulationis personarum," being a dilatory exception, must be pleaded initio litis, and is not, therefore, a ground of absolution from the instance.

Breach of condition of bond, what is a sufficient assignment of in a declaration.

An exception of insufficient assignment of breach of bond must also be pleaded initio litis.

Excussion of principal debtor, what is sufficient.

It is no bar to the commencement of action against the sureties by the creditor that there are still unrecovered assets of the principal debtor's insolvent estate, on which, when recovered, the creditor would have a right of preference.

Funds belonging to the principal debtor, but not within the jurisdiction of this Court, cannot be excussed, nor their non-excussion pleaded by sureties in defence.

The non-excussion of the principal debtor must be excepted initio litis before joining issue on the merits.

Sureties to the fisc for the collection of public revenue are not entitled to the beneficium excussionis, and, therefore, cannot plead the exception of non-excussion.

Fidejussores indemnitatis, who are not.

The creditor on a penal bond not bound to excuss principal debtor before proceeding against sureties.

A creditor is not required, in order to entitle him to recourse against sureties, to make demand on the principal debtor for payment of the debt when it becomes due, nor to give notice to the sureties of the debtor's default; nor are the sureties (not being entitled to the beneficium excussionis) discharged from their obligation where the creditor does not cause the bond to be immediately put in suit against the defaulting principal debtor, even though the sureties have thereby suffered loss, or though during such mora the principal debtor has become insolvent.

The words "shall and may" in legislative language are imperative, but the words "shall be lawful" in Ord. No. 31, *sect.* 5, *are discretionary.*

1837. May 23. Dec. 8.

Rogerson, N.O., *vs.* Meyer and Berning.

The declaration in this case set forth, *inter alia*, that the defendants, G. H. Meyer and B. C. Berning, were sued in an action of debt, and that they had, together with one J. A. Bartman, on the 1st January, 1834, made and entered into a certain bond or obligation in writing, and which said bond or obligation in writing was and is in the words and figures, or to the purport and effect following, that is to say,—the bond was then set forth *verbatim*, with the exception of the signatures, seals, and dates; and from its terms it appeared that in it Bartman had bound himself to the plaintiff in the penal sum of £500, and that the defendants had bound themselves as his sureties in the penal sum of £250 each, under certain conditions therein specified to be performed by Bartman.

The declaration further set forth the alleged breach of those conditions by Bartman.

In the summons served on Berning, he was individually, and without any mention of Meyer, commanded to pay to the plaintiff £250, "which he owes to the said R. Rogerson," &c., "upon and by virtue of a certain bond or obligation, in writing, bearing date the 1st of January, 1834, duly executed and signed by the said B. C. Berning, whereby he, the said B. C. Berning, bound himself in the penal sum of £250, to be paid to the said R. Rogerson, or his successor in his office, in case one J. A. Bartman should fail to perform certain conditions in the said bond or obligations mentioned," &c.

The summons served on Meyer was in *ipsissimis verbis*, except that Meyer's name was throughout inserted instead of Berning's.

The actions so commenced by these summonses had not been conjoined in any way, but the declaration was filed against both, as if they had been sued as co-defendants in one summons.

No other instance is known to be on record in which two sureties bound in the same deed were sued by separate and

1837. May 23. Dec. 8.

Rogerson, N.O., *vs.* Meyer and Berning.

distinct summonses, applicable to each alone, without any mention of the co-surety, and in which those sureties, thus separately sued in different summonses, were conjoined as defendants in one declaration.

The defendant Meyer did not except to the declaration, but filed a plea censuring it on the merits.

The defendant Berning excepted to the declaration as insufficient, and, as the causes of his exception, stated that the said declaration varies from the summons in the description of the bond or obligation in the said declaration mentioned, *and in the number of the defendants;* that although the defendants are sued as sureties who have not renounced the *beneficium ordinis seu excussionis,* it does not appear in and by the said declaration that the principal debtor is insolvent, and has been duly excussed, or even that he has been called upon for the debt alleged to be due; that the said bond or obligation, as set forth in the declaration, does not appear to have been duly executed; and also that the said declaration is in other respects uncertain, informal, and insufficient; and therefore prays that the same may be dismissed.

This day, *Musgrave,* for the defendant, in support of the exception, maintained that the bond must be considered, as therein set forth, as a several bond, to which the defendant Berning alone was party, and that as the bond set out in the declaration bore to be signed by two other persons as well as by defendant, there was a variance between the summons and the declaration in the description of the bond.

2ndly. That the defendant was in the summons sued individually, whereas in the declaration another defendant was joined, which is incompetent.

3rdly. That even if the summons had included both defendants, it would have been, and the declaration filed by the plaintiff is, informal and insufficient, inasmuch as it joins two defendants, who, if liable, are only liable in virtue of two distinct and several obligations, because it is not by law competent to join two defendants in such circumstances in one action.

4thly. That the declaration professed to set out the whole bond, whereas it omitted the signatures, seals, and dates affixed to the bond sued on, and therefore there was a variance between the declaration and that bond.

5thly. That although the defendant is sued (*Voet* 2, 13, *sec.* 1) as a surety who has not renounced the *beneficium ordinis seu excussionis,* the declaration does not set forth that the principal debtor is insolvent, and has been duly excussed.

The *Attorney-General,* for the plaintiff, maintained the contrary, and quoted *Maddox, Chancery Practice, vol.* 1, *p.* 39; *Pothier on Contracts, vol.* 1, *p.* 264.

The Court sustained the exception to the declaration solely on the ground of the variance between it and the summons, viz.: that from the description given in the summons of the cause of action, the bond on which the defendant was sued must be held to be a bond to which the defendant was the only party, and in which he was bound as principal debtor, whereas the bond set out in the declaration is stated to be executed by one Bartman as principal, and by the defendant and one Meyer as sureties. The Court held that the description in the summons could not be held to apply to the bond described in the declaration, and therefore that there was such a variance as rendered the pleadings defective. The Court gave no judgment whatever on any of the other points of exception taken by the defendant.

Exception allowed, with costs.

Thereafter the plaintiff discontinued the above actions against both defendants, and on the 13th June took out a summons against both defendants, "commanding that justly and without any delay they do each of them render to Ralph Rogerson, Esq., Collector of Taxes in Cape Town, on behalf of the Colonial Government of our said Colony, the sum of £250, which they owe to and unjustly detain from the said R. Rogerson in such behalf as aforesaid, upon and by virtue of a certain bond, bearing date 1st January, 1834, duly executed and signed by one J. A. Bartman and the said G. H. Meyer and B. C. Berning, whereby they, the said G. H. Meyer and B. C. Berning, bound themselves, respectively, in the penal sum of £250," &c., &c.

The declaration thereafter filed in this case set forth that the plaintiff was duly appointed Collector of Taxes for Cape Town and the district thereof on the 1st January, 1828, and has continued to hold the said office from thence hitherto.

That the said defendants, together with one J. A. Bartman, on the 1st January, 1834, entered into a bond to the purport and effect following, that is to say:

"Know all men by these presents that I, J. A. Bartman, auctioneer, residing in Cape Town, Cape of Good Hope, am held and firmly bound to Ralph Rogerson, Esq., Collector of Taxes, in the penal sum of £500, and that we, his sureties, G. H. Meyer and B. C. Berning, are each of us held and firmly bound in the penal sum of £250 each, to be paid to the said R. Rogerson, Esq., Collector of Taxes in Cape Town, or his successor or successors in office; for which said several payments we bind ourselves, and each of us by

1837. May 23. Dec. 8.

Rogerson, N.O., *vs.* Meyer and Berning.

himself, one and every of our heirs, executors, and administrators, firmly by these presents. Sealed with our seals. Dated the 1st of January, 1834.

"The condition of the above-written obligation is such, that if the above bounden auctioneer, J. A. Bartman, shall render an exact and true account, in writing, of the total amount of the money bid at every sale by auction made by him and of the several lots which have been there sold, and the price thereof respectively, and for that purpose shall produce all books kept by him relative thereto on the first day of every month to the said R. Rogerson, Esq., Collector of Taxes in Cape Town, and shall within two months from the date of every sale respectively made by him in Cape Town, and within three months from the date of every sale respectively held by him in the country, make payment of all sums of money imposed by way of duty by an Ordinance bearing date the 7th day of December, 1827, and with which auctioneers are thereby made chargeable, then this obligation shall be void and of none effect, or else shall be and remain in full force and virtue.

"J. A. BARTMAN,
"G. N. MEYER,
"B. C. BERNING.

"Signed, sealed, and delivered in the presence of

"H. A. TRUTER,
"N. H. E. SMIT."

That the said J. A. Bartman had not duly performed the conditions of the said bond, for that on the first days of the months of June, July, August, September, and October, 1834, respectively, the said J. A. Bartman did not render to the said plaintiff an exact and true account in writing of the total amount of the money bid at every sale by auction made by him during the months preceding the said first days of the said months respectively, and of the several lots which had then been sold, and the price thereof respectively, and did not for that purpose produce to the said plaintiff all books kept by him relative thereto on the said first day of the said several months respectively, but therein wholly failed and made default.

That the said J. A. Bartman hath not made payment within two months from the date of every sale respectively made by him in Cape Town, and within three months from the date of every sale respectively made by him in the country, during the months of May, June, July, August, September, and October, 1834, respectively, of all sums of money imposed by way of duty by an Ordinance bearing date the 7th December, 1827, but therein wholly failed and made default, to the amount of £1,440 2s. 8d. 1837. May 23. Dec. 8. Rogerson, N.O., vs. Meyer and Berning.

That the said J. A. Bartman became insolvent, and surrendered his estate, on or about the 28th October, 1834, and the said plaintiff has proved his said claim against the said estate, and upon the final distribution of the assets thereof, the sum of £403 15s. 11¼d. was awarded to the said plaintiff upon his said claim, and the sum of £1,042 18s. 8¾d. is still due and owing to the said plaintiff.

And the said plaintiff has, before the commencement of this suit, requested each of the said defendants to pay the sum of £250, according to the tenor of the said bond and the condition, but which they have hitherto refused to do.

Wherefore the said plaintiff saith, that by reason of the said obligation and such breaches thereof as aforesaid, and by reason of the premises, an action hath accrued to him to have and demand from each of the said defendants the sum of £250, the penalty in the said bond, &c.

The defendants filed separate pleas, which, although different in terms, were in substance the same.

1. They admitted the execution of the bond by them and Bartman, and the plaintiff's appointment as Collector of Taxes, and denied the several other allegations in the said declaration contained, as well as the conclusion in law therein and thereby taken.

2. As a special plea, the defendants pleaded that the plaintiff is barred from claiming the sum now demanded by reason of *laches*, which the plaintiff hath committed in that behalf, for that the plaintiff failed to follow up the terms of the Ordinance bearing date the 7th December, 1827, intituled, &c., &c., and referred to in the said bond.

And that the plaintiff did not duly call on the said J. A. Bartman, during the months of May, June, July, August, September, and October, 1834, respectively, to comply with the said regulations, according to the true intent and meaning thereof, and of the said bond.

That the said plaintiff did, without there being sufficient cause to forbear the same, fail or neglect to cause the said bond to be put in suit against the said J. A. Bartman, upon the first or any other of the alleged defaults of the said J. A. Bartman, as the said plaintiff was in duty bound to do.

And that the said plaintiff failed to give notice to the said defendants of any default being made on the part of the said Bartman to comply with any part of the aforesaid regulations, as set forth in the said Ordinance and said bond.

And that by reason of the premises, and of such *laches* committed, the defendants were freed from their liability as contained in the said bond.

1837. May 23. Dec. 8.

Rogerson, N.O., vs. Meyer and Berning.

In his replications to the defendants' pleas, the plaintiff denied that he had failed to call on Bartman to render his accounts and to make payment, as alleged in the pleas, and maintained that, even if he had failed to do so, the defendants were not thereby discharged from their liability under the bond.

The plaintiff admitted all the other facts alleged in the pleas, but maintained that the defendants were not thereby discharged from their said liability.

Postea.—At the trial the *Attorney-General* for the plaintiff, put in,

1. The bond sued on.

2. The account filed by the plaintiff in the insolvent estate of Bartman.

3. All the proceedings in the sequestration of the said insolvent estate.

4. A letter by the plaintiff to Wolff & Bartman, dated 2nd September, 1834, informing them that unless they forwarded to his office their books and catalogues of sales for the months of May, June, July, and August, and paid the duties due for the months of April, May, and August, previous to the 15th instant, he would report to the Government their neglect.

5. Reply to above by Wolff & Bartman, dated 19th September, 1834, informing plaintiff that they had addressed a memorial to the Government requesting time.

6. Memorial by Wolff & Bartman to the Governor, requesting him, for the reasons therein stated, to allow them a period of four months for the payment of their arrears by instalments.

7. Reply thereto by the Secretary to Government, dated 30th September, 1834, informing memorialists that the prayer of their application could not be acceded to.

8. Letter by plaintiff to Wolff & Bartman, dated 6th October, 1834, informing them that, unless they made immediate payment of the amount due by them, they would be prosecuted for the same.

9. Letter by plaintiff to defendants, dated 29th November, 1834, informing them of Bartman's failure of the conditions of the bond, and requesting immediate payment to him, on account of Government, of £250, being the amount for which they had bound themselves to Government.

10. Letter by defendants to plaintiff, dated 20th January, 1836, as follows:

"As sureties for Mr. Bartman severally in a sum of £250, in favour of your department, we humbly conceive that, as acting for Government, you hold a legal preference upon his estate for the amount of sums collected and unaccounted for by Mr. Bartman.

"We therefore request that you will be pleased to note your claim for such preference against the distribution account of the estate, we being ready, as ultimately liable for any loss, to indemnify you against all costs on that account, as we merely wish the preference to be claimed as by Government.

"G. H. MEYER,
"B. C. BERNING."

11. A bond of indemnity, dated 27th July, 1836, by defendants to Government, for the costs mentioned in their letter of the 20th January, 1836.

The above documents were all admitted.

The *Attorney-General* called Ralph Rogerson, plaintiff, who deposed: In January, and every other month of 1834, up to the date of his insolvency, Bartman failed to render his accounts and to produce his books, in terms of Ordinance No. 31. I have since got from Bartman accounts of all the sales held by him in 1834. Some of those accounts I received from his trustees after he was sequestrated. These accounts are perfect. They are regular in point of form. Bartman did not make payment of the duties for any month within the time prescribed by the Ordinance. He was always in arrear. When he failed, he was indebted for the whole duties for the months of May, June, July, August, September, and October, 1834. The balance due at the time of his insolvency was for £1,440 2s. 8d. A dividend has since been paid. I dunned him incessantly for payment. I threatened him, verbally and by letter, to prosecute him for the amount; but I never spoke or wrote to the defendants, the sureties, on the subject, before his insolvency. The first notice I gave to defendants was by the letter dated the 29th November, 1834. I took no steps against the defendants previous to his surrender on the 28th October, 1834. I ascertained the amount of the duties in arrear by accounts of the sales furnished to me after his insolvency by him or his trustees. I had no other evidence of the amount of these arrears except those accounts.

Johannes Arnoldus Bartman.—I was an auctioneer. After my insolvency, my clerk made up the accounts of the sales for the months for which I was in arrear, and after I had compared them with the vendue rolls, and sworn to them, they were given in to the Collector. These accounts were correctly made out, and the sum, for which the Collector claimed on my estate is the true amount of the duties which I was in arrear to Government.

Plaintiff closed his case.

Defendants called Thomas Hall.—I am trustee in the estate of Bartman, and also of Wolff & Bartman. I have not yet rendered a final distribution account of his estate. There are assets to the amount of upwards of £278, being the amount of the compensation money for his slaves, still to be recovered and distributed among his creditors. The Collector of Taxes has a preferent claim on those assets. The Collector of Taxes claimed on his insolvent estate for £500, as the amount of the penalty on the bond now sued. But the Master struck it out.

The defendants closed their case.

Adjourned to the 7th September.

This day, the *Attorney-General,* for the plaintiff, argued that the evidence made out a breach of both the conditions of the bond, and, therefore, that the defendants had been rendered liable for the full amount of the penal sums; but he gave up any claim in respect of the breach committed by the not rendering the accounts of sales on the first day of each month, as true and correct accounts had ultimately been rendered; and maintained that by the auctioneer's default in the payment of the duties now in arrear within two months of the date of the sales, the defendants were liable, to the extent of the sums for which they were bound in the bond, for the duties so in arrear, and that nothing, which had been done or omitted to be done by the Collector of Taxes was sufficient to release the defendants to any extent, and quoted *Pothier, pp.* 259, 261, 267, 268; *Wapenaar Practyk, c.* 1, *p.* 7; *Cens. For., part* 2, *lib.* 1, § 14.

Cloete, for the defendant Meyer, quoted *Voet,* 45, 1, § 13, *in fine.* He admitted that the insolvency did not bar the plaintiff from his claim against defendants for any duties which had been due in respect of sales held in Cape Town within two, and in the country within three months, preceding it; but he maintained that, if the Collector failed on the very day when, or at least the next day after, the auctioneer made any default in the payment of the duties due in respect of any sale, to make a demand on the auctioneer and on the defendants for payment, and immediately thereafter to commence the excussion of the auctioneer, that he thereby released the defendants. He maintained that the bond did not contain any renunciation of the *beneficium excussionis,* and that even if it should be held that sureties bound for debts consisting of liquidated amounts to the fisc were not, in a question with the fisc, entitled to insist upon the *beneficium excussionis,* even although it had not been expressly renounced, still that this did not apply to *fidejussores indemnitatis,* which he contended the defendants in this case must be held to be, and quoted *Voet,* 46, 1, 38; 45, 1, 13.

Musgrave, for Berning, maintained that he was now entitled to insist on an absolution from the instance at the present stage of the proceedings, in respect of this action having been brought against both the sureties, instead of a separate action against each, and quoted *Harrison's Digest, p.* 530; *Chitty on Pleadings, p.* 47. He maintained that as there was no positive and distinct allegation that any particular sale or sales had been made, the breaches of the bond had not been sufficiently assigned, and quoted *Douglas Reports,* 214. That under the bond the defendants were entitled to the benefit of the excussion. And that the allegation in the declaration that there had been a final distribution in the auctioneer's estate had been disproved by the evidence of the trustee; consequently, that the auctioneer had not been excussed. That no matter what the amount of the sum still remaining unrecovered in the auctioneer's estate, although it might still leave a greater balance due by the auctioneer than the amount sued on, the plaintiff was not entitled to commence his action until that amount was recovered by him. He argued that as the auctioneer's books had not been produced, there had not been the best evidence of the amount of the duties in arrear, notwithstanding the evidence of the auctioneer. He quoted *Voet*, 46, 1, 8, as to the nature of the obligation of *fidejussores indemnitatis,* which he contended the defendants must be held to be. He maintained that the plaintiff was bound to have elected whether he would go against the auctioneer for the duties or for the penalty, and that having claimed for the duties on the auctioneer's estate, he could not now claim for the penalties against the sureties, even although he had also claimed for the penalty on the auctioneer's estate. He quoted *Voet,* 50, 8, 4, § 5, to show that defendants could not be sued, as was done in the declaration, for the *penalty*. He contended that the indulgence which had been given to the auctioneer had been injurious to the sureties, had placed them in a worse situation than they would have been in if, at the commencement of the default, due diligence had been used for the recovery of the duties from the auctioneer, or even if notice had been given to the sureties; and, therefore, that in equity they must be held to be released. (*Pothier on Obligation, art.* 2, *p.* 264, *vol.* 1.) He maintained that the Collector of Taxes had no sufficient cause to forbear putting the bond in suit on the first default.

Cur. adv. vult.

Postea (8th December, 1837).—The majority of the Court (MENZIES and KEKEWICH, JJ.) held that the defendants, being "*simul debitores ex eadem causa,*" might

1837. May 23. Dec. 8.

Rogerson, N.O., *vs.* Meyer and Berning.

be sued in one action. (*Vide Voet,* 2, 4, 15, *and* 2, 13, 14, confirmed by the practice of the late Court, and by that of this Court during the last ten years, of including in one action the principal debtor and his sureties, even when they had renounced the *beneficium excussionis,* and including in one action sureties bound only *pro parte virili,* and a principal debtor bound by one deed and his sureties bound in separate deeds. *Vide Van der Linden, Inst.,* 420.)

2nd. That even if an exception might have been taken *initio litis* on the ground of the *inepta cumulatio personarum,* still, as it is a dilatory exception, it could only be pleaded *initio litis* along with the plea on the merits, and could not now be made the ground of an absolution of the defendants from the instance (*vide Cod.,* 4, 19, *l.* 19; *Voet,* 44, 1, 4, *and* 6; *Van Leeuwen Cens. For., p.* 2, *l.* 1, *c.* 26, §§ 19 *and* 21; *Pothier on Obligations, p.* 2, *c.* 6, *art.* 2, § 3 (410); *Van der Linden, p.* 415); and that as the colonial law was clear on this subject, and had not been altered by any Ordinance or rule, no regard would be paid as to what was the rule or principle of the English law on the subject. (*Sed vide Tidd on Practice, vol.* 1, *p.* 10.)

3rd. That the breach of the condition of the bond was sufficiently set forth (assigned) in the declaration. (*Vide Stephen on Pleading,* 384, 398, 400, 402, 404, and *Archbold on Pleading, p.* 235.)

4th. That even although an exception might have been taken on this ground, *initio litis,* still that as it was of the nature of a dilatory exception, it could only be pleaded *in initio litis* along with the plea on the merits, and could not now be made the ground of an absolution of the defendants from the instance. (*Voet,* 2, 13, 3–44, 1, 4, *and* 6; *Cens. For.,* 2, 1, 24.)

5th. That the sole object of the Legislature in requiring the auctioneer to give security is to provide for the public security and the due collection of revenue, and that the object of the Legislature, in framing the 5th section of the Ord. No. 31, was not to lay down equitable rules for regulating the mutual rights and obligations of creditors and sureties, but to provide as much as possible that the creditor, the public, should not lose any part of the public revenue.

6th. That the substance of the provision of the bond, therefore, is that the defendants are absolutely bound to make payment to the plaintiff of the sums of £250 (subject, however, to be restricted to such lesser sum as they can show to be the real amount of plaintiff's damage), except only in the event of the auctioneer's having duly made payment to plaintiff of all the duties with which he has become chargeable, in which event alone they are discharged from the obligation.

7th. That the auctioneer, the principal debtor, had been sufficiently excussed before the sureties were sued. (*Vide Voet* 46, 1, 15, 17; *Cens. For.*, 4, 17, 19.)

8th. That although it has been proved that there are assets of the insolvent estate to the amount of £278 still to be recovered and distributed, to which, when recovered, the plaintiff will have a preferent claim, this circumstance was no bar to the plaintiff's commencing this action. (*Pothier on Obligation, p.* 2, § 6, *art.* 2, § 3, (410), *p.* 264 (411), *p.* 265.)

9th. And that as the greatest possible amount of this sum has been ascertained, and the plaintiff has agreed to hold it as already received by him, and to deduct its amount from his claim, which is equally beneficial to the defendants as if he had recovered it by excussion of the debtor, there is no ground in equity on which the defendant, even if entitled to claim the *beneficium excussionis*, and even if this sum had been subject to the decision of the Courts of this Colony, can in respect of it now oppose the plaintiff's claim, for the privilege of *beneficium excussionis* has no other foundation than equity.

10th. That this sum of £278 is one in respect of the non-recovery of which want of due excussion of the debtor cannot be pleaded, because the Courts of this Colony have no jurisdiction or control over it, nor any means or power of enforcing its payment, seeing that it consists entirely of the compensation money due to Bartman's estate for the emancipation of his slaves, and that the funds out of which it is to be paid are not within this Colony, and that its appropriation and distribution is under the exclusive jurisdiction and control of the Commissioners in England appointed by the statute. (*Voet*, 46, 1, 15; *Pothier ut supra*—412.)

11th. That the defendants are not entitled to plead and found on the *beneficium excussionis* at this stage of the proceedings (*post litis contestationem*), not having done so *initio litis* before they joined issue with the plaintiff on the merits. (*Voet* 46, 1, 15—44, 1, § 4, 6; *Cens. For.*, 2, *tit.* 1, *c.* 26, § 19; *Pothier, ut supra* (410); *Cod.* 8, *t.* 36, *l.* 12.)

12th. That the defendants are not entitled to plead the exception *non excussionis*, because they are sureties to the fisc for a collection of the public revenue, and are not sureties for an illiquid debt; or if the debt was originally illiquid, that it had been rendered liquid, and its exact amount had been ascertained in the proceedings under the sequestration before this action was brought (*Voet*, 46, 1, 8, *and* 16, *in fine*); and because they are not *fidejussores indemnitatis*, as is clear from the definition of *fidejussores*

1837. May 23. Dec. 8.

Rogerson, N.O., *vs.* Meyer and Berning.

indemnitatis given by *Voet*, 46, 1, 8, 14, 38. That there cannot be a greater fallacy than to hold that because equity will not suffer the creditor in a bond of the nature of that in question to recover more than the actual amount of the loss occasioned to him by the default of the debtor, that therefore he is under any obligation to excuss the debtor, or to do anything whatever to diminish the amount of such loss before he proceeds against the sureties. The very use of a bond like the present is to entitle the creditor, the instant the default is committed, to claim, to the extent of his actual loss, the penalty from the sureties, without being obliged to take any other steps for the reparation of that loss. The plaintiff need not have excussed the debtor before commencing the action, nor have set forth in his declaration that he had done so. He took proceedings for the excussion of the debtor at the request and for the benefit of, and under a guarantee from, the defendants, who acknowledged that he was under no legal obligation to do so. (*Vide* their letter 20th January, 1836.)

13th. That the proposition maintained by the defendants, that the plaintiff was bound to elect whether he would proceed against the auctioneer for the duties or for the penalty, and that having claimed for the duties on the auctioneer's estate he could not afterwards sue the sureties for the penalty, even to the amount of the balance which he had failed to recover from the auctioneer, is not supported by equity nor by any principle or rule of law.

14th. That the argument maintained by Berning's counsel, that the sum claimed from defendants is claimed in the declaration as being the penalty in the bond, and that sureties are not liable to be sued for any penalty, is founded altogether on an erroneous interpretation or construction of the word *pœna*, in the passage quoted from *Voet* 50, 8, 4. (See also *Voet* 50, 8, 1, *and* 46, 1, 12.)

15th. That neither the Ordinance No. 31 nor the bond contain any provision, condition, or stipulation requiring the plaintiff, in order to entitle himself to recover against the sureties, to have made any demand on the auctioneer for payment of the duties as they become due, nor to give any notice to the sureties of the auctioneer's default; and that by no law in force within the Colony is any creditor required, in order to entitle him to recourse against the sureties of any class or description, to make any such demand on the debtor, or give any such notice to the sureties; and, therefore, that the pleas of the defendants, that they are discharged from their obligation by reason of the *laches* committed by plaintiff in not making such demand on the auctioneer, and not giving them such notice before the insolvency of the auctioneer, are ill founded. Besides, there is sufficient proof in the evidence of Rogerson and the letters of the 2nd September and 6th October, 1834, that repeated demands were made on the auctioneer.

16th. That the defendants have failed to support by sufficient argument or authority their defence: that they are discharged from their obligation by reason of the *laches* of the plaintiff in having failed or neglected to put, or cause to be put, the bond in suit upon the first or any other of the alleged defaults of the auctioneer, *as he was in duty bound to do.*

17th. That, although the bond was not put in suit at the commencement of the auctioneer's default, nor until after he had become insolvent, the defendants have utterly failed to show that the plaintiff has thereby placed the defendants in a worse situation than they would otherwise have been in.

18th. That even although the defendants had been proved to have suffered loss in consequence of the plaintiff's failure to put the bond in suit previously to the insolvency, still this circumstance would not have discharged the defendants from their liability, because it has been shown that the defendants are neither *fidejussores indemnitatis* nor are entitled on any other ground to the *beneficium excussionis,* and by law no *mora* on the part of the creditor, although during such *mora* the debtor becomes insolvent, discharges sureties who are not entitled to the *beneficium excussionis.* (*Vide Voet,* 46, 1, 38.) *Pothier on Obligation, p.* 2, *c.* 6, *art.* 2, § 6 (414).

19th. That there is nothing in the bond which imposes any obligation on the creditor to use any diligence or to institute any proceedings against either the debtor or his sureties, other or at an earlier period than he would have been otherwise required to do by the law on this subject.

20th. That there is no provision in the Ordinance as to the time or manner of putting the bond in suit, the non-observance of which by the plaintiff has the effect of discharging the defendants from their liability.

21st. That the provisions in clause 5 of the Ordinance, that in case of the auctioneer's making default it shall be lawful for the Collector to cause the bond to be put in suit, unless he shall find sufficient cause to forbear the same, do not make it imperative on the Collector in every case to put the bond in suit in respect of every default which should be committed, and immediately on its being committed.

22nd. That, admitting that the words "shall and may" in legislative language are imperative, yet the words "shall be lawful" are not imperative. On the contrary, they always imply a discretionary power, except when coupled with

1837. May 23. Dec. 8.

Rogerson, N.O., vs. Meyer and Berning.

other provisions excluding all discretion. (*Vide* § 4, 5, 11, 15, 24, 25, 29, 42, 43, 44, 46, 47, 50, of the Charter, which illustrate this.) And that in the Ordinance, so far from the terms in the context excluding the discretionary power implied by the use of the words "shall be lawful," a discretionary power is expressly given to him in the context by the words "*unless he shall find sufficient cause to forbear the same.*"

23rd. That this discretionary power as to the time when the bond is to be put in suit is expressly given to the Collector alone. If he exercised that discretionary power in such a way as his superiors considered improper or dangerous, they, of course, might have removed him, but so long as he was permitted to remain in office, the discretion was with him.

24th. That even if the terms used in the Ordinance be stretched to the uttermost, all that it can be held to enact is "that in the event of the auctioneer failing duly to make the payments at the prescribed periods, the Collector *shall* put the bond in suit." There is no provision as to the particular period within which he must do so. It is not enacted that he shall *forthwith* put it in suit. A default did take place, and the Collector has put the bond in suit.

25th. That the postponing the immediate enforcement of the payment of duties which might be instantly demanded may often be an act of sound discretion for the interest of the public revenue, and *that interest* is the only one contemplated in the Ordinance.

26th. That even supposing that by the provisions of the Ordinance he ought to have put it in suit sooner, and is therefore liable to censure or removal, or to make good to Government any deficiency which may have been occasioned by his improper forbearance, there is nowhere to be found in the Ordinance any provision, that in consequence of his failure to do his duty, the sureties are to be thereby discharged. Considering the object of the Ordinance as declared in its preamble, nothing could be more preposterous than to make the misconduct of the Collector a ground for discharging the sureties, and thereby diminish the security of the public and endanger the due collection of the public revenue.

27th. That the defendants' letter of the 30th January, 1836, cuts down all pleas as to the hardship of the defendants' case, and clearly shows their own opinion to have been that they had no claim to the *beneficium excussionis*, and that the plaintiff had neither done nor omitted to do anything in respect of which they could claim, either on the ground of *laches* or on any other ground, to be discharged from their liability. That in it they expressly admit their liability.

28th. That the objection taken by the counsel of Berning is groundless, viz., that no sufficient evidence has been produced of the amount of the duties due by the auctioneer, because the best evidence of it has not been given. The best evidence which the nature of the case admitted of was given. The auctioneer swore positively and distinctly as to the amount of the duties due by him. The books were produced in court by the trustee, and the defendants might have cross-questioned him from the books if they doubted the truth of his evidence.

The judgment of the Court was therefore given (Wylde, C.J., *dissentiente*) for the plaintiff against the defendants for £250 each, with costs.

Executors of Hoets *vs.* De Vos.

Arend B. passed a bond, January, 1826, *for* £150 *to J. H., and as security ceded and delivered in pledge a bond dated January,* 1821, *by Andries B. for* £175, *with defendant as surety and co-principal debtor. Arend B. surrendered. The* £150 *bond was proved in his estate and the* £175 *bond, ceded by his trustees to H., was now proceeded on to the extent of* £150. *De V. claimed a discharge on the ground that the* £175 *bond had not been proved on the estate of Andries B., who had surrendered September,* 1826, *and been rehabilitated June,* 1833; *but the Court gave for plaintiff, with costs.*

The declaration in this case set forth that one Arend Brink was indebted to J. Hoets, now deceased (whose estate is administered by the plaintiffs), in a sum of £150, by a notarial bond bearing date the 13th January, 1826, and as a security for the payment of the said sum of £150 ceded and delivered over as a pledge a certain bond bearing date the 5th January, 1821, due to him by one Andries Brink for a sum of £175, and for which sum the defendant had, in the said last-mentioned bond, bound himself as surety and co-principal debtor.

That the said Arend Brink, having surrendered his estate as insolvent, the said notarial bond for £150, which was then still wholly unpaid and due by him to the said J. Hoets, was duly proved in his insolvent estate; and that the said notarial bond of £175, due by the said Andries Brink to the said Arend Brink, so pledged to the

1837. Aug. 24. Sept. 8.

Executors of Hoets *vs.* De Vos.

said J. Hoets as aforesaid, was duly ceded and awarded by the trustees of the said Arend Brink to the said J. Hoets as a security for the said sum of £150. Wherefore, the plaintiffs say that an action has now accrued to them in their aforesaid capacity, as holders by cession and delivery in pledge of the bond bearing date 5th January, 1821, to have and demand of and from the said defendant, as surety and co-principal debtor, payment of the said bond for £175 to the extent of £150, being the amount due by the said Arend Brink to the late J. Hoets by the said notarial bond of the 13th January, 1826, together with the interest due thereon.

The defendant, in his plea, admitted the several facts as alleged by the said plaintiffs in their said declaration, and that the said Hoets once had a right of action for the recovery of the said bond of £175, or part thereof, against the said defendant as a surety *in solidum* and co-principal debtor in the said bond, but alleged that the said J. Hoets lost his aforesaid action thereof, and that the said plaintiffs are barred from bringing the present action against the said defendant, because the said Andries Brink, the principal debtor in the said bond of £175, having surrendered his estate as insolvent on or about the 28th September, 1826, the said bond, of which the said J. Hoets then was and since has been the legal holder by mortgage, has not been proved by him or by any one else in the said insolvent estate of the said Andries Brink, and that the said Andries Brink has been rehabilitated by order of the Supreme Court on the 7th June, 1833, and discharged from all debts due by him prior to his said insolvency.

The plaintiffs, in their replication, admitted the facts alleged in the plea, but denied that they were thereby barred from recovering the sum now claimed by them.

This day, *Brand*, for the defendant, in support of the defence made in his plea referred to the case of *Kotze vs. Meyer*, 7*th September*, 1830, (*ante*, *p.* 6), and of *Villiers vs. Cauvin*, 15*th December*, 1829, and quoted *ff. l.* 129, *lib.* 50, *De Regulis Juris*, *Carpzovius Defin. For.*, *p.* 2, *Con.* 19, *Defin.* 10; *Brunneman. Consilia*, *Consilium* 86; *Lyzenius ad Pandectas*, 2*nd vol.*, *Spec.* 81, § 8; *Pothier de Cont. et Oblig.*, § 377; and *Van Zutpen Utrecht Consultatien*, *p.* 454, 3*rd part*, 104, where it was decided that a creditor having a surety who has renounced the *beneficia excussionis et divisionis*, and who has subsequently obtained a pledge from the debtor or another surety, may release the pledge or the subsequent surety, without thereby releasing the first surety, or affording him any ground of defence against the creditor suing him for the debt.

Cloete argued contra, and quoted *Pothier*, § 414, 521. 1837. Aug. 24. Sept. 8. Executors of Hoets *vs.* De Vos.

In the course of the argument, it was stated and admitted that Arend Brink, the creditor in Andries Brink's bond for £175, and the debtor to Hoets, was surety in a bond for 2,000 rds., granted by Andries Brink in favour of W. D. Hoffman. That Hoffman filed his claim on this bond on Andries Brink's estate, and that both he and Arend Brink, in respect of this claim, signed as consenting creditors to Andries Brink's deed of rehabilitation. But although a claim had been lodged on Andries Brink's estate by Arend Brink or by Hoets, in respect of the bond in question, and both or either of them had refused to consent to his rehabilitation, he would, notwithstanding, have had a majority in number and value in his favour.

Cur. adv. vult.

Postea (8th September, 1837).—The Court gave judgment for plaintiffs as prayed, with costs. *Vide Vermaak vs. Cloete, 31st August,* 1836 (*ante, p.* 35). *De Vos vs. Brink, 23rd November*, 1837 (*post*).

Norton *vs.* Satchwell.

The signature of a third party at the back of an otherwise unendorsed promissory note creates no liquid liability either as endorser or surety (*Vol.* 1, *p.* 77). 1840. Nov. 19.

Baard *vs.* De Villiers.

De V. was surety on a bond which stipulated that the principal debtor should be liable to pay on one month's notice. The principal debtor surrendered; and without notice having been given to the surety, he was now called upon to pay the amount of the bond. Held *that the insolvency of the principal debtor purified the condition as to notice, and made the bond immediately demandable from the surety.*

In this case the defendant was a surety and co-principal debtor. Nov. 30. Baard *vs.* De Villiers.

The bond stipulated that the principal debtor should be liable to pay on getting one month's notice.

The principal debtor's estate was placed under sequestration on 31st May, 1839.

Hiddingh objected that defendant had not received a month's notice to pay.

1840. Nov. 30. — Baard vs. De Villiers.

Brand answered: the insolvency of the principal debtor purified the condition as to the payment on one month's notice, and made the debt immediately demandable from the principal debtor; in other words, that the insolvency of principal debtor was equivalent to one month's notice having been given to principal debtor. That notice to the principal debtor is sufficient to make the surety and co-principal debtor liable to pay on the day when the principal debtor is rendered liable.

The Court held this answer sufficient, and gave provisional sentence as prayed.

F. R. L. Neethling *vs.* Executors of Neethling.

W. H. N. executed a bond in 1822, to which plaintiff was a surety. In 1835, and several times thereafter, J. H. N. promised to release plaintiff from the suretyship, but died before fulfilling his promise. Held *that plaintiff could recover from J. H. N.'s executors the amount of interest paid by plaintiff from 1832 to 1836, which amount J. H. N. had promised should be repaid, and also the costs paid by plaintiff when summoned for such interest; it appearing to the Court that, but for such promise of indemnity, the plaintiff would have taken other measures to relieve himself from the obligation of suretyship.*

1841. Aug. 24. — F. R. L. Neethling vs. Executors of Neethling.

This was an action to recover a sum of £73 18s. 3¾d., under the following circumstances.—It appeared that Mr. William H. Neethling had, in 1822, executed a mortgage bond on a loan place called "Kleinberg," in the district of Tulbagh, in favour of the Lombard Bank, for a sum of £300, to which his uncle, Mr. Frederick R. L. Neethling was one of the sureties. In 1835, another uncle, Mr. J. H. Neethling, promised to release his brother from this suretyship, but he had failed or neglected so to do; and in 1836, Mr. Frederick Neethling was summoned for £72, being four years' interest then due on the capital, and which, with £1 18s. 3¾d. for costs, he paid; Mr. J. H. Neethling still promising to repay those sums to him, and bear him harmless from any loss on account of his suretyship. In 1838, however, Mr. J. H. Neethling died; and the South African Association for the Administration and Settlement of Estates having been by will appointed executors of his estate, the defendant, as secretary to that Association was now sued for the amount.

Brand appeared for the plaintiff, and *De Wet* for the defendant.

1841. Aug. 24.

F. R. L. Neethling *vs.* Executors of Neethling.

Michael Christiaan Ackermann Neethling called.—I am son of plaintiff, who is brother of the deceased J. H. Neethling, whose executors are the defendants in this case. I remember, in 1835, my uncle was at Stellenbosch, and had a conversation in my presence with my father. This was about ten or twelve months before my father was summoned for the interest mentioned in the declaration. My uncle then came on a visit. No one was present with them except myself. My father said to my uncle that he was anxious to be discharged from his suretyship in the bond mentioned in the declaration. My uncle said that as soon as he came to town he would take over the bond from the Bank to himself and then discharge my father. In 1836, my father was summoned for the payment of the interest on the bond. I came to town by my father's desire and paid the interest to the Bank, and the costs to Poupart, the attorney, on the 19th August. I produce the receipt. I brought a message from my father to my uncle, asking him why he had not paid the bond at the Bank and discharged my father from the suretyship, as he had promised. This was a few days before the return day of the summons. I gave my uncle this message. He replied that my father need not be afraid; that he was ill at the time, but as soon as he got well he would go to the Bank, pay the bond, and relieve my father. This was in my uncle's house. He was sick, and he requested me in the meantime to go to Poupart's and pay the interest and costs with the money I had brought, and come back to him. I had brought money with me for the purpose. After paying Poupart and the Bank, I returned to my uncle and showed him the two receipts I have produced, which he looked at, and then desired me to take them to Mr. Advocate Hofmeyr, as he was unwell himself and unable to do business, and that he would settle it with Mr. Hofmeyr. I took the receipts to Mr. Hofmeyr, the same day. My uncle said he would both pay the interest and costs to my father, who should not lose a single farthing. I was not acquainted with the circumstances of William Neethling at that time. My father did not apply to the principal debtor, William Neethling, because my uncle was always assisting the debtor, and had promised to pay my father. He always assisted my uncle Henry and his children. Some time in 1837, by desire of William Neethling, I proposed to my uncle to sell the place "Kleinberg" by private sale. I wrote a letter to my uncle, and I produce his answer to me dated 25th August, 1837. My uncle was not to receive from my father any consideration

1841. Aug. 24.

F. R. L. Neethling vs. Executors of Neethling.

for taking over the bond and releasing him. I do not know the reason why my uncle made this promise. No more interest was paid after I paid it in 1836. The bond itself was afterwards paid off through my uncle. My uncle was not at Stellenbosch since 1835. I know of no coolness which took place between my father and my uncle before the death of the latter. I do not recollect speaking to my uncle about the bond after 1836, although I frequently saw him. Nor did I write to him on the subject, because I left the matter in the hands of Mr. Hofmeyr, to whom I wrote about it, I think more than twice,—three or four letters. I was my father's general agent. No claim was after 1836 made upon my father by the Bank for interest.

John Hendrik Hofmeyr.—I remember in 1836 the last witness calling on me and bringing to me the two receipts, and leaving them with me. I afterwards had several conversations with the deceased upon that subject. He always said he would himself take over the bond from the Bank and pay plaintiff the interest he had paid. Deceased had already taken over the other mortgage bonds on William Neethling's place, "Kleinberg," with the exception of this bond. He afterwards applied to me, as being the brother-in-law of William Neethling, to endeavour to persuade him to sell off his place by private sale, and settle with deceased, who was the holder of bonds due by him to a greater amount than the value of the place. Deceased desired me, if I got the place sold, and received the price, to pay the bond to the Bank, and to pay plaintiff the interest he had paid. I did not succeed in getting the place sold; but in September, William Neethling did sell "Kleinberg" by private sale for about £1,100. Deceased, when I advised him, as I repeatedly did, not to assist William Neethling any more, always replied, "I know I will be a great loser by William, but I will pay all his debts, and have a memorandum with the receipts, to show my executors what I have done for this branch of the family."

Plaintiff put in the bond referred to in the declaration, and paid by the purchaser of "Kleinberg." Receipt by the executors, to the purchaser, for the balance of the price of "Kleinberg," dated 16th August, 1836. Receipt from Bank to plaintiff, dated 19th August, 1836. Letter from deceased to Mr. C. A. Neethling, dated 26th August, 1837, speaking of the "liberality" he had shown towards his nephew William.

Plaintiff closed his case. It was admitted that on the 19th August, 1836, deceased had a balance of £536 at his credit with the Government Bank.

Defendant closed his case.

The Court held it unnecessary to call on *Brand*, plaintiff's counsel, to support his claim, and called on defendants' counsel, *De Wet*, who maintained that the promise of deceased to pay the interest was *nudum pactum*, without a consideration, and gave plaintiff no right of action to compel the performance of the promise. Quoted *Pothier on Contracts de Politicitatione, and Voet*, 50, 12, 1. 1841. Aug. 24. F. R. L. Neethling *vs.* Executors of Neethling.

The Court unanimously gave judgment for plaintiff as prayed, with costs, and interest from the date of the first demand on defendants, and held that it was proved that the deceased, J. H. Neethling, in 1835, and again on the 19th August, 1836, and again in his letter to Mr. C. A. Neethling, in 1837, undertook to free his brother, the plaintiff, from all his liability on the bond, both as to what he might in future have to pay and as to that which he had already been called on to pay, namely, the interest paid in 1836. That the circumstances of the case, as disclosed by the evidence, was sufficient to prove that, but for the undertaking of indemnity to the plaintiff on the part of the deceased, the plaintiff would have taken measures against William Neethling to free himself from his liability as surety in the bond, and to compel Mr. Neethling to repay the £73 15s. 7¾d. interest, which he paid for him in 1836; and that this forbearance was a sufficient consideration given by him to give him a right of action to compel the deceased to perform his undertaking to indemnify him, the plaintiff.

Mrs. Robertson, born Borcherds, *vs.* Onkruyt.

W. was the principal debtor and O. surety and co-principal debtor, on a notarial bond in favour of R., containing a general mortgage of W.'s estate. The bond was never registered by R. on the estate of W., who afterwards surrendered. **Held** *(confirming Watermeyer vs. Theron and Meyring, ante, p.* 14*), that R. by such non-registration, lost her right of preference on W.'s estate, and thus discharged defendant, his surety. Further, that the fact that W.'s estate had not yet been liquidated made no difference in the principle to be applied, and furnished no ground of distinction between this case and that confirmed, supra.*

In this case the *Attorney-General*, for the defendant, who was a surety and co-principal debtor for and with one Wentzel, now an insolvent, pleaded in defence against the claim for provisional sentence that as plaintiff, by not registering the bond, which was notarial, and contained a 1842. Jan. 12. Mrs. Robertson, born Borcherds, *vs.* Onkruyt.

1842. Jan. 12. — Mrs. Robertson, born Borcherds, vs. Onkruyt.

general mortgage of the estate of the principal debtor, had lost her preference on the estate of that debtor, and could only be ranked as a concurrent creditor, and obtain, instead of the whole debt, only that dividend, if any, which may be awarded to the concurrent creditors; and that by so destroying the effect of the mortgage, she had discharged the defendant. Quoted the case of *Watermeyer vs. Theron and Meyring, &c.*, (12th February, 1833, *ante, p.* 14).

Cloete, contra, maintained that the fact that the liquidation of Wentzel's estate had not yet been made, distinguished this case from that quoted; as here the amount of the injury which the defendant would suffer by the non-registry of the bond had not been ascertained, as it had in the case quoted, and would not be ascertained until Wentzel's estate was wound up, when, perhaps, it might turn out that he sustained no damage; and, therefore, that plaintiff was entitled now to provisional sentence in full, reserving to defendant, after the liquidation of Wentzel's estate, to recover back from plaintiff the amount of any loss which he could prove he had sustained by the non-registration of the bond.

The Court held that there was nothing in this case which could make any legal distinction between it and the case quoted; and refused the provisional sentence. Costs to remain costs in the principal case.

Westhuyzen *vs.* Pope and Devenish.

Where J. signed a note "q.q." for certain sheep stated in the body of the note "to have been purchased on account of F. C.," and defendants bound themselves as sureties: Held *that they bound themselves for J. personally, and not for F. C., and that J.'s excussion was therefore sufficient to found this action against the sureties, without requiring the excussion of F. C., who, from the terms of the note, could not have been sued upon it as a co-obligant. The Court, moreover, being of opinion from the evidence that J. had no right, under the power of attorney held by him from F. C., to bind him to a sale on credit: and that, although this would not, not having been published and made known, have freed F. C. from action for goods so bought by J. and recognized by F. C., there was no evidence in this case of any such recognition.*

1842. May 17. — Westhuyzen vs. Pope & Devenish.

Plaintiff sued defendants in Circuit Court of Beaufort, "for payment of £92 13s. 8¼d., upon and by virtue of a promissory note, originally amounting to £210 16s. 1½d., made and signed by one John Johnstone, q.q., as principal debtor, in favour of plaintiff, dated 5th June, 1839, for the due payment whereof the defendants interposed and bound themselves as securities, together with interest," &c. The summons also set forth that plaintiff had obtained judgment of the Circuit Court of Beaufort on the 28th April, 1840, which sentence having been carried into execution, the sheriff made a return therein of *nulla bona.* The defendants, in their plea, denied all the facts alleged by plaintiff, and joined issue thereon, and for a further plea, averred that they signed the said promissory note as security for the principal debtor, F. Collison, who has not been excussed by the plaintiff, and that they, the defendants, are not legally liable to pay the sum claimed.

Plaintiff put in the note, which was as follows:

"Nieuwveld, 5th June, 1839.

"Six months after date, I, John Johnstone, promise to pay Mr. N. B. van Westhuizen, or order, at his farm Van Oswegen Fontein, the sum of 2810 rds. 6 sk., for value received in the purchase of sheep at the sale, on account of Mr. Francis Collison.

"J. JOHNSTONE, q.q.

"As Sureties:
"C. POPE,
"J. G. DEVENISH."

It was admitted that this note was in the handwriting of Johnstone and signed by him.

Plaintiff called John Baird, the auctioneer by whom the sheep mentioned in the note had been sold, who stated: I produce the vendue roll, showing that all the notes were entered in Johnstone's name. I was not responsible for the price to the seller; if I had been, I would not have sold goods to the amount of 2,810 rds. to Johnstone on his own credit. I would have refused his bid too, unless he had first produced sufficient securities. It was perfectly well known that Johnstone was residing on Collison's farm as his overseer or manager. I am plaintiff's agent in this case. Plaintiff has never made any application to Mr. Collison for payment. I did not consider Johnstone was buying on his own acount, and when he signed the note as q.q. for Collison, it was just what I expected. I believe everybody at the sale was under the same impression with myself.

William Kinnear.—I was plaintiff's attorney in the case against Johnstone, and recovered judgment against him. Subsequent to the judgment, and when the writ of execution was in the hands of defendant, Pope was deputy sheriff. I received from Pope on the 23rd May, 1840, £60; on 15th

September, £40; and on 15th March, 1841, £4 5s. 8½d. He paid it on account of Johnstone, who said this was all the money he had in his hands belonging to Johnstone. I gave him receipts, copies of which I produce. Copies admitted put in and read.

On the application of the parties, the case was removed to the Supreme Court. The defendant Pope, after the removal, became insolvent, and the plaintiff for the present did not insist against him.

This day (17th May, 1842) the trial came on in the Supreme Court.

Plaintiff put in the power of attorney (executed by the constituted attorneys of Collison, having full power to that effect) appointing Johnstone to be Collison's attorney, and, as such, to manage certain of the affairs in the manner therein set forth, dated 22nd March, 1838, and closed his case.

Defendant called John Galloway, formerly clerk of Collison, the nature and effect of whose evidence will appear from the judgment of the Court.

The *Attorney-General*, for plaintiff, maintained that the terms in which the note was framed were such as to make Johnstone personally liable, whether he was or was not authorized by Collison to sign q.q. for him or as his agent, and quoted *Paley on Principal and Agent, p.* 378–386. And that as Johnstone was personally liable, the defendants, who signed as his sureties, are liable to pay on his failure and excussion, even although the note was so framed that if Johnstone had authority to bind Collison it was sufficient to bind Collison, without the plaintiff's being bound to excuss Collison first.

2ndly. That Johnstone had no authority to bind Collison in any such transaction by any instrument in any form. (*Voet,* 17, 1, 11.) That the defendants, before signing, ought to have inquired and ascertained whether Johnstone had such authority or not, and as he had no such authority they have rendered themselves liable to plaintiff, whom, by signing as sureties, they led to believe that Johnstone had such authority. (*Thomson on Bills, p.* 227.) He referred also to the case of *Elliot vs. Albertus,* in this Court, 22nd February, 1833. He contended that if the note had been worded as it is, and signed not J. Johnstone, q.q., but signed J. Johnstone, agent for Francis Collison, or attorney for Francis Collison, or per procuration of Francis Collison, Johnstone, by so doing, rendered himself liable to pay, although he had the power so to sign from Collison, and to render Collison liable also on proof of the authority given by him.

Musgrave, contra, maintained that Collison having originally authorized Johnstone to purchase farms and sheep for him on credit, and recognized and confirmed his acts in so doing by paying his drafts for the price, and continuing him in the management until long after the purchase from the plaintiff,—and Collison's attorneys having after his departure from the Colony recognized purchases made by Johnstone on credit, by paying drafts drawn by him at Beaufort on them at Cape Town, expressly on account of purchases of cattle made for Mr. Collison, at a few days after sight,—held him out to the public as the agent of Collison, authorized to make purchases for him on credit, and had thus rendered himself liable to third parties, and consequently to plaintiff, for purchases made by Johnstone on account of Collison on credit; and, therefore, Collison was rendered liable to plaintiff in the bill drawn by Johnstone, and sued on in this action; and in support of this he also founded on the fact, that Collison's attorney, Galloway, had recognized the purchase from plaintiff, by wishing to take and mark the sheep of Snyman's, which Johnstone alleged were those he had purchased from plaintiff, and this notwithstanding the limitation in the power of attorney of 22nd March, 1838, of which no notice had been given to the plaintiff or third parties, and who could only judge of the powers Johnstone had by the acts he had done under his original authority, and afterwards, and which had been recognized and confirmed both by Collison and by his lawful attorneys after his departure from the Colony; and quoted *Smith's Mercantile Law, 2nd edit., p.* 56, 93, &c., &c.; and that the plaintiff must be held to have taken the note sued on, not as his (Johnstone's) personal obligation, but as an act done by him as the known and accredited agent of Collison, and on account of the latter, and consequently that the defendants must be held to have signed, and to have been received by the plaintiff, as sureties for Collison, who alone was bound by the note. That the letters q.q. affixed to the signature of Johnstone were equivalent to his having added the words "per procuration," either at full length or abbreviated, or the word "agent" or "attorney" of, and that the mention of Collison in the end of the note was sufficient to designate him as the party for whom Johnstone, either per procuration or as his agent or attorney, signed; and referred to the case of *Barlow, Cashier of the York Buildings Company,* mentioned in *Paley,* quoted by *Attorney-General; Hayes vs. Hesselton, 2 Campbell Nisi Prius, p.* 604; 1 *Campbell,* 40, *Ld. Galway vs. Marther and Smith.*

The *Attorney-General,* in reply, quoted *Byles on Bills, p.* 18.
Cur. adv. vult.

1842. May 17. — Westhuyzen *vs.* Pope & Devenish.

JUDGMENT.—The Court is unanimously of opinion that the promissory note in question made by Johnstone, and which the defendants Devenish and Pope signed as sureties, has, in law, the effect of rendering Johnstone *personally* liable to the plaintiff for the amount of the note, in conformity with the principles on which were decided, in this Court, the cases of *Ross and others vs. Munting*, 5th February, 1833; *Elliot vs. Albertus*, 28th February, 1833; *McDonald vs. Albertus*, 25th June, 1833; and that the defendant and Pope, by signing the note, became sureties *for him*, and, therefore, as he has been excussed by the plaintiff, are liable to pay the plaintiff the balance which he has been unable to receive from Johnstone. If the note had been so framed that by it Johnstone had rendered not only himself, but also Collison, his constituent, personally liable for its amount to plaintiff, so that he and Collison were co-obligants, bound *singuli in solidum*, then the defendant and Pope, by signing it as sureties, would have been sureties for the co-obligants, and notwithstanding Johnstone's failure to pay, and his excussion, could not have been called upon to pay the note until Collison had been excussed, and this, even although the plaintiff, after the note had become due, had acted so as to discharge Collison from his liability. The Court are of opinion that an agent, who, acting under either an express or legally implied authority from his principal, purchases goods on credit, may make a promissory note for the price, signed by him in such terms as will have in law the effect of rendering not only himself but also his principal personally liable *in solidum* for the payment of the price. But the Court is of opinion that Johnstone had no authority so to bind Collison by any note signed by him, in whatever form it might have been drawn. The written power of attorney under which Johnstone acted expressly *prohibited him* from making purchases for Collison *on credit*. It is true, that as this power of attorney was never published or made known to the public, this prohibition contained in it would not have freed Collison from liability for the price of goods purchased in his name by Johnstone, if he, Collison, or his constituted attorneys in his absence, had so conducted themselves, by sanctioning and recognizing purchases made on credit by Johnstone, as to give the sellers legal grounds for inferring that Johnstone had authority from his principal to purchase for him on credit. The defendant has failed to show that any acts had been done, either by Collison or by his attorneys in his absence, which could afford to the plaintiff, even supposing they had come to his knowledge, legal grounds for inferring that Johnstone had authority from Collison to purchase goods for him and to bind him personally to *pay any note* for the price made payable *six months after date* within the district of Beaufort. 1842. May 17.

Westhuyzen *vs.* Pope & Devenish.

For 1st. The written authority granted by Collison to Johnstone in 1838 to purchase for him the farm of which he was afterwards the manager, and to some extent or other the sheep and cattle exposed at the time of the sale of the farm, has not been produced, and the Court have no ground for holding that it empowered Johnstone to make any purchases for Collison except *at the particular sale* to which that writing referred, much less that its terms were capable of being stretched so as to furnish legal grounds for *implying an authority* from Collison to Johnstone to purchase sheep *for him in June*, 1839, on credit, and on a note promising that the price would be paid by Johnstone, in the district of Beaufort, *six months after date.*

2ndly. Although Johnstone was the publicly recognized manager of Collison's farm in Beaufort, the appointment of a person as manager of a farm is no legal ground for implying an authority from the owner to the manager to purchase stock to the amount of £200 *on credit.*

3rdly. With regard to the alleged fact, that on two or more occasions previously to June, 1839, Johnstone had purchased sheep and cattle on credit, and had given in payment bills drawn either on Collison or his attorneys, payable in Cape Town *at a few days after sight*, and which were *duly paid* by Collison's attorneys in Cape Town, —the evidence as to these transactions is very meagre; it does not show the amount of the purchases so made. But supposing that they were of such a nature as that from them the law would have implied an authority from Collison to Johnstone to purchase the plaintiff's sheep in June, 1839, on credit obtained by giving in payment a bill drawn by him on Collison or his attorneys, payable by them in Cape Town a few days after sight, the Court is of opinion that the transaction which actually took place between the plaintiff and Johnstone in June, 1839, namely, the purchase of sheep on credit obtained by him by giving in payment a note promising that payment of the price would be made by Johnstone in the district of Beaufort six months after date, is a transaction in its nature *so very different from the former* that no authority to bind Collison by it can legally be implied from the fact that Johnstone had authority to purchase sheep for Collison on credit obtained by giving a bill on Collison or his attorneys, payable by them in Cape Town a few days after sight. The giving of such a bill, payable a few days after sight, must have had almost necessarily the effect of bringing the purchase made by Johnstone to the knowledge of Collison or his attorneys within *a few*

1842. May 17. Westhuyzen *vs.* Pope & Devenish.

days after it took place, and thus enable them to take care that the sheep so purchased were received and appropriated by Johnstone to his master's use; while by such a transaction as that which took place between Johnstone and plaintiff in June, 1839, Collison and his attorneys might be kept in utter ignorance of the purchase of the sheep for at least upwards of six months from its date. If Johnstone had authority to bind Collison by such a note, payable six months after date, he must have had power *to do so by a note payable two or three years after date.* This is sufficient to mark the distinction between purchases in respect of which bills drawn on Collison or his attorneys, payable a few days after sight, were given, and purchases in respect of which notes payable by Johnstone, in the district of Beaufort, *six months after date* were given. An implied authority which will impose a legal liability on A to pay the price of goods purchased on credit in his name by B, and which have never been received or made available to A, is not to be inferred on slight grounds. It will not do for the seller in such a case to allege that from acts done by B and recognized by A, and which had previously come to his knowledge, he *supposed* that A must or might have given authority to B to do some other acts; he must be able to prove that such acts had been done by B and recognized by A as were sufficient to induce a third person, acting with due prudence and discretion, *bonâ fide* to *believe* that B had actually authority from A to enter into the very transaction in respect of which he, the third party, attempts to impose a liability in his own favour on A. This is necessarily a jury question. The Court, acting as a jury, are of opinion that the plaintiff had no such grounds for believing that Johnstone had authority to render Collison personally liable for the price of sheep purchased by Johnstone in his name, under the circumstances which actually took place in this case. The Court can attach no weight to the circumstance that, in 1840, when Collison's attorney was taking over the stock from Johnstone, the former wished to mark as Collison's the sheep pointed out by Johnstone as those which he had purchased from the plaintiff. An assent, however positively expressed, by Collison himself to receive and pay for sheep tendered to him by Johnstone as having been purchased for him on *credit* cannot be legally construed either as an implied authority previously given to Johnstone to bind Collison for the price of sheep to be purchased in his name on credit, nor as such a *postera ratihabitio* of a purchase made by Johnstone, on credit, of sheep which he had converted to his own use, and never delivered or made in any way available to Collison, as would render Collison liable to the seller for the price of those sheep. As the defendant Devenish only bound himself, along with Pope, as a simple surety, without renunciation of the *beneficium divisionis,* he is, of course, only liable for one half of the amount which the plaintiff has failed to recover from Johnstone.

Judgment for plaintiff for £41 1s. 6d. and costs.

The Court left out of view entirely the payments made by Pope on account of Johnstone. It did not appear in what character or capacity or from what funds they were made. But as the defendant Devenish was not a party to them, nor, as far as appears, even cognizant of them, they could have no effect on the question as to *his* liability. (*Et vide Devenish vs. Johnstone, post, p.* 82).

IN RE KOTZÉ.—LOW *vs.* TRUSTEE AND CREDITORS OF KOTZE.

K. in 1812 (*being married in community to Mrs. K.*) *passed a bond in favour of L. for* £250. *Mrs. K. died in* 1818. *In* 1820, *before his second marriage, K. executed a deed of Kinderbewys, for the maternal portions of the children of the first marriage. Afterwards he surrendered. The trustee of his estate ranked the Kinderbewys preferent to L.'s bond. It was objected for L., that the bond in his favour, being an obligation on the first joint estate, the children of the first marriage were liable to him for* £125, *being half the bond, and to that extent should be ranked posterior to him. The Court held that whatever claim L. might have against the children by action, if so advised, he was not entitled in the distribution of K.'s estate to any preference under the bond and over the Kinderbewys, and confirmed the plan of distribution accordingly.*

In 1816, *Laubscher had passed a bond in favour of L. for which the insolvent K. had bound himself as surety and co-principal debtor. This bond was registered against Laubscher, but not against K., the name of the surety being merely mentioned in the registration of the principal debtor's obligation in the usual way. K.'s trustee ranked the proof as concurrent, on the ground that there was, in fact, no separate registration of the surety's obligation; and preferred the children for the amount of their maternal portion under the Kinderbewys. Low objected to the distribution, but the Court, after inquiring into the practice of the late Court of Justice, and of the mode of registry of the Deeds Office, upheld the distribution, holding that there must be a separate and distinct register in the name of the surety also.*

1843. Aug. 8. Nov. 23.

In re Kotzé.—Low *vs.* Trustee and Creditors of Kotzé.

In 1812, Kotzé, the insolvent, then being married in community of property with his first wife, executed a bond in favour of Low for £250. His first wife died in 1818. In 1820, Kotzé, before his second marriage, executed a *Kinderbewys* in favour of his children of the first marriage for their maternal inheritance. In the plan of distribution of Kotzé's insolvent estate, the trustee ranked this *Kinderbewys* as preferent to Low's bond. The *Attorney-General*, for Low, now objected to this demand that the plan of distribution should be amended by Low being ranked for £125, being half the amount of the said bond, in preference to the children of the first marriage, on the ground that in the bond for £250 was a debt due out of the joint estate of Kotzé and his first wife, at the time of her death; the children, as representing her, were liable to pay him £125, being the one half of said bond, and consequently, to that extent, must be ranked posterior to him in the insolvent estate of their father, to enable him (Low) thus to obtain payment of the £125 due by them to him.

After argument, the Court held that whatever claim Low may have against the children of Kotzé's first marriage, for one half of the bond which, at the death of their mother, was a debt due by the joint estate of her then surviving husband (which might depend on circumstances, and as to which the Court now expressed no opinion), Low was not entitled, in the distribution of Kotzé's estate, to claim preference to any extent in virtue of this bond over the *Kinderbewys* which had been executed by Kotzé in favour of the children of the first marriage; and, *quoad hoc*, confirmed the plan of distribution, leaving it to Low, if so advised, to institute an action against the children to recover from them the £125 now claimed by him.

Low had also proved a debt upon a notarial bond dated 10th September, 1816, passed by Laubscher, and for which the insolvent bound himself as surety and co-principal debtor, which bond was registered against Laubscher, but not against the insolvent, the name of the surety being merely mentioned in the registration against the principal debtor in the usual way.

The trustee ranked this proof as concurrent, and awarded in preference to the children of the insolvent the sum of £409, leaving the balance of the assets to be divided among the rest of the creditors.

1843. Aug. 8. Nov. 23.

In re Kotzé.—Low *vs.* Trustee and Creditors of Kotzé.

Low objected to his being ranked as a concurrent creditor, and claimed a preference on his bond, as constituting a general mortgage over the estate of the surety (the insolvent), which he maintained was sufficiently registered by the mention of the surety in the registration of the bond against the principal debtor.

Musgrave and *Brand* argued that this mode of registration was not, by the Proclamation of 15th May, 1805, § 7, sufficient registration as against the surety, and that in practice no preference had ever been given, or even claimed, on the ground that any bond so registered as to the surety constituted an effectual general mortgage over the estate of the surety.

The *Attorney-General*, for Low, maintained the contrary, and also maintained that whether the registration was made against the surety in the very form originally prescribed by the Proclamation or not, yet that it was registered in the form which had been invariably used from the publication of the Proclamation down to the present day, and had invariably been considered as good registration.

On this it was suggested by the Court that this case should stand over until, by a reference to Sir John Truter, late Chief Justice, Mr. Watermeyer, late Commissioner for winding up the office of Sequestrator, and the records of that office, it should be ascertained whether, in practice, any preference on any such bond, so registered as to the surety as constituting a valid general mortgage against the surety's estate, had ever been claimed or awarded upon the surety's estate.

Postea (23rd November, 1843).—*Brand*, for the trustee, produced a letter from Sir John Truter, stating that during his practice and tenure of office as Chief Justice, from 1797 to 1827, he had never known one case in which, under the above circumstances, such a preference had been awarded, or even claimed; also a letter from Mr. Watermeyer, certifying the same in so far as his experience went; and the records of the scheme of distribution in the first case which occurred in 1803, after the appointment of the Board of Sequestration and of the new Supreme Court of civil and criminal justice, in which a bond by a surety was lodged as a claim against an insolvent surrendered estate. In that case no preference was awarded to or even claimed on the bond as a general mortgage, and it was expressly ranked as a concurrent debt.

The *Attorney-General* stated that he was not prepared to show any case in which a contrary course had been followed.

1843. Aug. 8. Nov. 23.

In re Kotzé.—Low *vs.* Trustee and Creditors of Kotzé.

It was admitted that before the decision of the Court in the case of *Executors of Lombard, in re Pallas,* no bond having sureties bound in it was ever registered as to the sureties, except in the way in which the bond in question was registered.

It was also stated by Mr. Zastron, of the Registrar of Deeds Office, that in all cases in which sureties executed a separate surety bond in favour of a creditor in a previous principal debt duly registered, such surety bond was never registered separately as the debt of and under the name of the surety, but was merely entered on the margin of the folio in which the principal debt was registered.

The Court (WYLDE, C.J., and MENZIES, J.,—MUSGRAVE, J., having been counsel in the case, declined himself as Judge) were unanimously of opinion that the thing required to be done by the Proclamation of 15th May, 1805, was—not that the substance of the bond should be entered on a public record, but that the debtor should be registered as being the debtor in a certain sum by virtue of a certain bond, the substance of which was stated in the registry. That the entry in the register in the present case was one exclusively appropriated for registering the debts of the principal debtor, and describing the instrument in virtue of which he was indebted; and that no mere incidental mention in the description of the bond of the persons who were sureties to it (especially as this description did not state what kind of sureties they were, or to what extent they had bound themselves) could be considered as a registration, in terms of the Proclamation, of the debt or obligation to which they were liable by virtue of the bond. That a different construction of the Proclamation, by which such a registration should be deemed sufficient to constitute a valid general mortgage, would frustrate all the objects for which the registration of such mortgages is required. And therefore overruled the objection and confirmed the plan of distribution, with costs against Low.

The Court did not consider it necessary to give any decision as to the effect of a separate and subsequent surety bond, registered by a description of its substance being written on the margin of the page on which the debt of the principal debtor is registered; nor as to the effect of a bond by a surety passed before a notary and duly registered, containing a clause binding his property generally according to law, in constituting a general mortgage on the estate of such surety.

BRINK *vs.* LOW, WIDOW NIEKERK.

Where during the community the husband had entered into a suretyship, for which he became liable, and had afterwards surrendered his estate as insolvent, the Court held that the surviving widow, who had received nothing out of the joint estate at her husband's death, but had since her husband's death acquired property of her own, and had not duly repudiated or abandoned her interest in the joint estate at the time of her husband's death, could be sued for half the amount of the suretyship. (*Vol.* 1, *p.* 210.) 1842. Nov. 24.

VILLIERS *vs.* VILLIERS.

In November, 1839, *J. de V. passed a bond in favour of H. for* £300, *plaintiff, defendant, and a third party binding themselves as sureties and renouncing the benefits of excussion and division, but guaranteeing each other for a third. In January,* 1842, *H. obtained judgment against the principal debtor, but did not proceed to execution, the sureties consenting to delay by a writing dated February,* 1842. *On the same day the defendant undertook, in writing, individually and separately, to indemnify plaintiff if called upon by H. for the* £300. *In March,* 1842, *the principal debtor surrendered. H. ceded the bond for value to defendant's mother, to whom plaintiff paid his share,* £100, *and now brought action to receive this* £100 *under the indemnity, and got judgment accordingly.*

It is competent for a defendant at any time before judgment to refer the case to the oath of the plaintiff, whether the matter referred have been specially pleaded or not.

The following were the facts proved in this case :— 1843. May 30.

Jacob de Villiers, on 16th November, 1839, executed a bond in favour of Hiebner for £300, in which bond the plaintiff, the defendant, and a third party bound themselves *in solidum* as sureties and co-principal debtors, renouncing the benefits *ordinis, divisionis,* and *excussionis,* but guaranteeing each other each for one third. In January, 1842, Hiebner obtained a judgment against the principal debtor, but did not issue execution on the judgment, being applied to on behalf of the debtor to suspend it, and having got a writing signed by plaintiff, defendant, and the third surety, dated 11th February, 1842, by which they gave their consent that Hiebner might withdraw or suspend proceedings against the principal debtor, without prejudice to his claim against the sureties. Villiers *vs.* Villiers.

1843. May 30. — Villiers vs. Villiers.

On the same day the defendant gave the plaintiff the following writing:—

"I, the undersigned, J. P. de Villiers, do hereby undertake to indemnify J. A. de Villiers if A. Hiebner shall call upon him for the payment of the £300.

"J. P. DE VILLIERS.

"Stellenbosch, 11th February, 1842."

Hiebner swore that he believed that if at the time he had issued execution against the principal debtor, he would have been able from his effects to have received his whole debt. After this, on the 25th March, 1842, the principal debtor surrendered his estate. Hiebner ceded the bond for full value (*as he swore*) *to the defendant's mother*, to whom, when demanded, plaintiff paid his share, viz., £100. Plaintiff brought this action against defendant to recover the sum of £100, in respect of the indemnity granted by defendant to him on the 11th February, 1842.

After the writing had been admitted by the defendant to be genuine, the Court expressed their opinion that it was sufficient to entitle plaintiff to judgment as prayed. Whereupon the defendant referred the whole case to the oath of the plaintiff.

The *Attorney-General* (apparently without having had an opportunity of consulting with plaintiff) objected to the oath being referred to plaintiff under the plea of the general issue, on the ground of surprise to the plaintiff, as the plea of the general issue suggested no allegations of fraud, to prove which (he supposed) was the object of the reference.

The Court held that it was competent for the defendant at any time before judgment to refer the whole cause to the oath of the plaintiff, and thus by it to substantiate any matter which was a complete defence to him against the action, whether that matter had or had not been pleaded by him as a defence in his plea.

Plaintiff was then sworn, and deposed: The paper signed by defendant dated 11th February was given to me by him for the purpose of inducing me to consent to the delay of execution by Hiebner against the principal debtor, and as being an undertaking by him to hold me harmless for the £300 in the bond. He undertook, if I would consent to the delay, to pay the whole, and that I should not lose a farthing; but for his undertaking then I would not have consented to the delay. He undertook to pay the whole £300, for which he had signed as surety. It is not true that he merely undertook to guarantee me whatever I should be called on to pay beyond my one-third share.

The Court gave judgment for plaintiff as prayed, with costs.

VAN DER BYL *vs.* MUNNIK.

H. passed a bond in favour of De W., and M. bound herself as surety, renouncing the benefits of order and excussion, and the S. C. Velleianum. H. surrendered. The bond debt was proved in his estate, and in the liquidation account the full amount awarded. The trustee had the amount in his possession, but declined to pay it to the mandatory of De W., on account of De W.'s death having put an end to the mandate. The trustee became insolvent, without payment of the amount or assets sufficient to meet it. Action was now brought against the surety, who defended on the ground that the amount might have been recovered from the trustee. HELD, *that a surety having so renounced the benefits of order and excussion is not relieved by such omission on the part of the creditor, provided his right of action be not impaired.*

Porter, A.G., claimed provisional sentence against defendant on a notarial bond which he put in for £91 11s. 7½d., with interest, executed by defendant as surety for one Dirk W. Hertzog, in favour of Pieter De Wet, of whose estate plaintiff is executor dative, in which bond she bound herself *in solidum* as co-principal debtor, renouncing the *beneficia ordinis divisionis et excussionis*, and the *Senatus Consultum Velleianum.*

1845. Nov. 25.

Van der Byl *vs* Munnik.

Brand, for the defendant, opposed the motion, and stated that Hertzog's estate had been surrendered as insolvent, and a claim lodged in it, at the instance of De Wet, for the debt on the bond now sued on; that in the liquidation of that estate, the full amount of her debt had been awarded to De Wet in respect of the said bond, and that the money for this purpose had been in the hands of Buyskes, the trustee. That the plaintiff, who then held a power of attorney from De Wet, applied to the trustee for payment; but that the trustee, who had become aware of De Wet's death, refused to pay it to the plaintiff, on the ground that his mandate from De Wet had ceased in consequence of De Wet's death. That the defendant had subsequently applied to the trustee to know what had been done, and had been informed by him that the plaintiff had applied for, and been refused, and that the trustee continued to hold the money. That afterwards the plaintiff had been appointed executor dative of De Wet, but Buyskes, the trustee, had previously become insolvent; and that no part of the amount in his hands, which had been awarded in payment of De Wet's debt, could be recovered by the plaintiff from his estate.

1845. Nov. 25. — Van der Byl *vs.* Munnik.

These facts having been admitted by the plaintiff's counsel, *Brand*, for the defendant, maintained that as the amount of the debt had been realized in the estate of Hertzog, and set apart for the payment of the debt due to De Wet, and as De Wet or his representative might have obtained it from the trustee if they had duly applied for it soon enough, and as its loss had been occasioned by the insolvency of Buyskes, an event in no wise attributable to her, she was thereby relieved from her obligation as surety now to pay this debt.

But the Court, on the principle on which the cases of *Overbeek vs. Cloete*, 31st March, 1831 (*ante, p.* 7), *Vermaak vs. Cloete*, 30th August, 1836 (*ante, p.* 35), and *Executors of Hoets vs. De Vos*, 24th August, 1837 (*ante, p.* 53), had been decided,—held that a surety who was bound as co-principal debtor, and had renounced the *beneficia ordinis et excussionis*, must be considered absolutely as the proper debtor in the debt for payment of which he had so become surety, in every respect except that he was entitled to claim the *beneficium cedendarum actionum*, and was therefore not released by the creditor omitting to take any steps by which he might, at one time, have recovered his debt from the original debtor, although when he demands payment from the surety the debt could no longer be received from the estate of the debtor, provided the creditor had not done any act which destroyed or impaired his power of ceding to the surety his (the creditor's) right of action against the original debtor, such as but for this act of his it would have been when he made his demand on the surety.

The defendant in this case, when she was informed by the trustee that he had refused to pay the money he had in his hands on account of De Wet's debt, ought to have taken steps under the provisions of the Insolvent Ordinance to compel the trustee to lodge the money in the bank as directed.

The Court therefore repelled the defence against the provisional sentence, and by consent of defendant gave judgment for the plaintiff as prayed, with costs.

Roos *vs.* Coetzee.

Undertaking of Suretyship, construction of.

1846. Jan. 12. — Roos *vs.* Coetzee.

Porter, A.G., for the plaintiff, stated that Cilliers had left a certain sum to his grandson Kruger, and had appointed one Roussouw and the plaintiff his executors and guardians of his said minor grandson. Cilliers died, and his said executors entered on the administration of his estate and of that portion of it bequeathed to his said grandson.

Kruger, the father of the minor, applied to the said guardians for a loan of his portion during the minority of his said son, and as a security offered them the following written undertaking, signed by the defendant and one Van der Merwe:

"We, the undersigned, as executors and guardians of the minor child J. G. Kruger, hereby declare to be willing to have made over unto us his inheritance which has devolved on him from his late grandfather Jan Cilliers, now under the guardianship and administration of Messrs. P. Roussouw and Tieleman Roos, should they wish to do so, whilst we are willing to take upon us the trouble which they otherwise would have.

"Warm Bokkeveld, 1st Nov., 1816.

"F. van der MERWE.
"J. G. COETZEE."

The guardians having refused to take this security the following undertaking was then annexed to it:—

"P.S. We, the undersigned executors, bind ourselves as surety (*borg*) and co-principal debtors (*meede principaale schuldenaren*) for the inheritance of the aforesaid child J. C. Kruger, which will be received by his father.

"1st November, 1816.

"J. G. COETZEE.
"F. van der MERWE."

The father afterwards became insolvent, and on the son attaining majority, the plaintiff, as his guardian, paid him the amount of inheritance, for repayment of which he now claimed provisional sentence against the defendant.

Brand, for the defendant, admitted all the facts above stated, but maintained that as Van der Merwe was insolvent, defendant was entitled to the *beneficium divisionis*, and could only be sued for one half of the sum claimed.

Porter, *A.G.*, *contra*, maintained that the effect of the undertaking last quoted, whereby the defendant and Van der Merwe bound themselves not merely as surety, but as *co-principal debtors*, was equivalent to an express renunciation not merely of the benefit *divisionis* as regarded the principal debtor Kruger, but of the benefit *divisionis* as regarded each other.

The authorities quoted on both sides were, *Voet*, 46, 1, 24; *Pothier*, 1 *vol.*, *p.* 263, 269.

After some argument, the Court seemed to consider the question as attended with some doubt, and wished for further

1846. Jan. 12. — Roos vs. Coetzee.

argument on it, and time to consider of their judgment. But the plaintiff alleging that Van der Merwe was insolvent and the defendant that he was solvent,—and as the defendant admitted that if Van der Merwe was insolvent, he was liable to be called on to pay the whole debt,—it was agreed that the parties should have time to ascertain the fact, and liberty thereafter to make such further application to the Court as they should think fit. And by consent the case was ordered to stand over *sine die.*

Postea (11th June, 1846).—By consent judgment for plaintiff for one half of the sum claimed, and the case to stand over as to the other half and the costs, *sine die.*

Openshaw & Unna *vs.* Stoll.

Guarantee, letter of.

1846. Feb. 24. — Openshaw and Unna vs. Stoll.

The plaintiffs' declaration set forth that on the 31st January, 1845,—in consideration that the plaintiffs would deliver to the defendant, to be forwarded to one Claasen, certain goods sold by plaintiffs to Claasen, amounting to £161 11s. 8d.,—the defendant undertook and promised the plaintiffs to accept a bill for the said sum, drawn by Claasen in favour of the plaintiffs payable six months after date (31st January, 1845), and to be accountable to the plaintiffs for the said sum of £161 11s. 8d. That the plaintiffs, confiding in the said promise and undertaking of the defendant, delivered the said goods to the defendant; but the defendant did not accept the said bill for £161 11s. 8d., or pay the said amount to plaintiffs. That Claasen did not pay the said sum of £161 11s. 8d., or any part of it. That his estate was surrendered as insolvent on the 19th June, 1845; and there are not assets in his estate to pay the said sum of £161 11s. 8d., or any part thereof. That the term of payment of said bill has long since elapsed, and the defendant has therefore become liable to pay the amount thereof, but refuses so to do. Wherefore the plaintiffs prayed that he might be condemned to pay the said sum, with interest from 31st July, 1845.

The defendant pleaded the general issue.

Plaintiffs put in letter from Stoll to Claasen, dated 31st January, 1845 (admitted), containing the following passage:

"At 11 o'clock, however, Mr. Unna called and said that the inquiry he made at Mr. Billingsley's (by your recommendation) had not been replied to in such a manner that, with the credit already given to you he could execute this new order, upon which I quite drily answered him that this

1846. Feb. 24. Openshaw and Unna *vs.* Stoll.

was very correct, and that he had better keep his goods; but having at the same time bethought myself that you were wanting for these same goods, on my considering the sense of your last order. At first, therefore, I agreed to the acceptance demanded of me, on condition that you should acquiesce in it; and lastly, *to show that I was not afraid, and to keep up your credit, I agreed without condition to accept for you,* for the amount of the goods this day put out for you. Therefore, after you have found everything correct, draw on me to the order of these gentlemen the amount at six months, and I shall accept."

Jacobus Nicolaas Meeser.—I am clerk to the plaintiffs. I was so in January, 1845. I recollect a quantity of goods being there sold to Claasen at Swellendam. These goods were delivered at the defendant's store, to be forwarded by him to Claasen. The bill of parcels now shown me is in my handwriting; it is the bill of parcels of these goods which were delivered to defendant; it amounts to £161 11s. 8d. The bill now shown me was enclosed with the bill of parcels. The envelope was unsealed when delivered to defendant.

"Cape Town, 31st January, 1845.

£161 11s. 8d.

"Six months after date please pay to the order of Messrs. Openshaw & Unna £161 11s. 8d., for value received, which place to account of

"To Mr. J. A. Stoll."

(N.B.—It was admitted that this blank bill was found in the papers of Claasen's insolvent estate unsigned.)

Cross-examined: Plaintiffs proved a debt against Claasen's estate. I proved the debt by the affidavit now shown me, on the promissory note of Claasen, now shown me, for £166 10s. 8d. This included the £161 11s. 8d., the amount of the bill of parcels, and £4 19s. for goods sold to him in February.

It was admitted that Claasen's estate was surrendered on the 19th June, 1845; and that plaintiffs will receive no part of the debt of £161 11s. 8d. from the estate of Claasen.

The plaintiffs closed their case.

Defendant put in letter dated 4th April, 1845, from plaintiffs to Claasen (admitted):

"Sir,—Not having heard from you since we sent you the goods through Mr. Stoll, we beg to hand you enclosed acceptance for the same, as well as for those sent you by Mr. Cross in Swellendam, as per statement at foot.

1846. Feb. 24. Openshaw and Unna vs. Stoll.

"We at first desired Mr. Stoll to accept for you, not being as yet sufficiently acquainted with you to make business go quite smooth; but since you appear to object to it, we beg to hand you *acceptance for your signature alone.* Have the goodness to return the same per next post, since we wish to close our books.

"We are, Sirs,

"Yours truly,

"OPENSHAW & UNNA."

Also letter from plaintiffs to Claasen, dated 25th April, 1845 (admitted):

"SIR,—Yours of the 14th inst. came to hand. Mr. Stoll tendered us your six months' bill on condition of two months' renewal, which amounts to eight months.

"As we have written you before, your own letter shows that you only desired us to give you eight months' credit in that letter, which we did not accede to.

"You will therefore oblige us by returning your note signed at six months, since we consider the amount due six months after the day of invoice.

"We are, &c.,

"OPENSHAW & UNNA."

And closed his case.

Ebden, for plaintiffs, contended that defendant's letter of 31st January, 1845, proved that he had given an unqualified guarantee to plaintiffs for Claasen's debt of £161 11s. 8d.; and that—as the defendant had pleaded the general issue, and not that there had been a waiver, release, or discharge of the guarantee—plaintiff was not entitled to found as a defence on the letters of the 4th and 25th April, as proving that plaintiffs had relinquished the guarantee, supposing they contained evidence of that.

The Court, without calling on *Porter, A.G.*, gave judgment for the defendant, with costs.

The Court held that the only evidence of the nature of the undertaking entered into by defendant to plaintiffs was to be found in that passage of the defendant's letter of the 31st January to Claasen, in which he says, "and lastly to show that I was not afraid, and to keep up your credit, I agreed without condition to accept for you for the amount of the goods this day put out for you." That this did not amount to an absolute and unconditional guarantee to pay to plaintiffs the price of the goods when it became due, if not then paid by Claasen, but was merely an agreement to accept a bill in favour of plaintiffs, for the price, payable at six months from the 31st January. That even although under this agreement the plaintiffs might have been entitled to call on defendant to accept not merely a bill drawn on him by Claasen in their favour, but to accept a bill for the price drawn on him by plaintiffs, yet that this obligation on the part of the defendant was qualified by the necessarily implied condition that a bill should be presented by the plaintiffs to the defendant for his acceptance in due time. That the plaintiffs had not so presented any such bill to defendant, or called on him to accept it until after they had, at the request of Claasen (as was proved by their letter to Claasen of the 4th April) taken from Claasen a promissory note signed by himself alone, in payment of the price of the goods, after which they had no right to call on defendant for an acceptance in virtue of his agreement with them, to which they had by their own act put an end. Consequently, that the plaintiffs had failed to prove that defendant had ever given them any guarantee of the nature of that alleged in the declaration, or had refused to do anything which he was legally bound to do when the plaintiffs made their demand on him.

Ogilvie *vs.* Norton.

Surety Judicatum Solvi.

Rule of Court No. 8, attachment under.

The facts of this case were as follows: On the 22nd February, 1844, the plaintiff took out a writ of attachment under the provisions of the 8th rule of Court against H. L. Davies, on a debt due by him to plaintiff. On the same day Davies was arrested on this writ by the deputy sheriff of Albany, but was liberated in consequence of the defendant having executed a bail bond for Davies in favour of the sheriff for £100, which contained the usual condition, as follows:

"The condition of this obligation is such, that if the above bounden, H. L. Davies, do appear by his attorney before the Judge of the Circuit Court next to be holden in and for the Division of Albany on the first day of the said Court, &c., then and there to answer William Ogilvie, of Graham's Town, wherefore he hath not paid to the said W. Ogilvie the sum of £90, *and shall stand to, abide, and perform the judgment of the said Court thereon, or render himself to the prison of the said Court*, then this obligation to be void; otherwise to remain in full force."

1845. May 22. — Ogilvie *vs.* Norton. On the 8th of April, the cause *Ogilvie vs. Davies* was called on in the Circuit Court, and no appearance being made for the defendant, provisional sentence was duly given against him by *default* for £113, and costs.

On the 9th of April, the plaintiff duly sued out a writ of execution, on which thereafter, on the 4th July, the sheriff made the following return:

"I have not found the within-named defendant, nor have I found any of his goods or chattels whereof I could cause to be made the exigency of the said writ, or any part thereof."

In consequence of which the plaintiff brought an action in the Supreme Court against the defendant, and in his declaration set forth the above facts,—that the defendant had not performed the condition of the bond, but had wholly withdrawn himself from the Colony, and that the sheriff had, on the 1st May, 1844, duly ceded to plaintiff the said bail bond; and therefore prayed that the defendant might be condemned to pay to him the said sum of £100, being the amount of the bail bond, together with the costs of suit.

In his plea the defendant pleaded, 1st, the general issue; 2nd, as a special plea, that on the 8th April, 1844, when provisional claim was made against Davies before the Circuit Court, as in the declaration mentioned, Davies surrendered himself, and made appearance in Court, and that thus the condition of the bail bond had been to all intents and purposes complied with, and hath, therefore, as far as defendant is concerned, become void; 3rd, the defendant pleaded, that should the Court consider the said special plea, to be untenable, the plaintiff is not yet in a situation to demand from the defendant the forfeiture of the said bail bond, nor entitled to the claim made, because the plaintiff hath not yet proceeded against Davies in execution by way of civil imprisonment, which he ought first to do, for that the said Davies may surrender himself in prison; and thus the said bail bond, in as far as regards the defendant, is void.

In his replication, the plaintiff joined issue with the defendant on his first two pleas; and as to the third, replied that under the circumstances in his declaration stated, more especially the circumstance that Davies has wholly withdrawn himself from the Colony, the plaintiff is not obliged to sue out, by means of edict or other process, a decree of civil imprisonment against Davies, as a condition precedent to a demand from the defendant of the amount in the bail bond.

After the pleadings were closed, the cause was removed to the Circuit Court of Graham's Town, in which, at the trial thereof, it was proved that on the first day of the Circuit in April, 1844, there had been a communing between the plaintiff's attorney and Davies, respecting Davies's signing on the record a confession of judgment, but that in consequence of some question raised as to the amount of interest due, he did not do so; that Davies was in Court when the cause of Ogilvie *vs.* Davies was called on, but did not answer nor make appearance in any way; that Davies remained in Court the greater part of that day; that he publicly remained in Graham's Town until the 22nd or 23rd of April, and was afterwards seen in Cape Town on the 2nd or 3rd May, from whence it was believed that he had sailed, as he had said he would do, to Ichaboe.

The further hearing of this cause was then removed to the Supreme Court. This day (22nd May, 1845) the case came on for argument, when *Cloete,* for the plaintiff, maintained, in answer to the second plea,—1st, that the personal presence of Davies in the court-room, *was not in law an appearance in Court;* and 2ndly, that no proof of his appearance could now be received to contradict the record, which stated that Davies made default of appearance. As to the third plea, he quoted *P. Bort on Arrests, p.* 582, § 16, *Voet* 2, 8, § 16, to the effect that a surety *judicatum solvi* cannot claim the *beneficium ordinis vel excussionis* of the principal debtor, the defendant; also *Pothier on Contracts, vol.* 1, *p.* 263.

Brand, contra, did not support the first and second pleas, but maintained that plaintiff, having allowed Davies to remain at large between the day of the judgment and the 23rd April, when he might have obtained a writ against him, had not suffered any damage which he could call on defendant to make good.

Ebden followed on the same side, and maintained that the condition of the bail bond amounted to no more than the obligation *de judicio sisti;* and that the plaintiff might, after obtaining judgment, have proceeded in execution against Davies himself; and, lastly, contended that it was not proved that plaintiff had sustained damage to the extent of £100, by the non-surrender to prison of Davies's body, in execution of the judgment, plaintiff had against him.

The Court gave judgment for plaintiff as prayed, with costs.

Devenish vs. Johnstone.

In an action by D., a co-surety, against J., principal debtor, to recover the amount paid under such suretyship, the defence was that J., the principal debtor, had paid to P., the other co-surety, who happened also to be a deputy sheriff, the full amount of the obligation, in satisfaction of a judgment recovered by the creditor against J., the principal debtor, thereupon. This payment was, however, made to P. after he had already made a return of nulla bona, and it was moreover admitted that P. had never accounted to the creditor for the sum so received. Held: *that no such payment made to P., although he was deputy sheriff, after he had made a return of nulla bona on the writ and parted with the possession thereof by returning it to the High Sheriff's office, was sufficient to discharge J., the principal debtor's debt to the creditor, nor to have barred J. from suing D. as a co-surety, P. not having paid or accounted with the creditor. Wherefore D. was entitled to recover in this action accordingly.*

1847. June 11. — Devenish vs. Johnstone.

This action originated in the following facts. In 1839, the defendant, who represented himself as the agent of Mr. Collison, purchased sheep from one Westhuyzen, in payment of which he gave him a promissory note of the following tenor:

"Nieuwveld, 5th June, 1839.

"Six months after date, I, John Johnstone, promise to pay to Mr. N. B. van Westhuyzen, or order, at his farm Van Oswegen's Fontein, the sum of 2,810 rds. 6 sk., for value received in the purchase of sheep at the sale, on account of Mr. Francis Collison.

"J. JOHNSTONE, q.q.

"As Sureties:

"C. Pope,
"J. G. Devenish."

In April, 1840, Westhuyzen recovered a judgment in the Circuit Court of Beaufort against defendant for the amount of this note, the writ in execution of which was lodged with the said Pope, then deputy sheriff of Beaufort, who afterwards transmitted it to the High Sheriff with a return of *nulla bona* endorsed thereon. Both before and subsequently to the return of the writ, Pope paid several sums to Westhuyzen's attorney, which reduced the balance due on the note to £82 3s. In 1841, Westhuyzen brought an action in the Circuit Court at Beaufort against Pope and the present plaintiff, as sureties to the said note, for the said balance of £82 3s. In defence against this action they pleaded that they had signed the note as sureties for Francis Collison, who was the principal debtor in it, and that as he had not been excussed for the debt, they were not legally liable to pay the sum claimed.

The cause was removed to the Supreme Court. Pope, having surrendered his estate as insolvent, proceedings against him were abandoned. The Court found (*vide ante, p.* 60) that Johnstone had had no authority from Collison to bind him; that he, Johnstone, was personally the principal debtor in the note; and that Pope and the present plaintiff were bound as sureties for him; and, as Johnstone had been excussed, gave judgment against the present plaintiff for £41 1s. 6d., being his one half of the balance remaining due on the note, with interest and costs. The present action was brought by plaintiff to recover from Johnstone this sum, with interest; and also the amount which he had paid Westhuyzen for costs and the amount of his own costs in the said action.

In his plea, the defendant, *inter alia,* pleaded that while the writ in execution of Westhuyzen's judgment was still in the hands of Pope, the deputy sheriff,—to wit, on the 26th day of December, 1840, he had paid to the said deputy sheriff, the amount then due upon the said writ, together with the interest and expenses, and thus the promissory note mentioned in the declaration had been duly satisfied.

The plaintiff put in the writ in execution of the judgment obtained by Westhuyzen *vs.* Johnstone, dated 28th April, 1840, having the sheriff's return of *nulla bona* thereon, dated 2nd September, 1840.

The defendant admitted that plaintiff had paid to Westhuyzen on account of this judgment £41 1s. 6d., as principal and interest, and £37 8s. 2d., the amount of the costs found due to Westhuyzen; and also that plaintiff had paid £13 7s. 7d. for his own costs in that action.

The plaintiff closed his case.

The defendant put in a copy of a statement of account between Johnstone and Pope, dated 26th December, 1840, and signed by defendant and Pope. Plaintiff admitted that this copy is correct, and that the original was signed by defendant and by Pope. In this account, Pope was debited in favour of Johnstone in the sum of 7,684 rds. 2 sk. 4 st., as the price of sundry cattle, goods, and merchandise, and for

1847. June 11. — Devenish *vs.* Johnstone.

cash advanced, the items of which were set forth. The account then proceeded as follows:

	£	s.	d.	Rds.	sk.	st.
"Brought forward				7,684	2	4
"Capital and interest of Van der Westhuyzen sentence	£191	2	6½			
"Your outlay	1	15	4			
	£192	17	10½			
"Paid by me to you ...	216	0	0			
	£23	2	1½	307	2	4
Cr.				799	5	2
"Amount of your account				9,149	4	2
				1,157	7	0

"Beaufort, 26th December, 1840.

"The above balance of 1,157 rds. 7 sk. settled by Mr. Johnstone's bill at six months.

"JOHN JOHNSTONE,
"CHARLES POPE."

Defendant closed his case.

Ebden, for the defendant, maintained that this account proved that the defendant had paid to Pope, who was admitted to have been in 1840 deputy sheriff of Beaufort, the full amount due to Westhuyzen by Johnstone in respect of the judgment obtained by Westhuyzen against Johnstone on the bill for which plaintiff was surety, and his alleged payment of the half of the balance of which to Westhuyzen, under the judgment obtained by the latter against plaintiff, was the foundation of the present action; and, therefore, that as the defendant had already paid the full amount to the deputy sheriff in satisfaction of Westhuyzen's sentence against him, plaintiff could not call upon him again to pay the half which he had improperly paid to Westhuyzen, who had already been paid in full.

Porter, A.G., for the plaintiff, maintained that even if the document in question could be considered sufficient to prove that any payment had been made by defendant to Pope, as deputy sheriff, in satisfaction of the sentence against defendant,—which he denied,—no such payment made to Pope, although he was deputy sheriff, after the latter made a return of *nulla bona* on the writ, and parted with the possession of the writ by returning it to the High

Sheriff's office, was sufficient to discharge defendant's debt to Westhuyzen, or to have barred defendant from suing plaintiff as surety for the half of it, if, as was admitted, Pope had never paid or accounted for the money received by him from defendant to Westhuyzen; and consequently, notwithstanding any such payment, plaintiff was now entitled to receive from defendant the amount which Westhuyzen by his action had compelled plaintiff to pay as co-surety for Johnstone.—And so the Court found.

1847. June 11.

Devenish *vs.* Johnstone.

Ebden maintained that plaintiff could not demand from defendant the costs which the plaintiff had incurred in defending the action brought against him by Westhuyzen, because as judgment had in it been given against the plaintiff, his defence must be held to have been groundless, and he ought to have paid Westhuyzen, without putting him to the necessity of bringing an action.

The Court were satisfied, from the circumstances which had been disclosed in this case, that the defendant had induced plaintiff to sign the bill in favour of Westhuyzen, as co-surety, by falsely representing himself as authorized by Mr. Collison to sign the bill as his agent and for his account; and that if plaintiff had not been deceived by defendant into a belief that Collison, and not Johnstone, was the debtor in the bill, he would not have signed it; and that he was therefore eutitled to recover from defendant the costs which in consequence of that action he had been compelled to pay. And therefore gave judgment for plaintiff, as prayed, with costs.

NOURSE *vs.* STEYN, WIFE OF GRIFFITHS.

Feb. 25. ,, 27.

Provisional sentence granted against a wife married out of community, who had bound herself in solidum, as surety and co-principal debtor for her husband (since excussed by insolvency) on a bond, in which she renounced her beneficia, without production of evidence to show that the wife was not unduly influenced by her husband in the execution of the bond, which was ex facie entirely for her benefit, and without requiring the appointment of a curator ad litem to act for the wife. (*Vol.* 1, *p.* 23.)

MENZIES' REPORTS.

[NEW SERIES.]

1828–1849.

VOL. II. PART II.

CHAPTER I.

PURCHASE, SALE, AND TRANSFER.

DREYER *vs.* ROOS.

Onus probandi. Delivery.

An acknowledgment of the receipt of the purchase price of goods "to be delivered" is sufficient to claim provisional sentence for the repayment of such price, the onus probandi the delivery being on the defendant. 1828. Feb. 29.

[Vol. I, p. 34.]

COMMISSIONER FOR THE SEQUESTRATOR *vs.* VOS.

Credit. Dominium. Insolvency.

G. sold and delivered on credit certain wine to W., whose estate was afterwards sequestrated. G. reclaimed within six weeks the wine or its proceeds. Held that the sale having been on credit, the dominium was vested in W., and G. was not entitled to reclaim or to a preference in W.'s insolvency. March 11.

[Vol. I, p. 286.]

ROBERTSON *vs.* THE SEQUESTRATOR.

Movables. Delivery.

1829. Jan. 15. *A bill of sale of movables, without delivery, gives no jus in re, and holder of such bill cannot claim movables attached in seller's possession.*

[Vol. I, p. 349.]

MURRAY, APPELLANT, *vs.* DE VILLIERS, RESPONDENT.

Onus probandi. Pleading. Rent.

March 17. *Sale of wine. Purchaser not in morâ for not ascertaining the quality before delivery of the whole quantity is completed. But the onus probandi of quality, bad or good, rests on the purchaser, when he takes part delivery.*

Actio redhibitoria is pleadable to the whole sale if part is of bad quality.

The purchaser having intimated his intention not to keep the wine, the seller held liable for cellar rent of wine pendente lite, the purchaser proving that he could have let his cellar on lease but for the stowage of the declined wine there.

[Vol. I, p. 366.]

DE WET *vs.* MANUEL.

Warranty. Actio redhibitoria.

1830. Dec. 28. *Sale of a slave made "voetstoots," or as she stood, without warranty, not reduceable actione redhibitoria, on account of mental infirmity of slave, of which seller was ignorant at the time of sale.*

[Vol. I, p. 501.]

IN RE TWYCROSS AND JENNINGS.

Immovable. Transfer.

1831. Feb. 22. *Where immovable property at the Cape was sold in London under a notarial agreement entitling transfer to be made at the Cape, the Registrar of Deeds here was directed to allow transfer accordingly.*

[Vol. I, p. 503.]

Stiglingh *vs.* De Villiers.

Sale, breach of contract of, is no defence against payment of price of what is delivered to buyer, only a ground for action of damages. 1831. July 12.

[Vol. I, p. 530.]

Fischer *vs.* Daneel.

An acknowledgment of the purchase of goods ex facie of the document to be delivered only under certain circumstances, the proof of which must be extrinsic, coupled with a promise of payment, is not a liquid document, and provision was refused, although in the summons plaintiff tendered performance of the condition. 1833. June 1.

[Vol. I, p. 567. Per Menzies and Kekewich, J.J.: Wylde, C.J., *dis.*]

Eaton, N.O., *vs.* Johnstone.

Compensation.

It is a good defence to a provisional claim on conditions of sale for the first instalment of landed property purchased at public auction, that the defendant holds a mortgage bond over the property, the amount of which bond he offered in compensation with the sum claimed. June 4.

[Vol. I, p. 90.]

Rens *vs.* Bam's Trustee.

Movables. Delivery. Arbitration: exception of submission to. Pleading. Letting and Hiring.

In an action against the trustee of an insolvent estate claiming certain property, the plaintiff alleged purchases from the insolvent on two occasions several months before the insolvency, and in proof thereof produced notarial agreements of sale and purchase, in which all his right and title in the movables were stated to be ceded and transferred by the insolvent to the plaintiff, and the plaintiff let to the insolvent, who hired the same, movables at a monthly rent for a time within which the insolvent should have the right of re-purchase at the price paid to him. And called evidence to show that on the premises of the insolvent, the property had been pointed out to a neighbour as having been sold to the plaintiff by the insolvent, and let to the insolvent by the plaintiff. The Court held that there was no proof of such a bonâ fide sale and real and bonâ fide delivery, as was in law sufficient to divest the insolvent of the right of property (jus dominii).

1835. May 29. — Rens *vs.* Bam's Trustee.

In this case, the plaintiff, in his declaration, stated that, on the 19th March, 1834, C. J. Bam sold and delivered to the said plaintiff certain movable property, and amongst other things one covered cart, one set of harness, and two horses, and the said C. J. Bam did also sell and deliver to the said plaintiff, on the 28th July, 1834, one dray and one open wagon, altogether of the value of £75, which sum the said plaintiff duly paid to the said defendant. That the said plaintiff afterwards hired out the said articles to the said C. J. Bam, and afterwards, to wit, on the 17th December, 1834, the estate of the said C. J. Bam was surrendered as insolvent, and the said defendant was duly chosen and appointed trustee. That the said defendant, as such trustee, hath possessed himself of the said property, and hath refused, and still doth refuse, to deliver it up to the said plaintiff. Wherefore he prayed that defendant should be condemned to deliver to the plaintiffs the said articles or pay him the value, viz. £75.

The defendant put in an exception and plea, and answer, in which he denied all and every one of the allegations, matters, and things as set forth in plaintiff's declaration, save and except that on the 17th December, 1834, the estate of the said C. J. Bam was surrendered as insolvent, and the defendant was duly chosen and appointed trustee thereof, which the defendant admits. And the defendant further averred that on the said 29th July, 1834, and not on the 28th July, as alleged in the declaration, the plaintiff purchased the open wagon mentioned in the declaration, and some other articles from the said C. J. Bam, all which are mentioned and set forth in an agreement entered into by the said C. J. Bam and the plaintiff, before the notary J. G. Borcherds, on the 29th July, 1834. And the defendant, as a further plea, stated that therein it is expressly stipulated and agreed "that in order to prevent expenses, if they, the appearers, should unexpectedly disagree as to the terms of this contract, to submit themselves to the arbitration of two good and proper men to be chosen by both parties as arbitrators." And the defendant further stated that the matter complained of in plaintiff's declaration is such a dispute as, by virtue of said agreement, should be submitted to the decision of arbitrators as aforesaid. And the defendant therefore proposes the exception of submission to arbitrators, and prays for an absolution from the instance with costs. Should, however, the Court decide the aforesaid exception to be inadmissible, in that case, the defendant subordinately puts the plaintiff upon the proof of his declaration, and prays that the plaintiff's claim be dismissed with costs.

In his replication, the plaintiff denied that, by anything in the said clause contained, he is barred from having or maintaining his action against the said defendant, and thereupon joins issue with the said defendant.

This day, after hearing *De Wet*, for the defendant, in support of the exception, the Court (WYLDE, C.J., absent) overruled the exception. Defendant to pay the costs of the exception, and of the replication.

Plaintiff then put in two receipts in the following terms:

"Received from Mr. P. Rens the sum of 800 rds., being in payment of a covered wagon, eight horses, and harness, a covered cart with four horses, and harness for four horses; I hereby acknowledging to be paid in full.

"C. J. BAM.

"The 19th March, 1834."

"Received from Mr. P. Rens the sum of 400 rds., being in satisfaction of a dray and a wagon for carrying goods, and I do hereby cede and transfer all the rights to and property in which I have had to the same.

"C. J. BAM.

"Cape Town, the 28th July, 1834."

And a notarial deed, dated 19th March, 1834, executed by the plaintiff and C. J. Bam. The plaintiff then called C. Buissinne, who proved that the two receipts were signed by Bam, that he saw Bam sign the said deed, and at the same time saw Rens give to Bam some money in Government notes, and also one or two notes of hand by Bam in favour of Rens.

The notarial deed was as follows:

"Appeared Rens of the one part and Bam of the other part, who declared 'that the said Rens has purchased, taken into possession, and paid for, from and to the aforesaid Bam, who has sold, delivered, and received payment for the same, one covered wagon, a set of harness for eight horses, eight bay horses, one covered cart with four bay draught horses, and a set of harness for four horses, for a sum of 800 rds. And the aforesaid Bam declared in

1835. May 29. — Rens vs. Bam's Trustee.

consequence thereof that he doth by these presents cede and transfer to the said Bam all the right and property which he has had up to this date in and to the said covered wagon, harness, horses, and cart. Furthermore, the appearers declared that they have entered into with each other the following contract of hire of the above-written horses, harness, wagon, and cart, viz.: the said Rens acknowledged that he has let, undertaking to deliver on hire after the passing of this deed, and the said Bam acknowledged that he has hired, to receive on hire after the passing hereof, for the term of four months, commencing on the 14th March, and terminating on the 14th July, 1834, the aforesaid horses, harness, wagon, and cart, at a monthly rent of 35 rds., which rent the aforesaid Bam by these presents undertakes to pay, promptly, on the 14th of each month, the aforesaid Rens having a perfect right, should the first-named fail in paying the said rent on the day it becomes due, immediately to annul the contract, and to take back his horses, harness, wagon, and cart. Further, the said Bam shall be bound and obliged to provide proper stabling and sufficient forage for the said twelve horses during the time agreed upon,—at the termination of this contract to return the said horses, harness, wagon, and cart, in good order to the hirer out, the aforesaid Rens, and in the event of one or more of the aforesaid horses unexpectedly dying, then to pay to the said Rens the value of such horse or horses so dead to such an amount as by a just valuation shall be found to be due. Moreover, they declared that they have covenanted with each other that the aforesaid Bam shall have the right, during the continuance of this contract, should he think fit, to repurchase the said horses, harness, wagon, and cart, for the like purchase amount of 800 rds., the said Rens binding himself, on receipt of the said sum of 800 rds., together with such rent as is then due and unpaid, to give back to the said Bam the said horses, harness, wagon, and cart. Finally, they declared that they do further determine, in order to prevent costs being incurred, that should they, the appearers, unexpectedly have any dispute as to the terms of this contract, then that they will submit themselves to the decision of two irreproachable persons to be chosen reciprocally for that purpose as arbitrators. And lastly, they have agreed to consider this contract as renewed after the 14th July next, and so on every four months, unless one or both of the contracting parties shall not have given notice of his or their intention to put an end to this contract fourteen days before the expiration of the period hereby fixed, and so on before the end of each four months.'

"For the fulfilment," &c.

On this contract the following memorandum was written:

"This contract renewed by us, the undersigned, by notarial contract passed before the notary J. G. Borcherds, and witnesses, dated 29th July, 1834, with the addition of a wagon for the carriage of goods, and a dray, and an increase of the capital to 1,200 rds.

"P. RENS,
"C. J. BAM.

"Cape Town, 29th July, 1834."

The plaintiff then put in the notarial contract, dated 29th July, 1834, executed by him and Bam, which (with the exception that it related also to four other horses, four sets of harness, one dray, and one open wagon, and in consequence increased the amount of the sum mentioned as the price to 1,200 rds., and of that mentioned as the hire to 45 rds.) was, word for word, the same as the contract of the 19th March; and called

Nicholas Jacobus Lotz: I know plaintiff and C. J. Bam. I recollect in March, 1834, Rens and Bam making an agreement about the sale and purchase of some horses and a wagon. I was sent for to Bam's stable by Mr. Rens, and went into the stable with them, and there Mr. Rens said to me, There stand eight horses with their harness, and a covered wagon standing before the door, and a cart which has gone out to the country, and these I have bought from Mr. Bam; but I have let them to Mr. Bam again. And Bam said, This is the case. I have sold them to Mr. Rens, and I have hired them back from him. Rens said, Mr. Bam, you must procure me that cart; and Bam said, upon his honour, the cart would be back next day, and it should then be sent before Mr. Rens's house. I said, Why have you sent for me? And Bam replied, It is only in case of the death of either party, that you may know that my cart, wagon, &c., had been sold to him. I then went out with them through the back passage, and Bam said, Neighbour, I am now satisfied; I have now sold my things, and if anybody should now prosecute me, "they will fish behind the net."

The *Attorney-General* here admitted that the plaintiff's other witnesses could not carry the case beyond what the evidence already given had done, except to prove that a delivery of the same kind had taken place of the additional articles mentioned in the deed of 29th July, 1834.

After hearing the *Attorney-General* on the effect of the evidence, the Court (Sir J. WYLDE, C.J., MENZIES and KEKEWICH, J.J.), without calling on the defendant, gave judgment for the defendant with costs to defendant, except

1835. May 29. — Rens *vs.* Bam's Trustee.

the costs of the exception and replication, which defendant was adjudged to pay.

The ground of the judgment was, that the plaintiff had failed to prove that, previously to the insolvency and sequestration of Bam, there had been such a *bonâ fide* sale, and real and *bonâ fide* delivery of the articles by Bam to the plaintiff, as was in law sufficient to divest Bam of the right of property (*jus in re*) in them.

Hare *vs.* Kotzé.

Action to compel transfer. Ratification. Conditions of sale: authority of auctioneer to vary.

Aug. 27. — Hare *vs.* Kotzé.

This action was brought by the plaintiff to have the defendant condemned to give him legal transfer of two lots of ground.

The declaration set forth that at a public sale held on the 15th July, 1834, by the auctioneer, M. C. Wolff, for account of the said defendant, of certain lots of land, situated, &c., the plaintiff became the purchaser of certain two lots for the sum of £81. And that although it was stipulated in the conditions of sale that the purchase money should be paid in three instalments, namely: one third in three months, one third at one year, and the remaining one third two years after the day of sale, yet that the plaintiff paid on the said 15th July, 1834, the whole purchase money in cash to the said auctioneer, M. C. Wolff, for account of the said defendant, of which payment the said defendant had due notice. And that the plaintiff hath performed, and is still ready and willing to perform, every part of his engagement as purchaser of the said two lots of land, and hath demanded of the said defendant to give him legal transfer of the same, which the defendant has refused to give.

In his plea, the defendant alleged that it was stipulated in the conditions of sale that the purchase money should be paid in three instalments as stated in his declaration, that the purchaser should pass notarial bonds for the two last instalments, payable to the said defendant, and that the transfer of the said property should be made according to the laws of this Colony, the purchase money having been previously settled to the satisfaction of the seller and auctioneer. That the purchase money was not settled to the satisfaction of the seller (the said defendant), but that the whole thereof was settled with the auctioneer alone, by the said plaintiff giving the said auctioneer an order on the Government Bank for the amount on the 15th July, 1834.

And the said defendant denies that he had due notice of such payment, or consented thereto, or concurred therewith. And the said defendant saith that the said auctioneer exceeded his authority, as agent for the said defendant, by accepting such order on the bank as aforesaid from the said plaintiff. And that the defendant hath never received any part of the said purchase money, either from the said auctioneer or from the said plaintiff, or from any person on his behalf, and therefore refused to give transfer until he should be paid the amount of the purchase money in manner stipulated in the conditions of sale.

At the trial, *Cloete*, for plaintiff, called

Michiel Wolff: I was an auctioneer, and on the 15th July, 1834, I sold by auction, on the defendant's account, some lots of ground near Rondebosch. A few days before the sale, defendant came to my office and settled the conditions of sale. I then told him that the conditions generally were that the payment should be in three instalments, but that sometimes the purchasers paid the whole amount at once in cash. At the commencement of the sale I read the conditions. Plaintiff became the purchaser of lots Nos. 1 and 2. He did not sign the conditions of sale. When I asked him to do so, and for his sureties, he told me to walk over with him to his house and he would pay me the amount, which was £81. I went with him, and he then signed a cheque on the bank for £81 in my favour, which he gave to me, and I gave him a receipt. I now produce that cheque. After I did this, I saw defendant either on the ground where the sale was or in his house, but I am sure on the same day, and I told him that plaintiff had settled with me by a cheque. Nothing further or about the amount was mentioned on that day. About a month or two months after, I met defendant in the street, and he told me he would call to settle accounts with me, and I said he might come whenever he liked. He was then and previously indebted to me in 70 rds. There was no other account between us except for this 70 rds., and the price I had received from Kotzé. I only used the words: "Hare has settled with me by a cheque," because I thought that Kotzé knew that instead of taking security for the price, Hare was going to pay the whole amount of the price. But I am not sure whether he did know this, and whether he might not have thought he was only going to pay the first instalment, and signed the bond for the other two. I never paid any of the money to defendant. He never came to settle with me before I became insolvent, which was not until more than three months after the sale.

Christiaan de Jongh: I was the clerk of Messrs. Wolff

1835. Aug. 27. — Hare *vs.* Kotzé. & Bartman. I recollect the sale to plaintiff. I heard Wolff ask Hare for his sureties, and he answered, "I have none, but walk over to my house and I will pay you with a cheque on the bank." The sale was entirely over before this. Defendant was present, but I do not recollect exactly where he was standing when Hare spoke. I saw Mr. Wolff after this receive the cheque from defendant. We then returned to the spot where we had made the sale. I then heard Wolff tell defendant "he has paid me with a cheque on the bank."

The plaintiff closed his case. The defendant called no witnesses.

The Court held that the evidence showed that the defendant was made aware that the plaintiff had paid the whole price at once with the cheque on the bank, and by his not objecting at the time had ratified the transaction.

WYLDE, C.J., held that the auctioneer, as agent for the seller, had such power to alter the conditions as to authorize him, without the knowledge of the seller, to vary the conditions from payment by instalments to instant payment in cash, and to bind the seller to that transaction. (*Vide Phillips on Ev., vol.* 1, *p.* 541; 2, *pp.* 84, 97.) But the Court proceeded on the other ground, and gave no decision on the last point.

Judgment for plaintiff, as prayed, with costs.

BLORE *vs.* CHIAPPINI.

Sale at public auction. Warranty by owner. Tender.

B., an auctioneer, sold to C. for account of T., 88 *boxes of cigars at public auction. At the sale, T. informed intending purchasers that the boxes contained* 1,000 *each. On delivery they were found to contain from* 800 *to* 810. *B. sued C., reckoning the contents at* 1,000. *C. tendered for the lesser number, which tender the Court sustained.*

1836. Nov. 3. — Blore *vs.* Chiappini. This action was brought by the plaintiff to recover from the defendant the price of 88 boxes of cigars, which had been purchased by the defendant at a public auction held by the plaintiff as auctioneer, at the rate of 20 rds. for each box, and which boxes were after the sale delivered to the defendant.

In defence against the action, the defendant, admitting the purchase of the 88 boxes of cigars at the price alleged in the declaration, pleaded that at the said public auction the plaintiff acted as auctioneer and as agent therein for

John R. Thomson, of and as representing the firm of Messrs. Thomson, Watson, & Co., who was personally present at the said sale, and caused the said boxes of cigars to be thus publicly sold. 1836. Nov. 3. Blore *vs.* Chiappini.

That at the said sale, and before the said 88 boxes of cigars were knocked down to the said defendant, the said J. R. Thomson, in answer to a demand made by and among the bidders at the said sale as to the number of cigars the said boxes contained, publicly declared that the said boxes contained each 1,000 cigars; that upon this assurance of the said J. R. Thomson as to the contents of the said boxes, the said defendant became the purchaser of the same.

That after the said boxes of cigars were delivered to the said defendant, he caused a survey to be held on the said boxes of cigars, when they were found to contain only between 800 to 810 cigars each box, and that the defendant did accordingly, on the 26th July last, tender to the said plaintiff the sum of £107, being calculated at the value of 810 cigars to each box, which the said plaintiff however, refused to accept.

This day defendant called evidence fully substantiating his plea, and the Court gave judgment for the amount tendered. Plaintiff to pay defendant's costs.

Farmer *vs.* Findlay and Chisholm, Executors of Durham.

Broker's Sale. Fictitious Invoice. Fraud.

F. sold to D.'s Executors, through M., a broker, certain ironmongery on an invoice which D.'s executor's afterwards repudiated. On evidence it appeared that the articles had been in store for a long time, and that the invoice was, in this respect, a fictitious one. The Court set aside the transaction, holding that the intended sale was one of fresh goods on a fresh invoice.

This action was brought by plaintiffs to compel the defendants to accept a bill of exchange for the price of certain goods, alleged to have been sold to and bought by them through the medium of a broker. 1837. Feb. 2. Farmer *vs.* Findlay and Chisholm, Executors of Durham.

The defendants pleaded the general issue.

The plaintiffs called Thomas Mosse: I am a clerk of plaintiffs. I made a sale to the defendants on account of plaintiffs, about the 2nd of August last, of an invoice of ironmongery, with which plaintiffs had entrusted me as a broker to dispose of. I presented the invoice for sale to

1837. Feb. 2.

Farmer *vs.* Findlay and Chisholm, Executors of Durham.

defendant, Findlay, and Mr. Robertson, a clerk in the late Mr. Durham's warehouse, and who is the manager of the concern. After they had looked over the invoice, Mr. Robertson asked me to call next morning. I told them I was acting as a broker. I called next morning, and after conferring with each other, they both agreed to take the goods at the invoice price, and requested me to make out a broker's note. I did so in my office, and then took it and delivered it to Mr. Findlay, and asked him to look at it. He did so, and said very well. I delivered the same day an exact duplicate of the broker's note to plaintiffs. In about half an hour after I had delivered the note to Mr. Findlay, Mr. Robertson brought it back to my office, laid it on the table, and said he declined the transaction. He said he had no objection to the goods, but declined having any transaction with the parties, and he gave me certain reasons for so doing. He left the note on the table. I had had several communications with Mr. Robertson previously to the day I delivered the broker's note. Mr. Robertson had objected to certain of the goods, a cask of saws, in the invoice, and before the sale it was agreed they should be taken out of the invoice. I produce the original invoice shown to Robertson and Findlay. He expressed that he was satisfied with all the articles, except those which I took out of the invoice. Findlay was then present.

Cross-examined: I am not a sworn broker, but I was acting as a broker on my own account. I acted solely as an agent for plaintiffs. I was to receive from plaintiffs a commission of one per cent. on the amount of the sale. Previous to and from the commencement of the bargain up to the delivery of the sale note, neither Findlay nor Robertson said that they would have no transaction with Messrs. Farmer. They did not know before the delivery of the broker's note that the goods belonged to plaintiffs. They had made no inquiry on that point. Robertson had asked me when I first applied to him whether the goods were landed. I told him a part were and that the rest would be landed in a day or two. I only knew this from one of the plaintiffs having told me so. He did not name the vessel.

Charles Matthews: I am storekeeper to Messrs. Farmer. I know that the goods were ready for delivery on the day Mr. Mosse brought the broker's note. They were then all on shore and warehoused. By ready I mean they were all in the warehouse, had all been landed. I immediately began to look out and put aside the goods in the invoice. The invoice now shown me is in the handwriting of Mr. McCrie, then a clerk of plaintiffs. Some of the goods mentioned in the invoice were not a fresh importation, but had been for some time in our stores. The nails were a fresh importation by the *London*, which was then discharging, but the goods in this invoice had not all been imported in the same ship, nor had come with the same invoice to plaintiffs. Some of the goods, *e.g.*, the files in cask 41, had been in store for twelve months. The saws had been received by another ship than the *London*, two or three months before, I think by the *Kersewell*. The spades had been about six months in the store.

1837. Feb. 2.

Farmer *vs.* Findlay and Chisholm, Executors of Durbam.

The Court stopped the case, and gave judgment for defendants with costs.

They held that the transaction into which defendants meant to enter was the purchase of an original invoice from the consignor to the consignee of goods fresh imported, and that a fraud had been committed on them by the plaintiffs in endeavouring to impose on them a fictitious invoice.

Vouchee *vs.* Van Ellewee.

Immovables. Transfer. Bond. Summons. Tender.

Nov. 7.

A bond in which the obligor undertakes to pay the purchase money of land on transfer being given is a sufficiently liquid document; the summons should tender such transfer forthwith.

[Vol. I, p. 18.]

Waters & Herron *vs.* Phillips & King.

Sale by broker on sample and invoice. Warranty.

Plaintiffs sold to defendants, through a broker, 184 chests Canton Bohea, to sample, at 9d. per lb., as per invoice, and 264 chests Fokeen Bohea, in the same way, at 1s. Samples were shown, sale completed, and invoices delivered. There was no mention of the F. B. in the invoices. Defendants then tendered 9d. per lb. all round. Plaintiffs insisted on 1s. for the F. B., or a relinquishment of the sale. Defendants then took delivery without mention of price. The Court found all 264 chests to be fine Canton Bohea worth 10d. per lb. That the defendants had bought on faith of sample and warranty combined, had taken delivery of the 264 under the plaintiffs' warranty that it was F. B., and were entitled, on discovering it was not, to refuse to pay for it as such. It, therefore, absolved defendants from the instance; but suggesting that on an action for F. C. B. at 10d. plaintiffs would recover, judgment was taken by consent for 9d. for C. B. and 10d. for F. C. B.

1838. May 17. — Waters & Herron vs. Phillips & King.

The plaintiffs sold to defendants, per broker, as per his note, "184 chests and half chests of *Canton Bohea, to sample,* at 9d. per lb. *as per invoice,* and 264 chests *Fokeen Bohea, to sample,* at 1s. per lb., *as per invoice.*" Samples were shown by the broker to defendants at the time of the sale. After the sale was completed the invoices were given to defendants. In the invoices all the tea was described as Canton Bohea; no mention was made in them of Fokeen Bohea. On seeing the invoices defendants wrote to plaintiffs that they doubted whether 264 chests were Fokeen Bohea, and offered to pay 9d. per lb. for all the tea, on condition that if upon examination by skilful tea brokers in London, the 264 chests should be certified to be Fokeen Bohea, they would pay 3d. per lb. additional for it; but if certified to be Canton Bohea, the price for the whole to be 9d. per lb.

Plaintiffs wrote in reply to defendants that the 264 chests were Fokeen Bohea, and stated their reasons for maintaining it to be such, and gave defendants the option to take the whole teas at the prices mentioned in the broker's note, or to relinquish the purchase altogether.

Next day the defendants sent to plaintiffs the following order for delivery:

"Messrs. WATERS & HERRON,

"Please deliver to the order of Mr. Calf 184 chests and half chests Canton Bohea, 264 square chests Fokeen Bohea.

"PHILLIPS & KING."

The whole of the teas were in consequence delivered by plaintiffs to and received by defendants.

Defendants tendered to plaintiffs £1,639 5s. 6d., being the amount of the price of the whole teas, calculated at 9d. per lb. The plaintiffs refused to receive this sum, and brought this action to enforce payment for the Canton Bohea at the rate of 9d. per lb., and of the 264 chests in dispute at 1s. per lb.

Defendants admitted their liability for the sum which they had tendered. It was admitted that both teas were in conformity to the samples which had been shown at the time of sale.

It was proved that the 184 chests and half chests were marked Canton Bohea, and the 264 chests F. Bohea.

It was proved that there are three kinds of tea, viz.: Canton Bohea, Fine Canton Bohea, worth 1d. per lb. more than the former, and Fokeen Bohea, which is superior in value to the Fine Canton Bohea.

1838. May 17.

Waters & Herron *vs.* Phillips & King.

The Court found that it was proved that the 264 chests in dispute contained Fine Canton Bohea and not Fokeen Bohea, as mentioned in the broker's note. That the defendants had not bought the tea by sample merely, but on the faith of the plaintiffs' representation that the 264 chests were Fokeen Bohea. That as the plaintiffs, on the defendants informing them of their doubts that the 264 chests were Fokeen Bohea, had maintained that they were Fokeen Bohea, and refused to allow defendants to reject the doubtful chests unless the defendants also gave up their bargain for the Canton Bohea, the defendants were entitled to send for and receive the 264 chests as warranted by plaintiffs to be Fokeen Bohea, and on their subsequently discovering that it was not such, to refuse to pay for it at the rate they had agreed to pay for Fokeen Bohea. Consequently, that the plaintiffs could recover nothing under this action, and the defendants must be absolved from the instance except as to the sum tendered. (*Vide Fisher vs. Permuta, Campbell's Rep., vol.* 1, *p.* 190, and the case at *vol.* 3, *p.* 461.

But the Court held that as the 264 chests were proved to have contained Fine Canton Bohea, worth 1d. per lb. more than Canton Bohea, the defendants were not entitled to retain it at the price of 9d., agreed on for the Canton Bohea, and that plaintiffs would in another action recover from defendants the price of the 264 chests calculated at 10d. per lb.

Whereupon, by consent, judgment was given for plaintiffs for £1,753 11s. 4d., being the price for the whole calculated at 9d. for the Canton, and 10d. for the Fine Canton, with costs to defendants.

Broekmann, Executrix of Durr, *vs.* Rens.

Action for re-delivery of transfer deed. Pleading. Læsio enormis. Evidence.

Læsio enormis must be specially pleaded.

1839. June 1.

Broekmann, Executrix of Durr *vs.* Rens.

The plaintiff in convention, as executrix of her deceased husband, Durr, brought an action against defendant for delivery to her, in her said capacity, of a deed of transfer in favour of Durr of a place called Weltevreden, which deed, she alleged, Durr had delivered to defendant *for a*

1839. June 1. — Brockmann, Executrix of Durr, *vs.* Rens.

certain purpose, to be re-delivered by defendant when such purpose should have been duly effected, and she alleged that said purpose had not been effected in the lifetime of Durr, and that the consideration on which the said deed was so deposited by Durr with defendant had wholly failed.

Defendant, in his plea, admitted his possession of the deed, but denied plaintiff's claim to have the deed re-delivered, on the ground that the said deed was delivered to him by Durr to be by the defendant retained until Durr should be enabled to give defendant a legal transfer of said place Weltevreden and tendered re-delivery of the deed on the plaintiff undertaking to give him legal transfer of said place.

And in reconvention alleged that Durr and the defendant, on the 20th April, 1839, had mutually agreed, the former to sell, and the latter to buy, the said place Weltevreden, for £625, to be paid in cash on the transfer being made, and that Durr had then delivered to defendant the said deed for the purpose of enabling the defendant to get transfer of the place made to him, and had undertaken to attend at the office of the Registrar of Deeds for that purpose, whereupon the defendant prayed that plaintiff might be condemned to give him transfer of said place, and tendered thereon to pay the stipulated price of £625.

As a plea to the defendant's claim in reconvention, plaintiff joined issue with defendant therein.

After the evidence had been led on both sides,

Cloete, for defendant, contended that he had proved that a valid sale had been made verbally by Durr to Rens.

Musgrave, A.-G., contra, maintained that no such contract of sale had been proved to have been made; and, secondly, maintained that although it had been proved that such a verbal contract had been made, yet that defendant was barred in equity from claiming performance of it, and that on grounds of equity the Court ought not to enforce performance in respect of the gross inadequacy of the price.

The Court held that it had been proved that a verbal contract of sale had, as alleged by defendant, been entered into between him and Durr, and held that the plaintiff, under her plea to the claim in reconvention, above set forth, was not entitled to lead evidence to show that the price stipulated by said contract was less than one half the real value of the property, or to claim that the sale should be set aside on that ground; and that certain evidence which the plaintiff had been permitted to lead as to the inadequacy of the price had only been admitted as proving a circumstance in the case tending to show the improbability of such a sale having been made by Durr as defendant alleged.

The Court, therefore, gave judgment for the defendant,

both as defendant in convention and as plaintiff in reconvention, with costs; but suspended execution for fourteen days, in order to give the executrix of Durr an opportunity of instituting, in proper form, an action against defendant for setting aside the sale on account of the inadequacy of the price to the value of the property.

1839. June 1.

Broekmann, Executrix of Durr, *vs.* Rens.

Postea (12th June).—In absence of the defendant's counsel, some discussion took place between the Court and the counsel for plaintiff, in consequence of which the Registrar was led by mistake to draw up an erroneous order, which the counsel for defendant now moved to have discharged, with costs. Order discharged, with costs.

Postea (8th August).—The *Attorney-General*, for plaintiff, moved to have the case re-heard as to the judgment for costs.

Cloete, for defendant, opposed the application as incompetent, on the ground that it was not alleged that this motion was founded on any fact or document *noviter veniens ad notitiam* since the judgment had been pronounced. (*Cens. For., part* 2, *Lib.* 1, *c.* 31, § 5, § 17; *Merula, B.* 4, *Tit.* 90; *Voet,* 42, 1, 28.)

This motion was withdrawn on the ground that no notice had been given, with liberty to the Attorney-General to move again on giving notice.

Postea (20th August, 1839).—Execution of judgment was stayed on payment of the costs of the action, and of this motion, until the issue of an action to be brought by plaintiff for setting aside the sale on the ground of *enormis læsio*, and on condition that plaintiff's declaration shall be filed before the last day of term. (*Vide infra inter eosdem,* 14*th November,* 1839.)

NORDENS *vs.* BARNES AND OTHERS.

Transfer: tender of, by summons, one day beyond stipulated time for, is bad.

The plaintiffs and defendants entered into a notarial contract, dated 1st April, 1838, whereby the plaintiffs agreed to sell, and defendants to purchase, a certain farm and flock of sheep belonging to plaintiffs, on the following terms and conditions, viz.: that in consideration of £1,500 to be paid by defendants to plaintiffs in three years from the date thereof, the said plaintiffs shall forthwith deliver over the said sheep to defendants, and further shall and will make a proper and legal transfer and conveyance of the said farm

Aug. 30.

Nordens *vs.* Barnes & Others.

1839. Aug. 30. — Nordens *vs.* Barnes & Others.

to defendants within twelve months from the date of the said deed, provided that on receiving such transfer the defendants shall pass a mortgage bond, mortgaging the said farm for the said sum of £1,500, or such part thereof as may be due at the time of such transfer, to be paid in three instalments of £500 each, with interest from the 1st April, 1838, the first instalment to be paid on 1st April, 1841, the second on 1st April, 1842, and the third on 1st April, 1843.

On the 8th February, 1839, plaintiffs took out the summons in this case to answer in an action to receive transfer and perform the conditions of the said agreement.

In their declaration, plaintiffs alleged that they had performed the conditions set forth in said contract to be performed by them, and are ready and willing to perform any such conditions as may still be required of them, and therefore prayed that the defendants may be condemned to receive transfer of the farm and to pass mortgage bond as stipulated in the said contract.

The defendants pleaded the general issue.

Cloete, for plaintiffs, contended that the demand in the summons (which was dated 8th February, 1839) was a sufficient demand by plaintiffs on defendants for performance to found this action, and that the tender made in the summons to give transfer on the 2nd April, 1839, was a sufficient tender by plaintiffs to perform their part of the contract.

Musgrave, A.-G., for defendants, contended that by the terms of the contract, the defendants, although they have the right of compelling the plaintiffs to give transfer *within* twelve months of the 1st April, 1838, on their granting the required mortgage, yet could not be compelled by plaintiffs to receive transfer before the arrival of the term when they were bound to pay the first instalment of the price.

The Court absolved the defendants from the instance, with costs, on the ground that plaintiffs had not proved any such performance, or tender to perform their part of the contract, as is sufficient to entitle them to maintain this action, inasmuch as they have proved no other tender of performance of their part except that made in the summons, in which they have only tendered to give transfer *one day after* the period *within* which they were by the contract bound to give transfer.

The Court expressed no opinion as to what would have been the case if the day on which, in the summons, the plaintiffs had tendered to give transfer had been within the period within which the plaintiffs were by the contract bound to have given transfer.

Harris *vs.* Trustee of Buissinne.

Immovable Property. Tradition. Jus in re. Insolvency. Hypothec.

Dominion of immovable property could by the law of Holland be conveyed only by transfer coram lege loci.

This rule of the law of Holland was introduced into this Colony with the rest of the laws of Holland on its first settlement in 1652, and has been acted on invariably ever since, except that by colonial laws the Registrar of Deeds has been subsiituted for the Magistrates before whom, in Holland, such transfers were by law required to be made.

An agreement of sale of immovable property, followed by delivery of possession by the vendor to the purchaser, gives the purchaser nothing more than a jus ad rem, and a personal claim against the vendor to convey the jus in re or dominium to him, by transfer coram lege loci.

On the order of the sequestration of the vendor's estate, no conveyance coram lege loci having been effected, the dominium became vested in the Master of the Supreme Court, and ultimately in trustees for the benefit of creditors.

Part of the purchase price having been paid by the purchaser to the vendor, the purchaser has a personal claim against the estate for damage sustained by non-fulfilment of the vendor's undertaking to perfect the sale by making legal transfer, and for restitution of the price, and is entitled for such personal claim to be ranked concurrently with the other personal creditors of the vendor, but has no right of preference whatever.

No conventional special hypothec can be constituted over immovable property except by writing coram lege loci.

Ord. No. 64.

1840. Feb. 11. „ 20. June 23.

Harris vs. Trustee of Buissinne.

The house in question in this case was duly registered as the property of Buissinne, in 1836.

On the 13th January, 1837, Buissinne and the plaintiff entered into a contract respectively to buy and sell the said house for £1,050, £400 of which it was stipulated should be paid immediately in cash, and for the balance, £650, the plaintiff agreed to pass a mortgage bond in favour of the directors of the Savings Bank.

Same day plaintiff paid Buissinne the £400 and obtained his receipt, and also paid the collector of transfer dues the dues on the sale of the house by plaintiff to him. On the same day he obtained possession of the house and premises, which he continued to occupy to the present time.

1840. Feb. 11. „ 20. June 23.

Harris *vs.* Trustee of Buissinne.

The plaintiff applied to Buissinne to give him transfer of the house, so that he might perform his obligation to execute a mortgage in favour of the Savings Bank. Buissinne being unable to give the transfer in consequence of the refusal of other mortgagees, whom he could not pay their mortgages, to consent to its taking place, did not comply with the plaintiff's claim. It was admitted that the plaintiff had attended at the Transfer Office on the 28th May and 11th June, 1839, to receive transfer and pass the mortgage, and that Buissinne, although duly warned to be present, did not attend. Thereupon the plaintiff took out the summons in the present action against him on the 17th June, 1839. On the 31st July, 1839, Buissinne surrendered his estate as insolvent, and it was placed under sequestration.

The declaration set forth the contract of the sale and the payment of the £400, and tendered performance of all the other covenants and conditions of the contract, and prayed that Buissinne, the defendant, might be condemned to give him a legal transfer.

The trustee of the insolvent estate took up the action, and pleaded that he was not liable to give transfer to plaintiff unless he should now pay to the estate the full amount of the purchase money, £1,050, without regard to the £400 paid to Buissinne before his sequestration, upon which he tendered transfer.

20th Feb.—*Cloete*, for the plaintiff, founded on the 11th and 79th sections of Ordinance No. 64 of 1829, and maintained that notwithstanding the non-execution of the deed of transfer before the insolvency the *jus in re* of the house has been completely transferred to and vested in plaintiff. He referred also to the Placaat of 10th May, 1829 (*Groot Placaat Boek, vol.* 1, *p.* 1953), and the Placaats therein recited; *Voet,* 41, 1, 38; *Van Leeuwen's Cens. For.*, 1, 2, 7, 6; and contended that although by the law of Holland the execution of the transfer *coram lege loci* and the payment of the fortieth penny were both essential to transfer the *dominium* or *jus in re* of immovable property, yet that the Placaats establishing this rule had not become the law of this Colony. That by the law of the Colony the payment of the duty was the only essential requisite to complete the transfer and convey the *dominium* to the purchaser, who had received actual delivery by obtaining the actual possession, and quoted *Proclamations of* 20*th July,* 1798, 22*nd September,* 1789, *and* 2*nd January,* 1818.

Musgrave, on the same side, cited *Van der Keessel, Thes.* 202, *Van Leeuwen's Rom. Dutch Law, p.* 381 (*English Ed.*).

C. J. Brand, contra, produced the first volume of the Registry of Deeds of the Colony from 1652, the date of the settlement, which, besides the registration of wills and other deeds, contains the original of a grant of land, dated 1658, and a deed of transfer dated 11th July, 1660, which commences as follows: "Appeared before Commissioners of the Council of the Fort of Good Hope, with the assistance of the Burgher Raaden on the part of the Freemen of the Cape of Good Hope, Jacob Cloete, of Cologne, Free Burgher, who acknowledges, with the previous knowledge of the Commander and Council aforesaid, in the place of *Schepenen*, for his heirs, to have sold," &c., &c. (*Vide* also *Statutes of India, Tit. Schepenen, § Penultima.*) And maintained that the law of Holland, requiring, as essential to their validity, the execution of sales of landed property *coram lege loci*, was introduced into the Colony along with the rest of the law of Holland from its very first establishment, and referred to the first volume of the Registry above mentioned in proof of this, and quoted *Grotius*, 2, 5, § 13, to show that the Placaat of Charles V, 10th May, 1529, merely declared and enforced what had previously been the law: "But immovable property, such as houses, lands, erven, were considered of old in many places of Holland not to be delivered unless the conveyance took place before the judge of the place where the property is situated. The conveyance, if made otherwise, was void, which has been made common throughout these countries in the time of Emperor Charles, to which the States have added that the conveyance should be entered in a book (registered), and if arising from a sale or exchange the fortieth penny be paid, for the use of the commonwealth: *Also* in pain of its being of no effect." And quoted *Voet* 6, 1, § 20, *Res litigiosæ; Burge, vol.* 2, *p.* 528. *Voet* 18, 6, 6. *Matthæus de Auction.* 1, 18, 15; 1, 20, 16. *Colonial Placaat,* 17*th August,* 1672. *Instructions to the Court of Justice,* 1803. *Ordinance No.* 39; *No.* 97. *Voet* 41, 1, 38, 42. *Voet* 42, 8, 18, *Plane si quis.*

1840. Feb. 11. „ 20. June 23.

Harris *vs.* Trustee of Buissinne.

Postea.—Musgrave, for the plaintiff, quoted *Loenius, Obs.* 256, *Cens. Forens.,* 4, 19, 5. *Burge,* 3 *vol.,* 530, 895; *vol.* 2, 447, 816. *Voet* 21, 3, 3; 44, 6; 21, 2, 5. *Vesey's Reports, vol.* 9, 100, 409. *Vesey Jun., vol.* 15, 345. *Van der Keessel, Th.* 633.

Brand, contra, quoted *Burge, vol.* 2, *p.* 529, *Ordinance No.* 64, § 7, as to what is sufficient legal process to be deemed compulsory.

Cur. adv. vult.

23rd June.—This day the Court gave judgment for the defendant on the following grounds:

By the law of Holland, the *dominium* or *jus in re* of immovable property can only be conveyed by transfer made

1840. Feb. 11. „ 20. June 23.

Harris vs. Trustee of Buissinne.

coram lege loci, and this species of transfer is as essential to divest the seller of, and invest the buyer with, the *dominium* or *jus in re* of immovable property as actual tradition is to convey the *dominium* of movables, and that the delivery of the actual possession of immovable property has no force or legal effect whatever in transferring its *dominium.* This rule of the law of Holland was not a mere fiscal regulation. It was with the rest of the law of Holland introduced into this Colony on its first settlement, and has been acted on invariably ever since, except that, by certain colonial laws, the Registrar of Deeds has been substituted for the magistrates before whom in Holland transfers were by law required to be made.

Consequently, the agreement of sale between Harris and Buissinne, and the delivery of the possession of the house by Buissinne to Harris, gave Harris nothing more than a *jus ad rem,* and a personal claim against Buissinne to convey the *jus in re* to him by transfer *coram lege loci.*

And, therefore, on the day on which Buissinne's estate was placed under sequestration, the *dominium* of the house in question was still vested in Buissinne, and then formed part of his estate, and that by the order placing his estate under sequestration this house became instantly and wholly vested in the Master, and ultimately in the trustee for behoof of the creditors of Buissinne.

On these grounds it followed that Harris had only a personal claim against Buissinne's estate for the damage which he has sustained by the non-fulfilment of his undertaking to perfect the sale, by making legal transfer of the house to Harris; and for restitution of that part of the price which he has paid, and in respect of this personal claim, he has no preference on the house in question, or on any other part of the estate, and is only entitled to be ranked concurrently with the other personal creditors of Buissinne.

Admitting it to be true that this house must pass to the trustee, subject to any hypothec which existed over it prior to the sequestration of the estate, still Harris had acquired no legal hypothec over the house prior to the sequestration, because no conventional special hypothec can be constituted over immovable property except by writing executed *coram lege loci,* and no agreement to grant a hypothec over immovable property, even when followed by delivery of actual possession of the immovable property is effectual to constitute any hypothec over such property, and the fact that Harris got possession of the house does not put him in any better situation than if he had never got possession of it. Therefore, the house in question passed to the trustee unburdened by any hypothec on it in favour of Harris, and Harris has no better right to compel the trustee now to transfer this house to him than he would have had to compel the actual delivery to him of 1,000 bolls of wheat, which Buissinne had sold to him, and the price of which he had paid, but of which he had not received actual delivery of possession before the sequestration.

1840. Feb. 11. " 20. June 23.

Harris *vs.* Trustee of Buissinne.

Harris can in this case derive no benefit from the fact that he had commenced an action for transfer of the house before the sequestration, and had thereby made the house *res litigiosa*, because the effect of litigiosity can never put a party in a better situation than he would have been in if that had been done on the day when the litigiosity commenced, which he claims, and which, by decree being given in his favour, would be adjudged to be done. Harris, therefore, can be in no better condition in respect of the litigiosity created by his action against Buissinne than he would have been if on the day he served the summons in that action on Buissinne the latter had transferred the house to him. Now, as the summons was served within sixty days before the sequestration, any transfer made on that day by Buissinne in favour of Harris, would have been null and void under the provisions of the Ordinance No. 64.*

The Court held that to sustain the claim of Harris would be to overturn the whole of the law of Holland, and of this Colony, as to the transfer of the *dominium* of immovable property, and deprive creditors of the protection which had been provided for them by the registry of deeds.

Judgment for defendant, with costs.

NOTE.—On the same principle, the Court held before the abolition of slavery, that inasmuch as registry in the slave register was required to transfer property in slaves, sale and delivery of possession of a slave by a person in whose name the slave was on the register to the purchaser, without registration effected in the latter's name, was wholly ineffectual in a question with the creditors of the seller.

[*Vide Hanekom's Trustee vs. Kotzé, vol.* I, *p.* 411.]

[*Et vide Smith's Trustees vs. Norden,* 23*rd February,* 1843, *post.*]

[*Van Aardt vs. Hartley's Trustees,* 28*th August,* 1845, *post.*]

* This portion of the judgment is, since the repeal of Ordinance No. 64 by Ordinance No. 6, 1843, no longer applicable.

Buyskes, Trustee of Buissinne, *vs.* Holl.

Conditions of Sale. Auctioneer. Written conditions altered by parol. Purchaser at sale of land discharged from obligation to find personal security for payment of instalments in terms of the conditions of sale by verbal agreement of auctioneer during the sale to exempt him from such obligation.

1840, Aug. 29. — Buyskes, Trustee of Buissinne, *vs.* Holl.

In this case, a verbal agreement proved by the auctioneer to have been made while the sale was going on between the seller and the purchaser, that he should not be required to find personal securities for payment of the second and third instalments of the price, was found sufficient to discharge the purchaser from the obligation imposed by the written and published conditions of sale to give such securities.

Terrington *vs.* Simpson.

Periculum rei venditæ nondum traditæ. Ship: sale and delivery of. Registry Acts. Bill of exchange: consideration for.

[The "Alert" Case.]

1841. Feb. 16. Aug. 25. " 27. — Terrington *vs.* Simpson.

This action was brought by plaintiff for payment of the following bill of exchange drawn by defendant in favour of plaintiff:

"Port Elizabeth, 4th Sept., 1840.

"£500.

"At thirty days after date pay to Captain Terrington or his order £500, being for part payment of his schooner *Alert*, as advised by

"Your obedient servant,

"J. P. Simpson.

"To Messrs. Simpson Brothers & Co."

Which had been duly protested both for non-acceptance and non-payment by the drawers.

In his plea, defendant admitted that he had made the bill of exchange mentioned in the declaration, but denied every other allegation therein contained, and for a further plea pleaded that the plaintiff is not the legal holder of the said bill for a valuable consideration, and alleged that on the 4th September, 1840, defendant entered into a treaty with plaintiff for the purchase of the schooner *Alert*, the property of plaintiff, then lying at anchor in Algoa Bay, with her tackle, &c., &c., and certain articles and stores said to belong to her, and that defendant then declared himself willing to allow the plaintiff the sum of £2,200 as the price of said schooner, her tackle, &c., &c., and stores aforesaid, provided the same should be found on a careful inspection, by some competent person to answer the description which had been given of them by the plaintiff to the defendant. That the said £2,200 was proposed to be paid upon the completion of the purchase in the manner following, by £100 in cash, three bills for £500 each, drawn by defendant in favour of plaintiff on Messrs. Simpson Brothers & Co., respectively at thirty, sixty, and ninety days after date, and the remaining £600 by a transfer to the plaintiff of a certain estate, which was valued at that sum. That the defendant deposited in the hands of the notary who was employed to prepare a bill of sale of the said schooner the said sum of £100 and the said three bills of exchange, which had been so conditionally proposed to be paid to plaintiff in part of the purchase money, to be by such notary handed over to the plaintiff, in the event of the said contemplated purchase of the said schooner being fully and finally arranged and completed. That before the said contemplated purchase was fully and finally arranged and completed, viz., on the said 4th of September, the said schooner was driven on shore. That the defendant was always ready and willing to complete the said contemplated purchase on the terms and conditions above mentioned, and its not having been completed before the schooner was so driven on shore was not owing to any neglect or default on the part of the defendant. That shortly after the said schooner was driven on shore, and before the said contemplated purchase was finally arranged and completed, the plaintiff, in the absence of the defendant, prevailed upon the said notary to hand over to him the said £100 and the said three bills of exchange, which had been so deposited with the said notary as aforesaid, and that the bill in the declaration mentioned is one of the said bills so deposited by the said defendant and so handed over by the said notary; and on these grounds prayed that the plaintiff's claim be rejected with costs, that the said schooner may be declared to have been at the risk of the plaintiff when so driven on shore, and that plaintiff may be adjudged to deliver up the bill mentioned in the declaration to defendant, to be cancelled.

In his replication, plaintiff also joined issue on the first plea. And as to the second plea replied that the said defendant, of his own wrong and without the cause by him in his said second plea alleged, neglected to pay the amount of the said bill of exchange. And further replied that he ought not to be barred from maintaining his said action,

1841. Feb. 16. Aug. 25. „ 27.

Terrington *vs.* Simpson.

because he denies all and every the allegations in the said second plea set forth, and joins issue thereon.

Plaintiff put in the bill of exchange sued on, and the notarial protests for its non-acceptance and non-payment, and notarial copy (admitted by defendant) signed by plaintiff and defendant, dated 4th September, 1840. "Memorandum of the mode of payment agreed to between W. Terrington and J. P. Simpson for the sale and purchase of the ship or vessel, the *Alert*, sold this day by the first-named to J. P. Simpson, viz.:

Cash	£100
J. P. Simpson's bill at thirty days' date	500
Do. do. sixty do.	500
Do. do. ninety do.	500
And a certain estate called Myrtle Grove, situated &c., &c., which is to be immediately conveyed to said W. Terrington, valued at	600
	£2,200

" W. Terrington,
" J. P. Simpson.

" Witnesses: J. D. Wielbach,
" J. Centlivres Chase."

And having endorsed thereon:

" Port Elizabeth, 4th Sept., 1840.

"Received from J. P. Simpson, in part payment of the ship the *Alert*, sold to him this day, £1,600, as under, viz:

Cash...	One hundred pounds.
Bill at thirty days	Five hundred pounds.
Do. sixty days	Five hundred pounds.
Do. ninety days	Five hundred pounds.

" W. Terrington.

" Witnesses: J. D. Wielbach,
" J. Centlivres Chase."

Plaintiff also put in the notarial bill of sale executed by him as sole owner of the *Alert*, in favour of the defendant, in due and legal form, dated 4th September, 1840, and closed his case.

After voluminous evidence led by defendant in defence, and plaintiff in replication,

On the suggestion of the Court, the *Attorney-General* for the defendant was first heard.

He maintained, first, that the *Alert* had not been delivered by plaintiff to defendant; second, that there had not been a comparison between the inventory and the stores, as stipulated and agreed on, and quoted *Burge* 2, 535; *Voet* 18, 1,

24; *Bell's Bank. Law*, 1, *Contract of Sale*, § 1, *p.* 444; and maintained that therefore the sale and purchase had never been completed. He then maintained that the effect of the Registry Acts, 3rd and 4th *Wm. IV, Cap.* 55, § 31, 34, was such as to prevent the *periculum navis venditæ* from passing to the purchaser until he shall have produced the bill of sale to the proper Collector of the Customs, or shall have delayed so long to do this after he had it in his power to do it, and shall make him deemed to be *in laches*, and quoted *ex parte Yallop*, 15 *Vesey; Coote on Mortgages, pp.* 333, 334, and the authorities therein quoted; and that no contract, either verbal or in writing, whereby a shipowner binds himself to sell a ship, and so soon as possible to execute every legal deed required by the Registry Acts, can be enforced by law, and therefore that plaintiff had neither given nor done anything equivalent to giving a legal valuable consideration for the bill sued on.

Cloete, contra, quoted *Voet*, 1, 8, 11; 41, 1, 34; 18, 6, 1, *and seq.*, *Burge*, 3 *vol.*, *p.* 470; *Holt on Shipping*, *p.* 142.

The Court held that when defendant left the *Alert* on the 4th September, 1840, the parties had arranged all the terms and conditions of the sale, and completed the sale as far as it was possible for them to do so before the execution of a bill of sale in terms of the Registry Act. And that the defendant then received actual delivery of the possession of the vessel, and took upon himself the ownership of the vessel, in so far as it was possible for him to do so before the completion of the requisites of the Registry Act, and that the charge of the ship was taken from her former captain and given to Mintor, and under him, in his absence, to the chief mate Archer, who made a new engagement with Mintor to act for a time as chief mate.

That when plaintiff executed the bill of sale, the sale was in every respect so far concluded as to enable him to do so, and that when he delivered it to Chase, it was held by Chase for defendant, and was as much under defendant's control as if defendant himself had it in his pocket. That after the execution of the bill of sale, plaintiff was entitled to receive, and Chase was entitled to give him, the cash and bills which had been put into his possession, to be delivered to plaintiff on the completion of the bill of sale, and that plaintiff had done everything which by law he was required to do to divest himself of the property of the ship, and to transfer it to defendant, and that it depended on defendant himself when he should complete the transfer of the property to him, by complying with the requisites of the Registry Acts, and that in respect of what had taken place, the

1841. Feb. 16. Aug. 25. ,, 27.

Terrington *vs.* Simpson.

periculum of the ship was by the civil law transferred to defendant, after at least the execution of the bill of sale, even if the price had not been paid, or delivered by defendant to Chase to be paid to plaintiff.

That as to the question, what is the effect of the Registry Acts on the present case, there is no doubt that no right of property, no *jus in re* passed or could pass, or be transferred by the buyer to the seller, until the bill of sale had been presented to the Collector of the Customs, and the other requisites of the Registry Acts complied with, which had not been done when the vessel in this case went on shore.

But that this effect of the Registry Act does not in the slightest degree interfere with, affect, or deprive of effect, the rule of the civil law *periculum rei venditæ nondum traditæ est emptoris,* because that rule contemplates the case, namely, when in respect of want of tradition no property in the thing sold had passed to the buyer.

It is no doubt *possible* that the Registry Acts go further, and contain words which may have the effect of rendering any agreement or contract, whether written or verbal, for the sale of a ship, or any undertaking or obligation to execute a bill of sale in the form required by the statute, and to comply with all the statutory requisites, and to pay a stipulated price, void and of no effect, so as even not to furnish legal ground for an action, at the instance of the owner of the ship, to compel the other party to perform his obligation and complete the sale, by performing the statutory requisites, and pay the price, or even to pay damages for failing so to do. In which supposed case, if the plaintiff, instead of having obtained bills for the price, were now suing defendant to complete the sale and pay the price, and consequently was obliged to found his action on the written documents, which have been executed by the parties, and the transaction proved to have taken place between them, it is *possible* that the effect of the statutory provisions would bar the action.

But it is not necessary to inquire whether there is any such provision in the statute or not, for the plaintiff in this case is not in the situation which has just been supposed. He is not in this action obliged to found on any of the written documents which have passed between the parties, or on any of the transactions which have taken place between them. This action is founded on a bill of exchange, in form a complete, legal, unexceptionable document, containing a legal obligation by defendant to pay the amount, against which the only defence which has been made, or under the circumstances of the case can be made, is, that the bill was granted without consideration; and therefore the only question the Court has to try is whether, at the time when the bill was granted and delivered to plaintiff, the latter had given or done that which is considered in law as equivalent to giving a legal consideration for the bill, without regard to the fact whether the consideration so given is now available or of any value to the defendant, at least provided it has not been rendered unavailable or of no value by the act of the plaintiff. The Court considered it to be proved that the plaintiff did give a valuable and legal consideration for the bill. He executed aud caused to be delivered to the defendant a regular bill of sale, in strict conformity with the provisions of the statute, and did everything that by the statute the seller of a ship is required to do in order to complete the sale. The completion of the sale, according to the provisions of the statute, after this, depended entirely on the defendant himself. By delivering the bill of sale, plaintiff put it out of his own power, as an honest man, to execute any bill of sale in favour of any other person. If he did so, he would have subjected himself to be tried and convicted of the crime of stellionate. He had, therefore, in as far as he could, divested himself of the property and put it in the power of the defendant absolutely and completely to divest him of it whenever he chose. The Court held that this of itself was sufficient consideration for the bill; but further in consideration of getting the bills for the price, he had given up the entire possession and charge of the ship to defendaut and to his servants, and removed his own captain. The Court held that this of itself, but still more when coupled with the delivery of the bill of sale to defendant, was a sufficient consideration to give him a right of action on, and entitle him to recover, the contents of the bills.

Judgment for plaintiff, as prayed, with costs.

25th August.—Another action was for £1,000 between the same parties, being the amount of the remaining two bills of exchange on Messrs. Simpson Brothers & Co., of Cape Town, given to plaintiff by defendant, in part payment of the *Alert*, but which Messrs. Simpson Brothers & Co. had refused to accept or pay.

(On these bills a provincial judgment of the Court had been obtained, and the money had been paid under security that it should be repaid in the event of that judgment being reversed on a trial by the Court.) Against this claim the defendant pleaded that these bills were held without any consideration for them having ever passed from the plaintiff or been received by the defendant, inasmuch as the sale of the *Alert* was never perfected. And further, that these

1841. Feb. 16. Aug. 25. " 27.

Terrington *vs.* Simpson.

bills of exchange were delivered by plaintiff to defendant, not absolutely, but subject to a certain condition to be fulfilled by plaintiff, and which condition he had broken, inasmuch as when the said bills were delivered, it was conditioned, agreed, and fully understood that notwithstanding the delivery of these bills,—the execution of a bill of sale of the schooner,—and any other matter done or transacted by the parties,—the schooner should remain in charge of the plaintiff and be safely kept at his risk until the 5th September, at which time the defendant should take over the charge and risk of it on himself; and that in case she should not be safely given over into his charge, the sale, whether perfected or not, should be taken to be null and void to all intents and purposes; and the bills should become of no effect whatever. But the schooner having come ashore and been wrecked, thereby became incapable of being given over to the defendant according to the true intent and meaning of the parties; wherefore the defendant prayed the judgment of the Court whether the claim of the plaintiff should not be rejected with costs. Should, however, the claim of the plaintiff not be rejected on these grounds by the Court, defendant further pleaded as a claim in reconvention, that while the schooner remained undelivered, she was allowed (by reason partly that the plaintiff negligently and improperly had not provided any adequate number of servants and seamen to man her, and by reason partly that certain of the servants and seamen of the plaintiff in charge of the schooner conducted themselves carelessly, negligently, and unskilfully, and with a want of due and proper attention) to drift on shore and become a wreck, and was thus lost in consequence of mere negligence and default of the plaintiff and his servants and seamen, or one or other of them; wherefore the defendant was entitled to claim in reconvention the value of the vessel, £2,200, which he claimed accordingly. And for a further plea, or claim in reconvention, the defendant alleged that during the negotiations for the sale and purchase of the *Alert* it was stipulated and agreed that, in case the defendant should take charge of her, two policies of insurance, one for £1,650 on the vessel, and the other for £600 on the freight, should be assigned and made over to him by plaintiff; and therefore he prayed that, if the Court should determine against him on the preceding pleas, he should yet be declared entitled to an assignment of all right, title, and interest in those policies.

Plaintiff put in the two bills sued on. Defendant admitted that they were drawn by him, had been duly presented, dishonoured, and their dishonour duly notified.

Plaintiff put in the memorandum of sale, dated 4th September, 1840, with the receipt endorsed thereon, and the notarial bill of sale which had been put in in the previous action, all of which were admitted by defendant.

Plaintiff closed his case.

Defendant called voluminous evidence in support of his pleas.

On the suggestion of plaintiff, the Court called on the *Attorney-General* to sum up first.

The *Attorney-General* argued, first, that there was no consideration whatever which Capt. Terrington in this case could maintain had been given by him for the bills, except that, in consideration of getting the bill, he had done that which amounted to a perfected sale of the ship by him to Mr. Simpson; and therefore, if previous to the wreck, the sale was not in the eye of the law perfected, no consideration had been given by Capt. Terrington for the bills, and therefore, that, as by virtue of the 31st and 34th section of 3 and 4 W. 4, c. 55, no bill of sale is valid for any purpose whatever, until it has been registered at the Custom-house, in the way prescribed by the said 34th section, the sale of the *Alert* by Capt. Terrington to Mr. Simpson cannot be in law considered to have been perfected. That which was done by Captain Terrington was not a consideration given by him for the bills sufficient to enable him to maintain action on the bills, and quoted *Coote on Mortgages, p.* 327; *Moss vs. Charwick*, 2 *East p.* 399; *Mestaer vs. Gillespie*, 11 *Ves. Jun., p.* 637; *Rolleston vs. Hibbert*, 3 *Term* 406, &c. He maintained that notwithstanding the difference of the terms used in the statute of 3 & 4 *Gul. IV, c.* 55, § 31 and 34, and the 34 *Geo. III, c.* 68, § 15, the 3 & 4 *Gul. IV*, made no alteration in the law as it previously stood; and that no agreement or bargain between Capt. Terrington and Mr. Simpson, for a sale to be afterwards made and perfected between them, according to the Registry Act, although proved by the clearest evidence to have been so made, would have given Mr. Simpson a right of action against Capt. Terrington to compel him to perfect the sale; and that, therefore, as Capt. Terrington had done nothing which gave Mr. Simpson a right of action against him for anything, he had done nothing which could be considered as giving a consideration for the bills. Secondly, he maintained that there was no evidence to prove that Capt. Terrington, or his master, on the 4th September, had given up the charge of the vessel to Mr. Simpson, or any person acting under him; and that neither he nor any person under him, on the 4th Sept., took charge of the *Alert*.

He argued in support of his plea or claim in reconvention, and also of his second plea in reconvention.

1841. Feb. 16. Aug. 25. „ 27.

Terrington *vs.* Simpson.

The Court, without calling on plaintiff's counsel to reply, gave judgment for plaintiff as prayed, and for defendant in reconvention on the first claim; and on the second claim in reconvention adjudged that defendant in reconvention (Capt. Terrington) shall, on satisfaction of the judgment in this case, and on receiving legal transfer of the place Myrtle Grove, execute such deed or deeds as shall be most effectual for conveying to plaintiff, in reconvention, all his interests in the policies of insurance specified in the claim in reconvention. Defendant in convention to pay the costs.

27th August.—In a third action between the same parties, the plaintiff alleged that he had, on the 4th September, 1840, at Port Elizabeth, purchased from defendant the farm or estate of Myrtle Grove, which the defendant undertook to convey to him on demand. That the price of the farm was fixed at a sum of £600, which plaintiff paid by allowing it to be held as part of the purchase price of a certain vessel, the *Alert*, sold to defendant, at the same time and place, for £2,200; and that the defendant had refused or neglected to give the transfer.

The defendant tendered issue, and pleaded that the undertaking to convey the farm was made under a condition suspensive or precedent, which had failed, inasmuch as when that undertaking was entered into, it was conditioned, agreed, and fully understood between them that Capt. Terrington should keep the *Alert* at his risk till the 5th of September, on which day it should be taken over by defendant; but that before that day she came on shore in Algoa Bay, and was wrecked. Should, however, the claim of the plaintiff not be rejected by the Court on this ground, the defendant further pleaded as a claim in reconvention, that on the 4th of September, while the *Alert* remained undelivered to him, by the mere negligence and default of the plaintiff and his servants and seamen, and for want of due and proper care on their part, she was permitted to drift on shore and become a wreck. Wherefore the defendant claimed in reconvention the value of the schooner, viz., £2,200.

Plaintiff put in the order of Court of 2nd of August, whereby it was ordered that the pleadings in the action should be declared closed; and that the said case, and likewise a certain other case (describing the preceding case), be set down respectively for trial, peremptorily on the 24th day of August instant, so that both cases may come on for trial on the same day. But the action on the bills of exchange aforesaid to have priority in order of hearing. By consent of parties, the evidence of one case to be applicable to both cases.

Parties closed their cases.

Judgment for plaintiff in convention as prayed, and for defendant in reconvention. Transfer to be given within fourteen days.

1841. Feb. 16. Aug. 25. „ 27.

Terrington *vs.* Simpson.

In the above two cases, the judgment of the Court proceeded on the same grounds on which they gave judgment for plaintiff in the action *inter eosdem* on the 16th February, 1841, *supra*.

And, further, MENZIES, J., held, more especially with reference to the action for the transfer of Myrtle Grove, that the 31 B. 4 § of the 3rd and 4th of Will. IV, c. 55, did not annul or render invalid for any purpose whatever the memorandum of sale of the 4th September, 1840, signed by both parties, or the agreement for the sale and purchase of the *Alert* by the parties respectively, whether considered as having been *constituted* by the said memorandum signed by both, or as being, by the said memorandum, by the evidence of Chase, and by circumstances proved by other of the witnesses,—proved to have been entered into by the parties; and that therefore the said agreement being valid and effectual, the plaintiff, who had before the wreck performed everything which under the agreement he could be required or it was possible for him to do, for accomplishing the performance and fulfilment of the agreement on his part, was entitled now to claim from the defendant that he should perform his part of the agreement, viz., should pay the bills and give transfer of Myrtle Grove, notwithstanding that in consequence of the wreck of the *Alert*, the defendant could now derive no benefit or advantage from the transaction; and that the plaintiff, by signing the memorandum and by executing the bill of sale, had given such a consideration to defendant as was sufficient to bar the defendant from now maintaining that the bills had been given by him to plaintiff, and the obligation to transfer Myrtle Grove to the plaintiff had been undertaken by him without any consideration for the same having been given by the plaintiff.

This opinion as to the effect of the statute had been formed even on the hypothesis that the Court was bound to construe its terms according to the law of England, and that by that law there was no distinction between the property of a ship sold and the property of a ship transferred, and therefore that the 31st section should be construed as if the word "sale" had been used instead of the word "transfer," and *a fortiori:* on the hypothesis that the Court was bound to construe the terms of the statute according to the law of this Colony, in which there is a distinction between the property

1841. Feb. 16. Aug. 25. ,, 27. — Terrington *vs.* Simpson.

of a ship sold and the property of a ship transferred, and according to which the word "transfer," in the 31st section, must be held to have been used in contradistinction to "sale."

N.B. by MENZIES, J.—An appeal was taken against the judgment in these cases, but after the appellant had taken the opinion of eminent English counsel the appeal was withdrawn.]

DENEYS & CO. *vs.* ELLIOTT & STILL, EXECUTORS OF GEORGE.

Executors, plene administravit. Accord and satisfaction. Pleading.

1841. Nov. 17. — Deneys & Co. *vs.* Elliott and Still, Executors of George.

In this case, the declaration set out that the defendants, in their capacity as executors of the deceased Edward George, formerly proprietor of George's Hotel, or otherwise upon their own personal and individual liability, were indebted to the plaintiffs in the sum of £91 10s. 7⅛d., for meat furnished by plaintiff at the request and by the order of the said defendants for the purpose of continuing the business theretofore carried on at the said hotel, between the 20th July, 1840, and 31st March, 1841, and that the defendants had taken upon themselves the administration of the estate of the deceased George as his testamentary executors, and had paid to the plaintiffs the sum of £65 9s. 4½d., on account of the said sum of £91 10s. 7⅛d., but have refused to pay the balance of £26 1s. 2⅝d.

The defendants pleaded, first, the general issue; second, that the defendants, in their capacity as executors, on or about the 7th April, 1841, paid to plaintiffs the sum of £69 13s. 5d., which the plaintiffs accepted and received in full settlement, satisfaction, and discharge of the debt in the declaration mentioned (if it shall be made to appear that any such debt there were), and of all demands in respect of such debt against the defendants in their said capacity; third, that previously to the commencement of this suit or notice thereof, they had, in their said capacity as executors, divided and specifically appropriated amongst the creditors of said George all and singular the goods, chattels, and effects belonging to the testator's estate which ever came to their hands in their said capacity to be administered.

The plaintiffs joined issue on the first plea, and replied to the plea of accord and satisfaction that they ought not in respect thereof to be barred from maintaining their action, because admitting, as they do admit, that the plaintiffs received the said sum of £69 13s. 5d. in full settlement, satisfaction, and discharge of any demand which they had against defendants in their capacity as executors aforesaid, they say that they gave such discharge and acquittal upon the representation then made by the defendants that the assets of the estate of the deceased were insufficient to pay all the debts due by the said estate, and that all the creditors of the said estate had accordingly agreed with the said defendants to receive a sum of money as a dividend *pro rata* of their respective claims in full satisfaction thereof, whereas, in truth, the assets in the said estate were or would have been sufficient to have paid the full amount of the demand now claimed by the plaintiff, if the said estate had been duly administered by the said defendants, and that, in fact, the defendants did pay to some of the creditors in the said estate the full amount of their claims. And replied to the third plea of *plene administravit*, that they denied the allegation therein set forth; and further, that even should the defendants prove all the facts then alleged, yet the plaintiffs say that the defendant Elliott did bind himself to pay to the said plaintiffs out of his personal estate, and individually, the full amount of the sum now claimed of the said defendants, notwithstanding the receipt granted by the said plaintiffs on the 7th April, 1841, for the said sum of £69 13s. 5d., should the plaintiffs claim the said amount, and therefore that (even if the defendants' several pleas or either of them be allowed) the said Elliott should be adjudged individually to pay the amount claimed out of his personal goods and chattels.

In their rejoinder, the defendants denied all the allegations of the plaintiffs contained in their replication to the second plea of accord and satisfaction, and join issue with them thereon. And as to the replication to the third plea of *plene administravit*, in so far as the same denies the allegations of the defendants in the same plea, the defendants joined issue with the plaintiffs thereon: "But as to the residue of the said replication, the defendants, in their said capacity, say nothing, submitting to this Court that they are not bound by law to answer the same; the certain matter therein set forth being irrelevant to the present action, and a ground of suit different from any in the plaintiffs' declaration mentioned, and being, moreover, a claim and demand incapable of being joined with that for which this action has been brought."

In their surrejoinder the plaintiffs denied that the said matters were irrelevant to the present action, or that they formed the ground of another action, or that the said matters were incapable of being joined to this action.

After the plaintiffs had called and examined William George and Margaret George, the son and widow of the deceased, defendants admitted that meat had been furnished to Mrs. George, from the 21st of July, 1840, to the 3rd March,

1841. Nov. 17.

Deneys & Co. *vs.* Elliott and Still, Executors of George.

1841, to the amount of £91 10s. 7½d., of which only £7 12s. 6⅜d. was furnished subsequent to 15th December, when, the hotel having been sold, Mrs. George went to live in lodgings of her own; and that the meat so furnished prior to the 15th December was furnished by order of the defendants, as executors; and the evidence of those witnesses also went to shew that the meat purchased after 15th December was furnished on the express or implied security of the defendants, or at least of the defendant Elliott.

Plaintiffs closed their case.

Defendants called Edward Norton: "I was employed by the trustees of Waters & Heron, creditors to deceased George, to attend a meeting of the creditors on the 11th March last. At that meeting his executors, the defendants, produced a balance sheet of the estate; the same now shown me and signed by them. (Put in and read.) I produce a resolution signed at that meeting by some of the creditors. (Put in and read.) The resolution was in the following terms: "At a meeting of the creditors of the late Edward George, it was resolved that the balance of the account-current, as rendered by the executors, of £633 17s. 3d., be divided amongst us according to our respective debts, and payable 7th April by Mr. Eagar, and to sign a receipt in full of all demands." Mr. Still stated that unless the creditors consented to this resolution they must surrender the estate.

[Defendants put in the receipt (admitted by plaintiffs) signed by the creditors, and among others by the plaintiffs, on the 7th April, 1841, as follows: "We, the undersigned, creditors in the estate of the late Edward George, acknowledge to have received from the executors, Messrs. Elliott and Forbes Still, the several sums of money set opposite to our respective names, being in full settlement of our original claim and full demand against the said estate and said executors."]

"The plaintiff Frederick Deneys attended the meeting. He objected to sign this paper, because he said he thought he had a good claim on the executors for meat supplied after the death of Mr. George. One of the defendants, who were both present, and I think Mr. Still, said, that signing the resolution would not affect his claim, if he had a just claim against the executors. Mr. Deneys did refuse to sign it at that meeting, and I believe did not sign it afterwards, until he had taken a legal opinion."

Defendants put in the following paper, signed by the defendant Elliott, which was admitted to have been given to plaintiff, when he signed the resolution, and before he received the dividend: "I, the undersigned, hereby declare, that by a payment of 12s. sterling, or so much as the same may be, per pound, made to J. F. & S. Deneys, on their claim for butcher's meat supplied, amounting in the whole to rds. 1,556 6 4, the said Messrs. J. F. & S. G. Deneys are not to be held as having relinquished or being barred from claiming the full amount of the account for butcher's meat supplied from 1st October, 1840, to 28th February, 1841, amounting to rds. 730 7 2, should they deem it advisable to claim the whole amount from the undersigned, either individually or in his capacity as executor of the estate of the late Edward George.

1841. Nov. 17.

Deneys & Co., *vs.* Elliott and Still, Executors of George.

"THOMAS ELLIOTT."

Defendants closed their case.

Plaintiffs, in replication, called Jacob Deneys to prove the allegations contained in their replication to the second plea of accord and satisfaction, but completely failed to prove any of them by the evidence of this witness, and closed their case.

Cloete, for plaintiffs, maintained, first, that the document signed by Mr. Elliott barred him from founding on plaintiffs signature to the resolution and receipt as barring plaintiffs' claim against him (Mr. Elliott), either as executor or in his individual capacity. Second, that Mr. Elliott must be held, when he signed this document, to have acted as one of the executors, and as such had power to bind his co-executor; and, therefore, that this document bound Mr. Still as much as it did Mr. Elliott.

The *Attorney-General* argued that the plaintiffs were barred from founding on the document signed by Elliott against either of the defendants, even although it might have been well pleaded, at least against Elliott, in replication to the plea that plaintiffs had received the sum of £69 in full settlement, satisfaction, and discharge of their debt and all demands, in respect of such debt or claim against the defendants in their said capacity, because it was not pleaded in replication to that plea, but merely in replication to the defendants' other plea of *plene administravit.*

The Court held that the last objection to the form of the pleadings was good; and that therefore plaintiffs could not found on Elliott's document in bar to the plea of accord and satisfaction maintained by Elliott. The Court also held whatever might be the effect to be given to Elliott's document, as qualifying the receipt granted by plaintiffs, it could only be founded on against Elliott, and did not bind Still to any extent whatever. And the Court further held that the receipt, except in so far as qualified by the document signed by Elliott, was a complete discharge to the defendants, both in their capacities as executors and individually; and therefore gave judgment for the defendant Still, with costs, and absolved Elliott from the instance, with costs.

Norden *vs.* Still and De Villiers, Trustees of Bonnin.

Auctioneer. Trustee. Insolvency. Pleading.

A trustee cognizant of and tacitly acquiescing for thirteen years in a purchase made in the insolvency by the auctioneer employed to sell the estate assets, cannot afterwards refuse transfer, even when such purchase is an illegal one.

Such purchases are not null and void, ab initio, but are voidable according to the circumstances.

These circumstances must be specially pleaded.

1842. Aug. 30. Norden *vs.* Still and De Villiers, Trustees of Bonnin.

This was an action to compel trausfer of a certain lot or erf of ground in New-street, Graham's Town, which the plaintiff in his declaration alleged that he had, in July, 1829, purchased of the defendants in their capacity as trustees in the above estate, but of which they had hitherto declined or neglected to give transfer.

The defendants pleaded that they had not sold the land in question to plaintiff, but to one W. E. Smith, by the plaintiff, the auctioneer and agent in that behalf, as would appear by reference to the vendue roll and conditions of sale.

In replication, the plaintiff admitted that the name of W. E. Smith was entered on the vendue roll, but alleged that the name of the said W. E. Smith was made use of and entered upon the vendue roll by the said plaintiff, who was the real purchaser of the said erf or lot of ground of his own mere motion, and entirely for his convenience; that the said W. E. Smith was an absolute stranger to the said purchase, and that the said W. E. Smith hath not, and never had, any right, title, or interest whatever in or to the said erf or lot of ground; wherefore he prayed judgment that the transfer be made to him as demanded.

The *Attorney-General,* for plaintiff, put in receipt for transfer dues paid by Mr. B. Norden on the erf in question, as the purchaser thereof, dated 30th November, 1837.

The following undertaking, by the first defendant, was also put in:

"I promise to pay the estate of S. Bonnin the sum of £16, being the purchase amount of a piece of ground, being erf No. 230, Graham's Town, bought by W. E. Smith, at the sale by the trustees of S. Bonnin, the same having now been sold to me for £18.

"Forbes Still.

"Cape Town, 29th Sept."

Witnesses were called by plaintiff to prove the sale to himself and the circumstances connected with it.

1842. Aug. 30. Norden *vs.* Still and De Villiers, Trustees of Bonnin.

Musgrave, for defendant, put in a certificate by the Civil Commissioner of Albany, dated 30th November, 1837, stating that the sum of 19s. 2¼d. had been received from Mr. Benjamin Norden, being six per cent. upon the purchase money of an erf of ground situated in New-street, Graham's Town, bought by him at a public sale held for and on account of the insolvent estate of Samuel Bonnin, on the 1st July, 1829, for the sum of £16. And a certificate by plaintiff, as auctioneer, certifying that Mr. B. Norden had been the purchaser of the erf in question at the sale held of Bonnin's estate in 1839.

The Court called on defendants' counsel, who maintained that the purchase on which plaintiff's claim is founded is illegal and null in respect of the Proclamation of 3rd September, 1813, which he maintained is still in force. And quoted *2nd vol. Burge's Colonial Law, p.* 459, 466, to show that by the Dutch law, the purchase was illegal and null. Also *Voet* 18, 1, 9 ; *Burge, vol.* 1, *p.* 26.

The *Attorney-General, contra*, maintained that the Ordinance No. 31 repealed the Proclamation of the 3rd September, 1813; and that it also repealed the common law imposing any restriction on auctioneers' purchases at auctions held by themselves. Thirdly, he maintained that it was not competent for the defendants, under the present form of his pleading, to state any illegality of the purchase on the ground of the plaintiff having made it at an auction at which he himself was the auctioneer. Fourthly, he maintained that the purchase in question, under all the circumstances attending it, was not a purchase made *clam*, and, as such, prohibited by the common Dutch law, Mr. Still being cognizant of all the circumstances.

The Court unanimously held that Mr. Still was cognizant of the fact that Mr. Norden purchased for himself, and immediately resold to Comely ; and this acquiescence, even tacit, in what had thus taken place, for so long a period of time, is, in law, equivalent to an express confirmation of the purchase; and, therefore, that, whether the purchase was one which by the common (Dutch) law was originally voidable in respect of certain circumstances attending it or not, the defendant Still could not now refuse to so stand by the contract, and to give transfer to plaintiff, the purchaser.

The Court held that the Ordinance No. 31 has repealed the Proclamation of the 3rd September, 1813.

The Court held that, by the common (Dutch) law referred to by defendant,—even supposing that the common law, in so far as it imposed any restrictions on auctioneers purchasing

1842. Aug. 30. — Norden *vs.* Still and De Villiers, Trustees of Bonnin.

at auction held by themselves was not repealed by the Ordinance No. 31, a question which it was not necessary at present to decide,—yet purchases made by auctioneers at auctions held by themselves are not absolutely null and void *ab initio,* but are only liable to be set aside in respect of certain circumstances under which they may have been made.

The Court held that, as the declaration merely set forth that the plaintiff had purchased the erf, and that, as the facts which alone it was necessary for plaintiff to prove in order to establish the purchase (namely, that he had been employed to sell the property by auction, and that, at the auction held by himself, he himself purchased it), not only did not show that the purchase was null and void *ab initio,* but were not such as would entitle the defendant to have the purchase set aside, without proving other facts than those alone which it was necessary for the defendant to prove in order to support his declaration,—the defendant was not now entitled, under his general denial in his first plea to claim to have the sale set aside as voidable in respect of the peculiar circumstances under which the plaintiff, as auctioneer, made this particular purchase.

In other words, that, under the general denial of the allegation in the plaintiff's declaration, a defendant may maintain a defence against a contract sued on, founded on the contract being illegal, and null and void *ab initio,* but may not maintain a defence against the contract sued on when it is not illegal, null and void *ab initio,* but only voidable in respect of certain concomitant circumstances.

And gave judgment for plaintiff, as prayed, with costs.

NORDEN *vs.* COLE.

Provisional sentence refused for the second instalment of the purchase price of a farm (sold payable in three instalments, transfer to be given on the last), the seller refusing immediate transfer notwithstanding an immediate tender of the other instalments.

1842. Nov. 1. — Norden *vs.* Cole.

This case which stood on the provisional roll, was to recover £312 10s., as a second instalment due upon an agreement for the purchase of a farm called Plathuis, in the district of Somerset, which had been bought by the plaintiff from one E. Howard in the year 1839, and since transferred to the defendant. One of the conditions of the agreement was, that transfer was not to be given until the whole of the purchase money should be paid off. After the summons had been issued the third instalment had become due, though the plaintiff now sought only to recover the second instalment. It appeared that the estate had passed through at least four hands from him who held the actual title; and the defence of the defendant as to the provisional judgment now sought was, that he should not be bound to pay any further instalments until a transfer of the farm was in the hands of the party to whom the payment was to be made. It appeared indeed, and was admitted, that some question might arise between the intermediate parties; but *Cloete*, for the plaintiff, insisted that, as the defendant had agreed to make the instalments without transfer until the whole had been paid off, and as the agreement was admitted, that the defendant could not resist the performance of the contract accordingly, although the plaintiff had only obtained transfer in April last.

The *Attorney-General*, for defendant, suggested that, in practice, the Court had been accustomed to interfere where it could be shown that there was any jeopardy to the purchaser of obtaining due transfer upon the purchase money being paid; and that in the present case it would be inequitable that the plaintiff should obtain so large a sum of the defendant's money when he himself, in respect of an intermediate interest, had to raise an objection as to the transfer to one of the intermediate parties through whom the defendant could only derive his title. And produced to the Court the copy of a tender made to the plaintiff that not only the instalment now sought, but the third also, would be at once paid off by the defendant upon a guarantee by plaintiff that the estate should be duly transferred to the defendant; to which, however, the plaintiff had not consented.

The Court (Chief Justice and Kekewich, J.; Menzies, J., absent on circuit) considered that this was sufficient cause for refusing the provision, and held that equity would interpose so as to protect the defendant from a payment of which he might wholly lose the benefit; that a condition of the agreement could not be enforced any longer than its performance was consistent with the agreement of a beneficial purchase for which the defendant had paid so large a consideration; that such equity had in many like cases been afforded; and that it was the constant practice to decree that the payment over of the purchase money, and the transfer of the estate for which it was a consideration, should be made contemporaneous acts. And accordingly refused provision, with costs.

B. Norden, Trustee of Smith, *vs.* M. Norden.

Purchase and sale. Compensation. Judgments. Insolvency. Dominium.

A sale of immovable property having been made by an insolvent before his insolvency, and the trustee having called on the purchaser to complete the contract and pay the instalments according to the contract. Held, *that certain judgments obtained by the purchaser against the insolvent before the actual sequestration might be pleaded in compensation in part payment of the purchase price.*

But notwithstanding this and tender in the action to give transfer of payment of the purchase money, the claim in reconvention, claiming transfer on payment of the difference between what was allowed in compensation and the purchase price, could not be maintained. The dominium (on the principle of Harris and Buissinne, ante) remained in the insolvent estate, and could be transferred only on full payment of the purchase price.

1843. Feb. 21. „ 24.

B. Norden, Trustee of Smith, *vs.* M. Norden.

The following facts were admitted by the parties in this case:

W. E. Smith was enregistered as proprietor of certain premises in Graham's Town, over which he had executed a mortgage bond for £500 in favour of the Guardians' Fund. Smith and his wife (now the Widow Smith) were married without community of property. On the 14th July, 1835, and on the 6th January, 1837, he executed two mortgage bonds for £350 and £666 16s. 6d. = £1,016 16s. 6d., in favour of his said wife. On the 12th September, 1839, Smith, by his agent, Kidson, and the defendant, Marcus Norden, executed an agreement for the sale and purchase of said premises, for the price of £1,150, upon the following, *inter alios*, stipulations and conditions: That Norden should pay the said price by six instalments of £100 and one instalment of £50; the first to be paid on the 12th December, 1839, and the remaining six on the same day in the six succeeding years, with interest thereon payable in a certain manner therein set forth. That upon and at the payment of the first instalment of £100 on the 12th December, 1839, Smith should be bound to release, or cause to be released, before the proper authority, the two mortgages upon the said premises, for £1,016 16s. 6d., in favour of his wife. That Norden should give good security for the payment of £550, being the six last instalments. That the £500 held on mortgage by the Guardians' Fund should stand and remain on mortgage so far as the said Smith is concerned.

That possession of the premises should be given upon the due signing and execution of these presents. That transfer of the premises should be given upon payment of the first instalment, that is to say on the 12th December, 1839. That upon free and unencumbered transfer being given by Smith, save and except the mortgage bond for £500 in favour of the Guardians' Fund, Norden should execute a mortgage bond over the premises for £550 in favour of Smith.

1843. Feb. 21. „ 24.

B. Norden, Trustee of Smith, *vs.* M. Norden.

Immediately after the execution of the above deed of sale, Norden received possession of the premises on the 14th December, 1839. Smith and his wife obtained from the Registrar of Deeds the following memorandum: "I, Susannah Smith, born Bolton, married without community of property with William Edward Smith, and duly assisted by my said husband, do hereby declare to have received from my said husband the above-mentioned two capital sums amounting together to £1,016 16s. 6d., with interest due thereon, and consent in the cancelling of the said sum of £1,016 16s. 6d. from the public debt registrations of this Colony. And I further declare never to have ceded the above two named bonds to any person whomsoever, and in the event of the same being found, to be null and void.

"Cape Town, December 17, 1839.

"SUSANNAH SMITH.
"W. E. SMITH.

"As witness: C. ZASTRON,
Acting Registrar of Deeds."

The first instalment was not paid on the 12th December, 1839. Mr. Reid, attorney for Smith, took out a summons against Norden for payment of the first instalment, offering, in the usual form, to perform the stipulation in the contract of sale incumbent on the plaintiff. The day of appearance inserted in the summons was the 13th February, 1840. But this summons was withdrawn by plaintiff, in consequence of his title deeds and diagrams being accidentally mislaid, or that he was unable to give transfer; which fact plaintiff was aware that Norden had knowledge of and meant to found upon. On the 13th February, 1840, Norden recovered provisional sentence against Smith for £227 19s. 8¼d., inclusive of costs, on certain debts due by Smith to third parties. On the 30th May, 1840, Norden recovered another judgment against Smith, £203 6s. 2½d. on certain debts due by Smith to third parties. On the 14th February, 1840, Mr. Barker, attorney for M. Norden, gave notice by letter to Mr. Reid, attorney for Smith, that Mr. John Norden would, on behalf of M. Norden, attend at the office of the

1843. Feb. 21. „ 24.

B. Norden, Trustee of Smith, *vs.* M. Norden.

Registrar of Deeds, on the 18th February, to receive transfer of the premises in question, and pass mortgage bonds, according to the contract of the sale dated 12th September, 1839. Nobody attended for Smith. None of the instalments were paid, nor did it appear that any further steps had been taken by either party before the death of Smith, which took place on the 3rd April, 1841. On the 16th June, 1841, Smith's estate was duly surrendered as insolvent, by his widow as the sole executrix of his last will. Only six creditors proved their debts against the estate, viz., the Guardians' Fund on the bond for £500, Benjamin Norden for £20, the widow on the two mortgage bonds in her favour for £1,016 16s. 6d., and three other creditors, for debts amounting in all to £20 9s. The latter appear to have taken no further share in the proceedings under the sequestration.

Benjamin Norden was appointed trustee. On the 14th September, 1841, the third meeting of the creditors was held before the Master, and attended only by the trustee and Mrs. Smith. After reading the trustee's report, which recommended that the premises in question should be peremptorily sold to the highest bidder, and the contract of sale with Marcus Norden, dated 12th September, 1839,

"It was resolved by the undersigned creditors then present that the terms of the said contract be fulfilled by the trustee on account of the estate, and that notice be given to the said Marcus Norden to complete the purchase of the immovable property accordingly, in the terms of the said contract.

"Widow Sus. Smith.
"B. Norden."

On the 12th August, 1842, the trustee took out the summons in the present action, calling on defendant to receive transfer, according to law, of the premises in question; and upon receiving such transfer to pay to the plaintiff £300, being the first, second, and third instalments of the price; and to comply with the further terms and conditions of the contract of 12th September, 1839.

The plaintiff's declaration set out the contract of 12th September, 1839, *verbatim;* the death of Smith; the surrender of his estate as insolvent; the plaintiff's appointment as trustee; that defendant had been duly put in possession of the property; and although Smith was, in his lifetime, and his widow and the plaintiff since his death had been, always ready and willing to perform all the matters and things stipulated in the said contract to be performed by Smith, yet that the defendant had refused and neglected to perform any of the matters and things stipulated therein to be performed by him; and more particularly had not paid any of the instalments of the price, although often requested so to do; wherefore an action had accrued to plaintiff to demand that the defendant be condemned to pay to the plaintiff the amount of such of the instalments as shall have been due at the time of the Court giving judgment in the case, with interest. And, further, generally to perform and specifically execute the contract according to its terms and provisions; the plaintiff being ready and offering upon his part to perform everything which, under and by virtue of the terms and conditions of the contract, the defendant is entitled to require; and prayed that the defendant might be condemned accordingly; or otherwise, that the said plaintiff might have such other relief as to the Court should seem meet.

Defendant's plea denied that Smith in his lifetime, or the widow and plaintiff since his death, had been ready at any time to perform the matters and things stipulated in the contract to be performed by Smith; and joined issue thereon, and prayed for judgment with costs. And for a further plea, denied that the defendant had refused or neglected to perform the matters and things stipulated in the contract to be performed by him. And joined issue thereon; and prayed for judgment with costs. And for a further plea, the defendant said that the plaintiff ought not to have his action, because, before the commencement of this suit, to wit, on or about the 1st October, 1841, the defendant tendered to plaintiff, in satisfaction and payment of the said several instalments of the said purchase money then due and owing by defendant, certain judgments recovered by the defendant in the Supreme Court against the said Smith in his lifetime, and before his estate had been surrendered as insolvent; which judgments had never been paid or satisfied by Smith or any person on his behalf; which judgments (those above mentioned in the narrative of the facts) were particularized in a schedule thereunto annexed; but the plaintiff refused to receive the same in satisfaction and payment of the said instalments. And the defendant further said that he had always been, and still is, ready and willing to pay the said instalments which are due and owing, provided the said judgments be allowed in account between defendant and plaintiff, and received in payment of the said instalments to the amount of the said judgments, and tendered the same accordingly; whereupon he prayed for judgment with costs. And for matter of claim in reconvention, the defendant prayed that the plaintiff may be adjudged to give transfer, and generally to do all matters and things stipulated to be done by Smith according to the terms and conditions of the

1843. Feb. 21. „ 24.

B. Norden, Trustee of Smith, *vs.* M. Norden.

contract; he, the defendant, being ready and tendering to perform all matters and things stipulated in said contract to be performed by him.

Plaintiff, in his replication and plea in reconvention, joined issue on the defendant's first two pleas; to the last plea (submitting to the Court that the said plea, being a plea of compensation, is not properly pleadable in this action, founded as it is on the contract in the said declaration mentioned) averred that he ought not, by reason of anything in that plea alleged, to be barred from having his said action; because he averred that all the said judgments in the said plea mentioned were recovered by the defendant against Smith in his lifetime upon or by virtue of debts which accrued to the defendant by purchase after the date of the said contract, and when he had full notice of the insolvency of the said Smith.

And for a further replication to the said third plea, averred that he ought not, by reason of it, to be barred from having this action; because the two mortgages on the premises in favour of Mrs. Smith, which are in the notarial contract in the declaration set forth mentioned and described, are still remaining wholly unsatisfied to and are of right demandable by her; and that she, and such mortgager as aforesaid, will be wholly deprived of her said debt of £1,016 16s. 6d., and will receive no part of the same, in case the defendant be permitted to set off and plead in compensation against the amount of the purchase money the said judgments set forth in the said plea.

And in answer to the claim in reconvention, plaintiff pleaded that, "protesting he is not bound by law to give such transfer, he always has been, and is now, ready and willing to give to the said defendant transfer of the premises upon the terms and conditions of the contract, and hath frequently offered to give such transfer, and has only declined to give such transfer as aforesaid because the defendant insisted and required that he should be allowed to set off the amount of the said judgments against the amount of the purchase money; and joined issue generally with defendant on his said claim in reconvention."

In their rejoinder and sur-rejoinder, the parties joined issue, both as to facts and conclusions in law respectively pleaded by them; and, in particular, defendant excepted to the second replication, as being insufficient in law and irrelevant.

After hearing the counsel for both parties in the action in convention, the Court unanimously found,—

1st,—That the plea of compensation pleaded by defendant in respect of the judgments recovered by him against

Smith was properly pleaded by him as a defence against the action in convention founded on the contract of sale.

1843. Feb. 21. „ 24.

B. Norden, Trustee of Smith, *vs.* M. Norden.

2ndly,—That the compensation now pleaded by defendant in respect of those judgments operated *retro* to the date of the judgment, and *pro tanto* extinguished Smith's claim for the instalments which had then, or might previously to the surrender of his estate, become due, as much as if defendant had paid the amount of the judgments in cash to Smith; and, consequently, that if Smith were now alive and solvent, and had brought the present action for the amount of the instalments claimed in it, the defendant's plea of compensation would have afforded him a good defence against the action, and entitled defendant to judgment.

3rdly,—That if the creditors, by their trustee, chose to take up the personal contract constituted between Smith and defendant by the deed of sale and attempted to enforce performance by defendant of the personal obligations, which by it he had bound himself to perform, whatever would have afforded to the defendant a good defence against Smith was a good defence against his creditors; consequently, that as the plea of compensation pleaded by defendant would have barred Smith's claim for the instalments now sued for, it was a good defence against the creditors.

4thly,—That the words "said insolvency" in the thirty-fifth section of Ordinance No. 64, meant the adjudication or surrender of the insolvent's estate as insolvent; and therefore, as it was proved that defendant had obtained cession of the debts on which he obtained judgments against Smith, prior to the surrender of his estate as insolvent, defendant was entitled to plead compensation thereon, although they had accrued to him after the execution of the contract of sale, and whether he knew at the time that Smith was *de facto* in solvent circumstances or not.

The Court held the second replication was irrelevant to, and insufficient in law as an answer to, the plea of compensation, even although the effect therein alleged would be produced by the Court sustaining the plea of compensation, which the Court held it would not, as no judgment given against the trustee, decreeing him to give transfer, could have the effect of depriving her of her hypothec over the premises which she possessed by virtue of her mortgage bond.

On these grounds they gave judgment for the defendant in convention, with costs.

The defendant prayed the Court, in addition to this judgment, to decree that the plaintiff should give transfer to the defendant, on the defendant's paying the balance of the price remaining due after crediting him with the instalments extinguished by compensation.

1843. Feb. 21. ,, 24.

B. Norden, Trustee of Smith, *vs.* M. Norden.

The Court refused this application, because they held that the only issue joined between the parties in the action in convention was whether the plaintiff could enforce payment from defendant of the instalments which the defendant pleaded were extinguished by compensation, on offering him transfer. Because the plaintiff had in his declaration tendered transfer only on condition of receiving full payment of all the price. And likewise the defendant had not in any part of his pleadings, in the action in convention, upon which the issue between the parties was joined, prayed that the plaintiff might be decreed to give transfer.

Postea (24th February, 1843).—After hearing the counsel for both parties in the action in reconvention, the Court unanimously gave judgment for the defendant in reconvention with costs.

They held that this case was in every respect precisely the same with that of *Harris v. Buissinne's Trustee;* and that, in conformity with the law as declared by judgment in that case, the purchaser of immovable property who has not obtained transfer before the surrender of the estate of the seller as insolvent, cannot by law compel the seller's creditors to give him transfer of the property purchased, although he may previously have paid the whole of the stipulated price to the seller, or may offer to do so to the creditors; and that he is only entitled to claim and rank on the seller's estate for the damage sustained by him by reason of the non-fulfilment of the personal obligation of the seller to give him transfer.

They held that creditors were not barred from maintaining this defence against the claim in reconvention, by reason of the resolution of the creditors at the third meeting; because the true meaning of that resolution was only that the sale should be completed by giving the plaintiff in reconvention transfer on condition of his paying the whole price without being allowed credit for the amount of the judgments. And because this resolution was, in so far as concerned the said plaintiff, *res inter alios acta;* and because no resolution or determination among creditors to take certain steps could be founded on by any third person who was no party to it, as barring them from altering their resolution and afterwards adopting a different course of proceeding.

That the defendants were not barred from maintaining this defence from having, in their action in convention, attempted to enforce payment of the whole price from defendant, by offering, in the event of his making such payment, to give him transfer.

And because even if all or any of the reasons on which he maintained that the creditors were barred from maintaining their defence against the claim in reconvention had been well founded, the plaintiff could not be allowed now to plead and found on them, because he had joined issue in the action in reconvention on defendant's plea without having pleaded any of such reasons in replication to it.

1843. Feb. 21. " 24.

B. Norden, Trustee of Smith, *vs.* M. Norden.

Van Aardt *vs.* Hartley's Trustees.

Tradition. Immovable Property. Jus ad rem. Insolvency.

A vendor who had not the dominium of a farm, but a jus ad rem, a right to claim conveyance, having sold the farm, or, in law, his right to the farm, and having thereafter surrendered his estate as insolvent without having obtained transfer coram lege loci, the trustee of his insolvent estate was held bound to effect transfer in favour of the purchaser. The jus ad rem had been sold and actually delivered before the sequestration.

The case of Harris and Buissinne's Trustee (vide ante p. 105) *is distinguished from this case by the fact that there the vendor who had become insolvent had the jus in re at the date of the sequestration.*

1845. Aug. 28.

Van Aardt *vs.* Hartley's Trustees.

Charles Hartley, an insolvent, had before his insolvency purchased certain portions of two places, called Zwakfontein and Tweefontein, from one Van der Merwe, and obtained actual possession of them. Before he got legal transfer of those lands from Van der Merwe, Hartley sold them to the plaintiff for £1,500, by a notarial deed of sale, dated 13th September 1842, whereby he bound and obliged himself to give legal transfer thereof to the plaintiff within twelve months from that date. The plaintiff satisfied and paid the said price of £1,500, to and on account of Hartley, in terms of the provisions of the deed of sale, and received actual possession of the lands from Van der Merwe, and subsequently before he had given legal transfer thereof to the plaintiff, Hartley became insolvent.

The trustees of Hartley refused to take any steps for giving the plaintiff such transfer, maintaining that on the principle of the case of *Harris vs. Buissinne,* the right to the lands which Hartley had acquired from Van der Merwe and sold to the plaintiff devolved and became vested in them, *ipso facto,* by virtue of the sequestration for behoof of all the creditors of Hartley; and therefore that the plaintiff had no right to claim transfer thereof from the trustees, and could only claim to be ranked as a concurrent creditor on Hartley's estate for repetition of the price

1845. Aug. 28. — Van Aardt vs Hartley's Trustees.

which he had paid to Hartley, unless the creditors should allow the transfer to be made to him on condition of his paying to the trustees the price for which he had bought the lands, notwithstanding he had already paid it to Hartley prior to the insolvency of the latter.

The plaintiff, in consequence, brought an action in the Circuit Court of Albany to compel the defendants to give him transfer, to which they pleaded, first, the general issue, and secondly and subordinately, that even if the facts alleged by the plaintiff were true, yet that by reason of the subsequent insolvency of Hartley they had a good defence against the action.

At the trial (12th April, 1845), the plaintiff put in the deed of sale referred to in the summons, and the defendants admitted all the facts alleged in it. Whereupon the Circuit Court removed the case to the Supreme Court.

This day, *Porter, A.G.*, for plaintiff, maintained that, as Hartley had himself only a personal right to the lands, the deed of sale so divested him of all interest in the lands that at the time he became insolvent there remained no interest in them which could pass to the trustees; and that the execution by Hartley of the transfer to plaintiff was necessary, not to divest Hartley of his interest in the lands, which were already completely transferred by the sale to Van Aardt, but merely as a form requisite to complete Van Aardt's real right. The decision in *Harris vs. Buissinne* was given solely because, in that case, the *jus in re* of the house, transfer of which was claimed from the trustees, had been vested in Buissinne, and as, by the law of the Colony, he could not divest himself of it except by a regular transfer, executed *coram lege loci,* it was vested in him at the time of the surrender of the estate, and consequently, by virtue of the surrender *eo ipso* devolved to the trustees for behoof of all the creditors.

C. J. Brand argued *contra.*

The Court gave judgment for plaintiff, as prayed, with costs.

Jenkins, Executor of Batt, vs. Maynard.

Diagram, expenses of. Action for recovery of. General plan. Conditions of sale.

Under what circumstances a purchaser at a sale of landed property is not bound for the expenses of a general plan.

1843. Feb. 14. — Jenkins, Executor of Batt, vs. Maynard.

This action was brought for a sum of £55 5s., being the amount of expenses incurred in preparing a plan or diagram, with subdivisions, of the estate called Sussex

Place, and adjoining lands, of which defendant became purchaser.

Plaintiff founded his claim on the following clause in the conditions of sale: "The purchaser shall pay the transfer dues to Government; also the expenses of the diagrams of the said property, of the transfer and mortgage bonds, of the stamps; of the said conditions of sale and also the expenses of a fresh survey, should it be necessary, of subdivisions and new diagrams, and all such other expenses as might be incurred to complete the said transfer."

Defendant pleaded the general issue.

Musgrave, for plaintiff, called,

Clark William Adams: I am an auctioneer. On the 20th October, 1841, I was employed by Mr. Jenkins to sell some property for him belonging to the estate of Mrs. Batt. Mr. Maynard bought five lots, being lots 9 to 13 inclusive, in one lot by the fall. They had previously been put up in five lots by the rise, and bought by separate persons. To the best of my belief, the plan now shown me is that which was exhibited at the sale. The plan, besides the five lots 9 to 13, constituting Sussex Place, contained also two lots of ground near it, but not adjacent, marked 15 and 16, and also two lots 14 and 15, bought by another person. There were no other plans or diagrams of those lots exhibited at the sale. This was the first sale in which I was required to obtain a new diagram to be made. On all previous occasions we had been able to give transfer from old diagrams, but here it was necessary to have a new survey of the property and a new diagram. As the new survey was expensive, I framed the conditions of sale, according to direction, for the express purpose of making the purchaser liable for the expense of the survey. If the conditions do not cover those expenses I made an error in framing them. I was never asked at the sale by any one what was meant by the expenses of the diagrams, or I would have told him. I was surprised that I was not asked the question. Other questions were put to me by bidders as to the servitude connected with Mr. Batt's tomb, and as to the goodness of the roof of the house. If the lots had been sold by the rise, the purchasers of each lot would have had to pay a proportionate share of the expenses of the diagram and survey. I produce the conditions of sale of the several lots, and of the general lot, all of which contain the following clause: "The purchaser shall pay the transfer dues to Government, being 4 per cent. on the purchase money; also the expenses of the diagrams of the property, the transfer and mortgage bonds, of the stamps, of these conditions of sale, and all the expenses of a fresh survey, should it be necessary, of subdivisions and

1843. Feb. 14. — Jenkins, Executor of Batt, *vs.* Maynard.

new diagrams, and all such other expenses as may be incurred to complete said transfer." I have seen the bill of the surveyor, Mr. Ruysch. I know it was above £50. I cannot identify it. I had not seen it before I made the conditions of sale; but before doing so I had seen, not the plan now shown me, but a rough outline of it. When I made out the conditions of sale, I thought the charge for the diagram would not have exceeded £10.

William F. Bergh: I am in the habit of attending sales of landed property as a commissioner of the Supreme Court. I would call the instrument now shown me a general plan and diagram of the estate. I have seen in conditions of sale clauses exactly similar to the seventh clause in the conditions produced. In fact, this seventh clause is a general clause which has been in use for thirty years. I have before seen the words "expenses of the diagrams of the said property" pertinently introduced, but they are generally included in the words, "and all such other expenses as may be incurred to complete the said transfer." If an estate formerly included in one diagram is sold in lots to different persons, the purchasers cannot get transfer of their respective lots without getting new diagrams made of their respective lots, unless the estate had been originally formed of separate lots, having separate diagrams, and it is sold precisely in the same separate lots in which it was separately purchased. In all sales of land by auction, by the Master or trustees, it is always stipulated that the expenses necessary to obtain transfer shall be borne by the purchasers, and not paid by the seller.

Mynardus Ruysch: I am a sworn land surveyor. I was employed by plaintiff to make the plan now shown me. The account now shown me is that which I rendered for making this survey and plan. The charges are my usual charges. I have been paid within a trifle. It was decidedly necessary for the sale that I should make this survey and plan, not only to subdivide the lots, but to ascertain the original boundaries. I had nine diagrams put into my hand to work upon, and I had first to ascertain the landmarks and boundaries of these nine pieces of land, and then to include them in one general plan, and I had then to subdivide this estate into seven new lots. If these seven lots had been sold to separate purchasers it would have been utterly impossible to have given them transfer and diagram of the respective lots without having had a general plan made; because the diagram of the lots must specify the extent and bearings of each.

Cross-examined: The boundaries and landmarks of the nine lots were not known before the survey. Had the plaintiff been able to point them out, a great deal of the expense of the survey would have been spared, viz., the £30 clear.

The plaintiff closed his case.

The defendant called,

Johannes George Steytler.—I have had a good deal of experience in the sale of immovable property by auction as a trustee, and I have known estates sold in lots different from any of which previous diagrams had been made, and of general plans being made to show lots by diagram. I understand a document on which the transfer can be effected, transfer could not be effected on the plan now shown me alone, without reference to the original diagrams, but when the estate consists of separate pieces which have never been included in the Register Office in one general diagram, and is sold in new lots, transfer with diagrams of those lots cannot be made without first having a general plan first made. From the words in the seventh clause I should have considered that in the event of the lots being sold separately, the purchasers must pay the expense of making the general diagram, but that if sold in one lot, the seller should pay those expenses. But the purchaser of the whole would pay all expenses except the plan. I go on the general practice, and also on the final words of the clause. Because it is not possible for the purchasers of several lots to get transfer of the lots without a general plan having first been made, and because one purchaser of the whole could get transfer of the whole, without the necessity of any general plan.

Cross-examined: The construction I would have put on the words, "also the expense of the diagrams of the property," is, that if any of the original diagrams had been lost, the purchaser was to pay the expense of getting new diagrams. To the additional words in the seventh clause I can attach no other or additional meaning than I would have attached to the clause if it had stood without them, and would have understood it to have applied only to new copies of former diagrams, if those were missing.

Fred. Godfrey Watermeyer: I have had much experience in the sale of landed property. When it was necessary to subdivide it into lots, I have a new plan made of it in order to effect the subdivision. I have read the seventh clause of the condition, and if I had been a purchaser of the whole property I should not have understood from them that I should have had to pay the expense of the general plan now shown me, which I do not consider to be a diagram. I should not consider that one purchaser of separate lots should pay for such a plan, unless expressly stipulated in the conditions of sale that the expenses were to be paid

1843. Feb. 14. — Jenkins, Executor of Batt, vs. Maynard.

either in whole or in part. Although I must admit that in this case such a plan must necessarily be made before each purchaser could get transfer of his lot.

Daniel Cloete: I have read the seventh clause in the conditions. I was formerly agent for the Sequestrator and for the Orphan Chamber, and have had experience in the sale of lands by auction. I have seen the plan now produced. From the usual construction given to the words in this clause, I should say that certainly defendant was not bound to pay the expense of making such a plan. I look upon such plans as merely a picture of the estate, for the information of the public, showing the relative extent and position of the property offered for sale, and not as the diagram which is required to be made in order to obtain transfer.

Richard Webber Eaton: I have had experience in the sale of land by auction as trustee and general agent. When I have had a property put up in lots, I have had plans of the description now shown me made out. From the construction generally put on the words used in the seventh clause, I should not think that a purchaser of the whole in one lot was thereby bound to pay any part of the expense of this plan. I consider all such general plans as necessary for the property to be put up for sale in lots, and therefore not properly to enable the purchaser of the lots to obtain transfer. I am of opinion that a plan showing the subdivision of the lots is in every case necessary for the sale, and that therefore it is not included in the words "and all such other expenses as may be incurred to complete the transfer," and it has never been my practice to charge it. I conducted the sale of George's half-way house. I had it before the sale surveyed and divided into twenty-five lots, and a plan thereof made out by Mr. Skirrow, and exhibited at the sale, and all were purchased by one person by the fall. Skirrow charged for that survey and plan £25. I made an express stipulation in that case that the purchaser of each lot should pay a certain specified sum, and that if one man purchased the whole of the lots, he should pay the sum total of those sums; and I accordingly received from the purchaser £29, being £4 more than the expense of the survey.

Henry Cloete: I am an advocate, and have had much experience in the sale of lands by auction. From the usual construction given to the words in the seventh clause, I consider that the purchaser is bound to pay every expense which is necessary to give him a proper title; and that, therefore, whether those expenses have been incurred before or after the sale, still, if necessary to complete the title, they must be borne by the purchaser. I consider the plan now produced to be a plan, and not technically a diagram, which I understand to mean either the original representation of the property as surveyed and granted, and which is affixed to the original grant of the property, or to an extract or copy of that; and that, as defendant was the purchaser of the whole, no general plan of the pieces of ground of which the estate sold was originally composed was necessary to enable him to obtain transfer, and consequently that he is liable for no part of the expense of making it. But where the estate sold consisted of pieces of ground having separate diagrams, and never included in one general diagram, and is at the sale subdivided into new lots, which are purchased by separate persons, a general plan of the whole must necessarily be made before the purchasers can obtain transfers with diagrams of the separate lots.

Thomas Sutherland: I have had much experience in the sale of lands as a trustee. From the construction usually put on the words used in the seventh clause, I am of opinion that a purchaser in the situation of the defendant would not thereby consider that he was bound to pay the expense of making such a plan as that now shown me, and that if the seller wished to have charged the purchaser with the expense he should have made an express stipulation to that effect in the condition of sale.

Defendant closed his case.

Musgrave referred to the eleventh (manuscript) condition in the conditions of sale, applicable to the whole five lots, and which are signed by the defendant as purchaser of those five lots, in which the plan now produced, and which was exhibited at the sale as described in the diagram: "The piece of ground on which the tomb is erected to the memory of Henry Batt, Esq., enclosed in an iron railing or fence shown in the diagram, with the letter — measuring from —— square roods, shall be reserved (with the right of a road to approach the same) to the executors of the said Henry Batt's relations, and descendants, or their agents, and if required with workmen or otherwise; the purchaser and future proprietors of Sussex Place shall be obliged to keep the said iron fence or railing in good repair," and which condition is also inserted in the condition applicable to lot 11, with this difference, that in the latter the words "marked on the diagram with the letter B," measuring ——; and argued that therefore whatever ambiguity there might otherwise have been as to the meaning of the words in the seventh clause, "also the expenses of the diagrams of the property," and as to whether they would, taken by themselves, have or have not been held to apply to and include in their meaning the plan produced; the evidence of Mr.

1843. Feb. 14. — Jenkins, Executor of Batt, vs. Maynard.

Adams showing that this was the only plan or diagram exhibited at the sale, and the description given in the eleventh (manuscript) condition must be held to have fixed the meaning of those words, and as proof of the intention of the parties that this plan should be included in the diagram in the passage above quoted; and that this word "diagrams" was intended by the parties to apply exclusively to this plan, seeing that the expenses of all diagrams to be made thereafter were provided for by the concluding words of the seventh clause.

The *Attorney-General*, *contra*, argued that *non constat* that the instrument described in the eleventh clause as the diagram must necessarily be the instrument prepared by Mr. Ruysch, and entitled "plan." And in support of this, founded on the facts that, in the seventh clause, the word used is "diagrams" in the plural, while in the eleventh clause the instrument there referred to is called "the diagram," and that "diagrams," of the said property, referred to new diagrams in place of or copies of previous diagrams which might have been lost or missing.

The Court were of opinion that the defendant was not bound to pay any part of the expenses of Mr. Ruysch's survey and plan, by reason of any of the divisions contained in the seventh clause, unless the words "also the expenses of the diagrams of this property" should be considered to be in law a sufficiently clear and unambiguous stipulation to that effect, either taken by themselves as they stand in the seventh clause, or together with the stipulation in the eleventh (manuscript) condition. Because they were of opinion that this general plan was not comprehended in the word "diagrams," in the end of the seventh clause, and that as defendant had purchased the whole property in one lot, the formation of a general plan was not necessary to enable him to obtain transfer, and therefore the expense of making it could not be included in the words, "and all such other expenses as may be incurred to complete the said transfer."

The Court were unanimously of opinion that the words "also the expenses of the diagrams of this property," whatever was the intention of the seller in introducing them into the seventh condition, were not a sufficiently clear and unambiguous stipulation that the purchaser should pay the expense of making this plan, to render the defendant liable to pay those expenses.

The majority of the Court were of opinion that the words in the eleventh (manuscript) clause, were not sufficient to explain the above quoted words in the seventh, so as clearly to make them applicable to the plan, and were in some degree, in coming to the conclusion, influenced by the argument of the Attorney-General,—that the word "diagram," in eleventh clause, did not necessarily refer, nor was intended by both parties to refer, to the plan in question.

MENZIES, J., was inclined to be of a different opinion, and held that the use of the unusual stipulation in the seventh clause, that the purchaser should pay "also the expense of the diagrams of this property," must be held to have put the purchaser on his guard that something more than the expense usually borne by purchasers should be borne by him, and that he must be held to have deliberately agreed to the eleventh condition, and therefore must have known that the plan which has been produced, and which was the only plan or diagram exhibited at the sale, was meant to be referred to and described as "the diagram," and so have intended in that condition it should be so referred to and described; and that, although this instrument ought properly to be called a plan, and that "diagram" is an improper and unsuitable appellation for it, still if the identity of the instrument to which the parties intend to refer is clear, the Court must give effect to these clearly expressed intentions and agreement respecting that instrument, however improper the denomination given to it by the parties. Now this instrument having been referred to and described in the eleventh condition as a diagram, the parties must be held to have understood that it was a diagram, and that this was its proper denomination; from which it follows that it may have been one of the things which the purchaser, by reason of the words in the seventh clause, "also the expenses of the diagrams of the property," bound himself to pay the expenses of. And if it can be shown that this was really the case, the purchaser is bound and liable to pay the expense of making it, although, properly speaking, it is not a diagram. His Lordship was of opinion that as the last clause of the seventh condition expressly bound the purchaser to pay all the expenses of making what are properly diagrams, and the expense of which is usually paid by purchasers, he must, when he bound himself to pay "also the expense of the diagrams of the property," have understood that he bound himself to pay the expense of some other instruments or documents; and as this plan, which the parties, in the eleventh clause, agreed to call a diagram, was the only thing in the shape of a plan or diagram exhibited or referred to at the sale, he must be held, by reason of these words, to have bound himself to pay the expense of making it.

The majority of the Court gave judgment for defendant, as prayed, with costs.

HAMILTON ROSS & CO. *vs.* BAM & CO.

B. & Co. ordered from India, through H. & Co., a quantity of cigars, of a sample bearing a particular label. There subsequently proved to be no such maker in India, and the local agents of H. & Co. bought, instead, boxes of cigars by other celebrated makers. HELD, *on a construction of the terms of the order, that it being shown that the quantity of the cigars delivered was equal to that of the labelled sample, the defendants were bound to take delivery accordingly.*

1844. Aug. 13. Hamilton Ross & Co. *vs.* Bam & Co.

The plaintiffs, in the declaration, alleged that the defendants addressed and delivered to them a letter of which the following is a copy:

"Cape Town, 7th November, 1843.

"Messrs. HAMILTON ROSS & CO.

"GENTLEMEN,—Referring to our communication of this morning, we have now to request you will offer for your account, through your agents, the following quantities of cigars. Ten chests, each 50 boxes, containing 250 cigars each, Van Zan Dyk's cigars, not to exceed $1\frac{1}{4}$ rupees per box. *Thirty chests, each* 50 *boxes, containing* 250 *cigars each, of Chinsurah cigars, green quality, same as sample box sent in charge of Capt. Roome, not to exceed one rupee per box.* Five or six boxes real Trichinopola cigars, 1,000 each, if to be procured at a reasonable rate. The said cigars to be shipped by the *Olivia.*

"The cost of the cigars, including shipping expenses, insurance, agent's commission, and other usual charges, to be paid by us in cash on their arrival at this port, &c., &c.; and a commission of 5 per cent. to be paid by us to you for your trouble and advance of funds in Calcutta.

"We are, &c.,

"J. H. BAM & CO."

That the plaintiffs did, in their capacity of factors, agents, or commission merchants, accept and agree to cause to be executed the said order; and did, without any deviation from the terms of the said letter or order, through their agent at Calcutta, procure to be shipped on board the said vessel *Olivia,* 40 chests of cigars, which duly arrived in Table Bay on the 10th May, 1844, of which defendants had due notice; but the said defendants while they have duly accepted and paid for ten of the said chests, have refused to accept or pay for the remaining thirty, alleging that they

1844. Aug. 13. Hamilton Ross & Co. *vs.* Bam & Co.

are not in quality conformable to their order, whereas the plaintiffs say that the said thirty chests of cigars are in all respects conformable to order. And the plaintiffs say, moreover, that even if the said cigars were not in all respects so conformable, yet that the plaintiffs performed, and caused to be performed, the utmost care and diligence to obtain cigars wholly conformable to the said order, and that no negligence or carelessness whatever in regard to the said cigars is chargeable upon the plaintiffs, or any person for whose use of due and proper care they were responsible; and that, under and by virtue of the agreement aforesaid, they are not accountable for any unknown and unsuspected defect in quality, which defect, however, the plaintiffs aver, does not exist. Wherefore they prayed that the defendant may be condemned to pay them £215 7s. 6d., the amount of the price, &c., &c., of the said cigars, of which they again tender delivery.

In their plea, the defendants denied all and every allegation in the declaration set forth, and joined issue thereon. The letter marked A, signed by defendants, referred to in the declaration, was put in and admitted.

The plaintiffs put in the examination, taken *de bene esse*, of William Roome, now absent from the Colony, in which, *inter alia*, he deposed as follows:

I am the master of the said vessel, the *Olivia*, of which plaintiffs are part owners and managers. I was present at the conversation referred to in the letter, and saw the draft of it written by the plaintiff Mr. Stein, and heard him read it aloud to defendants, who approved of its contents. From now reading the letter marked A, I have no doubt that it is a correct copy of that draft. I heard defendant say he would send the sample box mentioned in the letter, which he subsequently did, to plaintiffs' office, where I got it. On my arrival at Calcutta, I sent this sample box to Gillander & Co., who are plaintiffs' agents, by whom I was afterwards consulted relative to the execution of the order. It was ascertained that there was no such maker of cigars at Chinsurah or at Calcutta, or, so far as I know, anywhere else, as the party whose name was upon the label on the sample box sent by defendant. I do not remember the name on the label, but it was that of a native of India; and I was informed by Van Zandyk & Co. that such a person had been in the employment of the late Mr. Van Zandyk, and was now a circar in the employment of Bagshaw & Co., a mercantile house, and not cigar-makers. Van Zandyk & Co. expressed great indignation to me at the form of the label, which stated the person referred to in it to have been the late superintendent in the manufactory

1844. Aug. 13. — Hamilton Ros & Co. vs. Bam & Co.

of Van Zandyk & Co. Gillander & Co., after consulting with me, ordered from Van Zandyk & Co., not merely the ten chests of their own cigars mentioned in the defendants' order, but also the thirty chests Chinsurah cigars in reference to which the sample box was sent, the cigars in which box Van Zandyk & Co. stated were not their make, but that they thought they could supply an article of equal quality at the price limited; but afterwards they wrote that they could have those thirty chests ready in time for the *Olivia*. Gillander & Co. and I then gave an order to another maker at Chinsurah, on condition he would have them ready for the *Olivia*. He executed it at one rupee per box, to be sent from Chinsurah to the ship free of expense, and the thirty chests came down to the *Olivia* in time. With those cigars came down what I have no doubt whatever was the same sample box which I had brought down from defendant and sent up to Chinsurah [this was by a subsequent witness proved to be the box without the lid produced in court marked B], together with another box [proved to be that produced in court marked C], sent as a sample of the thirty chests. I, in the counting-house of Gillander & Co., compared these two samples, along with one of the partners and a native clerk of theirs whose department is to look after such orders, and who is a judge of the article; and I compared them again on board the *Olivia* with those in two of the chests taken indiscriminately, and I found the bulk as represented by those two chests equal to the sample sent, and the latter fully equal to the sample sent by defendants. This was also the opinion of the partners and of the native clerk. We considered both samples to be of the same tobacco. Those thirty chests were well and safely stowed, and were landed in good condition. It was after I happened to hear from Mr. Stein that defendants had refused the thirty chests that I mentioned to him that I had still on board the sample boxes marked B and C. I went off and brought them ashore for inspection.

Plaintiffs also produced and put in evidence two other boxes marked D and E, taken indiscriminately from two of the thirty chests in dispute, and called

Thomas Lawton, August Lewis Lichtwark, and John Kilcullin,—all of them dealers in and well acquainted with the quality and value of cigars, who swore that, in their opinions, the cigars in boxes C, D, and E, as well as those in sample box B, were Chinsurah cigars, and of the same sort or species. That the cigars in B, by exposure and long keeping, had been deteriorated in appearance, and that those in C, D, and E were now superior in quality and value to and more saleable than those in B; and that those in C, D, and E were, in the opinion of Lawton (who was by far the most extensive dealer in cigars of the three witnesses), superior, and in the opinion of the other two witnesses fully equal, in quality and value, to what those in B had been in their original state, and before their appearance had become deteriorated.

On the cross-examination of Lawton and Kilcullin, it was proved that Van Zandyk & Co. were the manufacturers whose name was most in favour with customers, and whose cigars fetched the highest price. By Lawton, that Gomez, by whom the thirty chests in dispute were made, had but only recently become famous as a maker, and ranked next to Van Zandyk; that they were the only two manufacturers whose cigars are asked after by the name of the maker; and that he had on several occasions seen, but never had dealt in or had in his possession, cigars labelled as having been made by a person professing to have been in Van Zandyk's employment. And by Kilcullin that he had found the cigars having the last-mentioned label on the boxes as common in the trade as Van Zandyk or Gomez's, and to be a good and saleable article; but that he could see no difference between such cigars and those in C, D, and E, and did not know that cigars so labelled were more saleable than Gomez's, and always himself bought cigars with reference to the quality of the sample shown, without reference to the maker's name.

Plaintiffs closed their case.

Brand and *Ebden*, for the defendants, moved for an absolution from the instance, on the ground that by the evidence of the plaintiffs' own witnesses it was proved that the thirty chests of cigars in dispute had been made by Gomez and not by the person who professed to have been formerly the superintendent or in the employ of Van Zandyk, who on the label of the box given by defendants to Capt. Roome as the sample was represented as the maker of the cigars contained in that box. That according to the true construction of the terms of the order it directed that the thirty chests should be in every respect the same as those in the sample box sent, and thus directed that they should be made by the same maker, and that it was for this very purpose that the sample box was sent. And that on this very ground, the defendants were entitled to demand cigars made by the maker whose name was on the label of the box, and the plaintiffs were not entitled to furnish them with, or compel them to receive, cigars made by any other maker, however good in other respects their quality might be.

The Court, without calling on the *Attorney-General*, held

1844. Aug. 13. — Hamilton Ross & Co. *vs.* Bam & Co. that the fair construction of the terms of the order, viz. "containing 250 boxes each *Chinsurah* cigars, green quality, same as sample box sent in charge of Captain Roome" was that they were to contain *Chinsurah cigars, green quality, same* IN QUALITY *as those in the sample box sent,* and not *by the same maker as those in the sample box sent.* And that if the latter direction had been intended to have been given, the words "by the same maker," or "of the same mark," or "brand," or "label" as the sample box ought to have been used. And therefore, seeing that at this stage of the case, the cigars in dispute had been proved by the plaintiffs' evidence to be of the same quality with those in the sample box, the defendants could not now obtain absolution from the instance, but must proceed to contradict, if they could, the plaintiffs' witnesses on this point. Whereupon defendants gave up the case.

Judgment for plaintiffs, as prayed, with costs.

[N.B.—The Court gave no opinion as to whether the defendants could have been compelled to receive cigars of the same quality with those in the sample box, but by a different maker, if their construction of the terms of the order had been proved to be the proper construction, even under the circumstances proved by the evidence of Capt. Roome.]

ASSUE *vs.* CURATOR OF ASSUE.

Burghership. Transfer. Minor.

W. A., a foreigner, without having obtained a deed of burghership and unable from poverty to obtained one, having become purchaser of a lot of ground, obtained permission from the Governor that transfer might be allowed to pass to him and a minor of ten years of age, believing that he would thus receive the ground to himself. The transfer was effected to W. A., as father and natural guardian of and in trust for his son, J. A. Thereupon W. A. erected buildings, partially from funds borrowed under a promise of mortgage, but was unable to effect a mortgage, the ground being registered in his son's name. The Court found that the son never was intended to have, and had not, any beneficial interest, and decreed that the deed of transfer should, in so far as it conveyed any interest to him, be set aside; and W. A. having thereupon obtained a deed of burghership, ordered the transfer to be effected in favour of the plaintiff.

1844. Aug. 30. — Assue *vs.* Curator of Assue. In this case the declaration set forth that the plaintiff purchased on 10th August, 1841, for £31 5s., a certain lot of ground from F. Deneys, who had on that day purchased it by auction, and that the plaintiff's name was inserted in the vendue roll, as purchaser; that he produced two securities, as required by the conditions of sale, and paid the first instalment of the price with his own money; that on going to the transfer office to pay the transfer duty, he was informed that in consequence of his being a native of China, and not having obtained a deed of burghership, transfer of the lot of ground could not lawfully be made to him. That from poverty, he was unable to pay for a deed of burghership; that by the advice of his friends, who informed him that in this way he could secure the ground for himself, he addressed a memorial to the Governor, setting forth the facts of his case, and praying that transfer might be allowed to pass to the name of his son, the defendant, then a boy of only ten or eleven years of age, the prayer of which memorial was granted. That transfer of the ground was accordingly made to his son in the following terms, "to and on behalf of William Assue (the plaintiff), as father and natural guardian of and in trust for his minor son, John Assue;" and the ground was mortgaged by him in that capacity in favour of the seller, for the second and third instalments of the price. That, acting under the belief that the ground was his own, he had erected on it certain buildings by means of his own funds and labour, and of funds borrowed by him under a promise that when the buildings were completed, he would mortgage them for the sums so borrowed; but that he has been prevented from doing so by reason that the title to the ground stands registered in the name of his son. That his son never had any funds of his own whatever, and that the plaintiff never made, or intended to make, any gift of the said ground or of any part of the purchase money thereof, or of the buildings erected thereon, to the said son, and therefore prayed that his said son, the defendant, may be declared to be a trustee for the plaintiff in regard to the title of the said ground, and that he may be condemned, by means of his said curator or otherwise, to give transfer of the said ground to the plaintiff, or that the said ground and the building thereon may be declared to be subject to the amount of the first instalment, which had been paid by plaintiff, and to the value of the buildings erected thereon, as the same shall be proved by the plaintiff; and that the defendant may be condemned to pay such amount to the plaintiff, and on his failing so to do that the plaintiff may be at liberty to issue execution against the ground for the recovery thereof, or that the plaintiff may have such other relief in the premises as to the Court shall seem meet.

The plaintiff proved all the facts set forth in his declaration to the satisfaction of the Court, and the *curator ad*

1844. Aug. 30. Assue vs. Curator of Assue. *litem* of the defendant stated that after making every inquiry he believed that they were true.

Whereupon the Court held that the defendant never was intended to have, and had not, any beneficial interest in the premises in question, and that the deed of transfer, in so far as it proposed to convey such interest to him, should be set aside; but on the application of the plaintiff postponed giving judgment, in order to give him an opportunity of procuring a deed of burghership.

Postea (6th February, 1845).—The plaintiff having produced a deed of burghership, the Court gave judgment that the transfer in favour of defendant be annulled and cancelled from the register, and that the Registrar of Deeds do transfer the piece of ground and premises in question in favour of the plaintiff, on condition that the plaintiff shall execute a mortgage bond thereon, in terms and in lieu of bond now registered as a mortgage on the premises, and which is to be cancelled.

NORDEN *vs.* SHAW.

Where a Kafir war prevented the defendant from fulfilling a contract to deliver Kafir gum, held that the plaintiff was nevertheless entitled to damages for breach of contract.

1847. June 21. Norden *vs.* Shaw. The declaration set forth that on the 12th December, 1845, the defendant, by his agent, A. Croll, sold to the plaintiff forty tons of gum, at the price of £20 6s. 8d. per ton, to be delivered at the stores of the defendant at Graham's Town, within five months next after the said 12th of December. That while the said contract was in progress of completion, but before the final completion of the same, to wit, on the 9th December, 1845, the plaintiff being then confident and certain that the said contract would be completed, and when completed would be fulfilled by the defendant, made an agreement with Manuel & Co., for the sale to them, at the price of £30 per ton, of the said gum, so to be delivered as aforesaid by the defendant to the plaintiff. That the defendant has wholly failed to deliver any part of the said gum, either at his stores or elsewhere, although duly demanded, whereby the plaintiff hath lost and been deprived of the gain and profit that he would have made had the defendant, by delivering the same to the plaintiff, enabled him to fulfil his contract with Manuel & Co (which, by reason of the default of the defendant, the plaintiff has been wholly unable to fulfil), and whereby the plaintiff has been otherwise deprived of large gains and profits which would have accrued to him from the delivery by the defendant of the said gum, and hath sustained damages to the amount of £400, wherefore he prays that the defendant may be condemned to pay him the said sum of £400 with costs.

The defendant, in his plea, admitted the sale of the forty tons of Kafir gum to the plaintiff, as alleged in the declaration, but averred that in conformity with the said contract, he on the 12th March, 1846, offered to Thomas Jarman, at Graham's Town, who was then the agent of the plaintiff, delivery of ten tons of the said gum, but which the said agent refused to accept. That he was ready and willing, and intended to have delivered to plaintiff, in terms of the said contract, forty tons of gum within the stipulated period, namely, before the 12th April, 1846, but that owing to the state of hostility in which the Colony on the frontier was placed in regard to Kafirland, from which the said gum was to come, and the commencement of hostilities in that part of the Colony about the end of March, 1846, he was entirely prevented from further completing his said contract of sale; in consideration whereof the defendant, on the 7th September, 1846, offered to the plaintiff £50 as and for damages which the plaintiff might in consequence have suffered, together with all costs incurred up to that time, but which the plaintiff refused to accept, and which sum the defendant again offers to pay, and prays that the sum may be declared by the Court sufficient in satisfaction of all claim of damages which on account of the breach aforesaid the plaintiff may have suffered.

In his replication the plaintiff admitted the tender of £50, but denied its sufficiency, and joined issue. Witnesses were called at the trial by both parties.

T. Jarman stated: By desire of the plaintiff, as whose agent I acted, I, in the beginning of January, 1846, demanded from the defendant delivery of the gum, which, he refused to make, alleging that he was not bound by the contract which Croll had made for him with the plaintiff. In the middle of March following, I met the defendant in the street; he told me he had reconsidered the case, and in order to avoid litigation would deliver the gum immediately. I understood him to mean the whole gum; he did not offer any specific quantity. I replied that in consequence of his previous refusal, I could not now accept the gum without first communicating with plaintiff. I did so, and received his answer by return of post, in consequence of which, about the end of March, and about a fortnight after he had offered to deliver the gum, I demanded delivery of the gum.

1847. June 21. — Norden *vs.* Shaw.

He said that in consequence of the approaching war with the Kafirs, he had not then a pound to deliver.

A number of witnesses connected with the Kafir trade, proved that considerable quantities of gum reached Graham's Town in January and February, and in the first two weeks of March, by wagons which had been sent in early in the year, and had commenced their return at least early in March; but that after the 14th March, it was almost impossible to bring any produce out to Kafirland, and that they and their connections in trade had been compelled to abandon large quantities of gum which they had in store in Kafirland.

Samuel Impey stated: I am clerk to the defendant. I know that he had contracts in November and December, 1845, with several traders in Kafirland, who had engaged to supply him with gum, in all amounting to about 350 tons. He received ten tons in March, 1846, which he delivered to Mr. Maynard in fulfilment of a contract he had made with him. Defendant received in all, I think, about sixty tons of gum from Kafirland during the months of January, February, and March, 1846. Defendant sold fifty tons of this gum to Messrs. W. & J. Smith, of Port Elizabeth, which was delivered to them in parcels, in the months of January, February, and March, 1846.

Charles John Manuel stated: I am a partner in the firm of Manuel & Co. In consequence of information I had received from my correspondents in London, that gum was on the rise, and that they expected to obtain for some gum of ours which they had in store £45 a ton, I, on the 9th December, made the contract with the plaintiff for the purchase of forty tons of gum at £30 per ton, to be delivered by him within a month from that date. He had delivered none of the gum before the 5th of February, when I received a letter from my London correspondents, informing me that gum had sold for £36 per ton, and was likely to fall lower. In consequence of this information I caused my broker, on the 7th of February, to cancel the purchase from the plaintiff, on the ground of his non-delivery of the gum within a month from its date. I received intelligence from London that the price of gum was falling up to April, and after that period that it was rising.

Evidence was also given as to the costs and charges of transporting gum from Graham's Town to Algoa Bay, and from thence by sea to Table Bay, and as to the value which the gum would have been to the plaintiff at Table Bay, for shipment to England, if the defendant had delivered it to plaintiff at Graham's Town within the stipulated period.

The *Attorney-General*, to show that even if it were proved that the defendant had been prevented by the Kafir war from delivering the gum, still that this would not deprive the plaintiff of his claim for reasonable damages for the non-fulfilment of the contract, quoted *Campbell's Reports, vol 2, p. 58. Note A.*

1847. June 21. — Norden *vs.* Shaw

The Court held, that as Manuel & Co. had cancelled their contract with the plaintiff two months before the expiration of the period previous to the end of which the defendant was not bound to have delivered any of the gum to the plaintiff, this contract must be thrown out of view altogether in estimating the amount of even the plaintiff's damages. They held that although the defendant had been prevented from delivering the gum solely by the Kafir hostilities, that fact did not afford a defence against the plaintiff's claim for damages. They held that it had been proved that if delivered by defendant in due time the gum would have been worth in Table Bay £1,200, being £30 per ton, and therefore gave judgment for the plaintiff, for £200 as damages, being the balance remaining after deducting from the said sum £1,200, £833 6s. 8d. being the price which plaintiff would have had to pay to defendant at £20 6s. 8d. per ton, and £166 13s. 4d., being the estimated amount of the charges of transporting the gum from Graham's Town to Table Bay, with costs.

FRY *vs.* REYNOLDS.

Sale of farm by extent. Contract of Sale how completed. Warrandice. Actio quanti minoris.

1848. Feb. 29. — Fry *vs.* Reynolds

The declaration in this case set forth that the defendant did, on or about the 7th August, 1847, purchase of and from the plaintiff his place called Vyge Kraal, for the sum of £1,500, to be paid by defendant granting a note for £200, payable six months, and another note for £300, payable twelve months from the date of the purchase, and the balance of £1,500 by a mortgage bond on the place.

That the plaintiff has already done and performed, and is still ready to do and perform, all such acts and things as are required to be done and performed by the plaintiff, and has demanded from the defendant to pay the said purchase money in manner aforesaid, which demand the defendant has refused to comply with; wherefore the plaintiff prayed that the defendant may be condemned to pay the said sums of £200 and £300 in manner aforesaid, and to pass a

1848. Feb. 29.

Fry *vs.* Reynolds.

mortgage bond by hypothecating the said place for £1,000, the plaintiff thereby offering upon the payment of the said sum of £500, and upon the execution of the said mortgage bond as aforesaid, to grant to the defendant a proper, valid, and legal transfer and conveyance of the said place. And, further, that the defendant may be condemned to pay the costs of suit.

In his plea, the defendant pleaded, first, the general issue. Secondly, and for a further plea, in case the plaintiff should succeed in proving the allegations in his declaration, but not otherwise, alleged that at the time of the said supposed sale, the plaintiff sold the said place to defendant as being in extent 600 morgen or 1,200 acres, whereas in truth the place contains only 441 morgen 502 square roods and 22 square feet. And that the said place was sold and purchased with reference to its said extent; and that had the fact as to its extent been known to the defendant he would not have purchased the place,—at all events, would not have agreed to give a greater price for it than £1,000. And the defendant further submitted that the said supposed sale was, for the reason aforesaid, not valid or binding upon the defendant; but should the honourable Court judge differently, then the defendant submits that he should only be compelled to pay for the place the said price of £1,500, less so much as fairly and reasonably to compensate for the aforesaid deficiency in extent, which compensation the defendant averred amounts to the sum of £500.

In his replication, the plaintiff joined issue with the defendant in both pleas.

N.B.—There was also an allegation in the plea that plaintiff had sold the place as being free from all servitudes, except a right of thoroughfare, whereas, in fact, it was burthened with a servitude of a much more onerous nature, and which greatly diminished the value of the place; but as the Court found it to be proved that the plaintiff had given to the defendant a true and correct description of the only servitude to which the place was subject, it is not necessary to report this part of the case.

At the trial it was proved that the plaintiff's place, Vyge Kraal, being for sale, the defendant, in June, 1847, employed Van Reenen, a conveyancer, and a friend of both parties, to purchase it for him, and in that month the defendant went over the whole place with Van Reenen. After several communings about the price, carried on through the medium of Van Reenen, plaintiff stated to Van Reenen that he would take £1,500 for the place, which Van Reenen told to the defendant. In consequence, by agreement, the plaintiff, defendant, and Van Reenen went to Vyge Kraal on the 31st July, and there the plaintiff and defendant occupied two hours in walking over the place by themselves. After which defendant said he liked the place. 1848. Feb. 29. Fry *vs.* Reynolds.

On the 3rd August, 1847, defendant wrote to plaintiff the following letter:

"MY DEAR SIR,—I could not write to you sooner. I agree to purchase your place, Vyge Kraal, for the sum of fifteen hundred pounds sterling, on the following conditions,—that you put me in possession of the place, the Government dues on which I will immediately or as soon as necessary pay, one third of the purchase money payable in twelve months, viz., £200 in six months, and £300 in twelve months, I passing notes to that effect, including everything in the place, with exception of your live-stock of cattle, cows, sheep, horses, and your furniture. But the poultry and farming implements I include in the purchase, together with your seed grain and all that is already in the ground. And I would wish to know what guarantee I shall have for the remainder of the purchase money to remain on mortgage, and for what period; also the butcher's contract to be made over to me. You will perceive that in this sum I have come up £100 higher than I first offered. But this is my highest figure.

"I am, my dear Sir,

"Yours faithfully,

"G. A. REYNOLDS.

"Of course, whatever you may wish to retain of the poultry for your own use you can freely do so, but it will be an advantage to me to have such kind of things accustomed to the place. If you have any good mules I will take them at a fair valuation, as also your cows. I would have been with you on Monday, had the weather permitted."

Defendant left this letter at Van Reenen's house, to be by him sent to plaintiff, which was done. Van Reenen afterwards, at defendant's request, rode to plaintiff's place to ask him for his answer to that letter. Plaintiff then said to Van Reenen, "Tell Reynolds I accept his offer, and consider the place sold to him;" and also said he had got the consent of Mr. de Smidt, who held a mortgage bond over the place for £1,000, that defendant should take over this mortgage bond.

Van Reenen, on the same evening, told defendant what plaintiff had said, and that he had accepted his offer; defendant then said, "I thank you, I am very glad."

1848. Feb. 29. — Fry *vs.* Reynolds.

On the 9th August, Van Reenen wrote the following note to defendant:

"9th August, 1847.

"DEAR REYNOLDS,—From the accompanying contract you will perceive that I have been instructed by Mr. Fry to accept your offer, and that the sale has been effected; please to scrutinize the same, and if it is in accordance to your terms, sign it and return the same to-morrow morning. I got him to give you a wagon, &c., &c.

"M. VAN REENEN."

The contract sent with the note was in the following terms:

"Agreement made and entered into this 9th day of August, 1847, between the Rev. John Fry of the one part and George Alexander Reynolds of the other part, as follows, viz.: The first undersigned engages to sell, and the second undersigned to purchase of and from the first undersigned, his place called Vyge Kraal, situated in the Cape Division, as the same is more fully described in the deed of transfer made in favour of the said John Fry on the —— at and for the sum of one thousand and five hundred pounds (£1,500), payable as under mentioned, and under the conditions following, that is to say:

"On condition that the said property shall be transferred to the second undersigned on or before the first of September next, the second undersigned binding himself hereby to receive and take transfer thereof upon the date aforesaid, and the second undersigned further binds and obliges himself, his heirs, executors, and administrators, to pay or cause to be paid to the said first undersigned as follows, to wit, two hundred pounds sterling at six months from the date of transfer, for which a promissory note is to be passed by the second undersigned to the first undersigned, a sum of three hundred pounds, for which another promissory note is to be passed at twelve months from the said date, and for the residue of the purchase money the second undersigned is to pass a mortgage bond under security of said property.

"It is further agreed upon between the parties, that possession of the said property is to be taken on the said 1st September next, from which said date the same is to be and remain at the sole risk of the second undersigned, who further engages to pay and defray the transfer dues to Government, as also all the expenses attendant upon the transfer and mortgaging of said property.

"Lastly, the first undersigned agrees to give and leave upon the said property the poultry now upon the said place, as also three ploughs, one wagon, trektouw and riems complete, six or eight spades and picks. For the due performance hereof, the parties declared mutually to bind themselves each to the other, their persons and property of every description, according to law."

Van Reenen swore that he wrote and sent to the defendant this note and the contract at the request of no one, but entirely on his own suggestion and without the knowledge of the plaintiff.

It was proved that on some day between the 3rd and the 10th August, defendant went to the office of the Surveyor-General and inspected the diagrams of the grants of two pieces of land now forming the place Vyge Kraal.

The clerk who showed him the diagrams added up the number of morgen contained in the two grants, and told him the amount was between 441 and 442 morgen.

Defendant then stated that he wished to know the extent of the place, that he had bought it and liked it, but as it had been sold to him as of a certain extent, he should like to have the full extent, so as to give him more freedom, upon which the clerk told him he might get Government ground lying contiguous to it, sufficient to make up the 600 morgen, at two shillings an acre.

On the 10th August the defendant called at Van Reenen's and said, "I want to speak with you about the extent of the place; it is not 600 morgen," and on Van Reenen asking him, "Who told you it was?" defendant said, Van Reenen had done so. Van Reenen denied this, and said he could not have done so, as he had never known the extent of the place, but that if he made any objection about the extent, he ought to go and speak to plaintiff, who had just left him to purchase another place. Defendant said, "Never mind, I will write to plaintiff to-morrow." Van Reenen said, "That is not fair, for by speaking to him now, you save him from getting into an unpleasant situation; for what can he do with two places?" Defendant then changed the subject, and began to talk of alterations he proposed to make on the buildings at Vyge Kraal.

On the 13th August defendant sent the following note to Van Reenen:

"13th August 1847.

"MY DEAR VAN REENEN,—I have had a fair copy made of the agreement which I have signed; yours I will keep as a copy.

"Yours faithfully,

"G. A. REYNOLDS."

1848. Feb. 29. — Fry vs. Reynolds.

The defendant sent with this note a copy of the agreement signed by himself and a witness, but on examining this copy, Van Reenen found that the words "in extent 600 morgen or 1,200 acres," which had not been in the original drawn by him, had been inserted in copy between the words "Vyge Kraal" and "situate."

Some days after this Van Reenen sent to plaintiff the copy of the agreement which the defendant had sent him.

It was proved that five or six days after the 31st July, defendant had told Bosenberg, a friend of his, that he had bought Vyge Kraal. It was also proved that in August, apparently after the 10th, but the exact dates were not proved, defendant had gone on three occasions to Vyge Kraal, had seen plaintiff's furniture in the act of being removed, had taken a carpenter with him and had a number of measurements made by him with a view to certain alterations on the house. That he had ordered the gardener to turn off the place some men who were taking up Hottentot fig plants for the purpose of carrying them away, and desired him to tell the men he, defendant, was the master of the place, and would not allow them to do so. That he had also caused to be cut, and took away with him from the garden, six cabbages and four cauliflowers.

It did not appear that after the 13th August there had been any communication between defendant and plaintiff until a day about the end of that month, when defendant and De Kock went to Vyge Kraal, where they found the plaintiff, when De Kock stated that a conversation took place to the following effect. Defendant said he had called to see if plaintiff had signed the contract. Plaintiff said he had not, because defendant had inserted in it 600 morgen, and that he could not deliver that quantity. Defendant replied, "But you have sold me 600 morgen." De Kock then said to plaintiff, "Did you tell Mr. Reynolds that the extent was 600 morgen?" Plaintiff said, "Yes; but I did not recollect; I had not looked at the title at the time." At De Kock's request he then went and brought the deeds of transfer, which proved the extent to be about 442. On going away defendant said, "Mr. Fry, I am ready to take transfer on the 1st September, but if you can't deliver me 600 morgen, it is no sale." Plaintiff replied, "I will go to town to-day, and see Mr. van Reenen."

Morkel, the butcher, proved that he had paid plaintiff £3 15s. per month, for permission to graze his slaughter cattle on the place on the way to town, under a verbal agreement, which either party might have put an end to at pleasure, and that on hearing of the sale, he had asked defendant if he would allow him to graze his cattle there on the same terms plaintiff had done. 1848. Feb. 29. Fry vs. Reynolds.

It was admitted that the creditor who held a mortgage bond for £1,000 over the place had consented to allow the defendant to take over the mortgage on his becoming the purchaser of the place.

The *Attorney-General*, for the defendant, maintained that the sale of the place had never been completed; that it had not been completed by the defendant's letter of the 3rd August, even although the plaintiff had accepted the offer therein contained, because its tenor shows that there were certain conditions referred to in that offer which still remained to be settled and defined before the sale and purchase could be completed; because till these were settled and defined, the parties had not yet come to any mutual agreement or consent as to the terms on which the sale and purchase were to be made, or in other words, as to what was to be done by each of the parties respectively.

These conditions were, first, as to the guarantee that £1,000 of the price should be allowed to remain on mortgage; second, as to the cession of the butcher's contract; third, as to the number of fowls which plaintiff was to be allowed to take away. That the fact that the sale was not, and was not understood by either of the parties to have been, completed by what had taken place before the 9th August, was proved by Van Reenen having on that day drawn up the contract dated 9th August, and sent it to defendant for his signature. And that defendant's signature to that contract did not complete the sale, because the condition that the place should be in extent 600 morgen had not been accepted by the plaintiff nor the contract itself signed by him. He admitted that such a mistake as had been made by the plaintiff as to the number of morgen, supposing that he believed it to be 600 morgen, and even if he had sold the place with reference to the number of its morgen, did not entitle the defendant, under the circumstances of the case, to claim the benefit of the *actio redhibitoria*, and that the defendant was only entitled, on the principle of the *actio quanti minoris*, to claim a reduction of the price proportionable to the value of the number of morgen less than 600.

Cur. adv. vult.

Postea (1st March, 1848).—The Court, on the grounds on which the case had been argued for the plaintiff by *Ebden*, gave judgment for the plaintiff as prayed, with costs.

They held that the contract of sale was perfected and completed by the defendant's letter of the 3rd August, delivered to plaintiff by Van Reenen, who *quoad hoc* was

1848. Feb. 29.

Fry *vs.* Reynolds

the defendant's agent, coupled with the plaintiff's unqualified and unconditional acceptance of the offer therein contained, expressed by him to defendant's agent, and according to the plaintiff's direction immediately communicated to the defendant by his said agent.

That the three conditions as to which the Attorney-General maintained that the parties had not come to any final agreement had reference to matters not essentials of, but merely accessories to, the contract for the sale and purchase of the place, and therefore the fact that they had not yet agreed as to them would not have had the effect of preventing the contract for the sale and purchase of the place itself, which had been entered into, from being valid and effectual. That these matters were considered by the defendant himself either as accessories and not essentials, or to have been sufficiently agreed on to enable the respective rights of the parties under them to be ascertained and enforced by law, was proved by the fact that the defendant had signed this contract of sale of the 9th August, although it contained no mention whatever, either as to any guarantee that £1,000 of the price would be allowed to remain for any certain time on mortgage, or as to the assignment of the butcher's contract. Besides that, it had been proved that plaintiff had got Mr. de Smidt's consent to allow defendant to take over the existing mortgage, that Van Reenen had been told this by plaintiff, and had communicated this to defendant at the same time he did the plaintiff's acceptance of defendant's offer.

That plaintiff had had no contract with the butcher which he could assign to defendant, or which could have enabled the plaintiff to retain to himself any interest in a profit arising from the place after its sale to defendant, who might then renew the agreement with the butcher or not, as he thought fit.

They held that it was placed beyond all doubt, both by the nature of the place sold, the real value of which consisted almost entirely in the buildings on it and the arable and garden ground adjacent to the buildings, and by the conduct of the parties themselves, that the place was sold by the one and bought by the other as it stood, and without any reference to the number of morgen of land by which the buildings and arable ground were surrounded; and that therefore, although the plaintiff in the course of conversation, when he had not the title deeds at hand, did accidentally, and without any intention to deceive or mislead the defendant, state to him that the place was 600 morgen in extent, it was clear that the defendant had not been induced by this statement to give a greater price for the place than he would have agreed to do if he had been told by plaintiff that its extent was 442 morgen. 1848. Feb. 29.

Fry *vs.* Reynolds.

That therefore this statement could not, in law, be considered as a warrandice that the place did contain 600 morgen, or as affording to the defendant any ground, in respect of the principle on which the *actio quanti minoris* is founded, for claiming from the plaintiff a deduction from the price of £31 12s., which was proved to be the value of 158 morgen of the contiguous sandy ground. (*Vide Herbert's Grot. Inleid., B.* 3, *section* 33, *note* 80.)

CHAPTER II.

LETTING AND HIRING.

GANTZ *vs.* WAGENAAR.

1828. Dec. 30.

Minority held a sufficient defence (MENZIES, J., *diss.*) *against a provisional claim on a lease entered into by a minor, with the assistance of his mother, not his legal guardian.*

[Vol. I, p. 92.]

DICK *vs.* HIDDINGH.

1830. Dec. 16.

Construction of clause in lease as to term of holding after a sale. Ejectment, action of.

[Vol. I, p. 499.]

NEETHLING *vs.* TAYLOR.

1834. Dec. 23.

Production of lease sufficient to entitle the lessor to claim provisional sentence for rent. Procurator in rem suam entitled to sue provisionally on such lease.

[Vol. I, p. 30.]

BIDDYS, APPELLANTS, *vs.* WARD, RESPONDENT.

Construction of clause in lease as to lessee's right to purchase during tenancy. Lessee cannot claim such right of purchase after receiving notice of termination of lease.

Dec. 30.

Biddys, Appellants, *vs.* Ward, Respondent.

This was an appeal by Biddys, plaintiffs in an action before the last Circuit Court of Graham's Town, against the judgment of that Court given in favour of the defendant, the now respondent.

The case depended entirely on the construction to be put on the following clause of the agreement between the parties:

"The first undersigned (the respondent) on his part doth covenant and agree to let to ——— (the appellants) his farm, &c., fully to use, occupy, and enjoy, for the space of six calendar months from the 1st of November, 1832, and so from one half year to the other, until the one party or the other shall give six clear months' notice of his or their intention to terminate this agreement, &c., &c.

1834. Dec. 30.

Biddys, Appellants, *vs.* Ward, Respondent.

"And the first undersigned doth further covenant and agree that, in case the second and third undersigned shall propose and make known to him their intention to purchase the aforesaid farm at any time during their occupancy thereof, he shall and will duly and promptly transfer to them the same, on their giving him sufficient security for the payment of the sum of one shilling and sixpence sterling for every English acre of land comprised in the aforesaid farm, which said purchase money shall be payable in four equal instalments at two, three, four, and five years from the date of purchase."

On the 5th of April, 1834, respondent gave appellants notice that on the 1st of November, 1834, they were hereby required to quit and yield up peaceable possession to respondent of his farm, &c.

On the 8th of October, the appellants gave notice to the respondent of their intention to purchase the farm on the terms stipulated in the deed.

The action brought by the appellants in the Circuit Court was to compel the respondent to complete the sale by giving transfer of the farm to the applicants.

The Circuit Court gave judgment for the defendant, with fifty shillings costs.

The Court affirmed the judgment with costs, holding that, according to the true construction of the lease, the applicants' right to purchase ceased the instant the respondent gave notice that the agreement was to terminate.

SMITH *vs.* HOWSE.

Location. Compensation. Cessionary. Pleading. Exceptio non qualificatæ. Title to sue.

An agreement by which the lessor (locator) of property makes over, cedes, transfers, and alienates for a term the rent of the property let, gives the cessionary a title to sue for such rent.

The lessee (conductor) is entitled to compensate against the claims for rent due prior to the cession, all liquid claims due by the cedent to the lessee before the cession; but as regards rents coming due after notice of the cession, he cannot compensate debts due to him before the cession.

1835. Aug. 31.

Smith *vs.* Howse.

In this case, the declaration set forth that on the 8th August, 1823, one J. Wyatt, by a written agreement entered into between him and the defendant, by which he let on

1835. Aug. 31. — Smith *vs.* Howse.

lease to the defendant certain premises in Port Elizabeth for the term of five years, for a yearly rent of £72, to be paid quarterly, under condition that the said J. Wyatt should make certain alterations on the premises, and also certain repairs, as they should become necessary, at his expense, and under this further condition that should the said J. Wyatt fail in performing and executing the repairs and alterations, as set forth in this agreement, then and in that case, it shall and may be lawful for the said J. Howse to cause the said repairs and alterations to be performed and executed, and to deduct the just and reasonable expenses of the same from the rent to be by him paid.

Thereafter the said J. Wyatt did, by a notarial act of cession, bearing date the 10th May, 1833, cede and transfer unto the said plaintiff the whole of the rent then due, and to become due by the said defendant for the said house and premises from the said 1st January, 1833, to the 31st December, 1834, and which amounts to the said sum of £144, and of which cession and transfer the said defendant had due notice on the 13th of May, 1833. Which said sum the plaintiff prayed that the defendant should be condemned to pay to him.

The defendant pleaded as matter of exception to the plaintiff's qualification, that the act of cession, or deed as set forth in the plaintiff's declaration, bearing date 10th May, 1833, does not give the plaintiff any legal authority, nor does it vest in the said plaintiff a legal right to sue him, the defendant, for the amount of rent now claimed, or any part thereof. Wherefore the said defendant prayed that he might be absolved from this instance with costs.

This day *Cloete* argued in support of the exception, and contended that the plaintiff had no title to sue, because the deed of cession by Wyatt to him did not contain a clause constituting a procuration *in rem suam*, and quoted *Wassenaar Jud. Praktyk* 2, *Cap.* 3, *page* 33.

The *Attorney-General*, *contra*, maintained that the following words in the said deed of cession, viz.: "He, John Wyatt, by signing these presents declares to make over, cede, transfer, and alienate unto the said John Owen Smith, for a term hereinafter specified, the whole of the rent of certain houses and tenements his, appearer's, property, situated in Port Elizabeth aforesaid, and which said houses are at present in the occupancy of the persons now to be named, and at the rent specified against each name, to wit," &c. (here, *inter alia*, the defendant and the premises in question and the rent of the same were specified) were sufficient to give him a title to sue; and so the Court held and overruled the exception, with costs.

Thereafter the defendant filed a plea, in which he admitted the lease of the premises to him as set forth in the declaration, and also the deed of cession in favour of the plaintiff, dated 10th May, 1833, and *quoad ultra* pleaded the general issue; and secondly, pleaded as a further plea, that even if all the allegations in the plaintiff's declaration were true, which the defendant denies, and the plaintiff be entitled to demand at law the sum therein claimed, yet that he, the said plaintiff, as cessionary of the said J. Wyatt, is liable to all counter claims or demands which he, the defendant, would be entitled to plead as a set-off against the said J. Wyatt; and the said defendant saith that prior to the said 10th May, the said J. Wyatt was and still is justly and truly indebted to him, the defendant, in the following sums of money, to wit (here sundry sums were specified).

Thereafter a rule had been made by consent that the Court should decide the point of law raised in the pleadings before calling on the parties to prove the facts at issue between them.

This day the counsel for the parties were heard on the said points of law.

Cloete, for defendant, quoted *Voet*, 16, 2, 4.

The Court held that the defendant was entitled to set off against the plaintiff's demand for rents, which had fallen due prior to the date of the cession to plaintiff, all liquid debts which had become due to defendant before the date of the cession, and that he had no right to plead compensation on debts due by Wyatt to defendant even before the cession as a set-off against rents, which have become due since the cession was notified to plaintiff on the 13th of May, and gave judgment for plaintiff for £99 8s., and costs, reserving to the plaintiff his claim for the rents which fell due prior to the 13th May, and to the defendant his defence against the same, in so far as he would, on that day, have been able to plead compensation thereon against Wyatt, the cedent.

VICTOR *vs.* COURLOIS.

Tacit relocation of a house originally let for a year, rent payable monthly, is a relocation from month to month.

Acceptance of notice to quit and treaty for a new lease is an abandonment of right of tacit relocation.

Where a landlord gives a tenant a certain time to determine whether he will take a new lease, and before the lapse of that time validly lets the house to a third party, the former tenant cannot keep possession, but may have an action of damages against the landlord for breach of contract.

1838. Nov. 27. — Victor *vs.* Courlois.

In this case the Court decided that the effect of a tenant being allowed to keep possession by tacit relocation, after the expiration of the original term, of a house originally let for one year, but at a rent of twenty-six rixdollars per month, is to renew the lease from month to month, and each time for the term of one month only.

That acceptance by the tenant of notice to quit and entering into a treaty for a new lease is an abandonment by the tenant of all right to possess by tacit relocation after the day notice to quit on which has been given and accepted.

That an agreement by the landlord to allow the tenant till a certain time to determine whether he will or will not take a new lease does not entitle the tenant to keep possession of the house against the third party, to whom the landlord has before the lapse of the time so allowed, and before receiving the tenant's answer, let the house by a valid lease, although it may give the tenant a right of action for damages against the landlord for breach of agreement.

The landlord quoted *Van der Linden's Inst., pp.* 161, 162, 164; *Kersterman,* 1 *Book, p.* 186.

The tenant quoted *Van Leeuwen's Rom. Dutch Law,* 4 *Book, p.* 392; *Grotius,* 19 *Book, p.* 337.

HERBERT *vs.* ANDERSON.

Ejectment. Action of.

Parol lease followed by possession, paramount to subsequent written lease.

Placaats which, being fiscal, have never been law in this Colony.

1839. May 30. — Herbert *vs.* Anderson.

Plaintiff's declaration stated that Osmond, being the proprietor of a certain house and premises in Simon's Town, then occupied by defendant by a certain agreement in writing, dated 12th December, 1838, demised the said house and premises to the plaintiff for the year 1839 on condition that if the plaintiff wished to obtain possession of the premises from the defendant he should give the defendant three months' notice to quit, to be computed from 1st July, 1839. That plaintiff, on 30th December, 1838, gave defendant notice of said demise of the premises to him, and required the defendant to deliver up the premises to him on the 1st of April, which the defendant had refused to do, and therefore prayed that he might be adjudged to deliver up possession of the premises to plaintiff. 1839. May 20. Herbert *vs.* Anderson.

The document was in the following terms :

"I, the undersigned, do hereby certify that I have let my store in Simon's Town, at present occupied by Mr. William Anderson as a commission and a wholesale store, to Mr. John Herbert, at the rate of fifty rixdollars a month for the year 1839, to commence on the 1st day of January, 1839 ; but with this condition, that should Mr. John Herbert wish Mr. Anderson, the present tenant, to give up the store, Mr. Herbert is to give Mr. Wm. Anderson three months' notice to quit, from the 1st day of January next.

"J. OSMOND.

"Simon's Town, 12th December, 1838."

Defendant pleaded the general issue. It was admitted that Osmond was the proprietor of the premises, and that the document founded on by plaintiff had been executed by Osmond. Defendant objected that this document, even if a prior or valid lease, was null, in respect that it was not written on stamped paper.

Plaintiff quoted the Proclamations 24th December, 1807, 26th May, 1815, 10th December, 1824, and contended that it was sufficient that the lease should be covered with a stamp when produced, as had in this case been done.

The Court held this was sufficient in the case of leases, and repelled the objection.

Musgrave contended that the document founded on by plaintiff was sufficient to constitute a lease of the premises, and to give him a title to sue for ejectment, and quoted *Voet* 19, 2, 2 ; *Burge Col. Law, 3rd vol., pp.* 127, 145 ; *Van Leeuwen Rom. Dutch Law, p.* 401. And maintained that this document was of such a nature as to fall under the description given of it in the declaration, viz., "by a certain agreement, in writing, bearing date the day and year aforesaid, demised." And further, that defendant had no title to possess the premises on which he could resist plaintiff's title and demand possession.

Cloete, contra, quoted *Voet* 19, 2, 2 ; *Codex Batavus, voce "Huur," sec.* 26 ; *Grotius Inl., Book* 19, *sec.* 2, *in notis ; Van der Linden, p.* 237 ; *Lybrecht's Not. Prac., 2nd vol., p.* 92 ; *Placaats,* 11*th June,* 1452, 1*st April,* 1580, 3*rd April,* 1677, 18*th April,* 1794, 22*nd January,* 1515, 28*th March,* 1677, 30*th September,* 1744 ; and maintained that the document in

1839. May 30. Herbert *vs.* Anderson.

question did not constitute a legal written lease, and therefore gave the plaintiff no title to sue for ejectment. That it was proved that Osmond had verbally let the premises to defendant for one year, 1839, and that, admitting that defendant had no written lease on which he could maintain possession of the premises against the proprietor, Osmond, still that being in possession he could not be disturbed in that possession by the plaintiff, who had no better title than himself.

Cur. adv. vult.

Postea, the Court gave judgment for defendant, with costs.

The Court held that the four Placaats—11th June, 1452, 22nd January, 1515, 1st April, 1580, 28th March, 1677, 30th April, 1677—were merely fiscal or revenue Ordinances of Holland, and had never become or been made law in this Colony. That although writing may be necessary to the validity of leases in the cases mentioned in *Van Leeuwen's Rom. Dutch Law*, 401, it is not by the law of this Colony required in leases of urban tenements, even when the term is a year, at least when followed with possession. That it had been proved that defendant and Osmond had entered into a verbal contract of lease of the premises for the year 1839, which verbal lease, for the reasons above mentioned, was a valid and effectual one, giving the defendant a title to retain and possess the premises during the year 1839; and thus that neither Osmond nor, *a fortiori*, the plaintiff, deriving right from Osmond only by a written lease made subsequently to the verbal lease by Osmond to defendant, could deprive defendant of the possession of the premises during the year 1839.

SMITH *vs.* GROENEWALD.

Action by tenant against landlord for damage by non-repair. Reconventional claim by landlord for arrear rent.

1839. Aug. 22. Smith *vs.* Groenewald.

The plaintiff in this case hired defendant's mill for six years, for £90 per annum, on condition that, during said period, defendant should keep the outside of the premises in good repair. After having possessed them for nearly two years, plaintiff surrendered possession of the premises to defendant on the alleged ground that defendant had failed to keep the premises in tenantable repair, and thereafter brought this action, claiming from defendant £400 damages for the loss he had sustained by the defendant's failure to fulfil the conditions of keeping the premises in tenantable repair. Defendant in convention pleaded the general issue, and in reconvention claimed £49 as being the arrears of rent due by plaintiff for the period during which prior to his surrendering the premises he had occupied them. 1839. Aug. 22. Smith *vs.* Groenewald.

Plaintiff defended himself against defendant's claim for these arrears, which he admitted had not been paid, on the ground that during the time he had been in occupation, defendant, although often requested so to do, failed to put and keep the premises in such repair as the plaintiff was by the terms of the lease entitled to insist he should do, by which plaintiff had been deprived of all the profit and advantage which otherwise he would have derived from the occupation of the premises.

After hearing the evidence adduced by both parties, and the arguments of *Attorney-General Musgrave* for plaintiff, who quoted *Van der Linden, p.* 257; and *Cloete*, for defendant, who quoted *Grot. Inl.* 3, 19, *S.* 12, *Voet* 9, 2, 12.

The Court gave judgment for Smith, the plaintiff, in convention, for £66 damages, and for Groenewald, the defendant in reconvention for £49, and condemned Groenewald to pay all the costs.

TRUTER *vs.* EVEREST.

Provisional sentence granted on an underhand contract of lease. The plaintiff lessor need not prove lessee's possession under the contract. 1842. Feb. 17.

[Vol. I, p. 32.]

VOWE *vs.* PEDDER.

The allegation of unliquidated damages for want of repairs is no defence to a provisional claim for rent on a lease, but if the lessee can make out a primâ facie case to satisfy the Court that in the principal case he will be able to prove damage, it will be a bar to provisional sentence. But proof that the repairs require a certain amount of money to be expended is no criterion that the lessee has sustained a corresponding amount of damage by failure to repair. 1843. Feb. 9.

[Vol. I, p. 33.]

J. M. Maynard *vs.* Usher.

Lease: penalty in. Title to sue. Placaat 9th May, 1744, not law in the Colony. It is therefore unnecessary to register or pay transfer duty on a lease for 99 years.

1845. Nov. 18.

Maynard *vs.* Usher.

The plaintiff's declaration set forth that on the 10th day of February, 1820, William Underwood, being then the proprietor of a certain piece of land called Waterloo, let on lease to one John Martemis a certain part of the same piece of ground, which said lease is in substance and effect as follows, that is to say,—

"By this indenture or lease, Captain William Underwood, proprietor of the estate situate at Old Wynberg called Waterloo, cedes unto John Martemis, lately a soldier in the 60th Regiment, and now living with him as his servant, a piece of ground in length 335 feet, and in breadth 109 feet, situate on a tongue of land between the two roads leading into Wynberg and opposite the Krakeel Water, which crosses the said road, on lease for 99 years, at the ground rent of one rixdollar per annum, on following conditions, namely: First, that in whatever tenement the said John Martemis may build for a residence no canteen or store shall be kept for the sale of wine, spirits, or public entertainment of any kind, or any article whatever, either by the said John Martemis, or any other person to whom he may hereafter consign the said tenement and ground, held by virtue of this lease, on pain of forfeiture of all right and claim to the aforesaid tenement or house and ground to the said Captain Wm. Underwood, or to the proprietor for the time being of the said estate of Waterloo; and further if either the said John Martemis or any other proprietor to whom he may sell or consign the said tenement shall keep a disorderly house or allow improper inmates within the same, then the said house and ground shall revert to the owner or proprietor of the estate of Waterloo, and this lease become null and void.

"On these conditions the said Capt. Wm. Underwood cedes to the said John Martemis the before described piece of ground, to be occupied by him or his assigns for the period of 99 years from the date of this instrument, on paying annually a ground rent of one rixdollar; subject, however, to the following obligation namely,—That whenever the said John Martemis shall wish to dispose of his right and title, held by virtue of this lease, and the buildings thereon, the proprietor of the estate Waterloo for the time being shall have the refusal of purchase at the price offered by any other individual.

"WM. UNDERWOOD,
"Capt. 21st Light Dragoons."

That the said John Martemis entered into and remained in possession of the said piece of ground mentioned in the said lease until February, 1832, when the residue of the lease aforesaid then unexpired was sold by the High Sheriff of this Colony, in execution of a writ against the said John Martemis, to the defendant, who has since remained in possession of the demised premises.

That on the 25th day of June, 1839, the said William Underwood sold and transferred to the said plaintiff the certain piece of ground aforesaid of which the part aforesaid had been as aforesaid let upon lease to the said John Martemis, whereby the said plaintiff became lawfully entitled to the reversionary interest in the demised premises, expectant upon the legal determination of the said lease, together with all privileges and rights arising out of the said lease, as by the deed of transfer, bearing date the said 25th day of June, 1839, reference being thereunto had, will appear; and that the said lease, admitting the same to have been for some certain space of time valid, is now by law wholly determined and void, for and in respect of the grounds and reasons following, or of one or other of them, that is to say, first, because the term which the lease aforesaid purported to create is a longer term than can by the law of this Colony be created by any lease not registered in the Deeds Registry Office, and in regard to which no transfer duty has been paid to Government, and because the longest term for which the lease aforesaid, which was neither registered nor paid any transfer duty, could by law be considered as enduring, has expired, to wit on or before the 10th day of February, 1845.

Secondly, because in a tenement erected for a residence by the said John Martemis on the said demised premises, a certain store or shop has been by the said defendant, or by his leave and licence, opened for the sale of divers articles, to wit, from the month of March, 1839, till the month of February, 1845, in which store or shop divers articles have been sold, and were in the daily habit of being sold, during the said space of time, contrary to the condition in that behalf in the said lease inserted and contained. And that, by virtue of one or other of the said grounds and reasons, the plaintiff is now, as the proprietor of the piece of land, of which part was comprised in the said lease, and by virtue also of the provisions of the transfer deed aforesaid, entitled to claim possession of the said demised premises. Wherefore the said plaintiff prays that the said lease may be declared to be absolutely at an end, and that the said defendant may be ordered to deliver up to the said plaintiff possession of the said demised premises.

1845. Nov. 18. — Maynard *vs.* Usher.

The defendant pleaded the general issue.

At the trial, all the facts alleged in the declaration were either admitted or proved, and in particular it was proved that one Joseph le Croes, to whom defendant had let a house and premises built on part of the ground let by Underwood to Martemis by the aforesaid lease, had, within the period set forth in the declaration, kept a shop on the said premises in which he had sold linen and haberdashery wares, groceries, and pastry, but no spirits or wine.

It was also proved that previous to the sale by Underwood to the plaintiff, of the place Waterloo, including the ground let to Martemis by the lease aforesaid, not only Le Croes but also a preceding tenant of Martemis had kept a similar shop and sold articles of the like sorts.

The defendant admitted that the lease to Martemis had not been registered in the land register.

The plaintiff closed his case.

Defendant put in the transfer, dated 14th June, 1839, by Hare, as agent for Underwood, to the churchwardens of Wynberg, of certain piece of freehold land, with building thereon, now called Waterloo, situated at Wynberg, being part of the property transferred and granted to Underwood on the 4th November, 1814, and 24th December, 1818, measuring 5 morgen 122 square roods 54 square feet.

It was admitted by plaintiff that the above mentioned piece of land is a part of the Waterloo estate of Underwood.

Defendant closed his case.

The *Attorney-General*, for plaintiff, quoted *Van der Linden's Inst.*, 236, 237; *Lybrecht's Not. Prac.*, 2, 94; *Placaat 9th May*, 1744, § 9; and maintained that this Placaat was in force in this Colony, and that therefore the lease was null, and that there was no usage in the Colony in opposition to this Placaat. And that Underwood himself, the granter of the lease, might have enforced this legal nullity. Secondly, he maintained that the lease was forfeited by the breach of its condition, in consequence of Le Croes having kept a shop in the house which Martemis had built for a residence. He maintained that *shop* and *store* are synonymous; and that Le Croes kept a store; and that his selling any article, no matter of whatever description or kind it might be, in this store, was a forfeiture of the lease.

C. J. Brand, contra, referred to the deed of transfer in favour of the plaintiff, by Hare as attorney of Underwood, of the whole of the land at Wynberg belonging to Underwood, which deed, after describing the property sold and transferred, contained the following clauses: "Together with all privileges and rights arising out of a certain lease originally granted by the appearer's constituent to J. Martemis on the

10th February, 1820 (copy of which is hereunto annexed.") And maintained that by reason of this clause in the plaintiff's title the lease was as effectual against him as it would have been against Underwood. And quoted *Cod.*, 4, 65, 1, 10, *Voet* 19, 2, § 1, to show that by the law of Holland, before the Placaat of the 9th May, 1744, was enacted, the longest lease was good against the granter himself and his heirs, and those legally representing him in the obligation of the lease, although it was a contested question whether a lease longer than ten years would be good against singular successors or creditors of the lessor. The Placaat was enacted to settle this question, but as it never became part of the law of this Colony (see *Discount Bank vs. Dawes*, *8th Sept.*, 1829, *vol.* 1, *p.* 380), the law of this Colony remained as it was before that Placaat was enacted,—the enactment of which proves that previously to its enactment its provisions were not law. Secondly, he maintained that by reason of the transfer of part of the place Waterloo to the churchwardens of Wynberg, the plaintiff was not proprietor of *that estate of Waterloo* in favour of whom the forfeiture was created, and therefore could not, at least by himself alone and without the intervention of the churchwardens, enforce the forfeiture. Thirdly, he maintained that the keeping such a shop as that proved to having been kept by Le Croes, did not fall under the fair construction of the clause of forfeiture, which was only intended to prevent canteens and stores for the sale of wine and spirits, or any places of public entertainment, and can never be construed as intended to prevent Martemis, for whose benefit the lease was made, and for whose welfare the lessor evidently felt an interest, from contributing to his support by keeping a shop for the sale of the produce of the ground, or of his own industry, or articles the sale of which could not tend to immorality or breach of the peace; and that this view of the case was corroborated by the fact that Martemis had been suffered to keep such a shop by Underwood.

The *Attorney-General* replied, and quoted *Van Leeuwen, Cens. For.*, 4, 22, 5.

The Court held that the Placaat was not in force in this Colony. That the lease was effectual against Underwood and those who represented him in the obligation of the lease,—which they held that the plaintiff did by reason of the clause in plaintiff's title referring to the lease. That the defendant's objection to the plaintiff's title to enforce the forfeiture was bad; but that on the grounds stated by the defendant, no act inferring a forfeiture of the lease had been committed by defendant, and gave judgment for the defendant, with costs.

1845. Nov. 18. — Maynard *vs.* Usher.

MENZIES, J., on the authority of *Voet* 45, 1, 13, doubted whether, even if the sale of articles proved to have been sold on the premises had been held to have been a contravention of the conditions of the lease, the Court ought to have enforced the penalty of forfeiture to its full extent, and whether they ought not rather to have mitigated it to what would have been sufficient to protect the actual *interest* which the plaintiff had to enforce the condition, namely, to interdicting the defendant from keeping such a shop on the premises in future.

RUBIDGE *vs.* HADLEY.

Tenant's right to deduction of rent for loss of beneficial occupation caused by the Queen's enemies.

1848. Oct. 9. — Rubidge *vs.* Hadley.

[Decided by MENZIES, J., at the Albany Circuit.]

This was an action to recover the sum of £60, being for one year's rent from 1st April, 1846, to 1st April, 1847, due by Benjamin Hadley to Robert Henry Rubidge, under and by virtue of a certain unexpired lease, executed by and between the said Benjamin Hadley and the said Robert Henry Rubidge, before the notary public James John Henry Stone, bearing date the 4th day of October, 1841, wherein the said Robert Henry Rubidge did demise, lease, and let, unto the said Benjamin Hadley, all and singular the estate, farm, or place, situated about seven miles from Graham's Town, and known by the name of Gletwyn, together with the dwelling-house, and houses and erections, and all other the premises thereon,—as also a certain lower location at Cottingham, situated in the district aforesaid, and commonly called Clarke's Party, to hold the same unto the said Benjamin Hadley, his heirs, executors, or assigns, for the full end and term of seven years, commencing from the 1st day of October, 1841, at and under the yearly rent of £60 sterling, payable by two equal instalments of £30 sterling each, the 1st day of April and the 1st day of October, in each year during the continuance of the said lease,—reference thereto being had will more fully appear: And which said property, demised as aforesaid, hath been since the said 1st day of October, 1841, and still is, used, held, and possessed by the said Benjamin Hadley, under and by virtue of the lease thereof executed as aforesaid, and the whole of the rent which hath accrued and grown due and become payable to the said Robert Henry Rubidge, in pursuance thereof, save and except the said sum of £60 sterling as hereinbefore demanded, hath been paid and satisfied by the said Benjamin Hadley, but which lastmentioned sum of money, although he, the said Benjamin Hadley, has been often requested to pay, refuses so to do.

The defendant pleaded the general issue; and for a further plea, that the plaintiff ought not to have this action, because he says that the defendant before the said 1st day of April, 1846, in the summons mentioned, was compelled by the force and violence of the Queen's enemies, who invaded this Colony, and were threatening the inhabitants in the vicinity of the place in the summons mentioned, and amongst others the defendant,—and that therefore the defendant, by a good and reasonable fear, was compelled to fly and depart, and remove himself and his family and servants, his goods, cattle, and chattels as time permitted, to a place of safety, to wit, to Graham's Town, and the defendant further saith that from the 1st day of April, 1846, to the 1st day of April, 1847, he was prevented from returning or occupying, or, except as hereinafter stated, making any manner of profit, use, or advantage of the said premises, or any part thereof,—and the said defendant further saith that he admits that he did from time to time, as the state of the country permitted, send his servants from Graham's Town to the place aforesaid for the purpose of cutting and bringing away for the use of the said defendant certain firewood growing and being in the said place, and which by the contract of lease or hire the said defendant was allowed to remove,—and the defendant further saith that the use, profit, or advantage by him derived by reason of the obtaining of such firewood as aforesaid was small and inconsiderable, and did not amount to near the one third part of the use, profit, or advantage which he would have derived from the said place, had he not, by the just and reasonable fear aforesaid, been compelled to abandon and forsake the said place or farm; but the said defendant further saith, that in order to avoid litigation and to satisfy all reasonable claims and demands of the said plaintiff, he did, on or about the 21st day of September, 1847, at Graham's Town, tender and offer to the said plaintiff to pay to him the sum of £20, being one third part of the rent or sum by the plaintiff demanded in this action, which sum the plaintiff refused to accept, but which the said defendant is really and willing to pay; and the matters aforesaid the defendant is ready to verify; wherefore he prays judgment if the said plaintiff ought to receive from the said defendant any greater sum than the said £20 so tendered as aforesaid before the commencement of this

1848. Oct. 9. — Rubidge *vs.* Hadley.

action, and he prays that the claim or demand of the said plaintiff, except as to said sum of £20, be dismissed, with costs.

James Honey examined by *Ebden,* for the plaintiff: I am a farmer. I occupied a portion of the farm under defendant at a rent of £20 a year. I paid him that sum to April, 1847. (On cross-examination the witness said the defendant had applied to him for his rent up to April, 1847.) I paid it rather than run the risk of a law suit. Defendant told me that he intended to dispute the rent, and I paid the money conditionally that defendant was to return it if he was not compelled by law to pay. I left the farm at the same time as the defendant. The Kafirs had made some attacks in the neighbourhood. It was never safe to return to the farm until April, 1847. I did not return during that period, and I made no use of the farm. I never during that period had a head of cattle upon it, nor was I able to cultivate. The defendant did not return during that period to my knowledge, excepting that he sent the cattle there once. They were there two days with armed herds, and 40 head of them were stolen by Kafirs.

By the Court: The farm is a dangerous farm. It will carry about 700 head of cattle. I had the grazing of about 60 head.

Jeremiah Honey sworn: I know the farm in question. I have lived within two or three miles of the farm for about twenty-seven years. I am a farmer and know defendant's farm well. A portion was let to my nephews, another portion was let by defendant to John Ford, who is dead. It was unsafe to remain on the farm after the commencement of the war. I was obliged to leave my place about the time defendant did. Just about that time my servant boy was shot dead by the Kafirs at Botha's Hill just by. It was never safe to return to the farm till April, 1847. I have not yet returned to mine. I know the defendant cut wood during the war. It was very dangerous to do so. I acted as his agent on one occasion when he was at Fort Beaufort. I paid him then about £6 in cash. The average price of wood during the war was 20 rds. a load.

Cross-examined by *Porter, A.-G.,* for defendant: The farm is a good farm. I was acquainted with the manner in which defendant managed it. I knew the number of cattle and stock he had on the farm. The farm must have been before the war worth to defendant at least from £300 to £400, besides the increase of stock. I calculate this from the milk, butter, and other produce that defendant used to sell.

Mr. Brumage, Mr. Brooks, Mr. Pankhurst, and Mr.

Orsmond, the market-master, were called to prove the number of loads of wood drawn by the defendant during the war, amounting in all to 43 loads. The defendant admitted 50 loads.

Defendant closed his case. The Attorney-General did not call any witnesses.

Ebden, for plaintiff, contended that inasmuch as the defendant had been proved to have received £20 from the under tenant Honey, and had proved on the estate of Ford, for £20, and had made £50 by the wood, the plaintiff was entitled to the full amount of the rent. There was no evidence as to any tender.

The Attorney-General applied to the Court to examine the witness who made the tender.

By the Court: Mr. Roberts, the attorney for the defendant, being called and sworn, said: I am the defendant's attorney. Mr. Haw called on defendant when I was present. He demanded £60 for the rent; I tendered £20. Mr. Haw dispensed with the counting of the money; he said he would take it for part. I said I offered it as a sufficient sum in discharge of the rent. Mr. Haw refused to take it.

Ebden, notwithstanding the tender, contended that the plaintiff is entitled to his full rent. The defendant has had the use of the farm, and has made more than the rent, and it would be a hard case, under such circumstances, that he should enjoy the money derived from the farm and the plaintiff lose his rent.

Porter, A.-G.: By the law of England losses for non-user of this kind fall on the tenant, by the law of Scotland they fall on the landlord, and also by the Roman-Dutch law, where such losses are occasioned by reason of extraordinary seasons of unfruitfulness, war, fire, and acts of God. (*Van der Linden*, 238, 239; *Grotius, Book* 3, *c.* 12, *sect.* 12; *Burge's Colonial Law*, 3, 686; *Voet L.* 19, 2, 23.) As to the wood, it was a mere easement thrown in for the convenience of the tenant; it was never contemplated that he was to pay rent for it; therefore the tender of £20 was more than sufficient.

Ebden, in reply: The cases quoted only apply where there was a total failure of occupation; here the defendant had occupied and made his rent out of the land, and he therefore ought to pay the full amount of rent, having made it from the property of the plaintiff.

Menzies, J.: This is an action to recover the sum of £60, being one year's rent of a farm from 1st April, 1846, to 1st April, 1847, let under a lease. It is proved that the defendant was compelled to leave the farm in April, 1846, by the Queen's enemies, and it was unsafe without danger

1848. Oct. 9.

Rubidge *vs.* Hadley.

of life to occupy it to 1847. It is necessary to look to the terms of the lease in order to see what was contemplated to be enjoyed. It is proved that this was a valuable farm, consisting of arable land, pasture land, and wood land; these three advantages were then clearly in the contemplation of the parties when the lease was executed. Now for the period for which it is attempted to recover this rent it is proved that the defendant was deprived of the arable land and of the pasture land, and had only the use of the wood land. It is clear by the law of this Colony that a tenant is entitled to demand the entire remission of his rent or an abatement of part, according as he has had no use of it during the whole or part of the time of lease, unless this had been occasioned by his own fault. All the authorities agree on the point, and I am therefore of opinion that the rent must be apportioned. It has been proved that the farm was worth to the defendant before the war from £300 to £400 a year; during the period stated it has been proved that he has derived a profit of £70 only, for I throw overboard altogether the sum he has proved against the estate of John Ford, which it is probable he will never receive. The rent is to be apportioned on the profit made, not on the gross amount received, and I am therefore of opinion, according to the law of this Colony, and looking to all the circumstances, that the tender of £20 made by the defendant was ample and sufficient remuneration for the use he had of the farm during the time stated. There must therefore be a judgment for the plaintiff for the £20, the plaintiff to pay defendant's costs,—the defendant intimating that from April, 1847, he was willing to pay the full rent.

MENZIES' REPORTS.

[NEW SERIES.]

1828–1849.

VOL. II. PART II.

CHAPTER III.
MANDATE.

COOKE *vs.* HOGUE AND ANOTHER.

A special power of attorney to sell goods and receive money gives no power to go beyond, nor to defend suits; and therefore an action brought against such attorney dismissed accordingly. 1828. June 16.

[Vol. I, p. 302.]

CHIAPPINI *vs.* GEORGE.

Mandatores liable to make good the expenses of the mandate each pro rata his own share, but not liable to make good the shares of insolvent mandatores. June 20.

[Vol. I, p. 303.]

NISBET & DICKSON *vs.* VENABLES.

English Assignees: capacity of. Proof by affidavits of assignees themselves and one of the bankrupts, of their appointment, not sufficient. June 23.

[Vol. I, p. 304.]

HEARTLEY *vs.* POUPART.

1829. Sept. 24.

Mandate ceases by the death of the mandant (principal). Proceedings in name of a dead person, after death, null, and set aside. Costs of attorney for proceeding in the name of a dead party not allowed where death known to him.

[Vol. I, p. 400.]

ROWLE'S EXECUTOR *vs.* MOSTERT.

1831. Dec. 1.

A bond executed in favour of a mandatory (agent) "or his administrators," may be sued upon by the administrator of the mandatary after death of the mandant (principal).

[Vol. I, p. 534.]

BRINK, q.q. BREDA, *vs.* VOIGT AND ANOTHER.

Dec. 29.

A judgment against a plaintiff suing as agent for another not executable against him personally unless so ordered.

[Vol. I, p. 537.]

ELLIOTT *vs.* ALBERTUS.

Agent and Principal.—Guarantee by Agent.

A debtor on a bill of exchange, about to leave the Colony, obtained from the person whom he constituted his agent an undertaking in the following terms, which he gave his creditor: "As agent for D. & B. P., the following acceptances which you hold of them at maturity will be paid by me." This was held by the majority of the Court to be an undertaking binding the agent personally, and a guarantee of payment of the bills by him, whether he has funds of his principal or not.

1833. Feb. 22. — Elliott *vs.* Albertus.

The following were the facts of this case. The plaintiff on 7th April, 1832, drew a bill on the firm of Messrs. D. & B. Philips, for £786 17s. 6d., payable six months after date, which was accepted by B. Philips, the partner resident in this Colony.

1833. Feb. 22. Elliott *vs.* Albertus.

The plaintiff indorsed this bill to McDonald. It having become known that B. Philips intended to leave the Colony, McDonald asked him for security that this bill would be paid when due, and on the 9th July, 1832, Philips gave him the following letter:

"Cape Town, 9th July, 1832.

"A. McDonald, Esq., Cape Town.

"Dear Sir,—As agent for Messrs. D. & B. Philips, the following acceptances which you hold of them at maturity will be paid by me.

"I have, &c.,

"J. ALBERTUS.

"1832.—October 7	... ...	£786	17 6
"1833.—January 7	... ...	786	17 6
"1832.—November 5	... ...	706	17 6"

McDonald stated that he had no conversation with the defendant personally on the subject of the payment of the bill or of this letter.

B. Philips left the Colony, and when the bill became due, McDonald presented it to defendant, and on his refusal to pay it, protested the bill, and demanded payment from plaintiff as drawer, and on receiving payment of it gave him a cession of the bill.

Plaintiff now sued defendant for payment of the bill, in respect of his letter on the 9th July, 1832, above quoted.

In his plea the defendant admitted that McDonald had applied to him to know whether the bill would be paid when due, and pleaded that, on the 9th July, 1832, he, the said defendant, having been appointed the general agent of the said firm of D. & B. Philips, during the intended absence from this Colony of B. Philips, the managing partner, passed the undertaking contained in the letter of 9th July, 1832; that in giving said undertaking in writing, the defendant passed such engagement in his capacity as the then agent of the said firm, but that he is no longer agent for said firm, the estate of which has been surrendered as insolvent, and trustees duly elected for the administration thereof, by reason whereof the defendant is not personally liable for the said claim. And that plaintiff was the drawer as well as the first endorser of the bill, and by the cession thereof to the plaintiff, his capacity as holder and drawer became merged, and that the plaintiff as joint debtor in said bill is not entitled to recover the amount, upon and by virtue of defendant's said undertaking.

1833. Feb. 22.

Elliott *vs.* Albertus.

The *Attorney-General*, for the plaintiff, referred to the case of *Ross vs. Muntingh* (*Vol.* 1, *p.* 39), and maintained that the letter of the 9th July, 1832, was a positive, unconditional, and unqualified undertaking by the defendant to pay the bill when it became due, whether he then had funds of D. & B. Philips in his hands or not, or then continued or had ceased to be their agent, and that the words "as agent" in the beginning of the letter had not the effect of freeing him from personal liability (*Bayley on Bills, page* 56, *note* 5, and 54; *Paley on Principal and Agent, cap.* 6, *and page* 298, 311); and maintained that as McDonald, in consequence of this letter, gave credit to Albertus, and thus forbearance to Philips, this had the effect of making the letter a guarantee, even although it were ambiguous in its terms. (*Bell's Commentaries on Bankrupt Law. Edit.* 1821, *vol.* 1, *p.* 390, 422.)

Cloete maintained the contrary, and quoted *Dig.* 45, 1, 99, 38, § 18, and maintained that however favourable the civil law might have been to the plaintiff's argument, yet that the law of Holland differs entirely from the civil law in this respect. (*Barels Advysen, page* 102; *Coren Observns.*, 258; *Van Leeuwen, Cens. For.* 4, 3, § 6.) He stated nothing in support of the second plea. (*Vide Chitty on Bills, Edit.* 5, *p.* 36, 226.)

Menzies and Kekewich, JJ., held that the circumstances of this case proved that although defendant had no communication personally with McDonald, yet that he gave the letter to McDonald to satisfy the desire for some additional security, expressed by him to Philips, and by Philips communicated to plaintiff, and consequently that the defendant must be deemed to have given the letter, not merely as a notice that he was to be agent for Philips, but as thereby giving McDonald security of some kind and to some extent or other, in addition to that already possessed by McDonald, which a mere undertaking that the bills would be paid at maturity, given by defendant *as agent*, and so expressed as to bind only his principal Philips, and not himself, would not have given. That the insertion of the words "as agent" did not necessarily prove that the obligation was granted with the object and intent of binding Philips, and not defendant personally, because the words "as agent" might have been inserted to show the character in which Albertus became a party to the transaction, and that it was on behalf of Philips, and not of Elliott, that he undertook the payment, and that it was as being agent of Philips, and not in consequence of any valuable consideration already received by him from Philips, that he did so. That in the law of Holland, as in that of England, it is a settled principle that the insertion of the words "as agent" do not *per se* necessarily in every case free the agent from personal responsibility. (*Vide Van Leeuwen Cens. For.* 4, 3, § 6 *and* 7; *Bayley on Bills*, 54 *and* 56; *Paley*, 294 *and* 211.) That there is no ground for holding that the words "as agent" have the effect of qualifying the positive personal undertaking to pay implied by the words "will be paid by me." That as McDonald, in consideration of getting this letter, gave forbearance to B. Philips, by allowing him to leave the Colony without futher security, want of consideration cannot be pleaded as a bar to the claim madé on this letter by McDonald or by Elliott, who by the cession is placed in the same situation that McDonald would have been in.

1833. Feb. 22.

Elliott *vs.* Albertus.

WYLDE, C.J., differed from the other Judges on nearly all the points above set forth.

The Court, by a majority, gave judgment for the plaintiff, with costs. (*Vide Westhuizen vs. Pope and Devenish*, 17*th May*, 1842. *Vol.* 2, *Pt.* 1, *p.* 60.)

McDONALD *vs.* ALBERTUS.

Agent and Principal. Guarantee. Bill of Exchange.

One of the acceptances referred to in the following undertaking by an agent on behalf of his principal, who was about to leave the Colony, "as agent for D. & B. P., the following acceptances which you hold of them at maturity will be paid by me," having fallen due after the return of the principal to the Colony, the Court, by a majority, held the agent personally liable, notwithstanding the principal's return.

June 7.

McDonald *vs.* Albertus.

Postea.—The Court by the same majority (WYLDE, C.J., *dissentiente*) on the same grounds gave judgment for the plaintiff against the defendant for the promissory note for £706 17s. 6d., due on the 5th November, 1832, last mentioned in the list in the defendant's letter of 9th July, 1832, with costs, notwithstanding that *Cloete*, for the defendant, maintained that the circumstance that the bill now sued for did not become due until the 5th November, 1832, while Philips had returned to this Colony on the 15th October, and that the estate of D. & B. Philips was placed under sequestration on the 17th October, made this case very different from that of *Elliott vs. Albertus*, where the bill sued for became due on the 5th October, before B. Philips returned to the Colony, and quoted *Heinneccius Wissel-*

1833. June 7. McDonald *vs.* Albertus.

regt, 3, *cap.* § 32, *note, pages* 187 *and* 284, *and cap.* 5, § 12, *note* 20, which is as follows:

"This follows from the general principle of mandates, *quod quis per alium facit ipse fecisse intelligitur,* so that thereby the person accepting the mandate cannot be sued in his own person for the same. However, it is clear that his mandate must be clearly shown, for otherwise the principal would not be responsible, but himself. On the same principle, if a principal draw a bill on his factor, without adding that it is in his capacity as his factor, and the latter accept the same as having power from his principal, the drawer, he will still be personally responsible, without being able to avail himself of his addition *as agent.*" See also p. 187, 4th chap., § 26, text.

"If the drawer promises to pay a bill of exchange, his engagement must be written under the bill, as follows: '*I accept and promise prompt payment.*' Sometimes a factor accepts as agent, when it is done in words to this effect or similar: 'In the name of my principal, N. N., and by virtue of his power, I accept and promise prompt payment.'" (*Pothier on Bills,* 2*nd vol.,* §§ 20, 25. *Sed. Vide Van der Keessel, Th.* 851.)

Silberbauer, q.q. Davis, *vs.* McDonald and Sutherland.

Mandatary. Insolvent. Pleading. Exception.

An uncertificated insolvent may be a mandatary.

Dec. 10. Silberbauer, q.q. Davis, *vs.* McDonald and Sutherland.

This action was brought by Silberbauer in the capacity of agent or mandatary of Davis.

The *Attorney-General,* this day, argued in support of the exception pleaded by the defendant, McDonald,—that at the time of filing the declaration, and hitherto, the plaintiff was and is an uncertificated insolvent, and dead in law, and cannot have or maintain his action against the defendant; and quoted *Van Leeuwen, Cens. For.,* 4, *c.* 24, *p.* 440, and maintained that no uncertificated insolvent could act as a mandatary, and quoted *Van Leeuwen, Cens. For.,* 4 *c.,* 24 §, *p.* 440; *Voet,* 5, 1, § 10.

Cloete, contra, quoted *Voet,* 42, 3, 10; 17, 1, 5; *Cens. For., part* 2, 1, 33, § 27.

The exception was overruled with costs, and defendant ordered to answer over in eight days.

Ryneveld *vs.* The Wine Depôt.

1833. Dec. 19.

Ryneveld *vs.* The Wine Depôt.

A "Negotiorum Gestor" suffered to appear in Court.

In this case the *Attorney-General* moved to make absolute a rule granted calling on the Wine Depôt Company or Association to show cause why a scheme of distribution should not be amended in terms of the Master's report.

Brand appeared, and stated that he had no power of attorney or other authority from the said Wine Depôt Company or Association to appear for them, but that he appeared as their *negotiorum gestor* to show cause against the rule.

The Court allowed him to appear in that capacity solely in consequence of the consent of the other party, and by no means admitted that he had any right to appear in that capacity if any objection had been made to his so doing.

Rule made absolute, with costs, unless cause to the contrary shall be shown before this day week.

Neethling *vs.* Taylor.

Procurator in rem suam entitled to sue for rent on a lease.

1834. Dec. 23.

[Vol. I, p. 30.]

Dickinson *vs.* Ley, q.q. Van Der Chys.

Mandatary. Summons must be directed against absent principal, though served upon agent within the Colony.

1835. Feb. 10.

Dickinson *vs.* Ley, q.q. Van der Chys.

Van der Chys, before leaving the Colony, executed a power of attorney in favour of Ley, whereby he constituted and empowered Ley generally, in his name and in his place, to conduct and execute, as well in as out of courts of law, all the affairs, without distinction, in which the interests of the appearer are in any way concerned, consequently also to receive moneys and to make payments, to settle accounts, to pass receipts, and to make good the same in all cases amicably, and in case of unwillingness to compel those unwilling by means of law, before whatever tribunal it may be, to that effect to commence actions at law, to appeal against those against him, or to prosecute and bring the same in review, &c.

1835. Feb. 10.

Dickinson *vs.* Ley, q.q. Van der Chys.

Dickinson, the legal holder of a bond passed by Van der Chys, and by which he mortgaged certain landed property belonging to him, situated in this Colony, sued Ley on a summons, which "commanded Ley, in his capacity as the general agent of Van der Chys, absent from this Colony, *that he render to Dickinson* £150, *which the said Ley in his aforesaid capacity owes to the said Dickinson, upon and by virtue of a mortgage bond passed and signed by Van der Chys,* &c. And unless he shall do so, then summon the said Ley in his capacity as the general agent of Van der Chys to appear and show wherefore he hath not done it, &c., and to show cause why the property mortgaged should not be declared executable."

Ley did not appear.

Proof was offered that Ley had accepted and acted under his appointment in the above quoted power of attorney.

But the Court was of opinion that the summons ought not to have been directed against Ley, and that the power of attorney and his acting under it were not sufficient to support the allegation that Ley, in any capacity, owed the sum in the bond; that the summons ought to have been directed against Van der Chys, and that service of it on his attorney, Ley, would have been good service, notwithstanding Van der Chys's absence from the Colony.

On hearing this opinion the plaintiff withdrew the case.

Nicholls, and Deacon, his Assignee, *vs.* Thomson, Watson, & Co.

Ship-agency.

A ship having been condemned as unseaworthy in one of the ports of the Colony, and sold by the agents on behalf of the owner, in an action brought by the assignees of the owner against the agents to account for the proceeds, the Court ordered the account rendered to be debated, notwithstanding that the charges in it to which objection were taken had been admitted in an account-current signed as correct and settled between the agents and the master of the ship.

A charge of 2½ per cent., made as commission on transhipment of certain oil forming the cargo of the ship, to another vessel, was reduced to 1½ per cent. after hearing the evidence of merchants on the subject.

A charge for commission for entering into a security bond to answer the adjudication of an action in the Vice-Admi-

ralty Court by the crew for wages, in regard of which the ship had been arrested, was wholly disallowed, the action having been dismissed and the bond thereby rendered null.

An account paid by the agents to the master as a balance alleged by him to be due on an account-current between him and the owner disallowed, as having no relation whatever to their agency. The agents had no right to take upon themselves, without authority, to admit the correctness of, and pay, claims by the master on account of transactions between him and the owner prior to their agency.

A payment to two of the crew of wages due to them, which they might have enforced out of the proceeds of the hull, was maintained as having been made beneficially for the plaintiff.

1835. Aug. 18. June 12.

Nicholls, and Deacon, his Assignee, *vs.* Thomson, Watson, & Co.

The plaintiff in this case was the assignee of the insolvent Nicholls, who was the sole owner of the bark *Castor*.

In September, 1831, the *Castor* had been condemned in Simon's Bay as unseaworthy, and the plaintiff brought this action to recover from the defendants the proceeds of the cargo and vessel, offering to allow a deduction for such commission-agency and disbursements as they could show themselves to be entitled to.

With their plea, the defendants filed an account of the proceeds of the vessel and cargo, sold by them in this Colony by the direction of the master, as they alleged, together with the application thereof.

To this account, the plaintiff, in his replication and debate, stated sundry objections.

In their rejoinder and counter debate, the defendants pleaded that, with respect to the first six of the objections made by the plaintiff, they were not bound now to debate the same, because the whole of the charges now objected to have been admitted as just and correct, and settled by and with the said master of the vessel.

This day, *Cloete*, for plaintiff, argued in support of the said six objections.

The *Attorney-General*, *contra*, argued in support of the exception made to those objections in the defendants' rejoinder, and produced an account-current made out by defendants as between them and the plaintiff, in which the sums referred to in those objections were placed to the debit of the plaintiff, and the balance brought out, and which account-current was signed by the said T. Litchfield, the master of the vessel.

1835. Aug. 18. — Nicholls, and Deacon, his Assignee, *vs.* Thomson, Watson, & Co.

The Court held that the plaintiffs were not debarred from proposing the said objections by reason of the account-current signed by Litchfield, and the settlement alleged to have been made between the defendants and Litchfield, and accordingly gave judgment to that effect. (*Vide Abbot on Shipping, Ed.* 1827, *pp.* 102, 107, 240, 241.)

Postea (3rd November, 1836).—The parties produced their evidence, and were heard in support of and against the plaintiff's objections to the defendants' account. The plaintiff had charged £100 as commission at 2½ per cent. on the transhipment of certain oil valued at £4,000, part of the cargo in Simon's Bay, from the *Castor* to the *Corsair*, in which it was sent to London. The plaintiff objected that the rate of commission charged was too high, and called the master, Litchfield, who stated: "I transhipped the oil myself from the *Castor* to the *Corsair*. Three or four of the men and five or six of the ship's apprentices assisted. The defendants had neither a partner nor a clerk present at the transhipment. Wools, their agent at Simon's Bay, assisted me in getting my men to work, and sometimes in getting men to hire. Whenever I wanted anything, I applied to him."

Two merchants of Cape Town, Messrs. A. McDonald, sr., and S. Townsend, swore that, in their opinion, 2½ per cent. was a fair and usual commission, and two others, Messrs. Billingsley and Pillans, that 2½ per cent. was an overcharge, and that 1½ per cent. was fully sufficient commission on such a transhipment.

The Court (Chief Justice absent) allowed only 1½ per cent.

On the arrival of the *Castor* in Simon's Bay, the vessel and her tackle, &c., had been arrested on a warrant issued by the Vice-Admiralty Court in an action brought by the crew against the master for recovery of their shares of the oil which the vessel had made, and for breach of contract. In order to obtain the release of the vessel, the defendants, with Mr. G. W. Prince, had entered into a security bond for £2,000 to answer the adjudication of the said action. The action was finally dismissed, and the bond thus rendered null. The defendants had charged £50 as commission at 2½ per cent. on the amount of the said bond. Plaintiff objected that they were not entitled to any commission on this transaction, and called Mr. G. W. Prince, who stated: "I am a merchant in Cape Town, and was one of the sureties in the bond in question. I received no value for doing so. The defendants had, on a former occasion, signed a similar security bond for me without receiving any pecuniary consideration."

The Court thereupon sustained the objection.

The defendants had debited the plaintiff in their account with the sum of £691 12s. 4d., as having been paid by them to Litchfield, as the balance due to him on his account-current as master with the owner of the *Castor* previously to her arrival in this Colony.

The plaintiff objected to this item *in toto*, and denied that he had been indebted in any part of the said sum to Litchfield.

The Court sustained this objection, on the ground that the payments alleged to have been made to the master had no relation whatever to the subject matter in which the defendants were the agents of the plaintiff, and that the defendants had no right to take upon themselves, without authority from the plaintiff, to admit the correctness of, and to pay, claims made by the master on account of debts alleged to have become due by the plaintiff to him prior to the employment of the defendants as agents. And that, under the circumstances of the case, the plaintiff ought not to be compelled to litigate in the Courts of this Colony with the defendants matters in dispute between the plaintiff and his shipmaster, arising out of transactions which occurred previously to the arrival of the ship here and the employment of the defendants as agents. But the Court sustained the right of the defendants to debit the plaintiff with £168 3s. 10d., which, it was admitted, had been paid by them to Shuker and Smith, two of the crew, as the wages due to them, because, as there was no express stipulation in the ship's articles respecting the wages of those two men, which were to be at the rate of so much per month, either as to the time when or the place where they should be payable, or as to what would render them liable to forfeiture, the claims of those men for their wages must be regulated by common law. And that therefore, as the ship had brought the oil she had made to the Cape, and as her hull, &c., had sold for more than was sufficient to pay the wages of those two men, they were entitled to have demanded and enforced payment of their wages out of the proceeds of the hull, &c., and consequently the defendants had acted beneficially for the plaintiff when they paid those men the amount of their wages. (*Vide Abbot on Shipping, Ed.* 1827, *part* 4, *cap.* 2 *and* 3, *pp.* 447, 451, 452.)

On these grounds, the Court dismissed the plaintiff's objection to this item of the account.

Trustee of Ziedeman *vs.* De Wet.

1836. Nov. 4.

Where on voluntary separation a mensâ, thoro, et communione, an attorney of the Court was appointed by the husband as his agent in the administration of the joint estate, the Court held that such attorney was entitled only to commission as agent, and not to fees as an attorney.

[Vol. I, p. 237.]

Moodie *vs.* The Registrar of Deeds.

Agent. Transfer.

A general power of attorney, cum specialibus potestatibus, without special authority to sell immovable property, does not authorize the sale and transfer of immovable property.

Circumstances in which a transfer by virtue of such a power together with a holograph letter of the principal was allowed by the Court, without prejudice to the principal's rights.

1840. March 12. — Moodie *vs.* The Registrar of Deeds.

On leaving this Colony in 1829, Mr. John Moodie executed, before a notary, a general power of attorney, *cum specialibus potestatibus*, in favour of his brother, Mr. Donald Moodie, but containing no power or authority to sell or transfer immovable property. After his departure, Mr. John Moodie wrote several letters to his brother Donald, desiring him in urgent terms to sell a certain landed property belonging to him, and to remit the proceeds. Mr. Donald Moodie accordingly sold it, and the purchaser now was anxious to obtain transfer, which Mr. Donald Moodie was ready to make, but the Registrar of Deeds refused to draw or register the deed of transfer, on the ground that Mr. Donald Moodie had no sufficient authority to enable him to sell and transfer lands. It was agreed on all sides that the power of attorney as it stood would not, *per se*, authorize Mr. Donald Moodie to sell or transfer the property, and that, therefore, if there was nothing else than the power, Mr. Donald Moodie would have had no title to give transfer which the Registrar of Deeds could recognize. But the Court (Kekewich, J., absent) held that the power of attorney, in conjunction with the holograph letter, gave Mr. D. Moodie such a *prima facie* title to give transfer as to entitle him to call on the Registrar to execute and register the deed of transfer, *valeat quantum*, and therefore ordered the Registrar to do so accordingly. The Court held that the execution and registration of the deed of transfer would in no case prejudice the rights of Mr. John Moodie, or his representative, supposing that it should afterwards turn out that the letters were not authentic, or did not, in conjunction with the power of attorney, give Mr. D. Moodie power to sell and give transfer of the lands, or involve the Registrar in any responsibility for having drawn and registered the transfer.

1840. March 12.

Moodie *vs.* The Registrar of Deeds.

HARRIS *vs.* RUTHVEN.

Mandate. Sale.

Variance between contract alleged and proof.

Authority by letter to purchase a wagon at a sale in which the principal wrote, "I expect the sale is at six months' credit," is exceeded by a purchase payable in cash or on delivery.

Aug. 11.

Harris *vs.* Ruthven.

Plaintiff, in his declaration, claimed payment from defendant of £107 2s., as being the price of a wagon and oxen, which he tendered to defendant, and which he alleged had been sold by him to George Ruthven, the son of the defendant, who was duly thereto qualified by said defendant, and for account of said defendant, for said sum of £107 2s., to be paid for in cash on delivery.

Plaintiff put in evidence the following letter from defendant to his son: "At the sale of Harris is a wagon complete for the road with all its gear for twelve oxen, and I hear he has a good span of oxen of a powerful strength. Should I not come by the time of the sale, and if you can buy this wagon, &c., &c., you had better, and send it to me at Mr. B. Muller's for goods, and we will establish a regular conveyance to and from Worcester. I shall attend chiefly myself to it. Not more than twelve oxen. Some friend will advise you of the worth, so as not to give more; the cheaper the better of course. If security is wanted I don't know, but I expect the sale is six months' credit." And called Adrian Marthinus Nel, the auctioneer through whom the sale had been made, who stated that the son having bid for the wagon, "I went to him and said I can't take your bid; I can't give you credit. He then showed me a letter, and said it contained an order from his father. It was in English; I did not read it. I said I don't know your father, you must give security to me from a resident in this village. This was spoken so loud that any person

1840. Aug. 11. — Harris *vs.* Ruthven.

could have heard it. Plaintiff then came up and said, 'I will be security for the wagon, I will take your bid, *upon condition that I shall keep the wagon until your father either pays me or gives me security.*' The wagon, and afterwards twelve oxen on the same terms, were then knocked down to him, and he signed the vendue roll."

The Court absolved defendant from the instance with costs, on the ground, first, that the bargain, as proved by Nel, was at variance with that alleged in the declaration, viz., that the sale was for *cash to be paid on delivery*, and that this variance between the facts alleged in the declaration and the facts proved was fatal to the action, even although the son had had authority to buy, on condition that cash should be paid on delivery; second, that the letter of defendant to his son did not prove and support the averment in the declaration that the son was duly qualified to make the purchase on the condition alleged in the declaration, but the contrary.

SMITH *vs.* SOUTHEY.

1841. May 20.

A commission agent who has rendered an account-current of his commission sales, showing a balance in favour of his principal, cannot be sued for such balance in a provisional case.

[Vol. I, p. 53.]

CHIAPPINI & CO. *vs.* JAFFRAY'S TRUSTEES.

Ownership. Iusolvency. Vindication of principal's goods in hands of factor. Vindication of proceeds of principal's goods in the hands of factor.

1. *On the insolvency of a factor, his principal is entitled to vindicate, as his own property, all goods which he can trace to have been consigned by him to the factor, to be sold by the latter as factor, which at the date of insolvency are in the factor's possession; the property in these goods forming no part of the factor's estate.*

2. *Where the factor had sold goods of the principal, and taken bills in his own favour in payment, which remain in the factor's hands at the date of the sequestration, the*

principal is entitled to these bills to the extent of the balance remaining due on account of the proceeds of the goods consigned to him and not paid, or remitted for before the insolvency.

3. *The factor having sold his principal's goods, and having been sequestrated before the price of the goods has been paid by the purchaser, the principal may sue for such unpaid price, although the goods had been sold by the factor in his own name.*

4. *The fact of the factor's having credited the principal with the price of the goods, as sold, in his books, does not affect the principal's rights as stated in* 2 *and* 3.

5. *An agreement that the factor should receive a del credere commission does not affect the rights of the principal.*

6. *The stating of an account-current between the principal and factor, and an action brought by the principal for the balance of this account-current before the surrender, does not affect the principal's rights.*

7. *The balance for which the principal was creditor, and the transactions with the factor, being greater than the amount of the bills and outstanding debts mentioned in* 2 *and* 3, *this amount is not subject to deduction on account of costs, charges, and commission of the factor.*

8. *Certain promissory notes by purchasers in favour of the factor, representing, in part, goods of the principal, the principal is entitled to a proportion of the proceeds of the notes corresponding to the amount of the price of his goods, as if they had been granted for the exact amount of the price of his goods.*

9. *Bills granted by an auctioneer to the factor are in the same position as bills by the purchaser directly in the factor's favour.*

The insolvent, Jaffray, was a merchant, and commission agent at Graham's Town. The plaintiffs had for some time before the sequestration of his estate consigned goods to him for sale, for which he was to receive a commission of 5 per cent., and 2½ per cent. *del credere.* It had been the practice of the insolvent to remit his own promissory notes at six months, monthly, for the amount of sales during the month, but the practice was changed, and he undertook to remit cash or produce, as he had the means to do so, sending monthly accounts of the sales effected by him.

1843. May 23. June 12.

Chiappini & Co. vs. Jaffray's Trustees.

Shortly before the date of the sequestration the insolvent had handed over to the agent of the plaintiffs the residue of their consigned goods which he had on hand. He had not remitted to them to the full amount of the goods sold by him. The position of the insolvent in regard to such goods consigned by the plaintiffs which had been sold was—1. There were accounts standing open in his books against purchasers of such goods. 2. There were bills of exchange and promissory notes in his favour given for such goods in his possession. 3. There were in his possession promissory notes in his favour by persons for goods consigned, of which some had been consigned by plaintiffs, some by other persons. The shares in these notes applicable to the goods which had been consigned by the plaintiffs were traceable from the books and accounts.

All the goods consigned to the insolvent by his several principals, including the plaintiffs, were sold by him in his own name, and the bills of parcels were made out and delivered in his own name, without mention of the consignors. The insolvent was in the habit of selling such goods out of his stores and by public auction. After making out the account sales of the several consignees monthly, he entered them into his account sales book, entered the amount of the sales of each to their credit in the journals, and then carried them to their credit in their respective accounts in the ledger under the head of "by merchandise sales," without any mention of the purchaser. Whatever amount was received for them he used as his own funds. At the same time he carried on the business of sale on consignment he did a considerable amount of business on his own account.

On the 17th December, 1841, an account-current was made out by the insolvent's bookkeeper between him and the plaintiffs, in which there appear all the sales made up to that time, with the charges and commission and *del credere*, showing a balance due to them by the insolvent as their agent. All the matters in issue in the present case were embraced in this account, and the sums for which the goods were sold were placed to the plaintiffs' credit whether or not they were at that date due by the purchasers. The plaintiffs sued the insolvent for the balance of this account-current in the Circuit Court of Albany in April, 1842, but the estate was surrendered before the day of appearance, and the summons was withdrawn.

Evidence of merchants was given to the effect that the manner in which the insolvent had kept his accounts in regard to his transactions with the plaintiffs was that in which mercantile accounts are kept by factors employed to sell goods consigned on a *del credere* commission, that these accounts were kept on a principle which enables the goods and transactions of each consignor to be kept clear and distinct from those of other persons, and that such factors generally sell in their own names. Where there is no *del credere* commission, the names of purchasers are specified in the account sales, but even then the purchasers' promissory notes are made in favour of the factor, the purchasers account with him, and he with the principal.

Porter, A.-G., for plaintiffs, quoted *Voet* 17, 1, 17; *Storey on Bailments, p.* 152, § 211, to show that the insolvency of the mandatary is equivalent to a revocation of the mandate by the mandant; *Bell on Bankruptcy, B.* 1, *part 3rd, cap.* 2, § 4, and the cases there cited, to show that goods consigned to factors do not on the principle of reputed ownership flowing from their temporary possession fall into the general estate of the factor, and become, on his insolvency, distributable among his creditors; and that the proceeds into which the goods are converted by the factor, even money, *e.g.*, guineas, if they can be clearly traced and distinguished as being the substitute for the goods, fall under the same rule and principle which would have regulated the consignees' right to the goods themselves. He also quoted *Scott and Surnan* in *Chitty and Forster's Equity Index on Bankruptcy, p.* 157, and maintained that by those authorities it was also clearly shown that plaintiffs were entitled to demand from defendant restitution of any sums which, since the surrender of Jaffray's estate, they had received from the purchasers of the goods consigned by plaintiffs, whether purchased on open account or for the price of which promissory notes had been given. Lastly, he maintained that other consignors had a claim to a certain share in some of the promissory notes (those set forth in schedule C), as representing to that extent their goods, had not the effect of preventing plaintiffs from tracing and proving that those notes were granted partly in payment of and to that extent representing the plaintiffs' goods, and therefore could not bar them from claiming a proportion of the proceeds of those notes corresponding to the amount of the price of the plaintiffs' goods for which those notes were guaranteed, and quoted *McCulloch's Commercial Dictionary, p.* 569.

Musgrave, contra, argued that whatever might be the law of Great Britain on the subject, yet that by the law of this Colony a different decision must be given from that contended for by the Attorney-General, and quoted *Burton on the Insolvent Law, p.* 143, to show that a consignor could

1843. May 23. June 12.

Chiappini & Co. vs. Jaffray's Trustees.

reclaim his consigned goods from the general creditors of the factor only when the goods are found in specie in the estate. (*Voet* 20, 4, § 13; 6, 1, §§ 8, 9, 10.) He also quoted *Paley's Law of Principal and Agent, p.* 182; *Burge's Colonial Law, p.* 82; and 2*nd Campbell Reports, p.* 83; and argued that upon the principle of those authorities, this case, under its peculiar circumstances, would, even in the law of England, receive a different decision from that contended for by the Attorney-General. He also maintained that the mode which had been followed in stating their accounts between plaintiffs and Jaffray constituted a novation of their original claim against him.

Ebden followed on the same side (by consent, and without its being admitted that defendant is of right entitled to be heard by two counsel).

Court adjourned.

The *Attorney-General*, in replication on the questions of law raised by defendants, quoted *Loenius, Cas.* 9, *note; Grotius Inleid., B.* 3, *part* 1, § 38; *Coren Observations* and *Note on Cas.* 25; *Bell's Commentary, Preface; Pardessus Comment. on the Lex Mercatoria, part* 5, *tit.* 1, *cap.* 10, § 1; *Voet* 14, 3, 7.

Musgrave was allowed to refer to *Matthæus de Auction., B.* 1, *cap.* 18, §§ 6 *and* 8; *Voet* 20, 4, § 13; 6, 1, §§ 7, 8, 9.

Cur. adv. vult.

Postea (12th June, 1843).—The Court gave judgment.

The Court (WYLDE, C.J., MENZIES and KEKEWICH, JJ.) were unanimously of opinion that the dealings and transactions between Chiappini & Co. and Jaffray were in the ordinary course of dealing and transacting business between a principal and his agent or factor. That it was proved by the authorities quoted—and particularly those from *Loenius Cas.* 9, *Grotius Inleiding, B.* 3, *part* 1, § 38 and *Note by Scorer, and Coren's Observ., Casus* 25,—that, whatever might formerly have been the Roman law on the subject, by the Dutch law, by which, and not by the Roman law, the Court were bound to decide the case, it was clearly established that, on the insolvency of a factor, his principal was entitled to vindicate and take as his own property all goods which he could trace to have been those consigned to the factor, to be sold by him as factor, which at the time of the insolvency were in the possession of the factor, because the property in those goods remained in the principal, and consequently they form no part of the factor's estate; that, to the extent of the balance remaining due by the factor to his principal, on account of the proceeds of the goods consigned to him for sale by his principal and not paid, or remitted for, previous to the factor's insolvency, when the factor has sold the goods of the principal and taken bills for the price, payable to himself, which remain in the factor's hands undiscounted at the date of his sequestration, the principal is entitled to those bills, and they form no part of the funds divisible among the general creditors of the factor; and this, although the goods have been sold by the factor in his own name and without a disclosure of or mention of the principal.

Thirdly,—That when the factor has sold the goods of his principal and been sequestered before the price of the goods has been paid by the purchaser, the principal is the creditor for such unpaid price, and preferable to the creditors of the factor, and may sue the debtors for the price in his own name; and this although the goods have been sold by the factor in his own name and without any disclosure of or mention of the principal.

Fourthly,—That the fact of the factor having in his books credited the principal with the price of the goods as sold, whether he has received bills for the price or given credit for them to the purchaser, does not alter or affect the right of the principal to the bills or to the unpaid price.

Fifthly,—That the agreement between the parties that Jaffray should receive a *del credere* commission makes no alteration in the law of the case.

Sixthly,—That the facts that an account-current was stated between Nicholls, as agent for Chiappini & Co., and Jaffray, and that he (Jaffray) was sued by Chiappini & Co. on this account-current for the balance before his surrender, do not alter or impair plaintiffs' right to the bills in question, or to the price of the goods remaining unpaid by the purchasers at the time of Jaffray's insolvency.

Seventhly,—That it is for the general balance arising out of the transactions between the parties in their character of principal and factor that the plaintiffs are entitled to claim the bills and the debts outstanding at the time of the sequestration, and that their claim to any particular bill or outstanding debt is not limited or restricted merely to the extent of the amount of net proceeds of the particular sale for which such bill has been given, or such outstanding debt incurred, which they would have been entitled to claim from Jaffray if solvent or not. Consequently, that as, in stating the account between the parties, the plaintiffs have only been credited with a balance consisting of the net proceeds of the sale of the consigned goods, after deduction of all costs and charges and of Jaffray's commission and *del credere* commission,—the defendants can claim no deduction from the amount of the bills and outstanding debts which, by this judgment, may be adjudged to the plaintiffs on the ground that they represent the gross amount of the proceeds of sales of the goods to which they relate without deduction of the costs and charges which, if solvent, Jaffray, in settling with plaintiffs, would have been entitled to deduct from such gross amount. The balance for which the plaintiffs are creditors of Jaffray has been struck in their favour after giving Jaffray credit for all costs, charges, and commission; and it is larger in amount than the whole amount of the bills and outstanding debts claimed by plaintiffs. Those costs, charges, and commission have, therefore, already been paid to himself by Jaffray, out of the proceeds of the sales of goods consigned to them by plaintiffs other than those to which the bills and outstanding debts now claimed relate; and defendants have, therefore, in these circumstances, no more claim to a deduction on account of costs, charges, and commission, from the amount of such bills and outstanding debts, than they would have had if previous to the sale of each lot of goods plaintiffs had remitted in cash to Jaffray a sum sufficient to cover all the costs, charges, and commissions incurred and chargeable on each lot.

Eighthly,—That it has been proved by Jaffray's books and the other evidence in the case, that the outstanding debts are due by the debtors, on account of the price of goods consigned by plaintiffs to Jaffray, to be sold for them as their factor or agent, and purchased from Jaffray by such debtors; that the bills were granted for the price of other such goods so consigned and sold; and that the bills in schedule C, to the amount thereof respectively specified in the third column of schedule C, were, in like manner, granted for the price of other such goods so consigned and sold, and are as clearly distinguishable as representing, to that extent, the plaintiffs' goods, as if they had only been granted respectively for the exact amount set forth in the third column of schedule C.

Ninthly,—The bills granted by an auctioneer to Jaffray for the price of plaintiffs' goods consigned to Jaffray, and sold by him through such auctioneer, are exactly in the same situation as, and must be considered and treated as if they had been, bills granted to Jaffray by the person who purchased the goods at the auction.

Tenthly,—The Court, therefore, find that, at the time of the sequestration of Jaffray's estate, the outstanding debts in schedule A, the bills in schedule B, and the bills in schedule C, to the amounts specified in the third column thereof, were the property of plaintiffs, and that they, and not the defendants, are entitled to sue the debtors for such of the said outstanding debts as have not by such debtors been paid to defendants; and that defendants shall deliver over to plaintiffs such of the bills in schedule B as remain in their possession unpaid, and account to plaintiffs, in the manner prayed in the declaration, for the amounts claimed by plaintiffs as specified in the third column of schedule C, in respect of such of the bills, set forth in such schedule, which are still unpaid and now in the possession of the defendants. And that the defendants shall account to plaintiffs for all such moneys which they have received on account of the outstanding debts in schedule A, of the bills in schedule B, and, to the extent aforesaid, of the bills in schedule C, as moneys had and received by them on account of the plaintiffs, and not as being assets belonging to, and arising out of, Jaffray's insolvent estate, to which plaintiffs have a preferent claim. And find the plaintiffs entitled to costs.

Roussouw's Trustees *vs.* Becker.

Account stated, effect of. Mandant and Mandatory. Vendor and Vendee.

The plaintiffs' declaration stated that this action was brought by them, as the trustees of Roussouw, to recover the sum of £303 4s. 1¾d., being the balance due by the defendant to Roussouw before he became insolvent, upon an account-current (thereto annexed) for goods sold and delivered between 1st January, 1845, and 17th March, 1847, by Roussouw, before he became insolvent, to the defendant, at his request, and for commission thereon according to agreement entered into between the defendant and Roussouw, that Roussouw was to be entitled to charge the defendant a commission of three per cent. on the cost price of goods supplied by him to the defendant, instead of a profit on the said goods, and for interest, &c. That the said account-current is made out by the said defendant, and signed by the defendant and the said Roussouw, and that defendant has thereby admitted the said sum of £303 4s. 1¾d. to be due to the said Roussouw as on an account stated and agreed to between the defendant and Roussouw. That, on the 13th July, 1847, after action brought, the plaintiffs received from the defendant, in part payment of the said sum of £303 4s. 1¾d., the sum of £236 17s. 0¾d., leaving a balance of £66 7s. 1d. still due by the defendant to the plaintiffs, which they prayed he might be condemned to pay to them, with interest *a tempore moræ*, and costs.

1847. August 10. „ 18.

Roussouw's Trustees *vs.* Becker.

In his plea the defendant denied his liability to the plaintiffs for the abovementioned sum of £66 7s. 1d., because the said Roussouw, on the 1st February, 1847, upon the mandate and authority of the defendant, and as his factor and mandatory, and in consideration of the commission or reward thereinafter mentioned, to be paid by the defendant to Roussouw, purchased from Venning, Busk, & Co. certain goods for and on behalf of the defendant, to the amount of £66 7s. 1d., and that before and at the time of the said purchase of the said goods, it was mutually agreed and understood between the said Roussouw, the said defendant, and the said Venning, Busk, & Co., that the said Roussouw should become and be deemed and taken to be, as between him and the said Venning, Busk, & Co., the purchaser of the said goods, and responsible to them for the payment of the price thereof, and further agreed and understood between the said Roussouw and the defendant, that for and in consideration of the trouble and responsibility taken by the said Roussouw in obtaining for the defendant in manner aforesaid the said goods, he, Roussouw, should be paid by the defendant the price to be paid by him, the said Roussouw, to Venning, Busk, & Co., with a commission or reward at the rate of three per cent. upon the said price. That after the receipt by the defendant, under the agreement and understanding aforesaid, of the said goods, the defendant, finding that the said Roussouw had notoriously fallen into insolvent circumstances, and had not paid and would not pay the said Venning, Busk, & Co. for the said goods, and deeming it to be for his credit, interest, and advantage that the said Venning, Busk, & Co. should not lose the price thereof, which might injuriously affect future dealings or transactions between the said Venning, Busk, & Co. and the defendant, he, the defendant, paid and satisfied Venning, Busk, & Co. the price of the said goods so as aforesaid purchased by Roussouw as the mandatory or factor of the said defendant, which said Venning, Busk, and Co., therefore, on the 27th April, 1847, and before the surrender of the estate of the said Roussouw as insolvent, tendered to the said Roussouw wholly to acquit and discharge him from all claim and demand whatever for or on account of the said goods, as fully as if he had paid them for the same, which acquittance or discharge the said Roussouw refused to accept. That the said sum of £66 7s. 1d. so paid by the defendant to Venning, Busk, & Co. is the same sum of £66 7s. 1d. claimed in this action by the plaintiffs. And the defendant thereby again tendered to deliver to the plaintiffs a complete release, acquittance, and discharge from the said sum by and from the said Venning, Busk, & Co. And that the said sum of £236 17s. 1d., admitted by the plaintiffs to have been received by them from the defendant, contained and included all such commission and reward as the said Roussouw or his trustees are entitled to claim for and on account of the said sums of £66 7s. 1d.

In his replication the plaintiff denied all the allegations of fact and conclusions of law as above pleaded by defendant in his said plea.

The evidence adduced by the parties proved that the insolvent Roussouw, who kept a retail store in Cape Town, had been in the habit of supplying the defendant and other shopkeepers in the country with the goods they required, by purchasing in his own name and on his own credit those goods, sometimes selected by himself alone, and at other times by those shopkeepers in his presence, from the wholesale houses in Cape Town, and afterwards forwarding them to his employers in the country, with bills of parcels made out in his name, as the seller of the goods to them, for which he charged the price at which he had purchased the goods, and three per cent. additional.

These transactions were always carried through the books of the wholesale dealers to the debit of Roussouw, as the purchaser of the goods, and in his books the wholesale dealers were credited with the amount of the goods as having been purchased by him from them, and his country employers in like manner debited as having purchased the goods from him; and in this way, also, bills of parcels of the goods were made out by the wholesale dealers in his name, and kept by him, and by him in name of his several employers, and transmitted to them with the goods. Roussouw had dealt largely in this way on behalf of the defendant, as well as others, with the wholesale house of Venning, Busk, & Co., who, in addition to the separate bills of parcels sent to him with each lot of goods, regularly at the end of each month sent him a general bill of parcels in his own name, of all the goods purchased by him during the course of that month, and for the amount thereof he granted them his promissory note at six months' date. The notes were always paid by Roussouw when due, neither the defendant nor any of Roussouw's other customers ever paying any part of the price to Venning & Busk. Roussouw sold all the goods purchased for the defendant by him to defendant, on a running account settled at the end of each year, the defendant paying cash to Roussouw from time to time, as the receipts from his shop enabled him to do. The three per cent. was not charged in each bill of parcels, but in the account-current on their total amount at the end of the year.

1847. August 10. " 18. — Roussouw's Trustees vs. Becker.

It was proved that on the 1st February, 1847, defendant went with Roussouw to Venning & Busk's, and there selected goods to the amount of £66 7s. 1d. These goods were laid aside by Venning & Busk's salesman, who afterwards caused them to be packed and addressed to Becker. It was perfectly well known to Venning & Busk that these goods, as well as others which on other occasions had been purchased by Roussouw, were intended for Becker. These packages were on the 3rd February delivered to Roussouw's son, who took them away in a wagon. A bill of parcels for them, which was headed "Mr. H. Roussouw for Mr. Becker, debtor to Venning, Busk, & Co.," was sent to Roussouw. It was proved that Roussouw had, on the 1st February, purchased from Venning & Busk goods for others of his country employers besides Becker, and that, by Roussouw's desire, whenever he purchased goods on the same day for more than one person, Venning & Busk put on the bill of parcels delivered to Roussouw after his name that of the person for whom he had bought them, in order to enable him correctly to enter the amounts in his books to the debit of the particular person for whom he had respectively bought them; but that this was only done when he bought goods for more persons than one in the same day. It was admitted that, in Venning & Busk's waste book, all the goods sold to Roussouw, for Becker, were entered as sold to Roussouw, except this particular lot, which were then entered as sold to Roussouw for Becker. But that in the ledger they were entered to the debit of Roussouw, without any mention of Becker, and that there was no account in Becker's name in the ledger.

Roussouw kept this bill of parcels, and sent a new one in his own name to Becker with the goods.

At the end of February, Venning & Busk sent to Roussouw the following general bill of parcels for his purchases during that month:

"Dr.

Mr. H. Roussouw,
To Venning, Busk, & Co.

1847				
1st Feb.	To goods...	£8	19	6
———	"	74	11	9
2nd Feb.	"	59	15	0
3rd Feb.	"	66	7	1
13th Feb.	"	4	4	0
		£213	17	4

Settled by your promissory note at six months, due 1st September, 1847."

With this bill of parcels a promissory note for its amount, in favour of Venning and Busk, dated 1st March, 1847, at six months, was sent, in order that it might be signed by Roussouw and returned to Venning and Busk.

This note was not signed by him before the 30th of March, when Roussouw held a meeting of his creditors, because, as Roussouw swore, he knew that he was likely to surrender his estate. He also stated that during that period Venning, Busk, & Co. had not asked him to return them the note with his signature, and that on former occasions similar promissory notes had remained with him unsigned for as long a period.

On the 17th March, the account-current referred to in the declaration was made out by, and signed by Becker, and it was admitted that the item of £66 7s. 1d., therein entered to his debit, was for the price of the goods purchased from Venning & Busk on the 1st February, and delivered on the 3rd to Roussouw, and contained in the general bill of parcels above referred to. About a month before the surrender of his estate as insolvent, Roussouw finding himself embarrassed, called a meeting of his creditors.

On the morning of the 29th or 30th March, on which day the meeting was held, Mr. Eaton, the clerk of Venning & Busk, called on Roussouw and asked him if there could not be an alteration made in the account of defendant, and whether he had made any settlement with Becker. Roussouw replied that Becker had been as usual debited, and Venning & Busk credited in his books for the goods he had bought from Venning & Busk.

Defendant afterwards told Roussouw that he had given a good-for or note to Venning & Busk for this sum of £66 7s. 1d., and asked him to take this item out of the general account between them, which Roussouw refused to do, stating as his reason that Venning & Busk were creditors in his estate for it.

The plaintiff also put in the following receipt, which was admitted to be signed by Venning & Busk :

"27th April, 1847.

"Received from Mr. Becker a settlement of goods purchased by him on the 3rd February last, namely, £66 7s. 1d., which settlement we hereby undertake to refund should Mr. Becker be legally called upon to settle the same with his former agent, Mr. N. Roussouw,

"For VENNING, BUSK, & Co.,

"FREDERICK TAYLOR."

1847. August 10. " 18.

Roussouw's Trustees *vs.* Becker.

Ebden, for the plaintiff, maintained that the goods in question were sold, and credit for the price thereof given, to Roussouw by Venning, Busk, & Co.,—that the goods were afterwards resold by Roussouw to defendant,—that there was no privity or connection whatever between Venning, Busk, & Co. and the defendant, and that Roussouw stood in no other relation to the defendant than as the seller of the goods to defendant as a purchaser from him, and as much so as if the defendant had bought goods out of Roussouw's retail shop without knowledge of or reference to the parties from whom Roussouw had derived the possession of such goods; consequently, that the defendant could not release himself from responsibility to Roussouw or his trustees in any other manner than by payment to the trustees of the price of the goods; the more especially as, by rendering and signing the account-current of the 17th March, 1847, the defendant had thereby admitted that he was then absolutely indebted to Roussouw in the balance therein brought down to defendant's debit.

The *Attorney-General,* for the defendant, *contra,* maintained, that although Roussouw may have stood in relation to Venning & Busk in the character of purchaser, and no other, and as such solely responsible to that firm, for the price of the goods, he yet, in so far as the defendant was concerned, stood in the relation of agent to the defendant as his principal, and not in that of the seller of the goods to defendant and his vendee, and therefore that the defendant, as principal in the transaction, was under no obligation to Roussouw, as his agent, to do anything more for him except to release him from any claim at the instance of Venning & Busk for the price of the goods which had been purchased by Roussouw from that firm and delivered by him to the defendant; consequently, that by reason of the transaction between the defendant and Venning, Busk & Co., and the discharge of their claim against Roussouw's estate, tendered by defendant to plaintiffs, the defendant was no longer liable for this sum of £66 7s. 1d. to Roussouw's estate,—and quoted *Seymour vs. Pychlow,* 1*st Barn. & Alder., p.* 14; *Smith's Leading Cases, vol.* 2, *p.* 199, *et seq.; Coren's Observations, No.* 25, *p.* 102; *Loenius, Case* 9; and the case of *Chiappini vs. Jaffray's Trustees,* decided by this Court 12th June, 1843. (*Vide last case.*)

The defendant also maintained that this action could not at present be maintained against the defendant because it was premature, inasmuch as even if Roussouw and Becker were to be held to stand in the mutual relation of vendor and vendee, Becker must be held to be entitled to have the same credit from Roussouw which Roussouw had from

Venning & Busk, namely, six months' credit from the 1st of March, and therefore that, as this credit did not expire before the 1st of September, the plaintiffs could not legally commence this action until after that date, and that although this was an action for the price of goods alleged to have been sold and delivered by the plaintiffs to the defendant, the defendant was entitled, under the plea of the general issue, to object that the plaintiff could not maintain his action because it was commenced before the expiration of the term of credit at which the goods had been sold, the price of which was now in dispute,—and quoted *Chitty on Pleading, vol.* 3, *p.* 769. He maintained that the documents sent by Roussouw to defendant, and called by the plaintiffs bills of parcels, could not properly be considered as bills of parcels for goods sold to defendant by Roussouw, first, because in them the defendant was stated merely to owe to Roussouw the several sums therein stated, and not to have bought from him the goods therein mentioned; and secondly, because if the transaction had really been one of sale by Roussouw to defendant, the bills of parcels rendered to defendant by Roussouw ought to have set out the whole price, whereas they only stated the price at which Roussouw had bought the goods from Venning & Busk, and did not add to it the amount of the three per cent. charged by Roussouw against defendant, which, if the transaction had really been of the nature of a sale, would have formed part of the price, and consequently would have been specified in those bills of parcels.

Postea (18th August, 1847).—The Court gave judgment as follows: They held that as the summons and declaration in this case stated that the sum of £303 4s. 1¾d. sued for was due and owing to the plaintiffs as and for the balance due on the account-current therein specially referred to, signed by the defendant, and whereby he admitted the said sum to be due to Roussouw as on an account stated and agreed between the defendant and Roussouw, this action is founded on the defendant's liability "as on account stated," and not on alleged liability "for goods sold and delivered." That the statement in the declaration describing the nature of the items of which the account-current was composed was surplusage, and did not in any way alter or affect the nature of the action. That in the account-current the defendant had expressly admitted that the said balance of £303 4s. 1¾d. was due to Roussouw. And, therefore, that whether, if the account-current had never been drawn out or signed by Becker, and if this action had been brought against him as for the price of

1847. August 10. „ 18.

Roussouw's Trustees *vs.* Becker.

goods sold and delivered to him, Becker would have been entitled to defend himself by maintaining that in a question between them Roussouw must be considered as only his mandatory, and not as the seller of the goods to him, and that he had discharged the sole liability under which he was to Roussouw as his mandatory by paying the £66 7s. 1d. to Venning & Busk, and thus freeing Roussouw from the liability which he, as Becker's mandatory, had incurred to Venning & Busk; still that by signing the account-current he had made his election to consider Roussouw as absolutely his creditor, aud not merely his mandatory; and having thus, admitted that he was indebted to Roussouw in this balance he could not now relieve himself from his liability to Roussouw for any part of his acknowledged debt by any transaction entered into with any third party without Roussouw's consent. (*Vide Starkie on Evidence, vol.* 2, *p.* 75.) The Court, therefore, without deciding any of the other questions which had been moved by the parties, and on the sole ground that the defendant in a stated account between him and Roussouw had acknowledged himself to be absolutely indebted on the 17th March to Roussouw in the sum sued for, gave judgment for the plaintiffs, as prayed, with costs.

CHAPTER IV.

PARTNERSHIP.

LOLLY *vs.* GILBERT.

Summons.

It is not necessary to bring an action in the name of a sleeping partner. 1830. June 17.

[Vol. I, p. 434.]

LUCK *vs.* CHABAUD.

Division, benefit of.

Beneficium divisionis continues between solvent and insolvent partners of dissolved firm. 1831. July 26.

[Vol. I, p. 531.]

HANCKE, Q.Q., *vs.* BREDA AND ANOTHER.

Agreement between partners limiting their respective liability of no effect against parties having previously contracted with them. 1832. Jan. 10.

[Vol. I, p. 539.]

DAVIS & SON *vs.* McDONALD & SUTHERLAND.

It is a good defence to a provisional claim against two late partners on a bill purporting to be drawn by the partnership that it had been drawn by one partner only after dissolution. 1833. June 4.

Evidence of dissolution, on provision, what is sufficient.

[Vol. I, p. 86.]

Iles *vs.* Jones, Gie, and De Villiers.

Partnership. Pleading. Practice.

Form of action between partners.

1836. Aug. 26. Nov. 26. 1837. May 16.

Iles *vs.* Jones, Gie, and De Villiers.

The declaration set forth that on the 26th November, 1827, the plaintiff and defendants entered into copartnership; and that on the 30th November, 1833, the said copartnership was dissolved by mutual consent, and that on taking a full and fair account of the profits and losses, and the several sums which were due and owing from the said partners one to the other respectively, there was found to be justly due and owing to the said plaintiff from the said defendant R. P. Jones the sum of £602 19s. 3¾d., from the said defendant J. C. Gie the sum of £383 12s. 4¾d., and from the said defendant J. de Villiers the sum of £61 18s. 3d. Wherefore, &c.

To this declaration the defendants excepted, and pleaded that the same is informal, irregular, and has been inartificially pleaded by the said plaintiff, inasmuch as the said plaintiff is not at law entitled, upon the allegation set forth in the said declaration, to demand from the said defendants the sums severally claimed from them; but that the said plaintiff is only entitled to demand at law a liquidation of the partnership accounts between the said plaintiff and the said defendants, and a general account of the said copartnership, wherein the said defendants say they are willing to enter with the said plaintiff. And upon these grounds the said defendants claim that the declaration of the said plaintiff be expunged, &c., &c.

This day, *Cloete*, for the defendants, argued in support of the exception, and quoted *Van der Linden's Inst., p.* 579.

The Court, without calling on the plaintiff, overruled the exception with costs, holding that the averment in the declaration amounted to an allegation of such a liquidation as entitled the plaintiff to demand the sums in payment as stated.

This day, 26th November, 1836, after the plaintiff had put in the account founded on by him, and closed his case, *Cloete* resumed the objection to the form of this action, which he had formerly stated in support of the exception, and contended that therefore the defendants must be absolved from the instance. But, although he showed that there was another form of action to which the plaintiff might have had recourse, he failed to show that either by the former law or by the rules of the Supreme Court, the plaintiff was precluded, or that it was incompetent for him to sue in the form which he had adopted. And therefore the Court refused the motion for absolution from the instance made by him, reserving all questions as to costs until the conclusion of the suit, and ordered accounts of the partnership to be made up by a referee to be named by the Court, if not fixed by the parties before the last day of term.

1836. Aug. 26. Nov. 26. 1837. May 18.

Iles *vs.* Jones, Gie, and De Villiers.

Postea (16th May, 1837.)—The referee found a balance of upwards £100 due to the plaintiff by each of the defendants Jones and Gie respectively, and that nothing was due to plaintiff by De Villiers.

This day, the Court, after hearing parties, found the plaintiff entitled to the costs of suit, including the costs of this day, from the defendants Jones and Gie, and liable in the like costs to the defendant De Villiers (*i.e.* two thirds and one third.)

STILL *vs.* NORTON.

Partnership: Dissolution of. Construction of Clause in Deed of Dissolution.

Compensation must be specially pleaded.

1838. May 22. „ 29.

Still *vs.* Norton.

F. Still and J. Norton, as partners, carried on business at Graham's Town, under the firm of Norton & Co., and at Cape Town under the firm of Still & Co.

They dissolved partnership by a deed dated 10th May, 1837, by which it was stipulated that Norton should pay to Still £7,000 as and for Still's share of the profits made by the firm of Norton & Co., and that Still should pay to Norton £2,500 as and for Norton's share in the profits made by the firm of Still & Co.; and which also contained this clause: "Section 7.—It is further agreed between the parties that all produce received or that may be received in Cape Town by the said F. Still belonging to the firm of Norton & Co., shall be sold and accounted for to the said John Norton."

This action was brought by Still to recover from Norton the sum of £4,500, being the balance of the said sum of £7,000 stipulated to be paid by Norton to him, after deduction of the said sum of £2,500 stipulated to be paid by him to Norton.

1838. May 22. „ 29. Still vs. Norton.

Norton denied his liability for any amount to Still in respect of a claim made by him in reconvention for the sum of £6,560 4s. 7d., as due by Still to him under and by virtue of the said seventh clause of the deed of dissolution above quoted, and consequently claimed from Still the balance of this sum, after deduction of the £4,500, for which he admitted Still had a right to have credit given to him.

In answer to this claim in reconvention for £2,060 4s. 7d., Still pleaded that he was only liable under and by virtue of the said seventh clause to the defendant in the sum of £654 15s. 2d., which he was willing to allow in diminution of the £4,500 claimed by him.

And thereupon issue was joined.

Still maintained that by the said seventh clause he was bound to account to Norton solely for such produce, being the property of Norton & Co., as had been received by him, Still, previously to, and as had remained unsold on the 10th May, 1837, the date of the deed of dissolution.

Norton maintained, and the Court found that by the said seventh clause, Still was bound to account to Norton for all such produce which had at any time been received by him, and which had not been accounted for by him by accounts of sales rendered by Still & Co. to Norton & Co., previously to the 10th May, 1837, whether such property had or had not been sold prior to that date. And gave judgment in favour of Norton for £2,078 0s. 9d., being the balance due, as ascertained from an account of such produce which Still by order of Court had put in, after deduction therefrom of the £4,500 claimed by Still in convention, with costs.

Still maintained that he was entitled to reduce this balance of £2,078 0s. 9d. by pleading compensation, in respect of other claims which he had against Norton.

But the Court held that as, in his plea in answer to the claim in reconvention he had merely denied the amount claimed to be the amount for which under the said seventh clause he was liable to account to Norton, and had not pleaded compensation on any ground to reduce the balance for which in such accounting he was liable, he was not in this action now entitled to plead compensation on any ground to diminish the balance, which the Court had found had been proved to be that for which he was, under said seventh clause, liable to account to Norton.

STILL *vs.* NORTON.

Deed of Dissolution: Construction of. Assignation.

Appeal to Privy Council refused until after definitive accounting.

The following were the facts of this case:

Forbes Still and John Norton, as partners, carried on business in Cape Town under the firm of F. Still & Co., under the management of Still, and in Graham's Town under the firm of John Norton & Co., under the management of Norton. Each firm kept a separate and distinct set of books applicable to its own transactions, in which the transactions between the two firms were respectively entered as if they had been transactions with third parties having no connection with either firm.

1838. Nov. 28. 1839. Jan. 12.

F. Still and John Norton, after thus carrying on business for some years, executed a deed of dissolution of copartnery, whereby, in consideration of £7,000 to be paid by Norton to Still, as and for Still's share in the profits of Norton & Co., Still assigned to Norton all debts and sums then due and owing to the firm of Norton & Co., and Norton undertook to pay all debts and sums of money then due by the said firm of Norton & Co.; and whereby, in consideration of £2,500 to be paid by Still to Norton, as and for Norton's share in the profits of Still & Co., Norton assigned to Still all debts and sums of money then due and owing to the firm of Still & Co., and Still undertook to pay all debts and sums then due by Still & Co.

At the date of the dissolution there was an open account in the books of each between the firms of Norton & Co. and Still & Co., on which it was alleged by Still, the plaintiff, that there was a balance due by Norton & Co. to Still & Co., to recover which balance Still brought this action against Norton.

The Court, by a majority (WYLDE, C.J., being of the contrary opinion), found that by virtue of the assignation, made by Norton in favour of Still, of all debts due and owing to the firm of Still & Co., and of Norton's said undertaking to pay all the debts and sums of money due by the firm of Norton & Co., without any stipulation having been made that the debts appearing from the books to be due from the one firm to the other should be excepted from said assignation, or said undertaking, or that they should be deemed or held to be in any situation different from that of any other debts due by the said firms to third parties, Still was entitled to demand and recover from Norton the balance which on an adjustment of the account between the two firms should

1838. Nov. 28. 1839. Jan. 12.

Still *vs.* Norton.

appear to have been due at the date of the dissolution by the firm of Norton & Co. to the firm of Still & Co., and that he was not barred from so doing by a clause in the deed of dissolution, whereby both Still and Norton did "remise, release, and for ever quit claim unto and discharge each other, &c., &c., of and from all manner and actions, cause and causes of action, suits, accounts, reckoning debts, and sums of money, claims at law and in equity, which we and each of us now hath or shall have or may or without these presents might have, claim, or demand, or be in any wise entitled to from or against the other of us by reason or in consequence of the said copartnership so hereby dissolved. Save only and except as to and respecting all or any of the covenants and agreements in these presents contained by either of the parties to be observed and performed, and to any means or remedies, &c., to be taken for enforcing the due execution thereof."

Because this cause of action did not arise from the copartnership, but from one of the covenants or agreements in the deed of dissolution, to enforce the due execution of which this action was brought.

Postea (12th January, 1839).—The defendant lodged a petition, and moved to have an appeal allowed.

The Court refused the application *hoc statu*, in respect that until the accounting had taken place between the parties, it was impossible to ascertain whether this judgment, even supposing it to have the effect of a final or definitive sentence against the defendant, was one for or in respect of any sum above £500, or even that it would have any effect whatever against the defendant.

After accounting between the parties, a large balance of several thousand pounds was found to have been due by Norton & Co. to Still & Co., for which balance judgment was given for the plaintiff, with costs.

FRASER *vs.* NORTON & CO., VIZ.: J. NORTON AND F. STILL.

1839. Aug. 30. ,, 31.

Fraser *vs.* Norton & Co., viz.: J. Norton and F. Still.

Mercantile Interest: Payment of. Custom of Trade, as to.

The partnership of John Norton & Co., of Graham's Town, consisted of John Norton and Forbes Still.

In 1835, the said John Norton, living then in London, had with the plaintiff the transactions specified in the following account-current which it was admitted had been signed by John Norton of the date it bears:

1839. Aug. 30. ,, 31.

Fraser *vs.* Norton & Co., viz.: J. Norton and F. Still.

"Dr. Messrs. JOHN NORTON & Co.,
To JOHN FRASER.

1835.		
Jan. 19.—To cash advanced from Mr. Norton	£70	0	0
Feb. 7.—To my acceptance to Mrs. Joseph at three months, and due 10th May	25	0	0
Feb. 7.—To shipment per *Agrippina*, per invoice annexed	82	17	5
	£177	17	5
"London, 7th February, 1835. "E.E. JOHN FRASER.	£177	17	5

"Agreed, JOHN NORTON & Co."

On the 8th of October, 1836, plaintiff wrote to Still & Co., which was the title of a partnership subsisting in Cape Town between the said J. Norton and the said F. Still (or, in other words, the Cape Town firm of the same partnership, of which Norton & Co. was the Graham's Town firm, and through which firm of Still & Co. all the English transactions of the partnership passed), enclosing a copy of the above account-current, with this addition, that it charged interest on each of the three items of which it was composed,—on the first bond from 19th January and 7th February, their respective dates, and on the second from the 10th May to 8th October, 1836; which interest, amounting in all to £20 1s. 4d., was added to the capital, and a balance of £197 18s. 9d. brought out against John Norton & Co.

In June, 1838, plaintiff sent out a power of attorney to his agents here to sue John Norton & Co. for £214 14s. 7d., as the balance due by them in the following account-current thereto annexed:

"Dr. Messrs. JOHN NORTON & Co.
To JOHN FRASER.

1837.			
Jan. 1.—To amount due per account rendered Messrs. F. Still & Co.	£197	18	9
1838.			
May 31.—To interest on do. to date $\frac{1}{511}$ ...	16	15	10
	£214	14	7

"London, 31st May, 1838.
"E.E. JOHN FRASER."

1839. Aug. 30. " 31.

Fraser *vs.* Norton & Co., viz.: J. Norton and F. Still.

In 1837, John Norton and Still had dissolved their partnership under both firms, agreeing between themselves that John Norton should discharge all the debts due by Norton & Co.

John Norton refused to pay the above amount to plaintiff's agents when demanded, who thereupon brought this action against J. Norton and F. Still, as having been the partners of John Norton & Co., for the said sum of £177 17s. 5d. of capital, with the usual and customary interest thereon.

After receiving service of the summons, John Norton tendered £177 17s. 5d., the capital, and £7 10s. 6d., being interest thereon at 5 per cent., computed from the 8th October, 1838, when a letter from plaintiff dated 9th June, 1838, had been received by him demanding payment of the £214 14s. 7d. to the 2nd August, 1839, being the date of the tender, together with £15 to cover payment of all plaintiff's costs and charges.

This tender was refused.

Still allowed judgment to go by default against him.

Plaintiff called Edward Eagar: I am a merchant, and during twenty years I have in this Colony been engaged in mercantile transactions with merchants in London. As far as my transactions go, I have always understood that interest was due on the balance of our account from the day on which the balance was acknowledged. That interest was due from the day the debt was due, whether that debt was a single transaction or a balance in several transactions, and I have always paid interest accordingly. I know that other houses besides my own have settled for interest with London houses on this principle, and I believe it to be a general practice. The traders in London from whom I have bought goods generally deducted six months' discount from the amount of the invoices, and charged interest from the date of the transaction. I have only had dealings with Mr. Home, of London, but I have always understood that the above principle is acted on by all houses.

Richard Webster Eaton: I have been a merchant in this Colony for many years, and have had transactions with mercantile houses in London, and I have frequently been trustee in the insolvent estates of merchants here who had traded with London. In transacting business with my correspondent in London, Mr. Ebden, interest was charged on both sides of the account on each transaction, and the balance of interest included in the general balance, which accumulated balance was charged with interest from the day it was carried to the new account. I always understood this to be the general custom, and I have never seen an account between merchants in which the principle was not acted on.

Ewan Christian, who had been a merchant in Cape Town, trading with London for twenty-five years, gave precisely the same evidence as Mr. Eaton, and added, "I should expect to pay interest on a balance sheet at any time from that date."

1839. Aug. 30. " 31. — Fraser *vs.* Norton & Co., viz.: J. Norton and F. Still.

William Gadney: I have been a merchant in Cape Town trading with London for many years. I have heard the evidence of the preceding witness, and I believe that the usual custom of trade is that which he has described it to be. But if a final balance were struck on the parties ceasing to have further transactions with each other, I should conceive that if the creditor made no demand for the balance for a length of time, then that the debtor would be entitled to object to payment of interest from the date of striking the balance. I am of opinion that if the plaintiff in this case had made a timeous application for payment of the balance as then (7th February, 1835) struck, he would have been entitled to interest from that date; but as he forbore for several years making any demand, the defendants are now entitled to object.

Plaintiff closed his case.

Defendant called no evidence as to the custom of merchants in charging interest on cases like the present.

The *Attorney-General* maintained that plaintiff was entitled to interest as charged in the account.

Cloete, contra, quoted *Chitty's Comml. Law, Vol.* 3, *p.* 310; *Voet* 22, 1, 1.

Cur. adv. vult.

Postea (31st August, 1839).—The Court held that plaintiff was entitled to charge interest on the three items in the account signed by defendant Norton, and dated 7th February, 1835, viz., on the first item from the 19th January, on the second from the 10th May, and on the third from 7th August (thus allowing six months' credit on the goods shipped per *Agrippina*) to the 31st December, 1835, and to accumulate this interest with the capital on the 31st December, 1835. That if the plaintiff had rendered a state of the account to or made a demand for payment of that accumulated balance on the defendant *tempestive* in 1836, he would have been entitled to charge interest on the accumulated balance from 1st January, 1836, but that as he had not done so he could only claim interest from the day his demand for payment became known to John Norton & Co., by plaintiff's letter of 8th October, 1836, to Still & Co. being communicated by the latter to Norton & Co., which was held by the Court to have taken place on the 31st January, 1837.

1839. Aug. 30. " 31. — Fraser vs. Norton & Co., viz.: J. Norton and F. Still.

The Court, therefore, gave judgment for plaintiff for £183 12s. 9½d., with interest thereon from 1st February, 1837, to 31st August, 1839, and costs.

TERRINGTON *vs.* SIMPSON.

Service. Affidavit. Sheriff's return.

1840. Nov. 2.

Service at the counting-house of a partnership firm is not service against one of the partners individually. Affidavit allowed to impeach the Sheriff's return.

[Vol. I, p. 135.]

HAUPT *vs.* SPAARMAN AND ANOTHER.

Service.

Nov. 30.

Personal service on one partner of an alleged partnership, not at the place of business of the firm, held to be no service as against his alleged partner.

[Vol. I, p. 135.]

MEINTJES & CO. *vs.* SIMPSON BROTHERS & CO.

Service. Pleading. Intervention.

Absent partners: Service of summons on. Pleading: Exception.

Partners absent from the Colony must be summoned (or required to intervene after summons) at the place of business of the company in Cape Town.

1841. May 20. July 12. — Meintjes & Co. vs. Simpson Brothers & Co.

In this case the summons was taken out against J. P. Simpson, Joseph Simpson, T. Jones, and T. G. Simpson, copartners, carrying on business under the firm of Simpson Brothers & Co. A declaration was filed against these four as defendants. But by an order at Chambers obtained by plaintiffs, they were allowed to withdraw "all proceedings had in this cause against T. Jones, T. G. Jones, and Joseph Simpson, and to continue the proceedings against John Price Simpson, now or lately carrying on business at

Cape Town jointly with Joseph Simpson, under the firm of Simpson Brothers & Co., and to amend their pleadings accordingly." Thereafter plaintiffs filed a new declaration against "John Price Simpson, who, jointly with Joseph Simpson (now absent from the Colony), lately carried on business in copartnership at Cape Town, under the firm of Simpson Brothers & Co."

Defendant, in his plea, pleaded that all and singular the several transactions (if any), &c., &c., for an account of which transactions and for the recovery of such sums of money as should appear to be due to the plaintiffs upon such transactions the plaintiffs' action has now been brought, were entered into by and transacted with one J. Simpson in the declaration mentioned, who is still living, to wit, at London, in England, and also with one E. P. Amyott, who is still living, to wit, at London, in England, and also with one Thomas Simpson, who is still living, to wit, at Devonshire, in England, jointly with the said John Price Simpson, and not by the said J. P. Simpson alone; wherefore, inasmuch as the said J. Simpson, E. P. Amyott, and T. Simpson are not joined as defendants in the said declaration together with the said J. P. Simpson, he prayed that the said declaration may be quashed or set aside, with costs.

The plaintiffs excepted that this plea and the matter therein contained in manner and form as the same are pleaded and set forth are not sufficient in law to quash or set aside the declaration, and that the plaintiffs are not bound in law to answer the same, and assigned as causes of exception to said plea, that it appears by the said plea that the said J. Simpson, E. P. Amyott, and T. Simpson, therein named, are now absent from the Colony, and resident beyond the jurisdiction of this Court. It is not stated in said plea that they or any or either of them have or hath any agents or agent in this Colony, who could legally represent them, or any or either of them, in the present suit.

Musgrave, for plaintiffs, argued in support of plaintiffs' exception to the plea, and quoted *Tidd's Practice, Last Edition, p.* 319; 3 *and* 4 *of Wm.* 4, *Cap.* 42; *Grant's Chancery Practice, p.* 31.

Attorney-General, contra, quoted *Collier's Law of Partnership, Edn.* 1832, *p.* 416, *Stair's Institute, Appendix to Edition,* 1832, *p.* 99; *Voet* 17, *tit.* 2, *section* 13.

Further hearing was adjourned.

Postea (12th July, 1841.)—The Court decided that the plaintiffs must call the absent partners specified in defendants' plea as parties to this action, that it was sufficient for them

1841. May 20. July 12. — Meintjes & Co. *vs.* Simpson Brothers & Co.

to do this by serving said partners with summonses calling on them to intervene as defendants in the action, and that service of their summonses at the place of business of the company in Cape Town would be good service on those partners, and that the *induciæ* of those summonses would be the same as if those absent partners had resided at said place of business in Cape Town.

Costs of the plea and exception thereto to be costs in the cause.

The Court would have stayed proceedings until the plaintiffs should have had time so to serve such summonses, but the defendant consented to waive the necessity of those summonses, and that plaintiffs should at once amend their declaration so as in it to make the absent partners defendants.

Declaration was ordered to be amended accordingly.

The case was afterwards settled.

JACOBSON *vs.* NORTON.

Pleading. Exception.

No consideration is necessary to support a promise to pay.

Causa debiti must be specifically set forth in a declaration. What is such an insufficient specification as to support exception.

A debt due by a partner is not in law considered as due to the firm, but as due to the other partners, who must recover in an action pro socio in their own names.

Where a partner promises to pay to his copartners jointly, each is entitled, without the concurrence of the other, to sue in his own name for his share.

1841. Nov. 18. Dec. 13. 1842. May 30. — Jacobson *vs.* Norton.

In this case the declaration set forth that, in 1835, the plaintiff, together with Messrs. Dunell and Kisch, carried on business as merchants in Cape Town; that in 1838, this copartnership was dissolved by common consent, at which time Mr. Kisch stood fairly and justly indebted to the plaintiff, on account of the said copartnership, in a large sum of money; that in the same year Mr. Kisch entered into partnership with the defendant, and carried on business with him under the style of H. B. Kisch and Company; that on or about the 5th day of September, 1840, the said

H. B. Kisch suddenly left Cape Town, and afterwards left the Colony, that the said defendant, either as such partner, or otherwise, proceeded, after the departure of the said H. B. Kisch, to settle and arrange the affairs of the said copartnership, and of the said H. B. Kisch, and, in order thereto, took on himself the administration of the partnership and private property of the said H. B. Kisch, and made sale of both to a considerable amount; that the plaintiff, under these circumstances, caused application to be made to the defendant for payment of the amount due to him by Mr. Kisch on account of the former copartnership of Jacobson, Kisch and Dunell; and that the defendant, on the 1st December, 1840, promised and undertook, in his individual capacity, to pay to plaintiff whatever sum should be found due and owing to him by Mr. Kisch on account of the said dissolved partnership at the time of the dissolution. And the plaintiff further alleged that at the time of the dissolution there was thus due and owing to him the sum of £1,526 0s. 3d. sterling, for the payment of which the defendant, under these circumstances, and by force of his promise and undertaking, had become liable; but which sum he had not paid, nor any part thereof, although often requested so to do. Wherefore an action had accrued to him to demand from defendant the said sum of £1,526 0s. 3d., or such other sum as might be found due to him at the time aforesaid by the said H. B. Kisch, together with the costs of suit.

To this declaration the defendant excepted, on the grounds, that the matters therein contained, in manner and form as alleged and set forth, were not sufficient in law to maintain the action; 1, that the said declaration did not set forth with sufficient certainty either the character in which the defendant assumed his alleged liability to pay the debt of Mr. Kisch; 2, or the manner in which that debt was found and ascertained to be due at the time mentioned; 3, or at what time the same was to be paid by the defendant; 4, that the said declaration did not contain any averment that the amount and particulars of the alleged debt were notified to defendant; 5, or that he was specially requested to pay it before the present action was commenced; that the said declaration did not show a sufficient consideration to support the demand as a personal demand against the defendant; that if the said demand had been founded on a sufficient consideration in law, Mr. Dunell should have been made a plaintiff in this action; and that the said declaration was, in other respects, informal, uncertain, and insufficient, which the defendant was ready to verify; wherefore he prayed that the same be set aside, with costs.

Musgrave, for the defendant, argued in support of his

1841. Nov. 18. Dec. 13. 1842. May 30.

Jacobson *vs.* Norton.

exceptions, and maintained that the legal promise founded on, even if made, was *nudum pactum, ex quâ non actio.* (*Van der Linden*, 190; *Pothier*, 2, p. 405; *Kienar vs. Waters.*)

The *Attorney-General, contra,* quoted the 18th Rule of Court; and in answer to the first ground of the objection, argued that the declaration expressly stated that the defendant "promised and undertook in his individual capacity," and that he was not bound to have asserted the capacity in which defendant proceeded to settle and arrange the affairs of the partnership (that between defendant and Kisch), and of the said H. B. Kisch, with more certainty than he had done, because he could not know with certainty in what capacity he acted. (*Chitty on Pleading, last Edit., Vol.* 1, *p.* 234.) Secondly, because defendant must know in what capacity he acted. Thirdly, that this part of the declaration was surplusage, and therefore certainty was not requisite. On the second ground of objection, he argued that the words "on account of the partnership" (*Chitty on Pleading, last Ed., p.* 153) was a sufficient specification of the grounds of debt, in terms of the 18th rule, and would have been sufficient in a declaration against Kisch; and that the words in the alleged promise, "whatever sum should be found due and owing," meant whatever sum was due, and should be shown by the plaintiff to be due. On the third, he maintained that the promise to pay what should be found due inferred an obligation to pay on demand what was due. On the fourth and fifth he maintained that what the defendant there insisted should have been done, the plaintiff was in the present case under no necessity of doing. On the sixth he maintained that even if it were true, which he denied, that the alleged promise would have been null and invalid without a sufficient consideration, there was a sufficient consideration, and that consideration was sufficiently set forth; and that the consideration appeared from, and was sufficiently set out by, the following words on the declaration: "That on or about the 5th September, 1840, the said H. B. Kisch suddenly left Cape Town, and shortly afterwards left the Colony; that the said defendant, either as such partner as aforesaid of the said H. B. Kisch or otherwise, proceeded after the departure of the said H. B. Kisch to settle and arrange the affairs of the said co-partnership and of the said H. B. Kisch, and in order thereto took on himself the administration of the partnership and private property of the said H. B. Kisch, and made sale of both to a considerable amount; that the said plaintiff, under these circumstances, caused application to be made to the said defendant for payment of the sum so as aforesaid due and owing, &c.; and that the defendant on or about the 1st

December, 1840, and at Cape Town, promised and undertook," &c. Quoted *Grotius, 3 B.*, 1 *Cap., section* 52, *and Voet* 2, 14. 9; *Louisa vs. Van den Berg*, 10*th September*, 1830, (*Vol.* 1, *p.* 471), to show that by the law of Holland *ex nudo pacto actio datur*. On the seventh exception he maintained that the debt which he sued for was one due to Jacobson, in his individual capacity, and not to him and Dunell, as partners; and that if he failed to establish the existence of such a debt, he would be non-suited, and if he established its existence, he would be entitled to judgment, without the joinder of Dunell with him as a plaintiff.

Musgrave replied, and the Court adjourned.

Postea (13th December, 1841).—The Court held that no consideration was necessary to support the promise alleged in the declaration as a ground of action; and that therefore it was not necessary in the declaration to set out any consideration as the inducement of the promise; consequently, it was unnecessary to decide whether on the face of the declaration the consideration which was the inducement of the promise was sufficiently set out.

The Court held that the first, third, fourth, fifth, sixth, and seventh grounds of the exception were not sufficient to support it.

On the second ground of exception, the Court held, that the object of this action was twofold,—first, to have it proved that the defendant, by reason of a certain promise made by him, was liable to pay to plaintiff whatever sum should be proved due and owing by Kisch to plaintiff on account of the dissolved partnership at the time of the dissolution; and secondly, to have it found what was the amount which was so due and owing by Kisch to Jacobson, and was to be paid by defendant to plaintiff; that the declaration, in so far as related to the first object, was properly framed; that in the event of the plaintiff establishing that defendant had bound himself by such a promise, he was entitled, by an action against defendant, to have the amount of the debt which defendant was so bound to pay found and determined; but that the declaration in such an action must be as specific as to the *causa debiti* as if the action were brought against Kisch himself; that the declaration, in so far as related to this part of the action, set out the *causa debiti* alleged to be due by Kisch, only by stating that the debt was due "on account of the dissolved partnership," without specifying how or in what manner it had so become due; that the declaration would on this ground have been exceptionable in an action against Kisch; and therefore defendant was entitled to except to it on this ground; and to this extent

1841. Nov. 18. Dec. 13. 1842. May 30.

Jacobson *vs.* Norton.

the Court allowed the exception, and ordered plaintiff to amend his declaration. Costs to be costs in the cause.

The plaintiff had amended his declaration by expunging the words "that at the time of the said dissolution the said H. B. Kisch stood fairly and justly indebted to the said plaintiff on account of the said copartnership in a large sum of money," and inserting in lieu thereof the words "that at the time of the said dissolution the dealings and transactions of the said H. B. Kisch with the partnership estate and effects had been such that the said H. B. Kisch would have been found (had a fair account between the partners been taken) to be liable to the said plaintiff in a large sum of money;" and by inserting after the word "Colony," the words "the said plaintiff having often previously endeavoured in vain to induce the said H. B. Kisch to come to a settlement with him regarding the demand aforesaid;" and after the words "caused application to be made to the said defendant" by inserting the words "for a settlement of the demand which the said plaintiff had as aforesaid against the said H. B. Kisch, but the amount of which demand at the time of the said application had not been exactly ascertained. And that the defendant, on or about the 1st December, 1840, being the day of the said application, and at Cape Town, promised and undertook in his individual capacity to and with the plaintiff to pay to him whatever sum should, upon an examination of the books and accounts of the said copartnership of Jacobson, Kisch, and Dunell, be found to have been due and owing to the plaintiff by the said H. B. Kisch in respect of his aforesaid dealings and transactions with the stock and funds of the said last mentioned dissolved copartnership at the time of the dissolution thereof." And that thereafter, on the 5th December, 1840, after such examination as aforesaid, there was found to have been due to the plaintiff by the said H. B. Kisch at the time of said dissolution, by reason of the dealings and transaction aforesaid, the sum of £1,526 0s. 3d., for the payment of which sum the said defendant became liable under the circumstances aforesaid.

The defendant pleaded the general issue.

This day, 30th May, 1842, the cause came on for trial.

After evidence led,

Musgrave, for defendant, moved for an absolution from the instance, on the ground,

1st. That the promise, agreement, or contract referred to in the declaration, and which was the ground of this action, was stated in the declaration to have been made by defendant to plaintiff, whereas if any contract, promise, or agreement is proved to have been made, the evidence shows it not to have been made to the plaintiff, but to Jacobson & Co. (4 *Barn. & Alder*, 374, *Gill vs. Douglas; Chitty, p.* 52; *Guidon vs. Robson*, 2 *Campbell's Report*, 303; *Voet* 5, *tit.* 1, *section* 82.)

2nd. He maintained that the plaintiff could not sue defendant on the alleged promise until the amount due by Kisch had been ascertained by a judgment against him, and that the plaintiff had failed to prove that any such judgment had been obtained. (*Van der Linden, p.* 577.)

The *Attorney-General, contra,* admitted that promise is laid in declaration as made to plaintiff, and not as a promise made to plaintiff and Dunell, nor as a promise made to Jacobson, Kisch, and Dunell. He founded on the dissolution of the firm of Jacobson, Kisch, and Dunell, more than two years before, and known to defendant, and on the fact of the promise being made to pay the debt of Kisch, who had been a partner of the firm, and that even if the promise had been made to pay Kisch's debts to Jacobson and Dunell, such a promise could not, in the circumstances of this case, be considered as a promise made to them jointly, but as a separate and several promise to each; and that if it had been made to them jointly, yet by the civil law, contrary to the English law, each with or without the concurrence of the other, was entitled to sue for the share due to him. (*Evans Pothier*, 2*nd*, *p.* 56; *Chitty*, 1, 307.)

The Court held that the debt due by Kisch was due to his partners, and not to the firm; and that no debt due by a partner (at least no debt incurred by him in that capacity, or arising out of the partnership concerns) is in law considered as due to the firm, but as due to the other partners; and payment of it cannot be enforced by an action brought in the name of the firm, but only by *actio pro socio,* brought in the name of the other partners, or such of them as have an interest, therefore that no promise made by defendant to pay the debt due by Kisch now in question would in law be construed to be a promise to pay it to the firm, and such promise must in law be construed to be a promise to pay this debt to his partners. Besides that, the evidence and the circumstances of this case are sufficient to prove that, if defendant did make any promise to pay Kisch's debt now in question, it was a promise to pay it to the other partners. That such a promise must in law be construed, not as made to the partners jointly, but a separate and several promise to each. And that, even if it had been made to them jointly, yet by the law of this Colony, each of them is entitled, without the concurrence of the other, to sue in his own name for the share of the debt due to him.

1841. Nov. 18. Dec. 13. 1842. May 30.

Jacobson *vs.* Norton.

The Court held that if defendant was proved to have made such a promise as that alleged in the plaintiff's declaration, the plaintiff was entitled to sue defendant for the performance of that promise without first having the amount of the debt due by Kisch ascertained by a judgment recovered against Kisch, but that plaintiff, before getting judgment against defendant in this case, was bound to prove the amount of the debt due to him by Kisch, in the same way he must have done on an action brought for it by him against Kisch, and that defendant was entitled to avail himself, in defence against this action, of every defence which would have been competent and available to Kisch in action brought by plaintiff against him in respect of the same debt. On these grounds, the motion for absolution from the instance was refused.

Defendant called evidence, after which

The Court held that the plaintiff had proved that defendant had made the promise alleged in the declaration, and therefore, and in respect of the grounds stated by the Court on refusing the motion for an absolution from the instance, the Court gave judgment for plaintiff for £1,526 0s. 3d., and costs, subject to such deduction as may be made by Thomas Hall, hereby appointed by consent of the parties to ascertain and determine the value of the stock of Jacobson, Kisch & Dunell, left in charge of J. B. Kisch, which was found missing and unaccounted for on his flight from the Colony.

Second. The amount of the balance of cash for which Kisch was accountable to his partners, and indebted to them, or either of them.

Third. The amount of the balance due to plaintiff by his partners on his private account with the firm.

Award to be made on or before the 30th June. Costs of the reference to abide the judgment of the Court. Witnesses to be sworn before the Registrar of the Court, as commissioner.

Weinert and Meyer *vs.* Kohl.

Partnership: What not sufficient proof of. Pleading: Exceptio non qualificatæ.

1844. Nov. 21.

Weinert and Meyer *vs.* Kohl.

The summons in this case was as follows: "Command Adolph Kohl that justly, &c., he render to Carel Weinert and Wilhelm Meyer, copartners, trading in this Colony under the style or firm of C. Weinert and W. Meyer, the sum, &c., which he owes to the said firm, upon and by virtue of a certain receipt or acknowledgment of debt, &c., made and signed by the said Kohl in favour of the said firm of C. Weinert and W. Meyer," &c.

1844. Nov. 21.

Weinert and Meyer *vs.* Kohl.

Ebden, for the defendant, pleaded the exception of *non-qualification* of the plaintiffs in respect that Weinert and Meyer were not copartners, nor trading together under any firm, as untruly alleged in the summons.

The *Attorney-General* produced the receipt sued on, which was in these terms:

"£83 10s. Received from Messrs. [Den Heeren] C. Weinert & W. Meyer, the value of £83 10s. in medicines, which amount I engage to pay on demand.

"A. KOHL.

"Worcester, 28th April, 1842."

Which he maintained contained *in gremio*, a statement that the plaintiffs were partners of a company trading under the firm of C. Weinert & W. Meyer; and that the defendant having thus acknowledged this to be the case under his hand, was barred from now objecting that they were not copartners.

The Court held that the terms of the document were not, *per se*, sufficient to warrant this construction; and therefore allowed the plaintiffs fourteen days to prove their qualification.

Postea (December 5, 1844).—Plaintiffs failed to adduce any proof, and the summons was dismissed, with costs.

ONKRUYD *vs.* HAUPT.

Partnership: Insufficient proof of.

On the 4th day of February, 1842, the plaintiff and certain other persons entered into a copartnership for distilling and vending spirits at Stellenbosch, under the style of "*De Stellenbosch Spiritus Maatschappy*," and on that day executed a deed of copartnership, which contained, *inter alia*, the following clauses:

1846. Aug. 27.

Onkruyd *vs.* Haupt.

"Art. 4.—The shares may also be ceded or transferred, either by purchase or otherwise. A purchaser shall not be admitted as a shareholder otherwise than in accordance with the stipulation contained in Article 7. After the admission, the certificate of share (*i.e.*, the share purchased) shall be cancelled in the books, and then only a share shall be granted to the purchaser, in conformity with Art. 5.

1846. Aug. 27. — Onkruyd *vs.* Haupt.

"Art. 5.—No person is considered as shareholder unless he has in his possession his certificate of share, and no one shall receive a certificate unless he shall have previously delivered his share in wine and signed a notarial deed of partnership of the tenor of this present deed.

"The certificate shall be duly registered by the secretary in the ledger, and be signed by a special commission to be chosen at the annual general meeting, and be of the following tenor:

"'Stellenbosch Spiritus Maatschappy.

"'The holder hereof being ——— is a shareholder in the company known by the denomination above mentioned, and is as such entitled to ——— share in the property of the joint shareholders. All in accordance with the articles of agreement, a notarial copy whereof, with the seal of the company, is hereunto annexed. This document may be transferred by transfer on the back hereof. The same, however, gives no right either to the original holder or to the person to whom the same is ceded or transferred, unless the same be registered by the secretary for the time being, and which is to be repeated as often as any cession or transfer takes place,' &c.

"Art. 7.—No person shall be allowed to be a shareholder unless he being proposed in an ordinary meeting of the committee of directors, eight members of the committee in a subsequent ordinary meeting of the committee, shall have signed their consent thereto in the consent book. The same shall also take place in case of the shareholder applying for a second share."

Carel Albrecht Haupt was duly admitted as an original holder of two shares, signed the deed of copartnership, delivered his share of wine, obtained the certificate of two shares, and had them duly registered on the 14th May, 1836. The defendant purchased one of C. A. Haupt's shares, and the consent of the committee to his being admitted as a shareholder was duly obtained and entered in the consent book. But the defendant denied—and the plaintiffs produced no evidence to prove—that he had signed the articles of copartnership, that the original certificate of the share purchased by him had been cancelled, and that he had obtained a certificate that he was a shareholder.

On the 29th of December, 1838, a meeting was held at which upwards of two thirds of the shareholders were present, who resolved to dissolve the copartnership, and wind up its affairs, and signed the following writing:

"We the undersigned, shareholders of the Stellenbosch Spiritus Maatschappy, having, in an expressly convened extraordinary general meeting held this day, resolved to dissolve the said Spiritus Company, this resolution is communicated to those who were absent on the occasion, and who are requested to state whether they are in favour of or against the resolution."

1846. Aug. 27.

Onkruyd vs. Haupt.

This writing was signed by upwards of two thirds of the whole shareholders. The defendant attended at this meeting, consented to the resolution, and signed the above writing.

The affairs of the company were afterwards wound up, and its stock and premises sold, when it was ascertained that there was a deficiency of assets to discharge the debts of the company, the proportion of which chargeable against each shareholder was £86 9s. 1¾d.

The plaintiffs having, as copartners, paid and satisfied the whole amount of this deficiency, now brought this action against the defendant to recover from him his portion of the deficiency chargeable against him, as being the holder of one share.

The defendant denied his liability, on the ground that he had never become a shareholder according to the provisions of the articles of copartnership.

The Court, in respect that there was no evidence that the defendant had signed the articles of copartnership—had obtained a certificate that he was a shareholder, and that the original certificate of the share he had purchased from Haupt had been cancelled,—held that the defendant had not been proved to have been duly admitted and to have become a shareholder in the copartnership; and this without reference to whether the meeting of the 29th December, 1838, was or was not a meeting duly constituted and empowered to dissolve the copartnership,—which the plaintiffs alleged and the defendants denied it to be. And therefore absolved the defendant from the instance, with costs.

CHAPTER V.

BILLS OF EXCHANGE AND PROMISSORY NOTES.

BILLS OF EXCHANGE.

VENNING, Q.Q., *vs.* VENABLES.

1828. Sept. 6. *Bill of Exchange,—notice to the drawer of non-acceptance by drawee necessary from original payee or subsequent holder; and such notice coming from third party having no interest in the bill is insufficient.*

[Vol. I, p. 315.]

EBDEN *vs.* LIESCHING.

1829. Jan. 15. Mar. 17. „ 19. 1830. June 1. *Bills of Exchange,—Foreign, after sight, must, within a reasonable time, be presented for acceptance, or put in circulation. What is reasonable time, guided by custom of place where drawn; if none, then by the circumstances of the case. [But not specially decided in this case, judgment being by consent.]—*SEMBLE, *three months a reasonable time.*

[Vol. I, p. 349.]

THOMSON & CO *vs.* ARCHER.

1829. Dec. 1. *In a provisional claim against the drawer, presentment of a bill of exchange must be proved, although the acceptor became insolvent before the bill was due.*

[Vol. I, pp. 61, 402.]

FRESHFIELD *vs.* HARRIES.

1830. June 30. *How far the allegation of nullity of the debt as arising from a gambling transaction is a defence to provision where the instrument of debt (being a bill of exchange or order) expresses no causa debiti. [Per* WYLDE, *C.J., and* KEKEWICH, *J.: Yes; per* MENZIES, *J., and* BURTON, *J.: No. Court equally divided; no judgment.]*

[Vol. I, pp. 84, 85.]

KENNEL *vs.* HARRIES.

Whether a defendant is entitled to refer to the plaintiff's oath to prove the nullity of the debt as being a gambling transaction, as a defence against a provisional claim on a bill of exchange. [Per MENZIES *and* BURTON, *JJ., Yes; per* WYLDE, *C.J., and* KEKEWICH, *J.: No. Court being equally divided; no judgment.]* 1830. June 30.

[Vol. I, pp. 85, 86.]

HOVIL & MATHEW *vs.* POULTENEY.

Proof of presentment of a bill of exchange by the production of a notarial protest for non-payment, in which presentment is alleged, cannot in a provisional case be negatived by parole evidence. 1832. Dec. 31

[Vol. I, p. 14.]

MOCKE *vs.* VAN BREDA.

Bill of Exchange. Composition. Civil Imprisonment.

After provisional sentence obtained by the holder of a bill against the drawer and acceptor, the drawer, on execution, surrendered his estate, and the acceptor returned nulla bona. The holder then took a composition of one half the amount of the bill from the drawer's estate, expressly reserving his right against the acceptor for the balance, and then prayed civil imprisonment of the acceptor, who objected that the composition freed him from further liability. HELD *not, and civil imprisonment granted accordingly.*

1833. Feb. 5.

Mocke *vs.* Van Breda.

This was a claim for civil imprisonment, in execution of a provisional sentence given against the defendant and Heuser, the former as the acceptor and the latter as drawer of a bill, of which Mocke was the holder by indorsation, and which had not been paid when due, the one paying the other to be discharged.

Heuser surrendered his estate, and plaintiff claimed on it for the whole amount of the bill and costs.

The plaintiff and the other concurrent creditors agreed to accept a composition of 10s. in the pound, the plaintiff expressly reserving his right against defendant for the balance.

1833. Feb. 5. — Mocke *vs.* Van Breda. The plaintiff, before claiming on Heuser's estate, had taken out a writ of execution against defendant, on which a return of *nulla bona* was made.

Plaintiff now restricted his demand against defendant to one half of the amount of the bill and costs.

Cloete maintained that, by accepting the composition, plaintiff had discharged the defendant from all further liability.

The Court overruled this defence, and gave decree of civil imprisonment.

McDonald *vs.* Sutherland.

Feb. 28. *Provisional sentence refused against the defendant, who, after protest for non-payment, had guaranteed the payment of a bill of exchange to the drawer, there being no proof offered of any demand on and refusal by the acceptor after such guarantee by the defendant.*

[Vol. I, p. 74.]

Davis & Son *vs.* McDonald & Sutherland.

June 4. *It is a good defence to a provisional claim against two late partners on a bill of exchange, that it had been drawn by one partner only, after dissolution.*

[Vol. I, p. 86.]

De Ronde *vs.* Zeyler.

Sequestration of acceptor does not dispense with necessity of presentment and notice of dishonour. The notice in the "Gazette" of the sequestration of the acceptor's estate is not sufficient.

June 29. — De Ronde *vs.* Zeyler. In this case the plaintiff claimed provisional sentence against the defendant, the drawer of a bill stated in the summons to have been drawn by the defendant upon, and accepted by, F. Heinenberg in favour of plaintiff, payable three months after date, and bearing date the 14th day of March, 1833, and which bill was not honoured by the acceptor, who had, previous to the day the said bill became due, surrendered his estate as insolvent.

The *Attorney-General*, for defendant, pleaded want of due notice. 1833. June 29. De Ronde *vs.* Zeyler.

Cloete replied by producing the *Gazette* of the 7th June, containing the notice of the sequestration of the acceptor's estate.

The Court, on the principle stated in *Chitty, p.* 272, held that the notice in the *Gazette* was not sufficient notice, and as there was no proof of either presentment to the acceptor for payment, or notice of dishonour to the drawer, refused provisional sentence, with costs.

De Ronde *vs.* Zeyler.

Parole evidence is not competent to prove the dishonour of a bill of exchange. Aug. 31.

[Vol. I, p. 61.]

Et vide Anderson *vs.* Hutton, *post, p.* 259.

Barry *vs.* Bailey.

It is a good defence against a provisional claim on a bill of exchange that the holder, who was the payee, had, after the drawing of the bill, been sequestrated as insolvent, and that, although since rehabilitated, no assignment to him had been made by the sequestration creditors. 1834. June 2.

[Vol. I, p. 83.]

Moore *vs.* Alexander.

In a provisional claim by an indorsee of a bill of exchange the summons must aver the indorsement. June 10.

[Vol. I, p. 122.]

Rens *vs.* Cantz, Faure, and Neethling.

Joint acceptors found liable only pro rata. [But overruled, Kidson vs. Campbell, post. See under Promissory Note, post.]

Aug. 26. Rens *vs.* Cantz, Faure, and Neethling.

This was a claim for provisional sentence by the indorser

1834. Aug. 26. — Rens *vs.* Cantz, Faure, and Neethling.

against three acceptors of a bill, drawn in the following terms:

"Stellenbosch, 16th Dec., 1833.

"Rds. 500.

"Three months after date you will please to pay in Cape Town, to the lawful holder of this my order, the sum of five hundred rixdollars, for value received, and place the same to the account of

"Your obedient servant,
"J. G. MECHAU.

"To Messrs. JACOB CANTZ,
"J. G. FAURE,
"C. L. NEETHLING.
"Indorsed, J. G. MECHAU."

Brand, for the defendant Faure, besides a plea of *novatio debiti*, which was clearly unfounded, pleaded that Faure was only liable *pro rata*, which *Cloete*, for the plaintiff, admitted.

WYLDE, C.J., started a doubt that three persons could not be joint acceptors; at least, that no judgment could effectually be given against them in one action brought against them all in that character.

MENZIES and KEKEWICH, JJ., had no doubt but that a bill might lawfully be drawn upon two or more persons, and that, if accepted, it would bind all who accepted it as joint acceptors; and that by the law of the Colony persons jointly bound as acceptors were liable only *pro rata*, and not *in solidum*. [The contrary was deliberately decided in the case of *Kidson vs. Campbell & Joosten, 12th April*, 1844—*post.*] *Vide Chitty on Bills*, § 2, *pp.* 215, 216; *Bayley on Bills, pp.* 24, 44, 139, 454; *Van der Linden, pp.* 203, 204.

The Court gave provisional sentence, with costs against all the defendants *pro rata*.

THOMSON & WATSON *vs.* ALLEN.

Qualified indorsation of bill of exchange when not entitling holder to sue.

Dec. 1. — Thomson & Watson *vs.* Allen.

Plaintiffs claimed provisional sentence on a bill of exchange against the drawer, the captain of a vessel called the *Calypso*, on which were written the following words, signed by the last indorsee: "Transferred to the order of Messrs. Thomson, Watson, & Co., to be recovered on account of Messrs. Crook & Naz, from Messrs. A. Chiappini, of Cape Town, the owners of the brig *Calypso*."

The Court, although no appearance was made for defendant, decided that the plaintiffs had no title to sue the defendant Allen on the said bill, and refused the provisional sentence. 1834. Dec. 1. Thomson & Watson *vs.* Allen.

RENS *vs.* VAN DER POEL AND ANOTHER.

A copy of the protest for non-payment of a bill of exchange need not be served on the defendant. [This point had been considered doubtful in Simpson vs. Fleck, Vol. I, p. 117.] Dec. 2.

[Vol. I, p. 118.]

RENS *vs.* VAN DER POEL AND ANOTHER.

It is not necessary in a provisional claim against the indorser of a bill of exchange to allege in the summons that the bill had been presented to the acceptor, and that payment had been refused. Dec. 2.

[Vol. I, p. 122.]

SIMPSON BROTHERS & CO. *vs.* ALLINGHAM.

Provisional sentence refused against the acceptor of a bill of exchange, payable at a particular place, because presentment at such place was not duly alleged in the summons and proved. Dec. 16.

[Vol. I, p. 62.]

JANTZEN *vs.* VAN DEN BURGH, EXECUTOR.

Bill of Exchange. Executor. Execution.

Where a provisional judgment had been given on a bill of exchange against defendant as executor, and execution had been taken out against him in his capacity, and a return of nulla bona made, the Court, on further application by the creditor, refused to allow execution to issue on the same sentence, with an alteration in its terms, against the executor, de bonis propriis, or to give a new provisional sentence against him personally.

On the 9th December, 1834, plaintiff claimed provisional sentence against defendant on a summons in the following terms: 1835. Feb. 3. Jantzen *vs.* Van den Burgh, Executor.

"Command B. A. van den Burgh, &c., &c., as executor of the last will and testament of the late Sarah van de

1835. Feb. 3. — Jantzen *vs.* Van den Burgh, Executor.

Kaap, &c., that justly, &c., he render to J. J. Jantzen, &c., the sum of 320 rds., &c., which he owes to and unjustly detains from the said J. J. Jantzen, upon and by virtue of a certain bill of exchange bearing date the 2nd, &c., drawn by one F. Coverneels in favour of one F. P. Dort or order, and accepted by the said C. A. van den Burgh, and due at a day now past, &c., &c."

The *Attorney-General*, for plaintiff, produced the bill of exchange sued on, which was in the following terms:

"Cape Town, 2nd October, 1834.

"SIR,—On the 24th November, 1834, please to pay to Mr. F. P. Dort, or order, a sum of 320 rds., with interest already due, and as yet to become due, as per notarial bond, for the amount due to me by the late Sarah of the Cape, widow of the late Christoffel Renke.

"F. COVERNEELS.

"To Mr. C. A. VAN DEN BURGH,
Executor in the estate of the
late Widow C. RENKE.

"Accepted, C. A. VAN DEN BURGH, q.q."

Indorsed:

"Cape Town, 19th November, 1834.

"Ceded and transferred to Mr. J. J. JANTZEN.

"F. P. DORT."

Judgment:

"The Court grants provisional sentence as prayed against the defendant as executor.

"9th December, 1834.

"T. H. BOWLES, Registrar."

A writ of execution was taken out in the following terms:

"We command you that of the goods and chattels which were of Sarah van de Kaap, &c., at the time of her death in the hands of C. A. van den Burgh, &c., &c., as executor of the last will and testament of the said S. van de Kaap, you cause to be made the sum of £24, &c., &c., which J. J. Jantzen, &c., by sentence, &c., dated 9th December, 1834, recovered provisionally against the said C. A. van den Burgh, as executor as aforesaid, together with, &c., costs and charges, &c., &c., whereof the said C. A. van den Burgh, as executor as aforesaid, is convicted as appears to us of record."

On this writ the Sheriff made the following return : 1835. Feb. 3.

Jantzen *vs.* Van den Burgh, Executor.

"The defendant having been required by me to satisfy the exigency of this writ, has declared that he possesses no goods or chattels belonging to the above estate, except a female apprentice, stated by him to be in the district of Graaff-Reinet.

"31st December, 1834.

(Signed) "J. STEUART, H. S."

Thereafter (this day) the *Attorney-General*, for plaintiff, moved for a rule on defendant to show cause why a writ should not be ordered to issue, in execution of the said provisional sentence, as against the proper goods and chattels of the defendant himself.

But this application having been opposed, the Court refused it, on the ground that whatever might ultimately be found to be the personal liability of the defendant in respect of the said bill of exchange, no such writ as that now prayed for could be issued in virtue of the provisional sentence which had been given against him *as executor;* and that the Court could not now alter the terms of the provisional sentence, or give a new provisional sentence against defendant personally. That the plaintiff might go on with the principal case, if he thought he could make out that the defendant was in law personally liable in respect of the said bill, and obtain judgment against him personally.

GEERT *vs.* VAN AS.

A bill or order payable on a contingency, respecting which extrinsic proof would be required, is illiquid. Aug. 26.

[Vol. I, p. 62.]

NORDEN *vs.* STEPHENSON.

The drawer of a bill of exchange is not provisionally liable to the acceptor, who has paid the bill; such payment may have been out of the drawer's own funds. Aug. 31.

[Vol. I, p. 63.]

GIE *vs.* DE VILLIERS.

1835. Dec. 23. *The possession of a bill of exchange by one of three joint acceptors, coupled with an acknowledgment on the face of the bill from the holder, does not afford such presumption of payment by this one only as to entitle him to sue the other two provisionally for their shares.*

[Vol. I, p. 63.]

Et vide NEETHLING *vs.* HAMMAN, Vol. I, p. 71, where the same principle was laid down as to a bond.

CARSTENS *vs.* HENDRIKS.

1836. Feb. 2. *Provisional sentence refused against one of the drawees of a bill of exchange, of whose acceptance, alleged to be by mark, the only evidence appearing ex facie of the document, was three crosses. The Court refused proof that one of these was the acceptor's cross or mark.*

HOLTMAN *vs.* DORMEHL.

1837. Aug. 13. *The liquidity of an accepted bill of exchange is not affected by the fact that it was not addressed to any one. [In the subsequent principal case judgment was given for defendant with all the costs of provision and principal case.]*

[Vol. I, p. 14.]

MULLER *vs.* VAN OUDTSHOORN AND CALLANDER.

Where the acceptor and the drawer and endorser of a bill of exchange are summoned, it is not necessary to produce proof of presentment or demand for payment having been made to acceptor.

1838. Feb. 1. — Muller *vs.* Van Oudtshoorn and Callander.

In this case, the Court gave provisional sentence against both defendants, the first the acceptor and the second the drawer and endorser of the following bill of exchange:

"Cape Town, 5th October, 1837.

"£50

"Three months after date please pay to my order the sum of £50, *value received*, which sum place to the account of

"Your obedient Servant,

"J. CALLANDER.

"To W. VAN OUDTSHOORN."

Although no protest was produced of any presentment or demand for payment having been made to the acceptor. 1838. Feb. 1. Muller *vs.* Van Oudtsboorn and Callander.

[*Et vide* WILLIAMS & CO. *vs.* FARMER, *post. p.* 238.]

BORRADAILES, THOMPSON, & PILLANS *vs.* MORKEL.

Blank endorsement of bill of exchange. Title to sue.

The plaintiffs in their summons claimed provisional sentence against defendant, on a bill drawn by A. here, upon B., of Plymouth, in favour of the defendant or order, and specially indorsed by defendant to C. or order, and by C. to D. or order, and by D. endorsed blank, of which plaintiffs alleged that they were the legal holders. Along with the bill, plaintiffs put in a notarial protest for non-payment, bearing to have been made at Plymouth at the request of E., merchant (agent of D.) against B., and a copy of a letter written by plaintiff's attorney to defendant, informing him that plaintiffs had yesterday received by the ship *Fairlie* the original bill and the protest for non-payment, and adding that defendant was therefore held liable for the amount. Nov. 13. Borradailes, Thompson, & Pillans, *vs.* Morkel.

The defendant did not appear.

The Court doubted whether, as it was proved by the protest that the last indorsation on the bill (that by D. in blank) had been originally made for the purpose of conveying the bill to another party than the plaintiffs, and that it had not come into their possession until after it had been protested for non-payment at the instance of the party in whose favour this indorsation had been made, the plaintiffs could found on that indorsation, though in blank, as entitling them to claim provisional sentence on it as being the lawful holders under and in virtue of that indorsation, whatever they might have been entitled to do if they had sued as the agents of D. (which in fact they were).

The *Attorney-General*, for plaintiffs, in consequence of this doubt, withdrew the case.

BREDA'S TRUSTEES *vs.* VOLRAAD.

Bill of Exchange. Pleading.

Declaration alleged a bill of exchange, which it was sought to set aside as an undue preference, to have been made by the insolvent in favour of defendant. On evidence, it appeared that the bill, which was an accommodation one, was actually made by insolvent in favour of one B., and by him indorsed and discounted for the insolvent by the defendant. HELD, *that the description declared on was sufficient to cover the transaction proved.* [*See the other branch of the case,* 21*st November*, 1839.]

1839. Dec. 6. — Breda's Trustees *vs.* Volraad.

In the second count of the declaration in this case it was alleged that the insolvent Breda was indebted to the defendant in the sum of £105, "*upon and by virtue of a certain promissory note, bill of exchange, or acceptance made by the said P. van Breda, the insolvent, in favour of the defendant.*" This bill or note it was not in the plaintiffs' power to produce, but it was proved that the payment made by the insolvent to the defendant, which the plaintiff sought to have declared to have been fraudulent under the provisions of Ordinance No. 64, had been made in payment of a bill or note for £105, held by the defendant, in which the insolvent was the actual debtor, it having been granted for his accommodation, and discounted to him by the defendant, having on it the name of one A. Beck as indorser.

The Court held that the above description in the declaration was sufficient to apply to and comprehend the bill or note spoken of by the witnesses, whether it had been accepted or drawn by the insolvent or Beck, it being sufficient that the insolvent had put his name as drawer, acceptor, or indorser on it, being a bill for his accommodation in such manner as to make it become due and payable by him to the defendant, who had discounted it to him.

WILLIAMS & CO. *vs.* WILLIAM FARMER.

Bill of exchange, foreign: Presentment at specified place of payment not necessary to entitle holder to judgment against acceptors.

1840. Nov. 2. — Williams & Co. *vs.* William Farmer.

Provisional sentence was claimed against William Farmer and Henry Farmer, designed as late copartners, trading at 9, Essex-street, Strand, London, and also in Strand-street, Cape Town, under the firm of W. & H. Farmer, upon a bill of exchange, dated Birmingham, drawn by plaintiffs under the firm of C. Williams & Co., upon and accepted by the said firm of W. & H. Farmer, 9 Essex-street, Strand, London, *payable at Messrs. Leckie Brothers & Co., No.* 14, *Birchin Lane, London.*

The Court (WYLDE, C.J., absent) held that proof of presentment for payment at Messrs. Leckie Brothers & Co. was not necessary to entitle plaintiffs to maintain this action, because the terms of the acceptance "payable at Messrs. Leckie Brothers & Co." can only be construed as having the same legal effect which they would have had in England, where the bill was drawn and accepted, and because by the 1st and 2nd Geo. 4, c. 78, previous presentment at the place so mentioned in the acceptance is not necessary to entitle the holder of a bill to maintain action on it against the acceptors for payment. 1840. Nov. 2. Williams & Co. *vs.* William Farmer.

Norton *vs.* Speck and Another.

An acceptance of a bill payable on a contingency requiring extrinsic proof is illiquid. Non-allegation of presentment to the acceptor in the summons is sufficient to bar provisional sentence against the drawer of a bill of exchange, on objection taken by the drawer that no such presentment to the acceptor had, to his knowledge, been made. Nov. 19.

[Vol. I, p. 65.]

Phillips & King *vs.* Ridwood.

Provisional sentence refused [Menzies, J., *diss.*] *against the drawer of a bill of exchange payable ten days after sight, in respect that there was no protest alleging presentment for acceptance or sight to the drawer, though a protest for non-payment was produced, dated six months after the date the bill was drawn.* 1841. Feb. 11.

[Vol. I, p. 66.]

Livingston, Syers, & Co. *vs.* Dickson, Burnie, & Co.

Bill of Exchange, Foreign: Notice of non-acceptance and dishonour of, what is sufficient.
Agent: What is a waiver of above, by.
Lex loci contractus, Lex loci solutionis. Evidence of Foreign Law.
Pleading: Objection to title of plaintiffs must be by exception, and not under the general issue. Variance.
Judicial notice of a British Statute for India and letters patent issued thereunder.

This was an action to recover the sum of £500, being the amount of a certain bill of exchange for five thousand Company's rupees, together with the charges, damages, and expenses incurred by reason of the dishonour of the said bill. May 25. June 24. Livingston, Syers, & Co. *vs.* Dickson, Burnie, & Co.

1841. May 25. June 24.

Livingston, Syers, & Co. vs. Dickson, Burnie, & Co.

The *Attorney-General* for the plaintiffs, and *Musgrave* for the defendants, having been heard on a previous day, the Court now proceeded to give judgment.

The Court held that it was proved by the evidence and the admission of the parties, that the bill in question was drawn in this Colony on Lowe & Co., merchants in Calcutta, in favour of the defendants, merchants, having their permanent domicile in this Colony, by Major Hay, an officer in the service of the East India Company, while on a casual and temporary visit to this Colony, and when he had his permanent domicile in India; and who, when he drew the bill, intended to return to India before it should arrive at maturity, and did actually return to India before it was presented for acceptance. That the defendants, in this Colony, endorsed the bill in blank, and sent it to their agent at Mauritius, to be sold, if an advantageous sale of it could be there obtained, and if not, to be forwarded by him to their agents in Calcutta. That the bill so endorsed in blank was sold at Mauritius by defendants' agent, Mr. Grant, to Messrs. Aiken & Co., the agents there of the plaintiffs, and by Messrs. Aiken & Co. transmitted to plaintiffs; that neither Mr. Grant nor Aiken & Co. made themselves parties to the bill by putting their names on it, or otherwise; and that after the sale, and before the bill was presented for acceptance, the blank indorsation was filled up in favour of plaintiffs, but whether by Mr. Grant, Aiken & Co., or by the plaintiffs, does not appear. That plaintiffs duly presented the bill for acceptance to the drawees; and, on their refusal to accept it, caused it to be duly protested on the 3rd July, 1838. That notice of the non-acceptance and protest of the bill was sent by plaintiffs from Calcutta in due time, through their agents, Aiken & Co., to, and received by, defendants' agent, Grant, at Mauritius, on the 25th August following, and by him forwarded to defendants by the earliest opportunity, in a letter addressed by him to them, and received by them on the 28th September following. That no ship which sailed from Calcutta after the 3rd July, when the bill was protested, reached this Colony until some time after the 28th September; and that the defendants had notice of the non-acceptance and protest in the manner above mentioned sooner than they could have received it direct from Calcutta.

That, on the 13th July, 1838, only ten days after the protest, and consequently long before the defendants could have known of the non-acceptance of the bill by the drawee, they wrote a letter to their agent, Mr. Grant, in which they stated as follows: "We have, however, some fear that the one on Lowe & Co., drawn by Major Hay, may not meet due honour, and be returned to you; and to guard you against any inconvenience, we are anxious to place funds in your hands to await the result, for which purpose we have enclosed," &c. (viz.: three good bills for rupees 4,300 in all).

1841. May 25. June 24.

Livingston, Syers, & Co. *vs* Dickson, Burnie, & Co.

That, on receiving notice of the non-acceptance and protest, Mr. Grant made no objection that the dishonour of the bill by non-acceptance had not been duly notified to him, or that notification to him, instead of to defendant personally, was insufficient; but offered to pay it immediately to Aiken & Co., provided they would give him a guarantee for repayment of the amount *in the event of the second of the set not being duly presented by the plaintiff for payment, or the dishonour by non-payment not being duly notified to him;* which conditional offer was refused by Aiken & Co.

That the bill was not presented for payment or protested for non-payment, or at least that no due notice of such non-payment and protest was ever given by plaintiffs or their agents to defendants or their agents.

In consequence of the defendants refusing to pay the bill, the present action has been brought by the plaintiffs to enforce payment from defendants; in defence against which, the defendants have pleaded two pleas, in the first of which they admit that they indorsed the bill, but deny every other allegation in the declaration; and, in the second, they plead "that, admitting the said bill of exchange to have been dishonoured, the defendants are discharged from their liability thereon by reason of the laches of the plaintiffs, and their not having given due and sufficient legal notice to the defendants of the dishonour and protest of the bill."

The Court held that the defence maintained by the defendants under their first plea—that they are entitled to a non-suit, because the plaintiffs, whose only alleged title to the bill is its indorsement to the order of "Messrs. Livingston, Syers, & Co.," have not proved either that they are the partners of, or that they are the only partners of, that firm; both of which facts, the defendants alleged, it was essential they should have proved to entitle them to judgment—was bad; and that it was unnecessary to determine or inquire whether, by the law of this Colony, persons who are the holders of a bill indorsed to a firm, and who sue on it, representing themselves as the partners of that firm, are bound to prove that they are so; or whether it is not incumbent on the defendants, if they deny this, to prove that the plaintiff are not partners, or that there are other partners; because by the law and form of pleading in this Colony, such an objection to the title of the plaintiffs to sue can only be competently taken by pleading it by way of exception before pleading on the merits; and therefore, as the defendants have not pleaded such exception *in limine* of the pleadings, they are now barred from insisting on it, and must be held to have acknowledged that the plaintiffs possess the title to sue under which they have brought this action.

The Court held that the defence maintained by the defendants under the second plea—that the plaintiffs have committed laches by reason of their not having given notice of the non-acceptance of the bill and protest for non-acceptance directly to the defendants, the notice given by them through Aiken & Co. to Mr. Grant not being due and sufficient legal notice thereof—was bad; and that the plaintiffs were entitled to give notice of the dishonour of the bill through their agents, Aiken & Co., and that the notice given by Aiken & Co. was as sufficient legal notice as if plaintiffs had given it by letter which they had caused to be written and dispatched by one of their clerks in their counting-house at Calcutta. That the circumstances of the present case are totally different from those which led to the judgment in the case of *Stewart versus Kennet*, as reported in 2*nd Campbell*, 177; and therefore, that the notice given by Aiken & Co., if given by them to a proper party, was due and sufficient legal notice.

The Court held that the notice of the dishonour and protest given by plaintiffs to Mr. Grant—having been given by them to him in order that the defendants should thus be informed of the non-acceptance and protest of the bill, and of the plaintiffs' intention to have recourse against the defendants for payment of it, and communicated by him to defendants before they could have received notice in any other way—was due and sufficient legal notice to them, even if the nature of the connection between defendants and Mr. Grant, as their agent, was such that notice of the dishonour given to him, and not communicated by him to defendants, would not have been equivalent to notice given to them directly. And, further, that the nature of the agency of Mr. Grant, with respect to the bill, was such, that notice of the dishonour duly given to him by plaintiffs was equivalent to notice duly given to defendants directly, or to a clerk in their counting-house. That the defendants' letter to Mr. Grant, of the 13th July, 1835, and the fact of their having remitted to him funds to enable him to retire the bill, proved that they contemplated, in the event of the bill being dishonoured, that recourse should be had on them through Mr. Grant; and, as a necessary consequence, that due notice of the dishonour to him should be equivalent to due notice to them.

But the Court held that even if the notice given to Mr. Grant, or through him to the defendants, had been bad and insufficient, yet that the powers derived by him from the defendants as their agent were such as to enable him, in a question with plaintiffs, effectually to waive the want of due presentment of the bill for acceptance, of due protest for non-acceptance, and of due and sufficient notice of such dishonour and protest; and that by his making no objection on any of those grounds when Aiken & Co. gave him notice of the non-acceptance and protest, and his offer to pay the bill under the condition of a guarantee of repayment in the event before mentioned, had effectually waived any objection founded on anything which plaintiffs had done or omitted to do with respect to the non-acceptance of the bill, and thereby now barred the defendants from pleading any such objections in defence against this action.

The Court held that the defence maintained by the defendants—that they were discharged from their liability in consequence of the laches of the plaintiffs, in not presenting the bill when due for payment, and protesting it for non-payment, or, which was equivalent, in not having given defendants due notice of such presentment and protest—was bad; although the law of this Colony, in all cases in which the rights and liabilities of the drawers and indorsers of bills are to be regulated by it, is, that the holder of a bill protested by him for non-acceptance, and of such protest on which due notice is given, is, in respect thereof, only entitled to demand from the drawer or indorsers that they shall give security for the payment of the bill in case it shall not be paid when at maturity by the drawer, and must, in order to preserve his recourse against them, present the bill when due for payment, protest it for non-payment, and give due notice of such presentment and protest; and although in consequence of the bill having been dated and drawn in this Colony, the law of this Colony must be held to be the *lex loci contractus.* Because the rule that, where the original parties to a bill have not expressly stipulated what are the conditions which the payee must perform in order to entitle him, in the event of the bill being dishonoured, to have recourse on the drawer, these conditions must be determined by the law of the place where the bill is drawn, as being the *lex loci contractus,*—is not an absolute and universally peremptory rule, but applies only in those cases, the circumstances of which are such as to infer a legal presumption that the parties intended that their contract should be ascertained and regulated by that law; and

1841. May 25. June 24.

Livingston, Syers, & Co. *vs.* Dickson, Burnie, & Co.

ceases to apply in any case in which the circumstances are such as to afford stronger grounds for presuming that the parties intended their contract to be ascertained and regulated by some other law, as for example by the *lex loci solutionis.*

That, even although where a bill on Calcutta was drawn in this Colony, and the drawer and original payee were both permanently domiciled in this Colony, it should be held that according to the law of this Colony, as being the *lex loci contractus,* the holder, in order to entitle him to recourse against the drawer, was bound, after protest for non-acceptance and notice thereof, also to present the bill when due for payment, protest it for non-payment, and give notice of the protest (a case which the Court was not called on now to decide, and on which, therefore, they abstained from expressing any opinion), it did not necessarily follow that the law of this Colony, as being the *lex loci contractus,* should regulate the decision of the present case. Because, in the case supposed, not only the original payee, but the drawer, had their permanent domicile in this Colony, and it was *here* that both parties contemplated that, in the event of the dishonour of the bill by the drawee at Calcutta, it should be paid by the drawer; and the law of this Colony was, therefore, not only the *lex loci contractus,* in respect of the bill being drawn here, but, as being the law of the permanent domicile of both parties, there were sufficient grounds for legal presumption that it was the law by which both the parties intended their contract should be regulated; more especially as, in so far as related to the payment of the bill, to be made by the drawer in the event of its dishonour at Calcutta, it was also the *lex loci solutionis.*

While in the present case, although the bill was drawn here in favour of the defendants, who had their permanent domicile here, yet the drawer was a stranger on a casual and temporary visit to this Colony, having his permanent domicile in India, to which, at the time the bill was drawn, he intended, and was known by the defendants to intend, to return, before any demand could be made on him to pay the bill in the event of its dishonour by the drawer; and therefore the law of Calcutta was not only, in so far as relates to his conditional obligation to pay the bill, the *lex loci solutionis,* but there was no legal ground for presuming that either he or the defendants, when the bill was drawn, ever contemplated or intended that the law of this Colony should determine the conditions under which, in the event of the bill being dishonoured, he, the drawer, should be liable to pay it. The more obvious, and therefore the legal, presumption, on the contrary, being, that both the parties looked to the law of India, which was the *lex loci solutionis*, not only as to the drawee, if the bill were accepted by him, but as to the drawer, if the bill were dishonoured by the drawee, as that which was to determine the nature and conditions of the drawer's liability to pay the bill.

The Court held that the defence maintained by the defendants—that, as the indorsement was maintained by them here, the law of this Colony, as being the *lex loci contractus* between the indorser and indorsee, must determine the nature and conditions of the liability of the indorser to the indorsee, —was bad, notwithstanding they had indisputably established that such was the rule of the French law, because the Court had been unable to find the slightest traces of the existence of any such rule in the laws either of Holland or Great Britain. The rule recognized by both the latter countries being, that, by indorsement, the indorser undertakes the same obligations in favour of the indorsee which, by drawing the bill, the drawer originally undertook in favour of the payee, and could not exact from the indorsee the performance of any condition which the drawer could not have insisted should be performed by the original payee, in order to enable the latter to recourse on the drawer.

Further, that the rule of the French law is founded on the presumption that the indorser and indorsee, at the time the indorsement is made, and the bill delivered to and received by the indorsee, mutually entered into a tacit agreement that the nature and conditions of the drawer's liability should be determined by the law of the place where these acts took place; and in every case in which, by the French authorities, this rule is declared to apply, the indorsee is always represented as having been present at the time and place at which the indorser has made the indorsement and delivery; and such presence is the foundation of the legal presumption that he agreed that the contract between him and the indorser should be regulated by the law of that place in which both the parties were at the time the contract was made, as being the *lex loci contractus.*

But the circumstances of the present case do not afford the slightest ground for any such presumption; because, although it is admitted that the bill was indorsed by the defendants in this Colony, still it was indorsed in blank, and was not delivered to or received by the plaintiffs, or any person representing them in this Colony. The bill was sent by defendants, blank indorsed, to their own agents in Mauritius, and was from them transmitted to the plaintiffs by their agent, and received by them in Calcutta. No mutual contract or agreement, therefore, was ever made in this Colony, between the plaintiffs and defendants; and, consequently, there is no ground for holding the law of this Colony to be the *lex loci contractus indorsationis.*

Neither can the mere fact of the delivery of the bill at the Mauritius by Grant to Aiken & Co., and the payment of the price of it by the latter to the former, neither of whom made themselves in any way parties to the bill, so identify the bill with the Mauritius as to make the French law, which is the law of that island, regulate the rights and obligations of any of the parties to it, as being the *lex loci contractus indorsationis.*

On all those grounds, the Court held that the question whether a presentment of the bill when due for payment, a protest for non-payment, and due notice of such presentment and protest were necessary in order to entitle the plaintiffs to have recourse on the defendants for payment, must be decided by the law of Calcutta; that the Court were bound judicially to take notice of the statute of the 13 Geo. III. c. 63, and the royal letters patent made in pursuance of its provisions, and that these furnished legal evidence that the law of England was the law of Calcutta, in so far as relates to bills of exchange.

That the concurrent testimony of the text-books of the law of England, and of the reported case quoted by plaintiffs, that it was not necessary for the holder of a bill who had duly protested it for non-acceptance, and given due notice thereof, afterwards to present the bill when due, for payment, protest it for non-payment, and give due notice of such presentment and protest, in order to entitle him to recourse against the drawer and indorser,—was sufficient *primâ facie* evidence that such is the law of England to warrant the Court in holding it to be so, without calling on the plaintiffs to give further evidence of the fact: more especially in the absence of any suggestion by the defendants to the contrary.

That the non-production of the second of the set of the bill by the plaintiffs is no ground for a non-suit, although the defendants may insist on having it given up to them, or to a guarantee from the plaintiffs that it has not been so used as to prevent or impair defendants' rights of recovery against the drawer.

That the specification of the place where the plaintiffs alleged that notice of the dishonour by non-acceptance had been given by them to defendants was surplusage; and therefore the variance between the allegation in the declaration and the evidence on this point was not such a variance as to entitle defendants to a non-suit.

On those grounds, the Court gave judgment for the plaintiffs, as prayed, with costs.

BORRADAILES, THOMPSON, & PILLANS *vs.* W. F. J. VON LUDWIG.

Bill of Exchange. Acceptor other than Drawee. Alteration in Signature. Variance.

L. P. drew a bill on, and accepted by, C. H. v. L., afterwards altered to W. F. H. v. L., the defendant, who admitted the altered signature to be his. Defendant now objected on the ground of the alteration, but the Court held him liable. Defendant then claimed absolution for variance between the summons which described the bill as drawn on him, whereas it was drawn on his father. But the Court held that unless defendant would swear that the alteration was subsequent to his unconditional acceptance (which he declined to do) he was bound.

1842. April 12.

Borradailes, Thompson, & Pillans *vs.* W. F. J. von Ludwig.

In this case provisional sentence was sought on a bill, which in the summons was stated to have been "drawn by L. Precipe upon, and accepted by, the defendant Wilhelm Frans Jacob von Ludwig."

From inspection of the bill, it appeared that it had been drawn originally on C. H. von Ludwig (the father of defendant), but that these initials had been altered to W. F. J.

It was admitted by defendant that he had accepted the bill, and that the signature to the acceptance was his.

Stadler, for defendant, objected that as the bill had been originally drawn on another person, he was not liable to pay it, notwithstanding he had accepted it.

But the Court held that by his acceptance he had rendered himself liable, and would have been so even if no alteration had been made in the initials before he accepted it.

Defendant next objected that he was entitled to absolution from the instance in respect of the variance between the summons and the bill, which was described in the summons as having been drawn on defendant, while, in fact, it had been drawn on C. H. von Ludwig, his father.

The Court held that if the alteration in the initials had been made before its presentment to defendant, or after its presentment with his knowledge before he accepted it, this alteration had in a question with defendant the effect of making the defendant the drawer on the bill, and that the fact of his having accepted the bill unconditionally was presumptive evidence that the alteration had so been made, unless the defendant would positively and distinctly aver that the alteration had been made subsequently to his

1842. April 12. — Borradailes, Thompson, & Pillans *vs.* W. F. J. von Ludwig.

having accepted the bill; and explain how he came to have accepted a bill which was drawn not on him, but on another person.

This the defendant, who was in Court, declined to do, and the Court, therefore, gave provisional sentence against him.

De Smidt *vs.* Blanckenberg.

Bill of Exchange. Composition. Ord. No. 64, § 81. *Costs of Counsel.*

Held (*confirming Hawk. vs. Breda, Mœser vs. Mulder*), *that no majority of consenting creditors can bind any minority of consenting creditors to take less than the full amount of a bill of exchange, unless such power have, by legal enactment, been given to such majority. Ord.* 64, § 81, *gives no such power.* [*Et vide Ord.* 6, 1843, § 106.]

1843. August 3. „ 17. 1844. Feb. 27. — De Smidt *vs.* Blanckenberg.

This was an action to recover the sum of £100 due on a bill of exchange.

The defendant pleaded that he had duly surrendered his estate as insolvent; that the plaintiff, as a concurrent creditor, had duly proved the debt in question upon the estate; that a composition of 10s. 6d. in the pound had been accepted by nine-tenths in number and value of his creditors, according to the provisions of the 81st section of Ordinance No. 64; that afterwards his estate had been released from sequestration, in due form of law, by an order of this Court; that all the creditors, except plaintiff, had been duly paid by the said defendant the several sums owing to them, under and by virtue of the said accepted composition; that the amount so due and owing to plaintiff had been duly tendered to him, and that he had refused to receive the same. Defendant admitted that plaintiff had not in any way signified his acceptance of the said composition, but averred that he was by law equally bound to accept the same, as if he had actually agreed so to do.

Plaintiff, in replication, admitted the fact alleged; but denied that he was, by law, equally bound to accept the composition as if he had actually agreed to do so.

Musgrave, for plaintiff, referred to the 81st section of Ordinance 64, which, he maintained, only authorized the release of the estate from sequestration, and no more, and did not provide that there should be a release of the debts of the non-consenting creditors on paying them the composition agreed on by the majority, nor enact, as in the case of the allowance of certificate, that the approval of the composition by the majority and release of the estate by the Court should be a bar against any suit brought by a non-consenting creditor. He maintained—in reply to the question put by defendant: "Could the plaintiff, after the release of the estate from sequestration on composition, petition on his debt for a new sequestration?"—that he could have done so; and quoted §§ 25, 27, Ord. 64; and quoted the *Scottish Bankrupt Act*, 54 *Gui. III.*, *c.* 137, § 59, to show that the effect of the composition sought by the defendant is expressly enacted. And quoted *Smith's Mercantile Law*, *p.* 489; 6*th Geo. IV.*, *c.* 16, § 133; *Harrison's Digest*, *p.* 432; 9 *Barn. & Cress.* 437, *Tuck vs. Tooke*, to show that the English Courts have given to that clause (133rd), which is in the same terms with the 81st section of Ordinance No. 64, the same construction which he contended should be given to the said 81st section; and to show that by the common law of this Colony the release did not bind non-consenting creditors, quoted *Van der Linden*, 502; *Placaat*, 19*th May*, 1544, *art.* 35, *vol.* 1, *p.* 327; *Bell*, *vol.* 2, *edit.* 1821, *p.* 507; *Blackstone*, 1, *pp.* 87, 493; and cases decided in this Court, *Meeser vs. Mulder*, 1*st August*, 1835, and *Summer vs. Hewson*, 31*st August*, 1839.

Ebden followed on the same side. Referred to *Ordinance of Amsterdam*, 1771, and *Bell Com.*, *vol.* 2, *p.* 481, *edit.* 1821.

Porter, *A.-G.*, *contra*, maintained that by the law of this Colony, before the 64th Ordinance was enacted, a composition agreed to by a certain majority was binding on the non-consenting creditors. He stated that a bankrupt law was not known in Holland before 1570; and to show that by Dutch law and by the former colonial law a composition bound non-consenting creditors, quoted *Placaat* 11*th December*, 1649, *vol.* 1, *tit.* 16; *Consultations*, 238, 3*rd vol.*, *p.* 626; *Nederlands Placaat & Law Dict.*, *Art. Insol. Boedel*; *Code de Commerce of Holland*, *book* 2, *tit.* 1, *part* 4; *Placaat* 7*th July*, 1708, § 19, *vol.* 5, *p.* 1274; *Sequestrator's Inst.*, §§ 27, 31, 35, 36; *Ordinance No.* 46, *No.* 64, § 1 repealing words; *No.* 88, *and No.* 64, § 81. And contended that the requisites required by this section, before application could be made to Court to release the estate, proved that some more important effect than the mere release was intended to be produced. Quoted *Bell. Com.* 54 *qu.* 3*rd c.* 137; § 59, 2 & 3 *Voet; c.* 41, § 113, *et seq.* 116, 121; to show that an acceptance of the offer of composition by a certain majority of creditors present at the meeting, and not of the creditors who have proved, is sufficient to bind the non-consenting. He then argued that the inconvenience, or rather impracticability,

1843. August 3. " 17. 1844. Feb. 27. — De Smidt *vs.* Blanckenberg.

of a system which recognized the release of an estate from sequestration on a composition which had not the effect of binding the non-consenting minority was such as to show that the colonial legislature could not have intended to sanction such a system. That the principle of election which prevails in England gives a different effect to Geo. IV. cap. 16, § 133, from what must be given to the 81st section here, where no such principle is recognized. That the case of *Tuck vs. Tooke,* quoted in *Harrison's Digest,* proves that in England a creditor who had proved his debt would be bound by the majority, although not present at the meeting, or not acceding. And that the effect of the words "superseding the commission," in the English Act, is different from that of the words "release the estate from sequestration," used in the colonial Act—the latter being much more limited in effect than the former; because the former annihilated the commission and all that had taken place under it, as if it had never existed, and therefore no creditor who had not expressly acceded to the composition could be bound by anything do neby the majority of the creditors acting under the commission; whereas the effect of the words "release the estate from sequestration" is merely to give back to the insolvent the estate exactly as it stood at the date of the release, and therefore subject to a composition agreed to by a certain majority of the creditors, acting under the sequestration.

Musgrave was heard in reply, and the Court deferred judgment.

Postea (17th August, 1843).—The Court gave judgment for plaintiff, with costs.

The Court held that the Instructions for the Sequestrator ceased to have effect in law, or any effect of any kind, after the abolition of that office on 31st December, 1827; consequently, that they were not in force, and did not require to be repealed by the 64th Ordinance in order to deprive them of effect. That no majority of consenting creditors could bind any minority of dissenting creditors to take less than the full amount of their debts, unless the power of so binding the minority were, by legal enactment, expressly given to the majority; and that the provisions neither of the 81st section or of any other section of Ordinance No. 64, or of any other law or ordinance in force within the Colony, could be legally construed as giving any such power to any majority of creditors. The same had been found, *Hanke vs. Breda and Heuser,* 10*th January,* 1832 (vol. I, 539), and *Meeser vs. Mulder,* 1*st August,* 1835.

Postea (27th February, 1844).—On a review of the

Master's taxation of the costs in this case, on the motion of *Ebden*, for the plaintiff, the Court held plaintiff entitled to claim, as costs, the fees of two counsel who had been retained and acted for him in the cause, and made order accordingly.

J. Norton & Co. *vs.* Bain.

Bill of Exchange. Notice of non-acceptance when it may begin.

B. not domiciled in the Colony, drew, February 7, 1843, a bill of exchange on K., of Liverpool, at 60 days' sight, in favour of D. N. & Co., who endorsed it to plaintiffs. The bill was not accepted nor paid, and was duly protested. The protests were sent to the Colony, and on December 7, 1843, plaintiffs gave notice to the maker (having been prevented from doing so previously by his absence from the Colony until shortly before that date). **Held**, *that this notice was sufficient.*

In this case the plaintiffs claimed provisional sentence against defendant, on a bill for £120, dated 7th February, 1843, payable sixty days after sight, drawn by defendant on R. Kirton, Esq., of Liverpool, in favour of D. Norden & Co., by whom it was endorsed to plaintiffs (the summons stated that the bill had been refused both for non-acceptance and non-payment), and produced notarial protests in due form of the non-acceptance and non-payment of the bill.

The question arose whether plaintiffs had given defendant such due notice of the dishonour of the bill as entitled plaintiffs now to demand payment from defendant.

The *Attorney-General*, for plaintiffs, contended that this was proved by the Sheriff's return, stating that on the 7th day of December, 1843, he had served the summons with defendant personally, and delivered to him a copy of the protests.

The defendant did not appear.

The Court adjourned the case until this day, in order that the plaintiff might show that notice of the dishonour given to defendant in manner aforesaid on *the 7th December was notice given in due time.*

This day the plaintiffs put in an affidavit sworn by himself, stating that "protest for non-acceptance arrived in this Colony in July, 1843, and that for non-payment in September following. That previous thereto the defendant (who has no domicilium in this Colony) has been absent

1844. Feb. 1. " 8. — J. Norton & Co. vs. Bain.

therefrom for several months, and that in consequence thereof notice of dishonour of said bill could not be served upon him. That the very first intimation plaintiffs had of defendant's return to the Colony was through the *Frontier Times* of 23rd November last, which arrived in Cape Town on the 29th November," whereupon the plaintiffs having been informed that the defendant contemplated leaving the Colony in a very short time, on the 1st of December caused a summons to be issued and dispatched with copies of both the said protests for service on defendant.

The Court held this notice of dishonour sufficient, and gave provisional sentence as prayed.

OPENSHAW, UNNA, & CO. *vs.* MRS. TRUTER.

Bill of Exchange. Allocation of debtors' payment by creditor.

Transference of a bill of exchange to a running account bars claim for provisional sentence on such bill.

1846. Feb. 2. — Openshaw, Unna, & Co. vs. Mrs. Truter.

Ebden, for the plaintiffs, claimed provisional sentence against the defendant for the sum of £70 4s. 10d., upon and by virtue of two bills of exchange, payable the one on the 30th January, 1845, and the other on the 30th March, 1845, drawn by one Van den Burgh, and accepted by the defendant, Catherine F. Truter.

The *Attorney-General*, for defendant, admitted her signature, and at first objected, but afterwards passed from the objection, that as the bills mentioned one Henry Truter, and not the defendant, as the drawer, the signature of the defendant below the word "accepted"—although perhaps it might imply some legal obligation on her to pay the bills—was not sufficient to entitle the plaintiffs to obtain provisional sentence against her *as the acceptor* of the bills, in which capacity alone she was sued in the summons.

He then objected that her acceptance had been for the accommodation of Van den Burgh, who, on the 30th January, 1845, had paid £10, and on the 14th May, 1845, £40 14s. 8d., expressly in discharge of those two bills; and that therefore she was at most only liable for the balance of £19 16s. 2d., which she had tendered, and which plaintiffs had refused to accept. And in support of his allegation produced the following letter, written by the plaintiffs to Van den Burgh:

"MR. H. VAN DEN BURGH.

"SIR,—Having sold to you, at various periods lately, goods with the understanding that you were to give us the acceptance of Mrs. Truter for the same, we beg to inform you that as you have not complied with this agreement (although the last goods were bought fully four months ago, and are consequently due), we have passed the two amounts, viz.: £10 paid on the 30th January, and £40 14s. 8d., paid on the 14th May, to the credit of your running account; and further that we consider the two bills of £35 and £35 4s. 10d., which were due on the 30th January and 30th March last, accepted both by Mrs. Truter, as yet unpaid.

1846. Feb. 2.

Openshaw, Unna, & Co. *vs.* Mrs. Truter.

"We are, Sir, yours respectfully,

"OPENSHAW, UNNA, & CO."

The plaintiffs admitted this letter, but denied that it afforded evidence that Van den Burgh and the plaintiffs had at the time so appropriated the two sums therein mentioned to the payment of the bills of exchange so as to prevent the plaintiffs from applying those payments to the discharge of the other debts due by Van den Burgh, sufficiently clear and liquid to bar their claim for provisional sentence on the bills.

But the Court held that the letter did afford such evidence, and judgment for plaintiffs for £19 16s. 2d., with interest; and *quoad ultra* refused provisional sentence, with costs to defendant.

PROMISSORY NOTES.

REITZ *vs.* DE KOCK.

Provisional sentence granted on a promissory note, payment of which was first demanded four years after it was due. 1828. April 1.

[Vol. I, p. 38.]

DISCOUNT BANK *vs.* HEIRS OF CROUS.

Where a promissory note was proved to be for the sole accommodation of the indorser, HELD *that want of notice to indorser of non-payment by maker will not discharge indorser.* 1829. March 30.

[Vol. I, p. 369.]

Eaton *vs.* Hitzeroth and Another.

1832. June 19. *Notice of dishonour of promissory note by maker may be given to indorser on the very day the note is due, and before such day has wholly expired.*

[Vol. I, p. 569.]

Ross and Others *vs.* Muntingh.

1833. Feb. 5. *Provisional sentence was granted on a promissory note against an executor, the maker, although the estate had been subsequently to the making of the note surrendered as insolvent.*

[Vol. I, p. 39.]

Rens *vs.* Horak.

Feb. 28. *Provisional sentence granted where the consideration of the promissory note was alleged to be usurious.*

[Vol. I, p. 40.]

Et vide Muller *vs.* Redelinghuys and Another, *post p.* 257; Freshfield *vs.* Harries, *ante p.* 228; Kennel *vs.* Harries, *ante p.* 229.

Cruywagen *vs.* Oliviera and Van Hellings.

Promissory note. What not due notice of non-payment. Protest for non-payment of inland note necessary to render indorser liable. No days of grace in this Colony.

June 25. — Cruywagen *vs.* Oliviera and Van Hellings.

In this case, provisional sentence was refused against the indorser of a promissory note, in order that the following questions of law might be decided in the principal case:

1st. Whether it was necessary to have a notarial protest for non-payment of an inland promissory note? (*Vide Searight & Co. vs. Lawton,* 14*th June,* 1844.)

2nd. If not necessary, whether notice of non-payment given on the third day after the day the note became due was sufficient?

This question involving the question, what, if any, are the days of grace in this Colony?—it was afterwards found that such notice was not sufficient, and that there were no days of grace in this Colony. (*Vide Trustee of Randall vs. Haupt,* 12*th July,* 1844; *vol. I, p.* 79.)

WOLHUTER *vs.* VAN HELLINGS.

Rule of Court No. 12. *Summons.*

The copy of a promissory note on which an indorsee claims provisional sentence must contain a copy of an indorsement through which title is acquired. 1833. Aug. 1.

[VOL. I, p. 116.]

SIMSON & CO. *vs.* FLECK.

Provisional sentence. Summons. Tender. Costs.

Plaintiff having withdrawn a provisional summons cannot proceed anew until the costs of the former summons have been paid. An offer of such costs into Court on the day of second summons is not sufficient.

Tender of costs, what is a bad.

Aug. 31. Simson & Co. *vs.* Fleck.

The plaintiffs having of new summoned defendant for provisional sentence on the same notes on which the plaintiff had formerly summoned him, but which former summons had been withdrawn, the *Attorney-General* objected to any proceedings being now had in this case, in respect that the costs of the former summons had not been paid or tendered.

The Court, in respect that there was no sufficient proof of tender of costs by plaintiffs, sustained the objection that plaintiffs were not entitled to proceed to-day, notwithstanding a payment of costs now made into Court, and were about to grant the defendant until next provisional roll day to plead to the provisional claim, when the plaintiffs withdrew the case. Costs to defendant.

The Court also held that the tender to defendant in this case, which was in the following terms, was insufficient:

"Take notice that we have withdrawn the summons issued in the above cause, &c., &c., and your costs thereon when made up and *taxed*, will be paid by 'you' (a mistake for 'us') *on demand.*"

In respect that the defendant was thereby improperly and peremptorily required to tax his bill of costs, before it had been seen by plaintiffs, and thereafter to demand the costs from the plaintiffs, instead of the costs being offered to him by the plaintiffs.

Steytler *vs.* Smuts.

1833. Dec. 2. *Provisional sentence granted on a promissory note, containing a penal stipulation, for the amount of the note, but not of the penalty.*

[Vol. I, p. 40.]

Hovil and Mathew *vs.* Saunders and Johnstone.

Rule of Court No. 12.

Dec. 2. *Non-description in the summons of the notes on which the provisional claim was founded is a bar to provisional sentence.*

[Vol. I, p. 121.]

Meiring *vs.* De Villiers.

1834. Feb. 1. *Presentment and non-payment of a promissory note are not provable by affidavit in a provisional case.*

[Vol. I, p. 75.]

So found in Anderson *vs.* Hutton and Another, same day. Farmer *vs.* Breda and Another. De Ronde *vs.* Zeyler, *vol. I, p.* 61. Trustees of Randall *vs.* Haupt, *vol. I, p.* 79.

[Vol. I, p. 75.]

Brink *vs.* Gough.

Promissory Note. Presentment for Payment. Costs. Tender.

Where a promissory note is not made payable at any specified place, and summons was issued against the drawer, without previous presentment, held that if defendant, on being so summoned, at once tendered the sum to plaintiff or attorney, he will not be liable for costs of summons.

But such a tender to the Sheriff's officer on service is bad, if not authorized by plaintiff.

Feb. 4. Brink *vs.* Gough. Provisional sentence being prayed in respect of a promissory note made by the defendant in favour of the plaintiff or order, payable three months after date, no place of payment specified,—the Court held that if the defendant, after being summoned, had tendered payment of the debt to the plaintiff or his attorney, he was not liable for the costs, even of the summons, if no presentment for payment had been made to him previous to the service of the summons (*vide Van der Linden Inst.*, *p.* 395); but that if such previous presentment had been made, a tender of the debt was insufficient unless the costs of the summons were also tendered. 1834. Feb. 4. — Brink *vs.* Gough.

And that an offer of payment to the Sheriff's officer who served the summons, unless he had been entrusted with the promissory note by the plaintiff to demand payment, was not a sufficient tender.

The case was postponed to allow the defendant to prove the alleged tender by him to plaintiff's attorney, and the plaintiff to prove presentment before service of the summons, but was afterwards settled extra-judicially.

Et vide REDELINGHUYS *vs.* THEUNISSEN, 1*st May*, 1835, *post p.* 258; ORLANDINI *vs.* POPE, 26*th February*, 1839, *post p.* 260; STEYTLER *vs.* DE VILLIERS, 13*th June*, 1846, *post p.* 286.

MULLER *vs.* REDELINGHUYS AND ANOTHER.

Provisional sentence granted against the maker and indorser in blank of a promissory note, notwithstanding proof tendered on their part that the holder had become possessed of the note fraudulently and for a usurious consideration. Feb. 18.

[Vol. I, p. 41.]

Et vide RENS *vs.* HORAK, *ante p.* 254.

CANNON *vs.* FORD.

Defence of novation against a provisional claim on a promissory note. June 2.

[VOL. I, p. 95.]

DIETERMAN *vs.* CURLEWIS.

Signature to a promissory note when denied may be proved instanter. June 30.

[Vol. I, p. 42.]

Et vide NORDEN'S TRUSTEE *vs.* BUTLER, *vol.* 1, *p.* 52.

Waters and Herron *vs.* De Roubaix.

1834. Aug. 26.

Provisional sentence granted against the maker of a promissory note, who alleged an error in the date of the note, but did not sufficiently satisfy Court as to such error.

[Vol. I, p. 42.]

Deneys *vs.* Daniel.

1835. Feb. 10.

Double costs as the penalty of a mala fide denial of signature and ability to write.

[Vol. I, p. 44.]

Redelinghuys *vs.* Theunissen.

Provisional Sentence. Service. Tender. Costs.

Service of summons is sufficient demand for payment.

Where service was not made until four months after due date of a promissory note specifying no place of payment, if the defendant tender payment of the note on presentment to be made to him thereof, such tender will save him from the costs of summons, but not when he only makes such tender in Court on day of hearing.

May 1.

Redelinghuys *vs.* Theunissen.

Provisional sentence being prayed in respect of a promissory note made by the defendant, payable, no place specified, to A. B., or order, twelve months after date, of which the plaintiff was the holder by indorsation, the defendant admitted his liability for the debt and interest, but objected to pay any costs, on the ground that no presentment for payment had been made to him before the summons was served at his dwelling-house, in his absence, on the 10th April, 1835 (four months after the note was due), and that he had this morning tendered payment of the note and the interest thereon, without costs.

The Court held that the service of the summons was itself a sufficient demand for payment. (*Vide Chitty on Bills, p.* 321, 5*th Edition.*) And that if the defendant had, immediately after receiving service, tendered payment of the note, *on its being presented to him,* he would not have been liable for the costs even of the summons. But that the tender made this morning was not sufficient to free the defendant from costs; and gave judgment for plaintiff as prayed, with costs.

Et vide Brink *vs.* Gough, *ante p.* 256; Orlandini *vs.* Pope, *post p.* 260; Steytler *vs.* De Villiers, *post p.* 286.

Wicht *vs.* Faure.

Promissory Note. Provision. Costs.

In this case the Court (Wylde, C.J., absent) held that the debtor on a promissory note payable to A.B., or order, is not liable to the costs of a notice to pay served on him by an indorser, the holder of the note. 1835. May 19.

Low *vs.* Oberholzer.

Provisional sentence granted on a promissory note not expressing any causa debiti, and where defendant did not take it upon himself to deny value given. Aug. 11.

[Vol. I, p. 43.]

Keyter *vs.* Viljoen.

A promissory note referring in its terms to an antecedent agreement, ex facie unconditional, cannot, in a provisional case, be invalidated by parole evidence that such agreement was conditional, and its condition unfulfilled. Aug. 31.

[Vol. I, p. 44.]

Brink *vs.* Napier.

*A variance between the promissory note indorsed Baumgardt, and the copy served, signed Baumgar*ett, *is immaterial; so also where the note described the payee as "Baum*b-*gardt or bearer," and the note was endorsed "Baumgardt," objection was taken to the difference of the letter* b; *but the Court found indorsation unnecessary.* 1837.

[Vol. I, p. 119.]

Anderson *vs.* Hutton and Woest.

Notice of dishonour of a promissory note is not provable by affidavit in a provisional case. Aug. 1.

[Vol. I, p. 75.]

[*Et vide* Farmer *vs.* Breda and Another; De Ronde *vs.* Zeyler, *ante p.* 230; Trustees Randall *vs.* Haupt, *post p.* 281.]

ORLANDINI *vs.* POPE.

Provisional sentence. Summons. Tender. Costs.

Where maker of a promissory note by first post after receipt of summons caused a tender to be made, held sufficient to free from costs.

Costs not prayed for on the day of order made may be afterwards prayed for, but no costs given for such second application.

1839. Feb. 26. „ 28. Orlandini *vs.* Pope. Provisional sentence being prayed by the plaintiff as payee of a promissory note made by defendant, payable two months after date, no place of payment specified, the defendant consented to judgment for the amount of the note; but objected to costs, on the ground that no presentment for payment had been made to him before the summons was served on him at Beaufort (his domicile); and that he had by the first post thereafter instructed his attorney, Merrington, to tender payment of the debt and interest to the plaintiff's attorney. Merrington, immediately on receiving these instructions, did, on the 4th January, tender a cheque on the Cape of Good Hope Bank, signed by himself, for the amount of the debt and interest, to the plaintiff's attorney, who had refused to receive it without the costs of the summons and service being also paid; at the same time stating that he did not object to the cheque as the form of the tender. The plaintiff did not deny this tender and refusal; but referred to the case of *Redelinghuys vs. Theunissen, ante p.* 258. [*Et vide Brink vs. Gough, ante p.* 256; *Steytler vs. De Villiers, post p.* 286.] The Court held this tender sufficient to free the defendant from costs; and gave judgment for plaintiff as prayed, without costs.

N.B. The defendant did not this day ask for his costs.

Postea (28th February).—The defendant's counsel stated that through oversight he had not asked for his costs on the 26th, and now prayed for them. Ordered that the plaintiff do pay defendant the costs incurred by him on and previous to the 26th inst.; but not the costs of this application.

SMITH *vs.* CAMPBELL.

Provisional sentence. Title to suc. Insolvency. Ordinance No. 64. *Ord.* 6, 1843, § 126.

Aug. 1. *It is (by the provisions of Ordinance* 64) *a defence against a provisional claim on a promissory note that the payee who had indorsed the note was a non-rehabilitated insolvent, who could therefore give no valid title to the plaintiff.* [But by Ordinance No. 6, 1843, section 126, such indorsation is good if made after the confirmation of the account and plan of distribution.]

[Vol. I, p. 96, and note.]

[*Et vide* STRETCH *vs.* CAMPBELL, *infra.*]

NORDEN *vs.* MAGADAS.

Provisional sentence granted on a promissory note given by an insolvent after sequestration under Ordinance 64, for a new debt contracted subsequently to such sequestration. No execution, however, could take place against his property while under sequestration, nor, semble, execution issue against person. 1839. Dec. 6.

[Vol. I, p. 45.]

HOVIL & MATHEW *vs.* WOOD.

Circumstances entitling the maker of a promissory note to the same defences against indorsees as against the payee in a provisional claim; 1. Submission to arbitration between maker and payee; 2. No value given by plaintiffs to payee at all, or until after due date. 1840. Feb. 6.

[Vol. I, p. 97.]

BRINK *vs.* MINNAAR.

Provisional sentence refused against the defendant, who had written his signature below the word "accepted," across a promissory note, although the maker of the note had first been excussed. Feb. 13.

[Vol. I, p. 76.]

STRETCH *vs.* CAMPBELL.

Insolvency. Ordinance No. 64, §§ 9, 49, 50. Consideration of note.

O., an uncertificated insolvent, carried on business after his insolvency with the knowledge, although not with the express permission, of his trustees, and sold goods to C., who knew of his insolvency. C. paid O. with two notes in his favour or order. O. endorsed the notes to S., who also knew of the insolvency. Subsequently S. took from C., directly, without O.'s name thereupon, two other notes in lieu of the first-mentioned notes, and now sued C. on one of them. C. pleaded no consideration; but the Court held that the delivery up of the first two notes was sufficient consideration to found this action.

SEMBLE: *If S. had sued on the notes originally given, it being proved that the insolvent had given valuable consideration for them, S. would have successfully maintained the action, even if the trustees had intervened and claimed on the notes.*

1840. Aug. 31. 1841. Feb. 4. " 27.

Stretch *vs.* Campbell.

In this case plaintiff, in his declaration, sued defendant for payment of a promissory note dated 1st May, 1839, for £49 7s. 6d., made by defendant, in favour of plaintiff, payable four months after date.

Defendant, in his plea, pleaded, first, that the said note was obtained by plaintiff from defendant without any legal consideration for the same; secondly, that the said note and another for the same amount, £49 7s. 6d., were obtained by plaintiff from defendant in lieu of two other promissory notes, the one dated 9th September, 1838, for £48 15s., payable on 9th March, 1839, the other dated 1st November, 1838, for £50, payable on 1st February, 1839, both made by defendant, in favour of and delivered to one Joseph Osmond, then and still being an insolvent person, and whose estate then was and still is under sequestration, and were afterwards indorsed and delivered to plaintiff by Osmond, while he was so insolvent, and could not lawfully transfer the same, and was known by the plaintiff to be insolvent.

Plaintiff, in replication, first joined issue on the first plea; secondly, pleaded that the second plea was not sufficient in law to bar and preclude him from having his action; thirdly, that even if otherwise said second plea should be held to be sufficient, the plaintiff ought not to be barred by it from his action in this case; first, because when the said two promissory notes in it mentioned were indorsed and delivered to the said plaintiff by Osmond, the said Osmond was not known by plaintiff to be such an insolvent as in the said plea stated, and joined issue upon such knowledge with the said defendant; and, secondly, because the said two promissory notes were both by the said defendant drawn in favour of, and made payable *to the order* of, the said Osmond, while the defendant knew that the said Osmond was such insolvent, and that the said Osmond had thereby sufficient authority from the said defendant to endorse and deliver over the said promissory notes to the said plaintiff so as to charge the said defendant in this action of the said plaintiff.

1840. Aug. 31. 1841. Feb. 4. „ 27.

Stretch vs. Campbell.

In his rejoinder, the defendant, *inter alia* unnecessary to be here set forth, pleaded that, admitting the defendant to have been well aware of the insolvency of the said Osmond when he made the said promissory notes in his favour, the said Osmond was, notwithstanding, as an insolvent, incapable in law of endorsing the same to the plaintiff, and that the said endorsement so made thereof by Osmond to plaintiff, while Osmond's estate was under sequestration, was, by virtue of the Ordinance No. 64, absolutely void and of no effect.

The evidence proved that Osmond's estate was surrendered as insolvent in July, 1837. That subsequently, and while the sequestration was pending, and he uncertificated, he carried on business openly and with the knowledge of his trustees, in buying and selling goods, and had dealings in the purchase of goods with one of his trustees. That he had received the two notes of the 9th September, 1838, and 1st November, 1838, from defendant for goods and other valuable consideration given by him to defendant, defendant then well knowing that Osmond was an uncertificated insolvent, and that in April, 1839, after these notes were due, he indorsed them to plaintiff in payment of goods bought by him from plaintiff. That there was every reason to believe, from the publicity of Osmond's situation and affairs, that plaintiff, when the notes were indorsed to him, knew that Osmond was an uncertificated insolvent.

Porter, A.-G., for plaintiff, maintained that an insolvent has such a right over property acquired by him after and during his sequestration as entitles him to alienate and dispose of it so long as his trustees do not interfere and oppose the alienation, and that no third party can plead the right of the trustee in bar of the effect of any alienation or cession made by the insolvent. In fact, that the provisions of the 49th and 50th sections of Ordinance 64 were intended and were effectual merely to enable the trustees to administer and apply the estate for the benefit of the creditors, and to prevent the bankrupt from doing anything to defeat the right of the trustees to any part of the estate which they thought fit to claim.

2ndly. That the trustees in this case, by having knowingly permitted the insolvent to trade, nay, having actually dealt with him, were themselves barred from objecting to the indorsation, and, consequently, no third party could object to its validity.—(*Cooke's Bankrupt Law*, 1788, *vol.* 1, *p.* 369; *Cowper's Reports*, *p.* 569.)

1840. Aug. 31. 1841. Feb. 4. ,, 27.

Stretch *vs.* Campbell.

He maintained that by the law of England the future property of a bankrupt is as absolutely vested in his assignees as by Ordinance 64 the future property of an insolvent in this Colony is vested in his trustees. (*1st James I, c.* 15, § 13; *6th Geo. IV, c.* 16, § 63, 64; *1st and 2nd Wm. IV, c.* 56, § 25; *and quoted* 7 *East Repts., p.* 53, *Kitchen vs. Burton; Drayton vs. Dale,* 2, *Barn. and Cress., p.* 293; *Lee's Nisi Prius, vol.* 1, *p.* 314; *Archbold, p.* 222, *Edit.* 1837; *Byles on Bills, p.* 261, *Edit.* 1834; *Webb vs. Fox, Webb vs. Ward,* 7 *Term Reports, Durnford and East, pp.* 96 *and* 391.)

He maintained that on the principle of the decision in the English cases, the defendant having, by making the note payable *to the order of the insolvent* (*or to the insolvent or order*), expressly undertaken to pay it to whomsoever the insolvent should make an order for payment, was thereby barred from now objecting to pay the plaintiff, who holds the order for payment of the note taken. He quoted *Chitty on Bills, p.* 115, as to the case of notes made payable to a married woman. (*Coates vs. Davis,* 1 *Campbell,* 484.)

2ndly. He maintained that even supposing plaintiff could not have recovered on the original notes, he was, notwithstanding, entitled to recover on the note now sued on, and that the giving up of the original notes was in law a sufficient consideration to sustain the note now sued on.

Musgrave, contra, quoted *Baillie vs. Bishop,* 1 *East's Repts., p.* 432, as to notes payable to a married woman, and quoted *Chapman vs. Black,* 2 *Barn. and Ald., p.* 589, to show that plaintiff could not recover on the note now sued on, if he could not have sued on the original one for which it had been substituted; and quoted the ninth section of Ordinance No. 64, to prove the indorsation was null. (*Willis vs. Freeman,* 6 *East, p.* 658.) He commented on *Drayton vs. Dale,* showing that in that case the plaintiff and his immediate author were ignorant of the fact that Clarke, one of the previous indorsers, was at the time of his indorsation an uncertificated bankrupt, and therefore had taken the note *bonâ fide.* He quoted *Nyas vs. Adamson,* 2 *Barn. and Ald.,* 229; *Tenson vs. Francis,* 1 *Campbell, p.* 19.

Ebden, on the same side, quoted the decision of this Court in the case of *Smith vs. Campbell, 1st August,* 1839 (*Vol.* 1, *p.* 96); *Puffendorff. Abridgment, vol.* 3, *p.* 920; *Smith's Bankrupt Law.*

Cur. adv. vult.

Postea (27th February, 1841).—The Court gave judgment for plaintiff, as prayed, with costs of all the proceedings, as well in the Circuit as the Supreme Court.

The Court held that the sole question was, whether the plaintiff had given, or done that which is in law equivalent to giving, a consideration for the note sued on. The Court held that even on the supposition that the indorsation of Osmond, while uncertificated, was insufficient to have conveyed to plaintiff any right or title to the document of debt, *i.e.*, the original notes themselves, or to convey from Osmond to plaintiff the debt which, by granting these notes, defendant had contracted and constituted in favour of Osmond; yet that, as by the possession of these original notes, he might have been able to have made some claim for their contents against defendant, or might have procured from the trustees an indorsation to supply the defective indorsation of Osmond; or in the event of their refusing to indorse them, and on tendering the notes to the trustees, might have been entitled to regain possession of the goods which he had sold to Osmond, and on payment of which Osmond had indorsed the note; the transaction, which defendant voluntarily entered into with plaintiff, by which plaintiff, in consideration of getting the new note, now sued on, agreed to postpone any claim he might have, in virtue of the original bills or of his possession of them, directly against defendant until the period of payment stipulated in the new note, and by which he gave up to the defendant the possession of the original notes, and thus gave up all claim against defendant founded on his possession of those notes, and all remedy which he might have against or through the trustees, was a legal consideration given by him for the note sued on, sufficient to support this action, and to enable him to recover its amount.

1840. Aug. 31. 1841. Feb. 4. " 27.

Stretch *vs.* Campbell.

The Court held that, even if the action had been brought for payment of the notes granted by defendant to Osmond, and although the indorsation of Osmond should be held not sufficient to bar his trustees from recovering from plaintiff, or any other person, the *ipsa corpora* of the notes, nor to prevent the trustees from suing and recovering from defendant the amount of those notes, yet that the defendant, by having given to Osmond, for a valuable consideration, notes by which he promised to pay a certain amount *to the order* of Osmond, rendered himself liable to pay this amount to the holder of them, to whom they had been indorsed, *at least* when such holder had given a valuable consideration to Osmond for them, and that judgment must, under those circumstances, have been given in favour of plaintiff against defendant, even although the trustees had intervened in the action, and also claimed payment of the amount of the notes; and this, without regard to whether the trustees' claim was sustained against defendant or not.

1840. Aug. 31. 1841. Feb. 4. „ 27. Stretch *vs.* Campbell.

The Court, in giving this judgment, held it to be proved that defendant knew Osmond to be an uncertificated insolvent when he gave the notes, and that it made no difference whether, when plaintiff took the notes from Osmond, he knew (which MENZIES, J., held it to be proved he did) that Osmond was an uncertificated bankrupt. (*Vide Ordinance* 1843, *No.* 6, § 49; *Still vs. Gilbert,* 5*th November,* 1840.) The Court gave no decided opinion whether, notwithstanding this judgment, the trustees would be entitled to recover the original notes from the defendant or not.

MENZIES, J., held that this judgment in favour of plaintiff was, *per se,* no bar to their doing so.

The Court ordered that the notes, originally granted by defendant to Osmond and given up by plaintiff to defendant when defendant gave him the note now sued, should remain with the record in the possession of the Registrar, until further order of the Court should, on motion, be made with respect to them.

COLLISON & CO. *vs.* EKSTEEN.

1840. Nov. 30. *It is sufficient consideration to support a provisional claim on two promissory notes for £70 each, given at the same time for coals sold, although the coals on one note alone had been delivered, and those on the other note rejected as bad, the plaintiffs denying the defendant's right so to reject, and defendant not being able to prove his right by the production of liquid proof instanter.*

[Vol. I, p. 46.]

ELLIOTT BROTHERS *vs.* BREDA AND ANOTHER.

Nov. 30. *Provisional sentence given in favour of a bonâ fide holder against an indorser in blank, who alleged want of consideration between him and an intermediate party to whom he delivered the note for a specific purpose to which it was not applied.*

[Vol. I, p. 47.]

DE KOCK *vs.* RUSSOUW AND ANOTHER.

1841. June 24. *The word "Accepted" written across the face of a promissory note, with a signature below it, creates no liquid liability.*

[Vol. I, p. 78.]

SUTHERLAND *vs.* ELLIOTT BROTHERS.

It is a good defence against a claim by the payee of a promissory note that other securities had been given in payment by the maker, and accepted by the payee. 1841. July 12.

Per MENZIES, J.—SEMBLE. *That usury is a good defence.* [*Sed vide Dyason vs. Ruthven, Feb.* 1860, *as to Usury.*]

[Vol. I, p. 99.]

TAYLOR *vs.* ELLIOTT BROTHERS.

An indorsee of a promissory note without value liable to the same defences as his indorser. Aug. 2.

[Vol. I, p. 101.]

C. G. H. BANK *vs.* ELLIOTT BROTHERS AND ANOTHER.

Boná fide indorsees of a note held entitled to provisional sentence, notwithstanding the defendant had a good defence against the payee. Aug. 26.

[Vol. I, p. 102.]

LEVICKS & SHERMAN *vs.* EKSTEEN.

Provisional sentence given against the maker of a promissory note, notwithstanding, an allegation of payment to the payee after the note became due, the note having been presented by the holder to the maker when long overdue. 1842. Nov. 17.

[Vol. I, p. 49.]

RAWSTORNE *vs.* WOLHUTER.

Provisional sentence refused to a boná fide holder, where, before the word "sixty," in the body of the note, had been inserted the words "one hundred and," by the payee, as it was alleged.

Porter, A.-G., prayed for provisional sentence on a note of hand for £160, drawn by C. P. Wolhuter, in favour of the late H. Sandenberg, and of which the S. A. Bank are now the legal holders. Dec. 12. 1843. Feb. 14. Rawstorne *vs.* Wolhuter.

1842. Dec. 13. 1843. Feb. 14.

Rawstorne *vs.* Wolhuter.

Musgrave objected to provisional sentence on the ground that the promissory note sued on had been altered by inserting the words, "One hundred &" before the words "sixty;" and consequently that the defendant was not liable for more than £60, even although plaintiff was a *bonâ fide* holder. He maintained that it was evident from the crowded state of the letters, that the alteration had been made; and produced defendant's affidavit to the truth of his allegation, and a receipt by the payee who was alleged to have made the alteration, acknowledging that the defendant had signed a promissory note for £60 for him, which he promised to take up when due. And quoted *Smith's "Mercantile Law," pp.* 161, 162.

Porter, A.-G., contra, admitted that the affidavit which had been read was presumptive evidence of fraud sufficient to have put Sandenberg out of court on an application for provisional sentence. This application, however, was not made by Sandenberg, but by the South African Bank, who had given their money for the note; and he maintained that at the time when Wolhuter had affixed his name to the note, which was in the handwriting of Sandenberg, there was so great a blank left before the word "sixty" as to allow of the insertion of the words "One hundred," and before the figures £60, the insertion of the figure 1, in such a manner as not to be discoverable by the exercise of ordinary caution on the part of the indorser; and therefore that the objection now taken by defendant could not be maintained against a *bonâ fide* holder, which the Bank was admitted to be. Quoted *Thomson on Bills, p.* 70: "If a person sign his name as maker, drawer, acceptor, or indorser to a bill or note in which the sum is left blank, he is liable for whatever sum the holder chooses to fill up; and if he subscribes a blank bill stamp, he will be liable for the highest sum (when filled up) to which the stamp is applicable. In the same way, if a person subscribes a bill or note, where the sum is written in such manner, or such blanks are left, as allow it to be altered to a larger sum without giving the document that suspicious appearance which would attract the notice of a person exercising ordinary diligence, the subscriber will be liable to any *bonâ fide* holder for the increased sum. The principle of this doctrine appears to be, that the parties to the bill or note, by drawing or subscribing it when in such a state as to enable the holder to alter the sum without risk of detection, have led third parties to believe, either that the increased sum was that inserted in the document at the time of drawing it, or that the whole sum was inserted afterwards, by virtue of an implied authority, in a blank left for the purpose. With the actual authority given, third parties have nothing to do; they are concerned only with the obligation presumable *ex facie* of the bill which the debtor has sanctioned by his signature. In the first of the cases now cited, the Court, adopting this doctrine, sustained both against the acceptor and indorser, to the full extent, a bill in which the sum had been altered from '*eight*' to '*eighty-four*' pounds, there being so much room for the alteration that it was made without giving the bill a suspicious appearance. In the second case cited, there being two bills, one in which the words '*four hundred and*' had been added before '*fifty-eight*,' without appearing suspicious, and the other, in which an alteration had likewise been made, but so as to have a crowded appearance, the Court sustained the first bill against the acceptors to the full amount, in a question with an onerous holder; but found the other bill at first, good only for the original sum, and on a reclaiming petition, suspended the charge on it altogether." And *Byles on Bills, p.* 184: "A customer of a bank, leaving home, entrusted to his wife several blank forms of cheques, signed by himself, and desired her to fill them up according to the exigency of his business. She filled up one with the words '*fifty pounds two shillings*,' beginning the word fifty with a small letter in the middle of a line. The figures 52: 2, were also placed at a considerable distance to the right of the printed £. She gave the cheque, thus filled up, to her husband's clerk to get the money. He, before presenting it, inserted the words '*three hundred*' before the word '*fifty*' and the figure 3 between the printed £ and the figures 52: 2. It was presented, and the bankers paid it. The Court held that the improper mode of filling up the cheque had invited the forgery; and, therefore, that the loss fell on the customer, and not on the banker."

Provisional sentence refused.

[*Sed postea* (14th February, 1843).—In the principal case the Court, finding from the evidence that there was no cause to doubt the genuineness of the note as a note for £160, gave judgment for plaintiff for that amount, with costs.]

TRUTER *vs.* HEYNS.

1843. Feb. 9.

Payment to the payee of a promissory note is no answer in a provisional claim by the bonâ fide holder.

[Vol. I, p. 49.]

VERSTER *vs.* O'REILLY.

1843. Feb. 28. *Where a promissory note is made payable in a certain time after notice, such notice cannot be proved by a mere memorandum that it had been given purporting to be written by a notary public on the note. But must be supported by affidavit to that effect.*

[Vol. I, p. 78.]

ATKINSON *vs.* NORDEN.

July 12. *It is a material variance between a promissory note and the copy served to describe the note as for "the sum of and ten pounds," instead of "the sum of one hundred and ten pounds," &c.*

[Vol. I, p. 120.]

THOMSON, WATSON, & Co. *vs.* MALAN.

Promissory note. Indorsation of note originally not payable to order. Cession.

Where a note not originally made to order has been ceded by the payee to A. or order, held, that a simple indorsation by A. was sufficient to entitle his indorsee to sue, without requiring a formal cession.

Aug. 3.

Thomson, Watson, & Co. *vs.* Malan.

This was a claim for provisional sentence on the following note:

"Rds. two hundred and sixty-six and five skillings.—I, the undersigned, promise to pay six months after date, to Mr. Joseph Brooks, for value received.

"Klein Drakenstein, 1st September, 1841.

"J. P. MALAN."

On the back of which was written:

"I hereby cede this note to J. C. Behr or order."

Signed "Joseph Brooks, without holding myself responsible."

Signed "J. C. BEHR"—"JOSEPH BARRY."

Brand, for defendant, quoted *Van der Linden, p.* 677, and maintained that although the note had been legally transferred from the original payee by a formal cession, yet that this cession, although made to order, did not entitle the cessionary to transfer the note by simple indorsation.

1843. Aug. 3.

Thomson, Watson, & Co. *vs.* Malan.

The Court held that the principle on which a cession, instead of a simple indorsation, is required to transfer a note not made payable to order from the original payee to a third party, is in order to make the third party a cessionary, and therefore liable to every objection or defence competent to the maker of the note against the original payee, and to deprive the third party of the privilege which indorsers of notes made payable to order enjoy; and, therefore, as Behr had been made a cessionary by Brooks, and thus stood in Brooks's shoes,—and as every third party subsequently acquiring the note through Behr acquired it only subject to the same conditions under which it passed to Behr,—the mode in which it should be passed or transferred from Behr to any third party could not possibly injure or affect the maker of the note in any way whatever; consequently, there is no legal principle or reason for requiring a formal cession, instead of a simple indorsation, to pass the note from the cessionary, to whom and *his order* the note had been ceded by the original payee. And gave provisional sentence, as prayed, with costs.

TWENTYMAN & WARNER *vs.* NORDEN.

The fact of a note being dated in Cape Town has not in law the effect of making it payable there.

Information received that the maker, resident at Caledon, had "given up his residence here, and has gone with his wagons into the interior, and expects to be away three or four months," does not relieve the holder from presentation at the maker's last residence.

Alteration in a note in its date from the 22nd to 30th, with the knowledge of the maker, does not discharge him from liability, and therefore does not make presentment to him unnecessary, nor even, as regards the maker's liability, where such alteration has been made without his knowledge.

A waiver on the 23rd, the first of the abovementioned dates, by the indorser of presentment to the maker does not bind such indorser, where, in fact, the 30th was the correct date of the note.

Waiver of presentment, what is not a sufficient.

The holder of a note or bill must present it for payment on the day it becomes due.

1844. Jan. 12. Aug. 20. „ 22. „ 29.

Twentyman and Warner *vs.* Norden.

This was an action brought by plaintiffs, indorsees and holders of the following promissory note:

"£276 17s. 3d., due 22nd December.

"Cape Town, June 30, 1843.

"Six months after date I promise to pay Mr. Benj. Norden or order, the sum of £276 17s. 3d., for value received in goods.

"(Signed) WM. HOMEWOOD."

and blank indorsed by defendant.

The plaintiffs had formerly claimed provisional sentence on it, when *Brand,* for the defendant, objected that the note had not, when due, been presented for payment to Homewood, and therefore that the plaintiffs were not entitled to demand payment from defendant as the indorser.

In reply, plaintiffs produced a protest by John Reid, notary public, which set forth that on the 23rd of December, 1843, "I, the notary, at the request of plaintiffs, repaired to Benjamin Norden, the indorser of the said promissory note, and exhibited the same to him, and informed him that Mr. Homewood, the maker thereof, resided at Caledon, and that I had lately been informed by letter from J. S. Needham, of Caledon, that the said Mr. Homewood had locked up his house, and had gone into the interior, and would not return for some time, and demanded payment thereof, whereupon he replied, 'This is payable upon the 30th December instant; it must have been made payable upon the 30th, before it was delivered to Twentyman & Warner.' That on the 2nd of January instant (the 31st December was Sunday, and the 1st January a holiday), I, the said notary, again repaired to the said Benjamin Norden, exhibited to him the said note, and demanded payment thereof, whereupon he replied, 'I wish to know the answer of the maker.' That I, the said notary, then presented the said note to Thomas Christian, Cashier of the Cape of Good Hope Bank, and G. Rawstorne, Cashier of the South African Bank, respectively, and received for answer from each, 'The maker has no funds in the bank.' That afterwards, on the same day, I, the said notary, repaired to the said B. Norden, and gave him notice of the answers so received by me, the notary, from the said Thomas Christian and Godfrey Rawstorne, all which being unsatisfactory," &c.

The plaintiffs maintained, first, that in consequence of the note being dated at Cape Town, and not made payable at any other place, it was by construction of law, made *payable at Cape Town,* as much as if those words had been expressly contained in it. Secondly, that where a note was made payable at a particular town, in which the maker could not be found when the note became due, presentment at the banks carrying on business in that town was equivalent to personal presentment to the maker.

1844. Jan. 12. Aug. 20. „ 22. „ 29. — Twentyman and Warner vs. Norden.

The Court held that the fact of the note being dated in Cape Town had not in law the effect of making it payable at Cape Town, and therefore it was unnecessary to give any decision in this case as to what would otherwise have been the legal effect of such presentment as had been made at the two banks.

The plaintiffs, thirdly, maintained that in respect of the circumstances concerning Homewood, stated in the first part of the protest, the plaintiffs were relieved from the necessity of presenting the note to the maker either personally or at his residence, and were entitled at once to demand payment from the indorser.

The Court held that those circumstances had not the legal effect attributed to them by plaintiffs, and refused provisional sentence, with costs.

The plaintiffs thereafter proceeded with the principal case.

The declaration averred that the two presentments of the note by Reid, stated in his evidence and in the protest to have been made on the 23rd and 30th December, were made on the 22nd and 29th December.

In the course of the trial it was proved, or admitted by the parties, that in June, 1843, plaintiffs sold to defendant a quantity of wheat;—that the defendant before receiving delivery of this wheat resold a portion of it to Homewood, who in payment thereof made the promissory note in question in favour of defendant, who indorsed it to plaintiffs in part payment of the wheat.

This note, including the words "due on the 22nd December," was proved to be in the handwriting of Mr. Burnie, a partner of defendant's son, and to have been delivered by him, then dated "22nd June," to Homewood for his signature, who took it away with him without having altered the date. Burnie had not seen the note since till shown him at the trial. It was admitted that the date had been altered to the 30th before it was indorsed and delivered by defendant to plaintiffs. No other evidence or explanation was offered by either party as to the time when or the person by whom the alteration had been made. Homewood had occupied, under a lease from Mr. Geering, a house and store in Caledon, during 1842 and 1843. On the 2nd December, Mr. Reid, at the desire of Dunell & Stanbridge, had

1844. Jan. 12. Aug. 20. " 22. " 29.

Twentyman and Warner *vs.* Norden.

addressed a letter to Homewood at Caledon, respecting a note of his then held by them, which became due in December; and by the post of the 20th he received the following letter from Mr. Needham of Caledon:

"Caledon, 19th December, 1844.

"J. Reid, Esq.

"Dear Sir,—Being authorized by Mr. Homewood to open all letters that may arrive here to his address during his absence, I beg to inform you, in reply to yours of the 2nd instant, which only arrived here per post of the 16th instant, that Mr. H. has given up his residence here altogether, and has gone with his wagons down the country to sell his merchandise, and he expects to be away about three or four months.

"I remain, &c.,

"J. S. NEEDHAM."

Mr. Reid received this note on the 23rd December, in order that, as a notary, he might, at the instance of plaintiffs, demand payment of it from defendant, and, if necessary, protest it. The notarial protest above quoted was put in.

Mr. Reid, in the course of the evidence given by him, stated: On the 23rd December, I presented the note to defendant at his place of business, and demanded payment. He took the note and looked at it, and said, "I can't pay it; the banks have not been liberal with their discounts lately, and I hope Twentyman & Warner will take my note at three months," and requested me to ask them to do so. I told him I had received a letter from Mr. Needham, of Caledon, in which he said that Homewood had locked up his place there, and gone away altogether. Defendant said, "I fully expected that I would have to pay this note." I said, "You see there has been an alteration in the date of this note; from the appearance of the figures I think the alteration has been made by yourself." He looked at it, and said, "Yes, it has been altered, but the figures are not mine; I could not write so well." He then produced a memorandum of Twentyman & Warner, I think, but I am not positive, in Warner's writing, and he said, "You see from this it must have been altered before I gave it to Twentyman & Warner." When he spoke about giving his own note at three months, he did not say "that he did so without prejudice," nor did he then say, "Mind I am speaking to you, not as a notary, but confidentially." I then went away. I told Warner of defendant's proposal about his note. Afterwards, I think on the Monday following, I again saw defendant, and told him Mr. Warner declined taking his note. Nothing more passed then, except that defendant complained it was unkind in him. On Saturday, the 30th December, I presented the note to him again, and said that, as the day of payment was the 30th, and as next day was Sunday, and Monday New Year's Day and a holiday, I would present it again on Tuesday. He said he would take no advantage of that. [See note at the end of this report.] I went to defendant on Tuesday, the 2nd January, and again demanded payment of the note. He said, "Will Mr. Warner not take my note?" I said he had declined. He asked me to go again to Warner and ask him, adding the words, "*Remember, I do this without prejudice.*" I went to Warner, who declined. I returned to defendant and told him so. He then said, "I request to know the answer of the maker." I replied, "Very well," and left him. I saw him again on the 2nd, and told him I had been at the two banks with the note, and that they had said they had no funds of Homewood. I saw defendant again on the 6th, when I went to demand payment of another note due by him to plaintiffs, but having no connection with Homewood's. He said he had not received a remittance to take up this, and at his request I agreed to assist him to do so. He then said, "Could you not also assist me to take up the other," meaning Homewood's, as I understood, as it was the only other note of his I had anything to do with. I said I could not. I neither made any presentment of the note to Homewood, nor did I write to him. Between the 23rd December and 2nd January I made no inquiries, except verbal, in Cape Town, as to where Homewood was. I took no other steps for this purpose before the 12th January, when I wrote to Needham on the subject. I did not in my protest mention all the particulars which I have now detailed of my conversations with defendant on the 23rd and 30th December and 2nd January, because I did not then think it would be necessary to do so. I considered the conversation which had taken place between us on the 6th January sufficient to prove the waiver by him of the want of due presentment which was all I considered necessary.

Defendant called witnesses to explain away or contradict some of Mr. Reid's statements, but as, in giving judgment, the Court proceeded on the assumption that Mr. Reid's statement was in every respect correct, it is unnecessary to report that evidence.

It was proved by the evidence of Geering, landlord of the premises which had been occupied by Homewood, in Caledon, that Homewood's lease of those premises expired in November last, and that he had been allowed by Geering to continue his occupation till the 4th December, when

1844. Jan. 12. Aug. 20. " 22. " 29.

Twentyman and Warner *vs.* Norden.

about midday he left them; that Geering knew of his intended departure a month before it took place; that he took with him four ox wagons loaded with goods, which had stood for five or six days in the public street before his house, while he was loading them; that Homewood said he was going on *togt* with these goods; that this was generally known in Caledon; he made no secret of it; it was public, everybody knew it. That when Homewood left Caledon on the 14th December, he had no longer any right to or in any part of Geering's premises, the key of which he delivered to Geering. That he said nothing to him of returning to Caledon. This evidence as to the notoriety of Homewood's intended departure was confirmed by the evidence of Major Barnes, the Resident Magistrate, and Mr. Needham, who added to the facts mentioned in his letter to Mr. Reid, that Homewood had told him before he left Caledon that he was going into the country to try to dispose of his goods, realize their value, and remit it to Cape Town.

None of these witnesses knew where Homewood now was.

Postea (22nd August).—The *Attorney-General* argued that the variance as to the dates was immaterial. 2nd. That the removal of the maker of the note from his former domicile, coupled with the fact that he had not since acquired any other domicile, freed the plaintiffs from the necessity of proving any presentment to him at Caledon, in order to render the defendant, the indorser of the note, liable to plaintiffs. And that as plaintiffs had obtained knowledge of those facts, it was unnecessary for them to have made any inquiry as to them, or after Homewood, seeing it was clear from the evidence that they could not by using any reasonable diligence discover where Homewood had gone to. 3rd. That defendant, by his conduct on the 23rd and 30th December, had waived the necessity of any presentment by plaintiffs to Homewood, and that what took place on the 6th January was a confirmation of the previous waiver. 4th. That the alteration in the date of a note is a material alteration, and if made without the knowledge or consent of the maker, renders the note invalid against him. That this alteration must be deemed in law to have been made without the maker's knowledge or consent, until the contrary be proved, which defendant, on whom the *onus* lay, had failed to do. Consequently, that as this alteration was admitted to have been made before the plaintiffs got it from defendant, the plaintiffs in a question with defendant were not bound to have presented the note to the maker.

Brand, for defendant, argued *contra*.

Cur. adv. vult.

Postea (29th August).—The Court gave judgment for defendant, as prayed, with costs. 1844. Jan. 12. Aug. 20. " 22. " 29. Twentyman and Warner *vs.* Norden.

The Court held that as the averments in the declaration as to the dates of the 22nd and 29th December are averments only that notice of dishonour had been given by plaintiff and a *waiver* given by defendant on those days, the variance between those averments and the evidence as to those dates is not material.

The Court held that under all the circumstances proved in this case, the legal presumption is, that the alteration in the date was made by or with the knowledge of Homewood, and consequently that there was no such invalidity of the note as was sufficient to discharge Homewood from liability for and on it, and consequently render presentment to him unnecessary. (*Roscoe on Evidence, p.* 193.)

The Court held that no authority has been shown for holding that any invalidity of the note as respects the maker, except that arising from a breach of the Stamps Acts, *even in England,* renders presentment for payment by the holder to the maker unnecessary; consequently, that presentment was necessary in this case to Homewood, even although the alteration had been made without his knowledge or consent.

The Court held that as, for the reason's given above, the 30th December must be held to be the day when the note became due by Homewood, nothing that passed between Mr. Reid and defendant on the 23rd could be a *waiver* by defendant of laches of plaintiffs, because plaintiffs could not *then* be in laches in respect of want of previous presentment for payment.

The Court held that what passed on that day between Mr. Reid and defendant, assuming Mr. Reid's evidence to be in every respect correct, is not sufficient to warrant the proposition that defendant on that day *dispensed* with due presentment for payment to Homewood by plaintiffs when the note should have become due.

The Court held that even if the note had been really due and payable by Homewood on the 22nd, there is no evidence that, before defendant said what he then did say, he had been informed by Mr. Reid, or knew, that there had not been due presentment, or equivalent to due presentment, to Homewood; consequently, that what he then said, even if it would otherwise have amounted to a *waiver,* cannot be held to have been a *waiver,* binding on him after he discovered that due presentment had not been made.

The Court held that what took place between Mr. Reid and defendant on the 30th December had no other legal effect than to make what afterwards took place between

1844. Jan. 12. Aug. 20. " 22. " 29.

Twentyman and Warner vs. Norden.

them on the 2nd January be deemed to have taken place, and have the same legal effect as if it had taken place, on the 30th December.

The Court held that what was said by defendant on the 2nd January, as to his note being taken in payment, being stipulated by him to be said "without prejudice," had not the effect of a *waiver* of due presentment, even if it would otherwise have had (which the Court considered it would not) that effect if that stipulation had not been used.

The Court held that what passed between Mr. Reid and defendant on the 6th January was with Mr. Reid *personally, and not as the agent for plaintiffs,* and could have no legal effect in a question between defendant and plaintiffs.

The Court held that the plaintiffs had, previously to the 23rd, ascertained that Homewood had removed from what had been his residence at Caledon, and that the house *there,* previously occupied by him, had ceased to be his residence; and that a presentment at that house, even although confirmed by a regular protest for non-payment, would not have been due presentment, to render the defendant liable.

The Court held that the plaintiffs, having ascertained that Homewood had removed from his previous residence, were bound to have made every possible and reasonable inquiry after him to endeavour to find out *where he had removed to,* unless Homewood had been proved to have *absconded,* or gone away under such circumstances that he could not have been traced from Caledon, *if an attempt to do so had been made.*

The Court held that it was proved that plaintiffs had made no inquiry whatever as to where Homewood had gone from Caledon; that Caledon was the place at which the inquiry ought to have been commenced; that Homewood proved *not* to have *absconded;* and that plaintiffs had failed to prove that inquiry, if commenced at Caledon, would not have enabled them to find Homewood personally within a reasonable time, if reasonable diligence had been used. (*Vide Chitty on Bills, 8th ed. pp.* 307, 400, 401, 387, 388.)

Note.—It having appeared that all or some of the notaries practising in Cape Town had acted upon a general but erroneous opinion, that because the maker or acceptor of a note or bill has the whole of the day (at least within business hours) on which it falls due, to pay it, therefore it was not competent to make the formal demand for payment, and protest it, until the day after that on which the note or bill became due, the Court stated that it is necessary for the holder of a note or bill to present it for payment on the day on which it became due, otherwise he will expose himself to the objection of want of due presentment.

1844. July 12. Aug. 20.

Twentyman and Warner *vs.* Norden.

KIDSON *vs.* CAMPBELL AND JOOSTE.

Joint acceptors, drawers, and indorsers are liable, singuli in solidum, unless the contrary is expressed in the bill. (Overruling Rens vs. Cantz and Another, ante p. 231).

Feb. 2. April 12. Aug. 9.

Kidson *vs.* Campbell and Jooste.

In this case, the plaintiff claimed provisional sentence on the following promissory note:

"Cradock, 9th August, 1843.

"£70.

"Three months after date I promise to pay to Messrs. J. P. Vester and C. J. Jooste, or order, the sum of £70, for value received, payable at the office of Mr. J. J. Stone, in Graham's Town.

"F. CAMPBELL."

and endorsed in blank by Vester and Jooste, of which he is the lawful holder, against Campbell, the maker, and Jooste as indorser.

The Court gave provisional sentence against Campbell, as prayed; but a doubt having arisen as to the extent of Jooste's liability, whether for the whole or only for a half, the case was postponed for further hearing. It was admitted that Vester's estate had been placed under sequestration, as insolvent, on the 1st November, 1842, before the bill became due.

Postea (12th April, 1844).—This day, *Porter, A.-G.*, quoted *Evans' Pothier, part* 2, 3, § 7, *note to pp.* 55, 11, and 62, to show that the general rule of this Colony is that *correi debendi* are liable only *pro rata.* He quoted *Bell, last Edition,* 1 *vol., p.* 345, § 4; *More's Edition of Stair, p.* 118, *App.;* and *Thomson on Bills,* 76 *and* 232; to show that, although the general rule in Scotland is the same with the general rule of the Dutch law, yet that joint drawers and acceptors are liable jointly and severally unless the contrary is expressed. He quoted *Pardessus on Mercantile Law, part* 3, *tit.* 3, *cap.* 2, § 4, *No.* 367, 182, to show that the law of France is in this respect the same

1844. Feb. 2. April 12. Aug. 9.

Kidson vs. Campbell and Jooste.

with that of Holland. And, in order to show that the law of Holland and of this Colony was the same with that of Scotland and France, he quoted *Heineccius on Bills of Exchange, edited by Reitz, pp.* 200, 279, 280, 5 *cap.* § *n.* 15; *Grotius cum Notis Schorer,* 3 *B.* 45, § 18, *n.* 12, 13; *Van der Keessel, Thes.* 595, 594; and *Uhl. Wissel Respons.,* 1 *vol., p.* 532, *Resp.* 69.

The Court ordered the case to stand over till the Bench should be full by MUSGRAVE, J., being present.

Postea (9th August, 1844).—In respect of the authorities last above quoted, the (*full*) Court found that joint acceptors, drawers, and endorsers are liable *singuli in solidum,* unless the contrary is expressed in the bill. And gave provisional sentence against Jooste, as prayed, with costs. Holding that the case of *Rens vs. Cantz, Faure, and Neethling,* 26*th August,* 1843 (*ante p.* 231), where it was found that three persons who had unconditionally accepted a bill drawn on them were liable only *pro rata,* ought not to be followed as a precedent, seeing that in it the point as to the liability of each of the defendants *singuli in solidum* had been given up by the plaintiff, and that the Court had not then had the above authorities brought under their notice.

BIRKWOOD *vs.* VAN ROOYEN.

Feb. 20. *Provisional sentence granted on a promissory note where the signature had been previously denied, and the plaintiff had then failed to prove the same, but refused on that account for the costs to which the plaintiff was put by such denial.*

[Vol. I, p. 50.]

DOBIE *vs.* LAWTON.

June 6. *Circumstances entitling the maker of a promissory note to claim that the question whether the holder of the note was liable to the same defences as the original payee should be tried in the principal case, viz.: agreement between maker and payee to renew, and action by plaintiff, the holder, on the basis of this agreement.*

[Vol. I, p. 103.]

Searight & Co. *vs.* Lawton.

It is a good defence against a provisional claim on a promissory note that the plaintiff, with other creditors, had entered into an agreement to give time to the defendant on certain condition. 1844. June 6.

Evidence: The Court refused to allow the plaintiff to prove instanter that two of the creditors had not signed.

[Vol. I, p. 105.]

Dickson, Burnie, & Co. *vs.* Lawton.

Provisional sentence refused on a promissory note given, on renewal of another promissory note, with respect to which the plaintiff, as well as the other holder of notes of the defendant, had agreed to give him time on certain conditions. June 6.

[Vol. I, p. 109.]

Borradaile & Co. *vs.* Lawton.

Circumstances as to agreement to give time amounting to a defence against a provisional claim or a promissory note. June 6.

[Vol. I, p. 110.]

Trustee of Randall *vs.* Haupt.

Affidavit held incompetent to prove indorser's waiver of due negotiation. July 12.

Presentment on the third day after that on which the note became due is not due negotiation in a question with the indorser.

There are no days of grace in this Colony.

[Vol. I, p. 79.]

[*Et vide* Cruywagen *vs.* Oliviera and Another, *ante p.* 254.]

Dickson, Burnie, & Co. *vs.* Harley.

Defence against the indorsees of a promissory note, that the note had been indorsed by the payee long after it was due, the circumstances being such as not to entitle the payee to provisional sentence. July 12.

[Vol. I, p. 112.]

Beukes *vs.* Van Wyk.

Notarial Protest. Tender. Costs. Evidence.

Where a note was made payable at a particular place "in the month of October," and notarial protest was made on the 22nd November, such protest held unnecessary, and costs thereof disallowed.

In such a case the 31st October must be deemed the day of payment.

Where a note is made payable at a particular place, on a particular day, and is presented on behalf of the creditor at that place and not paid, he is entitled to the fair costs of such presentment, although the notary have to travel a far distance to make it. But not if the note be duly paid.

1844. Dec. 12. — Beukes *vs.* Van Wyk.

The defendant had given to the plaintiff the following promissory note:

"I, the undersigned, acknowledge to be indebted to Mr. G. Beukes the sum of 230 rds., promising to pay in the month of October, 1844. Payable at Mr. Andries du Toit's, in the Voorste Nieuwveld.

"A. A. van WYK."

The plaintiff did not make any demand for payment at Du Toit's at any time in the month of October, or until the 22nd November, when he caused Mr. Kinnear, a notary public, to go there and present the note for payment. Kinnear's notarial protest set forth that on the 22nd November he repaired "to the dwelling-house of Mr. Andries du Toit, in the Voorste Nieuwveld, and then and there presented to him the said promissory note, and demanded payment thereof, when he replied, 'I have not, and never had, any funds to pay the same.'"

Thereafter, plaintiff obtained a summons against defendant, for payment of the above note, which was served personally on the defendant, in Cape Town, on the 7th December. Before the return day of the summons defendant tendered payment of the debt, and the previous costs, but refused to pay the expense of the notarial protest, which, in consequence of the great distance the notary had to travel, was upwards of £30.

Under these circumstances, the only question which was this day at issue between the parties was, as to the defendant's liability for the costs of the protest. The plaintiff maintained that Du Toit's answer, as set forth in the protest, must be held to prove that defendant had no funds at Du Toit's to meet the bill in the month of October.

The Court held that the notarial protest affords legal evidence of nothing more than that the bill was presented on the 22nd November, and payment refused; and that, even although it should be held to prove that Du Toit *said* he never had had funds to pay the note, that statement made by Du Toit was no evidence that he had not had funds.

1844. Dec. 12.

Beukes *vs.* Van Wyk.

Plaintiff then tendered an affidavit to that effect, made by Du Toit before Mr. Kinnear in his capacity as justice of the peace.

The Court held that an affidavit was not admissible evidence to prove this fact; and that if plaintiff considered the proof of this fact material to his case, he must proceed with the principal case, and prove it there.

The Court held that the 31st of October must be deemed to be the date of payment of a note bearing to be payable *in the month of October.* That where a note is made payable on a certain day, at a certain place, and payment is not demanded on that day at that place, the debtor is neither under any obligation to have, nor is there any legal presumption that he will have, the funds for payment of the note at that place after that day; consequently, after the lapse of the prescribed day, the holder of the note is not required to present the note at that place, and his making such subsequent presentment there will not be held to be a demand for payment made to the debtor. The taking of a notarial protest for non-payment at that place, after the prescribed day, must, therefore, be useless and unnecessary; consequently, the creditor cannot be entitled to demand the expense of making such notarial protest from the debtor.

The Court held that when the creditor causes a note to be presented *on the day it is payable at the place of payment,* and payment is refused, he will be entitled to the cost of a notarial protest for non-payment taken there, however much it may amount to, provided it be fairly charged according to the distance travelled; because, to entitle him to sue for provisional sentence he must prove this demand, and because a notarial protest is the only evidence of this demand which it is competent for him to give in a provisional case. And it is just the debtor should pay the creditor the expense of procuring that evidence, which the debtor's default to pay at the time and place prescribed has made it necessary for the creditor to procure in order to enforce payment. But if, when the note is presented at the time and place prescribed, the debtor has funds there and causes it to be paid, of course he will not be liable to the creditor for any expense incurred by the creditor in procuring evidence for the purpose of being made use of, *if payment had not been duly made at the time and place prescribed.*

1844. Dec. 12. — Beukes *vs.* Van Wyk. On these grounds, the Court held that the plaintiff is not entitled to provisional sentence for the costs of the protest; and gave judgment for plaintiff, for 230 rds., and costs as tendered, condemned him to pay the defendant's costs incurred since the summons, and refused provisional sentence for the costs of the protest, reserving right to plaintiff, if so advised, to proceed with the principal case for the recovery of those costs.

NORDEN *vs.* CAUVIN.

1845. May 29. *A promissory note payable "as soon as a bill of exchange referred to in it shall be discounted," is an illiquid document.*

[Vol. I, p. 80.]

JOHNSTONE *vs.* KOTZE.

Promissory Note. Presentment. Tender. Costs.

Where an accepted acknowledgment is made payable on presentation, the Sheriff's service of a summons for the amount is not such presentment, and where a defendant had under these circumstances tendered the amount of the note without costs, the Court upheld his right so to do.

Nov. 27. — Johnstone *vs.* Kotze. The plaintiff in this case claimed provisional sentence on the following document:

"Rds. 950.—I accept to pay to Mr. W. P. Low, or order, or presentation, the sum of Rds. 950, being for value received, for which this serves as an acknowledgment.

"H. P. KOTZE.

"Endorsed W. P. Low."

The *Attorney-General,* for defendant, alleged that this document, the verity of which he admitted, had never been presented to him for payment, nor any demand made upon it before the summons was served on the 18th, at his residence in the country, on his wife, during his absence in town. That on the 21st instant, he was informed by the Sheriff's officer in Cape Town that the summons had been served at his house in the country, whereupon he, on the same day, by the notary Maynier, notarially tendered the said sum of Rds. 950 to the plaintiff's attorney, who refused to receive it unless the costs also were paid. And therefore, while he admitted the debt, he maintained that not only was he not liable in costs, but was entitled to his costs. 1845. Nov. 27. Johnstone *vs.* Kotze.

Ebden, for plaintiff, maintained that even if there had been no previous presentment the service of the summons, although the Sheriff's officer serving it had not the document of debt in his possession when he served it, was a sufficient presentment to place the defendant *in morâ*, and consequently to make interest run from the date of the service; and that, as the defendant had not tendered the interest which had become due between the 18th and the 21st instant, the tender was an insufficient one, and did not relieve the defendant from the liability to costs.

The Court held that the service of the summons was not a presentment. The case was postponed till the 12th January, to give the plaintiff time to prove an alleged presentment to or demand on the defendant before the service of the summons.

VILLIERS *vs.* DE KOCK.

Promissory Note. Presentment.

Presentment to maker of note after summons is good, but unnecessary unless defendant on receipt of the summons alleged that on that day he had funds.

This was a claim by the plaintiff for provisional sentence against the defendant for £36 10s. 9d., in respect of a promissory note by defendant to plaintiff, payable on the 21st February, 1846, at the Colonial Bank. 1846. Feb. 28. Villiers *vs.* De Kock.

The summons was taken out and served personally on defendant on the 24th February.

Defendant did not appear.

Plaintiff put in the note and a notarial protest, dated 27th February, which set forth that on the 27th February, the notary presented the note for payment at the Colonial Bank to the cashier, who replied "no funds, nor had Mr. de Kock any funds in the Bank on the 21st instant."

The Court held that, as against the defendant, the maker of the note, the notarial protest, although showing that the presentment at the Bank had been made after the service of the summons, was good *primâ facie* evidence that defendant had had no funds there on the 21st, and that he need not have produced the protest at all to entitle him to provisional sentence, unless the defendant had appeared and alleged that he had funds in the Bank on the 21st, and had been injured by the non-presentment of the note on that day. (*Vide Story on Bills, p.* 414, § 335.)

Steytler *vs.* De Villiers.

Summons. Presentment. Costs. Tender.

Where the holder of a note not made payable at a particular place summoned the defendant without presentment, the Court awarded the costs to defendant; but, holding that defendant, immediately on service, should have tendered the amount on condition of the note being presented, which he had not done until the day of hearing, gave plaintiff the costs of the day.

There must be an actual presentment of such note, and not a mere letter of demand before summons.

1846. June 13.

Steytler *vs.* De Villiers.

Provisional sentence being prayed in respect of a promissory note made by the defendant, payable to J. A. Pesold, or order, on the 1st May, 1846 (no place mentioned), of which the plaintiff was the holder by indorsation. The defendant admitted the debt, but objected to pay the costs, on the ground of no presentment of it having been made to him by plaintiff for payment, and that he had this morning tendered the amount of the debt. He referred to the Sheriff's return, which showed that the summons had been served on his wife at his dwelling-place, in the district of Stellenbosch, in his absence, on the 4th instant, and that consequently he had no knowledge of the service of the summons for some days afterwards.

The plaintiff put in an affidavit, sworn by the clerk of his attorneys, setting forth that he had on the 25th May, 1846, put into the Government post, prepaid, a letter addressed to the plaintiff at Klapmuts (his residence), informing defendant that plaintiff was the holder of the said note, and requesting payment within eight days.

The defendant put in his own affidavit that the said note was never presented to him for payment, and that he was never asked to pay the same, and had received no intimation of where the said note was, except by the summons served on him.

The Court held that it was immaterial to inquire whether the defendant had received the letter of the 25th May, 1846, because the defendant was not obliged to regard any such demand (as it contained) for payment; the note itself not having been presented to him, which, as there was no place of payment specified in it, the defendant was bound to cause to be presented to the defendant personally, or at his place of business or residence. That under these circumstances the defendant was not liable to pay either the expense of the summons or of its service. But that on being made aware that the summons had been served at his residence, it was the duty of defendant, without any unnecessary delay, to have tendered to the plaintiff or his attorney to pay the debt *on the note being presented to him for that purpose,* and that as he had unnecessarily delayed making this tender until this morning, when the plaintiff had already incurred the costs of this day, he must pay these last-mentioned costs. 1846. June 13. Steytler vs. De Villiers.

The Court, therefore, gave judgment for plaintiff, as prayed, with the costs of this day only.

PHILLIPS & KING, Q.Q. PORCIA, *vs.* FARMER.

Interest on an English promissory note not specifying place of payment, is calculated according to the rate of interest due in England, and is reckoned until the date of payment in the Colony, and not until the date of receiving the capital in England.

In this case the Court gave provisional sentence in favour of the plaintiffs against the defendant, in virtue of a promissory note, dated London, 7th July, 1843, made by defendant in favour of Porcia, the plaintiff, payable twelve months after date, and not specifying any place of payment. 1847. Mar. 12.

Porter, A.-G., for plaintiff, claimed interest at the colonial rate of 6 per cent.; or, if the interest was awarded at the English rate, of 5 per cent., then that it should be continued until the period at which the principal remitted from this Colony arrived in London.

Brand, for defendant, maintained that plaintiff was only entitled to interest at the English rate of 5 per cent., and only until the principal was paid here.

And so the Court found.

HAW *vs.* CODRINGTON & MCMASTER.

What not due protest for non-payment as against indorser.

The plaintiff in this case claimed provisional sentence against Codrington as the maker of a promissory note for £33, falling due on the 24th September, 1847, in favour of McMaster, or order, and against McMaster as indorser. 1848. Feb. 1. Haw vs. Codrington and McMaster.

The Court gave provisional sentence against Codrington.

The summons was personally served on McMaster, for whom, however, no appearance was made.

The plaintiff put in a notarial protest, setting forth that

1848. Feb. 1.

Haw *vs.* Codrington and McMaster.

on the 24th September, 1847, the notary "at the request of Messrs. Herron & Co., then holders of the said promissory note, did address a letter to Edward Codrington, the drawer thereof, at Uitenhage, demanding payment of the same, and did put the said letter, on the 25th day of the said month, into the General Post Office at Graham's Town, but have not received any reply thereto. Wherefore I, the said notary, at the request aforesaid, have protested, and by these presents do protest, against the maker, &c., &c., &c. That afterwards, to wit, on the said 24th day of September, &c., I, the said notary, also at the request aforesaid, did take the said original promissory note to the residence of the said David McMaster, in High-street, Graham's Town, by whom the same is indorsed, and then and there speaking to the said David McMaster, I exhibited to him the said promissory note, and gave him notice of the dishonour thereof by the said Edward Codrington, wherepon he replied 'I hold myself responsible, but let Captain Codrington be sued; it ought to be paid.' Thus done and protested at Graham's Town aforesaid, the day, month, and year first before written."

Wylde, C.J., and Musgrave, J., took the objection that the note had not been duly presented for payment to Codrington, and therefore had not been duly protested for non-payment; and that when McMaster made the above-mentioned reply to the notary it must be held that he believed the note had been presented to Codrington and protested, and was in ignorance of what really had taken place; and refused provisional sentence.

Menzies, J., held that when he made the said reply McMaster must be presumed either to have been informed of what really had been done, or to have made the said reply without inquiring or caring whether the note had been duly protested for dishonour or not, and to have intended to waive such presentment and protest, provided Codrington should be sued; and that, therefore, provisional sentence should be given.

Kilian & Co. *vs.* Tredoux.

Mar. 13. *Provisional sentence granted on a promissory note, notwithstanding an error of due date appearing on the face of the document.*

[Vol. I, p. 51.]

Norden's Trustee *vs.* Butler.

Verity of defendant's signature to promissory note, if denied, may be proved instanter by parole evidence on the provisional claim. 1843. July 12.

[Vol. I, p. 52.]

[*Et vide* Dieterman *vs.* Curlewis, vol. 1, p. 42.]

Thalwitzer *vs.* Sparmann.

Summons defective when taken out on day note sued on became due.

In this case the Court found that a summons for payment of a promissory note could not legally be issued by and taken out from the Registrar of the Court on the day on which the note became payable, and therefore dismissed the case, with costs. Aug. 31. Thalwitzer *vs.* Spaarman.

Vide Voet, L. 5, *tit.* 1, § 27.

MENZIES' REPORTS.

[NEW SERIES.]

1828–1849.

VOL. II. PART III.

CHAPTER I.—SERVITUDE.

DE WET *vs.* CLOETE.

Servitude, by agreement.

Servitude Aquæductus, how constituted against singular successor of grantor. 1829. Dec. 3. 1830. Jan. 12.

Government: how far "dominus fluminum, and how far of rivulets.

Regulations made in pursuance of a judgment affirmed on appeal, such regulations being recognized by legislative authority, are sufficient to determine the rights of parties affected by such judgment and regulations.

[Vol. I, p. 405.]

[*Et vide* HAUPT *vs.* CLERK OF THE PEACE, STELLENBOSCH, *post.*]

HAWKINS *vs.* MUNNIK.

Servitude aquæ haustûs implies right of way to fountain, and cannot be impaired by a merely personal agreement. 1830. Sept. 2.

Hawkins *vs.* Munnik.

Where a river separates two properties there is a right of passage over a bridge, notwithstanding that the properties had formerly been one, and that in their sale or division the conditions were that a then standing bridge should be

1830. Sept. 2. — Hawkins vs. Munnik.

removed by the purchaser of the lower place, and that no bridge servitude should exist: the defendant having thereupon removed the bridge accordingly, but afterwards put up a temporary bridge. HELD: *that the personal agreement cannot limit the real right, the executors of the vendor, in transferring, having constituted, by the terms of such transfer, an unqualified right of servitude to the drink water.*

[Vol. I, p. 465.]

DICKSON, Q.Q. ELLIS, *vs.* BIDDULPH.

Personal Servitude. Habitatio. What does not amount to.

An authority by a proprietor of land to another person to reside there "as long as you may think fit to occupy it," does not constitute an irrevocable right of occupancy for life, but gives a right revocable on reasonable notice.

1835. Aug. 11. — Dickson, q.q. Ellis, vs. Biddulph.

This action was brought by the plaintiff to have defendant condemned to yield up to him possession of a certain erf in Bathurst, of which the plaintiff is the legal proprietor, and which he alleged the defendant occupied without any legal right or title, and without permission from the plaintiff; or that, if such permission was ever given, it had long since expired, and notice to yield up which to plaintiff within three months from such notice had been given to defendant seven months previously.

The defendant admitted the plaintiff's right of property in the erf, his own possession thereof, and that he had received notice to quit, but denied all the plaintiff's other allegations.

The defendant's claim to a right to occupy the erf was founded on the following letter addressed to him by plaintiff:

"Cape Town, July 14, 1820.

"DEAR SIR,—As my stay at the Cape has become uncertain, in consequence of my return to Parliament for the town of Boston, I shall feel obliged by your applying the 500 rds. to building the hut on my erf at Bathurst, which I shall consider as the dwelling of Mrs. Biddulph and yourself, as long as you may think fit to occupy it,—and, further, will undertake to defray all expenses of bringing the garden into cultivation, to be equally appropriated to the same purpose. My reason for this proposal is, that your sons may readily erect such a dwelling on your own erf within the period as will secure the right; whereas, if I should leave the Colony, even for a year in September, mine may be unoccupied beyond the regulated period, and I forfeit all claims thereunto."

1835. Aug. 11.

Dickson, q.q. Ellis, *vs.* Biddulph.

At the trial, the *Attorney-General* maintained that the plaintiff's letter to defendant, dated 14th July, 1820, gave the defendant no title of occupancy.

Cloete maintained that it gave the defendant and his wife a right of occupancy for life, and quoted *Voet* 13, 6, 1; and maintained that, even if defendant's title should be considered only as a *precarium*, still that the plaintiff could not reclaim it so long as defendant thought fit to occupy it; and quoted *Dig.* 19, 2, 4, and *Voet* 13, 6, 9.

The Court adjudged the defendant to yield up to the plaintiff possession of the premises on or before the 1st of October next, and (*Postea*, 23rd August, 1836) condemned defendant to pay the plaintiff's costs.

Cloete *vs.* Ebden.

An agreement by a vendor to give the purchaser "the free and uninterrupted use of the water for the mill-stream, during the period of four hours every alternate day," &c. "which right of water shall be a perpetual servitude on the aforesaid mill-stream and property;" the vendor himself possessing the right of damming up the water to a limited extent only, and leading a certain quantity therefrom, entitles the purchaser to claim only a right of servitude over the limited right in the stream such as the vendor possessed it.

Aug. 13.

Cloete *vs.* Ebden.

In this case, the plaintiff and defendant had entered into a written agreement, dated 21st November, 1834, for the sale by plaintiff to defendant of a certain piece of ground with the right of water therein mentioned, and which agreement contained the following clause:

"The said H. Cloete hereby further engages with the said J. B. Ebden, that the said J. B. Ebden shall have the free and uninterrupted use of the water from the mill-stream during the period of four hours every alternate day, by means of the present wooden pipe, or one of equal size, leading from the mill-stream or dam, to be conveyed from such pipe to a certain point, as shall be ascertained by *level*, on or within the boundary of the land so purchased, through the said Cloete's property, by means of a stone or paved channel, to be made at the expense of the said Ebden, which right of water shall be a perpetual servitude on the aforesaid mill-stream and property of the said H. Cloete."

This action was brought by the plaintiff to have the defendant condemned to receive transfer in terms of this agreement, and to pay the stipulated price.

In defence, the defendant pleaded that the plaintiff had, by the agreement, engaged that the defendant shall have the free and uninterrupted use of the water from the mill-stream during the period of four hours of every alternate day, and that such right of water shall be a perpetual servitude on the said mill-stream and property of the plaintiff. And that the plaintiff hath no sufficient, good, or legal right or title to convey transfer, make over, or guarantee to the defendant the said right of water or the free and uninterrupted use of water from the mill-stream in manner and form aforesaid; and that the transfer tendered by the plaintiff is therefore not sufficient, nor in the terms and under the conditions of the agreement aforesaid.

At the trial, the defendant called Frederick Hendricks, who stated: I am a brickmaker. I was employed by defendant in December last to make bricks on his premises (the ground purchased by him from the plaintiff). Defendant pointed out to me where I was to get the water. We were short of water sometimes. This water came from the mill-stream. The only water was that which came from the mill-stream, and when the mill was grinding we could not always get water. The pipe that leads to defendant's ground is from the mill-stream above the mill; and when the mill is working, sometimes the level of the water is so low that it will not run in the pipe.

Defendant put in a grant to plaintiff by the Landdrost and Heemraden of the Cape District, dated 15th August, 1818, of a right of damming up the Liesbeek to a certain limited extent only, and leading a certain quantity of water therefrom, and maintained that the effect of the clause in the agreement was to give defendant an absolute and indefeasible right of servitude of water from the Liesbeek through the mill-stream, which plaintiff was bound to guarantee; and that it was clear from the above grant that he could neither guarantee the perpetuity of such a right, nor even give at present any valid title to such a right of servitude.

But the Court held that the agreement conveyed to defendant nothing more than limited right of servitude over plaintiff's right to the water in the mill-stream, such as he possessed it; and that the transfer tendered by plaintiff was sufficient to convey to defendant the right stipulated to him by the agreement, and gave judgment for plaintiff, as prayed, with costs.

SAUNDERS *vs.* EXECUTRIX OF HUNT.

A question as to a disputed right of servitude may indirectly be tried by a personal action for damages, but the proper remedy is by a real action against all claiming right on the alleged servient tenement to have the servitude declared in favour of the dominant tenement, and the possessors and occupiers of the servient tenement interdicted from interrupting the enjoyment of the servitude.

1840. May 12.

Saunders *vs.* Executrix of Hunt.

In this action, the plaintiff claimed damages from defendant for the injury alleged to have been suffered by plaintiff in consequence of defendant having prevented a certain stream of water running through defendant's ground, and over which plaintiff claimed a real right of servitude, from running into plaintiff's ground, as in virtue of his alleged servitude he was entitled to have it run.

Defendant pleaded the general issue.

The plaintiff's object in bringing the action was not to obtain damages for the past, but to have his right to the servitude established by judgment of the Court, so that he might enforce it in future, and trusting that defendant would take the same view of the action, the plaintiff produced only the evidence which he considered sufficient to establish the existence of the right of servitude, and was not prepared with evidence, and therefore failed to prove that the defendant had done any thing to prevent the water from running into plaintiff's premises.

Whereupon *Cloete,* for defendant, claimed an absolution from the instance.

The Court held that there was no proof that the defendant, either by herself or by any person for whose acts she was responsible, had either directly herself, or by continuing what had been done by her predecessors, done any thing which had occasioned to plaintiff the injury for which he claimed damages from her, supposing that any such injury had been occasioned. That he had not proved that, even supposing he had the right of servitude which he claimed, and that it had been interrupted by the defendant's predecessors, the defendant had done or failed to do any thing, the commission or omission of which by her could be deemed to be such an interruption of the servitude as entitled plaintiff to claim damages for any injury thereby occasioned to him; and therefore absolved the defendant from the instance with costs.

The Court expressed an opinion, that although a question as to a disputed right of servitude might indirectly be tried by a *personal* action of the nature of the present, yet that

1840. May 12. — Saunders *vs.* Executrix of Hunt.

the plaintiff's proper remedy was by a *real* action against the possessor of, and all claiming right in, the alleged servient tenement, to have the servitude declared in favour of the dominant tenement, and the possessors and occupiers of the servient tenement interdicted from interrupting the enjoyment of the servitude.

PARKIN *vs.* TITTERTON.

Right of Way.

The proprietor of a piece of ground sold portion of the ground in seven lots, a plan being exhibited at the sale on which a road was marked, and the auctioneer stating that the road would run as exhibited on the plan. In course of time, the plaintiff became purchaser of all the lots. One of the lots only was transferred from the original owner. After the sale in 1841, *the proprietor sold the remaining portion of the ground, and gave transfer to the defendant's vendor, who transferred to defendant. No mention was made in either of the title deeds of any road or passage between the seven lots originally sold and the remainder. The defendant having obstructed the alleged road, the Court, on action brought by the plaintiff, gave judgment for the defendant, on the ground that the ground claimed for the road had never been transferred to the plaintiff or his predecessors, nor had any grant of a servitude been recorded in the Land Registry prior to the transfer to defendant's vendor, nor had it been shown that defendant when he received transfer had any notice or knowledge of the right of road promised by the original owner.*

1847. May 20. — Parkin *vs.* Titterton.

The plaintiff's declaration set forth, in substance, that plaintiff is now, and for the last fifteen years has been, possessed of seven plots of ground, being parts or subdivisions of an original erf, numbered 20, situated in the main street of Port Elizabeth, and that by reason thereof the plaintiff, during all the time aforesaid, ought to have had, and still of right ought to have, a certain way to pass and repass on foot and with horses and carriages from the said plots of ground and between them and certain other ground of the defendant lying adjacent thereto, towards the said main street; but that the defendant hath wrongfully and unjustly stopped up and obstructed the said way, so that the plaintiff is prevented from enjoying the said way, whereby the plaintiff hath sustained damage to the amount of £500.

Wherefore the plaintiff prays that the defendant may be condemned to restore to him the said right of way, and to remove all obstruction to the use thereof by the plaintiff, or to pay to the plaintiff the sum of £500, as damages, together with the costs of suit.

In his plea, the defendant pleaded, first, the general issue; and for a special plea pleaded that the plaintiff ought not to have or maintain his action, because he, the defendant, has purchased a certain part of the original erf No. 20, without any reservation whatever having been stipulated in the transfer thereof that the plaintiff ought to have any right of way whatever.

At the trial in the Circuit Court of Port Elizabeth, the plaintiff called

John Owen Smith, who stated: I was employed by the agent of Reid, the original grantee of the erf No. 20, to sell by auction the seven plots, being part thereof, which are now in possession of the plaintiff. I myself bought the plot No. 7, and the plaintiff's predecessors bought the other six plots. I produce the plan which was exhibited at the sale. All the explanations on the plan are in the handwriting of Reid's agent. The white line on this plan, drawn between these seven plots and the remaining part of the erf, is intended to represent the road claimed by plaintiff, and which has been shut up by defendant. I mentioned it at the sale as a road which was to run as represented on the plan. The six upper plots would have been valueless without that right of road, as the possessor would without it have no access to and from the main street. I obtained transfer of No. 7, and afterwards sold and transferred it to plaintiff. I believe the other plots have not yet been transferred from Reid, but the plaintiff is in possession of all the plots, and has built on some of them. I always used the road when I required it.

Charles Joseph Gray: I am a sworn land-surveyor. I have surveyed and measured the whole of erf No. 20. If the ground the property or in the possession of the plaintiff, and a road of any breadth as claimed by him, be deducted from the remainder of the erf, there will not remain the 107 square roods and 32 square feet transferred by Reid to F. Still, through whom defendant has derived his title to the remainder of the erf. There is access to all these seven plots, on their other side, from the adjoining erf No. 21, which is the property of the plaintiff.

Thereupon the Circuit Judge proceeded to and inspected the premises in question, when he found that in their present state the access to several of the buildings in plots Nos. 7 and 6 is from the ground claimed by plaintiff as the road

1847. May 20. — Parkin *vs.* Titterton.

in question; and that although it is physically possible to give all these seven plots access to the main street by a road or passage through plaintiff's adjoining erf No. 21, it would be very inconvenient, difficult, and expensive, in the present state of the ground, to obtain such access;—that if the road claimed be taken away, the plaintiff could not get access to certain of the entrance doors in the buildings on that part of his property lying adjacent to the road;—that there was no road or way made or marked out on the ground;—and that not only the ground over which plaintiff contended that the road claimed by him should run, but also a considerable portion of erf No. 20, between the ground claimed for the road and where the defendant's buildings are situated, was lying utterly waste and unenclosed.

The Court removed the case to the Supreme Court, in order that the parties might produce respectively the deeds of transfer in favour of themselves and their predecessors in their respective properties; with liberty to both parties to have the ground remeasured by competent surveyors.

Postea, in the Supreme Court, 20th May, 1847,

Ebden, for the plaintiff, produced the deed of transfer of the plot No. 7 by Reid, the original grantee of erf No. 20, to plaintiff's author, John Owen Smith, which described it, No. 7, as being bounded on the north (being that side which is adjacent to the road claimed) *by the remaining part of erf No.* 20.

The *Attorney-General*, for the defendant, produced the deed of transfer, dated 5th January, 1838, by the said Reid to Forbes Still, of a "certain lot of ground situated, &c., &c., being part of Lot No. 20, granted to the appearer by his title deed, dated the 25th August, 1821, measuring 107 square roods and 32 do. feet, extending north to lot No. 19, east to the street, west to reserved pasturage, and *south to other portions of Lot. No.* 20, as will further appear by the annexed diagram." Also the deeds of transfer of the said lastmentioned piece of ground by Still to W. Titterton, and by the latter to defendant, in both of which the piece of ground is described by a reference to the abovementioned deed of transfer and diagram of the 5th January, 1838.

The plaintiff did not allege that unless the breadth of the road claimed were added to his lot he would not have received the *quantity of ground* mentioned in the transfer of plot 7 to J. O. Smith; nor that if the ground claimed by plaintiff as the road were held to be included in defendant's property, he, defendant, would get a greater quantity than that mentioned in Reid's transfer to Still, namely, 107 square roods and 32 square feet.

It thus appeared, from the title deeds of both parties, that these lots were respectively bounded by each other, and that no mention was made in either of any road or passage running between them, such as Reid's agent had at the sale of the seven plots stipulated should be given to their purchaser. 1847. May 20. Parkin *vs.* Titterton.

The Court gave judgment for the defendant, with costs, on the ground that no transfer had been made to the plaintiff or his predecessors of the ground now claimed by him for the road, nor any grant of a servitude of road in their favour recorded in the Land Registry Office prior to the date of Reid's transfer of the remaining part of erf No. 20 to Still; and that it had not been proved that the defendant, at the time he received his transfer, had any notice or knowledge of the right of road promised by Reid to the purchasers of the seven plots.

Du Toit *vs.* Malherbe.

Servitude of Water. Evidence. Res Judicata. Decree of Landdrost and Heemraden. Error of fact.

Evidence. Admission of a Secretarial Copy of a Contract which ought to have been among the records of the district of Stellenbosch, but could not be discovered, on proof of the signature of the Secretary.

A decree of the Court of Landdrost and Heemraden regarding the right to water of co-proprietors is res judicata of a competent Court as regards these proprietors and their successors.

Even though there might be ground for supposing that the decree was founded, in part, on an error in fact, it would be res judicata until set aside in a regular action of reduction.

Such a decree is not to be considered as abandoned by the parties or rendered ineffectual by prescription because its arrangements, by which the parties should be enabled to enjoy the use of the water, were never adhered to nor carried into effect; the several parties having throughout enjoyed the proportions of the water to which by the decree they were found entitled.

June 14. Du Toit *vs.* Malherbe.

The declaration of the plaintiff set forth, in substance, that the plaintiff has for some time been and now is proprietor of the place Orleans, situated at Drakenstein, in the division of Stellenbosch, and, by reason thereof, before and at the

1847. June 14. — Du Toit *vs.* Malherbe.

time of the committing of the grievances by the defendant hereinafter mentioned,of right ought to have had and enjoyed, and still of right ought to have and enjoy, the benefit and advantage of the water of a certain stream having its source in the Drakenstein mountains, and which, after running past or through certain other places, ought to run to and past the place of the plaintiff; yet the defendant, who is the proprietor of a certain part of the place called Dekkers-valley, situated higher up on the said stream than the said place of the plaintiff, well knowing the premises, at divers times between the 1st of January, 1846, and the day of the commencement of this suit, wrongfully and unlawfully diverted from and out of the said stream the water therein running, or divers large quantities thereof, and stopped and hindered the water of the said stream, or much thereof, which ought of right to have been permitted to run and flow in its usual course to and through the certain places situate lower down on the said stream than the said place of the defendant, and, amongst others, to the said place of the plaintiff; by reason whereof the plaintiff, as such proprietor as aforesaid, is greatly injured, and has been deprived of the water necessary for the use of his family and cattle, and of the vineyard and garden on his said place, which, but for the said wrongful and unlawful acts of the defendant, he would have had and enjoyed, and hath sustained damages to the amount of £200, which sum he prays that the defendant may be adjudged by the judgment of this honourable Court to pay him, together with costs, &c.

The defendant pleaded the general issue.

At the trial, it was admitted that the plaintiff was the proprietor of the place Orleans, and the defendant of a part of the place Dekkersvalley; that both these places had been granted by Government to the predecessors of the defendant and plaintiff respectively between 1690 and 1700, and that the original grant of Dekkersvalley was about four years prior in date to that of Orleans, and it was stated by plaintiff, and not denied by defendant, that the water of this stream was derived in part from Government ground in the Drakenstein mountain, and also from two springs which were situated on Government ground when the grants of the two places were made, but which lastmentioned ground had afterwards been acquired from Government by the present defendant.

The plaintiff called

John van Blommestein, clerk of the Civil Commissioner of Stellenbosch, who produced the Record Book of the proceedings of the Landdrost and Heemraden of Stellenbosch for the year 1805, containing, under date the 4th

March, 1805, a report of the proceedings of that board respecting the rights to the water of the Palmiet River (the stream in question) of the different proprietors whose places were situated on that stream, a translation of which was put in and read.

1847. June 14.

Du Toit *vs.* Malherbe.

This witness also proved that he had searched for the original of the underhand contract, dated 23rd January, 1805, referred to in the report, which ought to have been among the records of the district of Stellenbosch, but had not been able to find it.

Plaintiff also called Petrus Borchardus Borcherds, Civil Commissioner of the Cape division, who stated: I knew the late Johannes Wege. He was secretary of the district of Stellenbosch; I often saw him write, and knew his writing and signature well. I believe the signature to the paper now shown to me to be his.

This paper, purporting to be a secretarial copy, signed by Wege, as secretary of the said district, of the said contract of the 23rd January, 1805, with a translation thereof, was put in and read.

The contract of the 23rd January, 1805, according to the secretarial copy thereof put in, commenced and was in substance as follows:

"We, the undersigned, J. Cilliers (the then proprietor of the present defendant's place, Dekkersvalley), J. R. Louw, the Widow J. de Villiers, P. B. Wolfard, and the Widow A. du Toit (the then proprietor of the present plaintiff's place, Orleans), declare to have contracted on the following conditions:

"1st. The water named Palmiet River, rising in the Drakenberg, and running near and through the places of the undersigned is settled by us, and for our benefit, according to the following periods, commencing with 1st October and ending the 30th April.

"2nd. The first contractor, J. Cilliers, though the former possessor of the place never made any lawful pretension to the water of the Palmiet River, shall retain the water thereof during forty-eight consecutive hours, on the 1st and 2nd October, for the irrigation of his ground, provided he allows, and which he shall be bound to do, during the whole period of forty-eight hours, a good stream of drink water to run down for the use of the other contractors, and, after the expiration of the said forty-eight hours, to let the same run, not partly but wholly, in its natural course" (on the ground that he possesses another and separate stream).

The 3rd, 4th, and 5th conditions provided that J. R. Louw and the Widow de Villiers, and P. B. Wolfard should in succession after Louw be allowed to retain the said water

1847. June 14. — Du Toit *vs.* Malherbe.

for periods, the two former of seventy-two, and the latter of sixty consecutive hours each, under obligation to let a good stream of drink water flow down during those periods for the places lower down.

"6th. The last contractress, the Widow Du Toit, shall in succession, after Wolfard, be permitted to enjoy the said water for a period of sixty consecutive hours, after which the leading out of the partnership water shall again be made *de novo* by the first undersigned, J. Cilliers, and afterwards by the other contractors, successively, in rotation according to the aforesaid stipulation."

After reciting some further stipulations, of no importance to the present case, the said secretarial copy proceeded as follows:

"Further, we bind ourselves, each on his part, strictly to fulfil the terms of this agreement, without making the least exception to any of the foregoing points, and in witness whereof we have under obligation, according to law, affixed our signature."

Five true copies were made hereof and placed in the possession of the contractors.

R. LOUW,
Widow J. DE VILLIERS,
P. B. WOLFARD,
Widow A. DU TOIT.

As Witnesses:

J. J. HAUPT,
J. ROOS.

"By strict examination with the original, in the office of the Secretary of Stellenbosch, the above was found to agree.

"J. WEGE, Secretary."

The report of the proceedings of the Landdrost and Heemraden set forth in terms and in substauce as follows:

"14th March, 1805.

"Present the Lauddrost, &c., together with the Heemraden, &c., &c.

"Firstly was read, &c., &c.

"Likewise was handed over by the said commissioned members the following report on the complaint of the Widow A. du Toit and P. B. Wolfard against J. Cilliers and J. R. Louw, purporting thus:

"'To the Landdrost, &c., &c.

"'President and Members.

"'An application having been preferred to you, dated 11th February last, for a judicial commission, at the instance of the Widow du Toit and P. B. Wolfard, proprietors of places in Dal Josaphat, to and against J. Cilliers and J. R. Louw, because the same have led out the greatest part of the drink water, to which they, the applicants, maintain to have full right,—the undersigned commissioners having on the 15th repaired there for the investigation of this complaint, and summoned before them the parties, who then also appeared, with the exception of the respondent, J. Cilliers. There was then handed over to them by the applicant, P. B. Wolfard, a provisional contract by him and the Widow du Toit with the respondents, Cilliers and Louw, as also the Widow J. de Villiers, mutually entered into, concerning the use of the Palmiet River, they, the applicants, desiring that the same should have effect, and complaining that the respondents, Cilliers and Louw, nevertheless arbitrarily detained the water, with request that the commission would make the necessary ocular inspection at their places, &c.

"'Also appeared before the commission the said Widow J. de Villiers, who represented that in the aforesaid contract the use of the water was allowed to her by mistake for only seventy-two consecutive hours, as proprietor of two places, while as such she was entitled to it for ninety-six consecutive hours, which was instantly admitted by the respondent Louw.

"'The commissioners then went first to the place of the Widow du Toit, where they found the orchard, vineyard, and kitchen garden very much parched, and she declared that she had had no water for the space of fifteen days, and would in consequence press at least twenty leaguers of wine less than usual.

"'2nd. To the place of P. B. Wolfard, where they found everything also very much parched, though not so much as at the Widow du Toit's place.

"'3rd. To the place of the respondent, J. R. Louw, where they found no want of water. It was then stated by Louw that the reason why his opponents had no water was to be imputed to themselves, because they did not bring the water of the river, which was divided and dispersed, into one course, and did not clear out the channel, in consequence of which the water could not possibly force itself through sand and stones to so great a distance to the lower proprietors, &c., &c., &c.

"'4th. To the place of the respondent, J. Cilliers, when Charles and Pieter Cilliers appeared before the commission, and represented that their brother, the said J. Cilliers, through sickness and weakness at present was not well in his senses, and thus not in a situation to be able in any way to transact business with him; that they had wished to speak to him about the present dispute, but that he had answered that he wished to trouble himself with nothing; whereupon the commission, not having been able to ascertain his, the said Cilliers', interests from himself, for the reason above stated, have examined the state of things on his place, and were not able to discover any waste of water.

"'There then appeared before the commission the son of the Widow Malherbe (N.B.—This person is the defendant in the present action), for and in the name of his mother, as being proprietrix of a part of the place of the said J. Cilliers, who represented that the said Cilliers had made no use before of the water of the Palmiet River, except for a piece of land which had been sold by him, on which the purchaser had placed a cellar and brandy still, and had used that water for his still; that this piece of land had been repurchased by Cilliers, and that the water which had been led to it afterwards flowed down to the piece of ground belonging to his mother, who had no other water than this; but that Cilliers had another and distinct, though not strong, stream, which flowed out of a separate kloof above his house, and that therefore if, as he, Malherbe, understood, no stream of drink water was to be allowed to Cilliers from the Palmiet River, and that he might only lead off the water from it during his rotation periods, then the course through which his mother would receive the water must dry up so much that the water could not reach her place until late in the day, and thus be productive of little advantage to her, whereupon the contractors present declared that they had no objections to Cilliers being allowed a stream of drink water, which the Widow might also use, provided that the same be afterwards made to take its course into the channel of the river by a certain course which they specified. To which proposed course Malherbe objected, but on behalf of his mother offered to bring back the water immediately after it had been used for her brandy still again into the ordinary course of the river, which offer appeared to the commission to be fair; and they have therefore, although the Widow Malherbe is not one of the parties to the suit, yet as she is greatly interested in the granting or not granting to Cilliers a stream of drink water from the Palmiet River on the days when it is not his turn to lead off the water from the river, deemed it right to report what is hereinabove mentioned as having been represented on her behalf.

"'That the commissioners having examined as far as possible the course of the Palmiet River, it appears to them that after a proper clearing of it by the parties, a moderate use of it can be made, even in this dry season, and therefore ought to be allowed, for the irrigation of the places of the parties; and they are of opinion that the parties ought to be directed each on his part strictly to act up to the agreement that was made by them, dated 23rd January, 1805, the original of which the commission herewith present, with these further stipulations, that the Widow J. de Villiers be allowed the use of the water for ninety-six instead of seventy-two consecutive hours, and that J. Cilliers be allowed to retain a stream of drink water on the days when, by the second article of the contract, it is not his turn to lead off the water, provided the Widow Malherbe, as proprietrix of a part of the place of Cilliers, be bound immediately after use to bring the same back to the ordinary channel of the river, &c., &c.

"'J. S. MARAIS.
"'P. ROUX.'

"After the reading whereof, and deliberation thereon, it has been thought proper to pronounce the following decision:

"Landdrost and Heemraden having heard the report of the commissioned members of the board, and, besides, having taken into consideration everything relating to the matter, and which in any manner could move them, doing justice in the name and on the behalf of the Batavian Government, direct that the parties, each on his part, do strictly act up to the contract made between them, under date 23rd January, 1805, concerning the water running down out of the Drakenberg, called the Palmiet River, with this exception, nevertheless, that to the Widow J. de Villiers, as comprehended also in that contract, shall be given the use of the water for ninety-six consecutive hours, besides that to the respondent, J. Cilliers, beyond the forty-eight consecutive hours allowed to him by the said contract, a stream of drink water be allowed to be led off, provided that care be taken that the Widow Malherbe, as possessing a part of his place, do bring back the said water immediately after the use of the same into the old course, with condemnation of the parties *pro parte* in the costs."

A great number of witnesses were then called and examined, both by the plaintiff and defendant, the effect of whose evidence was to satisfy the Court that each of the four lower proprietors at least, if not also the proprietor of Dekkersvalley, had always possessed secretarial copies of the contract of the 23rd January, 1805; that from the 14th March, 1805, the date of the judgment of the board of Landdrost and Heemraden, to the present day, the arrangements respecting the distribution of the water contained in the contract of the 23rd January, 1805, and as amended by the said judgment, never had at any time been

1847. June 14. — Du Toit *vs.* Malherbe.

adhered to or carried into effect, but that, notwithstanding this, from the said 14th March, 1805, down to the end of 1844, or beginning of 1845, the lower proprietors had always, by some other arrangement or arrangements, been furnished with and allowed to enjoy their fair proportions of the use of the water as calculated in the contract, or at least as much thereof as they required for their use; and that whenever, during that period, a fair proportion of the water was prevented from flowing down to the lower proprietors, the obstacle which prevented it was immediately removed as soon as the lower proprietors complained of the want of water to the proprietors of Dekkervalley.

That from the end of 1844 or beginning of 1845, the defendant in the dry season between October and April, when the water is required for irrigation, had prevented the lower proprietors from enjoying the use of the water in the proportions to which, as estimated in the contract, they were entitled, by sometimes turning off the whole of the water, at times when, under the terms of the contract and judgment, he was entitled only to a small stream of drink water, and at other times by constantly leading off, sometimes one half, and never less than one-third, of the stream, whereby, for want of the water, the lower proprietors, and particularly the plaintiff, suffered considerable damage; that on their going to his place and complaining to him, he at one time, when the field-cornet accompanied them, opened the dam he had made, so as to allow as much water as they required to run down for about ten days or a fortnight, when he again prevented a just and proper supply from running down. That on another occasion he allowed them, as an experiment, to put into the dam a plank, having six holes in it, and so placed as to allow one sixth of the water to run to his place, and the remaining five sixths to the lower places, but removed this plank before the end of three days; that when urged to comply with the conditions of the contract he admitted a knowledge of its existence, but wholly denied its validity to affect him, and maintained that he had an uncontrolled right to the use of the water, and was not bound to allow any more of it than he pleased to run to the lower places.

After the defendant had closed his case, the Court called on *Brand* to state the grounds on which the defendant maintained that the judgment of the Board of Landdrost and Heemraden of the 14th March, 1805, was null and of no effect as against the defendant.

Brand maintained, first, that this judgment was not intended to settle any questions as to the original rights of any of the parties to the use of the water, but merely to declare and enforce the provisions of a contract which had been made by certain parties against the parties who had made and signed it. That as the original of the contract had not been produced, and as from the secretarial copy of it which had been produced it appeared that, although it had been signed by four of the lower proprietors, it had not been signed by his predecessor, the then proprietor of Dekkers-valley, therefore this judgment could not have been intended to bind, nor could have the effect of binding, his predecessor, more especially as he had not appeared as a party before the commissioned members; or if it had been intended by the said board, and could, from its terms, be construed as having been intended to bind the defendant's predecessor, that it must to this extent be deemed to have been given through error, in consequence of the board having over-looked the fact that it was not signed, and believed that it had been signed, by Cilliers.

2ndly. That as it had been proved that the said judg-ment, from its date to the present time, had never, to any extent, been carried into effect, it must be held to have been abandoned by the parties, or, at all events, to have been put an end to by prescription, and therefore could not now be founded on or given effect to against any party, and that the plaintiff had alleged no other ground on which the defendant could be prevented from using the water of the Palmiet River to any extent he thought proper, without regard to the water of the lower proprietors.

The Court, without calling on the plaintiff's counsel to reply, held that from the terms of the judgment of the 14th March, 1805, it was clear that the object and intent of the suit instituted by the Widow Du Toit and P. B. Wolfard against J. Cilliers and J. R. Louw, and of the judgment given by the Board of Landdrost and Heemraden on the 14th March, 1805, was to obtain and give a judicial decision as to the respective rights of the proprietors of the places situated in the Palmiet River to the use of its water,—that this judgment had been given by that Court *tota re per-specta*, and having the original of the therein denominated "provisional contract" under their consideration, and that in it this contract was referred to merely as already specify-ing and setting forth the regulations according to which that Court deemed it to be just and lawful that the water should be distributed, and was not intended merely to give effect to a contract which had been made by some of the parties interested, without reference to the previous rights of those parties, or of other parties having a claim to the water, and, consequently, that the fact of Cilliers having, or not having, signed the said contract was of no

1847. June 14. — Du Toit vs. Malherbe.

consequence. That the Board of Landdrost and Heemraden being a competent Court for the decision of the matter in dispute between the parties, and Cilliers having been duly summoned to appear before the commission and having made default, the decision of that Court must be held to be, and be given effect to as, *res judicata* against Cilliers and his successors in the place Dekkersvalley, until a decree of reduction of it had been obtained in a regular action of reduction, even although there were grounds for supposing that it might have been given through a mistake as to the fact that he had not signed the contract.

2ndly. That the object and effect of the judgment of the Board of Landdrost and Heemraden was primarily to ascertain and declare the several proportions in which each of the places situated on the Palmiet River had a legal right to the use of the water thereof, and only secondarily to determine the arrangements by which each of the said parties should be enabled to obtain and enjoy the use of the said proportion of the water, and therefore, that as, up to the end of 1844, the several parties had always obtained and enjoyed the use of the proportions of the water to which they had been so found entitled, or as much thereof as they required, this judgment could neither be deemed to have been abandoned by the parties nor to have been rendered ineffectual by prescription, either determining the proportion in which the parties were respectively entitled to the use of the water, or as providiug the arrangements by which they might compel the defendant to allow them to obtain their said proportions of the water, if his conduct rendered it necessary for them to have recourse thereto; and therefore gave judgment for the plaintiff, for the amount of damages which it had been proved he had suffered by being deprived of the use of the water, and costs.

CHAPTER II.

MORTGAGE AND PLEDGE.

SMUTS *vs.* STACK AND OTHERS.

Delivery necessary to make effectual a special mortgage of movables. 1828. March 31.

[Vol. I, p. 297.]

VAN DER BYL AND ANOTHER *vs.* SEQUESTRATOR AND ANOTHER.

Legal hypothec enjoyed by the Government of this Colony upon the property of collectors of the revenue. Sept. 23.

Not diminished or impaired by Government taking sureties from such collectors.

Kusting Brieven, and also special conventional mortgages, for purchase money lent, or money for payment of purchase money, or mortgage taken over, when constituted "simul ac semel" the transfer of the property mortgaged, are privileged, and preferent to prior tacit or legal hypothecs, and this without being necessarily constituted in the deed of transfer itself.

[Vol. I, p. 318.]

VENDUE COMMISSARIES *vs.* BRINK.

Hypothec, tacit or legal, created by instructions not promulgated, of no force. Dec. 31.

Vendue, no legal preference on goods.

[Vol. I, p. 340.]

COMMISSARIES OF VENDUE *vs.* SEQUESTRATOR.

Hypothec of fisc on estate of pachter. 1829. March 19.

Preference of Vendue Commissioner by instructions of 1793 refused.

[Vol. I, p. 368.]

Crœser *vs.* Sequestrator and Another.

1829. June 5. *Special conventional mortgages, although for purchase money, but not constituted "simul ac semel" (i.e., on the same day) with the transfer, not entitled to the privilege of Kusting Brieven.*

Legal hypothec of Government upon the property of collectors not impaired by Government having taken sureties from them.

Legal hypothec of Government commences from date of appointment of such collectors.

[Vol. I, p. 330.]

Commissary of Vendue *vs.* Sequestrator and Another.

Hypothec of fisc for taxes.

June 2. *Preference of Vendue Commissaries refused.*

[Vol. I, p. 370.]

Brink *vs.* Joubert.

June 2. *Mortgage of slaves. Registration necessary, both in the Slave Register and the Colonial Debt Register: preference regulated by the last.*

Proclamation of 30*th January,* 1818.

[Vol. I, p. 371.]

Discount Bank *vs.* Dawes.

Sept. 28. *Preference. Notarial bond. General mortgage. No preference unless enregistered in General Registry Office.*

Special mortgage on a slave; no preference without such registry, although enregistered in the Slave Registry Office.

[Vol. I, p 380.]

Woutersen's Executors *vs.* Widow Palmer and Another.

1830. Feb. 23. *Jus retentionis, of mortgager, against mortgagee, available to enforce performance of reciprocal obligations constituted by mutual agreement: also of force against pledgee of mortgage bond.*

Pledge,—Pand ter minne,—by notarial bond of special mortgage bond, what effect, and how affected by anterior agreement between mortgagee and mortgager.

[Vol. I, p. 417.]

SEQUESTRATOR *vs.* THOMSON AND ANOTHER.

Hypothec, general, prior in date, preferent to posterior special on movables without delivery. **1830. Sept. 28.**

[Vol. I, p. 479.]

BLANCKENBERG *vs.* GUARDIANS OF LOND.

Hypothec. Pignus prætorium, prior, preferent to posterior general hypothec. **Sept. 29. Oct. 11.**

Minors not entitled to preference on bonds in their favour, granted by a person not their guardian.

[Vol. I, p. 483.]

WATERMEYER *vs.* HECKROODT AND ANOTHER.

Hypothec, special and general: general not lost by discharge of special: right of cession of second hypothecation. **Sept. 29. Dec. 9.**

[Vol. I, p. 477.]

MEINERT *vs.* NISBET AND DICKSON.

Pignus prætorium not destroyed by surrender of estate within twenty-eight days. **Dec. 30**

[Vol. I, p. 425.]

SCHEUBLE *vs.* VAN DER BERG AND ANOTHER.

Hypothec of landlords on invector et illaba as to property actually remaining in the landlord's house, without attachment to pignus prætorium (i.e., judicial arrest by messenger of the Magistrate's Court). **1831. Dec. 20.**

[Vol. I, p. 537.]

Cloete *vs.* Colonial Government.

1832. March 27. *Pignus nobilium: prætorium, by attachment is equivalent to tradition, and is preferent to pignus tacitum vell egale et generale of prior date, but without tradition.*

[Vol. I, p. 554.]

Osmond and Another *vs.* Widow Van Reenen and Another.

May 8. *Preference, of fisc on property of insolvent pachter.*

[Vol. I, p. 564.]

In Re Lutgens.—Neethling, q.q., Lutgens' Heirs, *vs.* Trustees and Creditors of Lutgens.

Fidei Commissum. Novation.

Where the executor of a fidei-commissary estate, and guardian of the fidei-commissary heirs, handed over the fidei-commissary estate to the fiduciarius, taking a bond from him in security, held that this was a novatio debiti, and destroyed the tacit legal hypothec antecedently possessed by the fidei-commissarii on the estate of such fiduciarius.

Registration of a fidei-commissum not necessary to entitle it to a hypothec.

1832. Dec. 31.

In Re Lutgens.—Neethling, q.q. Lutgens' Heirs, *vs.* Trustees and Creditors of Lutgens.

This day, *Cloete* showed cause in support of a rule, which he had obtained on the defendant, to show cause "why the distribution account as drawn out by the trustees shall not be amended, and preference adjudged to the said applicant, J. H. Neethling, as executor and testamentary guardian for the fidei-commissary heirs of the late J. W. Lutgens, for the amount of a certain bond passed by the insolvent for the sum of 52,598 guilders on the 21st September, 1813, and duly registered, by virtue of the legal tacit hypothec due to the said fidei-commissary heirs before the special mortgages of posterior date." In this case the Master had made the following report:

"Mr. Neethling, as executor under the last will of J. W. Lutgens, having proved a debt under this estate upon a notarial bond, dated 21st September, 1813, and duly registered on the 8th November, 1813, in the capital sum of 17,532 rds. 6 sk. 2 st., executed by the insolvent under a general mortgage of his whole estate, in respect of the inheritance of the insolvent and his children under his grandfather and grandmother's estate, which inheritance was burthened with *fidei-commissum*. The trustees have objected to award any preference in respect of the said bond, by reason, as they allege, of Mr. Neethling having surrendered the property under his guardianship to the insolvent himself, and having taken as a security the notarial bond before mentioned, by which they contend that Mr. Neethling has lost his right of preference as guardian, and can only be entitled to preference as a general mortgage after six special mortgages of a later date have been satisfied, to which they have awarded preferences over the claim of Mr. Neethling, by which order of preference Mr. Neethling has been deprived of the tacit legal mortgage claimed by him over the whole estate of the insolvent, and has only been awarded the sum of £170 2s. 0½d., by virtue of a first general mortgage.

"The trustees instituted an action against Mr. Neethling, for the purpose of obtaining a release of the estate of the insolvent from the burthen of *fidei-commissum* attached thereto by the aforesaid last will of his grandfather and grandmother, and that the bond passed by the insolvent on the 21st September, 1813, might be cancelled, both which claims were rejected by this Honourable Court with costs on the 6th September, 1831." (*Vide Lutgens' Trustees vs. Neethling*, 3rd March, 1831.)

The following are the clauses of the joint will of the deceased Johan W. Lutgens and his wife, dated 12th April, 1802, which have reference to the present question:

"Proceeding now to the election of heirs, the testator declared to nominate and institute his lawful wife the testatrix, jointly with the child procreated in lawful wedlock by his son, the late J. N. Lutgens, and named J. W. Lutgens (the insolvent), or the lawful descendants of the first dying by representative in equal shares, and in want of these, the longest living of them, subject to the following conditions: Whilst the testator burthened with a *fidei-commissum* the inheritance to be enjoyed by the aforesaid J. W. Lutgens (either at his decease, as well as in the event of a second marriage, or the demise of the testatrix, or in what manner soever) from his estate, until the third line of the descendants, viz., to the children of the said heir inclusive, with prohibition of alienation or estrangement, under what name or title soever. Wherefore, the testator did nominate and appoint, as administrators of the said moneys and guardians over the minor lawful descendants of the said heir, the hereundermentioned executors, directing them to demand and to receive the moneys due to the said J. W. Lutgens from the

1832. Dec. 31.

In Re Lutgens.—Neethling, q.q. Lutgens' Heirs, *vs.* Trustees and Creditors of Lutgens.

estate of the longest living testatrix, who shall, during her lifetime, keep such moneys under her administration, and pay the interest thereof at six per cent. per annum to the fidei-commissary heir, and having purchased for the whole proceeds thereof, either here or elsewhere, immovable property, or having secured it in any other safe manner, to see all such property or effects registered in the Colonial Office, or at such other place as is customary, *as specially bound and mortgaged in favour of them* who, at the death of the fidei-commissary heir, shall be entitled to inherit the expectancy of the said *fidei-commissum*, whilst such heir or heirs shall be at liberty to act with, and to dispose of the aforesaid property or revenue of the effects as they may think proper, subject only as aforesaid to keep the property for their lawful descendants *fidei-commissum* and unalienable."

By a codicil, dated 17th April, 1802, the testator and testatrix, "in accordance with the reservation made in respect to the appointment of testamentary executors, administrators of the estate, and guardians of our minor heirs or legatees, as also curators over the *fidei-commissum*, nominate and appoint, after the death of both of us, jointly with J. Smuts, J. H. Neethling, both with the power of assumption."

Neethling, after the decease both of husband and wife, administered the estate; but instead of securing the *fidei-commissum* by a special mortgage, he delivered over to the insolvent the whole amount of the paternal share of the joint estate (the widow had discharged the *fidei-commissum* on her half), and took from him a notarial bond, whereby he acknowledged himself indebted to J. H. Neethling, in his capacity as the testamentary executor and guardian of the minor heirs of the appearer's late grandfather (being eventually the appearer's late children and grandchildren), in the sum of 17,532 rds., being the capital of the inheritance left to him, the appearer, under *fidei-commissum*, which aforesaid sum will have to be paid either by him, the appearer, or after his death by his testamentary executor, or other administrator of his estate, to the said J. H. Neethling, his order, heirs, or assignees, on demand, and on behalf of his, the appearer's, lawful heirs, in compliance with the last will of the said testator Lutgens.

Cloete and *Neethling* maintained that the bond sued on was merely taken in order to liquidate and ascertain the amount of the *fidei-commissum*, and that, by the registration of this bond, the *fidei-commissum* might be registered, and that the preference here sought was claimed on the ground that, by law, fidei-commissary heirs have a tacit legal hypothec on the fidei-commissary estate for the amount of the *fidei-commissum*, and that in this case the whole of the estate of the fiduciaries (Lutgens, the insolvent) must be considered to be the fidei-commissary estate; and quoted *Van Leeuwen, Cens. For., p. 1, l. 4, c. 9, § 12.*

1832. Dec. 31.

In Re Lutgens.—Neethling, q.q. Lutgens' Heirs, *vs.* Trustees and Creditors of Lutgens.

Neethling maintained, further, that as the insolvent would be the guardian of his children, if any shall be procreated by him, and that as minors have a tacit legal hypothec on the estate of their guardian, he, as representing the future children, had a tacit legal hypothec on the general estate of the insolvent for the amount of the bond now sued on; and quoted *Inst. de Tutel., l. 1, t. 13, § 3; Van der Linden, Institutes, b. 1, ch. 5, § 2, p. 99.*

Cur adv. vult.

Postea.—The Court held that the insolvent cannot be considered as a tutor before the birth of his children; that at present he is merely a fiduciarius, liable to account to Neethling as fidei-commissarius; consequently, that his estate is not now affected by that tacit legal hypothec belonging to minors over the estate of their tutor.

2ndly. That although the father is the natural guardian of his children, the hypothec is only available for security of what fell under the guardianship; and here, as the grandfather appointed other guardians over the estate left by him, it never could come under the guardianship of the insolvent.

3rdly. That even if he were tutor, the bond is a *novatio debiti*, and no hypothec exists in respect of it. (*Voet,* 20,2,16.)

4thly. That registration of the *fidei-commissum* is not now necessary to entitle it to a hypothec. (*Van Leeuwen, Cens. For.*, 4, 9, 12; *Van der Keessel, Th.* 319.)

5thly. That although it be true that the fidei-commissarius has a tacit legal hypothec *in omnibus bonis a testatore relictis, pro consequendis fidei-commissis sibi relictis,* and that Mr. Neethling possesses the character and rights of a fidei-commissarius, there is no evidence to show that the effects of the insolvent now under distribution were in specie part of the estate of old Lutgens, the testator; consequently, there is no ground established on which the Court can award any preference on that estate in respect of this bond, or fidei-commissary obligation. (*Voet,* 20, 2, 21; *Cod.* 6, 43, *l.* 1 *and* 3, § 2; *Voet,* 30, 1, §§ 40, 41, 42, 43.)

6thly. The Court were inclined to be of opinion that, although the effects of the insolvent now under distribution had actually *in specie* formed part of the estate of the testator, still that by taking the bond in question, such a *novatio debiti* took place as discharged the fidei-commissary property of the hypothec (*Vide Voet,* 20, 2, 16, *in fine, et*

1832. Dec. 31. — *In Re* Lutgens.—Neethling, q.q. Lutgens' Heirs, *vs.* Trustees and Creditors of Lutgens.

contra, *Voet*, 20, 2, 24, *quæ confer;* and consider the effect of the decision of the Court, 6th September, 1831.)

(1st February, 1833.)—The Court on these grounds gave judgment against the claim of Neethling, and discharged the rule with costs.

In Re D. G. Van Reenen.—Van Reenen *vs.* Reitz and Breda.

Loan place: Effect of special mortgage of.

Question as to the value of special hypothec of the opstal of a loan place in competition with the special hypothec of the place after its conversion into a quitrent place, entertained but not decided by the Court.

1833. June 29. — *In Re* D. G. van Reenen.—Van Reenen *vs.* Reitz and Breda.

The place Kleinfontyn had been granted by Government as a loan place on 13th March, 1787.

On the 27th September, 1819, D. G. van Reenen, the person then having the legal right to this loan place (whatever that might be), granted, in favour of the Orphan Chamber, a *special mortgage of the opstal of the said loan place Kleinfontyn*, in security of a bond for 9,000*f.*, which had been granted by him to the Orphan Chamber on the 8th January, 1813.

This loan place was by Government converted into a perpetual quitrent place in favour of D. G. van Reenen on the 5th February, 1824. And on the 20th February, 1824, and 2nd March, 1827, this quitrent place, Kleinfontyn, was by the said D. G. van Reenen specially mortgaged in favour of Karnspek, now represented by Reitz, and M. van Breda respectively.

The question in this case was, what preference, if any, was the holder of the special mortgage of 27th September, 1819, entitled to, in competition with the holders of the special mortgages dated 20th February, 1824, and 2nd March, 1827.

After the counsel for both parties had been heard, the parties agreed to settle the question by an extra-judicial arrangement, so that no decision was given by the Court.

Menizes and Kekewich, JJ., were inclined to hold that the holder of the mortgage bond of 27th September, 1819, was entitled to a preference on the whole amount of the value of the place, under deduction of the additional value which the place had acquired by the conversion of its tenure from loan place to quitrent place.

Wylde, C.J., was inclined to hold that this preference should be limited at most to the value of the opstal or buildings on the place, and even to that extent he thought the claim of the holder of said mortgage bond to any preference very doubtful.

The *Attorney-General*, for the Orphan Chamber, had quoted the Proclamation of the 10th September, 1790, whereby it was enacted "that in future when any so-called loan places, or mere property in the opstals (buildings erected on) of the same shall be sold, either publicly or privately, or alienated, the purchasers, or those to whom the same are alienated, shall be bound of the true purchase money of the said loan places to pay to the Honourable Company the 40th penny, in the same manner as of all other immovable property."

Cloete, for Reitz and Breda, had maintained that the mortgage of the *opstal* could at most not be effectual for more than the value of the superstructures erected on the place, and referred to the *Memorie Instructif* of Governor Van Imhoff, dated 28th February, 1732.

The Proclamation dated 20th July, 1790.

The Instructions by Commissary-General De Mist to the bookkeepers of the General Land Revenue, 23rd July, 1793, § 14.

Circular letter by Government to the Landdrosts of the country districts and the Receiver of the Land Revenue, dated 8th July, 1809.

Dispatch by the Fiscal to the Governor, dated 28th June, 1811.

Proclamation of the 6th August, 1813.

The following is a translation of the title under which Kleinfontyn was held as a loan place:

"Permission is hereby granted to the landbouwer, A. B., to allow his cattle to lay and graze for the term of one whole year on the place ———, situated, &c., provided he does not thereby hinder in grazing any prior occupant, nor take this leave into any consequence (*i.e.*, founding any claim in consequence of this leave), being bound, moreover, to have this permission registered in the Secretary's office, and upon payment to the Company's chest as a recognition in favour of the Company of 24 rds.; and also provided he renew this permission within one month after the expiration thereof, under the penalties prescribed in that respect; and further being bound to deliver the tenth part of whatever crops are reaped upon the said place in this castle for the Lord or the Company, and also deliver this deed to the Landdrost. This done in the Castle of the Cape of Good Hope. Signed," &c., &c.

In Re Roux.—Ryneveld *vs.* Juritz.

Hypothec for price of medicines.

A medical man has no preference for medicines supplied before insolvency to an insolvent alive when his estate was sequestrated.

1833. Dec. 19. — *In Re* Roux.—Ryneveld *vs.* Juritz.

The Court decided that a medical man has no preference for medicines supplied to an insolvent alive when his estate was sequestrated for any period prior to the sequestration; and ordered the scheme of distribution to be amended in terms of the Master's report, with costs.

In Re Meiring.—Cloete *vs.* Aling.

Interest: Hypothec for. Custom. Ord. No. 64, § 40. [*No.* 6, 1843, § 33.] *Insolvency.*

The holder of a mortgage bond is entitled in preference on the debtor's sequestration, not to full arrears of interest which may be due on the bond, but only to interest for one year in addition to that for the current year.

Dec. 3. 1834. Feb. 28. Mar. 1. — *In Re* Meiring.—Cloete *vs.* Aling.

In the distribution account of the insolvent estate of Meiring, the trustees, under the 40th section of Ordinance No. 64, in respect of a mortgage bond dated 23rd June, 1820, passed by the insolvent in favour of De Villiers, awarded the whole amount of the capital and of one and the current year's interest due thereon previously to the surrender of Meiring's estate, together with the interest from that date up to the time of payment, and awarded the balance of the assets of this estate to Aling, the holder of a general mortgage bond next in date to that in favour of De Villiers, in part payment of the capital due to Aling. P. L. Cloete and R. A. Cloete, the sureties in Meiring's bond to De Villiers, and to which they had now acquired right by cession from De Villiers, objected to this mode of distribution, and claimed a preference in respect of the said bond for the whole arrears of interest due thereon previous to the surrender, viz., for four years and seven months; and obtained a rule on Aling to show cause why the said distribution account should not be amended, and the preference claimed by them awarded to them.

Postea (28th February, 1834).—*Brand* showed cause against the rule. He stated that before 1802 there was no Boedel Kamer and no Sequestrator in this Colony, but all executions of sentences and distributions of insolvent estates were conducted by the Secretary of the

Court, under the examination of two commissioners of the Court, and subject to the confirmation of the Court, and that while this was the case, it appears from the records that a preference for the interest on mortgage bonds was invariably allowed in express terms for one year and the current year, from 1736 to 1802, when the Boedel Kamer was instituted, and that the same rule was invariably followed and acted on from 1802 to 1814, by the Boedel Kamer, and after that period in like manner by the Sequestrator; and referred to *Voet,* 20, 4, § 27; *Groenwegen,* 20, 4, *l.* 18; *Ordinance, 26th October,* 1572, altered by the Ordinance provisionally passed in 1755, and finally passed 17th January, 1777, § 60, which enacted that "to creditors in an insolvent estate, upon whose debts interest runs, no interest shall be awarded than up to the day of the sequestrations being decreed. And creditors having debts secured by hypothec shall also have no interest on their claims than only for the current year and the year before, and with the further arrears of interest only be ranked in concurrence." (*Vide Hollandsche Jaarboek; Burton's Observations on Insolvent Ordinance, page* 147; *Voet,* 20, 2, § 3.)

Cloete argued that although the rule contended for *contra* had been introduced by custom to a certain extent, in cases of special mortgages, so that the creditor was only in such cases entitled to a preference for one and the current year's interest on the proceeds of the property specially mortgaged, yet that no such rule existed in cases of general mortgages, and that the creditor was entitled to a preference for *all* the arrears of interest due, no matter for how many years, on the proceeds of the property affected by the general mortgage; and quoted *Cens. For.,* 4, 11, 20, and argued that the Ordinance 1777 was only a local Ordinance of Amsterdam; and quoted the case of Van As, August, 1805, where to the creditor on a special mortgage preference was awarded for nearly three years' interest on a debt secured by special mortgage, and the case of Heurtly, whose estate was surrendered in 1827, where a preference for many years' interest was awarded, to show that the practice had not been universal.

He admitted that some lawyers in this Colony, and particularly the late Chief Justice, Sir John Truter, who had practised in the Court at Amsterdam, had considered this ordinance as law here; but that mistaken opinion could not make it law, and quoted *Van der Linden, page* 57, and the *Vol.* 6, *Consultations, 8th case, 25th December,* 1665.

Brand, in reply, quoted *Voet,* 20, 4, § 27; *Voet,* 1, 3, 37; *Van Leeuwen, Roman Dutch Law,* 4, 13, § 22; and argued that Van As's case was no precedent, because by it a preference was not given for more than a year and the current

1833. Dec. 3. 1834. Feb. 28. Mar. 1. — *In Re* Meiring.—Cloete *vs.* Aling.

year's interest prior to the date of the sequestration,—the rest of the interest allowed had accrued subsequently to the sequestration; and that the case of Heurtly was not in point, as it was not a case of mortgage. The interest was on the price of the Drostdy House at Tulbagh, sold but not yet transferred, by Landdrost and Heemraden, to whom the interest was awarded.

This day, 1st March, 1834, the Court discharged the rule, and confirmed the scheme of distribution, but without costs.

The Court held that the rule of the civil law, and of Holland prior to the year 1572, undoubtedly was "*prior in sorte prior est in usuris,*" but that the Ordinance of Philip, 1572, although it had never been promulgated or formally acknowledged as a binding law in the United Provinces (*Vide Consult., vol.* 6, *case* 8, 25*th December,* 1665), had shaken the rule of the civil law (*Voet*, 20, 4, § 27; *Groenwegen*, 20, 4, *adl.* 18), and that after its date the principle of the law of Holland came to be, that a preference should be allowed for interest only for a limited period of years, and that the different provinces and cities had by local ordinances fixed different periods of limitations, that at Amsterdam being one and the current year; consequently, when the law of Holland was introduced into this Colony, the principle of law respecting preference for interest introduced here was not *prior in sorte prior est in usuris,* but that *arrears of interest were entitled to a preference only for a limited period.* That although no written law or ordinance had been discovered by which the rule of Amsterdam was made the law of this Colony, yet that the invariable practice, which had prevailed in this Colony, without interruption, for ninety-eight years, and which there was no reason to doubt had prevailed ever since the establishment of the Colony, must be held as sufficient *primâ facie* evidence that the rule of Amsterdam had been duly made part of the law of the Colony. That equity also was against the claim of the sureties, because in consequence of the rule, which had so long subsisted in this Colony without variation, they must be held to have contracted on the faith that the mortgage would only be available to secure to them interest for one and the current year.

[Note. This was the last act of the Supreme Court under the 1st Charter, dated 24th August, 1827.]

THOMAS *vs.* BARKER.

Attorney: Lien for costs.

An attorney employed by an executor to recover a debt due to the testator has a preference on the amount of the judgment in the Sheriff's hands for his costs of this action, but has no preference for his account against the executor for other business done, not in connection with the testator's estate.

Hayward, now an insolvent, had been executor of the estate of Thomas. Prior to his insolvency, the heirs of Thomas had applied to the Court to have Hayward removed from his executorship, and interdicted from receiving any of the debts due to the estate, which application was granted. Hayward had previously obtained provisional sentence against a debtor to the estate for £100, which, at the time the interdict was granted, was in the hands of the Sheriff.

1834. Sept. 12. — Thomas *vs.* Barker.

This day, the *Attorney-General*, for the heirs, applied to the Court for an order that this money should be paid over to them. This was opposed by *Cloete* for Attorney Barker, who claimed a preference over it for the amount of an account for business done by him for Hayward, and quoted *Hullock on Costs*, 2, 52.

The Court (WYLDE, J.C., absent on circuit) were clear that for the costs of the provisional sentence Barker would have had a preference, but that those had been paid, and that as the account was not for business done for the benefit of Thomas's estate, but for Hayward personally, there was no pretence on which he could claim any preference on the sum in the Sheriff's hands; and granted the application of the heirs, with costs.

The Court held that it was unnecessary to decide, and therefore did not decide, whether an attorney has a lien on the amount of a judgment recovered in an action conducted by him as attorney, merely for the amount of his bill of costs in that action, or also for the whole amount of the bill due to him by his client on other accounts, and whether, if the account due by Hayward had been for work done by Barker for the benefit of Thomas's estate, he would have been entitled to the preference claimed by him.

In Re Wolff and Bartman.—The Colonial Government and Sandenberg, and Securities for Wolff and Bartman, *vs.* The Trustees of Wolff and Bartman.

The Colonial Government held to be preferent on the insolvent estates of auctioneers for the amount of the Government auction dues received by them and not duly paid.

[*Sed vide Act* 4 *of* 1861.]

1836. May 19.

In Re Wolfe and Bartman.—The Colonial Government and Sandenberg, and Securities for Wolfe and Bartman, *vs.* The Trustees of Wolfe and Bartman.

Wolff and Bartman had carried on business as licensed auctioneers, but had become insolvent, and surrendered their joint and separate estates. At the date of their insolvency, they were in arrear to Government, to a large amount, for auction duties, with which they had become chargeable under the 4th and 5th sections of Ordinance No. 31. A liquidation account of their joint and separate estates had been framed by their trustees; to which account the following objection was taken on the part of the Government, viz.:

"Clerk of the Peace Office,
"6th February, 1836.

"Sir,—As the liquidation of the joint and separate estates of Messrs. Wolff and Bartman are about to be submitted to the Supreme Court for confirmation, I beg leave to call your attention to the two claims, each of £500, proved on account of the Colonial Government at the special meeting held on the 19th ultimo, of which no notice has been taken by the trustees. I beg, therefore, that you will note my objection on the part of Government against the said liquidation being confirmed. I have also to object to the debts due to the Government for unpaid auction dues being ranked in concurrence, considering them entitled to preference.

"D. J. CLOETE."

The *Attorney-General,* for the Government, supported the objection taken for the Government to the scheme of distribution, in respect that, by being only ranked in concurrence for certain auction duties, instead of as preferent creditors, the Government were improperly deprived of a certain large sum of money. He quoted the *Ordinance No.* 31, §§ 3, 4, *and* 5, and contended that the duties imposed by the third section must be considered as taxes, the collection of which was, in respect of the fourth and other sections of the Ordinance, farmed out to persons taking out licence as auctioneers, and consequently that, for the arrears of those duties unpaid by the auctioneers, the Government were entitled to be ranked as preferent creditors, and quoted the case of *Van der Byl & Co. vs. the Sequestrator*, 23*rd September*, 1828 (*Vol.* 1, *p.* 318). He proceeded to argue that, by virtue of the fifth section of the Ordinance, and the fact of the failure of Wolff and Bartman to pay up the duties at the proper time, Government was entitled to be ranked on the estates of each for the penalty of £500. But it appearing that, although Government had claimed to prove a debt for this penalty, yet their claim to prove had not been allowed, and that no proceedings had since been taken by the Government to have the decision of the matter altered, and the debt allowed to be proved, he gave up this objection for the present, as of course the Government could not object that they had not, in the distribution, been ranked for penalties for which they had not as yet been allowed to prove, and for which they had as yet recovered no judgment.

1836. May 19.

In Re Wolfe and Bartman.—The Colonial Government and Sandenberg and Securities for Wolfe and Bartman, *vs.* The Trustees of Wolfe and Bartman.

Cloete, for the sureties, argued on the same side, and quoted *Voet*, 20, 4, 23.

Brand, contra, argued that neither Wolff nor Bartman were to be considered as collectors of taxes, but merely as a contractor, and that Government had not the same preference over the estates of contractors as over those of collectors. *Van der Keessel, Thes.* 420.

The Court sustained the objection, and ordered the scheme of distribution of the separate estate of Wolff and of Bartman to be amended, by ranking the Government as preferent creditors, on the separate estate of Wolff for £594 15s. 2d., and on the separate estate of Bartman for £1,440 2s. 8d., being the amount of duties due by them respectively as auctioneers, with costs.

Executors of Swart *vs.* All and Sundry.

Mode by which a bond remaining uncancelled in the Debt Registry may be cancelled, the bond itself being alleged to have been given up by the creditor and receipted; but having been mislaid, so that, after the death of both creditor and debtor, proof could not be given of payment so as to authorize cancellation in the Debt Registry.

The deceased Nicholas Vos, on the 11th December, 1807, executed a mortgage bond for 4,000*f.*, whereby he mortgaged his place Heuvels Kraal in favour of J. J. Vos.

May 26.

Executors of Swart *vs.* All and Sundry.

1836. May 26. — Executors of Swart vs. All and Sundry.

Payment of this bond having been demanded in 1814, Nicholas Vos, the debtor, applied for and obtained a loan of 4,000*f*. from the Lombard Bank, to enable him to discharge the said bond of 1807; and in security of the said loan, on the 15th September, 1840, executed in favour of the Lombard Bank a mortgage bond for that sum, mortgaging his said place Heuvels Kraal.

With the 4,000*f*. so received from the Lombard Bank, Nicolas Vos paid to J. J. Vos the amount of the said bond of 11th December, 1807, which was thereupon receipted by the said J. J. Vos, and given up and returned by him to the said Nicolas Vos.

Nicolas Vos died in July, 1824, and J. J. Vos had also died long ago. Thereafter the plaintiff, as executor of Nicolas Vos, desired to have the said bond of 11th December, 1807, cancelled from the Debt Register, which, however, he could not procure to be effected, being unable to produce the bond itself so receipted, or any written evidence of its having been discharged by J. J. Vos, the bond having been lost or mislaid by Nicolas Vos, so that it could not be found after his death.

Under these circumstances, the plaintiff applied for and duly obtained summons by edictal citation "against all and every person having or pretending to have any right, title, or interest to or in the said bond," which was fully described in the said summons, and, after having duly published the four edictal citations, filed his *intendit*, in which he set forth the above facts, and prayed the Court to order the said bond to be cancelled from the Debt Registry.

No appearance was made by any person as defendant; and the plaintiff having fully proved the above facts by two witnesses, one of whom saw the money paid to and the receipt written on the bond, and the bond delivered to N. Vos, by J. J. Vos, the creditor, and both of whom, long afterwards, saw the bond so receipted in the possession of N. Vos in his house; and also produced the records of the late Court of Justice, containing the usual publication, by order of the Court, at the instance of N. Vos, executor, dated 28th October, 1824, calling in all claims against the then deceased N. Vos, and showing that no claim had been lodged in respect of said bond of 11th December, 1807: the Court gave judgment for the plaintiff as prayed.

In Re Stoll.—Cloete *vs.* The Colonial Government.

An anterior conventional general hypothec is not preferent to the posterior tacit general hypothec of the Government over receivers of the public revenue.

1836. Aug. 26.

In Re Stoll.—Cloete *vs.* Colonial Government.

Cloete, for the applicant, moved to have made absolute a rule, calling on the Government to show cause why the liquidation account in this estate should not be amended by awarding a preference to the applicant in virtue of a notarial bond, dated 5th April, 1811, passed by Stoll as principal debtor, and by Cloete as surety, in favour of Serrurier, paid to Serrurier by Cloete, and ceded by Cloete to Serrurier on the 13th November, 1834, and duly registered on the 5th April, 1811, before the preference which was therein awarded to the Colonial Government.

It was admitted that the tacit legal hypothec, in virtue of which the Government claimed and had obtained preference for the debt due to it by Stoll, in his capacity of Receiver-General and Treasurer, commenced, and must be held to date back to the 9th April, 1819.

The question, therefore, was simply whether an anterior conventional general hypothec is or is not preferable to a posterior tacit general hypothec of the nature of that which by law Government has over the effects of the receivers of the public revenue for debts due by them to the Government in that capacity.

In support of the preference of the anterior general conventional hypothec, *Cloete* quoted *Voet* 20, 1, 14.

The *Attorney-General*, in support of the contrary proposition, referred to *Van der Keessel*, § 437.

In respect of which lastmentioned authority, the Court refused the rule, with costs.

The Master, as the Executor of Bohmer, *vs.* The Churchwardens of the Roman Catholic Chapel and Others.

Hypothec on Church property for moneys expended in its erection.

Nov. 24.

The Master, as the Executor of Bohmer, *vs.* The Churchwardens of the Roman Catholic Chapel and Others.

In this case, the Master, as representing the Orphan Chamber, who were the executors of the deceased Bohmer, having sued out and caused to be duly served edictal process against all and sundry having, or pretending to have, any right, title, or interest in certain immovable

1836. Nov. 24. — The Master, as the Executor of Bohmer, *vs.* The Churchwardens of the Roman Catholic Chapel and Others.

property, registered as the property of the Rev. P. Scully, formerly pastor of the Roman Catholic congregation in Cape Town, summoning them to hear certain claims made by him, as administering the estate of Bohmer, against the said immovable property, filed his declaration (*intendit*), which set forth—

That on the 7th September, 1821, the Governor of this Colony granted unto the said P. Scully, a certain piece of land, containing 228 square roods 101⅓ square feet, situate where the Roman Catholic chapel of Cape Town now stands, for the purpose of his causing to be built thereon a chapel for the Roman Catholic congregation of Cape Town and a dwelling-house for the minister thereof.

That between the 15th April, 1822, and the 3rd January, 1825, the said J. W. Bohmer did, at the special instance and request of the said P. Scully, pay, lay out, and expend, in, for, and about the building and erecting of the said chapel and dwelling-house, the sum of 6,577 rds., and which sum, or any part thereof, the said P. Scully or any person in his behalf never paid or satisfied to the said Bohmer. That the said chapel and dwelling-house have been long since completed, and that in great part by the said sum so advanced and expended thereon by the said J. W. Bohmer as aforesaid, and have always been used by or appropriated to the use of the Catholic congregation at Cape Town and the minister thereof.

That the said P. Scully hath long since left this Colony, and there is no person within the same to represent him and administer his real or personal estate, and that by reason of the premises and of the said money having been expended as aforesaid on the immovable estate of the said P. Scully, and for the benefit and advantage thereof, the said plaintiff has a claim against the said immovable property for the said amount of 6,577 rds., together with the interest thereon from the 1st May, 1825.

Wherefore the said plaintiff prayed that the said immovable estate of the said P. Scully, or such part thereof as may be sufficient to pay the said claim, may be sold under the decree of this Court, and that such part of the purchase-money thereof as may be sufficient to satisfy the said claim may be directed to be paid to the said plaintiff, in his capacity aforesaid, together with his costs of suit, or that the said plaintiff may have such further or such other relief as he may be found legally entitled to have in the premises, &c.

Appearance was made for the present pastor and churchwardens of the Roman Catholic congregation, who filed a plea, in which they admitted the grant of the ground to Scully in the manner and for the purpose set forth in the declaration, the fact that the chapel and house had been erected, and had been used by the congregation and the minister thereof, but denied every other allegation in the declaration, and joined issue thereon.

1836. Nov. 24.

The Master, as the Executor of Bohmer, *vs.* The Churchwardens of the Roman Catholic Chapel and Others.

Appearance was also made for A. Chiappini, F. de Lettre, M. Donough, and the widow Mabille, who filed a separate plea, in which they stated that they joined in the suit for their own interest; that they admitted all the allegations in the declaration, and further that over and above the sum of 6,577 rds. advanced by Bohmer, and expended in behalf of the said Roman Catholic chapel in the manner as stated in the plaintiff's declaration, the late F. L. Mabille and the said Bohmer, duly qualified by the then churchwardens of the said Roman Catholic congregation, did on the 19th April, 1826, borrow from the Lombard Bank the sum of £375, which also they, the said churchwardens, expended in behalf of and for the erection of the said Roman Catholic chapel and dwelling attached thereto, and for which debt also the ground upon which the said chapel now stands was especially mortgaged by a bond in which the said A. Chiappini, F. de Lettre, F. L. Mabille, J. W. Bohmer, M. Donough, and one J. Heenrich, since insolvent, became sureties *in solidum* under renunciation of the *beneficia ordinis*, &c., &c., and that they or their representatives are liable at all times to be called upon to pay and discharge the same; and therefore they, for their interest, consent in the claim made in the aforesaid declaration, and pray that in the event of the said landed property of the Rev. P. Scully, or the erf upon which the said Roman Catholic chapel and dwelling-house are built, being sold in execution, so much of the proceeds thereof be set apart and applied to the discharge of the aforesaid sum of £375, with the interest, &c.

A separate plea was also filed by M. Donough, joining in this suit for his own interest, in which he admitted all the allegations set forth in the declaration. And further stating that over and above the sum of 6,577 rds., expended by the said late J. W. Bohmer, as in the said declaration alleged, he, the said M. Donough, hath also, at the special instance and request of the said P. Scully, and also of the churchwardens for the time being of the said Roman Catholic chapel, paid, laid out, and expended divers sums of money in, for, and about the building and erecting of the said chapel and dwelling-house, amounting by balance to a sum of 1,257 rds. 7 sk. 2 st., as appears from an account, which the said M. Donough prays may be considered as herein literally inserted, and which sum of 1,257 rds., 7 sk., 2 st., is still unsatisfied, and for which the said chapel and dwelling-house is tacitly mortgaged.

1836. Nov. 24.

The Master, as the Executor of Bohmer, *vs.* The Churchwardens of the Roman Catholic Chapel and Others.

Wherefore the said M. Donough consented to the claim made in the declaration, and made a similar conclusion to that in the last plea.

After hearing the written and parole evidence adduced by the parties, the Court made this order:

"It is ordered that, in the mean time staying all further proceedings, the case do stand referred to the Master to hear any objection which may be stated by the defendants, the pastor and churchwardens of the said Catholic chapel, as to the correctness of the account of the late J. H. Bohmer against the said Catholic church, dated on the 1st day of May, 1825, and certified as correct by the then churchwardens of the said church; and further to hear any objections that may be stated by the said parties against the account of M. Donough, and to report as to the nature and effect thereof; and further to report what funds, if any, may hereafter in any and what way be raised from the sale of the materials, or by the use, management, or appropriation of the said ground and buildings thereon, without affecting or changing the original purposes for which the grant was made."

Postea.—The Master reported that after having compared the accounts with the vouchers and documents submitted in proof thereof, he found the sum of 6,577 rds. 5 sk. 2 st. to be the balance due to the estate of the late J. W. Bohmer, and the sum of 1,252 rds, 7 sk. 2 st. to be the balance due to M. Donough for moneys advanced and expended by them in and about the erection and maintenance of the said Catholic chapel; that he also found A. Chiappini and M. Donough tendering and willing to pay for the hire of the aforesaid ground and buildings thereon the annual rent of £75 during the period there shall be a resident pastor, provided the said period does not exceed four years, and provided the temporalities of the same are under their management as the curators appointed by an order of Court, dated 10th July, 1832.

After hearing the parties on this report, the Court found that the immovable property of the said Patrick Scully stands charged with a preferent hypothec for the sum of £483 5s. 6d. to the estate of the late John W. Bohmer, and that the same stands also charged with a hypothec for the further sum of £93 19s. 4½d., to Matthew Donough; and for and towards satisfying the said hypothecs, order and adjudge that possession of the said immovable property be delivered over to the said Antonio Chiappini and Matthew Donough, upon and under the terms and conditions of the tender made by them, and referred to in the Master's report thereon. And as to costs, do adjudge that the said defendants (the pastor and churchwardens of the congregation) be condemned to pay the plaintiff's costs incident to and chargeable upon the issue between the plaintiff and defendants from the date of filing their plea in the said case, with the costs of the application to the Court. 1836. Nov. 24. — The Master, as the Executor of Bohmer, *vs.* The Churchwardens of the Roman Catholic Chapel and Others.

The Court refused the application made for Donough that the said defendants should be condemned to pay his costs.

In Re Mostert.—Smit *vs.* Jurgens.

A bond of anterior date, but not duly registered until after a bond of posterior date had been registered, postponed to latter.

On the 10th of March, 1824, the insolvent granted a bond in favour of Smit, mortgaging certain slaves, and on the 16th March, the bond was produced at the Slave Registry, and a certificate of the mortgage was taken out; but this bond was not registered in the Public Debt Register until the 21st of November, 1832. 1837. Feb. 14. — *In Re* Mostert.—Smit *vs.* Jurgens.

The insolvent, on the 6th April, 1827, granted a bond in favour of Jurgens, which bond was registered in and at the Slave Registry on the 18th, and in the Public Debt Register on the 20th of April, 1827.

The trustee preferred Jurgens's bond.

The Court (Kekewich, J., absent) confirmed this preference and the provisional liquidation account, with costs.

In Re Liesching.—Agents of Von Bihl *vs.* The President and Directors of the Lombard Bank, the Master of the Supreme Court, representing the Orphan Chamber, the Widow Van der Poel, and the Trustee.

Minor's hypothec on property of guardian.

A and B were guardians of a minor, B being the administering guardian. A granted a mortgage bond specially hypothecating certain property to B as administering guardian, which bond was, on B.'s departure from the Colony, delivered as an asset of the minor's estate to C, who had been constituted administering guardian. A having become insolvent, the question arose whether, for the amount of this bond, there was a preference by virtue of the legalis hypotheca tutelæ on the insolvent estate, taking preference of special mortgages prior to the mortgage in question. The Court held that the estate of A was not subject to any tutorial hypothec until after excussion of the administering guardian duly constituted, and then for the balance not recoverable from him: that the mortgage bond passed for the debt in favour of the administering guardian was therefore to be postponed in order of preference to the special hypothec of anterior date.

1837. Nov. 28. 1838. Feb. 20. „ 27.

In Re Liesching.—Agents of Von Bihl *vs.* The President and Directors of the Lombard Bank, the Master of the Supreme Court, representing the Orphan Chamber, the Widow Van der Poel, and the Trustee.

In the insolvent estate of Liesching, the following report was made by the Master:

"The agents of Captain von Bihl, of Java, object to the distribution of the assets of the abovementioned estate, by reason of the trustees not having awarded preference to the claim of Captain von Bihl over the property of his guardians. It appears that Dr. Liesching, senior, and J. J. Ziegler were appointed guardians of Von Bihl in the year 1809.

"The guardians received from the executors after the death of Von Bihl, senior, the sum of 14,656 rds.

"Dr. Liesching, senior, and Ziegler were in partnership as apothecaries.

"The account of the guardians was closed on the 31st December, 1822, with a balance of 30,414 rds. 2 sk. in favour of the minor, shortly after which Ziegler left the Colony, and died at sea. Previous, however, to his leaving the Colony, he had been appointed agent of Captain von Bihl, who was then of age, and before his departure he assumed the late P. Woutersen as von Bihl's agent."

(N.B. This is incorrect. Woutersen was substituted by Ziegler as tutor, and not as agent. *Vide infra*).

"In February, 1823, Woutersen received from Ziegler in payment of the abovementioned sum—

	Rds.	sk.	st.
"A mortgage bond passed by G. Zoin in favour of Captain von Bihl, amounting to	6,666	5	2
"An underhand bond of Dr. Liesching, senior	19,947	5	1
"The balance being due from Woutersen	3,799	7	3
	30,414	2	0

"On the 21st October, 1831, Dr. Liesching executed a mortgage bond in favour of Von Bihl to the amount of the underhand bond above mentioned, subject, however, to such deductions as might be made therefrom, should the account be hereafter reopened, either by consent or by decree of the Court.

1837. Nov. 28. 1838. Feb. 20. „ 27.

In Re Liesching. —Agents of Von Bihl *vs.* The President and Directors of the Lombard Bank, the Master of the Supreme Court, representing the Orphan Chamber, the Widow Van der Poel, and the Trustee.

"After the insolvency of Dr. Liesching, the trustees of the estate and the agents of Von Bihl submitted the matter of account to arbitration, and the arbitrators awarded to A. von Bihl a sum of 23,953 rds. 7 sk. 2 st., with interest on 19,947 rds. 5 sk. 1 st., from the 9th February, 1836, giving him legal hypothecation or mortgage on the estate of the said F. L. Liesching, senior, as having been his guardian, and as having in that capacity administered his inheritance. This award was confirmed by a decree of the Court on the 17th May, 1836. In the private estate of Dr. Liesching, senior, the trustees have awarded to the agents of Von Bihl a preference in respect of his tacit legal mortgage on the property of his guardian from 1809, when the insolvent took upon himself that office. But in the estate of Dr. Liesching & Co. they have not awarded the same priority of ranking, but have preferred the mortgage creditors of a later date. In the estate of Dr. Liesching & Co. there are two pieces of landed property, the one being a house and premises in Loop-street, and the other a store and premises in Shortmarket-street. The former became Dr. Liesching's sole property in April, 1800, and the latter the joint property of Dr. Liesching and J. J. Ziegler in October, 1802. The partnership between Dr. Liesching and Ziegler was dissolved in 1816, and the two sons of Dr. Liesching joined their father, and carried on the business under the firm of Dr. Liesching & Co. Dr. Liesching transferred one half of the house and premises in Loop-street to his sons in September, 1819, and Ziegler transferred his share in the store and premises in Shortmarket-street also to the sons of Dr. Liesching at the same time.

"On the 27th August, 1819, the father and the two sons mortgaged the house in Loop-street to the Lombard Bank for £270, and the trustees have awarded the first preference in respect of this bond.

"On the 17th September, 1819, the same parties granted a second mortgage on the same property to the Orphan Chamber for £375, and the trustees have awarded the second preference in respect of this bond.

"On the 24th September, 1819, the same parties granted a third mortgage on the same property, and a first mortgage on the store in Shortmarket-street, to Dr. Wehr for £500, which was ceded on the 24th December, 1827, to J. V. Karnspek, and by him ceded to the Widow van der Poel on the 16th May, 1834.

"The trustees have awarded the next preference in

1837. Nov. 28. 1838. Feb. 20. „ 27.

In Re Liesching.—Agents of Von Bihl *vs.* The President and Directors of the Lombard Bank, the Master of the Supreme Court, representing the Orphan Chamber, the Widow Van der Poel, and the Trustee.

respect of this bond, and the balance of the said landed property, amounting to £487 16s. 3d., they have awarded to the agents of Von Bihl, and allowed them to rank in concurrence for their balance.

"Against this plan of distribution the agents of Von Bihl object, and claim the first preference on the whole property by right of their tacit legal mortgage on the estate of Dr. Liesching as guardian of Von Bihl."

This day, *De Wet,* for the agents of Von Bihl, was heard in support of a rule which he had obtained, calling on the respondents to show cause why the liquidation and distribution account, as framed by the trustees, on the insolvent estate of Liesching shall not be amended, and why preference shall not be awarded to the said applicants on the proceeds distributable in the said insolvent estates, before the different sums of £310 10s., £453 15s., and £552 10s., awarded by the said trustees to the respondents respectively.

He maintained, first, that neither by the underhand bond for 19,947 rds. 5 sk. 1 st, dated 7th March, 1823, nor the mortgage bond, dated 21st October, 1831, granted by Dr. Liesching to and received by the agents of Von Bihl, was a novation constituted of the debt previously due by Liesching to Von Bihl in his tutorial capacity, and in security of which Von Bihl had a tacit legal hypothec over all Liesching's estate, and quoted *Van der Linden's Institutes, p.* 269; *Cod.* 8, 42, *l.* 8; *Pothier ad Pandectas, vol.* 4, *p.* 252; *Dig.* 46, *tit.* 2; *Voet* 20, 2, 18. He maintained that, as there had been no act of acquittal or discharge or receipt for the tutorial debt, this proved that no innovation of it had been made by the bonds subsequently granted by Dr. Liesching. That the mortgage bond was taken merely as a security over the property therein mortgaged, better than that afforded by the tacit legal hypothec, in respect that it prevented the property so mortgaged being alienated.

He objected also to the mortgage bond, in respect of which preference has been awarded to the Lombard Bank, on the ground that it had been granted by Dr. Liesching and his sons some days before the latter had got transfer of their share of the property mortgaged by them.

Cloete, for the Lombard Bank, argued *contra,* and stated that no claim whatever had been filed on the insolvent estate by the applicants, in respect of the debt due to Von Bihl by Dr. Liesching in his tutorial capacity, but only on the two bonds granted by him.

He maintained that the first bond, *i.e.,* the underhand bond, was granted by Liesching in his individual capacity, and not in his tutorial capacity, and at a time when the tutory had expired by the majority of the minor.

[N.B.—It was admitted on all hands that Von Bihl was more than twenty-one when this bond was granted, but it was disputed whether he had then attained his twenty-fifth year. From the deed by which Ziegler assumed Woutersen as co-tutor of Von Bihl on the 6th of March, 1823, previous to his, Ziegler's, departure, and the day before the bond of the 7th March, 1823, and the terms of the latter, it was clear that both Ziegler and Liesching considered that the guardianship still subsisted. It is true that there was a notarial power of attorney executed on the 17th September, 1821, by Von Bihl, then an officer in the Dutch army in Batavia, by which he constituted Woutersen as his attorney and general agent.]

1837. Nov. 28. 1838. Feb. 20. „ 27.

In Re Liesching.—Agents of Von Bihl *vs.* The President and Directors of the Lombard Bank, the Master of the Supreme Court, representing the Orphan Chamber, the Widow Van der Poel, and the Trustee.

And quoted *Voet* 49, 2, § 3, to show that novation had taken place by the granting and receiving the two bonds. (*Pothier de Novatione, Note by Van der Linden to* § 594.) He argued that from the very nature of the underhand bond, which was a negotiable instrument, it was clear that it must have been given in payment, and not as an additional security, and that this view of the case is confirmed by the terms of the mortgage bond, on which he commented, or that at all events the mortgage bond itself constituted a novation of the tutorial debt. And contended that a claim having only been filed on the bond, the applicant could not now claim a preference in respect of a hypothec not legally belonging to such a bond, although such a hypothec may belong to a debt which existed previously to the bond, for the further security of which the bond had been granted, and might have been claimed, if a claim had been filed on the estate specifically on that debt.

The *Attorney-General*, for the Master of the Supreme Court, followed on the same side, and quoted *Van der Linden, p.* 181. And, admitting that the underhand bond did not constitute a novation, but was merely a temporary voucher given by Liesching to his co-tutors, to show the amount of his debt to the tutorial estate at its date, he contended that the mortgage bond itself constituted a novation of the debt, and also quoted *Voet* 20, 2, 19.

Brand, for the trustee, and *Hiddingh* for the Widow van der Poel, followed on the same side.

De Wet replied.

Cur. adv. vult.

(February 20, 1838.)—In consequence of a doubt which had occurred to the Court as to the manner in which the estate of the minor had been administered, the argument was this day resumed, and De Wet, for Von Bihl, produced a liquidation account of the estate, dated

1837. Nov. 23. 1838. Feb. 20. „ 27.

In Re Liesching.—Agents of Von Bihl *vs.* The President and Directors of the Lombard Bank, the Master of the Supreme Court, representing the Orphan Chamber, the Widow Van der Poel, and the Trustee.

1st November, 1818, and an account, dated 7th March, 1823, between Liesching and Ziegler, and maintained that the debt due by Dr. Liesching was due by him in his capacity of tutor, and not of a debtor, to whom money belonging to the estate had been lent by the administrating guardians.

Cloete argued *contra*, and quoted *Voet* 26, 7, 1; and maintained that Ziegler had been the *administrator* or administrating guardian of the tutorial estate, and in proof of this produced and referred to the notarial deed, dated 6th March, 1823, executed by Ziegler, by which he assumed Woutersen as his co-tutor and administrator of the estate of Von Bihl, and an acknowledgment by Woutersen, dated 9th March, 1823, to the following effect:

"Received from Mr. J. J. de Ziegler, as one of the guardians and *late administrator* of the moneys of the ward A. von Bihl, the following mortgage bonds and private bonds, viz.: 1st, the mortgage bond for 6,666 rds. 5 sk. 2 st.; 2nd, a private bond of Dr. Liesching, senior, containing the obligation to pass in lieu thereof, within four weeks, a mortgage bond to the satisfaction of the co-guardians for 19,347 rds. 5 sk. 1 st.;" and quoted *Voet* 20, 2, 16, *in fine*, 26, 7, 8, and produced a notarial deed, dated 6th March, 1823, whereby Ziegler in his capacity of one of the guardians over the person, and administrators of the inheritance of the minor, assumed to himself and appointed as administrator and co-guardian Mr. Pieter Woutersen, and whereby the latter accepted the said assumption, and undertook the duties of guardian and administrator.

Brand followed on the same side, and quoted *Voet* 27, 8, § 6.

De Wet replied that Mr. Ziegler, being out of the Colony, and more especially as it is not known where he is, or whether he is insolvent, or whether he is solvent, or whether he is dead, he must be held to have been excussed.

Cur. adv. vult.

Postea (27th February, 1838.)—The Court were unanimously of opinion that Ziegler had been the administrating guardian of Von Bihl, and that on the 6th March, 1823, he had appointed Woutersen to be the administrating guardian, and that Woutersen had accepted that office, and continued to act in that capacity during the rest of the minority. That at the time Woutersen undertook the office of administrating guardian in the place of Ziegler, it was proved by the account between Ziegler and Von Bihl, dated 31st December, 1832, that Ziegler then had under his administration as administrating guardian, and as such was bound to account for, and hand over to his successor, assets of the estate of his ward to the amount of 30,414 rds. That previous to this, and on the 6th February, 1823, Liesching was indebted to Ziegler, either in his private capacity or as administrating guardian (but not as having himself received, or having had under his administration as one of the co-tutors, and as assets of the estate of the ward) 10,278 rds., and that on the 6th February he became indebted to Ziegler in another debt, arising in the same way, to the amount of 9,669 rds.; total 19,947 rds. That afterwards he settled this debt with Ziegler by granting the bond of the 7th March, 1823, and delivering it to Ziegler, who thereupon handed it over to Woutersen, then the administrating guardian, as part of the assets which had been under his administration, and that Woutersen received it as such. That, under those circumstances, it was not competent to Von Bihl to sue Liesching *actione tutelæ*, or to claim any tutorial hypothec over his estate, until (*Voet* 27, 8, 6; 26, 7, 1) he had first excussed Woutersen, the administrating guardian, and after such excussion, then only for such balance as could not be recovered from Woutersen; and that although it was competent for Von Bihl, or his representative, now to sue Liesching's estate for the amount of the bond, still it was not such a debt as (*Voet* 20, 2, 16; 26, 7, 8) *venire potest in judicium tutelæ:* or was secured by the *legalis hypotheca tutelæ* and therefore found that the agents of Von Bihl are not entitled to any preference in virtue of the *legalis hypotheca tutelæ*, and that the prior special mortgages are preferable to the mortgage bond of the 21st October, 1821, executed by Liesching in favour of Von Bihl; and confirmed the distribution account, with costs.

In Re Carter.—Leibbrandt and Geyer *vs.* Dickson and Burnies.

Preference in insolvency. Bond for future advances. Liquidation account, amendment of. Registration. Stamp on bond.

A bond for uncertain amounts to be advanced in future, and containing a special and general mortgage is a valid bond, in preference, if duly registered.

Where a bond for £500 already advanced on security of a special and general mortgage, and for future uncertain advances was registered as a special bond for £500, without any mention in the registry of the future advances or of the general clause; held that as no particular form of registry is prescribed by law, such registration is sufficient; although it is at the same time very desirable that regulations should be framed for the more specific registration of such bonds in future.

Where such bond was stamped originally for £500, no objection to the bond can be taken on this ground, the stamp law making no provision for stamps on bonds for uncertain amounts.

Per MENZIES, J.: *Non-registration, or a wrong registration, where it is the fault of the Registrar of Deeds, founds an action of damages against him, but deprives the creditor of preference.*

1837. Dec. 19.

In Re Carter.—Leibbrandt and Geyer *vs.* Dickson and Burnies.

Cloete argued in support of the rule which he had obtained, calling on the Messrs. Dickson & Burnies to show cause why the liquidation and distribution account should not be altered and amended, on the ground that Dickson & Burnies had been allowed to prove for a greater amount than the insolvent was truly indebted to them; and secondly, that, even if their claim was correct as to amount, they had been unduly preferred to the applicants. The Master's report was as follows:

"That in this estate the trustees have drawn out a provisional account of the distribution of the first assets, in which they have awarded a preference to Messrs. Dickson, Burnies, & Co., and to R. J. Jones, which preferences are objected to by S. Leibbrandt and J. D. Sertyn, widow and executrix of the late G. F. Geyer, concurrent creditors under the said estate.

"The objections of the opposing creditors against the preference awarded to Dickson, Burnies, & Co. are, first, because their account-current with the insolvent runs from January to November, 1836, the latter date being six months after the surrender of the estate; second, because the bond passed by the insolvent in favour of Dickson & Burnies, cannot be held to afford any preference beyond the sum therein expressed, nor for any sums subsequently advanced to or debts contracted by the insolvent, in favour of the said Dickson & Burnies.

"The bond passed by the insolvent in favour of Dickson, Burnies, & Co. is dated 22nd August, 1835, and is registered in the Public Debt Register on the 27th of the same month.

"It contains a special mortgage and a bill of sale of the

brig called the *Cape Breton* for the amount of £500 already advanced to the insolvent prior to the date of the bond, together with all further sums to be advanced to him, and further secured by a general mortgage.

1837. Dec. 19. — *In Re* Carter.—Leibbrandt and Geyer *vs.* Dickson and Burnies.

"Subsequent to the passing of this bond, various transactions have taken place between Dickson, Burnies, & Co. and the insolvent, and sums of money to a large amount have been awarded by them to the insolvent, or paid on his account, the balance due to them, after various payments credited in account, being £1,547 2s. 9d. For the whole of this balance, the trustees have awarded a preference to Dickson, Burnies, & Co., by virtue of the general mortgage in their said bond, but the objecting creditors admit them only to be entitled to preference for the amount of money expressed in the said bond, namely £500, and deny them any right to preference under the general mortgage."

After hearing *Cloete* on the first objection, it was ordered by consent that the Master should examine the vouchers, and report as to the nature and origin of the articles placed to the debit of the insolvent in the account-current after the date of the sequestration, for the balance appearing to be due to them on which the respondents have claimed and been ranked.

He then proceeded to argue in support of his objection to the preference awarded the respondents in virtue of the bond passed in their favour by the insolvent on the 22nd August, 1835, and registered on the 27th August, 1835. He produced the debt register, from which it appeared that this bond was registered as a mortgage only of £510, without any mention of future advances, and maintained that, even although the mortgage, if it had been differently registered, might have been valid for the amount of advances made subsequently to its date (which he denied), still as it was registered only as a mortgage for £510, it constituted only a valid mortgage for that sum, and quoted *Kerstenaus Woordenboek, Appendix, p.* 610, *van Hypothec; Burton on Insolvent Law, p.* 136; *Van Leeuwen, Cens. For.*, 4, 11, 15; *Voet* 20, 1, 12; *and Discount Bank vs. Dawes, 8th September*, 1829. (*Vol.* 1, *p.* 380.)

He contended that none of the items placed to the debit of the insolvent in the said account were payments or advances made in respect of any causes or transactions specified in or contemplated by the bond, but in respect of totally distinct and separate causes and transactions. The only payments and advances contemplated in the bond being such as should be made on account of the vessel the *Cape Breton*, which vessel was immediately afterwards totally wrecked.

1837. Dec. 19. — *In Re* Carter.—Leibbrandt and Geyer *vs.* Dickson and Burnies.

The *Attorney-General, contra,* denied that the further advances and payments specified or contemplated by the bond were only such as should be made in respect of the *Cape Breton.* He contended that registration of general conventional mortgages was not necessary to make them effectual over movables, and preferent to more recent general conventional mortgages and to all concurrent creditors; and quoted the *Dutch Consultations,* 1 *vol., Cons.* 232; *Voet* 20, 1, 20; 20, 4, 30; *Non obstante Van Leeuwen's Cens. For.*, 4, 11, §§ 1, 15.

Musgrave followed on the same side.

He maintained that, even if the bond had not been duly registered by the fault of the Registrar, this should not deprive it of any privilege which it would have had if duly registered. (*Sed vide Voet* 20, 1, 11, *in fine.*)

He also maintained that, as this bond was registered according to the form invariably used in the Colony (no particular form of registration having been prescribed), it was entitled to all the privileges to which by law bonds in virtue of registration are entitled. That it was as much entitled to preference as if it had been set forth word for word in the register, and therefore the only question is whether a general conventional mortgage may effectually be created by a notarial bond for an uncertain sum, *e.g.*, advances and payments, which may thereafter be made to any amount, not specified, or limited, in the bond, by the creditor to the debtor in the bond, which will give an effectual right of preference over movables in the possession of the debtor, when the *concursus creditorum* takes place.

He maintained that by the Roman law a general conventional mortgage for *an indefinite* sum was equally valid and effectual, and enjoyed the same preference as a similar bond for a *certain* sum. That this rule of the Roman law has never been altered by any legislative enactment in the law of Holland, except indirectly by the Placaat of 1665, depriving all bonds of preference, unless a duty of 2½ per cent. was paid on them when passed. That the Court found in the case of the *Discount Bank vs. Dawes,* that the Placaat of 1665 had never been in force in this Colony, nor had any similar rule been provided by any law at any time passed by the legislature of this Colony. That therefore this question must now be decided according to the rule of the Roman law. (*Vide In re Lond, Brink vs. the Guardian of Lond, 29th September,* 1830, *Vol.* 1, *p.* 483.)

Further consideration of the case was postponed until the Master should report as ordered.

[N.B.—No argument was founded on by either party as to the amount of the stamp on which the bond in question was written. *Vide* Proclamations of 24th December, 1807, p. 73; 22nd May, 1812, p. 191; 26th May, 1815, p. 338; 30th April, 1824, p. 648; 10th December, 1824, p. 679. Originally the bond had been stamped as above £500 and under ——, and after proceedings had been commenced, had been covered by the highest stamp.]

Postea (6th February, 1838).—The Master presented his report, showing, as was admitted by *Cloete* for the creditors, that the objections taken by them to the several items in the account of Dickson & Burnies were groundless, with the exception of the fourth and the last items.

The report stated, "that the fourth item, under date the 31st of July, 1836, amounting to £200 19s. 6d., was a bill dated the 1st of March, 1836, drawn by the insolvent on Rowland Winbourne, of London, at sixty days after sight, and indorsed by Dickson, Burnies, & Co., for the accommodation of the insolvent. It was returned dishonoured and paid by Messrs. Burnies & Co., of London, for the honour of the said endorsers."

Cloete contended that although the endorsation was made before Carter's sequestration, yet that as the bill was not paid by Dickson & Burnies until after the sequestration, this could not be considered as an advance made by them before sequestration; and that no advance not made before sequestration could be held to be an advance which was covered by the security created by the bond.

The *Attorney-General* and *Musgrave* argued *contra*.

Postea (27th February, 1838).—Judgment was given.

The Court were unanimously of opinion that the bond, in virtue of which preference has been awarded to Dickson & Burnies, was granted not only in security of the previous advance of £500, but for all further sums to be advanced to him, and whether in respect of the vessel, the *Cape Breton,* or in respect of any other transactions or concerns; that such a bond for uncertain amounts to be in future advanced is by the law of this Colony valid (*vide Voet* 20, 1, 20; 20, 4, 30); and that both a special and general mortgage may be by such bond validly constituted in security of such future advances; and that such mortgages will be entitled to the same preference which mortgages granted in security of a certain sum previously advanced are entitled to, provided the solemnities which are by law required to entitle such mortgage to preference have been complied with.

That all the items to the debit of the insolvent in the account-current between him and Dickson & Burnies, for the balance of which a preference has in respect of the bond been awarded to the latter, are advances of the nature of

1837. Dec. 19.

In Re Carter.—Leibbrandt and Geyer *vs.* Dickson and Burnies.

those contemplated in the bond, and for the security of which it was granted, and that the insolvent had become indebted to Dickson & Burnies in respect of all those items prior to his insolvency.

That the law does not require that, in order that effect may be given to general conventional mortgages of movables, 2½ per cent. or any other duty should be paid to Government; and therefore that no objection arises against this bond in respect of no such duty having been paid on it. (*Vide Discount Bank vs. Dawes.*)

That the law requires, as essential to their validity as preferent debts, that general conventional mortgages constituted by notarial deeds should be registered at the office, and by the officer appointed for that purpose, but has not specified in what form the registry is to be made, nor what particulars of the bond are to be specified in the registry.

That this bond has been registered in the usual way, and therefore is not objectionable, although the general mortgage of the property of the insolvent is not mentioned, which indeed must be unnecessary, as, according to the notarial style in use in this Colony, every notarial deed creating a special mortgage always contains *in fine* a general mortgage of the debtor's property; and also is therefore not objectionable, although the entry in the registry does not mention that the mortgage was not only for £500, but also for future advances. Although it would be desirable that a regulation should be made, requiring the entry in the registry to specify that the bond was in security of future advances, when such is the case.

[N.B.—MENZIES, J., was of opinion that, if the registry by the fault of the Registrar had been omitted to be made at all, or had not been made in the form prescribed by law, then, although the creditor would have had an action of damages against the Registrar, he would have lost his preference *in concursu*. *Vide Voet* 20, 1, 11, *in fine.*]

That although this bond was not originally written on a stamp sufficient to cover the sum now claimed under it, yet that it was written on a stamp sufficient to cover the sum of £500, and as the stamp laws make no provision as to bonds in security of uncertain sums to be in future advanced being written on any stamp, no objection could be made to the bond in question, on the ground that the stamp on which it was written was not of sufficient value to cover the amount now claimed under the bond, even if the bond had not been covered with a stamp, which, taken together with the stamp on which it was originally written, was in amount sufficient to cover the amount claimed under it; and *quoad hoc* found that Dickson & Burnies were entitled to the preference which had been awarded to them by the distribution account, which to this extent they accordingly confirmed, with costs.

In Re Carter.—Leibbrandt and Geyer *vs.* Dickson and Burnies.

Ship Mortgage.

A bond specially hypothecating shares in a ship belonging to the port of Cape Town, duly registered in the Custom-house on the day it bears date, and likewise registered in the Public Debt Registry two days after its date, held valid, although the proper endorsement of the particulars of the mortgage was not made until after the debtor's insolvency, the vessel being absent from Table Bay at the date of the mortgage, and the endorsement having taken place within thirty days of her return.

1838. Feb. 13. „ 27.

Postea (13th February, 1838).—For the facts which gave rise to this branch of this case, *vide* the report of the other branch given in the last case.

The report as to the last item in the liquidation account disputed between the parties, viz., the sum of £460, being the proceeds of the sale of the insolvent's shares in the brig *William,* placed, and as the creditors allege improperly placed, to the credit of the insolvent in the account, was as follows:

"It appears that Dickson, Burnies, & Co. advanced to the insolvent, prior to the 1st of January, 1836, two sums of £500 each, and which are included in the prior account beween the parties, and form part of the balance brought forward in the account-current before referred to. Shortly after the time of making those advances, the insolvent executed a bond in favour of the said Dickson, Burnies, & Co., specially mortgaging his shares in the brig *William.* The bond is dated the 29th March, 1836, and was duly registered at the Custom-house on the same day, and in the Public Debt Register on the 31st of that month."

It was admitted that the trustees had sold the insolvent's shares in the *William* to Dickson & Burnies, who had accordingly given credit for the price in the account.

The facts as to the *William* are, that prior to the 15th February, 1836, the *William* was registered as of the port of Poole. On that day she was duly registered *de novo* as of the port of Cape Town, as the property of the insolvent

1838. Feb. 13. ,, 27.

In Re Carter.—Leibbrandt and Geyer *vs.* Dickson and Burnies.

for thirty-two shares, of John Blore for sixteen shares, and of John Henry Dunn for sixteen shares.

On the 29th March, 1836, the insolvent executed a bond, mortgaging his shares to Dickson & Burnies, and on the same day the mortgage bond was duly produced to the Collector of Customs at Cape Town, and the particulars thereof duly entered by him in the registry book, in terms of 34th section of the 3rd and 4th *Gul. IV, c.* 55.

The vessel was then absent from Cape Town, but within thirty days of her return to Table Bay, viz., on the 23rd September, 1836, the proper endorsement of the particulars of the mortgage was duly made on the register by the Collector in terms of the said 34th section.

Cloete, for the creditors, maintained that Dickson & Burnies were entitled to no preference on the vessel, or the proceeds of the sale of the insolvent's share, in respect of the said mortgage bond. First, because the mortgage had not been duly constituted, in the manner prescribed by the 34th section of the said statute, prior to the sequestration, seeing that at the date of the sequestration, and for many months afterwards, the endorsation on the ship's register had not been made, as required by the statute, to constitute a valid and effectual mortgage. Second, that this bond was null and void, in respect that it had been granted by the insolvent, not being compelled thereto by legal process, within sixty days preceding the making of the order for the sequestration of his estate, and had the effect of preferring one creditor to another.

The *Attorney-General* and *Musgrave, contra,* contended that, in virtue of the provisions of the 35th and 36th sections of the said statute, the vessel being absent from her port of registry at the time the mortgage was produced to the Collector of Customs of the said port, and entered by him in the book of registry, the ship's register having been produced to him, and the endorsation thereon prescribed by the statute having been duly made by him within thirty days after her return to her port, a valid and effectual mortgage had been constituted on the insolvent's shares; and second, that, in virtue of the provisions of the 42nd and 43rd sections of the said statute, the provisions of the 7th section of the Ordinance No. 64 were rendered inapplicable to, and insufficient to invalidate the mortgage, notwithstanding it had been executed within sixty days of the insolvency, in manner alleged.

Cur. adv. vult.

Postea (27th February, 1838).—The Court held that a valid mortgage had been constituted over the brig *William* by the bond of the 29th March, 1836, and that all the legal solemnities had been duly complied with, and that, therefore, in virtue of the provisions of the 42nd and 43rd sections of the statute 3*rd and* 4*th Gul. IV, c.* 55, this mortgage was not liable to any objection, or to be set aside in respect of the provisions of the 7th section of the Ordinance No. 64. That Dickson & Burnies were entitled to the preference, which had in respect of this item of their claim been awarded to them by the distribution account, which they accordingly confirmed with costs.

1838. Feb. 13. „ 27.

In Re Carter.—Leibbrandt and Geyer *vs.* Dickson and Burnies.

Spangenberg's Trustee *vs.* Cousins.

Lien claimed by a bookkeeper on the books of his insolvent employer, for moneys lent and advanced, refused.

1839. May 28.

Spangenberg's Trustee *vs.* Cousins.

Spangenberg died, and his estate was placed under sequestration as insolvent. His books were in possession of Cousins, who had been in Spangenberg's employment as his bookkeeper.

Cousins claimed and was ranked on the estate for the sum of £5 odd as his wages as bookkeeper; and for £51 for money lent and advanced by him to Spangenberg. The trustee applied to him to give up the insolvent's books. He maintained he had a lien over the books, and refused to give them up unless both debts were first paid to him, or a guarantee given by the trustee that he should have a preference for both debts.

The trustee tendered the amount of the wages, which being refused, he applied to the Court, by motion, for an order on Cousins to give up the books to him, which the Court granted, being of opinion that he had no lien of any kind for his debt of £51, and that as a tender had been made of the wages, it was unnecessary to determine whether he had any lien for the wages, or if he had, whether such a lien, although it might entitle him to preference in the distribution of the estate, could entitle him to withhold the books from the trustee.

Menzies, J., held it could not have done so.

In Re Pallas.—Executors of Lombard *vs.* The Registrar of Deeds.

Order on Registrar of Deeds so to enregister a notarial bond that by a reference in the Registry to the name of the surety and principal debtor, it should appear that he had executed the bond as a surety and joint principal debtor.

1840. May 30. — *In Re* Pallas.—Executors of Lombard *vs.* The Registrar of Deeds.

The executors moved the Court to make an order on the Registrar of Deeds to enregister in the Debt Registry a notarial bond, in which D. Pallas as principal debtor, and the Widow Pallas as surety *in solidum* and joint principal debtor, in security of a certain debt, bound their persons and their respective properties according to law for the payment thereof, in such manner as to make it clearly appear on the Registry that the widow was surety *in solidum* and joint principal debtor, and had bound her person and property as aforesaid in security of the debt.

The Debt Registry is, and has always been, kept in the form of a ledger, in which each article or account is headed with the name of the respective debtor, and under this heading the debtor is in the left page debited *articulatim* with the amount of the several bonds granted by him to his several creditors, and credited in the opposite page with such sums as he may have paid in extinction or diminution of each bond.

The bonds are shortly described by the name of the creditor and their date, &c., and mention is made of any special mortgage contained in the bond. Where there are sureties, the entry mentions that certain persons, naming them, are sureties, but does not in any way specify the nature or extent of their suretyship obligation. No entry is made in the Registry under the names of the respective sureties, and it is impossible to ascertain from the index of the Debt Registry whether any person is or is not a surety in any bond therein registered against the principal debtor.

The Court ordered that the said bond be enregistered in the Public Debt Registry so that by a reference in the said Registry to the name of the said Widow Pallas, it shall appear that she has executed the said bond as such surety and joint principal debtor as aforesaid. (*Vide infra, Leewner vs. Trustee of Magodas:* next case.)

The Court expressly abstained from giving any opinion as to the effect which the registration now ordered to be made would have in making the bond effectual as a general mortgage over the estate of the said surety.

In Re Magodas.—Leewner *vs.* Trustee of Magodas.

An uncertificated insolvent, Ordinance 64 being then in force, purchased immovable property which was mortgaged by the vendor to A, for £925. In order to enable the vendor to effect transfer, the plaintiff paid off the mortgage, and the insolvent, on receiving transfer "simul ac semel" and "pari passu," executed a bond in plaintiff's favour for the amount.

The Court confirmed the Master's decision. The trustee of the estate claiming to have the house sold, the plaintiff claimed that he should be allowed to prove his bond in the sequestration, and the Master having refused to admit the proof, the debt having been contracted subsequent to the sequestration.

1840. June 12. Aug. 25. Nov. 26.

In Re Magodas.—Leewner *vs.* Trustee of Magodas.

The estate of Magodas was placed under sequestration in 1835. The sequestration was not worked out, but allowed to stand still, nor did Magodas obtain his certificate. While this sequestration remained so pending, Magodas, although uncertificated, purchased a house previously mortgaged by the seller to A, for £925. It was alleged by Leewner that in order to enable the seller to give transfer and Magodas to pay the price, he (Leewner) had out of his own funds paid said sum of £925 to A, who thereupon discharged his mortgage, whereupon the seller executed transfer in favour of Magodas, and Magodas executed a mortgage bond for £925 to Leewner, and that all these acts were done not only on the same day, but *simul et semel* and *pari passu.*

Proceedings under the first sequestration having thereafter been revived (*vide supra*), the trustee claimed this house as part of the estate of Magodas, and was taking measures for having it sold.

Leewner then claimed, but the Master refused to allow him, to prove his debt on the bond under the sequestration, on the ground that the debt had been contracted subsequent to the date of the sequestration.

The Court, this day, confirmed the Master's judgment, and found that Leewner was not entitled, under the 41st section of Ordinance No. 64, to prove his debt under the present sequestration; but on his application granted an interdict (*vide infra*) against the sale of the house, to remain in force until the Court shall have given judgment in an action to be brought by Leewner against the trustee within fourteen days, to have it found and declared that he had a valid and effectual hypothec over the said house in virtue of his said mortgage bond, unless previously recalled on the application of the trustee.

Thereafter, 25th August and 26th November, 1840, the plaintiff accordingly brought an action against defendant to have the said mortgage in his favour declared a valid and effectual hypothec over the house.

The facts alleged by him as to the nature and particulars of the transaction were all proved and admitted as alleged.

Brand, for plaintiff, quoted the *Cod.* 8, 18, 7; *Burge Col. Law, 3rd Vol., p.* 347; *Voet* 20, 4, § 18; and maintained that there was no distinction in law between the

1840. June 12. Aug. 25. Nov. 26.

In Re Magodas.—Leewner *vs.* Trustee of Magodas.

mortgage in favour of plaintiff, and a kusting-brief granted by Magodas to the seller, and that notwithstanding his insolvency he might lawfully, on receiving transfer, have passed a kusting-brief to the seller for the price, which would have been valid; and quoted Ordinance No. 64, sections 9, 49, 50. (*Vide Van der Byl and Meyer vs. Sequestrator in re Buissinne*, 23*rd September*, 1828, *Vol.* 1, *p.* 318.) He also maintained that the house only passed to and was taken by Magodas *cum onere*, and that the price due to the seller and paid by the plaintiff was an *onus* on the house at the time the transfer was made to Magodas, and that therefore the house only became part of the estate of Magodas *minus* the amount of and subject to the mortgage bond.

Cloete, contra, quoted *Van Leeuwen's Cens. For.*, 4, 11, §§ 15 *and* 16; *Kesterman's Dictionary, Voce Kusting-brief; Van der Byl and Meyer vs. Sequestrator*, 23*rd September*, 1828, to show that there was no analogy between the mortgage bond in question and a kusting-brief, and argued that, even if entitled to the privileges of a kusting-brief, still it was rendered absolutely null by the 9th and 49th sections of Ordinance No. 64; and quoted *East's Reports, Kitchen vs. Burton, Bam. and Cross., Vol.* 2, *p.* 293; *Drayton vs. Dale.*

The Court gave judgment for plaintiff as prayed, with costs.

Oberholster *vs.* Holtman.

A mortgage of land extends to all buildings erected on the land after the date of the bond.

An undertaking to grant a first mortgage bond "on my newly-built house and store" is not fulfilled by granting a mortgage on a certain house and premises, marked No. 5, *together with such other buildings as are now erected on the above landed property; there being a prior mortgage on the property described, simply as "a certain house and garden marked No.* 5." *A second mortgage of the same property, only, is thus created.*

1840. Nov. 24.

Oberholster *vs.* Holtman.

The defendant in this case, on the 1st February, 1840, duly executed before the Registrar of Deeds a mortgage bond for £150 in favour of Stuckeris, whereby he mortgaged to him a certain house and garden, marked No. 5 (therein described), belonging to defendant.

Defendant had previously borrowed from plaintiff £875, for which he granted to him the following obligation, dated 24th August, 1839:

"I, the undersigned, acknowledge to have received from

——— Oberholster £875, &c., &c., under a mortgage bond of the first mortgage of my newly-built house and store, which bond I promise to send by the first opportunity."

On the 15th September, 1840, when the bond in Stuckeris's favour still stood on the Register undischarged, defendant duly executed and caused to be registered a bond for £875, containing a mortgage of the same property mortgaged to Stuckeris, and tendered it to plaintiff, who refused to receive it.

Plaintiff now sued defendant on said obligation, dated 24th August, 1839, demanding that defendant should be condemned either to grant to him a mortgage bond under first hypothecation of said property, or to repay him the said sum of £875.

Defendant, in defence against this action, maintained that as in the bond to Stuckeris, the property mortgaged was described "as a certain house and garden marked No. 5," and as in the bond to defendant, dated 15th September, 1840, the property was described "as a certain house and premises marked No. 5, *together with such other buildings as are now erected on the above landed property,*" this bond in favour of plaintiff, although second in date, must be held as the first mortgage on the new house and store, and therefore was sufficient implement of his obligation, dated August, 1839.

The Court held that as Stuckeris's mortgage extended over all buildings erected after its date on the land mortgaged in A, his bond was the first mortgage bond over the new house, and consequently that by executing the bond in plaintiff's favour, defendant had not fulfilled his said obligation, by which he had bound himself to grant a mortgage bond, which should have the first preference over the new house and store; and gave judgment for plaintiff as prayed, with costs,

Defendant to pay off and discharge Stuckeris's bond within fourteen days; and in default thereof defendant was decreed to pay £875 as prayed to plaintiff.

HAUPT *vs.* HANCOCK.

Priority of Mortgage. Pignus Prætorium.

Movable property, delivered to a mortgage creditor to be sold in payment of the mortgage debt, and sent to a public sale for such purpose, cannot be seized in execution of a judgment in an action in which proceedings were commenced before the delivery.

1841. Feb. 19. — Haupt *vs.* Hancock.

On the 15th October, 1840, Blackburn obtained a judgment in the Court of Resident Magistrate of Port Elizabeth, against Johnstone, and took out a warrant of execution returnable 30th November, 1840. Blackburn had obtained an interlocutory judgment for this debt on the 5th October. On the 6th October, Johnstone executed the following writing: "I, the undersigned, do hereby empower Mr. D. Haupt to dispose of my household property now in Port Elizabeth, and to receive the proceeds therefrom, which he will place to my credit on account of my debt to Mr. P. J. Haupt, of Cape Town, being for a certain mortgage bond passed by me in favour of the said P. J. Haupt.

"N. J. JOHNSTONE."

On the 8th October, Haupt removed certain articles of furniture from Johnstone's premises, and on the 6th November sent them to a public sale, where on the same day Hancock, the messenger of the Magistrate's Court, seized and took possession of them as being the property of Johnstone, in execution of the judgment obtained by Blackburn.

Thereupon the plaintiff brought an action in the Magistrate's Court against Hancock, to restore the furniture or to pay its value. The Resident Magistrate of Port Elizabeth gave judgment for plaintiff, with costs. Against this senteuce the defendant appealed. But the Court (WYLDE, C.J., MENZIES and KEKEWICH, JJ.), after hearing *Musgrave* for the appellant, and without calling on *Cloete* for the respondent, affirmed the sentence, with costs.

MULDER *vs.* CREDITORS OF LACABLE.

Hypothec for Wages.

A workman in a wagonmaker's shop has not the preference for wages to which a domestic servant is entitled.

1841. Nov. 30. — Mulder *vs.* Creditors of Lacable.

In this case, the question was, whether the Master ought to have ranked Mulder, who was a workman in the wagonmaker's shop of the insolvent, as preferent for the wages of four months' work, performed in the wagonmaker's shop which the Master refused to do, by reason of the claimant's service not having been of a domestic nature, and consequently not entitled to preference. Claimant argued that he was entitled to this preference, and quoted *Burton's Insolvent Law, p.* 147; *Van der Linden's Inst., p.* 178; *Loenius Dec., case* 33; *Voet* 20, 4. § 37.

Brand, contra, quoted *Van Leeuwen's Cens. For.*, 4, *c.* 11, § 19; *Carpzovius, b.* 1, 28, § 24; *In re Brink.—Klaassen vs. the Creditors, 12th April,* 1837. (*Vide supra.*)

1841. Nov. 30. Mulder *vs.* Creditors of Lacable.

The Court rejected the claim of preference, and confirmed the Master's report, with costs.

SUTHERLAND *vs.* ELLIOTT BROTHERS.

Ownership. Cession. Tradition.

A cession of securities by a debtor to a creditor who has made advances, accompanied by delivery, with the object that the creditor might recover payment of the securities and apply the amount received in extinction of the debt, vests in the creditor absolutely all right and title in the securities, subject only to an equitable right in favour of the trustees of the debtor's insolvent estate, of compelling the creditors to account with them for the sums received.

The securities in question being bonds in the debtor's favour, the Court would, on proof of negligence or dilatoriness on the part of the creditor to recover them, interpose to compel him to take steps for so recovering them, or enable the trustee to recover them.

1842. Feb. 10. Sutherland *vs.* Elliott Brothers.

Sutherland made an advance of money to the firm of Elliott Brothers, and in security they placed in his hands certain bonds due to them, on which they endorsed acts of cession in the following form:

"We, the undersigned, do hereby cede, transfer, and assign to Mr. T. Sutherland, or his order or assigns, for value received, all our right, title, and interest in this bond of J. N. Wood, for the sum of £130, with interest thereon from the 9th October, 1839; and we further bind ourselves, as sureties and principal debtors *in solidum*, for the payment of any deficiency in consequence of the said J. N. Wood having become insolvent.

"ELLIOTT BROTHERS.

"Cape Town, 3rd February, 1841."

There were circumstances proved or admitted which clearly established an agreement between the parties that Sutherland might recover payment of these bonds, and apply the amount so received by him in extinction of the debt due to him by the Elliotts in respect of his advances; and that, in the event of his so recovering, or otherwise

1842. Feb. 10. Sutherland *vs.* Elliott Brothers.

receiving the full amount of his debt, he should be bound to cede such of the bonds as still remained unpaid to the Elliotts.

This day, *Porter, A.-G.*, for the trustees of the insolvent estate of Elliotts, applied by motion for an order on Sutherland, in virtue of the right vested in them by the 50th section of Ordinance No. 64 of 1829 (Ordinance for regulating the due collection, administration, and distribution of insolvent estates),* to deliver up the bonds still in his possession, offering to allow him a preference on the proceeds of these bonds in the liquidation of the estate.

Cloete, for Sutherland, contended that he could not be compelled to deliver up, or rather to re-transfer, the bonds to the trustees, except in so far as his debt had been paid and on tender to him of the balance still due.

The Court (Sir J. Wylde, C.J., Menzies and Kekewich, JJ.) refused the order with costs, and held that the above recited cession had the effect of vesting absolutely all right and title in and to the bonds in Sutherland; subject to an equitable right in favour of the trustees, as representing Elliott, of compelling Sutherland to account with them for the sums he had received in payment of the bonds, and to apply the sums so received in extinction of his debt; and when that was extinguished, to re-transfer the remaining bonds to them.

They were also of opinion that if Sutherland had been negligent or dilatory in recovering payment of the bonds, the Court would have interposed at the instance of the trustees, and compelled him to take steps for recovering payment of the bonds or enabling the trustees to do so.

Singleton, in the Matter of the "Black Swan."—Ex parte Smith.

Hypothec of Seamen for Wages.

Attachment of ship by consignees of goods which have been sold in a foreign port to repair damage caused by stress of weather.

Edictal Citation.

Sale of ship under process of Admiralty Court, where the ship had been attached for seamen's wages, with the consent of the Supreme Court.

* Note.—This section vested in the trustees all the present and future estate, movable and immovable, personal and real, of the insolvent, and answered to the 48th section of Ordinance No. 6 of 1843, the present insolvent law.

Tradesmen who had furnished articles necessary for the safety of the ship of such a nature that the master might have granted a bottomry bond for the price, entitled, with the consent of the master, representing the owner, to be paid out of proceeds in the hands of the Sheriff paid to him out of the Admiralty Court, after the satisfaction of the decrees of that Court.

A seaman who had been prevented by a rule of form from joining with the other seamen in the action for wages in the Admiralty Court not entitled, without the master's consent, to be in like manner paid in preference from the proceeds in the Sheriff's hands, the master having no authority to grant a bottomry bond for seamen's wages.

1842. Feb. 10.

Singleton, in the Matter of the *Black Swan.*—*Ex parte* Smith.

The *Black Swan* had been arrested by process of the Supreme Court to answer the claims of certain consignees in this Colony of goods shipped in her which had been sold in a port in South America, into which she had been driven by stress of weather, to pay the expenses of repairs necessary to enable her to complete her voyage to this port. For these claims the consignees brought actions against the owner of the *Black Swan*, who was absent from the Colony, and proceeded by edictal citation. While these actions were pending, certain of the seamen attached the vessel by process of the Admiralty for wages claimed by them.

The Supreme Court, by consent of the consignees, and on condition that the balance of the price of the ship, after payment of the wages, costs, and expenses of selling the ship, should be paid out of the Admiralty Court to the Sheriff, to be held by him subject to the attachment of the consignees, allowed the vessel to be sold under the process of the Admiralty Court. The vessel was accordingly sold and said balance paid to the Sheriff.

Certain tradesmen in Cape Town who had before the arrest by the consignees supplied anchors, &c., &c., necessary for the supply of the ship, and of such a nature that the master might have granted a bottomry bond for their price, *and whose claims were admitted by the consignees to be preferent on the proceeds of the ship*, applied to the Court, by motion, for an order on the Sheriff to pay the money due to them out of the balance in his hands. They *produced the consent of the consignees*, and a certificate by the master of the vessel that the alleged furnishings had been made by them, that the sum claimed by them was due, and that he consented to payment being made as prayed.

The Court granted the motion, holding that as the master had the power of granting a bottomry bond over the ship for

1842. Feb. 28. — Singleton, in the Matter of the *Black Swan.*— *Ex parte* Smith.

the price of such furnishings, he had an equal right to direct the application of a part of the proceeds of the ship to defray them, and held that, *quoad hoc,* the consent of the master that the price thereof should be paid out of said proceeds was equivalent to a consent to the same effect by the owner of the ship, and on this ground granted the application. (*Vide note, infra.*)

This day, *Ebden,* for the assignee of Smith, a seaman, who had been prevented by some rule of form in the Admiralty Court from joining in the action for wages with the other seamen, produced a certificate in the form of an affidavit by the master that the wages claimed by Smith were due, and moved for an order on the Sheriff to pay Smith's wages out of the proceeds in his hands. The consignees consented to this. The Court were of opinion that the master had not the power of granting bottomry bonds over the ship for wages due to the seamen, and therefore that his consent and certificate had not necessarily the same effect which they had attributed to them as to the price of the furnishings to the ship above mentioned, and doubted whether the consent of the master was in this case of wages equivalent to the consent of the owner, and whether in respect of it the Court could, on motion, order any part of the proceeds to be applied in payment of seamen's wages, until such wages had been constituted a debt against the owner by the decree of some competent Court. But it was unnecessary to decide this question, because the consignees, in order to save the expense which would be incurred in constituting this debt, consented to pay these wages out of their own funds, by allowing the amount of the wages paid by the Sheriff to the applicant in diminution *pro rata* of the sums which might be now ordered to them out of the proceeds by the judgment of this Court.

The Court on this condition granted the order applied for.

[Note by Menzies, J.] The decision of the Court in favour of the persons who furnished the supplies above mentioned ought to be well reconsidered before being followed as a precedent, because it may be doubted whether, because the master had the power to grant bottomry bonds over the ship for certain purposes, he has therefore a power of disposing of the proceeds of the ship, after she has been sold for similar purposes.

In Re Hercules Sandenbergh. — Mathyssen and Curators of his Children *vs.* Trustees of Sandenbergh.

Minors in a foreign country, according to the laws of that country as well as of the Colony—held entitled, equally as minors in the Colony would be, to a tacit hypothec on the estate of the administering guardian for the amount of a legacy under their grandfather's will, the interest of which was during their father's lifetime payable to him.

1843. Nov. 30. Dec. 14.

In Re Hercules Sandenbergh.—Mathyssen and Curators of his Children *vs.* Trustees of Sandenbergh.

In this case the Master reported—

"That the plan of distribution framed by the trustees has been objected to by the following parties, on the ground of their being ranked as concurrent creditors, and considering themselves entitled to preference for the reasons hereafter stated: 1st. By G. H. Maasdorp, as agent to Sir Clement Sandenberg Mathyssen, who has proved a debt of £1,411 13*s.* 4*d.* for legacies arising out of the estate of the late Clement Mathyssen, of which estate the insolvent was the administering executor; and for which reason Mr. Maasdorp contends that he is entitled to preference under this estate. The trustees, after awarding to the mortgagees on the landed property payment of their respective bonds in preference, and having set aside a sum of £427 3s. 5d. to meet the issue of cases expected by them to be preferred, have distributed £2,624 17s. 11d. among the concurrent creditors, seventy-eight in number, the whole of whom will be interested in any alteration made in the order of preference in respect of the beforementioned claims set up by the objecting creditors."

Brand restricted his objection to the sum of £1,000, being the capital of the legacy, and gave up the objection to the extent of £411 13s. 4d.

It was admitted that this sum of £1,000 was, by codicil of 15th September, 1807, attached to will of 26th May, 1777, bequeathed, by old Mathyssen and his first wife, to Sir Clement Sandenberg Mathyssen, in the following terms:

"We bequeath to him a sum of 40,000f., which shall be placed at interest by the executors, and the interest to accrue thereon shall also be placed at interest during the minority, whilst we declare it to be our will and desire that he, on his becoming of age, shall enjoy no more than the interest of such capital to which it shall be augmented, whilst the capital itself shall devolve as a free and unincumbered disposition on his child or children, or their lawful descendants; but in case of his dying without issue, the

1843. Nov. 30. Dec. 14.

In Re Hercules Sandenbergh.—Mathyssen and Curators of his Children *vs.* Trustees of Sandenbergh.

said legacy, together with its augmentation, shall devolve in full and free property on his brothers or their lawful descendants."

It was admitted that Hercules Sandenbergh and his brother were appointed ultimately by old Mathyssen to be his executors and guardians of his minor heirs and legatees, and that Hercules was the administering executor and guardian.

It was admitted by the *Attorney-General*, for the sake of argument, that Sir Clement Sandenberg Mathyssen had certain children, and that those children were minors.

He also admitted that if these minor children of Sir Clement Sandenberg were now in this Colony, there could be no doubt that they were entitled to the preference claimed by virtue of the tacit hypothec over the guardian's estate. But he denied that this privilege of tacit hypothec was possessed or enjoyed by persons not residing in this Colony, although they are in a state of minority, both according to the law of the country in which they are domiciled and according to the law of this Colony. And therefore that the children are not entitled to the preference claimed. (*Story's Conflict of Laws, p.* 52; 1 *Burge on Colonial Law, p.* 113.)

Brand, contra, referred to the decisions of the Supreme Court in the case *In re W. Liesching*, and also in the case of *The Children Oosterze,* in which the Court enforced the hypothec.

Adjourned.

Postea (December 14, 1843).—The Court unanimously ordered the liquidation account to be amended, and the preference for the sum of £1,000 claimed to be awarded. And by a majority (MUSGRAVE, J., *dissentiente*) gave costs to the minors.

The following are the grounds on which this judgment was given:

The claim which is the subject of the present proceedings has been made by the agent of Sir C. Mathyssen, the father, and as such, the natural guardian of his minor children, on whose behalf the claim is made.

Sir C. Mathyssen is domiciled in Holland. It is admitted that these children were born in Holland, are now resident there, and are under twenty-one years of age; and that, according to the law of Holland, the *lex domicilii,* they are now in a state of minority. The age of majority in Holland being twenty-five.

The claim made for them is that,—by virtue of the hypothec which, by the law of the Colony, is given to minors over the estate of their guardians to enable them to obtain out of it the amount of the property of the minors which was under the administration of their guardians,—they are entitled to a preference on the estate of Sandenbergh, the insolvent, for £1,000 which was left, under *fidei-commiss.*, by their grandfather to them, under provision that their father should enjoy the interest thereof during his life, and placed by him under the administration of the insolvent and his brother, who, it is admitted, were ultimately appointed by him his executors, and the guardians of his minor heirs. And it has been admitted that the insolvent was the administrating guardian, that during his administration, and up to the period of his insolvency, he has been domiciled in this Colony; and that the funds placed in *fidei-commiss.* under his administration were received by him in this Colony, and have been mingled with the rest of his estate in this Colony.

1843. Nov. 30. Dec. 14.

In Re Hercules Sandenbergh.—Mathyssen and Curators of his Children *vs.* Trustees of Sandenbergh.

The respondents are the concurrent creditors of the insolvent.

The counsel for the respondents could not deny that such a hypothec in favour of minors over the estate of the guardian as that alleged by the claimants exists in the law of this Colony, and that no law or authority can be shown which restricts this hypothec to minors who have been born in this Colony and are domiciled there when the hypothec is sought to be enforced. He has, therefore, been unable to found his defence against the claim merely on the facts that the children were not born in this Colony, have never been in it, and have been and are domiciled in Holland, and has been obliged to rest his defence against their claim solely on the following argument:

That all questions as to personal *status* must be determined by the law of the country in which the person is domiciled, without regard to the law of any other country in which that person happens to have property of *a personal nature* situated. That, when the personal *status* of a person has been determined by the law of the domicile, the courts of other countries will, in respect of a principle of *comitas inter gentes,* which has generally been recognized in civilized States, decide questions which may arise before them in which his personal *status* is involved, according to the law of his domicile, although it may be different from, and conflicting with, their own law. That this principle of *comitas* is recognized by the law of this Colony, and that, in respect of it, the Courts of this Colony (at least in cases where *real* property situated in this Colony is not concerned) will determine the personal *status* of any party concerned in any cause before them according to the law of his domicile, although different from, and so conflicting with, the law of this Colony. And therefore that, as the

1843. Nov. 30. Dec. 14.

In Re Hercules Sandenbergh.—Mathyssen and Curators of his Children *vs.* Trustees of Sandenbergh.

claimants in this case are domiciled in Holland, this Court ought not to have, and cannot legitimately pay, any regard or have any recourse to the law of this Colony in determining whether the claimants possess the *status* of minors, or, if they are to be deemed minors, what are the rights and privileges which, as such, they are entitled to:—consequently, the Court cannot give effect to the claim for preference made by them in respect of the hypothec which the law of the Colony has given to minors on the estate of their guardians.

If the arguments of the respondents were sound, it is evident they have stopped short of the legitimate conclusion from them, which would have been—"and therefore the Court must determine whether the claimants are minors by the law of Holland, and if they are so, award to them all such rights and privileges as by the law of Holland are given to minors in Holland."

To this conclusion (legitimate if his arguments were sound) the counsel for the respondents refused to advance; and the proposition on which he rested his defence, although he attempted, by the exertion of great ingenuity, to veil its true nature from the Court, was really nothing else than this,—"That as the Court could not decide questions as to the *status* of persons domiciled in another country according to its own law, it could not and would not inquire what their *status* was by the law of their domicile, or give any effect to any *status* they possessed under it."

It is true that when the courts of this Colony are called on to decide causes brought before them involving questions as to whether any person does or does not possess any particular personal *status* which is recognized in the law of the Colony as a legal *status*,—*e.g.*, whether A B is a minor or major, married or unmarried, parent or child, legitimate or illegitimate, sane or insane,—they will, acting *according to the undoubted law of the Colony, in very many cases* decide those questions according to what is the law of the country in which A B was domiciled *at the time the events occurred which created, or out of which arose, the alleged status of A B,* although the law of that country be, on that subject, in conflict with the law of this Colony.

It cannot be laid down that the courts of this Colony would so decide *in every such case,* because cases can be supposed which, there is reason to believe, have never yet been brought before the courts of this Colony, and as to the law regulating the decision of which doubts are entertained by some of the best authorities on the subject. By the present law of the Colony, the age of majority is twenty-one years. Suppose that, by the law of Holland, minority continues until the age of twenty-five years, would the courts of this Colony sustain as valid a deed, *inter vivos*, disposing of personal property situated in the Colony or a power of attorney authorizing the institution of an action against an inhabitant of this Colony for recovery of a debt executed in Holland, by a person domiciled in Holland, and aged twenty-three? Or, if the law of Holland prohibited marriage by any person under the age of twenty-five, without consent of his parents,—would the courts of this Colony *set aside* a marriage entered into in this Colony, without the consent of his parents, by a young man aged twenty-three, domiciled in Holland, who touched at Table Bay in a Dutch ship on his passage from Batavia to Holland, or who had acquired a temporary domicile here, *sine animo remanendi?* (*Vide Greeff vs. Verreaux,* 21*st March,* 1829, *vol.* 1, *p.* 151.)

Had the law of Holland been, that the age of majority there is fifteen years, and had the claimants in this case claimed the privilege of the hypothec given to minors by the law of this Colony to protect them against the loss of their property which had occurred by the mal-administration of the insolvent during the period *after they have attained the age of fifteen years and before they were twenty-one,*—it would have been a question well worthy of consideration, whether the respondent could not have successfully resisted this claim, on the ground that the claimants, during the above period, were majors by the law of their domicile; and although they would have been held to be minors by the law of this Colony, had they been domiciled here, this Court must decide their majority according to the law of their domicile, and therefore hold that during the above period they must be deemed to have been majors, and consequently not entitled to that hypothec to which, by the law of this Colony, minors alone are entitled.

There the question would have been,—are the claimants according to the law of this Colony to be deemed to be majors or minors?—and not, what are the privileges to which, by the law of this Colony, persons are entitled who, according to the law of that country by which the question as to their *status* is to be determined by this Court, are declared and deemed to be minors?

In fact, it is a mistake to maintain, in the literal sense of the words, that the courts of this Colony ever do, or ought to, decide whether a person is a minor or a major according to the law of any other country. Such questions are, in truth, invariably decided by the law of this Colony, which is, that *every person under the age of twenty-one years shall be and be deemed and considered by the law of*

1843. Nov. 30. Dec. 14.

In Re Hercules Sandenbergh.—Mathyssen and Curators of his Children *vs.* Trustees of Sandenbergh.

this Colony to be a minor,—unless being domiciled in this Colony he shall have obtained his majority by marriage *venia ætatis*, or in some other manner specified in the law of the Colony as having that effect;—or, *exceptis excipiendis*, being domiciled in another country, shall have attained the age prescribed as the age of majority in the law of that country; or shall there have attained the *status* of majority in some other way prescribed in that law. But whether this view of the question be true or not is of little matter, for in this case there is no conflict whatever of laws. It is admitted that, by the law of Holland as well as by the law of this Colony, persons under the age of twenty-one are *in statu minorem ætatis*, and are deemed and treated as minors. On what principle, then, can it be maintained that the claimants, who, both according to the law of their domicile and to the law of this Colony, are of such age as to be minors, are not entitled to the privileges which the law of this Colony has bestowed on minors? The respondents are here driven to maintain either that all persons who are not domiciled in this Colony are to be considered as majors whatever their age may be, and whatever the law of their domicile may be,—a position which is not only utterly inconsistent with the foundation of his whole argument (namely, that all questions of personal *status* are to be decided by the *lex domicilii, i.e.*, that a person is to be deemed by foreign courts to be a minor if by the law of his domicile he is there deemed to be a minor), but one which, if followed up and acted upon to the full extent to which, if true, it ought to be carried, would lead to the most absurd and dangerous consequences,—or they must maintain that persons who, by the law of this Colony, are deemed to be in a state of minority, are, in consequence of being domiciled in a foreign country, and although they are also deemed to be minors by the law of that country, deprived of, and not entitled to, the privileges which the law of this Colony has bestowed on minors in general,—a position in support of which no law of this Colony, nor any authority in the law of this or any other country, can be adduced.

The Court expressed no opinion as to the respective rights of the respondents and of the claimants' father, during his life, to the future interests of this sum of £1,000; nor as to the respective rights which, in the event of the deaths of the claimants and of their father without issue, the respondents and the brothers of Sir C. Matthyssen, and their descendants (to whom, in such an event, a reversionary interest in the funds under the *fidei-commissi*, was given by the will) might ultimately have to the capital.

Walker and Others *vs.* Norden.

Cancellation of conveyance, coram lege loci, made by widow of grantee, non habente potestatem, at the suit of certain persons who had acquired rights to certain shares and subdivisions of the land granted.

1843. Dec. 12.

Walker & Others *vs.* Norden.

The defendant had been summoned before the Circuit Court of Albany on 29th September, 1842, by the plaintiffs, being members of a party of settlers commonly called Smith's party, and as such entitled to and interested in certain shares and subdivisions of the land allotted as the location of George Smith, deceased, and party of settlers in Albany, by grant to the said George Smith, dated 20th November, 1823, to show wherefore a certain deed of transfer made and executed at Cape Town on the 28th July, 1842, before the Registrar of Deeds of this Colony to and in favour of the defendant by one G. D. Brunett, as the agent of one Mary Smith, acting or pretending to act as the executrix testamentary to the estate of her deceased husband, the said George Smith, should not be cancelled and annulled by reason that the said George Smith was not entitled to the whole of the aforesaid location, but only to a part thereof, the said plaintiffs having acquired right to certain shares and subdivisions thereof under the grant aforesaid.

Defendant, in his plea, admitted that he has obtained transfer of the land in dispute from Mrs. Smith in her capacity of executrix, and that in virtue of that transfer he opposes the claim of the plaintiffs.

The case was removed to the Supreme Court.

This day, plaintiffs put in the grant by Government to George Smith, dated 20th November, 1822, the transfer by Brunett, as attorney of the Widow Smith, in favour of defendant, dated 28th July, 1842, and the power of attorney granted by the Widow Smith to Brunett, dated 6th June, 1842, and called

William de Smidt: I am clerk in the Surveyor-General's department. I produce from that office a general plan of the location granted to George Smith, signed by William Smith, land-surveyor, which is a duplicate of the original grant, dated 20th November, 1823, but having certain subdivisions marked on it as allotted to certain persons therein named, including the plaintiffs. Also separate diagrams of the lots marked on the general plan as having been allotted to the parties named therein.

Plaintiffs put in a certificate by the Master of the Supreme Court, dated 8th December, 1843, that no will of any person called George Smith is to be found in the

1843. Dec. 12. — Walker & Others *vs.* Norden.

register of wills except one dated 24th December, 1831. That by this will Thomas Phillips and Mr. Waddel were appointed executors, and that no letters of administration have been granted to either of them, and that no letters of administration have been granted to the Widow Smith as executrix of the estate of her deceased husband; and closed their case.

Brand, for the defendant, admitted that he could produce no evidence of any letters of administration having been granted to the Widow Smith as executrix of the estate of her deceased husband.

After hearing *Brand* for the defendant, the Court were of opinion that the plaintiffs had proved such an interest in the land in question as entitled them to have cancelled, on the ground of its being null and void, any deed in favour of a third party, which, if allowed to remain on record and considered as valid, might prevent them from or be an obstacle to their establishing and making effectual their interest in and claim to the said land against the representatives of the deceased George Smith; and gave judgment for the plaintiffs, declaring the transfer in favour of defendant, dated 28th July, 1842, null and void, as having been made by the Widow Smith *non habente potestatem*, with costs.

In Re Blommestein.—Executors of Van der Poel *vs.* Marais and Others.

A became a tutor of minors in 1827. *In* 1829 *he became the purchaser of property then burdened with four special mortgages. The first in favour of V. d. P.; the second and third in favour of V. d. B., and the fourth in favour of P: altogether amounting to* £1,200. *In* 1830, *A received transfer, and pari passu and simul ac semel granted four bonds to the mortgagees in lieu of the four bonds in their favour which had been granted by A's vendor and which were then cancelled. In* 1837 *it was agreed between A and V. d. P. that the latter should pay off all the mortgages and advance him a further sum of* £550, *A executing a bond in his favour of* £1,750. *This was done. On A's evidence the Court held that V. d. P. was entitled to preference before the minors, who had a tutorial hypothec for the amount of* £1,200, *the bond to that extent representing and coming in the place of the four bonds existing at the time of the transfer to A, which would have been entitled to preference before the tutorial hypothec. It was admitted that in respect of the loan of* £550 *the tutorial hypothec had preference before the special mortgage to that amount.*

1844. Aug. 27. Dec. 14.

In Re Blommestein.—Executors of Van der Poel *vs.* Marais and Others.

The facts of the case were the following: On the 1st January, 1827, the insolvent, Blommestein, became the testamentary guardian of the wife of the first defendant and of the two other defendants, as being the minor heirs of the late Abraham de Villiers; and as their guardian administered the inheritance of the defendants, whose claims against him, arising out of such administration, amounted to £1,136 1s. 10¾d., for which they duly proved on the insolvent estate, and claimed a preference, by virtue of their legal hypothec, over all debts contracted by the said insolvent subsequent to the 1st June, 1827, when the insolvent's guardianship, and consequently the tutorial hypothec, commenced. On the 3rd of November, 1829, the insolvent purchased the place Weltevreden from one Melander, which was then burdened with four bonds by which it was specially mortgaged;—the first for £300, in favour of Van der Byl, but which had been ceded by him to the Widow van der Poel on the 6th January, 1828; the second for £150; and the third for £375, of both which Van den Berg was the legal holder and the fourth for £375, held by Poleman.

It was agreed between the insolvent and Melander and the creditors in those bonds, that the insolvent, on receiving transfer of the place, should take over those four bonds; and accordingly, on the 30th August, 1830, when the insolvent received transfer of the place, he granted four bonds specially mortgaging it in favour of the Widow van der Poel, Van den Berg, and Poleman, for the sums respectively due to them on the four bonds above specified, which were at the same time cancelled.

In 1837, by means of transactions, and under the circumstances detailed in the evidence at the trial, it was agreed between the Widow van der Poel and the insolvent, that she should pay off the said four bonds, dated 30th August, 1830, amounting in all to £1,200, and lend him a further sum of £550, on the insolvent executing in her favour a bond of £1,750, especially mortgaging the place Weltevreden. This bond was executed 23rd May, 1837, when the abovementioned four bonds were paid and cancelled.

In the ranking of the creditors of the insolvent, the plaintiffs admitted that the defendants, in virtue of their tutorial hypothec, were entitled to a preference on the proceeds of the place Weltevreden, before the above bond dated 23rd May, 1837, in so far as concerned the £550 which was then lent by the Widow van der Poel to the insolvent, but

1844. Aug. 27. Dec. 14.

In Re Blommestein.—Executors of Van der Poel *vs.* Marais and Others.

claimed a preference before the tutorial hypothec of the defendants, for the balance of £1,200 secured by said bond, on the ground that it represented and came in the place of the four bonds of the Widow van der Poel, Van den Berg, and Poleman, which would have been entitled to a preference before the tutorial hypothec.

The defendants admitted the preference claimed by the plaintiffs for amount of the bond for £300 which had belonged to the Widow van der Poel herself; but objected to it in so far as claimed for the remaining £900, being the amount of the bonds of Van den Berg and Poleman.

The Court ordered this question of preference to be tried in the shape of an action brought by the plaintiffs against defendants, to have their right to the preference claimed declared and enforced by a judgment of the Court.

Plaintiff called

Petrus Canzius van Blommestein: I am an insolvent. On buying my place Weltevreden, I took over four bonds amounting to £1,200. In May, 1837, I applied personally to the plaintiff, Van der Poel, as the agent of his mother, the Widow van der Poel. I told him there were so many mortgages on my estate that I was anxious to have them all in one, as it was troublesome to me to be paying the interest at so many different times. He said he would give me the 70,000f., which was the amount I asked for. I told him verbally what mortgages there were on the place. It was proposed that the existing bonds should be ceded to Mrs. van der Poel, on her making the loan. The agreement was concluded between Mr. van der Poel and me that day. Next day a power of attorney was sent to me to sign. I signed it, and appointed in it Mr. Serrurier my attorney. I signed it in Stellenbosch, to which I had returned after my conversation with Van der Poel. It came enclosed in a letter from Van der Poel. I had told Serrurier to send me a power of attorney for me to sign. The rest of the transaction about the loan of the mortgages was transacted by Serrurier as my agent.

Jan Serrurier: I occasionally acted as agent for Mr. Blommestein some years ago. I recollect in 1837 getting some instructions from him in regard to a loan he was to get from Mrs. van der Poel. I got these instructions from Blommestein himself. I was to pass a bond for 70,000f. to Mr. van der Poel, and to receive 58,000f. in cash, which, with 12,000f. which Blommestein already owed her, made up the 70,000f. I got the power of attorney now shown me from Blommestein, and the bond now shown me is the bond which I passed, dated 23rd May, 1837. (Power of attorney and bond put in.) I think, I am almost certain, that

I received 58,000f. in cash from Van der Poel on the 20th May, when I paid off all the previous mortgage bonds, with the interest then due thereon. The receipt on the bond of Poleman for £375 and the two bonds of Van den Berg's are dated 20th May, and the date of the cancellation made on them was the 23rd. I got the bonds from the creditors when I paid the money, but I am not sure whether I gave them to Mr. Zastron or to Mr. van der Poel, for cancellation. The balance of the money I deposited in the Discount Bank to the credit of Blommestein. I paid Poleman and Van der Berg with the incidental money which I had received from Van der Poel.

Carel Mauritz Zastron: I am clerk in the Deeds Registry Office. The bond now shown me is one passed by Serrurier as agent for Blommestein in favour of Mrs. van der Poel for £1,750, dated 23rd May, 1837. The power of attorney annexed is dated 20th May, 1837. It was drawn out by Mr. Woeke, one of the clerks in the Registry Office, for the party to sign. At this time there were five bonds registered on Blommestein's place, Weltevreden, for £1,450. I produce the register book, and a copy made from it of the registry of the above five bonds. These bonds were cancelled on the 23rd, the day the bond for 70,000f. was executed. I got them for cancellation at the time the new bond was given for the 70,000f. I have no recollection of any conversation with Van der Poel about taking a new bond for the whole, instead of taking cession of the old bonds.

Cross-examined: I may have desired him to do this, but I have no recollection.

Plaintiffs closed their case.

Defendants called no evidence.

The cause of the debt stated in the Widow van der Poel's bond for £300, dated 30th August, 1830, was as follows:

"Arising from a debt taken over by him, the appearer (Blommestein), and for which the property hereunder mentioned was mortgaged."

The same *causa debiti* was stated in the other three bonds of Van den Berg and Poleman.

Terms of receipt written on Widow van der Poel's bond:

"Received from Mr. J. Serrurier the sum of Rds. 88, being interest from the 6th January, 1837, to the 18th May, 1837, and the capital taken over by mortgage bond of this date.

"Cape Town, 23rd May, 1837. Signed, J. van der Poel. Cancelled 23rd May, 1837."

Terms of receipt written on Van den Berg's two bonds:

"The contents hereof, being Rds. 2,000, with 1 year 3

1844. Aug. 27. Dec. 14.

In Re Blommestein.—Executors of Van der Poel vs. Marais and Others.

months and 12 days' interest, amounted up to this date, to Rds. 2,154 5 2 paid to me on this day, and consent to the cancellation.

"R. T. van den Berg, Cape Town, 20th May, 1837. Cancelled 23rd May, 1837."

Terms of receipt written on Poleman's bond:

"The contents of this bond discharged, with the interest of 13 months and 3 days paid to me on this day with £399 11s. 3d.

"Cape Town, 20th May, 1837.—J. H. Poleman. Cancelled 23rd May, 1837."

Causa debiti stated in bond for £1,750, taken by Mrs. van der Poel, dated 23rd May, 1837:

"Arising from a debt due by the appearer's constituent (Blommestein) to the said widow of the late C. van der Poel, as appears by a mortgage bond bearing date the 20th August, 1830, and partly from money duly lent and advanced."

Porter, A.-G., argued in support of the plaintiffs' claim, and maintained that although the fact that a stranger's money lent without any contract or stipulation has been employed in paying off prior preferent mortgagees will not place that stranger in the shoes of the mortgagees, nor entitle him to the same preference, yet, on the other hand, if the stranger stipulates with the borrower, even without the knowledge or consent of the mortgagees, that he is to have the same preference with the mortgagees whose debts are to be paid off by this money, he is entitled to such preference, and that when the party advancing the money to pay off mortgagees is himself a prior or subsequent mortgagee, that circumstance, without any special contract or stipulation, is sufficient to entitle him, by operation of law, to come into the shoes of the mortgagees paid off with his money; and in support of this quoted 3 *Burge, p.* 209; *Voet* 20, 4, 34. That Mrs. van der Poel was a prior mortgagee when she advanced this money with which the subsequent mortgagees were paid off, and that by paying them off and taking receipts from the creditors, she, by the operation of law, took for the time the place of those creditors and became the creditor in *their debts* as they stood before the payment of them with her money. And that by their subsequent cancellation, and taking the new bond, she did not destroy or impair the right which she had so acquired in a question with other creditors in the situation of the defendants here. And that there was no legal distinction between the present case and that which would have existed if Mrs. Van der Poel had taken cession of the other mortgage bonds on paying them, and had afterwards cancelled the ceded bonds on getting a new bond for the total amount, in which case she would no more have lost her preference in respect of the ceded bonds than in respect of her own original bond for the amount of which the defendants admit she is still preferent. (*Domat* 3, *tit.* 1, § 6.)

Cloete followed on the same side, and quoted *Voet* 20, 4, § 34, *Van der Keessel, Thes.* 641, *Cod.* 8, *tit.* 42, § 8.

Brand, contra, commented on *Voet* 20, 4, § 35, and maintained that the plaintiffs' counsel had relied on the old civil law, and not attended to the distinction between it and the modern law of Holland, which, he maintained, did not recognize under any circumstances the right of a mortgage creditor to succeed *without cession* to the preference enjoyed by a prior mortgagee, whose debt the former paid off; and founded on the fact that the receipts for payment of the bonds were dated 20th May, and that in the receipts on the two bonds of Van den Berg, he had added the words, "and I consent to the cancellation thereof," which fact, he maintained, was absolutely inconsistent with the idea of there being any intention to cede those bonds to Mrs. van der Poel; and quoted *Voet* 20, 4, 32, to show the legal distinction which he alleged existed between Mrs. van der Poel's own bond, which is expressly referred to (and the mortgage in it thereby, *i.e.*, by the mere reference to it, preserved), and the other bonds of which no mention whatever is made in the bonds of the 23rd May, 1837. He also quoted *Burge* 3, 215, 787, *Cod. Civil, Nap., Art.* 1278, and maintained that the terms of the receipt on Mrs. van der Poel's own bond proved this alleged distinction. He maintained that to sustain the preference claimed by plaintiffs in respect of the bond of 23rd May, 1837, would be to destroy the utility of the registration of deeds. That the defendants seeing this bond registered as of 1837 were entitled to hold that, being subsequent to the date of their tacit hypothecation, it could not interfere with their hypothecation.

Ebden followed on the same side, and quoted *Pothier, vol.* 1, *pp.* 380, 390, 385, on novation and its effects. And argued that here it was impossible to deny the bond of 1837 was a novation, not only because there was by it a new creditor introduced, but because the former bonds were annihilated by being cancelled. (*Burge, vol.* 30, *pp.* 783, 784, 785.) He added that although the defendant may have erroneously, which he thought had been done, given up the claim to preference over the £300, for which Mrs. van der Poel had held a bond in her own right, that fact cannot be considered as barring the defendants from now maintaining any argument with respect to the other bonds, which, if good at all, would be equally good as to Mrs. van der Poel's own bond.

1844. Aug. 27. Dec. 14.

In Re Blommestein.—Executors of Van der Poel *vs.* Marais and Others.

The *Attorney-General* replied, and quoted *Domat.*, 3, 1, 6.
Cur. adv. vult.

This day, 14th December, 1844, the Court gave judgment for plaintiffs, ordering that the plaintiffs should, in virtue of the bond of 23rd May, 1837, be ranked on the estate of the insolvent for the sum of £1,200, as claimed, in preference to the claim of the defendants, with costs.

The Court held that the decision of this case depended on, and must be regulated by, the principles on which the cases of *Van der Byl and Meyer vs. the Sequestrator,* 23*rd Sept.*, 1828 (*vol.* 1, *p.* 318) *and of Leewner vs. Brink, Trustee of Magodas,* 25*th August,* 1840 (*ante, p.* 344) had been decided.

That, as according to those decisions, and indeed according to the admissions of the defendants, the bonds granted by the insolvent to the Widow van der Poel, Van den Berg, and Poleman would, if they had still existed, have been preferent to the tutorial hypothec of the defendants; and as the bond of 23rd May, 1837, had been substituted for those bonds in such a manner that the place Weltevreden was never freed from mortgage, to the extent of their amount, for a single instant, so that the tutorial hypothec could, for a single instant, have attached to or have been made effectual against the place, as being wholly unencumbered,—no distinction could be drawn between this bond and the four bonds for which it had been substituted as to the legal preference. That as those four bonds were not cancelled until the new bond had been executed on the 23rd May, the fact that their amounts had been paid to and receipts taken from Van den Berg and Poleman, on the 20th May, was of no consequence to the decision of the case; more especially as during the interval they were in the custody of Serrurier, who, *quoad hoc,* must be deemed to have held them as agent of the Widow van der Poel.

That no particular form is requisite to giving a bond, executed under circumstances similar to those in which that of 23rd May, 1837, was executed, the preference which has now been awarded to it. Proof of the nature and circumstances of the transaction is sufficient.

Ogilvie and Mandy, Executors of McKenny, *vs.* Rorke.

A notarial deed duly registered, acknowledging a debt, and for the securing thereof purporting to assign, &c., the debtor's right, title, and interest in a farm, and agreeing that in case of non-payment, the said farm, &c., shall and may forthwith be made and declared executable, constitutes no valid hypothec whatever on the farm.

The debtor's interest in the farm is executable in a judgment on such notarial bond.

1845. Aug. 1. — Ogilvie & Mandy, Executors of McKenny, *vs.* Rorke.

The plaintiffs claimed provisional sentence for £416 9s. 7d. in virtue of a notarial bond executed by the defendant, and that certain landed property therein mentioned be declared executable.

The bond, after constituting the personal obligation to pay, contained the following clause:

"And for the better and more effectually securing to the said W. Ogilvie and S. D. Mandy, &c., or to the indorsee and legal holder thereof, the due and punctual payment of the said sum of £416 9s. 7d., on the 6th day of August, 1844, he, the said B. Rorke, hath assigned, transferred, and set over, as by these presents he doth assign, transfer, and set over, unto them, the said W. Ogilvie and S. D. Mandy, and their, &c., &c., or to the indorsee or holder hereof, all his right, title, and interest in and to a certain farm, situated, &c., known by the name of Oxkraal, the property of the said B. Rorke, together with all and singular the buildings thereon, consenting and agreeing that in case of nonpayment, *the said farm, &c., shall and may be forthwith made and declared executable* for the amount due or to become due, and doth further bind generally his person and property, &c.; which I attest.

"J. J. STONE, Notary Public."

This bond was duly registered in the Registrar of Deeds' office.

No appearance was made for the defendant.

The Court gave provisional sentence as prayed; and declared the said farm *called Oxkraal to be executable to the extent of the right, title, and interest* which the said B. Rorke may have therein.

The Court declared that the above deed constituted no valid legal mortgage or lien whatever on the said farm; and that if the intention of the parties had been to mortgage it effectually for the said debt, the notary was highly censurable for having, through negligence or ignorance, professed to have done so by the above deed.

Trustees of Randall *vs.* Norden.

Hypothec.—Title Deed, Deposit of.

The Court refused to try, on motion, the right of a creditor to retain, as against the trustees of an insolvent estate, the title deeds of land deposited with the creditor in security of a debt due to him.

1845. Dec. 10. — Trustees of Randall *vs.* Norde. *Ebden*, for the trustees of Randall, put in an affidavit by W. M. Harris, one of the trustees, setting forth that he had been informed by B. Norden, the respondent, that Randall, before his estate was placed under sequestration, had lodged in the hands of the said respondent the deed of transfer and diagram of a certain erf and building at Port Elizabeth, which had been transferred to Randall by one Berry; and that the respondent has refused to deliver the said title deed to the applicants. That at the date of Randall's sequestration the said property stood, and still stands, unregistered in the name of Randall; and that, in conformity with a resolution of Randall's creditors, the applicants have sold the said property to H. Southey for £135; but by reason of the detention of the said title deed by the respondent, the applicants are unable to give transfer of the property to Southey, by reason whereof the estate of Randall has been damnified.

Ebden, therefore, prayed the Court to grant an order on the respondent to deliver the said title deed to the applicants.

The respondent appeared, and stated that the title deed had been deposited with him by Randall, in security of a debt due to him by Randall, and refused to give up the deed unless payment of his debt was first made to him.

The Court, without expressing any opinion whatever as to the validity of the right of hypothec, or retention, claimed by the respondent, held that it was not competent for the Court summarily to try and decide the question as to respondent's right to keep possession of the title deed; and that the applicants could only establish their right to compel the respondent to deliver up the title deed in an action regularly brought against him for that purpose; and refused the motion, with costs. (*Vide Van der Linden's Gewysden; et vide Phillips & King vs. Norton's Trustees,* next case; *Trustee of Wilson vs. Preuss and Seligmann—Watermeyer's Reports,* 1857. *In re Matthews—Buchanan's Reports,* 1868, *p.* 251, in which the above case was not, however, cited.)

Phillips & King *vs.* Trustees of Norton.

A clause in a deed in which, among other things, title deeds of a house were deposited in pledge with the plaintiffs, provided that among other things it should be lawful for the plaintiffs to receive the interest, dividends, rents, and profits, if any, accruing on the bonds, shares, title deeds, and other securities in the schedules. **Held**: *that this had the effect of creating an assignment of the rents of the house in favour of the plaintiffs, which was not defeated by a deed of assignment to which the plaintiffs were parties conveying the debtor's estate to trustees in trust for creditors.*

Whatever may be the legal effect of a deposit of title deeds in security of a debt in a deed to which the creditor was a party, conveying the debtor's estate to trustees in trust for creditors, a clause by which creditors holding securities agreed to deposit the securities which the trustees for the purpose of relegation "on the special trust and confidence that the respective proceeds shall be paid over to the extent of their several and respective preferences by virtue thereof," in virtue of which the title deeds which were mentioned in one of the schedules as among the securities deposited with the creditor were actually delivered over, constituted a transaction by which it was stipulated that the creditor holding the title deeds should have a first preference over the proceeds of the land held upon the title deeds as well as over the proceeds of the securities.

Quære: *Does a written pledge of the title deeds of immovable property, followed by the delivery of the title deeds to the pledgee, or the actual delivery of such deeds without writing, in security of a debt, create any right or interest in such deeds, or in or to the property to which they are related, which would be effectual against any third party, having obtained a jus in re or a jus ad rem to such immovable property?*

1846. Feb. 10.

Phillips & King *vs.* Trustees of Norton.

On the 10th January, 1842, in consideration of large advances of money, by way of acceptances, previously made by the plaintiffs, Messrs. Phillips & King, to the firm of John Norton & Co., John Norton and the partners of that firm executed a deed in which, *inter alia*, it was declared that, for securing the repayment of all such sums of money as they had, before the date of said deed, advanced or had become liable to pay for or on account of John Norton & Co., together with certain commissions thereon, the said John Norton individually *did thereby deposit with and*

1846. Feb. 10.

Phillips & King vs. Trustees of Norton.

assign, transfer, and set over to the said plaintiffs, &c., by way *of special mortgage, pledge, hypothec, or otherwise as might be more available in law, all the right, title, interests, claim, property, and demand which the said John Norton had in and to* (amongst other things set forth in the schedule annexed to said deed, marked A) *twenty shares or certificates of shares,* belonging to the said John Norton, in the Cape of Good Hope Steam Navigation Company; *and the lease of certain house and premises in the High-street, Graham's Town,* made by the said John Norton to Henry Nourse, dated 29th October, 1841, at the annual rent of £80.

The said deed further declared that as and for a further security for the repayment of the said advances and commission thereon, the said John Norton *did thereby mortgage, pledge, and hypothecate to and deposit with the said plaintiff's* (amonst other things set forth annexed to said deed, marked B), *two transfer or title deeds belonging to him, whereby the said John Norton was constituted the owner of the erf No.* 17, *Graham's Town, with the buildings thereon erected, which were then let on lease by the said John Norton to Levicks & Co., at the yearly rent of* £200.

And by the said deed the said John Norton did also individually covenant and agree with the plaintiffs, that if at any time before the final settlement of accounts between Norton & Co. and the plaintiffs, it should be found by the plaintiffs that the securities mentioned in schedule A were insufficient to secure the claim and demands of the plaintiffs, *that then and in that case the said John Norton would, on demand of the plaintiffs, specially mortgage, pledge, and hypothecate so much of the immovable property mentioned and set forth in the title deeds specified in schedule B, aforesaid, as might be deemed sufficient by the said plaintiffs.*

And by the said deed it was further provided that, pending the repayment to the plaintiffs of the whole of the advances and commissions in the said deed mentioned, and the re-conveyance, re-assignment, and delivery by the plaintiffs to the said John Norton of the securities in the said schedule mentioned, *it should and might be lawful to the said plaintiffs to receive the interest, dividends, rents, and profits, if any, accruing upon the bonds, shares, title deeds, and other securities in the said schedules mentioned,* during the period for which the same should remain mortgaged, pledged, or hypothecated.

The shares of the Steam Navigation Company, and the lease of the house between Norton and Nourse, the two transfer or title deeds of the erf No. 17, were delivered by John Norton, at the time of the execution of the said deeds, to the plaintiffs, who afterwards received certain of the rents of both the Graham's Town houses.

The affairs of the said John Norton having afterwards become temporarily embarrassed, a deed was on the 15th February, 1844, executed between him and sundry persons, his creditors, and the defendants, whereby—in order to prevent, as much as may be, the diminution of his estate in pursuing rigorous measures for the recovery of their debts —he offered, and his creditors agreed to accept the offer, to convey his whole estate to the defendants in trust for his creditors; and whereby he, accordingly, *inter alia,* assigned, transferred, and set over to the defendants, all and singular the shares, farms, lands, &c., &c., respectively mentioned and referred to in the several schedules thereunto annexed, marked A, B, C, and D, to the defendants upon trust, *inter alia,* to sell and dispose of the same, and with the proceeds to pay off and discharge the incumbrances and preferent claims thereon, and thereafter to pay the residue thereof unto and among the several concurrent creditors of the said John Norton who shall have executed these presents.

The deed also contained the following clause:

"And it is hereby declared and agreed by the several creditors, parties hereto, who severally hold securities of the said John Norton, for the payment of their respective claims, that they will, when required, deposit the said securities with the said, &c. (the defendants), for the purpose of realization, upon the special trust and confidence that the respective proceeds shall be paid over to them, to the extent of their several and respective preferences by virtue thereof."

This deed was executed by the plaintiffs and by all the creditors of John Norton. Schedule A referred to in the deed contained an inventory of his immovable property, schedule B of his movables and other assets. Schedule C was intituled—

"Preferent creditors in the estate of John Norton, in addition to those whose bonds are deducted from the estates specially pledged as per Schedule A."

In this schedule the plaintiffs were inserted as creditors holding the securities therein specified, being all those specified in schedules A and B annexed to the deed of the 10th January, 1842, including the twenty shares in the Steam Navigation Company, the lease of the house in Graham's Town to Nourse, and the title deeds to the erf and buildings in Graham's Town let to Levicks & Co. And at the end of the list of those securities there was written the following memorandum:

"Balance of Phillips & King's account to be paid in full out of the above securities."

Schedule D was intituled—

"Concurrent claimants against the estate of John Norton, who hold no security."

The plaintiffs gave up the title deeds of the erf and buildings let to Levicks & Co. upon a receipt which set forth that they were "received by the defendants subject to the deed of hypothecation in the possession of Messrs. Phillips and King."

The defendants sold the shares for the net sum of £26 10s. 1d.,—received £145 18s. 5d. on account for the house let to Nourse, and £267 5s. on account of rent for the house occupied by Levicks & Co., which they also sold and transferred for the net sum of £878 6s., making in all a sum of £1,275 19s. 6d. received by them. The balance due to plaintiffs by Norton & Co., for their advances and commissions, much exceeded the said sum of £1,275 19s. 6d., for which the plaintiffs brought this action against the defendants as being so much money had and received by the defendants to the use of the said plaintiffs.

In their plea, the defendants admitted that plaintiffs had a right of preference for the two abovementioned sums of £26 10s. 1d. and £145 18s. 5d., payment of which they tendered, but denied that the plaintiffs had any legal right of preference upon the said two other sums of £207 5s. and £878 6s.

All the facts above set forth were admitted between the parties.

In support of the plaintiffs' claim to the £207 5s. rent received by defendants from Levick & Co., the *Attorney-General*, for the plaintiff, maintained that the clause in the deed of 1842 which provided *that it should be lawful for the plaintiffs to receive* the interests, dividends, *rents*, and profits, if any, accruing upon the bonds, shares, title deeds, and other securities, in the said schedules mentioned, *during the period for which the same should remain mortgaged, pledged, and hypothecated*, had the effect of a legal assignation in favour of the plaintiffs of the rent, &c., therein mentioned, which assignation was completed (if it required anything to complete it) by the intimation thereof given to Levicks & Co., independently of the fact of rent having, in virtue of it, been received from Levicks & Co., and that the words "*rents accruing upon the title deeds*" must be construed to be rents accruing from the premises to which the title deeds related, seeing that otherwise these words must be held to have been used without any meaning having been intended to be conveyed by them,—a presumption contrary to the principles of legal construction; and that those words were intended to bear the meaning which he contended should be given to them was evident from the context. On these grounds he maintained that the plaintiffs had as good a right to claim that £207 5s. as they had to claim the £145 18s. 5d., the rent of the house occupied by Nourse, to which the defendants admitted that the plaintiffs were entitled.

Brand, for the defendants, maintained the contrary, and further argued that the difference between the terms made use of in the deed applicable to the property specified in schedule A and that specified in schedule B proved that it was the intention of the parties that the plaintiffs should not have the same right to the rents of the house occupied by Levicks & Co., which he admitted was given them to the rents of the house occupied by Nourse, even supposing, which he denied, that the "*rents*" mentioned in the clause founded on by the plaintiffs could be held to mean the rents of the house occupied by Levicks & Co.

With respect to the claim of the plaintiffs to the £878 6s., the net price for which the house, the title deeds of which had been hypothecated to the plaintiffs, was sold,—the *Attorney-General* argued that—without being under the necessity of maintaining that the hypothecation of the title deeds of immovable property in security of a debt, followed by delivery thereof to the creditor, constituted any right in favour of the creditor which would be effectual against the creditors claiming in virtue of a sequestration of the debtor's estate as insolvent, or against any third party,—it was clear that such a hypothecation and deposit of the title deeds was effectual as against the debtor himself, who hypothecated and deposited them, so that, however great the inconvenience he might be put to by the want of them, he could not force the creditor to give them up without first discharging the debt in security of which they had been deposited; and that as the trust deed executed by Norton was a voluntary one, executed by him before any sequestration of his estate as insolvent, the defendants in virtue of it were not in the situation in which they would have stood if they had been trustees of the sequestrated estate of Norton, but were merely his agents, or mandatories, and therefore represented him, and could be in no better situation with respect to the plaintiffs than he himself would have been, and consequently could not have forced the plaintiffs to give up the title deeds to enable them to sell the property; and as the plaintiffs had only given up the title deeds and consented to the sale on the express condition that they were to have the same preference on the proceeds that they had on the property, the defendants had no better right to retain those proceeds from the plaintiffs

1846. Feb. 10. — Phillips & King *vs.* Trustees of Norton.

than they could have had to have compelled them to give up the title deeds and to have sold and transferred the property without the plaintiffs' consent; and must therefore be held to have received the price of the property for the use of the plaintiffs. (He quoted *Abbot on Shipping, Shee's Edit., pp.* 72, 77; *Burton's Compendium of the Law of Real Property,* 515; *Coote on Mortgages, p.* 220; *Van Leeuwen's Roman-Dutch Law, p.* 123; *Voet,* 41, 1, 42; *Voet,* 1, 20.)

Brand, for the defendants, maintained the contrary, and quoted *Neostadius Decisiones,* 28 *and* 29; *Matthæus de Auctionibus,* 1, 20, 16. He also maintained that the express provision in the deed that Norton should, on demand of the plaintiffs, specially mortgage, pledge, and hypothecate so much of the immovable property mentioned and set forth in the title deeds specified in schedule B as might be deemed sufficient by the plaintiffs, proved that Norton and the plaintiffs never intended to create, nor thought they had created, any mortgage over, or any interest in the premises the title deeds of which were referred to by them. That the trust property had been conveyed to the defendants not merely as the agents of Norton, or trustees for behoof of the plaintiffs, but as trustees for all the parties to the trust deed, in order to dispose of the same and distribute the proceeds among those parties to the extent of their several and respective *preferences.* That by the term *preference* was meant such legal rights of preference as were at the time of the execution of the trust deed already fully and completely constituted and completed, and not any of inferior right or interest, which the plaintiffs might have previously had, in virtue of which they might, if Norton had remained solvent, have, by legal proceedings, obtained a legal right of preference over the trust property.

The Court held that the question between the parties depended on, and must be decided solely according to, the legal effect of the provisions of the trust deed of 15th February, 1844, which must in law be deemed to have been a *transaction* entered into by the parties for the adjustment of the interests which they were to have in the assets realized by the trustees. That the schedules A, B, C, and D, annexed thereto, and referred to therein, must be held to be, and have effect given to them as if they had been, inserted *verbatim in gremio* of the deed. That from the tenor of the deed and of schedule C, it was clear that all the parties to the deed understood and agreed that the plaintiffs, in virtue of the deed of the 10th January, 1842, followed by the actual delivery to them of the title deeds and other securities mentioned in schedules A and B, had acquired a right of preference of some kind or other over the property to which those title deeds and securities related, which they could have enforced by legal proceedings, or of the supposed benefit of which they could not be deprived without legal proceedings, if at all. And that in consideration of the plaintiffs giving up the deeds and securities in their possession, and allowing the trustees to realize the value of the property to which they related, it was stipulated and provided that they should have a first preference over the proceeds for the whole amount of the debt in security of which the deed of 1842 had been executed in their favour; and that therefore—whether they really had, in virtue of that deed, and of what followed thereon, acquired any preference, or not, previous to the execution of the trust deed—they were now entitled to the two sums claimed by them.

The Court held that the clause founded on by the Attorney-General had the effect of creating such an assignation of the rents accruing on the house occupied by Levicks & Co. as could not have been defeated by the trustees or other creditors claiming under a subsequent deed of the nature of the trust deed of 15th February, 1844. That the obligation on the part of Norton, in the deed of 1842, to grant the plaintiffs a special mortgage over the lastmentioned house enabled the plaintiffs at any time to have, by legal proceedings, compelled Norton to execute that special mortgage, and pending those proceedings to have obtained an interdict which would have prevented him from, in the mean time, granting any transfer or mortgage of that house which could have defeated their special mortgage over it.

The Court expressly abstained from giving any opinion on the point whether a written mortgage of the title deeds of immovable property, followed by delivery of the deeds to the mortgagee,—or the actual deposit of such deeds (without writing) in security of a debt,—could or could not create any right or interest in such deeds, or in or to the property to which they related, which would be effectual against any third party having obtained either a *jus in re* in, or a *jus ad rem* to, such immovable property.

The Court gave judgment for plaintiffs, as prayed, with costs.

NORDEN *vs.* SOLOMON, Q.Q. THE ASSIGNEES OF CHARKE.

Jurisdiction of Supreme Court to declare and make effectual a hypothec over property within this Colony, forming part of the estate of an English bankrupt, in favour of a creditor whose debt had existed prior to the date of the bankruptcy. Where by the law of the Colony a hypothec has been acquired affecting the property of a bankrupt within the jurisdiction of the Supreme Court, the hypothec can be made effectual by an action in this Court in favour of the creditor of an English bankrupt whose debt existed prior to the bankruptcy. Notwithstanding the English bankruptcy, the Court has jurisdiction to try whether a hypothec claimed by a creditor has been acquired prior to the bankruptcy over any of the bankrupt's property situated within the Court's jurisdiction.

1847. Feb. 11.

Norden *vs.* Solomon, q.q. The Assignees of Charke.

The plaintiff brought this action against the defendant, as agent for the assignees of Charke, to have it declared that he was entitled by the law of this Colony to a tacit hypothec over the vessel *Justitia*, of which Charke was the owner at the time of her bankruptcy, for certain sums which as agent for the *Justitia* he had expended on the account prior to the date of the bankruptcy, and to have the proceeds of the said vessel (which had been sold, and the proceeds paid into Court by consent of all parties concerned) adjudged to him.

In bar of this action, the defendant pleaded that the amount claimed by the plaintiff was a debt due to him by Charke before and at the time of his bankruptcy; that Charke, while domiciled in England, had been rendered a bankrupt in England, and his estate had been assigned, under the English Bankrupt Statute, to assignees, whose agent the present defendant is; and that in virtue of Charke's said bankruptcy at and in the place of his said domicile, England became, and now is the *locus concursus creditorum,* in regard to all the creditors of Charke, and therefore that the defendant is bound to resort to the proper court or courts in England, under the control and direction of which the estate and effects of Charke are now being administered, and there to assert his rights and claims against the said estate, together with all preferences and hypothecations to which he may lawfully lay claim; that this Court ought not to try or determine whether the plaintiff has a tacit hypothec over the vessel *Justitia,* nor to order distribution here of any of the assets of the said bankrupt estate; and that all such matters and questions are properly and of right triable and determinable in England, and not elsewhere. Wherefore the defendant opposed to the plaintiff's claim the exception "*Ne continentia causæ dividatur,*" and prays that he may be absolved from the instance.

In support of this plea the *Attorney-General,* for the defendant, this day quoted the authorities, and repeated the arguments referred to, and used by him on the 17th November, 1846, in opposing the plaintiff's motion for a writ to arrest the *Justitia, jurisdictionis fundandæ causa.*

But the Court held that if, prior to Charke's bankruptcy, the plaintiff had by the law of this Colony acquired a hypothec affecting this vessel or any other property of Charke now situated within the limits of the jurisdiction of this Court, he was entitled to make that hypothec effectual, by an action in this Court; and that this Court had also jurisdiction to try the question whether the plaintiff had acquired prior to the bankruptcy any hypothec over any of Charke's property situated within the jurisdiction of this Court; and that the sale of the vessel and the payment of the proceeds into this Court, by consent of the parties concerned, was equivalent to an arrest, at the instance of the plaintiff, of the vessel, *jurisdictionis fundandæ causa* under a writ of this Court. And therefore repelled the exception, and rejected the defendant's claim for an absolution from the instance.

NORDEN *vs.* SOLOMON, Q.Q., ASSIGNEES OF CHARKE.

Hypothec for advances made for furnishings to vessels in a foreign port. Indefinite payments appropriated to items of debt best secured.

An agent of a ship claiming a balance of account against the ship in which account were included disbursements for the benefit of the ship which would by law have entitled a creditor for such disbursements to a hypothec, and likewise charges and money advanced which would not have entitled a creditor to a hypothec, the Court, without deciding whether his character as agent did or did not deprive him of the hypothec which, if not agent, he would have had, and whether such hypothec extended to anything beyond necessary repairs effected on the block of the vessel, i.e., to money expended on tackle, apparel, furniture, provisions, and seamen's wages: held that inasmuch as all these claims for which a hypothec could be pretended together amounted to a less sum than that received by the agent on account of the agency of the ship, he was bound to apply such amount, indefinitely received, for the benefit of the ship, in the first place to discharge the claim secured by hypothec, which was accordingly extinguished.

1847. Feb. 16.

Norden *vs.* Solomon, q.q. The Assignees of Charke.

The declaration set forth that J. Charke, as owner of the schooner *Justitia*, was, prior to the date of the bankruptcy, indebted to the plaintiff in the sum of £274 7s. 10d., being the balance of a certain account-current thereto annexed for divers disbursements and sums of money expended by the plaintiff as the agent in this Colony for the said vessel, for necessary repairs effected upon the said schooner in this Colony, at the request of the master of the said vessel, and for various ship's supplies and stores furnished by the plaintiff, as agent, for the use of the said schooner at the like request, and for money laid out and expended for procuring guano licences, paying Customs duties, seamen's wages, and other disbursements for the said vessel at the like request, and for certain reasonable and customary commissions due and of right payable by the defendant to the plaintiff as said agent in respect thereof; for which said sum the plaintiff maintains that he is by the law of this Colony entitled to a tacit hypothecation upon the said vessel; whereupon the plaintiff prays that it may be ordered by the judgment of this Court that he be paid in full of his said debt out of the proceeds of the said vessel, which have been brought into Court by consent of the plaintiff and of the defendant.

The defendant pleaded the general issue.

By the different accounts put in by plaintiff, as admitted by the defendant, after sundry amendments and corrections consented to by plaintiff, it appeared that the sum total which had been expended by him on account of repairs to the said vessel, tackle, apparel, and furniture, provisions, and seamen's wages, amounted to £824 3s. 9d.; that the remainder of the amount for which he claimed credit in his account was entirely composed of money expended in procuring guano licences, Custom-house charges connected with procuring freight for the vessel, commission, and sundry miscellaneous charges, all appertaining to a ship's agency, but for which it could not be pretended that by law any hypothec was constituted over the vessel; and that the amount which during the period of the agency he had received on account of the vessel was £1,558 11s. 9d.

Ebden, for the plaintiff, in support of his claim for a hypothec over the vessel for money expended on repairs to the vessel, her tackle, apparel, and furniture, on provisions, and in paying seamen's wages,—quoted *Inlied. Grotius*, 2, *cap.* 48, § 13, *p.* 262, *Herbert's Translation; Van der Linden's Inst., p.* 607; *Van Leeuwen's Roman-Dutch Law, p.* 385; *Abbot on Shipping, part* 2, *cap.* 3, § 10, *pp.* 108, 111, 116; *Pandects, Lib.* 20, *tit.* 4, l. 5 *and* 6; *Voet* 20, 2, 9; *Van der Keessel, Thes.* 417.

1847. Feb. 16.

Norden *vs.* Solomon, q.q. The Assignees of Charke.

The *Attorney-General, contra,* maintained that the hypothec extended only to necessary repairs effected on the block of the vessel, and quoted *Van der Keessel,* 417. To show that it did not extend to provisions, he quoted the case of the *Duke of Bedford,* 2, *Hagg. Reports, p.* 294. He denied that there was any hypothec for money expended in paying seamen's wages, or that a bottomry bond could be granted for money borrowed to pay them. (*Vide* the opinion of this Court *in re* the *Black Swan,* 28th February, *ante p.* 350.) He quoted *Hussy vs. Christie and others,* 9 *East p.* 426, to show that the money advanced by plaintiff having been advanced by him in his capacity as agent for the owner of the vessel, he could claim no hypothec for it, unless he had obtained an assignation of their debts and hypothec from the persons who had made the repairs or furnishings for the vessel, and to whom the defendant had paid the money expended by him. Lastly, he quoted *Voet,* 46, 3, 16; *Burge, 3rd vol. p.* 831; and maintained that as the plaintiff had received £1,558, indefinitely, on account of the owner of the vessel, without any appropriation of it to the discharge of any particular items expressly made or tacitly consented to by the owner, the plaintiff was bound in law to apply it in the first instance to extinguish that portion of the debt due to him for which he had the best security, namely, that for which he had a hypothec over the vessel, and that as the total amount of this portion of his debt, even allowing it to include moneys expended on the vessel's tackle, apparel, furniture, and provisions, and in paying seamen's wages, only amounted to £824 3s. 9d., this sum was far more than extinguished by the amount which plaintiff had received.

Ebden, in reply, denied this last proposition, and quoted *Rocca, p.* 119, and *Barels on Maritime Law.* He maintained that the hypothec over the vessel is a cumulative remedy, and therefore that the plaintiff's argument, founded on the plaintiff's agency for the owner of the vessel, was unfounded; and quoted *Harrison's Digest, p.* 2001.

The Court held that the plaintiff could not possibly claim any hypothec over the vessel for the amount of any of the items in his account not comprehended in the sum of £824 3s. 9d., referred to by the Attorney-General; that the defendant would have been by law entitled to a hypothec over the vessel for the money advanced by him under the circumstances of the present case, for necessary repairs to the vessel, if not deprived of the same by the fact of his having been the agent of the owner; but that it was unnecessary to give any decision as to whether the hypothec extended to moneys expended on the vessel's tackle, apparel,

1847. Feb. 16. — Norden vs. Solomon, q.q. The Assignees of Charke.

furniture, and provisions, and in paying seamen's wages, or as to the effect of his character as agent in depriving him of any hypothec which, if he had not been agent for the owner, he would have had; because the utmost he could claim on all those items added together was only £824 3s. 9d., which was extinguished by the greater amount which he had received indefinitely on account of the vessel, and which, therefore, he was bound to apply in the first place to the discharge of this claim of £824 3s. 9d., in so far as it was secured by a hypothec over the vessel.

On these grounds the Court gave judgment for the defendant, and ordered the whole proceeds of the vessel which had been paid into Court, being £198 3s., to be paid to the defendant, less the sum of £25, which, by consent of defendant, was ordered to be paid to plaintiff on account of his costs.

MUNICIPALITY OF GREEN POINT *vs.* POWELL'S TRUSTEES.

Preference. Municipalities have none for Arrears of Rates. Ordinance No. 4, 1839.

1848. June 14. Sept. 12. — Municipality of Green Point vs. Powell's Trustees.

Brand, for the applicants, objected to the plan of distribution framed by the trustees of the insolvent, in so far as they had refused a preference to the Municipality for the arrears of road rates assessed on his landed property at Green Point under the provisions of section 31 of Ordinance No. 4, 1839, due by the insolvent prior to the sequestration of his estate,—and had ranked the Municipality only as concurrent creditors, in consequence of which no dividend had been awarded to the Municipality.

Further hearing postponed.

Postea (14th June, 1848).—This day, *Brand* resumed his argument, and maintained that the Municipality had, by reason of its nature, and without any express enactment to that effect, the same rights and privileges which, by the Dutch law, the towns had in Holland, and *municipia* had under the Roman law, and that by the Dutch and Roman law every such community had a preference for the taxes which by its constitution it was legally empowered to levy; and quoted *Van der Linden, Inst., p.* 178; *Voet,* 20, 2, 8; *Locnius, Cas.* 17, *p.* 125.

The *Attorney-General*, for the trustees, argued *contra.*

Postea (12th September, 1848).—WYLDE, C.J., and MENZIES, J., gave judgment, that the Municipality was merely the creature of the Ordinance No. 4, 1839, and consequently that it possessed no power or privileges except such as were expressly given to it by the provisions of that Ordinance which created it, among which the right of preference claimed was not one. On this ground they overruled the objection made by the Municipality to, and confirmed the distribution account, with costs.

1848. June 14. Sept. 12.

Municipality of Green Point *vs.* Powell's Trustee.

Before going on circuit, MUSGRAVE, J., had authorized the Chief Justice to state for him, that he still had such doubts on the case as would have prevented him from concurring in the judgment given by the majority of the Court.

BRINK'S TRUSTEES *vs.* SOUTH AFRICAN BANK.

Pledge. Jus retentionis.

The pledgee of a bond, pledged by writing, and delivered to him in security of a sum specified in the writing, has no jus retentionis of the bond against the creditors of the pledgee in respect of any other debt due by him to the pledgee.

1848. Aug. 22. Dec. 30.

Brink's Trustees *vs.* The South African Bank.

The declaration in this case set forth that on the 19th May, 1847, Stephanus Brink was possessed, as his property, of a certain mortgage bond, dated 25th January, 1844, executed by the Rev. S. P. Heyns, in favour of the said Brink, for £1,000; and in security thereof specially mortgaged a certain house and garden, situated in Table Valley. That the said Brink obtained from the defendants a loan of £600, and for the security of the repayment thereof, made and executed the following writing:

"South African Bank, Cape Town,
10th May, 1847.

"£600.

"Four months after date, I promise to pay Mr. Godfrey Rawstorne, Cashier of the South African Bank, and at the South African Bank, the sum of £600 sterling, value received, for the security of which I do hereby pledge the annexed mortgage bond of £1,000, passed by the Rev. S. P. Heyns, D.D.; and, moreover, do bind my person and property according to law; and I do further declare that nothing has been or will be received, either by myself or by any person on my behalf, in part or in full payment of the said sum of £1,000, being the amount of the security pledged, without the previous knowledge of the chairman and directors of the said bank, as long as the aforesaid bond shall be so mortgaged.

"S BRINK."

1848. Aug. 22. Dec. 30.

Brink's Trustees vs. The South African Bank.

That the said G. Rawstorne was and is the cashier of the said bank, and that he was named in the said writing solely as representing and acting on behalf of the said bank, and does not pretend to have any interest whatever in the said loan or pledge.

That whilst the said bond remained pledged as aforesaid, for the security of the said sum of £600, the said Brink surrendered his estate as insolvent on the 2nd August, 1847; and that the plaintiffs had been confirmed as trustees of the said insolvent estate.

That on the 5th July, 1848, the plaintiffs tendered and offered to the defendants to pay to them the said sum of £600, with all interest due thereon, in case the defendants would receive the same and deliver up the said bond, so pledged as aforesaid, which tender and offer the defendants refused to accept, claiming certain other moneys to be paid to them before they would give up the said bond.

That under and by virtue of the deed regulating the joint-stock company trading under the firm of the South African Bank, the defendants, as trustees thereof, are the proper persons to be sued in this action on behalf of the said joint-stock company.

Wherefore the plaintiffs prayed that the defendants, in their capacity as aforesaid, should be condemned to come to an account with the plaintiffs, and upon payment of the said sum of £600, with all interest due and owing thereon, to deliver to the plaintiffs the said mortgage bond, and to pay the costs of this suit.

In their plea, the defendants admitted the several allegations and matters of fact stated in the declaration, and pleaded that before and subsequent to the said 9th May, 1847,—the date when the said bond was pledged to the defendants,—the said Brink was and became indebted to the defendants on six promissory notes therein specified and described, made or endorsed by Brink in favour of the defendants; all which sums, amounting together to the sum of £503 16s. 3d., are unsecured, unsatisfied, and unpaid; for the payment whereof the defendants alleged that they are entitled to retain, or take, or employ so much of the balance of the said bond after payment of the said sum of £600 with interest as shall be sufficient to pay and satisfy the defendants for the said sum of £503 16s. 3d., with interest due thereon.

Wherefore the defendants offered and tendered to come to an account with the plaintiffs, and to deliver up the said bond upon payment of the said sum of £600, with interest due thereon, and upon the further payment of the said sum of £503 16s. 3d., with interest due thereon.

At the trial, a consent paper was put in, signed by the attorneys of both parties, whereby it was admitted on the part of the plaintiffs that all the promissory notes made or endorsed by the insolvent Brink, and mentioned in the plea of defendants, have been duly proved in his insolvent estate by, and are still due and owing by the said estate to, the defendants.

(As the judgment given by the Court was in respect of a general principle, and was in no wise affected by certain special facts and circumstances which were admitted or proved by the parties respectively, it is unnecessary to set them forth.)

The plaintiffs called the insolvent.

Stephanus Brink: I executed and gave to defendants the writing, dated 19th May, 1847. The Bank had previously, and then had, paper of mine in their hands which they discounted for me. Before or after the execution of this writing nothing whatever passed between the Bank and me about this writing and the pledge of the bond therein made being also to be in security for the payment of those discounted notes, or of others to be by the Bank afterwards discounted for me. I never pledged the bond except in security for the sum of £600.

The plaintiffs closed their case.

The defendants called no witnesses.

The *Attorney-General*, for the plaintiffs, maintained that although by virtue of the *Cod.*, *lib.* 8, *tit.* 27, *l.* 1, the defendants had a *jus retentionis* against Brink himself, which entitled them to refuse to restore the pledge to him unless he should first pay or tender to them not only the amount of the debt for which the bond had been pledged, but also the amount of any other debts due by him to them for which no pledge had been given, yet that they could not exercise the right of retention against his creditors after his insolvency, and must give up the pledge on receiving payment merely of the debt for which the pledge had been given. Because the *jus retentionis* of the pledge for other unsecured debts given against the debtor himself, was given on the ground that the creditor holding the pledge was entitled to oppose the *exceptio dolï mali* to the claim of the debtor for the restoration of the pledge to him on payment merely of the debt for which the pledge had been given, while he refused to pay other debts then justly due by him to that creditor. And because this *exceptio dolï mali* could not be pleaded against the other creditors of the original debtor claiming, after his insolvency, that the pledge should be given up to the general body of the creditors, on paying to the creditor holding the pledge the amount of

1848. Aug. 22. Dec. 30.

Brink's Trustees *vs* The South African Bank.

the debt for which it had been pledged, seeing that the insolvency did, by operation of law, instantly divest the insolvent debtor of his whole estate, and vest it in the general body of the creditors, represented by the trustees, subject only to such real rights in or over it which had been constituted in favour of third parties prior to the insolvency, and without any other condition or qualification than that the proceeds of the said estate should be distributed equally, *pro rata*, amongst the personal creditors of the insolvent. He referred to the following authorities: *Burton on Insolvent Law, p.* 145, 146; *Van der Keessel, Thes.* 435 *and* 450; *Van Leeuwen, Cens. For., lib.* 4, *tit.* 37, §§ 1 *and* 2; *Voet,* 13, 6, 10; 16, 2, 15; 20, 6, 16; 41, 1, 42; *Carpzovius, Const.,* 40, *defn.* 3; *Cujacius on the Code, lib.* 8, *tit.* 27, *p.* 1,114, 1,115; *Faber, lib.* 8, *tit.* 16, *defn.* 4; *Grotius, Inleid.,* 3, 19, § 16; *Storey on Bailments,* § 305; *Kent's Commentaries, vol.* 2, *p.* 584; *Adams vs. Claxton,* 6 *Ves. Junr., p.* 229; *Henley on Bankruptcy, p.* 294; *Cooke on Mortgages, p.* 491; *Smith's Merc. Law, p.* 461; *Stair's Instit., b.* 3, *tit.* 4, § 23; *Bell's Comment, vol.* 1, *p.* 684; 2*nd, p.* 22.

Brand and *Watermeyer, contra,* maintained that, according to the true construction of the *lex unica* of the *Code, lib.* 8, *tit.* 27, the *jus retentionis* was given not only against the debtor himself, but also against all persons deriving any right from or through him, and consequently against all his personal creditors, save and except a *secundus creditor hypothecarius,* that is to say, a posterior creditor in whose favour a second mortgage of the thing pledged to the first creditor had been duly constituted; because by such second mortgage he had acquired a real right in the thing pledged, in virtue of which he was preferent to any personal debt due by the common debtor to the creditor to whom the money had been first pledged;—and that the *secundus creditor hypothecarius* was mentioned not as *one* instance of the rule that the *jus retentionis* could not be enforced against the creditors of the common debtor, but as being the single excepted case in which the *jus retentionis* could not be enforced against a creditor of the common debtor, in like manner as against the debtor himself. They referred to the *Pandects, lib.* 20, *tit.* 4, *l.* 20; *Van Leeuwen, Cens. For., lib.* 4, *tit.* 10, § 37; *Faber, lib.* 8, *tit.* 16, *defn.* 2; *Carpzovius, part* 2*nd, tit.* 25, *defn.* 25; *Christinæus, vol.* 4, *decis.* 169; *Huber, Prælectiones, b.* 20, *tit. C.; Voet,* 13, 7, § 6; 16, 2, § 20; 42, 7, § 5; 20, 4, § 37; *Leyser, vols.* 3 *and* 4, §§ 175 *and* 231; *vol.* 7, *p.* 515 *and* 560; *Hollandsche Regt. Book, p.* 245, § 1,205; *Grotius, Inleid., b.* 2, *part* 48; *Van der Linden, Inst., p.* 178; *Pothier on Pledges, cap.* 2, § 47; *Muhlenbruch, Doctrina*

Pandect., 2*nd vol.*, *p.* 208; *Burge, vol.* 3, *pp.* 236, 585; *Code Napoleon, art.* 2,082; *Mackeldey's Mod. Civ. Law, vol.* 1, *p.* 384; *Kent's Comment., vol.* 4, *p.* 176; *Storey's Equity Jurisprud., vol.* 2, *p.* 248, § 1,010; 270, § 1,034–5; *Zande's Decisions, b.* 3, *tit.* 10, *dec.* 7; *Van der Berg's Consult., vol.* 1, *com.* 36; *Præzius and Brunneman on the Code, b.* 8, *tit.* 27.

1848. Aug. 22. Brink's Trustees *vs.* The South African Bank.

Postea (30th December, 1848).—The Court, for the reasons founded on by the plaintiffs, gave judgment for the plaintiffs as prayed, with costs.

SMITH *vs.* RANDALL'S TRUSTEES.

A power of attorney authorizing an attorney to appear before the Registrar of Deeds, to acknowledge a debt due on the purchase money of land, and to pass a "schepenkennis" or mortgage bond in favour of the vendor, is a power authorizing the attorney to insert in the mortgage bond any clause which, by the established usage and custom of the Colony, it is the practice to insert in similar bonds, and therefore an authority to insert for a bond, specially hypothecating immovable property, a clause of general mortgage.

1848. Dec. 20. Smith *vs.* Randall's Trustees.

In this case, the Master reported that the plan of distribution framed by the trustee in the insolvent estate of Randall was objected to by Mr. John Owen Smith, a creditor, on the ground that a preference of £138 11s. 10d. was allowed by the trustee to the executors of the estate of the late Thomas Williamson, and that the sum of £91 12s. 10d. has been awarded to them on account of the said preference, alleged to be due upon and by virtue of a certain bond passed by William Tennant, as agent of the insolvent, on the 30th August, 1839, for the sum of £500, whereby the said William Tennant specially mortgaged a piece of ground with the buildings thereon, the property of the said insolvent, and further, generally, his property of every description. Whereas the said William Tennant was not at the time of passing such general mortgage legally empowered so to do.

The case having been set down for argument, a paper containing the following statement of facts admitted between the parties was put in:

In September, 1838, the insolvent purchased from the executors of the estate of Thomas Williamson, a house and premises situated at Port Elizabeth, for £700.

By deed of sale, Randall agreed to pay £100 cash by the

1848. Dec. 20.

Smith *vs.* Randall's Trustees.

1st October, 1838, and to execute a notarial bond with two sureties for the balance, to be paid in six equal instalments.

This arrangement was, however, subsequently altered, for Randall, having paid off £200, executed on the 30th August, 1839, through his agent, William Tennant, the bond now before the Court for the balance of the purchase money, £500, secured by second mortgage of the house and premises (which had in January previous been pledged under first mortgage to the Master of the Supreme Court for £400), and general mortgage of Randall's person and property, in the usual form.

The power of attorney under which Tennant acted, and which was, according to the custom of the Deeds Registry Office, preserved there and annexed to the said bond, was as follows:

"Know all men, that I, Nathaniel Randall, have made, ordained, nominated, constituted, and appointed, as by these presents I do make, ordain, nominate, constitute, and appoint, William Tennant, Esq., to be my true and lawful attorney and agent for me, and in my name and behalf to appear at the office of the Registrar of Deeds in Cape Town, and there to acknowledge that I am well and truly indebted unto Thomas Pullen and William Ward, executors of the late Thomas Williamson, of Port Elizabeth, in the true and just sum of £500, being the balance due by me in the purchase of a certain lot of ground with the buildings thereon, being a subdivision of the original erf No. 2, situate in the Main-street, in the residency of Port Elizabeth, and thereupon, for me and in my name, to pass a schepenkennis or mortgage bond, binding the said property to the said Thomas Pullen and William Ward, as executors of the late Thomas Williamson, in manner agreed upon by a certain deed of sale, as executed before G. M. Bruuette, Esq., notary public, and witnesses at Port Elizabeth, on the 21st September, 1838, as a security for the payment of the said sum of £500, with such interest as shall accrue thereon, at the rate of 5 per cent. per annum, commencing from the 1st October, 1838, and for effecting the premises, to sign and execute all papers and writings, and to do and execute everything that shall be required to be done and executed on my behalf as fully and effectually to all intents and purposes as if I was personally present.

"Promising to approve, allow, and confirm all that my said agent, the said William Tennant, shall lawfully do by virtue of these presents.

"Given under my hand at Uitenhage, this 2nd day of August, 1839.

"NATHANIEL RANDALL."

On the 4th February, 1842, the Attorney Reid, acting under a power similar to that of Tennant, and according to instructions from Randall, executed a mortgage bond, containing the usual general as well as special mortgage in favour of Mr. Rishton, which he transmitted to Randall, from whom he received no objections.

On the 10th June, 1842, Randall personally executed a notarial bond of general mortgage in favour of the objecting creditor, Smith, for the sum of £288 8s. 4d., which was duly registered on the 1st July following.

On the 18th May, 1843, Randall's estate was put under compulsory sequestration, and the several bonds mentioned, with other debts, were duly proved.

With the exception of the premises thus mortgaged to the Master and the estate of Williamson, the landed property of the insolvent realized enough to pay off their respective mortgages, but the erf in question realized barely sufficient to pay off the first mortgage due to the Master, leaving a balance of only £25 18s. 2d., to be applied to the payment of Williamson's bond, which, at the period of Randall's insolvency, had been reduced to £166 10s., and the amount of £25 18s. 2d. was accordingly awarded by the trustees to Williamson's estate in their distribution account.

The trustees next proceeded to award a sum of £91 12s. 10d., being the balance remaining in their hands of the general assets of Randall's estate, to the estate of Williamson, as a preferent claim, due by virtue of the clause of general mortgage contained in the bond executed by Tennant. And this preference is now objected to by the said creditor Smith, upon the ground that the said William Tennant was not authorized to grant such general mortgage as aforesaid.

The parties also put in the following paper, which was admitted to be the correct results of an examination of the powers of attorney filed in the office of the Registrar of Deeds, and the bonds executed thereunder, which they had procured to be made:

All the bonds registered in the Registrar of Deeds' office contained a clause of general mortgage in addition to the special hypothec, with the exception hereinbefore mentioned.

Prior to the year 1800, no power of attorney to pass a mortgage seems to have been registered; but from that period the powers are pretty regularly filed with the mortgage bonds.

The earlier powers are notarial, and vary from one another according as they are drawn up by different notaries.

1848. Dec. 20. ,, 30.

Smith *vs.* Randall's Trustees.

The powers for 1804 are a fair sample of the form and wording most in practice.

In this year there are six powers; the first, passed before T. B. Hoffman, authorizes the agents to execute a special mortgage of certain property, "according to local custom," *naar costume locaal.*

The second, also passed before Hoffman, empowers the agent to do "what shall be required," *gerequireerd werden zal.*

The third, passed before D. P. Haupt, directs the agent "to do all that is necessary and required," *alles te doen en verrigten hetgeen nodig and gerequireerd werden zal.*

The fourth, passed before C. J. Goertz, authorizes the agents to do "all that may be necessary," *asles te doen en te verrigten wat noodig weezen zal.*

The fifth and sixth powers, passed before Hoffman, authorize the agent to bind his constituent's person and property in addition to the special mortgage, "*uitsgarders voorts generalyk haar persoon en goederen.*"

In the year 1805, out of eight powers only one contains an authority to grant a general mortgage upon the person and property of the principal.

In 1806, out of seven powers, none contain such authority.

In 1812, out of eleven powers, only one, and in 1820, out of eighteen, none.

The powers of attorney executed in 1839, the date of Randall's power to Tennant, have been carefully examined, and the following is the result of an investigation of the first 14 volumes, containing 150 bonds, all containing the clause of general mortgage, and passed by virtue of powers of attorney.

Of the 150 powers, only 119 are filed, 31 being wanting, in consequence, perhaps, of their being general powers, which are not usually filed at the Debt Registry.

Out of 119 powers filed, 19 contain a regular authority, empowering the agent to bind his principal's person and property in addition to the special mortgage.

The remaining 100 powers make no mention of the principal's person or property, but merely contain the usual concluding clause to powers, "to do all that is requisite and necessary to be done," or refer to the *costume locaal.*

Two or three powers are from firms or companies, which will perhaps account for the absence of the clause authorizing a general mortgage, and two or three more refer to the conditions of the agreement of sale of the property mortgaged, which are not filed, and may or may not have stipulated for the general as well as special mortgage.

Much difference of form is to be observed in the powers drawn up by different notaries, or coming from different localities.

Those passed before G. M. Brunette are chiefly to execute mortgages in favour of the Orphan Chamber, and usually contain a clause, authorizing the agent to perform "all such other agreements as are required to be stipulated in mortgage bonds effected in favour of the Guardian Fund."

Eighteen powers passed before the notaries J. G. Borcherds, M. J. H. Borcherds, Korsten, Roselt, Chase, De Villiers, Barker, De Wet, Barnes, W. S. Buissinne, and Poggenpoel, do not contain the clause of general mortgage. And it may be remarked that the underhand powers from Graaff-Reinet, which are numerous, generally well drawn, and the greater portion apparently prepared by the same hand, do not contain the clause in question.

Thirteen powers, executed by the notaries G. Jarvis, Oertels, Moorrees, Berrangé, and Buyskes, with one exception by Jarvis, all contain a clause directing the agent to grant a general as well as special mortgage.

N.B.—Several powers, executed by the abovementioned notaries, as also before Messrs. Cadogan, Bergh, Auret, Plovier, and Ford, are wanting.

The parties also put in the following written statement, the truth of which they admitted:

Mr. Woeke, chief clerk in the office of the Registry of Deeds, states that during a period of about twenty years, he recollects about six instances, in which parties executing a mortgage bond have refused to grant more than the special mortgage, objecting to the clause of general mortgage.

These were all cases in which the mortgagers appeared in person.

The plaintiffs also put in the deposition of the insolvent, Randall, taken under a commission issued by the Court, pursuant to a mutual consent of the parties, in which he, *inter alia*, stated:

"I do remember employing Mr. William Tennant as my agent to pass a mortgage bond in favour of the estate of the late Thomas Williamson. I have no doubt this paper, marked A, is a copy of the power of attorney I then executed.

"Ward was one of the executors in Williamson's estate. We were very friendly, and he often pressed me to buy the house. *The agreement was that I was to pay £100 and have transfer on passing a mortgage for the remaining part of the money on the property.*

"The paper marked B, now produced, I have no doubt is

1848. Dec. 20. " 30.

Smith *vs.* Randall's Trustees.

a copy of the mortgage bond executed by virtue of the power of attorney aforesaid. I have, however, never seen it before, to the best of my recollection. The house was considered ample security for the balance due.

"I did not contemplate that any other property was to be mortgaged as security. If I had seen the mortgage bond, of which the copy is before me, after its execution, if that part of it which made other property answerable had caught my eye, I might have objected to it. I should have considered that the executors had no right to that security, as I considered the house sufficient, and that it was not the arrangement at the sale.

"When I granted the power of attorney aforesaid, I did not know or think it was the usage in the Deeds Registry office that special mortgages of fixed property had added to them a clause, binding generally person and property. I have seen it in different documents since.

"I considered, when granting the said power, that the estate of Williamson would not have any preference, except on the house mortgaged. I felt so confident that the house was good security for the balance, because I had on one occasion £200 profit offered, and subsequently £400 profit, upon the original amount purchased for.

"I remember Mr. J. O. Smith coming to me and demanding a considerable sum which I owed him. I requested time. He said, 'Answer me one question: Is there any general mortgage bond against you?' I told him there was not, but there was a mortgage on one or two of my houses, which I named, pointing to the house I purchased of Williamson as one, naming one at the north end of Port Elizabeth, and another house at Uitenhage. Mr. Smith then said, 'If that is the case, I will take your bond and let the debt stand over.'"

This day, the *Attorney-General,* for Smith, in support of the objection, quoted *Van der Linden, Inst., p.* 177; *Storey on Agency, cap.* 2, §§ 21, 61, 70, *and* 76; and maintained that the power of attorney in favour of Tennant did not authorize and would not be legally construed as authorizing him to execute the general mortgage. That the effect of the power of attorney must be determined according to its legal construction, and could neither be limited nor extended by any erroneous interpretation which had been put on similar powers in the office of the Registrar of Deeds, however long the period during which such erroneous interpretation may have been acted upon in that office. That Randall had never either expressly adopted, ratified, or confirmed the general mortgage executed by Tennant. That even if he had intended to do so, he could not effectually ratify or confirm tacitly, or indeed in any way, except by appearing in person before the Registrar, or by a power of attorney executed before a notary or the requisite number of witnesses, authorizing some person to appear for him before the Registrar and ratify and confirm the mortgage; or at least by a deed of ratification executed before a notary, or duly witnessed, signed by himself and transmitted to the Registrar of Deeds.

Brand, contra, quoted *Van der Linden, Inst., p.* 193, and founded on the custom of the Deeds Office, as proved by the investigation, showing that a clause of general mortgage was invariably inserted in every bond specially mortgaging immovable property, except when specially objected to at the time of passing such bond, and that a power of attorney similar to that in question had always been considered, both by the notaries in this Colony and by the Registrars of Deeds, as empowering the agent to insert this customary clause of general mortgage in such bonds.

He further maintained that the power of attorney in question must be construed as authorizing Tennant to insert in the bond, specially mortgaging the house, every clause which by usage and custom established in the Colony it was the practice to insert in bonds of that kind, and consequently the clause of general mortgage. That a power of attorney executed by A, authorizing B to bind A as a surety, and containing a general instruction to A to renounce the legal benefits to which a surety is entitled, would be held in law to authorize the agent specially to renounce each of those legal benefits severally, although a general renunciation of the benefits would by law have been ineffectual to deprive the surety of his right to claim them, while a special renunciation of them severally bars the surety from claiming them, because, except when there is an express agreement to the contrary, in every suretyship bond a special renunciation of the benefits severally is universally inserted.

He also maintained that when the conditions of sale of immovable property stipulated that the purchaser should, on receiving transfer, execute a bond hypothecating the property sold for the two last instalments of the price, the seller would be entitled to insist that, in the bond hypothecating the property, there should be inserted the usual and accustomed clause, constituting a general mortgage, and that no instance could be shown in which the general mortgage clause had not been inserted in such bonds.

Postea (30th December, 1848).—The Court gave judgment. The Court held that the extent of the powers granted

1848. Dec. 20. " 30.

Smith *vs.* Randall's Trustees.

to Tennant must be ascertained solely from the legal construction of the terms of the power of attorney executed by Randall, and could not be explained, qualified, or affected in any way by the parole evidence of Randall as to the extent of the power which he really intended to have granted to Tennant. The inexpediency of allowing written instruments to be explained or qualified by parole evidence was well illustrated in this case, in which Randall had sworn that the arrangement as to the sale and purchase of the house entered into between him and Ward was, that he, Randall, was to pay £100 of the price and have transfer on passing a mortgage bond on the property for the remainder of the price, while it was expressly stipulated in the deed of sale that on or before the 1st October, 1838, Randall should pay £100 of the price, and deliver to the said Ward *a notarial bond with two sureties for* £600, payable in six half-yearly instalments.

The Court held that, according to the legal construction of the power of attorney in question, it authorized Tennant to insert in the mortgage bond binding the property every clause which by the established usage and custom of the Colony it was the practice to insert in similar bonds, and that the result of the investigation in the office of the Registrar of Deeds proved that it was the invariable usage, custom, and practice of the Colony to insert in every bond specially hypothecating immovable property, a clause of general mortgage of all the property of the person executing the bond, except when the insertion of the clause of general mortgage was objected to at the time of passing the bond; and therefore repelled the objection and confirmed the liquidation account, with costs.

MENZIES' REPORTS.

[NEW SERIES.]

1828–1849.

VOL. II. PART IV.

CHAPTER I.

SUCCESSION EX TESTAMENTO.

[TESTAMENTARY SUCCESSION.]

PRINCE, Q.Q. DIELEMAN, *vs.* ANDERSON AND OTHERS.

Mutual will. Re-marriage of survivor. Kinderbewys. Guardianship of second husband. Judgment, confession of. 1829. March 26.

A widow re-married, out of community of property, to a second husband, held (on the objection of the second husband) incompetent to appear in Court to confess judgment for the amount of a kinderbewys executed before the second marriage, by which the paternal portions of the children of the first marriage had been ascertained.

[Vol. I, p. 176.]

PRINCE, Q.Q. DIELEMAN, *vs.* BERRANGE, *alias* ANDERSON.

Children, education of.

Surviving parent is obliged, under clause of mutual will giving usufruct of children's portion, to defray expenses of their education out of the interest of their portion, and if 1830. June 24. Sept. 1.

1830. June 24. Sept. 1. *such interest is exceeded, survivor must make good the balance.*

Kinderbewys: relief granted to surviving spouse from effects of error in calculating kinderbewys, in which there had been entered the value of a slave who was afterwards declared by the Privy Council to have been free.

[Vol. I, p. 435.]

LUTGEN'S TRUSTEES *vs.* LUTGEN'S EXECUTORS.

Mutual will. Fidei-commissum. Power of surviving spouse to revoke.

1831. March 3. *L. and his wife created, by mutual will, a fidei-commissum in favour of their grandson and his children, at the same time empowering the survivor to cancel the fidei-commissum, and to give the capital sum to their grandson, free and unencumbered, on certain specified conditions of prudent behaviour and marriage. L. died. The surviving widow, by codicil, provided for the cancellation of the trust on conditions other than those referred to in the mutual will.* HELD, *that on the ground of such variance, the codicil was void.*

[Vol. I, p. 504.]

BRINK, Q.Q. BREDA, *vs.* VOIGT AND ANOTHER.

Mutual will and codicil: heirs and legatees, appointment of, under.

1831. Dec. 29. *Spouses, by mutual will, appointed the survivor sole heir, subject to the usual condition of education, &c., of the children of the marriage until majority or marriage, when their paternal or maternal portions should be paid out to them. By mutual codicil, under the reservatory clause, they thereafter excluded two daughters from heirship, awarded them their legitimate, and directed that, in lieu of such daughters, the daughters' children should be heirs of the testators. Action was brought by the husband of one of the daughters to have the codicil declared void, on the ground that it contained an institution of heir, and derogated in this respect from the appointment of heirs in the mutual will.* HELD, *that the codicil was valid, inasmuch as the testator's daughters took under the mutual will merely as legatees for whatever sum was left them over and above their legitimate portion, and that it was open to the testators to charge such legacies by codicil.* 1831. Dec. 29.

[Vol. I, p. 537.]

RICHERT'S HEIRS *vs.* STOLL AND ANOTHER.

Inheritance of minor grandchildren. Compensation.

Compensation allowed of inheritance of minor grandchildren with debt due by their father to their grandfather; the father, who died before the grandfather, having, during the lifetime of both, acknowledged the deed, and expressed in writing his willingness that such debt should be deducted from the inheritance he was to receive. HELD, *that this was a discharge by the father, pro tanto, of his claim under the will, and bound his representatives.* 1832. June 7.

[Vol. I, p. 566.]

CAFFIN ET UXOR *vs.* HEURTLEY'S EXECUTORS.

Mutual will, construction of.

Where the testator, married in community of property, by his will bequeathed to his wife, in the following terms, in a notarial will: "One moiety or half part, or share of HIS *property, together with the houses and the whole of* HIS *furniture, situate Nos.* 8 *and* 35, *Dorp-street, Cape Town, with the* WHOLE *of the slaves" (these houses and the slaves, in fact, forming part of the property in community); and further desired that "the whole of* HIS *property, both real and personal, with the exception of the houses, furniture, and slaves hereinbefore mentioned, should be sold by public auction;" and afterwards made a codicil wherein he altered his will as follows: "I, R. H., for certain good reasons, do hereby cancel and make void such part of my will as applies to my present residence in Dorp-street, No.* 8, *as also my furniture and slaves given to my wife, J. S. H.; and I direct that the same shall form part of my general property; the same to be disposed of by my executors named in my said will, and* THAT MY WIFE SHALL BE ENTITLED TO ONE MOIETY 1832. June 14.

1832. June 14. OR HALF PART OF MY PROPERTY, BOTH REAL AND PERSONAL." *The Court* HELD (MENZIES, J., dis.) *that by virtue of the matrimonial community, the wife was entitled to one half of the common property, and under the codicil to one fourth more, being the moiety of his property left her by her husband, in addition to the matrimonial half.*

[Vol. I, p. 178.]

WIDOW CLEEUWICK *vs.* BERGH AND ANOTHER.

Mutual will, construction of. Acknowledgment of discharge by heir. Error, relief for. Interest, enjoyment of bonâ-fide possessor.

*C. and his wife, by mutual will, instituted the survivor sole heir on the usual condition of giving the children of the marriage an education, &c., and of maintaining them until majority or marriage, and then paying them such portion as they might be entitled to in equity and according to the condition of the estate. The survivor, in case of re-marriage, to make inventory and sale, and pass a bond "for the moiety of the whole of the proceeds" in favour of the children. The wife died. The husband caused an inventory to be made, and the joint estate taxed at Rds.*44,360. *The only child of the marriage married, and received Rds.*11,090, *and under the belief that that was all he was entitled to receive, gave an acknowledgment in writing in full of all demands for maternal inheritance. Subsequently, he brought an action for Rds.*11,090 *more, and obtained judgment, but with interest reckoned only from the date of summons; the Court holding the father to have been a bonâ-fide possessor during the interval, and therefore not liable for interest perceptæ et consumptæ ante litem constitutam.*

1832. Dec. 13. " 20. — Widow Cleeuweek *vs.* Bergh and Another.

The plaintiff's declaration set forth "that on or about the 20th September, 1800, T. F. Cleeuweek and his wife, C. M. Peusch, did duly make and execute their mutual last will and testament in writing, and which was never afterwards by them revoked, and which, among other things, contains the words following, that is to say:

[A] "Now proceeding to the election of heirs, the testators hereby declare reciprocally, that is the first dying, to nominate and to institute the survivor as their sole and universal heir or heiress, and such to all the property which may be left, as well movable as immovable, whether in possession or in expectancy, without any exception, to be entered upon and possessed for ever as free personal and indisputable property, all on this condition, however, that the survivor shall be holden and obliged to give the children who are already born, or who may yet be procreated in the present marriage, an honest and christian education, and to maintain them until their becoming of age, previous marriage, or other approved of state, when such sum of money shall be paid to each of them, as a father or mother's portion, as shall be found to be due in equity, and according to the condition of the estate.

[B] "The survivor shall, however, in case of re-marriage, be obliged, previously to the solemnization thereof, after a notarial inventorisation of the estate, and a public sale of the effects of the same, to pass a bond for the moiety of the whole of the proceeds of the estate in favour of the children, and to lodge the same in the hands of two good and impartial men to be chosen as superintending guardians, to which the predeceased in that case institutes his or her children, or, in case of their previous death, their lawful descendants as their representatives in equal shares, without it, however, being necessary for the same to be paid out to them previously to the period aforesaid, as the testators are desirous that the survivor shall remain in the full and undisturbed possession of the estate, in order the better to maintain and educate the minors from the usufruct of their respective shares of inheritance until the aforesaid period.

[B] "And the said testator or testatrix did likewise nominate and appoint the survivor of them as executor or executrix of their said will. That the said C. M. Peusch departed this life on or about the 14th July, 1814, leaving the said J. F. Cleeuweek, and L. F. Cleeuweek her only child, her surviving. That the said J. F. Cleeuweek did, in contemplation of entering into a second marriage, which was afterwards duly had and solemnized, and under the provisions of the said will, on or about the 5th January, 1817, cause the joint estate of himself and his said first wife C. M. Peusch to be duly inventoried and taxed, and the valuators thereof taxed the value thereof at 44,360 rds. That on the 6th November, 1815, the said L. F. Cleeuweek, the son, was duly married to the said plaintiff, and he was thereupon entitled, under the provisions of the said will, to have had such sum of money paid to him as a mother's portion as should be found to be due in equity and according to the condition of the estate, but which the said L. F. Cleeuweek did not then demand. That immediately upon such taxation as aforesaid, to wit, upon the 5th January, 1817, the said

1832. Dec. 13. „ 20.

Widow Cleeuweek vs. Bergh and Another.

L. F. Cleeuweek became entitled, under the provisions of the said will, to demand and have from his said father, the said J. F. Cleeuweek, a moiety of the whole of the proceeds of the said joint estate, that is to say, 22,180 rds.; yet the said J. F. Cleeuweek did never pay to the said L. F. Cleeuweek the sum of 22,180 rds.; bnt only paid to him the sum of 11,090 rds. That the said J. F. Cleeuweek and the said defendant M. J. Muller, with whom the said J. F. Cleeuweek intermarried for the second time, duly executed their mutual last will and testament in writing, and a codicil thereto, and which have never been revoked, whereby they nominated the said defendant M. A. Bergh, with the longest liver, executor or executrix of their said will and codicil. That on or about the 28th May, 1829, the said J. F. Cleeuweek departed this life, leaving the said defendant M. J. Muller him surviving, and upon or shortly after his death, the said defendants, as executor and executrix of his said will, took upon themselves the burden of the execution thereof, and entered upon the administration of his estate; and the said plaintiff is entitled to demand 11,090 rds., being the balance due to him by his said father under the provisions of the said will, with interest, &c."

In their plea, the defendants admitted the facts alleged in the declaration, but pleaded "that the late L. F. Cleeuweek became of age on or about the 6th November, 1815, and that the said J. F. Cleeuweek paid to the said L. F. Cleeuweek on the 10th January, 1817, the sum of 11,090 rds. as for his maternal inheritance, which was all that in equity and according to the condition of the estate the said L. F. Cleeuweek could claim from the said estate. And the said defendants, for a further plea, say that the said L. F. Cleeuweek did acknowledge on the 10th January, 1817, to be fully and satisfactorily paid the amount of his maternal inheritance upon the receipt of the said sum of 11,090 rds., and that the said L. F. Cleeuweek did on the same day release the estate of the said J. F. Cleeuweek from all further claim for or arising from his said maternal inheritance; and the said defendants say that the said plaintiff is not entitled in law to claim any relief against the said deed of acquittal and discharge granted by the said L. F. Cleeuweek from the said defendants in their capacity as executor and executrix of the last will and codicil of the said J. F. Cleeuweek deceased."

In her replication, the plaintiff maintained that the said L. F. Cleeuweek did not give such acknowledgment to the said J. F. Cleeuweek as in the plea mentioned, but the acknowledgment hereinafter mentioned, that is to say: "I, the undersigned, L. F. Cleeuweek, do certify that I have been fully paid by my father, J. F. Cleeuweek, for my maternal inheritance to the amount of 11,090 rds., as well by taking over movables at the price they were valued at, as by an underhand bond passed by my said father in my favour and behalf. I therefore declare to have no further claim, and to have passed this to serve there and where my father may think advisable." That the said acknowledgment or receipt was given by the said L. F. Cleeuweek under the supposition that the sum mentioned therein was the true sum which he was justly and legally entitled to demand and have, and was never intended by him to give up or waive, and does not waive, any portion of the inheritance due to him, and was given by him through ignorance and error, and is void in law."

The defendants, in their rejoinder, denied "that the acknowledgment or receipt given by the said L. F. Cleeuweek on the 10th January, 1817, was given through ignorance or error of the said L. F. Cleeuweek, and was not intended to give up or waive every other claim for inheritance, and the said defendants join issue thereon."

The Attorney-General and *De Wet*, for plaintiff, maintained that by law, if the Widow Cleeuweek had died intestate, leaving a surviving husband and an only son, the estate in communion between her and her husband would have been divided equally between her husband and her son; that the clause in the will (marked A in declaration) distributed the joint estate of the testator and testatrix in the same way in which the law would have divided it if they had died without a will; and, secondly, that even if this were not the case, the second clause in the testament (marked B in the declaration) gave, by the express will and provision of both parents, the son, in the event of the father's re-marriage, a right to one half of the whole estate in communion between the testator and testatrix—(*vide Caffin et Uxor vs. Heurtley's Executors,* 14*th June,* 1832, *Vol.* 1, *p.* 178); and, thirdly, maintained that the receipt was given by the son in error, he having been led to suppose that he had, under the will, a right to a quarter of the estate only, instead of to a half, to which he was by law and the provision of the will entitled, and that this receipt having been given in error could not have barred the son, and consequently cannot bar his representative, the present plaintiff, from now claiming the full amount to which he was by law and the provision of the will justly entitled, and quoted *l.* 7 *and l.* 8, *ff. de jur. et fact. ign.* (22, 6).

Cloete, for the defendants, maintained that, admitting as he did that, by the law of this Colony, if the father's first wife had died intestate, her husband would only have been

1832. Dec. 13. „ 20.

Widow Cleeuweek *vs.* Bergh and Another.

entitled to one half of the estate in communion, and the son would have been entitled to the other half, yet that by the clause in the will (A), it was not provided that the son should have that share which he would have been entitled to if his mother had died intestate, but only that he should have what would be his legitimate portion of his mother's inheritance,—that of which she could not by will deprive him, and which by the law of the Colony is only one third part of his mother's half share of the goods in communion.

2ndly. That whatever might have been the effect of the clause B, if the father had re-married during the minority of the son, yet that as the son was actually of age two years before his father's re-marriage, he was only entitled to that share to which under the will (clause A) he would have been entitled on the day he came of age, namely, one third of his mother's half of the estate in communion, and that he could make no claim whatever under clause B.

3rdly. He maintained that if clause B be construed with reference to the context, the words "after a notarial inventorisation of the estate, and a public sale of the effects of the same, to pass a bond (bewyzen) for the *moiety of the whole of the proceeds of the estate*," must be construed as meaning one moiety of the mother's half of the estate, and not as the moiety of one half of the whole estate in communion. (*Van Leeuwen, Ctns. For.* 1, 3, 8, § 25.)

4thly. That the receipt and the docquet on the account of the joint estate would have barred the deceased L. Cleeuweek from now making the present claim, and consequently barred the present plaintiff, his representative, from making any such claim. (*Van Leeuwen, Cens. For.* 4, *c.* 40.) And that the said receipt could not now be set aside on any pretended ground of error on the part of L. Cleeuweek as to legal extent of his right under the will. (*Voet* 12, *tit.* 6, § 7; *Voet* 4, *tit.* 6, § 18.)

Attorney-General, in answer to the last point argued by defendant, quoted *ff.* 22, *tis.* 6, *l.* 7—8.

Cur. adv. vult.

Postea (20th December, 1832).—The Court unanimously gave judgment in favour of the plaintiff as prayed, with interest from the date of the summons and costs. (*Vide Reis vs. Executors of Gilloway, 1st September,* 1834, *Vol.* 1, *p.* 186, *et infra.*)

The Court held that the clause B came into operation on the re-marriage of the father, whether the children were then majors or minors; that on the re-marriage of the father, if the son had previously become major and received his share under clause A, he would be entitled to one half of the whole estate at the time of the re-marriage, under deduction of what he had received under clause A. 1832. Dec. 13. „ 20. Widow Cleeuweek *vs.* Bergh and Another.

KEKEWICH, J., dissented from the limitation of the interest, and wished to have given it back to the time of the settlement between the father and son.

The other two Judges (WYLDE, C.J., and MENZIES, J.), held that the father was a possessor *bonâ fide*, and therefore ought not to be made liable for interest *perceptæ* and presumed to be *consumptæ ante litem constitutam.* (*Voet* 41, 1, 29, 30, 33.)

REIS *vs.* EXECUTORS OF GILLOWAY.

Mutual will, construction of. Liquidation account, re-opening of.

Where a widow who had been married in community of property received her matrimonial half, and for several years continued to receive certain usufruct bequeathed by her husband, according to a liquidation account framed by the executors named in a will, made by her late husband and herself, the Court, by a majority (WYLDE, C.J., *and* KEKEWICH, J.; MENZIES, J., dis.) *held that after her death her executor was entitled to impeach this account, as based on an erroneous construction of the will; and the account being in consequence re-opened, the Court unanimously* HELD *that certain legacies which the testator (who had been previously married) had bequeathed to his god-children in a will, made jointly with his first wife, specially reserved in his present will, which legacies had been charged against the joint estate, should be charged against the testator's separate estate; and held, further, that a certain amount chargeable during the marriage against the joint estate had, by the terms made use of in the will by the testator, "expressly desiring that the same may be strictly observed by* HIS *testamentary executors," become chargeable on his separate estate.* 1834. Sept. 1.

[Vol. I, p. 186.]

DE SMIDT *vs.* BURTON, N.O.

Mutual will, construction of. Usufruct. Minor's inheritance. Community of property.

Where, in the terms of a mutual will made by two persons married in community, the survivor was entitled to the 1841. May 28.

1841. May 28. *usufruct of the inheritance of a minor child, under the burden of maintaining and educating the minor, and the mother, surviving, had for some years allowed the interest of the minor's inheritance, except a small annual amount for his maintenance, to accumulate in the hands of the Master of the Supreme Court, as guardian of the minor, who at the same time administered his property; the Court* HELD *that the plaintiff, who had married the widow in community, and who had also for several years after his marriage with her allowed the interest to accumulate as before, was entitled to bring an action for the recovery of the interest accumulated both before and after his marriage, as being property of the community.*

[Vol. I, p. 222.]

HORAK'S HEIRS *vs.* THE WIDOW HORAK.

Mutual will. Estoppal by acquiescence. What is not a revocation of will. Will, attestation of.

Acquiescence by the heirs of a testator in the widow's entering on the administration of the estate of her deceased husband, and continuing therein until after the sale and final liquidation thereof, does not bar such heirs from coming into Court to set aside a notarial deed in which the testator professed to have reinstated the executrix as executrix after having by codicil revoked the mutual will whereby she had been originally appointed.

Where a testator a few days before his death called in a notary, and declared to him his "wish to have a former codicil annulled, and to hold his testament executed by him with his wife, as of full force," and the notary "certified" this to the Court; the Court held that this notarial instrument did amount to a de-præsenti revocation of the first codicil.

SEMBLE: *the signature of a testator and witnesses not indispensably necessary to the validity of a will.*

1833. Dec. 27. — Horak's Heirs *vs.* The Widow Horak.

J. A. Horak and his wife, the defendant, on the 27th November, 1806, executed a mutual will, whereby they severally nominated each other to be the executor or executrix of the first-dying.

On the 24th March, 1831, J. A. Horak duly executed a notarial codicil, whereby he revoked his said will of 27th November, 1806, and died on the 28th June, 1831.

After the death of her said husband, the defendant, on the 2nd July, 1831, produced and caused to be registered at the office of the Orphan Chamber the said will of 27th November, 1806, and codicil of 24th March, 1831, and also the following instrument dated 25th June, 1831.

"I, the undersigned, J. P. de Wet, notary public, certify that I have, on this the 25th June, 1831, repaired to and in the presence of J. A. Horak, who was lying sick in bed, still perfectly in possession of his knowledge and senses, and his utterance intelligible, and who declared to me, the notary, in the presence of the aftermentioned witnesses, to wish (or desire) to have the act of date the 24th March of this year, before me the notary and witnesses, annulled, and to hold his testament executed by him with his wife of full force, and an act formed hereof by me, the notary, which is this.

"Thus certified at the Cape of Good Hope in the presence of F. W. Stoedel and Carel W. Liesching, as witnesses.

"Quod Attestor,

"J. P. de Wet."

The defendant, alleging that the effect of this last-mentioned instrument was to render null and void the codicil of 24th March, 1831, styled herself the executrix of the last will, and administratrix of the estate of her deceased husband, entered upon the administration of the said estate, and disposed by sale and otherwise of various parts thereof.

The plaintiffs, as being some of the heirs of the said J. A. Horak, brought, in July, 1833, an action against the defendant, in which they alleged that the said instrument, dated 25th June, 1831, was not written in the presence of the said J. A. Horak, nor read to or attested by him, and maintained that it was not a legal or valid instrument at law either as a last will, codicil, or other testamentary disposition, or as a sufficient declaratory act, and that they were entitled to have the same set aside as informal and invalid.

The defendant filed an exception and subordinate plea, in which she first excepted to the declaration, and maintained that the plaintiffs were barred from maintaining this action against her, because, immediately after the demise of her husband, she, by virtue of the said mutual will of 27th November, 1806, and also of the said notarial act dated 25th June, 1831, duly enregistered, had, on or about the 1st July, 1831, in her capacity of sole executrix of the said will, entered upon the administration of the estate of her said husband, and continued therein with the acquiescence and approbation of all the plaintiffs, until after the

1833. Dec. 27. — Horak's Heirs vs. The Widow Horak.

sale and final liquidation thereof on the 15th May, 1833, which she was ready to verify. Wherefore, before answering to the plaintiffs' declaration, she proposed against all and every the plaintiffs, the exception of homologation and acquiescence, and prayed that the same might be adjudged with costs.

And, secondly, in case the Court should overrule the said exception, she answering subordinately to the declaration said that she admitted all the allegations contained therein, except the averments that the said instrument of 25th June, 1831, was not written in the presence of the said J. A. Horak, and that the same is not a legal and valid instrument at law, both of which she denied.

And for a further plea maintained, that although the said instrument was not read over to or attested by the said J. A. Horak, yet that the same was not thereby rendered null and void, because the said instrument was dictated by the said J. A. Horak, then on his death-bed and unable to write, to the said notary, who immediately drew up the same at his house, at his express desire, in the presence and hearing of the witnesses thereto, and of all the said plaintiffs, and that the said J. A. Horak, on the following day, confirmed the said instrument, by inquiring of his children or one of them, whether they were satisfied with the declaration therein contained.

In their replication, the plaintiffs denied that the defendant entered on the administration of the estate with the acquiescence consent and approbation of the plaintiffs, and maintained that even if they had so acquiesced, such acquiescence would not in law be a bar to this action, and denied all the allegations contained in the defendant's subordinate plea.

The Court, after hearing *Hofmeyr* for the defendant, overruled the exception of homologation, without calling on the plaintiffs to reply, holding that none of the facts alleged, even if proved, would have the effect of barring the plaintiffs from setting aside the notarial deed of 25th June, 1831.

The *Attorney-General*, for the plaintiffs, put in the codicil of the 24th March, 1831, and maintained that as it was admitted in the plea that the paper sought to be set aside was not written in the presence of J. A. Horak, nor read to or attested by him, the said paper could not be deemed to be or sustained as a codicil or as the act of the deceased; and, secondly, that although the contents of this writing should be held *pro veritate*, it did not amount to a present revocation of the former codicil, but merely an expression of a desire, wish, or intention that it should be revoked at some future time. He contrasted the words of the codicil of the 24th March, 1831, drawn by the same notary for the purpose of revoking the will, with the words of the certificate of 25th June, 1831. In the former, the words were, "who declared to revoke and annul a certain mutual will (describing it), as also another will (describing it), not wishing or desiring that the same or any of them, after the passing of these presents, shall be of any force or effect, but, on the contrary, shall be considered as if never at any time passed." He argued also on the fact that the instrument of 1831 commenced with the words, "I, the undersigned, *certify* that I proceeded," &c., and concluded "thus certified," and not as in the usual form of notarial acts "thus passed."

Hofmeyr argued *contra,* and quoted *Van Leeuwen, Cens. For.,* 2*nd Part,* 1*st B., C.* 29, § 12, § 20; *Lybreght, Vol.* 1, *p.* 29; *Van Leeuwen's Rom. Dutch Law, B.* 3, *C.* 2, *Voet* 28, *tit.* 1, § 23, and *Groenwegen ibi cit.; Neostadius,* 1*st Decis.* § 14; *Van der Linden, Caus. Celeb.* 25.

The Court, without calling on the plaintiffs to reply, gave judgment for the plaintiffs with costs, on the second ground taken by the plaintiffs, viz.: that the contents of the instrument of the 25th June, 1831, did not amount to a *de præsenti* revocation of the codicil of the 24th March, 1831, and consequently that it was ineffectual to revoke the latter, and decided no other point, although all the judges held that the signatures of the testator and witnesses were not indispensably necessary to the validity of a will.

(*Vide* as to the necessity of the notarial act being read over to and approved of by the testator. *Voet* 28, *tit.* 1, 28.)

Orphan Chamber *vs.* Cloete.

Construction of Fidei-commissum. Accretion.

L. obtained from Government, on freehold tenure, the grant of a farm, with extent and boundaries described. By mutual codicil L. and wife bequeathed this farm to their son, H. O. L., for a certain sum, under fidei-commissum. On their death H. O. L. entered into occupation, and, with his wife, made a mutual will, instituting as heirs the survivors jointly with the children of the marriage. H. O. L. died, and his widow, who continued in occupation, subsequently obtained, in her own name, from Government, a grant of ground adjoining, and in part surrounding, the original freehold place. She died, leaving, besides daughters, one son, who, as sole heir male, took possession, under sentence of the late Court of Justice, on payment of a certain sum to the other heirs. The question then arose whether the grant to the widow had so accresced to the original grant as to require payment of a proportionate sum by the son. HELD, *that there was no accretion.*

1833. Aug. 28. „ 31. — Orphan Chamber *vs.* Cloete.

By a codicil, dated 19th October, 1781, to their mutual will, P. Laubscher and his wife, Susannah Eksteen, bequeathed "to their son, H. O. Laubscher, at the decease of us both, the place upon which we now reside, named Roodebloem, situated between Cape Town and the Salt River, for a sum of 40,000*f.*, *under the condition that this place shall always remain and devolve on our and his family,*" &c. This place, Roodebloem, so bequeathed, was a freehold place, held under a grant specifying the extent and boundaries thereof. P. Laubscher and his wife died, and Roodebloem was entered upon and possessed by their said son, H. O. Laubscher, until his death. H. O. Laubscher and his wife, Susannah van Breda, had one son and four daughters, and on the 28th March, 1802, made a mutual will, whereby they instituted, as their heirs respectively, the surviving spouse jointly with the children born during the marriage, in all the property to be left by the first deceased, movable and immovable, &c., nothing excepted, to be possessed by the surviving spouse as his or her property without interference, but under obligation to educate, until they became of age by marriage or otherwise, when such proportion of the estate shall be given them for father's or mother's portion as the survivor shall conscientiously deem reasonable and proportionable to the value of the estate. H. O. Laubscher died, and his surviving widow continued to possess the freehold place Roodebloem until her death. On the 28th November, 1807, the said widow obtained from the Governor of the Colony the following grant of Government ground, adjacent to and surrounding on three sides the original freehold place Roodebloem, and much exceeding it in extent.

"I hereby grant unto Mrs. Susanna van Breda, widow of the late H. O. Laubscher, at her request, a piece of 93 morgen, 63 roods, 72 feet of land, situated in the Cape district, at the place called Roodebloem, extending, &c., &c., &c., with full power and authority henceforth to possess the said piece of land in perpetuity; and, if she chooses to dispose of it with the approbation of Government, subject to all such duties and regulations as are either already, or shall in future be established respecting such lands."

Previously to 1817, a general survey of the whole lands between Cape Town and Wynberg was made by the

Surveyor Thibault, by order of Government,—and on its completion, separate diagrams of all the different places contained in it were, by order of Government, made from it, and lodged in the office of the Surveyor-General, as of record. A diagram had in consequence been framed, dated 16th June, 1817, which contained the original freehold place Roodebloem, and the land adjacent to and surrounding it, which had been granted as aforesaid to the widow, as forming one place; but in this diagram, the boundaries of the original freehold place were marked by dotted lines.

The widow died in the beginning of 1818, without having made any alteration in the mutual will of 28th March, 1802, and thereupon the Orphan Chamber assumed the administration of all the joint estate of the widow and her deceased husband. It was admitted by all parties that, notwithstanding the *fidei-commissum*, the value of Roodebloem formed part of the assets of the said joint estate, to be distributed equally among all the children in terms of the said will of 28th March, 1802; but a question arose whether, under the *fidei-commissary* bequest in the codicil of 1781, P. Laubscher, the only son, and therefore the only heir male of the said H. O. Laubscher the institute, was, as such, entitled to claim and take the *fidei-commissary* estate of Roodebloem, on paying into the estate its appraised value, or whether all the joint heirs, not only of the said institute, but of his father and mother who created the *fidei-commissum*, had not, in virtue of the words therein contained, viz., "shall always remain and *devolve in our* and his family," all of them such an equal right to Roodebloem, as to entitle them to claim that it should be put up for sale amongst them all, and be awarded to the highest bidder of them, on payment of the price into the estate of the said H. O. Laubscher and his wife.

The Orphan Chamber brought an action before the late Court of Justice to have the claim of the said joint heirs declared to be valid, and to have it carried into effect. In this action they obtained judgment, as prayed, on the 13th August, 1818, in which the place in dispute is described merely "as the place Roodebloem, situated in the Cape district, between Cape Town and the Salt River." This judgment having been brought under appeal by the son, P. Laubscher, the Court of Appeals, on the 26th April, 1819, reversed the judgment appealed from, declared the appellant to be the sole heir male of his father, and as such to be entitled *to the farm* Roodebloem; and decreed him possession of the same, upon the condition of his paying to the other heirs of his deceased father and mother the sum of sixty thousand guilders, and decreed all costs to be paid out

1833. Aug. 28. „ 31. Orphan Chamber vs. Cloete.

of the estate of the said H. O. Laubscher and wife, now deceased. This judgment was allowed to become final.

In the present action, the question was raised whether the said P. Laubscher was, by virtue of this judgment, entitled, in paying the said 60,000*f*., to claim, not merely the original freehold place Roodebloem, as it existed in 1781 when the *fidei-commissum* was created, but also the piece of land adjoining and surrounding it, of which the widow had obtained the grant above set forth in November, 1807, or whether he was not liable also to pay to the estate of his father and mother an additional sum of 16,000*f*., as the agreed on value thereof, in order to entitle him to take the said piece of land so granted.

Cloete, for the defendant, maintained that the land granted to the widow immediately accresced to the *fidei-commissary* estate of old Roodebloem, and that, after this grant, she, being the heir in possession of the *fidei-commissary* estate, could not have alienated the land granted to her, and that the same result followed from the proclamation of the 23rd December, 1814, and the diagram of 16th June, 1817, made out from Thibault's survey. That the new land, having thus become an integral and inseparable part of the old Roodebloem, must be held to have been included in the sentence of the Court of Appeals.

Cur. adv. vult.

Postea (31st August, 1833).—The Court held that the lands granted to the widow did not accresce to the original *fidei-commissary* estate. That the proclamation of 1814, and the diagram of 1817, had not the effect of consolidating the right of property in this land with the *fidei-commissary* land,—and that the sentence of the Court of Appeals applied solely to the *fidei-commissary* land, and not to the lands granted to the widow,—and, therefore, dismissed the objection.

Batt *vs.* Widow Batt.

Will, construction of. Onus probandi. Fidei-commissum. Will valid, though contains no direct appointment of heir. Executors: devise to, upon trust.

1835. Aug 28. Nov. 5. Batt *vs.* Widow Batt.

The late Henry Batt was a native of England, and had been married to his widow, the defendant, in England. On the 12th May, 1832, in this Colony, he made his last will, containing, *inter alia*, the following provisions:

"1st. I do declare to give, devise, and bequeath all my

estate or estates, lands and tenements, chattels and effects, movable and immovable, both real and personal, and of whatsoever nature or kind, and all that are situated in Africa, to my executor or executors hereinafter mentioned, or the survivor of them, or the executor or administrator of such survivors, upon the terms and trusts, as follows: Also the following bonds and landed property, to wit,"—here was inserted a list of 21 bonds due to him, and their respective amounts; and also a list of 14 lots of ground, houses, shares in the theatre and in the Commercial Hall, 40 stukvats, 37 leaguers in a certain store, a quantity of sherry wine, and other articles; and after this list the will contained the following words: "*All the above mentioned are included in the bequest to Mrs. M. Batt, and understood that Mrs. Batt, of the above mentioned, is to pay all the outstanding debts of the estate.*"

On the margin of the will, opposite to the above list, the following memorandum was written: "My debts at the Cape are as follows: Mrs. M. Batt, my present wife, holds a bond of mine for £5000, and Mrs. B. Sheppard for Rds. 10,000, or £750. This is all *I owe* in the WORLD, and I believe my outstanding debts, furniture, &c., would nearly pay this.

"E. E.

"H. BATT.

"June 19, 1832."

"2ndly. Should it, by any unforeseen accident, happen *that both me and Mrs. Batt were to depart this life at the same time*, then it is my express will and desire that the executor or executors shall dispose of all *this* property in the following manner (excepting what I may hereafter leave to my father and two sisters), viz., all the movable property to be sold for cash only, and the first payments of 10 per cent. for the landed property, to be paid three months after the date of sale, and the other payments of 10 per cent. per annum to bear interest from the date of sale; the amount or amounts arising from the sale *of one estate* to be divided equally to the undermentioned persons, viz." (here followed the particular bequests to different persons, which it is unnecessary to insert).

"3rdly. And I do further nominate, constitute, and appoint as my true and *lawful executors and trustees*, Mrs. M. B. Batt and J. D. Jackson, of Cape Town," &c., &c.

"4thly. All my slaves belonging *to the estate* to be manumitted after our deaths (that is after mine and Mrs. Batt.)"

5thly. I do hereby bequeath (*being well understood should Mrs. Batt, my wife, survive me*) to my father and

1835. Aug. 28. Nov. 5.

Batt *vs.* Widow Batt.

two sisters all the money I now have, or may hereafter have in the Bank of England, as also " (here followed a list of sundry bonds over property situated at the Cape and in England, and of sundry houses in England, none of which were mentioned in the lists in the first clause, and all of which he bequeathed to his father and sisters, to be equally divided, share and share alike).

The will contained no appointment or nomination of heirs.

The testator, Mr. Batt, died on the 31st May, 1833, leaving at the time of his decease sundry bonds to the value of £515 12s. 6d., and also divers promissory notes, bills of exchange, and other negotiable documents, the lawful property, and in the possession of the said H. Batt, amounting to a sum of £1,276 7s. 6d.; and also divers pieces of land and other immovable property, to wit, &c., &c.; and also divers articles of household furniture and other estate and effects, both real and personal, none of which were expressly specified in the list in clause first, nor in the list of property bequeathed to the testator's father, nor in any other part of the will.

The plaintiffs, as the heirs *ab intestato* of Batt, brought this action against the widow, as his executrix, to recover from her the said bonds, bills, household furniture, and other estate and effects, as specified in an inventory annexed to the declaration, on the ground that they had not, in and by the said last will and testament, been specifically given or bequeathed; and that with regard to them no testamentary disposition had been made by the testator, H. Batt; and consequently that, as regards the said estate and effects, the said H. Batt died intestate, and the said plaintiffs are entitled to the said residuary property, as his only legal heirs *ab intestato.*

The defendant put in the following plea: And the said defendant, for plea or answer to the declaration of the said plaintiff, saith that she ought not to be condemned, &c. Because she says she admits the truth of all the matters and things in the said declaration contained, save and except that this defendant denies that the said testator did leave any property, regarding which no testamentary disposition has been made, or that he died intestate as regards any part of his property; and, on the contrary thereof, the said defendant saith that, under the said will and by the true construction thereof, the said defendant is entitled to all his property, not specifically bequeathed to other persons than the said defendant, subject to the payment of the debts of the testator; and thereupon joins issue with the said plaintiffs, &c.

This day *Brand*, for the plaintiffs, opened the pleadings,

when the Court, being of opinion that it lay with the defendant to show what property was conveyed by the will to her, 1835. Aug. 28. Nov. 5. — Batt *vs.* Widow Batt.

The *Attorney-General,* for the defendant, proceeded to argue that the effect of the first clause of the will was to convey the whole of the testator's property, as well in England as in Africa, as well what is specified in the list inserted in the first clause, as what was omitted or afterwards acquired by the deceased, to the executors nominated by the will, "upon the terms and trusts, as follows;" and that the words in the end of this clause, "all the above mentioned are included in the bequest to Mrs. M. Batt, and understood that Mrs. Batt, of the above mentioned, is to pay all the outstanding debts of the estate," were sufficient to create, and did create, a declaration of the testator that the bequest made to his executors of the whole of his property, as above mentioned, with the exception of such property as is specifically bequeathed to other persons, was *upon trust for the use of, and to be paid to, Mrs. Batt;* and he argued that the marginal memorandum as to his debts, on the first page of the will, the words and effect of the second clause, and of the expressions of the fourth clause: "All my slaves belonging *to the estate* to be manumitted *after our death* (that is after mine and Mrs. Batt);" and the effect and words of the fifth clause, particularly the words, "I do hereby bequeath (being well understood should Mrs. Batt, my wife, survive me) to my father and two sisters all the money I now have in the Bank of England," &c., &c., were sufficient to explain the latter paragraph of the first clause, if it were considered as ambiguous; and to show that the construction and effect, for which the defendant contended, were the construction which should be put on, and the effect which ought to be given to that paragraph, and quoted *Roberts,* 1 *vol.* 4, 8, §§ 5 & 6.

Brand and *Stadler* argued *contra.*

Brand began by stating that there was no nomination of heirs in this deed; and seemed prepared to maintain that, therefore, this deed was entirely invalid and of no effect; but on being asked if he intended seriously to maintain this argument, he immediately abandoned it. (*Vide Voet* 28, 1, 1; 28, 5, 1; 29, 7, 1; *Van der Keessel, Th.* 290.)

Cur. adv. vult.

Postea (5th November, 1835).—The Court gave judgment for defendant with costs, on the grounds above set forth, as maintained by the defendant.

Children of Fehrzen *vs.* Widow Horak.

Collation. Adiation.

A. and B. claimed certain inheritance from the Estate of their grandfather, jure representationis their deceased parents. The grandfather's widow and executrix wished to compensate with such inheritance a debt paid by her, on account of the grandfather, for A. and B.'s father, for a suretyship debt. But the Court gave judgment for plaintiffs on the ground that there was no proof of A. and B.'s adiation of their parents' estate, which fact alone could found compensation.

1837. Sept. 8. — Children of Fehrzen *vs.* Widow Horak.

The deceased J. A. Horak had a daughter named Hester Adriana Horak, who was married in community of property to J. A. Fehrzen. The plaintiffs were the children of that marriage. The plaintiffs' mother died on the 7th November, 1823, and their father on the 5th June, 1823. The plaintiffs' grandfather, the said J. A. Horak, died on the 28th June, 1831, leaving assets to a large amount. The defendant is his widow and executrix. The plaintiffs brought this action against the defendant in her capacity as executrix of J. A. Horak, to recover from her £1,050, which they claimed as the amount of inheritance due to them as heirs of their said grandfather, out of his estate.

In her plea the defendant admitted all the facts alleged in the declaration, but alleged that on the 22nd May, 1823, her deceased husband, J. A. Horak, became bound as surety *in solidum* for the said J. A. Fehrzen, the plaintiffs' father, in a mortgage bond for 111,000*f*, passed by the latter in favour of one J. M. Horak, dated 4th January, 1822. That a judgment was recovered on this bond against Fehrzen, and a claim, in virtue of the said bond and judgment, was duly filed in the estate of Fehrzen, which, after his decease, intestate, had been, on the 25th June, 1829, surrendered as insolvent by the late Orphan Chamber, and that by the liquidation account of the said estate, confirmed by the Court on the 1st March, 1832, nothing was awarded to the said J. M. Horak.

That on the 4th February, 1833, the said J. M. Horak ceded the said bond and suretyship of the late J. A. Horak to and in favour of one A. Brink, D. son, and that on the 6th May following, the said defendant, having been married in community of property with the said J. A. Horak, and as his widow and executrix, was obliged to pay, and did pay, for principal and interest due upon and by virtue of the said bond and suretyship, the sum of Rds.6,162 2 4, which said sum the said defendant is entitled to deduct from the said sum of £1,050, as the portion of the inheritance which would have become due to the said Hester Adriana Horak, advanced as aforesaid by the late J. A. Horak to the said J. A. Fehrzen in his lifetime, by being security for him to the amount aforesaid, and which the defendant was obliged to pay as executrix of her said husband as such surety as aforesaid, and the payment of which said sum, the said defendant submits, must be deemed and taken in law to be an advancement of inheritance to the amount aforesaid, of Rds.6,162 2 4, or if the said sum is not in law to be deemed an advancement as aforesaid, then the said defendant says the same must be deemed and taken to be a payment on account of the said J. A. Fehrzen, and for which the estate of the said Hester Adriana Horak is liable, as the said Hester Adriana Horak was married in community of property with the said J. A. Fehrzen, and must be deducted from the said sum of £1,050, the balance whereof the defendant hath always been ready and willing to pay, and hath tendered the same to the said plaintiffs, and now pays the same into Court.

In their replication the plaintiffs admitted the facts, but denied the conclusions of law contained in the plea.

This day the *Attorney-General* argued in support of the defence taken in the plea, that the sum of Rds.6,162 2 4 therein referred to must be deemed and taken to be a payment on account of the said J. H. Fehrzen, and for which the estate of the said Hester Adriana Horak is liable, by reason of her having been married in community of property with the said Fehrzen, and must be deducted from the sum claimed, and quoted *Voet* 23, 2, 80. He gave up the defence pleaded, that the payment of the said sum was to be considered as an advancement.

But the Court held that, admitting that the payment of the bond by defendant created a debt against the joint estate, or separate estates of the father and mother of the plaintiffs, which was now due by and recoverable from their heirs, if they have any, still that, as the plaintiffs claim all their share of the inheritance of their grandfather, solely as being the heirs of their grandfather, *jure representationis*, and not as being the heirs of their own father and mother, or either of them, and as it has not been proved that the plaintiffs, by any *aditio hæreditatis*, or otherwise, have made themselves, or can be deemed in law to be, the heirs of their father and mother, they were not, merely as being the children of their father or mother, liable for the debts of either parent, and therefore the defence set up against their claim for what was due to them as heirs of their

1837. Sept. 8. — Children of Fehrzen *vs.* Widow Horak. grandfather was untenable. (*Vide Voet*, 38, 17—*ad Senatus Consultum Tertullianum*—§ 4.)

The Court gave judgment for plaintiffs, as prayed, with costs.

[Cons. *Richert's Heirs vs. Stoll and Richert*, Vol. 1, p. 566.]

KOTZES *vs.* KOTZE'S TRUSTEES.

Community. Re-marriage. Transfer. Dominium. Insolvency. Trustees. Costs de bonis propriis.

D. J. K. married J. M. S. in community. By mutual will they bequeathed to their sons certain farms, to devolve upon them on the death of the longest liver, who was to enjoy the usufruct. The wife died, the husband re-married and enjoyed the usufruct until his death, after which event the second joint estate was surrendered. The trustees in the insolvency refused transfer to the sons of the first marriage on the ground that the farms had come into the second community. But the Court ordered transfer, and condemned the trustees personally in costs.

1838. Feb. 22. Aug. 2. — Kotzes *vs.* Kotze's Trustees. The declaration in this case set forth *inter alia* that the plaintiffs were the only two sons of D. J. Kotze and his first wife, J. M. Smuts. Their said parents by a joint codicil to their mutual will, dated 17th May, 1812, declared to bequeath to their sons already born, or that might still be born, their places called Verloren Vlei, Matroosfontein, and half of the place called Afgunst, for a sum of 20,000*f*, under the express condition that the longest living of the testators shall always have a free and undisturbed use of the same, and that the said places shall not devolve upon them until the death of both the testators. That upon the death of the plaintiffs' mother, their surviving father, D. J. Kotze, continued to have the free and undisturbed use of the said places until his death on the 11th August, 1828. That on the 25th May, 1830, the estate of the said D. J. Kotze, jointly with that of his second wife and surviving widow, C. M. van Zyl, was surrendered as insolvent, and that the defendants were appointed trustees of the said joint estate. That the defendants have refused to give the plaintiffs transfer of the said places, in terms of the said codicil, although the plaintiffs have tendered to the defendants payment of the said sum of 20,000*f*. Wherefore the plaintiffs prayed that the defendants might be condemned to give them transfer of the said places, on payment of the said sum of 20,000*f*.

In their plea, the defendants admitted the facts alleged in the plea, but denied the plaintiffs' right to maintain this action. Because the defendants say that the joint estate of the said D. J. Kotze and his first wife, J. M. Smuts, having ever remained in the possession of the said D. J. Kotze, even after his second marriage with C. M. van Zyl, up to the time of his, D. J. Kotze's, decease, he, the said D. J. Kotze, has rendered that joint estate, as well as his estate with his said second wife, liable for the debts of the said joint estate of him, D. J. Kotze, and his first wife, J. M. Smuts. And because the defendants further say that the title to the possession of the said places by the plaintiffs has been affected, and the legacy of said places been rendered null and void, by the insolvency of the estate of their, the plaintiffs', said father, D. J. Kotze, and his second wife and surviving widow, C. M. van Zyl, inasmuch as there are still unsatisfied debts contracted by the late D. J. Kotze and his first wife, J. M. Smuts, for which their joint estate is still liable.

At the trial, *Cloete,* for the plaintiffs, put in the will, and codicil referred to in the declaration, and a deed of kinderbewys executed by the testator before his second marriage in favour of the children of his first marriage, and quoted *Cens. For.* 3, 11, 7; *Voet,* 28, 3, 11. He admitted that the joint bequest would have been invalidated by the insolvency of the joint estate, at the time of the predecease of either spouse, but that nothing else could invalidate it. He quoted *Cens. For.* 43, 23, 24,; *Voet,* 24, 3, 33; *Cens. For.* 4, 23, 25, and maintained that, as soon as the kinderbewys was executed, *communio bonorum* between Kotze and his first wife was severed. That by his second marriage he entered on a new community of property. That although, as he admitted, there were some creditors of the joint estate of Kotze and his first wife who had not made their claims against the joint estate, or whose debts had not been inserted by Kotze in his inventory of that estate before its liquidation, yet that the claims of those creditors could not be brought against the children or other representatives of the deceased spouse, who have succeeded to her half, but against the survivor and his estate held in community with his second spouse, and now under sequestration. He maintained that even special mortgages made by the surviving father over the property in question would not have been effectual to defeat the *jus dominii* in it, which became vested in the children by the joint will, and the predecease of the first wife. He stated that, by a codicil to the joint will of Kotze and his second wife, a certain piece of landed property was

1838. Feb. 22. Aug. 2.

Kotzes vs. Kotze's Trustees.

bequeathed by him to one of his daughters for a sum far below its value, and that if this piece of land was made assets of the joint estate of Kotze and his second wife, that joint estate would actually be solvent; and in support of this, he produced the minutes of a meeting of creditors of the joint estate of Kotze and his second wife, by which the majority of the creditors allowed the daughter to take the piece of land bequeathed to her, on her paying 5,000*f*, and stated that he was prepared to prove that this piece of land was worth 15,000*f*.

Hofmeyr, contra, stated that there was no calling in the claims of the creditors of the joint estate of Kotze and his first wife before he executed the kinderbewys. That the kinderbewys was a mere private act of his own, was never given over by him to the superintending guardian, and that the first joint estate has never been liquidated.

Here the Court stopped the argument, and ordered the defendants to frame and lodge an account of the sequestrated estate of Kotze and his second wife, as far as administered, but excepting and excluding from the same "the places Verloren Vlei, Matroosfontein, and the one half of the place Afgunst." This account to be lodged with the Registrar on or before the 20th April next, and notice thereof to be given to plaintiffs.

Further hearing adjourned till the first trial day in next term.

Postea. (2nd August, 1838).—Having considered the account rendered by defendants in terms of said order, the Court gave judgment for plaintiffs as prayed, with costs against the trustees personally.

Wilhelmina *vs.* Robertson, Executor Dative of Robertson.

Will, Attestation of.

R. on his deathbed sent for a notary, and showed him a paper writing which he declared to be his last will, in the presence of two witnesses. It was unwitnessed, and contained a legacy to the plaintiff. The notary informed R. of the informality, suggested the preparation of a new will, and took short-hand notes of the testator's intentions. Suddenly the testator died before these notes were extended. The legatee brought an action for her legacy, and the Court, after hearing the evidence of two witnesses as to its acknowledgment, upheld, as the declaration of the testator's will, the paper-writing which he had first produced to the notary.

1839. Aug. 29. „ 31. — Wilhelmina *vs.* Robertson, Executor Dative of Robertson.

The declaration set forth that W. Robertson died within the jurisdiction of this Court on the 21st March, 1839, and that defendant has since been duly appointed his executor dative;—that by a certain private and underhand paper-writing, written and signed by the said W. Robertson, dated 31st January, 1833, Haasdendal, the said W. Robertson declared the said paper-writing to contain his last will and testament, and therein, *inter alia,* declared to have bequeathed to the said plaintiff certain movable property, &c., &c.

That on the 21st March, 1839, and at Haasdendal aforesaid, within this Colony, the said W. Robertson, then being on his deathbed, but in perfect soundness of mind, memory, and understanding, produced to John Reid, a notary public, duly admitted, &c., &c., the said paper-writing, and declared the same to contain his last will and testament, touching and concerning all the matters and things therein mentioned, and did, moreover, especially declare with regard to the said legacy to be paid out and delivered to the said plaintiff, as set forth in the said paper-writing, that he desired the same to be secured to the said plaintiff in the most absolute manner; and that after the said John Reid, as a notary public, had received the said paper-writing as containing the express declaration of the said W. Robertson making and securing the aforesaid legacy to the said plaintiff, and while the said notary public was preparing the minute of a notarial will to be by him passed and executed, the said W. Robertson departed this life, and thereby confirmed this said paper-writing in so far as the same was expressly confirmed and declared to be the last dying will of the said W. Robertson to the said notary public; and that the said paper-writing, as so confirmed and declared by the said W. Robertson to be his last will and testament to the said notary public, is in law sufficient and valid to entitle the said plaintiff to claim the effect of the aforesaid legacy; wherefore the plaintiff prays that defendant, in his aforesaid capacity, may be condemned to deliver over and pay to the said plaintiff the following property, &c., &c., with costs.

In his plea, the defendant admitted that the said Mr. Robertson did, in his lifetime, write and sign the paper-writing in the declaration mentioned, and declare the same to be his last will and testament in the presence of the said John Reid, but denied any other fact and matter in the

1839. Aug. 29. „ 31.

Wilhelmina *vs.* Robertson, Executor Dative of Robertson.

said declaration alleged. And, for a further plea, the defendant saith that the said paper-writing is not a good and valid last will and testament under the law of this Colony.

Plaintiff called John Reid: I am an attorney of the Supreme Court and a notary public. On the 21st day of March last, I was sent for, and went to the house of the deceased Mr. Robertson, on the Camp Ground, and saw him about four in the afternoon. I found him sick in bed, but in the perfect possession of his senses; he was aware of the dangerous state in which he was, and he said he did not wish me to go home again, lest some accident, by which I understood his death, might take place in the interim. He pointed to a writing-desk, which he said contained his last will, and told me to open it. I did so, and found a pocket-book, which he said contained the will. I opened the pocket-book and found the paper now shown me (that referred to in the pleadings), in the same state in which it is now; it was not under an envelope. He said: "This is my will, and I wish a codicil should be made to it." I first had a conversation for about an hour with him on medical subjects, and then he said he wanted to make some alteration in it by a codicil. I read the whole of this paper-writing to the deceased, and left the room for the purpose of acting on his instructions; after I had been out of the room for about a quarter of an hour, a servant came and told me he was worse; I went to him found him insensible, and in ten minutes he died. When he told me the alterations he wished to have made in the codicil, there was no person but myself in the room. When I read the paper to Mr. Robertson, and came to that part which refers to plaintiff, he told me that if the legacy to her could be put in stronger terms, I was to do it.

Cross-examined: When he asked me to make a codicil, I told him that, as the will was not witnessed according to the laws of the Colony, I apprehended it might be invalid, and advised that the contents, with the exception of the omission of certain parts, which the abolition of slavery, and other circumstances, which had occurred since its date, had rendered unnecessary, should be embodied in a new and formal instrument. I made a minute at the time in short-hand of all that passed between him and me on the subject of the will, and the alterations he directed, which I afterwards extended into the paper I now produce, and which I swear contains the truth. He died of apoplexy brought on by his incautiously getting out of bed.

Plaintiff closed his case.

Defendant called no witnesses.

1839. Aug. 29. " 31. Wilhelmina *vs.* Robertson, Executor Dative of Robertson.

Plaintiff quoted *Van der Linden, p.* 126, and the cases *inibi cit. case* 25; *Van Leeuwen, Cens. For.*, 3, 2, § 9 *and* 10; *Holl. Consult., Vol.* 4, *case* 309, *Vol.* 3, *case* 108, *Vol.* 1, *case* 93.

Attorney-General, for defendant, stated that his client only wished the general principle to be decided, and argued that, except in certain privileged cases, of which this was not one, the presence of a notary and *two witnesses* at the acknowledgment is an essential solemnity to render valid any writing, even admitted to be written and signed by the deceased, and to have been acknowledged by him on his death-bed to be his last will. In like manner, that no nuncupative will, or instructions given to make a will, is effectual, unless made or given in the presence of a notary and two witnesses. (1*st Victoria, c.* 26, and quoted *Van der Linden, p.* 125.)

Further hearing postponed. Parties to be allowed to call further evidence.

Postea (31st August, 1839).—Plaintiff called Leentje.—I was in Mr. Robertson's service. I was in attendance on him the day on which he died. I know Mr. Reid. I was in the room when he came to Mr. Robertson, who was very sick; but he could speak and was in his perfect senses, and talked sensibly and did not wander. I was in the room when Mr. Robertson sent for a writing-case, out of which Mr. Reid took a paper by desire of Mr. Robertson, who said, when Mr. Reid had got the paper, "This is my testament, this is my will." Mr. Reid looked at it and said, "There are no witnesses." Mr. Robertson said, "Never mind, it is my will; it is my testament." We were then desired to leave the room. I remained near the door and heard Mr. Reid read the paper. During the time Mr. Reid was doing so, I heard my master say "yes, yes, yes," as the different sentences were read. After it was read, Mr. Reid called us, and I went into the room; Mr. Robertson was then in his perfect senses, and continued so to the last moment.

Betje.—I was in the service of Mr. Robertson, and was in the room on the day of his death. After Mr. Reid came, I heard Mr. Robertson tell my father to bring the writing-case, in which the paper was. My father did so, and Mr. Reid took out a paper, and Mr. Robertson said it was his testament. He had said to Mr. Reid, "If you open that desk, you will find my will," and when Mr. Reid did so and took out the paper, Mr. Robertson said, "That is my will." He asked Mr. Reid to read it, but he said there were no witnesses. Mr. Robertson said, "I don't care for that, my will stands good; go on and read it;" and Mr.

1839. Aug. 29. „ 31.

Wilhelmina *vs.* Robertson, Executor Dative of Robertson.

Reid then told us to leave the room, which we did. Mr. Robertson was then in his full senses.

On hearing the above witnesses, the defendant not making any further opposition, the Court unanimously found the paper, founded on in the pleadings, to be the valid last will and testament of Mr. Robertson, and gave judgment for plaintiff as prayed, with costs. (*Vide Ord.* 15 *of* 1845, *Section* 3, *as to Attestation of Wills.*)

Van der Spuys *vs.* Maasdorp, Executor of Domus, and Aploon.

Action to set aside a will on the ground of imbecility and consequent curatorship.

A father cannot by will, by placing his daughter under curatorship, deprive her after majority of the administration of her affairs, and the power of making a will.

1839. Nov. 7. „ 14.

Van der Spuys *vs.* Maasdorp, Executor of Domus, and Aploon.

P. N. Domus and his wife, S. N. de Wet, in their joint will, dated 22nd July, 1794, *inter alia* declared "to prelegate, make, and bequeath *to their now imbecile daughter M. N. Domus,* 15,760*f.*," and also appointed her to be one of the joint heirs of the longest liver of the said spouses. And further directed that the share of inheritance devolving on the said M. N. Domus, as well as the said prelegated sum of 15,760*f.* "shall remain under the administration of the Orphan Chamber, until such time as they (the Chamber) shall be convinced, or it shall be declared by the Judge, that the said M. N. Domus is possessed of her senses and understanding;" and also appointed the Orphan Chamber, after the death of the longest liver of the said spouses, to be *guardians of their said unfortunate imbecile daughter.*

By a codicil dated 14th September, 1811, the said spouses revoked the above appointment of the Orphan Chamber, and appointed the defendant Maasdorp, to be the executor of their said will, administrator of their said estate, and guardian of their said *imbecile* daughter. P. N. Domus died, and was survived by his wife. Thereafter the defendant, Maasdorp, presented a petition to the late Court of Civil and Criminal Justice, setting forth his said appointment as executor administrator and guardian, and having annexed thereunto a copy of the said codicil, in which he stated "that some doubts have arisen in the mind of the petitioner as to the right and competency of the testators in respect of their appointment," and thereupon prayed the

Court to confirm his appointment as curator over the *imbecile* M. N. Domus.

1839. Nov. 7. ,, 14.

Van der Spuys *vs.* Maasdorp, Executor of Domus, and Aploon.

On considering this petition and the copy of the codicil, without any further evidence, and without calling or making M. N. Domus a party in any way to the proceedings, the Court made an order, dated 4th September, 1817, appointing the defendant, the petitioner, *as curator over the imbecile M. N. Domus, with such power as by law appertains to curators over persons requiring superintendence.* On the 23rd August, 1820, the said M. N. Domus made a will bequeathing certain parts of her property to the plaintiffs.

This will commenced as follows: "On this, the 23rd August, 1820, before me, P. C. van Blommestein, Secretary of the district of Stellenbosch, practising as a notary public, and in the presence of the hereinafter named commissioned officiating Heemraden as witnesses, appeared the major Miss M. N. Domus, known to me, the Secretary, and to the commissioned Heemraden, *in bodily health, in full possession of her senses and faculties of speech,* and fully able to make a testament, as appeared at the passing of these presents, signifying a desire to dispose by will of these goods, so doing without being thereto advised or induced by any person," &c., &c.

The will was subscribed by the said Secretary and M. N. Domus, in presence of and attested by A. Brink and J. C. Briers, officiating Heemraden, and by it the defendant Maasdorp was appointed her executor.

On the 8th of July, 1834, and 26th of August, 1836, M. N. Domus, in virtue of the reserved power to that effect in her said will, executed two codicils thereto before the Notary Auret and witnesses, the said notary having, by direction of the defendant, called on M. N. Domus to receive her instructions for the first codicil which she gave him. The second codicil was drawn by the said notary from a note given him by defendant of what the codicil was to contain, which note the notary showed to M. N. Domus before he made out the codicil, and conversed with her respecting it, when she said it was according to her desire. Defendant was also present at the execution of both codicils. The other defendant, Aploon, was a legatee under the codicils.

M. N. Domus died on the 24th June, 1839, and thereafter the plaintiffs, as heirs at law of the said M. N. Domus, and also, as it would seem, as heirs under said will of 23rd August, 1820, brought this action, in order to have the said codicils set aside and declared null and invalid, as having been made and executed by the said M. N. Domus when *she was of unsound mind,* and had been adjudged and

1839. Nov. 7. " 14. — Van der Spuys *vs.* Maasdorp, Executor of Domus, and Aploon.

declared to be of such unsound mind by an order or decree of the late Court of Civil and Criminal Justice of the 4th September, 1817, whereby the defendant Maasdorp had been appointed her guardian, and which appointment continued of power and effect until the death of the said M. N. Domus.

The defendants pleaded, firstly, the general issue; secondly, they denied that M. N. Domus had been adjudged and declared by said decree or order to be *of unsound mind;* and thirdly, they averred that the said decree had been given without any inquiry or examination whatever into her state of mind, and also without her having been a party to any suit or application for obtaining said decree, and that it had been passed *causâ incognitâ* and *inauditâ parte.*

Cloete, for the plaintiffs, put in the above-mentioned wills and codicils, both of P. N. Domus and his wife, and of M. N. Domus, and the petition of Maasdorp with the order of the late Court of the 4th September, 1817, quoted *Burge's Colonial Law*, 4 *vol.*, *p.* 328, and maintained that in respect of this evidence, the burden of proving M. N. Domus to be sane at the time of executing the codicils, was now laid on the defendants who maintained their validity.

But the Court held that neither the will of the father nor the order of the 4th September, 1817, given, as it was, *causâ incognitâ et parte inauditâ*, were *per se* such *prima facie* evidence of M. N. Domus's insanity as to relieve the plaintiffs from the burden of proving her to be insane. Thereupon, the plaintiffs and defendants proceeded to call several witnesses as to her state of mind, and as to the facts above set forth.

After which *Cloete*, for plaintiffs, quoted *Burge's Colonial Law*, 4 *vol.*, *c.* 7; *Williams's Law of Executors*, *p.* 33; and maintained that he had proved that Miss Domus, from 1803 till 1825, laboured under such imperfection and imbecility of mind as rendered her incompetent to make a will, and that this threw on defendants the burden of proving her sanity in 1834 and 1836, which they had failed to do.

2ndly. He quoted *Voet* 28, 1, 11, and maintained that the codicil of 1834 was null, as it had not been *dictated* by Miss Domus, but merely assented to by her on being read over to her.

3rdly. He maintained that Miss Domus having, whether properly or improperly, been placed by the late Court under curatorship, could not, while that curatorship was suffered to subsist, make a will without the leave and authority of the competent magistrate or tribunal, even with the consent of her curators, and quoted *Van der Linden Inst.*, 128; *Grotius, Inl.*, 2, 15, 5; *Voet*, 28, 1, 34.

Brand argued *contra*, and quoted *Voet* 27, 10, 7, "*cujus etiam rei.*" 1839. Nov. 7. „ 14. Van der Spuys *vs.* Maasdorp, Executor of Domus, and Aploon.

2ndly. That even if the curatorship had been legally appointed, still that the codicils in question were valid, as being in favour of relatives and perfectly rational. (*Voet* 28, 1, 34, "*ac ex novellæ.*")

Lastly. That Miss Domus had not been proved to labour under such mental incapacity or imperfection as to disable her from making a will. (*Voet* 28, 1, 32; *Williams's Law of Executors, Vol.* 1, *p.* 34. *Jurisprudentia Forensis*, edited by *Van der Linden*, *p.* 419.)

Cur. adv. vult.

Postea (14th Nov., 1839).—The Court gave judgment for the defendants with costs. They held that a father could not by will place a daughter under curatorship so as to deprive her, after majority, of the administration of her affairs, or of the power of making a will. That the decree or order of the Court had been given or made *causâ incognitâ et inauditâ parte*, and was therefore null and of no effect. That even if the act or order had been valid, it only restricted her from acting without the consent of her curator. Consequently, that the codicils having been made with the full knowledge and consent of the curator were valid, notwithstanding the existence of the order and the curatorship. That Miss Domus had not been found to have been of unsound mind, and therefore incapable of disposing of her effects by will.

In re Herron; Waters, Applicant.

Ord. 104, §§ 3, 6, 7. *Master. Registration of will. Notary. Protocol.*

On the death of testators who have made notarial wills, the original will must be taken from the notary's protocol, and be enregistered with the Master; and even if more wills than one by the same testator be so offered, the Master is bound to enregister the same, leaving the question of their relative validity to be decided by the Court on action.

Musgrave, for Waters, moved for a rule on the Master to enregister in the Register of Wills, in terms of the 7th section of Ordinance No. 104, a document purporting to be a copy of a will made by Herron, deceased, before the late 1840. April 13. *In re* Herron; Waters, Applicant.

1840. April 13. In re Herron; Waters, Applicant.

Notary Cadogan and witnesses, and which notarial will was now in the protocol of the said Cadogan, in the possession of his partner, the Notary Reid, and by which will the said *Waters* and another were appointed executors of said will. The Master objected to this on two grounds: 1st. Admitting that the paper sought to be registered was a true copy of the notarial will in the protocol, he maintained that by the provisions of the said 7th section, the Master would only be required to enregister, and could only enregister, the original of wills, even although notarial copies, and admitted to be *true* copies, and therefore that if this will were to be enregistered at all, it could only be legally enregistered by enregistering the original deed in the protocol of Notary Cadogan, out of which the Master alleged that he could not obtain it, except under an order from the Court.

And 2ndly. That as there was evidence to show, and, indeed it had been admitted, that what is commonly called the *gross* of the will in the protocol had been delivered to the deceased Herron, either in the form of a duplicate signed by Herron and by the notary and witnesses, according to the practice of some notaries, or of a copy signed by the notary, and verified by his notarial attestation, according to the more general practice, the gross so delivered must be considered and held to be the original of Herron's will, and that which could alone be enregistered as such, and that as this *gross* had not been found in the repositories of the deceased, it must be presumed that he had destroyed it, and thus entirely revoked and cancelled the will made by him before the notary Cadogan; or, at least, that the said will in the protocol could not be enregistered, or in any way given effect to, as the will of the deceased, unless the said *gross* were produced uncancelled, or its non-appearance accounted for in some other way, by evidence that it had not been destroyed by the deceased with the intention of revoking and cancelling his will. It was stated by the Master, that in no case since the passing of the Ordinance No. 104 had the original of any notarial will inserted in the protocol of the notary been enregistered, but that such notarial wills had invariably been enregistered by the registration of the *gross*.

The Court held that the copy produced by the applicant was not entitled to be enregistered as the will of the deceased, but that under the provisions of the 3rd section of the Ordinance No. 104, every notary in whose protocol or possession there was at the time of the death of any person, any deed being, or purporting to be, or intituled, the last will, codicil, or other testamentary instrument of such deceased person, was bound, and on failing to do so could be compelled, under the provisions of the 6th section, to deliver or transmit the same to the Master, who, under the provisions of the 7th section, was bound to enregister every such deed or instrument in the original in the Registry of Wills, even although two or more such deeds or instruments, executed at different times by the same person, should be delivered or transmitted to him, leaving the validity or legal effect of every such deed or instrument to be afterwards decided by a competent Court. The Court therefore ordered the Notary Reid to take from the protocol of the Notary Cadogan, the notarial will (*authenticum*) which had been executed before said Cadogan by the deceased Herron, and to deliver the same to the Master, and that the Master should enregister the same in the Registry of Wills. It was not necessary to decide, but the Court expressed an opinion, that the mere fact of the destruction by the testator, much less the mere non-appearance of the *gross* which he had received from the notary, was not *per se* sufficient to destroy or impair the validity of any notarial will (*authenticum*) inserted and existing in the protocol of the notary at the time of the death of the testator; and the Court suggested that every notarial deed, being or purporting to be the last will or codicil of any person who had died since the passing of the Ordinance No. 104, and now in the protocol of any notary, should be taken from the protocol and delivered and transmitted to the Master, to be by him enregistered in the Registry of Wills.

OOSTHUYSEN WESSELS *vs.* EXECUTORS OF RENSBURG.

Mutual will. Acquittance and discharge. Estoppel.

C. J. S. and A. R. spouses, by mutual will appointed the plaintiff, in case they both died without issue, heir of the whole joint estate on the death of the longest living. S. died. His widow re-married M., and executed a second mutual will with him, revoking the former mutual will of herself and her deceased husband in so far as regarded the substitution of the plaintiff as heir to her share of the joint estate, declaring the plaintiff only entitled to the share of her late husband on her decease under a certain deduction. She afterwards paid over such half to plaintiff, and took from him a full written discharge. **HELD,** *that this barred the plaintiff from an action to set aside the second mutual will and to claim under the first.*

1840. Aug. 27.

Oosthuysen Wessels *vs.* Executors of Rensburg.

C. J. Snyman and his wife, A. M. J. Rensburg, married in community of property on the 19th January, 1811, executed a joint will, in which they appointed the longest liver sole and universal heir in his or her estate, and in the event of them both dying without issue, they appointed the plaintiff their sole and universal heir of the whole estate to be left by them, to be entered upon and possessed by him after the death of the longest liver.

Snyman died. His widow married Muller, and jointly with him executed a will, dated 25th January, 1823, in which she appointed the defendants her executors, and expressly revoked her will of 19th January, 1811, in so far as regarded the appointment or substitution of the plaintiff as heir to her share of the joint estate, and declared that plaintiff, by virtue of said will of 19th January, 1811, should only be deemed entitled to claim and demand the share of her said deceased husband, which share she declared should be paid over to plaintiff after her decease, under deduction of the Trebellianic portion.

Thereafter, on the 7th September, 1830, the said Mrs. Muller paid over to plaintiff the amount of the share of her deceased husband in the joint estate, and obtained from him the following acknowledgment:

"7th September, 1830.

"I, the undersigned, as heir in the estate of the late C. J. Snyman, acknowledge to have received my share of inheritance out of the abovementioned estate, from Mr. M. A. Muller, and that I have nothing to claim from said estate of whatsoever nature. This I have given as an acquittal in full for the said inheritance, in presence of the undersigned witnesses.

(Signed) "W. OOSTHUYZEN WESSELS."

The Court held that this deed barred the claim made by the plaintiff in the present action against the defendants, the executors of the said will of A. M. J. Rensburg, of the 22nd January, 1823, to have the revocation of her former will set aside, and to be declared sole heir of the *whole of the joint estate* of Snyman and his wife, existing at the death of Snyman, and as such to receive out of the estate of the deceased Rensburg, afterwards Muller, the amount of her share of said joint estate, and gave judgment for defendants.

[*Vide Van Renen vs. De Wet, Executor of Neethling, 10th May*, 1839, *post, p.* 470]

Sandenbergh, Husband of Zibee, *vs.* Executors of Zibee.

Fidei-commissum. Legitimate portion.

Widow Z. appointed her daughter Z., married to plaintiff, her sole heiress, subject to a fidei-commissum that the daughter should enjoy only the interest during life, and that on her death the interest should go to, 1, The plaintiff; 2, The children of her daughter; and on their death the capital to be divided among the grandchildren of Z. Plaintiff, in right of his wife, claimed her legitimate absolutely, and interest on the balance during life, which the Court awarded.

1841. Nov. 30. Dec. 13.

Sandenbergh, Husband of Zibee, *vs.* Executors of Zibee.

The facts of this case were that the deceased Widow Zibee, the mother of plaintiff's wife, by her last will nominated the plaintiff's wife to be her sole and universal heiress in all her property, movable and immovable, without exception, under condition that the whole inheritance should remain entailed under *fidei-commissum*, under the express stipulation and condition that the said plaintiff's wife should only enjoy and apply as she may think fit, during her lifetime, the interest of the capital of said inheritance, and that after her death the said interest should be enjoyed, first, by plaintiff if he survived; secondly, by the children of plaintiff's wife; and thirdly, "after the death of the said grandchildren of the said testatrix, the capital of her inheritance in proportion to the number of such grandchildren shall devolve in full and free property on the grandchildren of her said daughter," thus substituting as her heirs the *grand-grand*-children of the testatrix.

Plaintiff claimed in this action that under this will his wife, who was the only child and sole heir of the testatrix, should, as such, be found entitled absolutely and unconditionally to her *legitimate* portion of the estate of her mother, being one third share of the net amount thereof, and also to the interest annually accruing on the remainder of the estate still to be left under the *fidei-commissum*.

The defendant's maintained that plaintiff was entitled to claim only either her legitimate portion without the interest of the remainder, or the interest of the whole without her legitimate portion, and that she must elect which she would take.

Cloete, for plaintiff, quoted *Van der Linden, p.* 135; *Van der Keessel, Thes.* 316; *Loenius, Decis.* 85; *Alers' Rules and Definitions, p.* 76; *Voet,* 5, 2, 64, and 36, 1, 52.

Brand, for defendants, stated that in his opinion the law

1841. Nov. 30. Dec. 13.

Sandenbergh, Husband of Zibee, *vs.* Executors of Zibee.

was clearly with the plaintiff, and that defendants had only defended the case in order to have the judgment of the Court thereon.

Cur. adv. vult.

Postea (13th December, 1841).—The Court, in respect of the law as laid down in *Voet* 5, 2, 64, gave judgment for plaintiff as prayed, costs to be paid out of the estate before liquidation thereof.

GNADE *vs.* EXECUTORS OF PITON, AND BEUGEVONT, WIDOW AND EXECUTRIX, AND BEALE, EXECUTOR OF J. N. GNADE.

Pleading. Exception. Mortgage bond. Tacit hypothec.

Mr. and Mrs. G., by mutual will, instituted their children (of whom plaintiff was one) their heirs. Mrs. G. survived and acted as executrix of the estate. Plaintiff obtained judgment against her in that capacity for the amount of his inheritance. Mrs. G. borrowed certain moneys from one P., and passed to him a bond hypothecating a house and premises. This action was brought by the plaintiff to have it declared that he had, by virtue of his tacit hypothec, a preference before P. as mortgagee.

It was objected by defendant that plaintiff should have proceeded to execute the judgment obtained; but the Court held it was optional with him to do that or bring this action.

1842. Feb. 3.

Gnade *vs.* Executors of Piton, and Beugevont, Widow and Executrix, and Beale, Executor of J. N. Gnade.

The plaintiff's declaration set out that the deceased J. N. Gnade and his widow, the defendant, made a mutual will, which was confirmed by his death, whereby a certain amount of inheritance was bequeathed to plaintiff and the other children of the testator and testatrix; that after the death of the testator, his widow the testatrix entered on the administration of his estate as executrix testamentary; that the plaintiff afterwards obtained against her, in her said capacity, a final judgment of the Supreme Court for £204 3s. 6d., with interest and costs, as the amount of the sum bequeathed to him under the will. The plaintiff further stated that the defendant, the said Widow Beugevont, after the death of her husband, "for the purpose of securing the repayment of certain moneys borrowed by her from one J. D. Piton, now deceased (whose executors were defendants in this action), specially hypothecated to the said Piton certain three houses and premises (therein specified and described), of which houses and premises the said J. N. Gnade was at the time of his death the registered proprietor," by three mortgage bonds, dated, &c., and duly registered, and thereafter assumed the defendant Beale as co-executor. And that the plaintiff being entitled under the said will to a tacit hypothec over and upon the estate of the said testator for securing the payment of the inheritance to him by the said will given and bequeathed, and being unable to obtain from the said defendants, the Widow Beugevont and Beale, in their said capacities, any part of the said inheritance adjudged to him as aforesaid by decree of the Supreme Court, an action has accrued to him against the defendants the executors of Piton, to demand that the said mortgage bonds respectively may be cancelled and set aside, so far as they affect the interest of the plaintiff in the said houses and premises, or either of them,—or that the tacit hypothec of the said plaintiff may be declared to be preferent to the said mortgage bonds respectively as a charge upon such interest as aforesaid on the said houses and premises. And also an action against the defendants, in their capacity of executors of Gnade, to demand that they shall be barred and foreclosed from all right and title to said houses, &c., and that the same may be declared executable; and the said plaintiff accordingly prays, &c., &c.

1842. Feb. 3.

Gnade *vs.* Executors of Piton, and Beugevont, Widow and Executrix, and Beale, Executor, of J. N. Gnade.

The defendants executors of Piton excepted to the declaration in so far as it related to them, that it is informal and inartificially pleaded, inasmuch as the facts and allegations set forth therein are insufficient in law for the plaintiff to maintain his said action against him; and that the said facts and allegations, even if they were true in fact and admitted by the defendants, do not entitle the plaintiff to deduce therefrom the conclusion at law which he has drawn therefrom, or to pray for judgment in manner and form as he hath thereof complained.

Plaintiff joined issue on the exception.

Cloete argued in support of the exception, and maintained, first, that the present form of action was improper and incompetent, and that plaintiff having obtained a judgment against the executors of Gnade, ought to have executed that judgment by taking out a writ of execution for attaching the houses and premises in question, and thereafter, in *concursu creditorum* before the Master, have claimed, in virtue of his alleged hypothec, to be preferred on the proceeds thereof for his debt.

The Court held that although the plaintiff might have adopted the course of proceeding suggested by the defen-

1842. Feb. 3. — Gnade *vs.* Executors of Piton, and Beugevont, Widow and Executrix, and Beale, Executor of J. N. Gnade.

dants, it was equally competent to him to endeavour to establish and render effectual his alleged hypothec by the present form of action.

2nd. *Cloete,* for defendants, maintained that the plaintiff, although entitled (as he admitted him to be) to the privileges of a legatee, and as such to a hypothec over the property of the testator preferent to the claims of the heir, and of any person claiming through the heir, yet was bound in an action for establishing and making effectual his hypothec against the mortgage bonds held by defendants to have expressly alleged in his declaration that the bonds had been granted to Piton by the widow in her capacity as heir, and for money advanced to her as such, whereas the terms which he had used in his declaration, viz., "And that the said defendant Delia, &c., after the death of her husband, and for securing the payment of certain moneys borrowed by her from one J. D. Piton, did specially mortgage and hypothecate to the said Piton the said houses," were ambiguous and capable of being so construed as to imply, or at least not to exclude, an intendment that she had executed the mortgage bonds in her capacity as executrix and administratix, and in the *bonâ fide* administration of the estate, as she might lawfully do; and as in this case the plaintiff's hypothec would be ineffectual against the defendants' mortgage bonds, the declaration was therefore informal, because its terms in a material point admitted of a double construction, and because, according to one of the constructions of which it was susceptible, the facts alleged did not warrant the conclusion in law drawn from them; and referred to the case of *Moll vs. Executors of Van der Berg, 29th May,* 1840.

The Court held that the plain and obvious meaning of the words in question, more especially when viewed in connection with the context, was that the defendant, the widow, had executed the bonds in her private capacity and for the security of money lent to her for her own use, and therefore the fact as alleged by those words was sufficient to warrant the conclusion in law drawn in the declaration; and that the defendants, if they did not admit this allegation to be true, ought, instead of excepting to the declaration, to have pleaded and denied this allegation and averred the contrary.

Exception dismissed.

Costs to be costs in the cause.

This case was not afterwards brought before the Court.

Britz *vs.* Britz's Executors.

Mutual will. Adiation.

B. and his wife, by mutual will, left to their son a farm, on the death of the longest liver. **Held**, *that the survivor could not, after having adiated, alter this disposition by his separate will.*

1842. Feb. 28.

Britz *vs.* Britz's Executors.

Cornelis Jacob Britz and his first wife executed a mutual will, which, after appointing the survivor universal heir, and directing all their estate to be sold, and disposing of the proceeds in the manner therein set forth, contained the following clause: "From this sale, however, are to be exempted, 1st. The place of residence of the testators, Doornkraal, &c., &c., of which the survivor may take possession for the sum of 11,000*f.* (£275), being obliged, however, to cause the said place to devolve on the child of the testators, Hans Britz, or in case of his predecease, leaving children, on his eldest son for the same sum."

It was found that the surviving husband could not, by will made by him after the death of the testatrix, revoke this bequest; and on his death, his executors were adjudged to transfer this place, Doornkraal, to his grandson, the plaintiff, the eldest son of the said Hans Britz, then deceased, on the plaintiff's paying to them the said sum of £275. (*Vide Censura Forensis*, 3, 11, 7; *Voet*, 28, 3, 11.)

[For a fuller report of this case, see *Buchanan's Reports*, 1868, *p.* 312.]

In re Wium.—Serrurier *vs.* Children of Wium.

Kinderbewys. Legitimate and filial portions. Insolvency. Ord. 6, 1843, § 83.

On a question whether children claiming under a mutual will in the form given infra are entitled on the death of the mother, the first dying, to claim their share of maternal inheritance calculated according to the value of the estate at the death of the mother, or at the date of their majority, or at the date of the sequestration of the survivor's estate. **Semble**, *the shares of heirs major at the death of the first dying must be calculated according to the value of the estate at that date, but they have no right of preference. The shares of heirs minor at the death of the first dying must be calculated according to the value of their estate* *when they attain majority.* SEMBLE, *that where children entitled only to their legitimate receive from the survivor their filial portion by deed executed when liabilities exceed assets, such deed is, under Section* 83, *Ord.* 6, 1843, *liable to be set aside as an undue preference.*

1844. May 30. June 13. Aug. 13.

In re Wium.—Serrurier *vs.* Children of Wium.

Wium and his wife executed a joint will on the 15th June, 1807, containing the following clause: "———— declared to nominate and to institute each other, that is, the first dying the survivor, to be her or his sole universal heir or heiress of all the property to be left by the first dying, movable and immovable, without any exception, to be taken and possessed by the survivor as free and own property, without being called in question by any person; provided the survivor shall be bound and obliged to maintain the children already or still to be procreated during the wedlock, honestly and in the Christian religion until their majority or marriage or other approved state, when to each of them shall be paid over, for or in place of father's or mother's portion, such a sum of money as the survivor shall conscientiously, and according to the condition of the estate, find to belong to them. But in the event of the survivor inclining to a second marriage, he or she shall be bound and obliged,—after having previously caused the estate to be inventoried and valued prior to such marriage being solemnized, to secure the said portion of the children (kinderbewys) in the hands of two good and irreproachable men, without, however, being compelled to pay the same sooner than before mentioned."

The wife died on the 14th December, 1832, leaving eight children, six of whom were majors and two minors, who respectively attained their majority on the 6th October, 1835, and 9th January, 1838. No inventory and appraisement of the joint estate was made by the surviving spouse until the 23rd June and 1st July, 1842, and his estate was placed under sequestration as insolvent on the 11th July, 1842. At the dissolution of the marriage in 1832 there were fifteen slaves belonging to the estate. In the inventory these slaves were appraised at the value which had been put on them by the appraisers under the Compensation Act, viz., Rds.19,400, but it was admitted that the compensation money actually received was only Rds.5,400. The trustee of the insolvent estate of the father, in ranking the claims of the children who were majors as well as those who were minors at the death of their mother in 1832, ranked them all for their share of their maternal inheritance calculated according to the appraised value of the slaves, and not according to the amount of the composition received.

Serrurier, a creditor, objected that no separation or appraisement of the estate having taken place before the compensation was fixed and awarded, the share of the children must be calculated according to the amount of the compensation received, and not according to the appraised value.

1844. May 30. June 13. Aug. 13.

In re Wium.—Serrurier *vs.* Children of Wium.

Under these circumstances, the question was raised whether the children were entitled to claim their share of their maternal inheritance, under such a will as that in the present case, calculated according to the value of the estate at the death of the mother, or at the date of their majority, or at the date of the sequestration, or at what other date.

After some argument, the case was ordered to stand over for further hearing.

Postea (13th June, 1844).—This day *Brand*, for the children, maintained that the children majors at the time of their mother's death were entitled to their shares of her half of the estate, calculated according to the value of the estate at the time of her death (*vide Voet* 5, 2, 65; *Voet* 23, 2, 128); and maintained that the same was true as to the children who did not become majors until after the mother's death. That by law they are entitled to claim the same amount, whatever it may have been, which became due to the majors; and quoted *Burge,* 1, 305; *Voet* 28, 8, 6. That minors at the time of their mother's death, subsequently becoming majors, are entitled to have two inventories made, one according to the value of the estate at the death of the mother, and the other on their coming of age, according to its then value; and that they are entitled to select by which of the two inventories their share shall be calculated. And this not only by the law in a case of intestacy, but also under the provisions of a will, such as that in question. And lastly, that whether the minor children could or would not legally have compelled their father to give them more than their share of the estate calculated according to its value at the date on which they attained their majority, yet that the father, acting under the *conscientious* discretion given him by the will, having given them their share calculated according to the value of the estate at the mother's death, or at some time other than at the date of the majority, and the children having been satisfied with what he had given them, neither his creditors nor any third party have any right to question or interfere with this exercise of his discretion, and that the objecting creditor is not entitled to question the father's act done in the exercise of this discretion, although by it he gave the children more than they could legally demand or force him to pay; and although this act, thus giving the children an

1844. May 30. June 13. Aug. 13.

In re Wium.—Serrurier *vs.* Children of Wium.

amount to which they were not by law entitled, was done by him within sixty days of his insolvency (under Ordinance No. 64), or after his liabilities fairly calculated exceeded his assets fairly valued (under the 83 § 6—1843). The heirs major at their mother's death also maintained that by virtue of a tacit hypothec they had a preference over the other creditors of their father for shares of their maternal inheritance to the same extent that the children who were minors when their mother died had.

The *Attorney-General, contra,* maintained that the father could not under the will, give the children less than the *legitimate portion,* but was only bound to give them the *legitimate portion,* and not bound to give them the *filial* portion of the mother's estate, under whatever calculation it may be estimated. He maintained that even if the inventory with the distribution account were to be held to be a *kinderbewys,* which he denied, yet that, not having been made in payment of or delivered to the children, it could not be considered as a valid and effectual act,—that it would not have been binding on the children, and therefore could not bind the creditors who represented the father; and therefore that anything done on or by it could not be considered to be a valid and effectual exercise by the father of any legal faculty or power given him under the will (supposing any such faculty or power to be so given to him, which he denied), of giving the children a filial instead of merely a legitimate portion of their mother's estate, which last he contended was all that by the will he was legally bound to give them. (*Vide Voet* 5, 2, 65.) He further maintained that any deed done by the father within sixty days of his insolvency, having the effect to give the children anything more than they could by law compel him then to give them, was reduceable at the instance of the creditors under the provisions of Ordinance No. 64. That as no inventory or appraisement had been made before June, 1842, the shares of all the children could only be calculated according to the value of the estate at that date. That the heirs major at the death of their mother had no hypothec whatever, and consequently no preference for the amount of their shares, for which they must be ranked as concurrent creditors.

The Court, without proceeding to judgment, expressed an opinion that the shares of the heirs major at the time of the mother's death must be calculated according to the nature of the estate as at that date. That those major heirs had no hypothec or right of preference for their shares. That the shares of the heirs minor at the time of the mother's death must be calculated according to the value of the estate as at the dates when they respectively attained majority. And that in the calculation both as respected the major and the minor heirs, the amount of the compensation ultimately received for the slaves must be taken as their estimated value. That unless the parties came to some arrangement on these principles, they would call on the heirs to show on what grounds they maintained that, under the will, they had each a legal right to a filial share of their mother's estate, instead of merely a right to claim each a child's legitimate portion, which the Court were inclined to think they had not, seeing that the father could not, by any deed executed within sixty days of his insolvency, give the children, to the prejudice of the creditors, anything more than they had then a legal right to compel him to give them.

1844. May 30. June 13. Aug. 13.

In re Wium.—Serrurier *vs.* Children of Wium.

Postea (13th August, 1844).—The parties consented that the claim for preference by the major heirs should be waived, and that they should be ranked as concurrent creditors; and that preference being awarded to the two heirs who were minors at the time of their mother's death, for their respective shares according to the appraisement and valuation of June, 1842, less the difference between the amount of the value at which the slaves had been appraised and that of the compensation money subsequently realized, viz., to each of them the sum of 1,047 rds. 2 sk., or £78 10s. 10½d., with interest from the periods stated in their proof of debts. The costs incurred in both cases by Mr. Serrurier to be paid out of the insolvent estate.

Judgment as by consent.

In Re Kemp.

Insanity. Curatorship. Will.

1844. June 4.

In re Kemp.

This day a memorial was presented to the Court by T. J. Mathew and G. T. Kemp, setting forth, that on the 16th of May, 1843, the estate of E. Kemp, formerly of Uitenhage, was placed under curatorship, on the ground of the insanity of the said Kemp, and the memorialists were appointed respectively, Mathew curator of his estate, and G. T. Kemp of his person. That since the said date, the said E. Kemp has partially, if not entirely, recovered his reason, and has expressed a wish to make his will, and memorialists have therefore requested three medical men to examine him, who have given their opinion that the said

E. Kemp is at the present time perfectly sane. Wherefore your memorialists pray, that this Honourable Court may be pleased to make an order, after due inquiry, that the said E. Kemp is of sufficiently sound mind to make a will, or otherwise as to this Honourable Court shall seem right in the premises.

The Court expressed an opinion, that if the memorialists moved for it, it was competent for the Court to hear evidence, and inquire whether Kemp had so completely recovered his sanity as that he should be freed from all curatorship. The memorialists stated that this was not their object, and that they only sought that the Court should either allow Kemp to make his will in their presence, in accordance with the authority of *Voet*, or should after inquiry find and declare that Kemp at the present time enjoyed such a lucid interval, or was so sane, as to be legally competent to make a will.

The Court held, that as this Court, as the supreme tribunal of the Colony, might hereafter be called to adjudicate on the validity of any such will, whether made in their presence or in virtue of any such declaratory finding, the application of the memorialists ought not to be granted, lest the Court should hereafter be obliged, on fresh evidence, to set aside their own act, and because the authority quoted refers only to the Provincial Courts and Magistrates, and not the Supreme Court, and refused the application; recommending the parties to have recourse to the Resident Magistrate, or one or more justices of the peace, before whom Kemp might execute his will (as had been done in the case of one Beyers), and to have the will subscribed, as witnesses, by as many medical men convinced of the testator's sanity as they could procure.

BEKKER *vs.* MEYRING, BEKKER'S EXECUTOR.

Insanity. Witness to will. Ord. 72, § 39. *Ord.* 104, § 7. *Evidence. Master. Appeal from Circuit Court. Res inter alios acta. Pleading. Exception.*

Certified copies of wills registered with the Master are evidence without the production of the registered originals. So held on appeal.

Where the ground of objection in the Court below (reserved for the decision of the Supreme Court, and decided ut supra) was merely that such certified copy was not evidence, held that the appellants could not in this Court now go farther, and object that the instrument produced was not a regular and duly certified copy.

Where on the appeal the appellant sought, as one ground of setting aside the judgment of the Circuit Court, to object that some of the heirs interested in the will had not been made parties to the appeal, held that this should have been excepted in the Court below, initio litis; and that although there are certain matters in bar, of which this Court will take notice, although not pleaded below, and will in respect thereof reverse the judgment of the Court below, yet that this was not one of those cases.

And where one of the appellants founding on this objection was the executor, held that it was his duty to have tempestive called on the other heirs to intervene in the action below.

Moreover, it is not essential that all parties interested in a will should be made parties to a suit brought by one or more of them; but the decision of the Court being, as regards parties not intervening, res inter alios acta, cannot bind them re judicatâ.

1844. Nov. 26.

Bekker *vs.* Meyring, Bekker's Executor.

This action was brought in the Circuit Court of George in March, 1844.

The defendant, P. J. Meyring, jun., in his capacity as executor to the estate of the late M. Bekker, and P. J. Meyring, sen., as heir, and claiming and interested in supporting the will of the said M. Bekker, were summoned, at the instance of Jurie Bekker, plaintiff, to show cause why a certain will executed by the said M. Bekker, who departed this life on or about the 22nd of November, 1842, should not be set aside, and declared by the judgment of this honourable Court to be null, illegal, and void, on the ground that the said M. Bekker, at the time he executed the said will, was not in his sound and proper senses, and was legally incompetent to execute any will. Also on the ground that the said will was executed in the absence of those who, upon the face of the said will, purport to be the attesting witnesses; and, further, on the ground that the said Bekker, at the time stated in the said will that he executed it (the said will), could not, and did not sign the said will, but that one Daniel Boshoff held the hand of the said M. Bekker, in which was a pen, and by which process the said will was so signed.

The defendants, in their plea, pleaded "that the said plaintiff ought not to have and maintain his said action against the said defendants, for they denied all and every allegation set forth in the summons, and joined issue with the said plaintiff thereon."

1844. Nov. 26. — Bekker *vs.* Meyring, Bekker's Executor.

At the trial, *Ebden*, for plaintiff, put in a certified copy of the will (*i.e.*, certified by the Master of the Supreme Court, Keeper of the Registry of Wills).

Ryneveld, for defendant, objected that the original will should be produced, as the best evidence.

The Court reserved this point for the decision of the Supreme Court, the case to proceed subject to that decision.

Thereafter, the Court, on hearing the evidence, gave judgment that the will be set aside as prayed, *on the first ground assigned in the summons*, with costs, subject to the decision of the Supreme Court upon the point reserved; execution to be stayed until further order.

Appeal prayed by defendants, and allowed.

The following memorandum was, by order of the Court, endorsed by the Registrar on the record :

"No notice was given to the Court of the value of the matter at issue, either on the face of the summons, or otherwise before the trial commenced; but the Judge has allowed the appeal, because it was said by some of the witnesses who were examined that the testator had about Rds. 4,000 (or £300) at interest when he died; and he has suggested the bringing the appeal to a hearing before the Supreme Court on the evidence which was taken before him, a copy of which will be filed on record in that Court on his return to Cape Town.—(Signed) THOS. J. DICKSON, Acting Registrar."

A copy of the Judge's notes of the evidence had accordingly been filed on record, and was this day produced, together with the certified copy of the will.

The *Attorney-General*, for appellant, in support of the objection founded upon the production of a certified copy of the will instead of the will itself, quoted section 39 of Ordinance No. 72, and section 7 of Ordinance No. 104; and maintained that this section did no more than order the original will to be enregistered, and did not make it a public instrument, or alter the law of evidence as to whether the original must, or a certified copy may, be produced as evidence of the will. Quoted *Voet* 22, 4, 7; *Van der Linden*, 257; *Merula*, *b.* 4, *tit.* 66, *ch.* 4, § 2; *Domat, Civil Law*, *tit.* 6, § 10.

Ebden, contra, quoted *Phillips*, *vol.* 1, 384; *Starkie*, *part* 2, § 34; *Voet* 22, 4, § 2; *Van der Linden*, *p.* 257.

The Court held that by virtue of the provisions of sections 7 and 8 of Ordinance 104, testaments, so soon as enregistered by the Master of the Supreme Court, as therein prescribed, became public archives or records, not afterwards to be removed from the registry in which they are kept for preservation (*vide Voet* 22, 4, § 2); and that copies of them, duly authenticated or certified by the Master, the Registrar, or keeper of these records, and entrusted by law to grant copies thereof, are, without further proof, as full and sufficient evidence of the tenor and contents of such testaments as the original itself if produced would have been; and repelled the objection.

The Court held that the only objection made by the defendants in the Circuit Court was, that a certified copy had been produced instead of the original; and that, therefore, the appellants could not now in this Court object that the instrument produced was not a regular and duly certified copy. (*Voet* 49, 7, 2.)

The Court held that the evidence fully supported and warranted the judgment which had been given by the Circuit Court.

The *Attorney-General* maintained that the judgment of the Circuit Court must be set aside, in respect that the conclusion of the summons was,—"that the will should be set aside and declared by the judgment of this honourable Court to be null, illegal, and void;" and that all the parties interested in the will had not joined as plaintiffs in the action, and had not been by the plaintiff made parties to the cause as defendants; consequently, that judgment could not legally be given as prayed by the plaintiff, seeing the will could not be set aside and declared null and void without prejudicing parties who had not had an opportunity of being heard in support of their interest in the will. He alleged that several brothers and sisters of the plaintiff were entitled to bequests under the will, and that the Court must therefore presume that they had an interest in supporting the will, and could not inquire whether it was not their interest as well as that of the plaintiff, as being heirs of the deceased, *ab intestato*, to set aside the will.

The defendant, the executor, alleged also that he was prejudiced by those parties not having been made defendants, because he had paid to some of them the shares due to them under the will, and that if it were set aside, he might be forced to pay plaintiff part of the amount paid them, which the judgment given against him in an action to which they were not parties would not enable him to recover back from them.

Ebden, contra, maintained that, even if it had been competent for the defendants in the Circuit Court to have pleaded as an exception against the plaintiff's action, that it should be dismissed in respect that all parties interested in the will had not either joined the plaintiff, or been by him made defendants,—that this exception was a dilatory exception, and not having been pleaded *in initio litis,* could

1844. Nov. 26. — Bekker, *vs.* Meyring, Bekker's Executor.

not have been pleaded against the plaintiff after issue joined on the merits, even in the Circuit Court, and *a fortiori*, not now in this Court of Appeal. That even if the defendant could in appeal plead any new exception which he had not pleaded in the Circuit Court, he could plead no such new exception unless it were apparent on the face of the record, or arose directly out of the record. That in no part of the pleadings or in the judgment, which he contended alone constituted the record [*vide* Charter, § 41], was there anything stated which could inform or even suggest to the Court that there were any other parties having any interest in the will except the plaintiff and defendants; consequently, that the defendants could not found this exception on anything stated in or arising from the record; and could not travel out of the record and allege new facts on which to found the exception which they now contended they were entitled to plead. He maintained that if it were competent for the defendants to refer to the will as a part of the record in order to establish the existence of other parties interested in it, the plaintiff must equally be entitled to refer to it for the purpose of proving, as a reference to it would prove, that the other parties stated by defendants to be interested in the will were his, the plaintiff's, brothers and sisters, and, as such, co-heirs with him of the deceased, *ab intestato*, having precisely the same interest as he had to set aside the will which, by the bequest therein made in favour of the defendant Meyring, sen., of half of the deceased's estate, deprived those parties of half of the amount which would devolve to them if the will were set aside; consequently, that they had no interest whatever to support the will.

The Court held that in so far as the defendants had any personal interest in objecting to the form or competency of the action, in respect that all the parties interested in the will had not been made parties to the cause, either as co-plaintiffs or as co-defendants, they could not now, in this Court of Appeal plead, and could not even in the Circuit Court after issue joined on the merits, have pleaded, this objection, which was of the nature of a dilatory exception, and therefore could only be pleaded *in initio litis*, and not afterwards, in the inferior court, and not having been pleaded there, could not be pleaded at all in the Court of Appeal. (*Voet* 44, *tit.* 1, § 6; 49, *tit.* 1, § 2.) And that, in so far as the defendant the executor might be prejudiced by the consequences of the judgment which might be given in this cause, in which the persons to whom he had made payments under the will had not been made parties, his proper remedy was to have called on those parties to have intervened and defended their interest; and that not having used his remedy *tempestive,* he could not now insist on delaying, much less defeating, the plaintiff's action on that ground.

The Court held that there were cases in which, although an otherwise valid objection fatal to the action had not been pleaded in the inferior Court,—and, consequently, although the defendant was barred from pleading it in the Court of Appeal as part of his case,—it would not only be competent, but sometimes would be the duty of the Court of Appeal, on discovering its existence, either by their own inspection of the record, or by having it pointed out to their notice by the defendant, to give effect to that objection, and reverse the judgment of the inferior Court on that ground:—*e.g.*, suppose that by the Charter, the Circuit Courts had been expressly excluded from and prohibited to exercise any jurisdiction whatever, in any case whatever, respecting the validity of any will, and that the parties in this case, ignorant of the provision of law, had litigated, and the Circuit Judge, through inadvertence, had given judgment respecting the validity of the will in question, and that this judgment had been appealed against, solely on the ground that the Circuit Court had admitted and decided on incompetent evidence,—it would, notwithstanding, be the duty of the Supreme Court to reverse the judgment of the Circuit on this ground.

Or if, in an action brought in the Circuit Court by A against B to have a certain deed of transfer declared to be null and void, erased from the register of transfers, cancelled, and destroyed, it should come to the knowledge of the Supreme Court,—on an appeal by B on the ground that the Circuit Court had given judgment for A as prayed, in respect of incompetent evidence,—that the deed of transfer not only conveyed the lands therein mentioned to B for his life, but to C in fee,—it would not only be competent, but it would be the duty of the Supreme Court, although they held the appeal to be ill-founded on the grounds on which it had been rested, either to reverse that part of the judgment which directed the erasure, cancellation, and destruction of the deed, on the ground that it would prejudice C, who had not been made a party to the action,—or to stay proceedings until notice should be given to C, in order that, if he thought fit, he might now intervene as a party to the action, and defend his interest.

But this case is totally different from either of the two classes of cases of which examples have just been given.

The Court have postponed giving judgment until they should have had an opportunity of inquiring whether, by

1844. Nov. 26.

Bekker *vs.* Meyring, Bekker's Executor.

the Roman-Dutch law, there was any rule or provision requiring, under pain of nullity of the action, that in every action for setting aside a testament as null, all the parties having any interest in or under that testament should be made parties to the action; and they have found that, so far from there being any such rule or provision, it had been made a question in that law, whether in an action for setting aside a testament as *inofficiosum* (the effect of which by the old law was to cut down all legacies bequeathed in the testament), it was competent for the legatees themselves to insist on intervening in the action as defendants, to protect their interests, or themselves to appeal against a judgment setting aside the testament on that ground, given in an action to which they had not been parties;—and although the question is decided in their favour in both cases, yet the very existence of the question, and the ultimate recognition of the privilege in favour of the legatees, *when they claim it*, establishes that it was not competent for the original defendant, either in the inferior Court or in the Court of Appeal, to have objected to the validity of the action, or of the judgment of the inferior Court, on the ground that all parties interested in the testament had not been made parties. (*Vide Voet* 5, 1, 35; 49, 1, 3.)

Neither can it be maintained that the judgment in this case ought to be reversed, in whole or in part, or stayed because it cannot be sustained and carried into execution without necessarily prejudicing the interest of parties who have not had an opportunity of protecting their interest by reason of their not having been made parties to the cause. For the judgment which has been given merely declares *that the will shall be set aside as prayed*, (*i.e.*, that it shall be declared to be null, illegal, and void), on the first ground assigned in the summons, but does not adjudge (what indeed would have been *ultra petita*) that the original deed shall be cancelled, erased from the register, and destroyed.

The deed, therefore, will continue *in esse*, notwithstanding the judgment; and the judgment cannot prejudice the other parties named in the will (even supposing they have an interest in supporting it), unless it can be pleaded as a *res judicata* against them; which, most assuredly, having been *res inter alios acta*, it cannot.

The judgment appealed against cannot have any effect against them which it would not have had if those words had been expressly added to the judgment which the effect of the law is to imply, viz., *that the will be set aside in so far as the interest of the two defendants under it is concerned, and no further.* Many parallel cases might be adduced in illustration. For example, if C, the indorsee of a promissory note, should sue A, the alleged maker, for payment, and A should defend himself on the ground that his signature was forged, C could not object to judgment for A on that ground being given in the Circuit Court, or afterwards by this Court on appeal, on the ground that B, the payee and endorser, had not been made a party to the action, and would be prejudiced by the judgment, because if C should thereupon recover payment from B, and re-deliver the note to B, the latter might, notwithstanding the judgment given between C and A, sue A for payment, who could not plead *res judicata* against B, and would be condemned to pay B, unless he should be able of new to establish his defence of forgery in the action between B and him.

1844. Nov. 26.

Bekker *vs.* Meyring, Bekker's Executor.

In consequence of the above findings, the Court held it to be unnecessary to pronounce any decision on any of the other questions which had been raised by the parties.

And for the reasons above stated, affirmed the judgment of the Circuit Court appealed against, with costs.

SHAW, CHILDREN OF, *vs.* TRUSTEES AND CREDITORS OF.

Proclamation of the 12*th July*, 1822. *Testament.*

It is not necessary, to make a will good under the Proclamation, expressly to declare that the testation is under its provisions.

The facts of this case were as follows: John Edward Shaw and Anne Shaw, both natives of Ireland, were married at Dublin in 1814, and in 1820 came to this Colony as settlers. In 1841, John E. Shaw died, leaving the said Anne Shaw and eight children procreated of this marriage him surviving. In 1845, Anne Shaw surrendered her estate as insolvent. The defendants were respectively the trustees of her insolvent estate and creditors who had proved debts against it.

1847. June 8.

Shaw, Children of, *vs.* Trustees and Creditors of.

The plaintiffs were five of the minor children of the marriage, who brought this action through their curator *ad litem*, to recover from the defendants, out of the insolvent estate of their mother, who had taken possession of the whole of her husband's property, the amount of their paternal inheritance; which, according to an inventory made by her after her insolvency of the joint estate of her deceased husband and herself, as at the date of his decease, was alleged to be £242 2s. 11d.

The defendants pleaded the general issue; and specially

that on the 26th July, 1823, the deceased J. E. Shaw in this Colony "made his last will and testament in a form and of a tenor and effect which under the laws and customs of England would be a good and valid disposition of his estate; which will or devise hath not been revoked or in any manner made void, and by which not any of the said plaintiffs are heirs or legatees, or entitled to any matter or thing whatever," &c., &c. And that under and by virtue of the proclamation of the 12th July, 1822, the said J. E. Shaw was lawfully entitled to make his said will in manner and form and to the effect as the same was made by him.

At the trial, the plaintiff called the said Anne Shaw to prove the amount of the joint estate of her deceased husband and herself, as at the date of his death; but as on her cross-examination she proved that her husband was a natural-born subject of the United Kingdom of Great Britain and Ireland, and that his marriage with her had taken place before he came to this Colony, the Court directed the parties, before proceeding further, to argue the question of law raised in the pleadings founded on the Proclamation of the 12th July, 1822.

Whereupon the defendants put in the will made by J. E. Shaw on the 26th July, 1823, which was admitted by the plaintiffs, and by which the testator devised all his property to his wife, subject to the burden of supporting the two children then existing of the marriage, except certain landed property which he devised to his eldest son on attaining his majority.

Brand, for the plaintiffs, then argued that as Shaw had not in his said will expressly stated that he intended by it to avail himself of the provisions of the Proclamation, he must be presumed, notwithstanding the will, to have intended the succession to his estate to be regulated by the general law of the Colony.

The Court held this argument to be ill-founded; and without calling on the defendants to reply to it, gave judgment for the defendants, with costs.

Bresler *vs.* Kotze's Executors.

Will, construction of. Fidei-commissary institution, extent and effect of. "Children," meaning of word: how construed.

Where a testatrix directed that in the event of her daughter opposing a fidei-commissary disposition of a child's portion in her favour, and demanding her legitimate portion free and unencumbered, the residue of the said child's portion, after deducting the legitimate portion, should go to and devolve upon the children of the said daughter, the grandchildren of the testatrix: HELD, *that this direction extends only to such children as were alive at the death of the testatrix, and not to those born after her death.*

On the 12th August, 1841, the Widow Kotze executed her will, by which she nominated and appointed her seven children, of whom Susanna, then the widow Bresler, now Mrs. de Kock, was one, to be her sole universal heirs to all her estate; and in case of the decease of one or more of them in the lifetime of the testatrix, then the *legitimate descendants* of such child or children shall come into his, her, or their place by representation. The testatrix further declared that she hereby burthened with the entail of *fidei-commissum* the inheritances respectively of her heirs named J. M. Kotze, D. G. Kotze, and the said Susanna, in manner according to law, and to the effect that, upon the decease of them, the aforesaid heirs, their said inheritances shall devolve free and unencumbered on their *legitimate descendants by representation*, &c., &c. The testatrix, moreover, declared it to be her will that in case her aforesaid heirs should oppose this her disposition, with intent to prevent the same from taking effect, then and in that case it was her will that the opposing heir be instituted as heir in the legitimate portion only, to which children are by law entitled from their parents, subject, moreover, to the deduction of all such sums of money as he or she shall happen to be indebted to the estate of testatrix, declaring to revoke and annul, in that event, his or her institution as heir as aforesaid, and that the residue of his or her inheritance shall have to go to and to devolve *on his, her, or their children* (the grandchildren of the testatrix).

She then appointed the defendants to be the executors of her will, administrators of her estate, and of the inheritances burthened with the entail of *fidei-commissum*, and guardians over such of her heirs as shall be minors at the time of her decease.

The testatrix died on the 12th August, 1841. And at the time of her death her daughter Susanna was still a widow, with six children, then all minors, by her deceased husband Bresler, to wit, the plaintiffs F. R. J. Bresler and J. C. J. Bresler, now married in community of property with the plaintiff J. Leibbrandt, three others who are still alive and minors, and Christoffel F. H. Bresler, who died a minor, unmarried and intestate, on the 18th August, 1847. On the 31st August, 1841, Susanna married

1847. Nov. 30. 1848. Jan. 12.

Bresler vs. Kotze's Executors.

her present husband, A. J. de Kock, in community of property. It was alleged—and there seemed grounds for presuming, although it was not proved—that it was her knowledge of this second marriage being about to take place, and her dislike to it, that induced the testatrix to burthen Susanna's inheritance with *fidei-commissum.*

On the liquidation of the estate of the testatrix by the defendants, it was found that the amount of the inheritance under *fidei-commissum* to which Susanna became entitled under her mother's will was £1,480. On the 19th June, 1842, Susanna had a son named Maximilian, and on 28th February, 1845, another child by her present husband, De Kock. At some time previous to the 13th July, but whether before or after the birth of the said Maximilian was not positively proved, De Kock, in his capacity of husband of Susanna, opposed himself and his wife to the *fidei-commissary* disposition aforesaid, by claiming and demanding from the defendants his wife's legitimate portion out of her mother's estate free and unencumbered, which portion, being £720, one half of the said sum of £1,480, was on the 13th July, 1842, paid by the defendants to De Kock, who on that day duly executed a discharge for the same, in which he renounced all claim on the part of his wife to her *fidei-commissary* inheritance under the will.

After they attained majority, the plaintiffs maintained that, in consequence of De Kock and his wife opposing themselves to the *fidei-commissary* disposition by claiming and demanding her free and unencumbered legitimate portion of £720, her nomination as heiress of the remaining half of the *fidei-commissary* inheritance became and was revoked, cancelled, and annulled, and that this remaining half, viz., £720, thereupon devolved to and became vested in her said six children by Bresler, share and share alike. And that, upon the death of their brother Christoffel, his share thereof devolved to his five surviving brothers and sisters of the full blood, whereby the shares and proportions respectively of the said brothers and sisters became one-fifth each of the said sum of £720. And the plaintiffs respectively demanded payment from the defendants of their said one-fifth shares, and on their refusal to pay the same, brought the present action to have them condemned to pay the same with costs, as well in their capacity as executors as individually.

In their plea, the defendants maintained, that both by the terms of the will and by law, the direction of the testatrix,—that in the event of her daughter Susanna opposing the *fidei-commissary* disposition of a child's portion in her favour, and demanding her legitimate portion free and unencumbered, the residue of the said child's portion, after deducting the legitimate portion, should go to and devolve upon the children of the said Susanna, the grandchildren of the testatrix,—is not limited to those of her children only, who were alive at the decease of the testatrix, or at the date of her opposing the *fidei-commissary* disposition and demanding her legitimate portion, but extends to all the lawful children of the said Susanna who were alive at those dates,—have since been born,—and may yet be born of her body; and therefore maintained that the residue aforesaid, instead of any part of it being now paid over to the plaintiffs as prayed, should remain under the administration of the defendants until the death of the said Susanna, or until she shall have arrived at an age at which in law she may be considered unable to procreate any more children, and when the exact number of her children, the grandchildren of testatrix, may be ascertained, and their several portions fixed; defendants nevertheless offering, in the mean time, to pay annually the interest of the said residue to the children of the said Susanna, in such portions as at the time of payment there shall be living children of the said Susanna.

The defendants further maintained, that if the Court should decide that those children only of the said Susanna who were alive at the time of her said opposition to the will and claim for her legitimate portion are entitled to the residue aforesaid, then that her child Maximilian, by her present husband, is also entitled to a share therein. And lastly, they maintained, that the share which had devolved upon her son Christoffel should by law not accrue to the shares of the remaining children, but must, according to the law of intestate inheritance, be divided in the following proportions, to wit, one half thereof to his said mother Susanna, and the other half to his brothers and sisters (Maximilian included) equally.

The *Attorney-General*, for the plaintiffs, argued that the words "*his or her children*" must be construed as if the will had expressly stated "the children in existence at the date of the will, and as may be procreated before the death of the testatrix." That the revocation and annulment of the *fidei-commissary* institution consequent on Susanna's opposing it and claiming her legitimate portion free and unencumbered, drew back to and had effect from the date of the death of the testatrix, without reference to the date of such opposition and claim; and that the question between the parties must be decided as if, on the day after her mother's death, Susanna had renounced

1847. Nov. 30. 1848. Jan. 12.

Bresler *vs.* Kotze's Executors.

the *fidei-commissary* inheritance, and claimed her legitimate portion. Consequently, that although such renunciation and claim might have been made after the birth of Maximilian, no distinction could be made in his favour between his case and that of his brothers and sisters of the full blood, whether at present in existence, or who may hereafter be born.

He quoted *Roper on Legacies, 2nd vol., p.* 248, and maintained, that if the fund in dispute did not immediately vest in the children who were in existence at the death of the testatrix, then it must be held that the testatrix intended that the interest thereof should accumulate, and that the Bresler children should derive no benefit whatever from it before their mother's death or becoming from age incapable of child-bearing, because in that case the defendants would have no legal right to pay over the interest accruing in the mean time to the children in existence, as offered in their plea, but must have accumulated it with the capital, to be divided with it among the children who had been born before the mother's death or incapacity for child-bearing,—an incredible supposition. He quoted *Voet* 18, 17, § 30; *Voet* 36, 1, § 22, 26, 32; *Godfrey vs. Davis, 6th Vesey, p.* 43; *Roper on Legacies, vol.* 1, *p.* 33; *Roberts on Wills, vol.* 1, *p.* 437. He contrasted the words in the clause of the will which created the *fidei-commissum* in favour of Susanna, and on her death to devolve on her *legitimate descendants by representation,* and those in the clause providing for the disposal of the surplus over the amount of the legitimate portion in the event of Susanna's opposing the *fidei-commissary* disposition, where the words used are "shall devolve *on her children,*" contending that the former necessarily implied that the testatrix contemplated a remote succession, and the latter, that she contemplated a succession to take place immediately after her death.

Brand, for the defendants, argued *contra,* and quoted *Voet* 28, 5, § 12, 13; *Van Leeuwen, Cens. For.*, 3, 5, § 8, 9, 10; *Hollandsche Consult.* 98; *New do. do.* 26, 27, 127; *Kersterman's Addition to his Dutch Vocabulary, p.* 454.

Postea (12th January, 1848).—The Court held that defendants had failed to show that there was any general rule established in the law of Holland, that the institution of the children of a daughter as heirs in a will so framed as the one under consideration was, must necessarily in every case be construed to extend not only to such children as were alive at the death of the testator, but to all such as might be born at any time after his death; and that the cases specified in *Voet* 28, 12, § 12 and 13, &c., so far from proving the existence of any such general rule, were there mentioned and treated of as exceptions from the general rule; that when the word "*children*" was used generally, as in the present case, the judge in construing it must be guided by his opinion as to the intention with which the testator had used it, to be gathered from the context of the will and the peculiar circumstances of the case. That in this case it appeared to the Court, both from the context of the will and from its peculiar circumstances, that the residue of the *fidei-commissary* inheritance, after deducting the amount of the legitimate portion, should devolve on Susanna's children who were in existence at the death of the testatrix. And on the authority of *Van der Linden, Inst. p.* 160, the Court held that the share of Christoffel Bresler, on his dying intestate, devolved, one half to his mother and the other half, equally between them, to his brothers and sisters of the full blood. (See also *Tennant's Notary's Manual, pp.* 137 and 319.)

1847. Nov. 30. 1848. Jan. 12.

Bresler *vs.* Kotze's Executors.

The Court therefore gave judgment for the plaintiffs as prayed, except as to the share of their brother Christoffel, of which they adjudged one half to his mother, and the other half to be divided equally between his brothers and sisters-german. And by consent ordered the costs on both sides to be paid out of the mother's half of the share of the deceased Christoffel, and in so far as such costs might exceed the amount of that half, then out of the other half.

LUDWIG *vs.* LUDWIG'S EXECUTORS.

Mutual will: what does not revoke.

A mutual will by a husband and wife is valid and effectual as the will of the surviving husband, notwithstanding his having married a second wife in community of property.

A will is not invalidated by parole evidence that the testator declared himself to be intestate.

1848. Dec. 20.

Ludwig *vs.* Ludwig's Executors.

The facts of this case were as follows: On the 17th February, 1840, Baron Ludwig and his first wife, Alida, previously the Widow Altenstaedt, executed a mutual will before a notary. The said Alida died on the 23rd February, 1840, leaving one daughter by her former marriage, and four children by her husband Baron Ludwig. The mutual will was then duly enregistered, and her estate was duly administered under and according to her said will.

1848. Dec. 20.

Ludwig *vs.* Ludwig's Executors.

On the 8th June, 1847, Baron Ludwig married Eliza Griffith in community of property, and on the 27th December, 1847, died, leaving the said four children of his former marriage him surviving, but without any issue by his second marriage.

The mutual will having been, as above mentioned, placed in the register of wills, and no copy of, or document alluding to it, having been found in the repositories of the testator, its existence was unknown to, or forgotten by, his children and friends, and he was by them, and by the Master of the Supreme Court, believed to have died intestate, and accordingly, the defendants, P. M. Brink and the surviving widow, were appointed executors dative of his estate in regular form. These executors liquidated the joint estate of the testator and his surviving widow, and were proceeding to distribute his half of it according to the law of intestate succession, when the existence of the mutual will became known. An application was made to the Supreme Court to have it enregistered of new as the will of the testator, but the Court refused the application holding that a second registration was not required by law, and was unnecessary.

In this will the surviving spouse was appointed reciprocally as the executor or executrix of the will of the predeceased spouse, but there was no nomination of executors of the will of the surviving spouse on his or her death.

As the defendants had completed the liquidation of the estate, it was, in order to save expense, agreed upon by all parties that the defendants should be considered as if they had been appointed executors dative of this will, or alleged will, of the testator.

By the provisions of the will, the plaintiff, who was one of the sons of the first marriage, for certain reasons therein contained, was instituted as heir only to his legitimate portion as one of the children of the testator, and the defendants accordingly framed a plan of distribution of the testator's estate, and in it assigned to the plaintiff only his legitimate portion, instead of his filial portion.

The plaintiff therefore brought this action against the defendants, and in his declaration alleged the facts above set forth, and prayed that it might be declared by the judgment of the Court, that the will aforesaid was in law the will only of the said Alida, the first dying of the spouses, and that the said Baron Ludwig died intestate; that his estate ought to be administered as that of an intestate; and that the plan of distribution thereof aforesaid should be amended by awarding to the plaintiff a filial instead of his legitimate portion, for the following grounds and reasons: 1st. Because after the execution of the said mutual will, the said Baron Ludwig never made or executed any manner of will or testamentary writing whatever; 2ndly. Because according to the proper construction and true intent and meaning of the said will, and of its several provisions, it only took effect as the will of the first dying spouse (who proved to be the said Alida) and never was valid or effectual as the last will of the survivor, the said Baron Ludwig; 3rdly. Because the said will, even if it had after the death of his first spouse continued to be his will as such survivor, was wholly revoked and avoided by his secand marriage in community of property, whereby such a change was wrought in his circumstances as by law amounted to such revocation; 4thly. Because the said Baron Ludwig, after his second marriage, deemed, considered, and openly declared himself to be intestate, and to have no existing will; and was so considered by his family and others.

The defendants pleaded the general issue.

At the trial the parties admitted all the facts above narrated.

The *Attorney-General* was proceeding to call witnesses to prove the allegations on which the fourth reason for the invalidity of the will was founded, but the Court without hearing the defendants' counsel stopped him, on the ground that such evidence was inadmissible, as being utterly irrelevant, seeing that the clearest parole proof that the testator had declared that he considered—or even, if that were possible, that he had really and truly believed—himself to be intestate and to have no will in existence, would in law have no effect whatever in invalidating, to any extent, a will which had been legally executed by him, and had not afterwards been revoked.

In support of the second reason set forth in the declaration, the *Attorney-General* maintained that the will in question, being the mutual will of the two spouses, was a contingent will, depending on the chance of predecease, and intended to be only the will of the first dying, and that such a will may lawfully and effectually be made.

He founded on the clause in the will providing that "in order to ascertain the portions of the heirs instituted on either side, within six weeks after the death of either of them, their joint estate shall be inventoried, &c., and the property not specially disposed of by these presents shall be appraised by two persons, one to be chosen by the survivor, and the other by their children;" and the fact that no provision was made for any mode of appraisement after the death of the survivor;—and on the fact that the will contained no nomination of any executors of the will of the

1848. Dec. 20.

Ludwig *vs.* Ludwig's Executors.

survivor, while the testator and testatrix were reciprocally nominated as executor or executrix of the will of the predeceasing spouse,—as clearly showing that the will was intended to apply to and regulate only the estate of the predeceasing spouse, and not that of the survivor. He referred to the clause in the will in which "the testator further declared it to be his will and desire, in case he should be the first dying," that the insignia of certain German orders which had been conferred on him by German Princes should after his death be returned to the respective Chancellors of those orders, and to the fact that no directions whatever were given as to the disposal of those insignia in the event of his being the survivor, and maintained that the direction that the insignia should be sent to the German Chancellors is one in its nature totally unconnected with the contingency or condition of his being the first dying, and therefore this condition ought to be read parenthetically and construed as governing not merely the disposal of the insignia, but as intended to overreach and govern the institution of heirs and other testamentary dispositions of the will.

In support of the third reason set forth in the declaration, he referred, first, to the rule of the law of England previous to the passing of the statute of Victoria, namely, that when a woman married, her marriage operated in law as a total revocation of any previous will (*Williams on Excutors, 1st vol., p.* 103); and that although marriage by itself did not operate as the revocation of the previous will of a man, yet that marriage with the birth of a surviving child did so operate. That now, by the statute of the 1*st Victoria, cap.* 26, § 18, it was enacted that every will made either by a man or a woman shall be revoked by his or her subsequent marriage. He referred to the *Mirror of Parliament, vol.* 1, 1837, 1838, *p.* 383, and *Peckius de Testamen., cap.* 45, *No.* 1 *to No.* 9; and maintained that a man's marriage in community of property works such a change in his condition and circumstances as is by the Roman-Dutch law deemed sufficient to operate as a total revocation of his previous will. He quoted *Van der Linden, Inst. p.* 156; *Burge, vol.* 4, *p.* 512; *Van Zutphen, Hollandsche Practyk, p.* 574; and *Voet,* 4, 5, § 1,—28, 3, § 12.

The Court, without calling on *Ebden* and *Watermeyer,* counsel for the defendants, held that the plaintiff had failed to produce any authority sufficient to prove that a mutual will by a husband and wife is not valid and effectual as the will of the surviving husband on his death, even although he shall, subsequently to executing that will, have married a second wife in community of property. And gave judgment for defendants. Each party to pay their own costs.

CHAPTER II.

SUCCESSION AB-INTESTATO.

[INTESTATE SUCCESSION.]

ROCHE BLANCHE, HUSBAND OF PAS, *vs.* THE WIDOW OF J. J. PAS AND THE CURATOR AD LITEM OF J. J. P. ROCHE BLANCHE.

Deed, what not due execution of. Testament.

A and B made a will which was informally executed and admittedly void. Plaintiff and his wife (daughter of A and B) had subsequently to their death signed a paper approving, as far as they were concerned, of this informal will. But it being proved that they acted in ignorance, the estate of A and B was declared intestate.

1838. Nov. 29.

Roche Blanche, Husband of Pas, *vs.* The Widow of J. J. Pas and the Curator *ad litem* of J. J. P. Roche Blanche.

J. J. Pas and his wife the defendant had a daughter Margaret married to plaintiff, by whom she had a son, the second defendant.

J. J. Pas died on the 30th November, 1836. Thereafter his widow, in respect of a will, dated 19th November, 1836, alleged to have been executed by J. J. Pas in favour of plaintiff's son, and appointing his widow executrix, and of a certain writing, dated 27th January, 1837, signed by plaintiff and his wife, obtained letters of administration from the Master of the Supreme Court, as executrix testamentary of the deceased. Thereafter the plaintiff brought this action to have it declared that the said J. J. Pas died intestate, and that plaintiff, in right of his wife, was heir to the separate estate of said Pas.

It was admitted by defendants that the alleged will, which had been drawn by and executed under the direction of an ignorant person, one Needham, a justice of the peace at Caledon, was null and void, in respect that it had not been attested by the proper number of witnesses required by law. But the defendants pleaded that plaintiff and his said wife were barred and foreclosed in law from disputing or calling in question the validity of said will, by reason that plaintiff and his said wife had, on the 27th January, 1837, signed the writing above mentioned, whereby they agreed, allowed, and consented, in as far as regarded

1838. Nov. 29. — Roche Blanche, Husband of Pas, *vs.* The Widow of J. J. Pas and the Curator *ad litem* of J. J. P. Roche Blanche.

themselves, that the said will of the 19th November, 1836, should be as valid in law as if the same had been drawn by a notary or witnessed by seven persons, at the same time thereby ratifying and confirming all that was contained in the said will. This writing, which was put in by defendants, was in English.

At the trial it was proved by J. P. Eksteen that he had signed said writing as a witness after seeing it signed by plaintiff and his wife. That Needham brought it to them ready drawn out to be signed by them. That he did not hear that writing read over to them or explained, nor did he know its contents, but that Needham told them it was their will.

Needham stated that the said writing was written by him at the request of plaintiff's wife, who said she had orders to that effect from her mother, the first defendant, and that she wished it to be so drawn up as that her son the second defendant should be heir to the property according to the will. That plaintiff had never given him any instruction to draw up this writing, that he had not read this writing to plaintiff (who does not understand English), before he signed it. That he had explained the nature of it to him, but did not translate the whole of it to him, only explained its purport.

The Court adjudged that the deceased Pas died intestate, and ordered the costs of all parties to be paid out of his estate.

Spies *vs.* Spies.

Succession, intestate.

The North Holland law, including the Political Ordinance of the States General of 1st *April,* 1580, *and the Interpreting Ordinance of* 13*th May,* 1594, *is the law of this Colony in intestate succession.*

1846. Aug. 27. — Spies *vs.* Spies.

This action arose out of the following circumstances:

Anna Barbara Klein, widow of J. Rockenbach, died in this Colony on the 13th October, 1832, intestate, and leaving neither children, parents, brothers or sisters, nor any of their descendants alive. At the time of her death there existed,—

1. Two of her aunts, Carolina Spies, the plaintiff, and Susannah Spies, the mother of Kasper Michael, the plaintiff.

2. Tobias Wolf, son of her predeceased aunt A. M. Spies.

3. Two grandchildren of her predeceased uncle A. C. Spies, through his daughter J. C. Spies.

4. Nine grandchildren of her said uncle A. C. Spies, through his son E. B. Spies.

5. One grandson of her said uncle A. C. Spies, through his daughter A. B. Spies.

6. One granddaughter of her predeceased paternal uncle E. L. Klein.

It did not appear from the pleadings, or the statements of counsel, whether J. E. Spies, G. E. Spies, and A. B. Spies, the son and daughters of the said uncle A. C. Spies, were themselves alive at the death of their cousin the Widow Rockenbach.

The aunt Susanna died on the 27th October, 1833, and was represented by her only son and heir, the plaintiff, Kasper Michael.

Questions having arisen whether the estate of the deceased intestate Widow Rockenbach should be distributed solely between her two surviving aunts *per capita,* or whether the children of her predeceased uncle and aunt were entitled to share equally, but *per stirpes* with the two surviving aunts; and lastly, whether the grandchildren of the predeceased uncle and aunt—if their parents J. C. Spies, G. E. Spies, and A. B. Spies, had also predeceased the widow—were entitled to share *per stirpes,* as their said parents would have been entitled to do if they had survived the widow,—this amicable action was brought in order to obtain the decree of the Court on those questions.

The Counsel for both parties, *Brand* and *Ebden,* admitted that by the Placaat of 10th January, 1661, the law of North Holland, including the Political Ordinance of 1st April, 1580, and the Interpreting Ordinance of 13th May, 1594, was made the law of this Colony. (*Vide Tennant's Notary's Manual, p.* 132.)

The Court, in respect of the 28th section of the said Ordinance of 1580, and of the authority of *Van der Linden's Institutes* (*B.* 1, *C.* 10, § 2; *p.* 163, *Engl. Ed.*), and the 51st Consultation of the *Nederlandsche Advys Book,* adjudged that the estate of the Widow Rockenbach must be distributed with reference to the state of her next kin as on the day of her death.

2nd. That, for this purpose, it must be divided into as many shares as she had aunts surviving on that day, and uncles and aunts who, having predeceased her, had left children surviving on that day.

3rd. That her said aunts were each entitled to a share *per capita,* and her said cousins to the remaining shares *per stirpes.*

1846. Aug. 27. Spies *vs.* Spies.

4th. That the children of her surviving aunt who had since died, and the children of such of her said surviving cousins who had since died, were now entitled, as the heirs of the said deceased parents, to such share as those parents would respectively have been entitled to claim if they were now alive.

5th. That the children of her cousins, whose grandparents and parents had predeceased her, were not entitled to claim any share of her estate.

Judgment was given accordingly. All costs to be paid out of the estate.

CHAPTER III.

EXECUTORS.

HORN *vs.* LOEDOLFF ET UXOR.

Whether non-lodgment of a claim in the estate of a deceased person is a bar to creditors claiming from executor still having assets. [Not decided; but in *Moore's Executrix vs. Le Sueur, post,* held not.] 1830. Jan. 12.

[Vol. 1, p. 403.]

BRINK *vs.* ESTERHUIZEN.

Executor having distributed estate, his liability ceases. 1830. Sept. 16.

[Vol. 1, p. 473.]

SMUTS *vs.* HAUPT'S EXECUTORS.

When a bond stipulates three months' notice it does not become payable on demand on the debtor's death; but notice must be given to his executors. 1833. Dec. 17.

[Vol. 1, p. 70.]

MUTER & STONE *vs.* SPANGENBERG.

Executors. Title to sue. Ordinance 104.

Executors not having taken out formal letters of registration not entitled to sue.

Cloete this day, in support of his clients' title as executors of Scoon to sue the defendant, produced the will, by which they were appointed executors. 1834. June 3. Muter & Stone *vs.* Spangenberg.

To this it was objected by the *Attorney-General* for the defendant, that the will had not been registered in the

1834. June 3. — Muter & Stone vs. Spangenberg.

Orphan Chamber before the abolition thereof, in terms of the 16th Article of the Instructions, and that although it had yesterday been enregistered in the Register of Wills, yet as the plaintiffs had not obtained letters of administration, they were not entitled to sue as executors.

Summons dismissed with costs.

FOUCHE *vs.* MEYER, AS EXECUTOR, AND CILLIERS, AS WIDOW AND EXECUTRIX, OF THE LATE P. J. FOUCHE.

Surviving spouse. Mutual will. Executrix. Exceptionon qualificatæ.

A surviving spouse appointed executrix under a mutual will, but who has not yet acted in that capacity, may decline to act.

1835. Aug. 13. — Fouche vs. Meyer, as Executor, and Cilliers, as Widow and Executrix, of the late P. J. Fouche.

This action was brought against Meyer, as executor, and against Cilliers, as widow and executrix, of the late P. J. Fouche.

The widow filed the following plea: "The defendant M. Cilliers denies the qualification or capacity of executrix of the late Philippus Jacobus Fouche, assigned to her by the said declaration, and by which she is sued, and saith she is not such executrix as aforesaid, and thereupon joins issue with the said plaintiff, and prays that the costs of suit may be paid to her."

Cloete, for the plaintiff, in order to prove the capacity of the defendant Cilliers, as executrix, produced the joint will of the deceased Fouche and his wife, dated 29th June, 1825, whereby the testators nominated and appointed "the survivor of them as the executor of this their will, administrator of their estate, as well as guardian of their minor heirs," &c., &c., and a codicil thereto, dated 29th June, 1828, whereby the testators, "in virtue of the reservatory clause in their will, declare to nominate and appoint Messrs. J. H. Meyer and J. de la Harpe as the executors of this our will, and guardians over our minor heirs, grant to them all such powers as can or may, according to law, be granted to them, and especially the power of assumption and surrogation, under promise of approbation and ratification under pledge according to law."

And another codicil, dated 11th May, 1831, whereby the testators declare "the first codicil to this our will, wherein we have appointed Messrs. J. de la Harpe and J. H.

Meyer, as executors and guardians over our minor heirs, to be null and void, desiring that the same shall not have any force or effect, and appoint in their stead, and we, the undersigned testators, do declare thereto to nominate and appoint Mr. A. M. Meyer and our eldest son, P. J. Fouche, to be executors of our estate, administrators of the same, and guardians over our minor heirs, granting to the said A. M. Meyer and P. J. Fouche all such power and authority as can or may, according to the law," &c.

1835. Aug. 13.

Fouche *vs.* Meyer, as Executor, and Cilliers, as Widow and Executrix, of the late P. J. Fouche.

Cloete maintained that, notwithstanding those codicils, the defendant continued to be a joint executrix with the others by the last codicil.

The *Attorney-General* maintained, first, that although there was no express revocation in either of the codicils of the appointment of the survivor to be executor, yet that the new appointment of executors in the codicils had the effect of revoking the appointment of the survivor; and secondly, that, even although such appointment were not revoked, yet that the defendant might decline to act as executrix; and as she had never acted as such, and now signified her refusal to accept the office, she could not be compelled to be a party to this action.

As the plaintiff was not prepared to prove that defendant had ever acted as executrix, the Court, without deciding the first point raised by the Attorney-General, in respect of the second ground of defence stated by him sustained the exception, with costs.

In Re Hoets.—Executors of *vs.* Heirs of.

Ord. No. 104, § 20. *Letters of administration. Executor. Master, power of to withhold letters of administration under above section. Interdict.*

H. died, leaving a close will, and appointing certain executors. His heirs objected to the issue by the Master of letters of administration on the ground that they intended to have the will set aside "for want of solemnities required by the law of this country in closed or sealed wills." The Master withheld letters of administration; but on application by the executors, the majority of the Court (Wylde, C.J., *and* Kekewich; Menzies, J., dis.) *held that such an objection was not one of those referred to by Ordinance* 104, § 20, *and directed the Master to grant letters of administration accordingly.*

Postea, the heirs (before taking any legal proceedings by action) applied for an interdict to restrain the executors administering until the question of the validity of the will had been decided. But the Court unanimously refused the interdict, intimating, however, that after summons issued or declaration filed, an interdict would be granted on proof of injury to the estate from the executor's administration.

1836. May 27. " 30. " 31.

In re Hoets.—Executors of *vs.* Heirs of.

Cloete, for himself and three others, alleged to have been appointed by the will of the deceased Hoets the executors of his will, produced the following affidavit:

"H. Cloete, L.son, of Cape Town, maketh oath and saith that deponent was present on the 25th instant, at the office of the Master of the Supreme Court, when a sealed packet was delivered to the said Master by or on the part of Mr. J. N. Ley, as having been *curator* to the person and one of the curators of the estate of the said late J. Hoets; that the seals having been removed by the Master, the same was found to contain the last will of the said late J. Hoets, with a notarial deed of superscription attested by the notary J. N. Meeser and witnesses, bearing date 8th day of July, 1831, and a further notarial codicil, bearing date 15th September, 1834.

"That after a perusal and examination of the said documents, the Master of the said Court declared, upon the application of this deponent, as one of the executors named in the above-mentioned will, that the said will and codicil would be duly registered, and that letters of administration would be immediately granted to the executors named in the said will and codicil.

"That the deponent, together with his co-executors, J. G. Blankenberg, J. H. Lezar, and W. Udemans, upon the assurance that the said letters would be issued the instant they were drawn out on stamp, and understanding that none of the heirs of the said late J. Hoets resided in the house in which the deceased had died, deemed it essential for the interest of the estate to cause seals to be placed on the stores, rooms, wardrobes, presses, strong-box, and other places, which might contain articles of value belonging to the estate.

"That in the afternoon of the same day, the deponent having called at the office of the Master of the Supreme Court, he was then informed that the said letters of administration would not be granted, by reason of a letter received by him on the part of some of the heirs in the estate, setting forth that they objected to the said will and codicil, upon the ground of certain alleged but undefined legal informalities, and that the Master of the Supreme Court has this day appointed Messrs. J. C. Chase, P. M. Brink, and J. N. Ley, as *curators bonis* to the said estate.

1836. May 27. " 30. " 31.

In re Hoets.—Executors of *vs.* Heirs of.

"H. CLOETE, L.SON.

"Cape Town, 27th May, 1836."

And moved the Court that the Master of the Supreme Court should be ordered by the Court to grant them letters of administration in respect of the will of the deceased, which they had lodged for registration with the Master, in terms of the Ordinance No. 104.

It appeared that the following letter from the attorney of the children of the deceased, objecting to such letters of administration had been lodged with the Master:

"Cape Town, May 25, 1836.

"SIR,—I have the honour to inform you, on behalf of the children of the late John Hoets, that they intend (and that I have been instructed accordingly) to set aside the will of the said late J. Hoets, on account of the want of the solemnities required by the laws of this country in closed or sealed wills; and as the question is intended to be brought before the Supreme Court before the end of this term, I beg you will be pleased not to grant letters of administration to the executors appointed by the said will until the Supreme Court shall have decided thereon.

"I have, &c.

"J. P. DE WET, Attorney.

"To CLERKE BURTON, Esq.,
"Master of the Supreme Court."

Cloete objected that this letter was not sufficient, under the Ordinance No. 104, § 20, to warrant the Master to withhold letters of administration, as it did not specify *in gremio* any particular objection sufficient in law to render the will null, or bar the claim for administration, on which the objectors ground their opposition. [WYLDE, C.J., expressed his opinion to be in favour of *Cloete's* objection. MENZIES, J., was of the contrary opinion. KEKEWICH, J., did not express his opinion.] No decision was given on this point, as the parties stated they were prepared at once to argue on the objections to the validity of the will.

Brand then objected that the will was invalid, in respect that being a sealed will, the notarial superscription was not attested by the signature of any notary; and secondly, that at the time, when even the first part of it was said to have

1836. May 27. „ 30. „ 31.

In re Hoets.—Executors of *vs.* Heirs of.

been executed, the deceased was in such a state of blindness as legally to incapacitate him from executing a testament in the manner, in which this testament had been executed, and quoted *Voet* 28, 1, 26, 28, 37.

Cloete, contra, maintained that the want of the subscription of the notary was not such a defect as to violate the will, and that the notary might now affix his subscription. That whatever in the ordinary case might have been the effect of the want of the notary's subscription on the envelope, yet in this case this deficiency could not affect the will of the testator, because, within the envelope which wanted the notary's subscription, there was another envelope properly sealed and attested, and subscribed by the deceased, the witnesses, and a notary, in which the testament was enveloped, which circumstance was sufficient to cure the defect in the outer envelope, and that the two subsequent codicils, although not enclosed in that inner envelope, referred to and were connected with that testament, in such a way as to render them valid, notwithstanding the defect in the outer envelope enclosing them. He denied the fact of the testator's blindness.

Brand replied. The inner envelope mentioned had no doubt once been duly sealed, witnessed, and subscribed, and if it had been found sealed when the outer envelope was opened, might have been sufficient for the validity of the will enclosed in it; but the fact was, that this inner envelope was, in opening the outer envelope, found to be open, with all the seals broken, so that it was of no use, and could not have any effect in authenticating any papers then found within it; the identification and authentication of which as the will of the deceased, and as being the will originally enclosed in the inner envelope, therefore depended wholly on the effect of the outer envelope, which, wanting the subscription of the notary, was deficient in a legal solemnity essential to its validity, and was consequently totally inoperative.

The further hearing was postponed until the 30th instant.

This day (30th May, 1836), the *Attorney-General* for Mr. Rynier Hoets, one of the children of the deceased, maintained that the will was void for three reasons, and that the deceased therefore died intestate. 1st. That at the respective times when the deceased made all the testamentary documents produced, he was not in a state of mind in which he could legally make any will. 2nd. That at the said times he laboured under such a degree of blindness as legally to incapacitate him from making a closed will. 3rd. That even if he had mental and bodily capacity to make a will, still that this will was void by reason of the want of the notary's superscription; and in support of the two first reasons, he tendered affidavits.

1836. May 27. „ 30. „ 31.

In re Hoets.—Executors of *vs.* Heirs of.

Cloete objected that the other parties could only now be permitted to support the objection taken in their letter, and could not now make or support any other objections.

The Court here intimated that it was desirable that the question as to the meaning and effect of the 20th section of the Ordinance No. 104, which was mooted on the 27th instant, should be argued and determined in the first instance.

The *Attorney-General* and *Brand* for the other heirs of the deceased then contended that the attorney's letter was sufficient to warrant, and make it the duty of the Master to withhold the letters of administration, even if it had been more general than it is, and maintained that the objection referred to in the attorney's letter to the Master, and which the Attorney-General had now stated as the third objection to the validity of the will, was an objection to that deed, in respect of the statement of which by writing lodged at the office of the Master, the 20th section of the Ordinance No. 104 had provided that letters of administration shall not be granted, until the validity and legal effect of such deed shall have been determined by the judgment of some competent Court, or until the objection shall have been withdrawn, and that this objection had, for the purposes of the said 20th section, been sufficiently specified in the attorney's letter of the 25th of May.

Cloete argued *contra.*

Menzies, J., entirely concurred in both the propositions maintained by the Attorney-General and Mr. Brand, and held that this was one of the class of cases to which the provisions of the 20th section had particularly been intended to apply.

Wylde, C.J., and Kekewich, J., held that the objection to the validity of the deed referred to in the attorney's letter was not an objection of the nature of those to which the provisions of the 20th section applied, and that the only objections to which those provisions applied were objections which did not relate to the validity of the deed as a deed, but which, on the assumption that the deed was a valid deed, related to the validity or effect of the clause in such deed, in virtue of which clause the parties whose claim to letters of administration was opposed claimed the right to have such letters granted to them, or to objections personal to such claimants. The Chief Justice stated that in his opinion, even if the ground on which the deed, by virtue whereof any person claimed to be the testa-

1836. May 27. „ 30. „ 31.

In re Hoets.—Executors of *vs.* Heirs of.

mentary executors of any person deceased, was objected to as not in law sufficient to warrant and support such claims, was that such deed was a forgery, and although such objection were supported by the strongest affidavits, that still such an objection, stated in writing, and lodged at the office of the Master, would not be sufficient to stop the granting of letters of administration to the persons claiming under such deed. They also held that, if the objection referred to in the attorney's letter had been a sufficient objection, the statement of it was not sufficiently specific.

The judgment of the Court was (MENZIES, J., *dissentiente*) that the Master be ordered forthwith to grant letters of administration to the executors named by the testator, in respect that the objection, as stated in the letter of the 25th May, lodged at the Master's office, is not sufficient to stay the grant of such letters.

Postea (31st May, 1836).—The *Attorney-General* moved for an interdict upon the following notice of motion:

"Gentlemen,—Please to take notice that this Court will be moved, on behalf of R. C. Hoets and the other children of J. Hoets, Esq,, deceased, on the morning of the 31st instant, or so soon after as counsel can be heard, at which time you are to show cause (if any) to the contrary, why you and each of you shall not be interdicted by the order of this Court from interfering or intermeddling with the estate of J. Hoets deceased, on the ground that by virtue of the closed will and codicils, by virtue whereof you have obtained letters of administration, are not in law sufficient to warrant and support such appointment, and also for the following amongst other reasons:

"1st. Because at the time of the making all the writings testamentary, the said J. Hoets was of unsound mind, memory, and understanding;

"2nd. Because the said Hoets, at the time of making the said deed testamentary, was in such a state of blindness that he could not in law make a closed will; and

"3rd. Because the superscription will is not signed and attested by the notary before whom it professes to have been passed, and is therefore wanting in its legal solemnities,—the said interdict to have effect and stand good, until the validity or invalidity of the said testamentary deeds shall be decided by this Court.

"To H. CLOETE, L.son, J. G. BLANKENBERG, J. H. LEZAR, and W. UDEMANS, executors of the said late J. HOETS, or Messrs. TRUTER and MEESER, their attorneys."

1836. May 27. „ 31. „ 31. *In re* Hoets.—Executors of *vs.* Heirs of.

MENZIES, J., was of opinion that, as the effect of the judgment given by the majority of the Court on the 30th May was to find that, in virtue of the deed which had been lodged with the Master as the last will of the deceased, the respondents were entitled to have letters of administration granted to them, notwithstanding the objections which had been stated to the validity of that deed, that the allegation of the facts on which those objections were founded, or of any other, which being proved on the trial of the cause would be sufficient to set aside the deed as invalid, although supported by the strongest affidavits as to the truth of such allegations, was not *per se* a sufficient ground for interdicting the respondents from exercising the office of testamentary executors. That to found an application for such an interdict, it would be necessary to produce affidavits showing that, from circumstances personal to the respondents, their being permitted to exercise the office of executors while the question as to the validity of the deed was pending would be injurious or highly dangerous to the interests of those having claims on the estate of the deceased, and that, except some case of extraordinary emergency were shown to exist, the Court would not entertain any application for an interdict, even supported by such lastmentioned affidavits, until the applicants had filed their declaration, or at least served the summons in an action for setting aside the deed as invalid.

The other two Judges took the same view of the case.

The Court therefore refused the application with costs.

But at the same time intimated an opinion that a very slight case only would be required to be made out to support an application for an interdict to restrain the respondents from paying away or disposing of the funds of the estate, during the pending of the proceedings for trying the question as to the validity of the deed, in any way which might be prejudicial to the interests of any of the parties in whose favour such question might ultimately be decided.

Klerk, Executor of Bantjes, *vs.* Mostert.

Interest. Executor. Heir, overpayment to. Estoppal.

Where an executor overpaid the estate heirs, held that they were bound not only to reeoup to the executor the amount so overpaid, but likewise the interest thereon.

1838. Nov. 30. — Klerk, Executor of Bantjes, *vs.* Mostert.

Mrs. Andrews died in 1800, leaving her estate indebted to her daughter, married to Ackerman, Rds. 2,072, for her paternal inheritance, and having appointed Bantjes her executor. In 1804, Bantjes remitted to Ackerman Rds. 333, and also informed him of the total amount due to him. Some correspondence took place prior to 1806 between Bantjes and Ackerman about remitting the balance to Ackerman, but it was not remitted.

Bantjes and his wife appointed the plaintiff the executor of their will, and died, the former in 1814, and the latter prior to 1816.

The plaintiff administered their estate as executor, and in the inventary thereof entered the balance still unpaid to Ackerman as a debt due by the estate.

The plaintiff liquidated the estate in 1816 and 1817, when he paid over in equal portions (viz., Rds. 4,210 to each), to defendant in right of his wife, and to one F. J. Bantjes, who, with defendant's wife, were the sole heirs to the estate, the whole amount of the net proceeds, without retaining any part to discharge the debt due to Ackerman.

In 1835, the heirs of Ackerman demanded from, and were paid by, the plaintiff the balance, being Rds. 1,739, which had been due to Ackerman, with as much of the interest thereon from 1800 as could by law be claimed, namely, an amount equal to the capital, in whole amounting to Rds. 3,478.

The plaintiff in this action sued the defendant for one half of the said accumulated sum of Rds. 3,478, in respect of the overpayment which he had made to defendant in 1816, 1817.

The defendant admitted his liability to repay plaintiff one half of the capital sum which had been paid by him to Ackerman's heirs, but refused to pay one half of the interest which had been paid thereon, on the grounds—first, that Ackerman could have claimed no interest from Bantjes in his lifetime, and, therefore the interest which plaintiff had paid to his heirs had not been due by Bantjes' estate to them, and had been paid by plaintiff in his own wrong; secondly, that plaintiff by not remitting or retaining out of Bantjes' estate in 1816, 1817 the amount due to Ackerman or his heirs had committed a breach of duty, by reason of which he was barred in law from now claiming from defendant and his co-heir any sum which he had paid on account of interest for the period since 1816, even although Ackerman's representatives were entitled to enforce payment of that interest from the plaintiff. 1838. Nov. 30. Klerk, Executor of Bantjes, *vs.* Mostert.

The Court held that both the positions maintained by defendant were untenable, and gave judgment for plaintiff as prayed, with costs.

Brand *vs.* Neethling's Executor.

Executor, acquittance to. Liquidation account, action to re-open and debate. Error, relief against. Læsio enormis. Restitutio in integrum, to minor.

Where an heir, on attaining majority, gave the executor a receipt and acquittance, but afterwards found that the account framed by the executor, on the basis of which she had been paid, was wrong, and ten years after majority brought an action to re-open and debate such account on the ground of læsio enormis and her right to restitutio in integrum, the account was opened and amended accordingly.

A. Munnik and his wife, E. M. Hurter, by their joint will, dated 7th May, 1811, appointed the plaintiff's wife (with whom plaintiff is married in community of property) and her brothers and sisters their sole and universal heirs, under burden of certain legacies, and also appointed the late J. H. Neethling (whose executor the defendant is) and one C. Gie to be their executors and guardians of their minor heirs. The said E. M. Hurter died in June, 1811, and the said Munnik in November, 1815, when the said Neethling and Gie assumed the management of the estate as executors and *quoad hoc* guardians of plaintiff's wife and her brothers and sisters, then minors, and under the natural guardianship of their father, J. G. Munnik. Gie died in 1818, and Neethling became the sole executor and guardian aforesaid. 1839. May 10. Brand *vs.* Neethling's Executor.

In 1816 he and Gie had framed a provisional account dated 7th September, 1816, which was signed by the said J. G. Munnik. Plaintiff's wife became of age on the 26th June, 1829, and on the 13th January, 1830, said Neethling paid her Rds. 7,711, as and for her share of her inheritance under said will, which he alleged to have been ascertained by the said provisional liquidation account, and obtained from her a notarial deed dated 13th January, 1830, *inter alia* setting forth that she having attained the legal age of majority, "however, as far as need be assisted by her father, J. G. Munnik,

1839. May 10. — Brand *vs.* Neethling's Executor.

and her maternal uncles, Messrs. Hurter and De Wet, declared after having had the desired inspection of the will, &c. (dated 7th May, 1811), as also of the statement and inventory of the estate, framed 4th November, 1815, extract of vendue rolls of 12th and 13th December, 1815, and further documents belonging to the estate, likewise the provisional account of the estate framed, &c., on the 7th September, 1816, and afterwards examined and approved by her said father, whereby is appertaining to the heirs a sum of Rds. 53,981, of which one seventh part, Rds. 7,711, appertains to her as collateral inheritance. She, the appearer, further declared to have received from said Neethling as the only surviving testamentary executor, the beforementioned sum of Rds. 7,711, and *acquitting and discharging the said J. H. Neethling, on her part, from all further claim and demand respecting that administration, with indemnification under obligation* according to law, under the renunciation of the exceptions revision of account and *error calculi.*

(Signed) "A. F. W. MUNNIK.
"J. G. MUNNIK."

J. H. Munnik, one of the brothers of plaintiff's wife, became of age in March, 1837, and suspecting that the liquidation account of 1816 was not correct, refused to receive his share of inheritance according to it, brought an action against the said J. H. Neethling to account for the administration and for the inheritance due to him, Munnik, in which he proved the said liquidation account to be erroneous and untrue to the extent of many thousand rixdollars, and recovered judgment against Neethling for a much larger sum than that tendered by him.

Whereupon the plaintiff brought the present action against the defendant, executor of the said J. Neethling, now deceased, and in his declaration set out all the errors and omissions in the liquidation account of 1816, which, in his wife's brother's action had been proved to exist, alleged that his wife had signed the acquittance in error and ignorance, and trusting to the repeated representations of the guardian, the said J. H. Neethling, that the said liquidation account was correct, without either having examined or perused the vouchers belonging to the said account, as untruly alleged in said acquittance; and without having been duly made acquainted with the meaning of the said acquittance, except by the representation of the said J. H. Neethling that the same was a receipt for her inheritance, and that by reason of the premises, and of the *enormis læsio* of the said plaintiff's wife in her inheritance,

1839. May 10. Brand *vs.* Neethling's Executor.

by reason thereof, the plaintiff is entitled by law to a *restitution in integrum* of and relief from the effect of the approbation of the said liquidation account given by his wife, and of the said receipt and discharge so granted by her under the error, ignorance, and false representation aforesaid; and to have the said account of September, 1816, reopened and debated, and to recover such amount as shall therein appear to have been due to her.

In the plea the defendant admitted the existence of all the errors and omissions alleged in the declaration to exist in the liquidation account of September, 1816, according to which plaintiff's wife's share of the inheritance had been calculated and received by her, and every other allegation therein contained, except that plaintiff's wife signed the receipt of acquittance in error and ignorance as to the correctness of the account, without having perused the vouchers, &c., and without having been duly made acquainted with the force and effect of the said deed; and save and except that she suffered *enormis læsio,* and save and except that plaintiff is by law entitled to *restitutio in integrum* and relief from the effect of her said approbation of said account, and from the receipt and discharge, all which defendant denies.

And for a further plea defendant says that the several alleged causes of action within said declaration mentioned did not, nor did any of them, occur within four years next before commencement of the suit. Wherefore, &c.

Plaintiff called Johannes Gerhardus Munnik: I am the father of plaintiff's wife. The deed of acquittal executed by her dated 13th January, 1830, is signed by me; my daughter was not present when I signed it; nobody but Mr. J. H. Neethling was present. I read the deed and then signed it without any explanation from him. My daughter's signature, and no other, was at it when I signed it. I did not see her sign it, nor did I know she had signed it before I saw her signature to the deed. Not long before I signed the deed, I had been with plaintiff's wife at Mr. Neethling's. She was then of age, and he, in presence of her uncles, Hurter and De Wet, showed her the liquidation account and an account showing what her share was. He read to her parts of both those documents, but showed no vouchers. Neither she nor I examined the account. We trusted to Mr. Neethling that everything was correct in every respect. Her uncles were merely present, and did not examine the accounts. I do not think the will was read to my daughter. The liquidation account itself was not shown her, only a notarial copy thereof, which she signed. I allowed her to sign the notarial

1839. May 10. — Brand *vs.* Neethling's Executor.

copy without examination, because Mr. Neethling was so clever and honest that I trusted to him that all was correct. I was never present with my daughter at any other investigation of the accounts. When I signed the liquidation account in 1816, I read it over from beginning to end, but no vouchers were shown me. When I signed it, it had on it none of the alterations and erasions which now appear on it. I had had various money transactions with Mr. Neethling. He discharged the mortgage in a bond which I had granted in favour of the estate. I was very much in his power.

The plaintiff closed his case.

Defendant called no witnesses.

Defendant maintained, first, that plaintiff could not set aside the deed of discharge unless he proved *enormis læsio,* which, he contended, had not been proved. (*Voet* 4, 1, § 11.) Secondly, that such restitution as was now sought could only be claimed within four years of the act against which it was claimed. (*Voet* 4, I, § 16 ; 44, 3, § 7.)

Brand, contra, maintained that *enormis læsio* had been proved, and that under the circumstances of this case plaintiff was not restricted to the period of four years, and quoted *Voet* 4, 1, § 20.

The Court found that the plaintiff was entitled to open up the account as prayed, and gave judgment for plaintiff (for the sum agreed on between the parties) for £589 11s., with costs.

Van Reenen *vs.* Executor of Neethling.

1839. May 10. — Van Reenen *vs.* Executor of Neethling.

The plaintiff in this case was married in May, 1831, to a sister of the wife of the plaintiff in the preceding case, and now sought *restitutio in integrum* against a deed of receipt and discharge executed by him on 22nd March, 1833, in favour of the said J. H. Neethling of his wife's share of the same inheritance. This deed was in the same terms with that in the preceding case. It set out that plaintiff had read all the documents therein referred and approved of the same. And further declared "that he, the plaintiff, having had some objection to the calculation of the estate with respect to the doubtful debts and interest, now by way of a transaction on the law suit pending on that account before the Supreme Court to renounce the same and as in case of (uitkoop) buying out. And declares now to have received as the whole and only inheritance appertaining to his wife out of the said estate from said J. H. Neethling, Rds. 7,711,

1839. May 10.

Van Reenen *vs.* Executor of Neethling.

being the amount awarded her in the present liquidation account, 7th September, 1816, and whereupon the undersigned declares by the receipt of the said sum and interest to be satisfied in full for his wife's share as heiress in said estate as far as concerns the said J. H. Neethling, and therefore, under renunciation of revision of account and *error calculi*, to acquit and discharge Mr. Neethling from his administration and from all further responsibility, and further declaring, on account of said transaction and agreement, to renounce all means of relief of which he might otherwise have availed himself."

The declaration in this case alleged the same facts and claimed the same relief as the declaration in preceding case had done, and defendant's plea was to the same effect with his plea in the preceding case, except that he did not plead that four years had elapsed since the causes of action accrued before the action was commenced.

The only witness examined was Marthinus Melt van Reenen, whose evidence was as follows: I am brother of the plaintiff. I remember to have had a communication on the part of my brother with Mr. Neethling in 1833. There were sentences at that time against my brother for debts, for which my mother was surety, and writs of execution on them against both were in the hands of the sheriff. My brother had no means to discharge those debts, he therefore desired me to go to Mr. Neethling and endeavour to get the money which was due to him for his wife's inheritance. I went to Mr. Neethling and asked him for the money, and he said, "Oh, you can come now after you have been summoned; you see, that is the way. You young men will never listen." I said, "Mr. Neethling, we have not time to enter into the merits of the case, as the sentences are about to be put into execution; therefore help me, otherwise my mother will be exposed." He said, "How have you an authority to receive the amount?" I again asked him to give me money to discharge the sentence, and he then wrote an authority to be signed by my brother, authorizing me to receive the money. I got my brother to sign it and returned to Mr. Neethling and said, "I hope you will now have no further objection to meet this demand." He then said to me, "Mr. de Wet has been your brother's advocate; you must bring me a certificate that he has been paid his fees." I then went and got a certificate to this effect from Mr. de Wet. I then returned to Mr. Neethling, and he said, "It is not over yet;" and produced a paper, saying, "Get your brother to sign this, and then I shall pay him." I said, "Are you going to pay me with money or a cheque?" I said this because it was

1839. May 10. — Van Reenen vs. Executor of Neethling.

then near the time the bank closed. He said, "I shall give you a cheque on the bank." I said, "Then I must make haste," and went to my brother, who was sitting by my mother, and said to him, "Andries, sign this, as Mr. Neethling seems to make all sorts of excuses; and if you don't sign this, the bank will be shut, and my mother will be exposed." He said, "Give me pen and ink." I did so and he signed it. He was going to read it, but I said, "No, you cannot read it; there is no time to be lost; the bank will be shut and my mother exposed." He signed it without reading it. I then took it to my cousin, Oloff Ferzen, and said, "Sign this as a witness." He did sign it, and I also signed it as witness. I then took it to Mr. Neethling. He looked over it, and then he gave me a cheque on the bank. I had not read the document before my brother signed it, nor until within these few days. I declare upon my oath that I ran with the document to my brother, without reading it, and that I did not give my brother time to read it before he signed, and that the witness Ferzen had no time to read it. The deed now shown me is that which my brother and I signed before getting the money from Mr. Neethling (the deed of transaction on which the defence is founded). This document was not written in my presence. Mr. Neethling was previously aware that my brother was in great difficulty for money. The time which intervened between my going for the certificate and bringing it to Mr. Neethling might be about half-an-hour or three-quarters.

Defendant's counsel here gave up the case.

Judgment for plaintiff, as prayed, for £512 10s. (the sum agreed on between the parties), with costs.

Vide Chitty's Equity, Index 19; 1*st Eden*, 64, *Salkeld vs. Burrand; Van der Linden*, 467, 275; *Voet* 2, 15, 21; *Oosthuysen vs. the Widow Muller, Executrix of Rensburg*, 27th August, 1840, *ante*, *p.* 425.

Master of the Supreme Court vs. Executors of Van der Poel.

Ord. 104, *Sect.* 33. *Executor's account. Master. Executor.*

The Master has such an interest in testate and intestate estates as to require the executor to file accounts. And this on motion, and not by action.

1842. May 6. — Master of the Supreme Court vs. Executors of Van der Poel.

The *Attorney-General*, on the part of the Master, moved for a rule on the respondents to show cause why they should not lodge an account of the administration and distribution of the estate of the deceased Mrs. Van der Poel, whose executors they were, in terms of the 33rd section of Ordinance No. 104, and maintained that as it was the duty of the Master, under the Ordinance, to tax and assess the remuneration to be paid to the executors in every case where remuneration is sought or taken by executors, and to levy a fee of £4 per cent. on the amount of such remuneration, he had as Master such an interest in the said estate as to entitle him to call for an account of the administration and distribution of it. That independently of this particular duty in consequence of the superintendence of the administration of estates, testate and intestate, which is attached to his office of Master, and as being the person in whose office the accounts of the administration and liquidation thereof are by law appointed to be deposited, he was entitled as Master to apply by motion to the Court for a rule to confirm the provisions of the Ordinance without a regular summons.

1842. May 6.

Master of the Supreme Court *vs.* Executors of Van der Poel.

Cloete, contra, maintained that the Master had no interest in the estate which entitled him to make this application. And that even if he had, it was not competent for him to proceed in this form on merely giving notice of motion, but was bound to have proceeded by a regular summons.

2nd. He denied that either the Master or the Resident Magistrate, if not held to be persons having an interest in the estate, had any title on any other ground to make the motion.

The Court had no doubt of the Master's interest and title to make the application in the form which he had adopted, but of consent allowed the motion to stand open till next Court day.

The case was not again brought before the Court, the respondents having lodged in the Master's office the accounts applied for.

[By Act 16 of 1864 this point was legislatively affirmed.]

In Re Wicht.—Heydenrich *vs.* Curators of P. J. Sandenberg.

Where H., S., and S. acted as executors and guardians, and one S. surrendered and the other S. made a cessio bonorum, —**Held** *that H. was entitled to act as sole executor and guardian.*

The Widow Lategan executed, in virtue of a reservatory clause in her testament, a codicil dated 13th August, 1814, nominating and appointing, as executors of her testament and guardians over her minor heirs and legatees, C.

1843. Nov. 30.

In re Wicht.—Heydenrich *vs.* Curators of P. J. Sandenberg,

1843. Nov. 30. — *In re* Wicht.—Heydenrich *vs.* Curators of P. J. Sandenberg.

Mathyssen and J. P. de Wet. By another codicil, dated 2nd April, 1818, she appointed J. C. Lehman, together with Messrs. C. Mathyssen and J. P. de Wet, executors of her testament and guardians over her minor heirs and legatees. On 30th December, 1821, she executed a codicil containing the following clause:

"Together with Mr. C. Mathyssen and J. P. de Wet, I nominate as co-executor and guardian of my minor heirs Mr. J. C. Lehman."

And on the 25th September, 1824, a codicil containing the following clause:

"I further nominate as co-executors and guardians of my minor heirs the aforesaid B. G. Heydenrich, with the same power and authority as I have granted to my said executors Mathyssen, De Wet, and Lehman."

And on the 13th September, 1826, a codicil by which she released J. P. de Wet and J. C. Lehman from the office of executors of her testament and administrators of her estate, and nominated in their stead Messrs. H. A Sandenberg and P. J. Sandenberg as executors of her testament and guardians over her minor heirs.

The widow died, and either before or after her death Mr. Mathyssen died. The two Sandenbergs and Heydenrich acted as her executors, Pieter J. Sandenberg acting as administrating executor and guardian. In 1842, H. Sandenberg died insolvent, and soon afterwards P. J. Sandenberg obtained a writ of *cessio bonorum*. On the 1st November, 1843, Heydenrich applied to the Court to have certain bonds and moneys belonging to the estate of the widow, now in the hands of the curators of P. J. Sandenberg, paid over to him as sole surviving solvent executor and guardian. This demand the curators refused to comply with, until a proper indemnity and discharge should be granted to them by Heydenrich. The Court referred the matter to the Master for his report, who reported that the sum in bonds and money in the hand of the curators amounted to £1,220 6s. 7½d., of £597 14s. 3d. of which one Richard Brook was entitled to demand immediate payment, leaving £622 12s. 4½d. for distribution in certain proportions, between Mei and Bressida, subject to the benefit of the survivorship, and suggested that payment of his share should immediately be made to Brook and the remainder should be placed in the Guardian's Fund on account of the parties interested therein.

On considering this report and hearing parties, the Court, on the 21st November, ordered that P. J. Sandenberg, as having obtained a writ of *cessio bonorum* (*vide Villiers and Stuckeris*, 16*th June*, 1829, *p.* 377), be removed from the office of executor and guardian; that the curators should forthwith pay into Court the whole amount and balance in their hands (which was immediately done), and that the costs occasioned by the application should be paid out of the estate; and postponed any decision on Heydenrich's application to have the funds paid over to him until parties should be heard as to Heydenrich's right to act as sole executor and guardian after the death and removal from office of all his other colleagues.

1843. Nov. 30.

In re Wicht.—Heydenrich *vs.* Curators of P. J. Sandenberg.

This day, the *Attorney-General*, for Heydenrich, quoted the *Dutch Consult., vol.* 6, *p.* 196; *Stair's Inst.*, 1, 6, 14, and 1, 12, 13; *Hargrave's Notes on Coke and Littleton*, 113, 146; and maintained that he was entitled to act as sole executor and guardian.

No appearance was made for any other party.

The Court were unanimously of opinion that Heydenrich had fully established his right to act as sole executor and guardian; but, before ordering the remainder of the money in Court, after satisfying the claim of Brook to be paid over to him, referred to the Master to report under what conditions as to security, if any, this money should be paid over to him.

Moore's Executrix, Appellant, *vs.* Le Sueur, Respondent.

Ordinance No. 104, §§ 30 *and* 32. *Executor.*

Executors having still funds in hand are liable to creditors, although they have not lodged their claims in due time.

This was an application to the Court to review and set aside the sentence of the Resident Magistrate of Cape Town, in a case in which the respondent was plaintiff and the appellant defendant, on the grounds that the Resident Magistrate refused to receive evidence tendered on behalf of the defendant previous to the promulgation of the said judgment. 2nd. That the said Court refused to entertain the defendant's counterclaim. 3rd. That the said judgment is contrary to law and to the evidence adduced.

1844. Aug. 1.

Moore's Executrix, Appellant, *vs.* Le Sueur, Respondent.

The summons was at the instance of the plaintiff as Collector of Taxes, against the defendant as executrix of her deceased husband, Edward Moore, and claimed from her in that capacity £19 11s. for taxes due and payable by the said deceased to the Colonial Government from 1st January, 1831, to the 31st December, 1840.

1844. Aug. 1.

Moore's Executrix, Appellant, *vs.* Le Sueur, Respondent.

Defendant's agent admitted that the assessment from 1831 to 31st December, 1840, was a correct account of the taxes payable by the deceased during that period; but objected, in virtue of the provision of the 30th section of Ordinance No. 104, to the plaintiff's right of action,—no claim having been filed for said taxes in the estate of deceased, notwithstanding the notice given by defendant in the *Government Gazette* to creditors to lodge their claims on the deceased's estate within the period specified in terms of the 30th section of Ordinance 104; and put in the *Gazette* of 30th October, 1840, to prove said notice.

The Magistrate then (5th July), deferred judgment, and on 17th July, gave judgment for plaintiff for £19 11s. and costs, £1.

Ebden, this day, for the appellant, argued that the effect of the 30th and 32nd sections of Ordinance No 104, was absolutely to deprive a creditor who had not filed his claim within the period for so doing so notified in the *Government Gazette,* in terms of the said 30th section, of all right of action thereafter against the executor. (*Vide Horn vs. Loedolff, 3rd December,* 1829, *ante, Vol.* 1, *p.* 403.)

The Court held that the 32nd section protected the executor only against claims made by persons who had not duly lodged their claims in respect of property or funds *bonâ fide* distributed by him, after the expiration of the period prescribed in the notice, and did not affect or alter his liability in other respects, or as to property or funds in his hands still undistributed; and that therefore the appellant in this case could not maintain the objection which she had taken, unless she had pleaded *plene administravit,* and that she had no assets of the estate in her possession; neither of which she had done. And overruled the objection.

Southey *vs.* Dormehl's Executor.

1844. Sept. 12.

Where defendant as executor had given notice to creditors to lodge claims in terms of the 30*th section of Ordinance No.* 104, *the plaintiff, who had lodged his claim, was held entitled to claim payment of his bond without giving the usual notice.*

[Vol. I, p. 22.]

END OF VOL II.

LONDON: PRINTED BY WILLIAM CLOWES AND SONS, LIMITED,
DUKE STREET, STAMFORD STREET, S.E., AND GREAT WINDMILL STREET, W.

Lightning Source UK Ltd.
Milton Keynes UK
UKHW012046060220
358307UK00001B/204